BRITISH POLITICS
AND THE AMERICAN REVOLUTION

BRITISH
POLITICS
AND THE
AMERICAN
REVOLUTION

CHARLES R. RITCHESON

GREENWOOD PRESS, PUBLISHERS
WESTPORT, CONNECTICUT

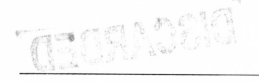

Library of Congress Cataloging in Publication Data

Ritcheson, Charles R.
    British politics and the American Revolution.

    Reprint. Originally published: 1st ed. Norman :
University of Oklahoma Press.
    Bibliography: p.
    Includes index.
    1. Great British--Politics and government--1760-1789.
2. United States--History--Revolution, 1775-1783--
Causes. I. Title.
DA510.R5 1981   941.07'3   81-1808
ISBN 0-313-22953-8 (lib. bdg.)   AACR2

Reprinted in 1981 by Greenwood Press
A division of Congressional Information Service, Inc.
88 Post Road West, Westport, Connecticut 06881

Printed in the United States of America

FOR MY PARENTS

PREFACE

THE EIGHTEENTH-CENTURY conflict between the North American Colonies and Great Britain was a clash of rights. Neither side possessed a monopoly on love of parliamentary institutions or civil liberties. Both firmly grounded their arguments in a common political heritage. Britain was committed to the principle of parliamentary supremacy as the only safeguard against absolute monarchy. Americans asserted they were not to be taxed for revenue except by their own representative assemblies. The failure to reconcile these two positions would mean the destruction of the first British Empire.

The task facing British politicians at the close of the Seven Years' War was an unprecedented one. The antiquated colonial system had not worked well. The Colonies had behaved badly. Jealous and squabbling, they had repeatedly ignored or only partially fulfilled urgent requisitions from the mother country for troops and money. They had persisted in trading with the enemy's West Indian islands even during a struggle which had as its stake their very existence. With the end of the war, the mother country had to cope with the additional problem of absorbing the great new conquests into the Empire, of coordinating them with the older colonies, and of protecting them both. Pontiac's revolt in 1763 had underscored the need for military occupation of the back country. Surely, British reasoning ran, the colonists could not expect the mother country to assume the whole financial burden of imperial defense. Britain already labored under an unparalleled debt, much of it contracted to finance a war fought largely in the colonists' behalf. The Americans could not object to bearing a fraction of the cost of their own protection. But imperial defense was a sphere of action outside the competence of individual colonial assemblies. It would therefore have to be undertaken by Parliament. Since the requisition system had proved inadequate and altogether unsatisfactory, a new method of defraying the increased expenditures would have to be found. That Parliament possessed no authority to devise a new imperial system and to finance it as they saw fit appeared to be a position so patently absurd that it needed no serious refutation. Such logic buttressed Grenville's classic concept of empire: a supreme center and subordinate parts. This concept of empire did not belong to that statesman alone, however. It was that of the great majority of the British political nation.

As the controversy developed, colonial leaders, justifying their resistance with British precedents, denied the validity of revenue laws passed by Parliament. When no lasting abatement of efforts to derive a revenue from them was forthcoming, Americans proceeded to a complete denial of Parliament's supremacy. Franklin, Jefferson, and John Adams proclaimed that the Colonies were bound to Britain only through the person of the King. American petitions appealed to George III for relief from parliamentary measures and for deliverance from evil ministers who had "interposed" themselves between his Majesty and his loyal subjects in the Colonies. This "federal" idea, had it been implemented, would have saved the empire; but it could not be made to work in the eighteenth-century political framework. In Britain, the American argument seemed outlandish and even pernicious. It implied a limiting of the supreme power of Parliament and an enlargement of the scope of royal activity. Neither Parliament nor the would allow it.

The monumental work of Sir Lewis B. Namier has g far to dispel the clouds of misunderstanding gathered abc the figure of that unfortunate, neurotic, but thoroughly whiggish monarch George III. Habitually mistaking obstinacy for perseverance and honest differences of opinion for "faction," he had no lust for absolute power. He possessed no wish to enslave the colonists. Venerating the British Constitution as the most perfect revelation of a mode of government, he aimed to "purify" politics. He desired to regain what he considered to be his rightful place in British politics: as active executive of the state, the source of all power and honor. Seeking to tyrannize over nobody, he went to fantastic lengths to keep himself free of chains. To extirpate "party," to allow no group of selfish, grasping men—those who disagreed with him—to "give him the law," to preside in a firm and harmonious union with Parliament over a united nation was his plan. And it is a fact of considerable irony that the King managed to attain a position at the center of politics by expelling the Old Whigs, whose frequent and sporadic incursions upon the royal powers under the first two Georges had created a false dawn of the modern British party system. Taking the means of patronage, which Walpole and the Pelhams had monopolized for half a century, into his own hands, the King made himself the heir of the Old Whigs.

For ten years, George III, aided by his Friends and, not a little, by the misguided zeal of Chatham in 1766, fought his battle. Fleeing from the Old Whigs to Grenville, he was forced to return to those he had dismissed. On he went to Chatham and to Grafton. These years of chaos were brought to an end only with the formation of the North Ministry. But an empire was lost. By committing himself to the role of an active agent in domestic politics, the King was unable to rise above that scene, as Americans asked, to serve as a symbol of imperial union.

The American problem was the first fully developed issue in British politics since the lingering death of Jacobitism. Its impact was twofold. As American radicalism grew, it combined with a domestic radicalism, the outward manifestation of which was the scapegrace John Wilkes. The result was a powerful conservative reaction. Centered about the King and dedicated to upholding the Whig doctrine of parliamentary supremacy, this conservatism became the seedbed of a new Tory party which would reach full development in the next century.

Secondly, the American problem produced in Britain an amazing development in imperial thinking—in the very concept of empire. As the struggle over rights reached revolutionary proportions, the British government retreated from Grenville's ideal of a mercantilistic empire of supreme center and subordinate parts. The first indication of such a withdrawal was not the repeal of the Stamp Act. It was North's Conciliatory Proposition. The next faltering step came with the Howe Peace Commission. Finally—too late and all lost—the Carlisle Commission, formed under the unrelieved pressure of Burgoyne's surrender and the fear of French intervention, represented the acceptance in elemental form of the idea of a federal empire or commonwealth of nations.

When embattled Americans rejected the terms held out by Carlisle and his colleagues, reaction in Britain against any devolution of authority within the empire was great. Indeed, after the Peace of 1783, the reaction extended to questioning the worth of an empire at all. There followed a strong resurgence of mercantilism. Then came the wars with revolutionary France; and the conservatism aroused by the American war increased tenfold. In the new century, however, Britain would crush the French menace. The Industrial Revolution would free her of the fear of an empire of manufacturing competitors. She would possess her modern party system; and her monarch, removed from the center of domestic politics, would become a symbol wherein all members of the empire might find union on terms of equality. Her American experience had pointed out the only way in which Britain, as a free nation, could build and keep an empire of free men.

SHOULD I attempt to pay tribute to, or even to name the many friends and colleagues who have given their assistance and encouragement to me while writing this book, the list would be long indeed. I must mention Professor Samuel Eliot Morison of Harvard. He remains for the author—as he must for all his former students—a constant encouragement and inspiration. Professor Keith G. Feiling of All Souls College, Oxford (retired), and Mr. Alfred B. Emden, principal of St. Edmund Hall, Oxford (retired), have ever given freely of their friendly counsel and great learning.

To my friend and colleague Professor Donnell M. Owings goes my deep appreciation for his unstinting devotion to, and excellent performance of, a tedious task: the reading of the manuscript. To Mr. and Mrs. Charles R. Spackman, of Portland, Oregon, go profound thanks for aiding and abetting my work.

I am indebted to the Trustees of the British Museum and to the officials of the Public Record Office for permission to make use of the extensive manuscript sources listed in the bibliography. I must also make acknowledgment to the Right Honorable the Earl Fitzwilliam and the trustees of the Fitzwilliam settled estates for my use of the papers of the Marquis of Rockingham and Edmund Burke on deposit at the Public Library, Sheffield. For the use of the papers of the fourth Earl of Sandwich, I owe a special debt of gratitude to the Viscount Hinchingbrooke, M.P., whose gracious hospitality and illuminating conversation aided me immeasurably.

Finally, it would be no exaggeration to say that without

the constant and unfailing aid and encouragement of my wife, this book would not now be in the reader's hands.

CHARLES R. RITCHESON

Kenyon College
January 5, 1954

CONTENTS

Illustrations

BRITISH POLITICS
AND THE AMERICAN REVOLUTION

CHAPTER ONE

THE AMERICAN PROBLEM
AND THE
GRENVILLE MINISTRY

GREAT BRITAIN emerged from the Seven Years' War possessing the most extensive empire since the days of Rome. The great subcontinent of India had been torn from France, and French and Spanish commercial competition practically destroyed. The greatest conquest, however, was that of Canada and the Mississippi Valley, whereby Great Britain established her unquestioned supremacy on the North American continent. The vast hinterland beyond the older seaboard colonies promised untold riches in raw materials, an indefinitely expanding empire, and unlimited markets for British trade. This territory the British government had chosen to retain in preference to the conquests in the West Indies, the French Sugar Islands, Guadeloupe, and Martinique. By doing so, Great Britain committed herself to a policy of westward expansion and of exploitation of the interior of North America; to fail to do so would be to fail to justify the retention of Canada and the Mississippi Valley.

The home government was now faced with a problem of staggering proportions. How were the new conquests, with a large body of alien people, the French Canadians, to be assimilated? How co-ordinated with the older Atlantic seaboard colonies into a coherent imperial system? This question involved a yet more fundamental one. What was the proper and constitutional relationship between the mother country and her Colonies?

The internal political development of the Colonies had been such that an amazing degree of self-government had been achieved by 1763. Usually this had been at the expense of the royal prerogative. As early as the middle of the eighteenth century, the usurpation of royal power by the colonial assemblies and their undermining of the system of colonial government by royal instructions had begun to cause serious alarm in London. The expulsion of France from the North American continent had now cleared the way for a reckoning between Great Britain and her Colonies. British politicians, among them the Earl of Halifax and Francis Bernard, generally thought that the moment had come for a readjustment of the imperial relationship. A reorientation of the Colonies about the mother country, they felt, should now be undertaken.[1]

A second cause of British dissatisfaction with the old colonial system was also in evidence. The mercantile theory had produced a body of Laws of Trade and Navigation designed to secure to Great Britain a monopoly of colonial trade. In practice, however, habitual and flagrant violations by the colonists had seriously undermined these palladia of mercantilism.[2] Even during the war colonial fortunes had been made by trade with the enemy's West Indian islands.

There was yet a third consideration which emphasized the need to reform the old colonial system as it had existed prior to 1763. When the home government had desired aid in troops

[1] E. Channing and A. C. Coolidge (eds.), *Barrington-Bernard Correspondence*, 42–45, 53, Francis Bernard to Lord Barrington, December 15, 1761; May 1, 1762.

[2] Additional Manuscripts, British Museum (hereafter Add. MSS) 38335, f. 217. Charles Jenkinson computed that 250,000 families were then living in North America. Theoretically, they would consume 6 pounds of tea annually. In 1763, however, only 182,000 pounds came from England, from January 1 to November 17, leaving a total of 1,318,000 pounds imported illegally.

or money from the Colonies in order to prosecute the struggle against a common enemy, a letter from the secretary of state setting forth the amount of the aid "requisitioned" and the purpose for which it was to be used would be sent to the colonial governors. Such "requisitions" would then be presented to the assemblies, who were expected to take action upon them. This system of imperial finance had been shown to be thoroughly unsatisfactory and inadequate during the Seven Years' War. Each colony had feared it would contribute more than its rightful share to the common defense. As a consequence, urgent requisitions had often gone unanswered, or only token aid been given. In the end, the elder Pitt, the great director of the war with France, was able to cajole the Colonies into giving effective assistance only by promising to reimburse them for a major portion of their expenditures.

Under these conditions, how was an imperial structure, including both new conquests and the established colonies, to be created? What was to be the relation of the various parts of the empire to the mother country? How was the British trade monopoly to be preserved? The need for a general imperial reorganization was obvious, but how was it to be financed?

These issues, which troubled the imperial relationship, also figured in the British domestic political scene. Indeed, the American problem from 1763 until the colonies were hopelessly lost to the empire was strongly conditioned by political developments inside Great Britain. In turn, that problem reacted upon domestic politics, bringing a change in imperial thinking, a modification of the mercantile view of empire, and the development of something approaching the "federal" view. Moreover, this American problem helped prepare the ground for the growth of the modern British party system.

The death of King George II and the succession of his grandson George III, in October, 1760, marked a watershed in British political history. The advent of the young King, determined to take his rightful place as the active chief executive of the kingdom, spelled the end of the half-century of Whig political domination. Sir Lewis B. Namier has brilliantly portrayed George III's capture of the Old Whig "system" of patronage which had allowed that party to monopolize the political stage under the first two Georges.[3] By doing so, George III thrust himself into the center of British politics. Furthermore, he threw into sharp perspective the degree to which the assumption and the facts of the Old Whig dominance in the latter years of his grandfather's reign had outrun the constitutional balance of power established in the last years of the seventeenth and early years of the eighteenth century.

From his accession, George III's battle was against "party" or "faction," against groups of men who sought to "give him the law." During the first decade of his reign, he fled from one combination of men to another, but he could find no sanctuary from "faction." In the end, the young King was forced to create and lead his own political group, his "Friends" whom he viewed as the proper answer to "party." In reality, the "Friends," in combination with certain splinter groups of the Old Whig party, represent the origin of the modern British party system. The King's position as a party leader with the free exercise of the royal powers was naturally stronger than that of any would-be competitor.[4] Men such as Pitt, the Duke of Bedford, the Duke of Newcastle, or Grenville could be charged with factious conduct, but the King was a center in whom both the ambitious and the patriotic might find a common head.

The opportunity to crush "faction" seemed at hand when the young King succeeded to the throne. Pitt, the great genius of the war, had lost the support of the Tory country gentlemen.

[3] L. B. Namier, *England in the Age of the American Revolution;* and *The Structure of Politics at the Accession of George III.*

[4] Add. MSS 38200, f. 121; printed in N. S. Jucker, *Jenkinson Papers,* 90, Tom Ramsden, Latin secretary to the King and political agent of Sir James Lowther, to Charles Jenkinson, November 20, 1762.

They had sustained him throughout the war, but growing tired of the expense and satisfied with the victory already achieved, they had declared for peace. By the end of 1762, the Tories, leaving the dead to bury the dead and forgetting their fathers' hatred of "Hanoverian rats," were counted as supporters of the King's and Bute's administration.[5] The first great royal victory, then, was the dismissal of Pitt, that "blackest of hearts" who had refused to work with the King's friend the Scottish Earl of Bute. Pitt's wartime ally, the Duke of Newcastle, leader of the Old Whigs and ever eager to grasp and hold power, congratulated himself for the moment on having divorced his fate from Pitt's.

Having betrayed Pitt, however, Newcastle now engineered his own fall. The furious onslaught against the Old Whigs, led by the King's agent *pro tempore*, Henry Fox, proved that the King regarded them, not Pitt, as the real enemy. Every office holder, great or humble, who owed preferment to Old Whig patronage was summarily turned out of place, and Old Whig power was broken forever. For half a century, the Old Whigs had preached that opposition to the "present system" was factious and disloyal. They had now to hear their own words from other mouths. Furthermore, the Duke of Newcastle, by refusing to resign with Pitt, had created an almost insurpassable gulf between Pitt's friends and his own. In addition, he had lost valuable men, for instance, Lord Barrington, who chose to follow Newcastle's earlier example and remain in office rather than join an unlucrative opposition. While apologizing "with the greatest heartbreaking" to erstwhile patrons, many found it expedient "to join in with the stream."[6]

[5] Add. MSS 38458, f. 23, Shute Barrington to Jenkinson, December 16, 1762. Barrington told his friend of the election of Sir William Bagot, a Tory, for Oxford University: "As I conclude that he will continue to act with the tories whose principles he adopted early, I congratulate you on having gained an additional vote; which tho' not necessary will render future victories more complete."

[6] Hinchingbrooke Papers; extracts quoted in Namier, *The Structure of Politics*, II, 354–55, Earl of Sandwich to the Duke of Cumberland, November 10, 1762.

George III's Friends soon became as real a political factor as the Old Whigs themselves or as the groups centered around the Duke of Bedford and George Grenville.

The Grenville Ministry which took office in April, 1763, was a legacy of that pompous and vague idealist the Earl of Bute. It was formed under Bute's tutelage and was designed to achieve two purposes. First, it was to allow him, hidden behind a ministry with which ostensibly he was unconnected, to continue his intimate relationship with the King. The immense personal unpopularity which had come to him as a result of his brief ministry dictated such a move. Secondly, the Grenville Ministry was designed to protect the King from the Old Whigs who had held George II in "captivity." Bute chose George Grenville to be his successor as first lord of the Treasury, and was content to see his own friends in small, lucrative offices outside the cabinet. The Scot had hoped to place his young protégé, the Earl of Shelburne, as secretary of state for the Southern Department, but Grenville flatly refused to acquiesce in turning out his own brother-in-law, the Earl of Egremont. Shelburne, deprived of his chance to act as Bute's check on Grenville, was accordingly made first lord of trade.

Bute's plan to garner support from all groups who would give it led to offers to the friends of the Duke of Bedford. The Duke, on bad terms with Egremont as a result of a squabble during the negotiation of the peace, refused office himself but gave his blessing to his friends. Lord Gower consequently became the new chamberlain; the Duke of Marlborough took the privy seal and Lord Sandwich the Admiralty. Further in keeping with the policy of flouting "party" groups, offers were held out to Sir George Savile, later to become a trusted lieutenant in the Rockingham Whig group, and to the Old Tory Prowse. Lord Henley, soon to become Lord Northington, continued as lord chancellor, and was thus the only real King's Friend in the cabinet.

The choice of the new ministry was manifestly an effort

to stamp out "party," but in seeking to do so, Bute and the King had laid the groundwork for the emergence of a new party system. The Old Whigs and Pitt had been condemned to wander in the wilderness; they were soon to overcome their reluctance to oppose the King's ministers.

With these colleagues and under these conditions, George Grenville began an administration which was to make America a problem of the first magnitude in British politics. It is much to Grenville's credit that he saw the importance of this problem and undertook to solve it. He alone among British statesmen, before the outbreak of the American Revolution, offered a comprehensive plan which demonstrated true imperial statesmanship and a deep understanding of the British Constitution. That old attitudes and doctrines could no longer be applied successfully to the American Colonies had to be established by the events of the next decade.

Even before he came to power, certain suggestions and basic decisions had been brought forward which preconditioned Grenville's American policy. Soon after the Peace of Paris, Governor Dinwiddie of Virginia had written to his friend and first lord of the Treasury, Lord Bute.[7] The Governor assumed that Canada and the West would be retained and that rapid settlement of that area would follow. To secure the new conquests, Dinwiddie recommended the creation of a military government along the frontier, with the Colonies bearing the expense of a three-year military occupation of the territory. The cost, he estimated, would be thirty thousand pounds sterling per annum. This sum should be raised in the Colonies by a "Stamp Duty on all Bonds, obligations, and other Instruments of Writing . . . similar to that Duty in Great Britain." He predicted that the Colonies would cheerfully acquiesce in such a plan since the revenue was to be devoted to the cost of their own defense. The Governor's paper included, indeed, all the elements of Grenville's later plan. The Indians were to be

[7] Add. MSS 38308, ff. 297–301.

secured in their land titles and pacified, the Indian trade regulated by the imperial authority, western expansion allowed in an orderly fashion, and a military force established to insure the execution of the plan and to protect the Colonies from Indian attack or foreign invasion.[8]

A more important guide for Grenville in the formation of his American policy was the Board of Trade Report of November 11, 1761, the Mohawk Valley Report.[9] It had been approved by the Privy Council, and instructions based on it had been issued to royal governors. Originally drawn up by Egremont and approved by Halifax, both of whom were now in Grenville's cabinet, the report became a basis for Grenville's plan.

The report sharply criticized indiscriminate granting of Indian lands, a practice to which many colonial governors had become addicted as a means of accumulating personal fortunes. Great discontent among the savages had thus been caused. The practice was an open violation of the compacts with them wherein Great Britain had guaranteed their hunting grounds and wherein "they had yielded to Us the Dominion but not the property of those Lands." It was therefore deemed highly expedient to order colonial governors to stop white settlement on Indian lands; and any idea of establishing new colonies before the rights of the Indians had been clarified was "a measure

---

[8] The urgency for supplying the new conquests with military protection as a method of integrating them with the rest of the empire is stated by C. E. Carter, "The Significance of the Military Office in America, 1763–1775," *American Historical Review*, Vol. XXVIII (April, 1923), 475–88. See also Add. MSS 38335, ff. 1–5, "Hints respecting our acquisitions in America." The author was undoubtedly William Knox. See Knox, *Extra Official State Papers*, 28–29. Both Knox and Dinwiddie argued powerfully for wholesale reforms of the established colonial system.

[9] W. L. Grant and J. Munro (eds.), *Acts of the Privy Council (Colonial), George III*, I, 494–501. See also C. E. Carter, "British Policy toward the American Indians in the South," *English Historical Review*, Vol. XXXIII (January, 1918), 37–56; "Observations of Superintendent John Stuart and Governor James Grant of East Florida on the Proposed Plan of 1764," *American Historical Review*, Vol. XX (July, 1915), 815–31.

of the most dangerous tendency." The report is not to be construed as a perpetual prohibition of westward expansion but as a temporary suspension until the conclusion of the war. At that time, the whole question of Indian-white relations, including a reform of the Indian trade, could be canvassed.[10]

Yet another decision of far reaching consequence had been made before Grenville's rise to power. During the Bute Administration, steps had been taken to maintain ten thousand British troops in the American West, and it had been generally understood that the American Colonies would shoulder at least a part of the expense. When the army estimates, including the force for America, had been moved in the House of Commons in March, 1763, they had passed with even Pitt's blessing, his only complaint being that the estimates did not provide Britain with a greater military establishment.

Accepting these decisions, Grenville now determined to create an imperial system embracing the new acquisitions and the older colonies alike. From his first assumption of office, he was preoccupied with absorbing the new conquests into the empire, settling a satisfactory financial basis for so doing, and, indirectly, creating better order among the older colonies by pulling them more firmly into the imperial orbit of the British Constitution.

In essence, the Grenville plan was to create an orderly administration for the new conquests, financed in part by the older colonies. These would receive protection from the imperial military occupation of the West, and would therefore be paying—or helping to pay—for services rendered. Probably Grenville was already beginning to question the constitutionality

---

[10] See Grant and Munro, *Acts of the Privy Council*, I, 502–506, wherein the Privy Council annulled three acts of the North Carolina Assembly which attempted to impose the tenure of judges during good behavior. The governor was sharply reprimanded: if governors continued to disobey their instructions, "the Dependence of those Colonies upon the Authority of the Crown and the Just Government of the Mother Country already too much relaxed, will stand upon a very precarious foot."

of the requisition system which provided a source of funds for the Crown independent of the control of Parliament. At any rate, the irksome and ineffective requisitions would be abandoned, and an American revenue derived by redrawing the Acts of Trade and Navigation in such a way that they would cease being merely safeguards to the British trade monopoly but would also produce a revenue. Grenville's plan was therefore more conservative than the suggestions of Bernard, the governor of Massachusetts, who was calling for a wholesale revamping of the colonial governments. Violent changes in the existing apparatus of government would be avoided. At the same time, the Colonies would be drawn gradually into a well-ordered, mercantilistic empire.

Grenville's plan was firmly based upon the spirit of the British Constitution. The colonial view that the assembly was a miniature Parliament within its own borders, with all the rights and privileges possessed by its prototype, had not as yet been formally enunciated by American political leaders. When it was, it came as a distinct shock, not only to Grenville, but to the overwhelming majority of British statesmen and politicians. To these latter, colonial assemblies were constituted by the Crown's special grace and favor, and possessed no authority except that exercised under the supreme power of Parliament. In the time ahead, both American and British politicians were to seek to justify their stands by historical appeals to the Glorious Revolution. Time after time, colonial assemblies, in dispute with their governors and the ministry, were to appeal to the principle put forward in 1688: the supremacy of the legislative body over an encroaching executive. Eventually, Parliament was to intervene in colonial affairs, and American radicals were to be forced to drive their argument on to the final assertion of the integrity of their legislatures against all encroachments, even Parliament's. As a last resort, they were to appeal to the royal prerogative for protection against Parliament. This colonial position would be, however, in British eyes indefensible. It would be the Colonies who denied the fundamentals of the Glorious Revolution and sought to re-establish the royal power after it had been finally defeated in Great Britain. The conflict between Great Britain and her Colonies was a tragedy in the classic sense; it was a conflict of rights. These were arguments of the future. As Grenville methodically began to formulate his plan to create an imperial system, he had no suspicion of the turbulent stage upon which Anglo-American relations were about to embark.

To the Secretary of State for the Southern Department, Lord Egremont, and to the President of the Board of Trade, Lord Shelburne, fell the task of formulating the ministry's western policy. In May, 1763, Egremont, on account of his senior position, took the lead by requesting of Shelburne a complete report. Shelburne immediately fell to work collecting all available information. Meantime, in June, he sent to his chief an interim report based on the Mohawk Valley Report.[11] It called for assuring to the Indians their hunting grounds, and for subsequent creation of new colonies in the west after a boundary line had been run and land been procured by imperial purchase. Until then, only the newly won lands of Nova Scotia and the Floridas should be formed into new governments.

In mid-July, Egremont informed Shelburne that his report had been approved and ordered the Board of Trade to prepare papers for the creation of these new colonies. He also suggested that the Indian lands be put under the province of Quebec for purposes of the administration of justice. Shelburne countered with a recommendation that the commander-in-chief of the military forces in that territory be given a royal commission for that end, but no agreement was reached.

Implementation of the new policy was prevented by a series of unfortunate incidents. In May, 1763, Pontiac struck

[11] See R. A. Humphreys, "Lord Shelburne and the Proclamation of 1763," *English Historical Review*, Vol. XLIX (April, 1934), 241–64.

and for a time carried all before him. What had been so long feared had happened. The Indians had found a leader with great organizing powers and the spark of military genius. At this crucial moment, when a firm and decisive settlement of the western question was urgently necessary, Egremont died, leaving to Halifax the burden of both Departments of State. Finally, on September 3, Shelburne, outraged by what he considered to be royal bad faith in an abortive negotiation to bring his new hero, Pitt, into office, resigned as president of the Board of Trade. He was succeeded by a hanger-on of the Court, the Earl of Hillsborough. Thus, at this delicate conjuncture, the direction of American affairs underwent a complete change.

Under great pressure himself, Halifax ordered Hillsborough to draft a proclamation promulgating the policy already settled by Egremont and Shelburne.[12] Using Shelburne's plan of such a proclamation, the new President of the Board of Trade soon drew up his own. Shelburne had intended to provide for the creation of three new governments, Nova Scotia and the two Floridas. As inducements to prospective settlers, English law and the speedy calling of an elective assembly were promised. Having embodied these provisions, Hillsborough then added a recital of the boundaries of the province of Quebec, thereby including this province in the provisions for the civil government of the three new colonies. The Alleghenies were selected as the temporary boundary line between the Colonies and the lands reserved to the Indians. Trade with the Indians was to be free, but traders were to obtain licenses from a governor and to bind themselves to abide by imperial regulations. Egremont and Shelburne had never settled their difference over the administration of justice in the Indian reservations; Hillsborough now completely overlooked the point, and no provision was made at all. Time was pressing, however, and the King signed and dated the document October 7, 1763. It was not, indeed, until mid-year 1764 that the Board of Trade

[12] *Ibid.* Corrects C. W. Alvord, *The Mississippi Valley.*

was able to present a comprehensive plan for the imperial control of Indian affairs.[13]

The rebellion of Pontiac was to have an important indirect result. It not only underlined the need for a new system of Indian regulations, but it again demonstrated the hopeless inadequacy of a scheme of imperial finance based upon requisitions. When hostilities commenced, General Amherst, commander-in-chief in America, called upon the Colonies for aid, telling them that since it was primarily a colonial struggle, no reimbursement for their expenditures was to be expected. Had any doubts remained in the minds of the British politicians concerning the efficacy of requisitions, they were now removed. Only four colonies, New York, Virginia, Connecticut, and New Jersey, made even a gesture of compliance. The others, most of them relatively safe from attack, refused to send any aid whatsoever. In this conflict, as in the Seven Years' War, it fell largely to the lot of the mother country to protect the Colonies.

Grenville, having left the "western" aspect of his problem to Egremont, Shelburne, and the Board of Trade, had immersed himself in another facet of it. The Seven Years' War had seen Great Britain's public debt doubled to about £130,-000, 000, with an annual interest of over £4,000,000. Grenville knew that an imperial system which included the management of Indian affairs, the erection of new colonies, the purchase of land from the Indians, and the military protection of the new acquisitions demanded new sources of revenue. The British public, however, was taxed already to the breaking point, the

[13] The Board of Trade informed Superintendent Johnson in August, 1763, that a plan for the imperial management of Indian affairs was under consideration and asked for his suggestions. He accordingly sent the deputy agent, George Croghan, to England, and it was not until the following July that the report outlining the new plan was made. There was to be an independent imperial department of Indian affairs, and the new plan would cost about twenty thousand pounds a year. Indian trade and prices were to be strictly regulated. Only the Crown would acquire land from the Indians. The cost was the great disadvantage which prevented the immediate execution of the plan, and the ministry decided to wait until the American revenue was settled.

indicative land tax standing at four shillings in the pound. It would be unfair, Grenville believed, to ask subjects in Great Britain to undertake to pay from their own pockets the cost of maintaining an army whose primary function was to protect the North American colonists. And when the British exchequer was being defrauded of thousands of pounds a year through the illicit trade of those same colonists! Before the war, the army in America and the West Indies had not cost above £100,000 per annum. Now, however, with ten thousand troops to be maintained in North America, and thirty-four hundred in the West Indies, the cost had soared to £320,000. To defray at least a part of this cost, Grenville resolved to tax Americans for revenue, for he believed it just that they should contribute to the cost of their own defense.

It soon became evident what direction Grenville's plan was taking. Always thorough, he now began a period of intensive research utilizing the services of his undersecretaries, particularly those of Charles Jenkinson. He also conferred frequently with Richard Jackson, the colonial agent who served as solicitor to the Board of Trade.

Jenkinson wrote on May 21, 1763, at the command of the Lords of the Treasury, to the Commissioners of the Customs in London, asking them to investigate why the revenue arising from duties imposed on America and the West Indies by the Acts of Trade had fallen so far below what might reasonably be expected. A month later, the commissioners reported.[14]

They declared that the most obvious cause of the deficiency was the fraudulent evasion of the Laws of Trade, particularly that of 25 Charles II. This had imposed duties, upon export from colony to colony, on white sugar, brown and white muscovado, tobacco, indigo, ginger, fustic, dyewoods, and certain other articles. The amount collected under the act for the past thirty years came to only £35,216 7s. 9d. This low sum proved habitual fraud by ships supposedly clearing out for Great Brit-

[14] Add. MSS 38335, ff. 144–47.

16

ain, but in reality proceeding to other colonial ports. The situation was, however, beyond the remedy of customs officers, and the only solution would be the imposition of further checks and restraints by Parliament.

The commissioners also took note of the Molasses Act (6 George II), which heavily taxed several articles of foreign produce when imported into the Colonies: rum and spirits at 9*d*. per gallon; molasses and syrups at 6*d*. per gallon; and sugar at 5/- per hundredweight. To enforce these duties more officers had been appointed, but during the past thirty years, the act had produced only £21,652 10*s*. 11¼*d*., a sum insufficient to pay even the cost of collection. The commissioners then reiterated a principle which they had laid down in a report of May, 1759: if these high duties were continued, smuggling and illicit trade would persist and could not be prevented because of the long and sinuous coastline of North America. They then proceeded to outline their plan. All American customs officers were to be required to reside constantly in America. This, in conjunction with a wartime Act of Parliament giving commanders of royal ships in American waters additional powers in dealing with vessels suspected of engaging in illegal trade, would go far to suppress smuggling. Those fees and perquisites which tended to entice customs officers into collusion should be replaced by poundages based upon the amount of revenue collected.

The Lords of the Treasury accepted this report and took the only steps which they felt authorized to take without direct parliamentary action. They ordered the commissioners to write at once to all officers absent from their posts and to direct them to return by August 31 on pain of dismissal. They were also to prepare instructions for all officers in America and the West Indies, calling on them for the strictest attention to duty and requiring regular and constant correspondence with the home government. To change established fees into a poundage and to embody the other points in the commissioners' plan would require an Act of Parliament, but in the meantime, the Lords of the Treasury asked the commissioners to recommend new checks and restraints.[15]

Secretary of State Egremont was also asked to write to the colonial governors conveying His Majesty's command that all support and assistance be given to officers of the revenue. He accordingly dispatched a circular letter referring to smuggling as an "iniquitous practice [which] has been carried to a great height in America." In it he called on the governors to see that the Laws of Trade were vigorously enforced. Illicit trade, he declared, had led "to the diminution and impoverishment of the public revenue, at a time when this Nation is labouring under a heavy Debt, incurred the last War for the protection of America."[16] Here then is the first official indication that the ministry had ceased to regard the Laws of Trade and Navigation as merely commercial regulations, and now intended them to become, in addition, a source of revenue.

Grenville fell to work immediately to tighten the system of trade laws, cut expenses, and produce his revenue. By October, it was decided to amend the Molasses Act in line with the report of the Commissioners of the Customs. At the same time, the commander-in-chief in America and the governors were forbidden to incur debts, the money for which had not previously been appropriated by Parliament or approved by the Treasury Board.

Charles Jenkinson, to whom fell the task of redrafting the Molasses Act, began laborious researches lasting well into 1764. Long hours were spent studying the Laws of Trade and Navigation; questionnaires were dispatched to the colonial governors to get information on colonial commerce. He requested of William Wood, secretary of the London Board of Customs, lists of all enumerated articles since 1710; and of John Free-

---

[15] *Ibid.*, ff. 154–56, Treasury minutes, July 22, 29, 1763.

[16] Chatham Papers, Public Record Office, 96, copy. In footnote references to the Chatham Papers the Arabic numeral refers to the bundle number in this collection. See Bibliography.

GEORGE III

mantle in the London Customs House, he asked a statement of the net produce for the past fifteen years of the duties of the chief Laws of Trade. Significantly enough, Jenkinson also asked for a statement of the amounts arising from the stamp tax in Great Britain. Moreover, in his search for sources of revenue, he did not neglect to consider the colonial postal system. It could have been a clever move since the American post existed already under imperial supervision, but the report of Anthony Todd of the London Post Office was discouraging.[17]

One result of Jenkinson's research was the Revenue Act of 1764, presented to the Committee of Supply in March, 1764. This act lowered the duty on molasses to three pence per gallon. Thus made more practical, the Molasses Act became perpetual. New duties were laid on foreign sugar, indigo, coffee, wines, silk, calicoes, cambric, and French lawns. It was thought that these would produce twenty-five thousand pounds a year, while the repeal of certain drawbacks was to save an additional twenty thousand pounds annually. Parliament's purpose was clearly stated in the act, it being considered just and necessary to raise a revenue from America for "defending, protecting, and securing the same."

Grenville by no means considered forty-five thousand pounds a year to be an adequate American contribution to the cost of her own defense. Part of the deficit was to be made up by extending the Mutiny Act to America. The colonists would then have to provide barracks for the troops and certain items of supply. Even so, a new and hitherto untapped source of funds was necessary.

[17] Add. MSS 38202, f. 23; printed in Jucker, *Jenkinson Papers*, 254, William Wood to Jenkinson, January 10, 1764. On the basis of Wood's report, Jenkinson calculated a revenue of £75,000 per annum on tea alone, should it be subjected to a tax of 1/- per pound. Colonial importations of foreign sugar (estimated at fifteen thousand hogsheads) when taxed at 2/6d. the hundredweight would yield £16,875 a year. Likewise, nine million gallons of molasses, the estimated annual importation, would, when taxed at a rate of 2d. per gallon, give £75,000 a year, all in all a total estimated revenue of £166,875. See Add. MSS 38335, ff. 223-24; ff. 66, 78, Anthony Todd to Jenkinson, January 28, February 2, 1764.

When the Revenue Act of 1764 had been presented to Parliament, Grenville had also stated that an extension of the Stamp Act to America might become necessary.[18] As early as 1722, an American stamp act had been suggested, and, periodically, the proposal had been renewed. In use in England since William III, it had been found to be an easy and self-executing device and one that did not require a large addition to the personnel of the customs. It had been suggested to Lord Halifax in 1757 by Henry McCulloh, and to Lord Bute by Governor Dinwiddie some years later. The idea of a stamp act for America was thus not a Grenville invention, but Grenville determined very early in his administration to investigate the practicability of its application to the American Colonies.

The Stamp Act of 1765 had its origin in a draft bill and a paper on the subject submitted to Jenkinson for Grenville's consideration by Henry McCulloh, formerly a political dependent of the Duke of Newcastle and an inveterate speculator in American land grants.[19] McCulloh, old and unemployed in 1763, was not unacquainted with the American Colonies. He had made three trips there and had twice held places in the colonial customs services, experience which gave some support to his pose as an expert in American affairs. While Jenkinson was deeply engaged upon his research into the problem of increasing the American revenue, McCulloh's second plan for an American stamp act arrived. This attempt to bring himself to the notice of government was unsolicited but opportune. Particularly attractive to both Jenkinson and Grenville must have been McCulloh's estimate that a stamp act would produce a revenue of £60,000 to £120,000 annually.[20] McCulloh soon

[18] Wm. Cobbett and J. Wright (eds.), *Parliamentary History*, XV, 1426. In his search for a revenue, Grenville did not overlook the West Indies. The 4½ per cent export duty was extended to the Ceded Islands, Granada, the Grenadines, Tobago, St. Vincent, and Dominica.

[19] For detailed information concerning McCulloh's land speculations, see Charles G. Sellers, Jr., "Private Profits and British Colonial Policy," *William and Mary Quarterly*, Third Series, Vol. VIII (1951), 535–51.

[20] W. J. Smith (ed.), *Grenville Papers*, II, 273–74.

found the principle of his bill approved and himself employed as a government consultant charged with the task of redrafting his proposed act more in accordance with the ideas of the ministry.

In autumn, 1763, he was given a colleague and a competitor for the dubious honor of writing the law which was to stir up such bitterness in the North American Colonies. The name of the second consultant has not come to light, but that he played an important role in the preparation of the American Stamp Act is clear.[21] In early September, Jenkinson ordered the two men to consult together "on a Plan for a general Stamp Law throughout America and the West Indies."[22] Work on a stamp act for the Colonies therefore proceeded simultaneously with Jenkinson's labors on the Molasses Act.

It was deemed expedient that McCulloh and his colleague work separately, only occasionally meeting for conferences. In October, Thomas Whately, Jenkinson's fellow secretary to the Treasury, replaced him as the immediate superior of the two consultants. Jenkinson's own work, no doubt, had become so heavy that it was felt wise to divide the labor on the American revenue. Soon McCulloh and his colleague were in disagreement on the nature of the act. McCulloh was the more optimistic, believing that an eventual revenue of £500,000 an-

[21] For detailed information concerning McCulloh's connection with the Stamp Act, see my "The Preparation of the Stamp Act," *William and Mary Quarterly*, Third Series, Vol. X (1953), 543–59. In this same article, I identified McCulloh's anonymous colleague as John Tabor Kempe, attorney-general of the province of New York. It has subsequently been established, however, that Kempe was not in England during the period of the preparation of the act, and therefore could not have been the second consultant. Kempe did, however, transmit to the home government an extensive list of legal documents, forms, etc., representing his suggestions of proper objects of taxation under the projected Stamp Act. See Add. MSS 36226, ff. 361–72. For the problem of the identification of the author of this document, see the article to which reference has been made.

[22] Add. MSS 35911, ff. 17–37, a bill for services rendered presented to the Treasury by the anonymous consultant and extending from September 8, 1763 to January, 1765.

nually could be derived from America.[23] The great point of difference, however, was in their plans for the disposal of the revenue to be raised. McCulloh favored application of such funds not only to the cost of colonial defense and presents to the Indians but also to the creation of a colonial civil list.[24]

No copy of the draft act written by McCulloh's anonymous colleague has been discovered, but both his and that of Mc-Culloh were considered by Grenville and the Treasury Board on November 19, 1763. McCulloh then had the mortification of seeing his own bill rejected as the basis for further work while that of his brother consultant was accepted. Apparently the latter's plan was more moderate than McCulloh's, and was, consequently, more in accord with Grenville's own views, namely, that the new revenue should be applied solely to the cost of colonial defense. The tremendous constitutional implications inherent in establishing a colonial civil list were thus avoided.

After the important meeting of the nineteenth, McCulloh's successful rival, conferring often with officials in the London Stamp Office, fell to work redrawing the bill, a task which engaged him for several months. Just as he was about to bring his bill to completion, however, he was informed, on March 10, 1764, that the Stamp Act would not be introduced during that session of Parliament. His work was accordingly halted.

The day before this surprising message was received, Grenville had presented his budget to the House of Commons. In his speech, he referred to the heavy cost of the recent war and to the reasonable expectation that America contribute to her own defense. The speech came as a surprise to many supporters of the ministry. During the winter, persistent and well-founded

[23] Add. MSS 36226, ff. 356–60, minutes of a conference with McCulloh, October 12, 1763.

[24] Add. MSS 35910, ff. 136–59, "A State of the several articles proposed by M. McCullo to be Stamp'd and Duties thereon." See also Add. MSS 35910, ff. 204–205, McCulloh's preamble to the Appropriation Clause.

rumors had suggested that a stamp act was in preparation and would be introduced with the budget. Now, however, Grenville contented himself with introducing the resolutions upon which the new version of the Molasses Act, the Revenue Act of 1764, was to be based. In addition, he merely announced that a stamp act for America might become necessary at some future date.

Underlying Grenville's hesitation to proceed with the Stamp Act must have been a conviction that the ministry possessed inadequate information concerning the application of a stamp act in America and a desire to wait until that lack could be remedied. Furthermore, in Grenville's own thinking, as well as in his talks with men conversant with American affairs— Richard Jackson; William Allen, chief justice of Pennsylvania, then visiting in London; John Huske, originally from New Hampshire but now a merchant in London and a Member of Parliament; and others—the great question of the constitutionality of a colonial stamp act must have arisen. Grenville well knew that the act was an innovation. It was therefore of the greatest moment that Grenville, strict constitutionalist that he was, put himself in an unimpeachable position. Before him was the British pattern: taxes imposed by the consent of the governed expressed through their representatives, the members of the House of Commons. Grenville must have hoped to extend a variation of that pattern to America. He postponed the Stamp Act, not only to receive more information from the Colonies, but also to give America an opportunity to express her consent through the various colonial legislatures.[25] A prece-

[25] Add. MSS 38202, f. 23, William Wood to Jenkinson, January 10, 1764, referred to above. Wood suggested a year's postponement of "every-[th]ing which may have been thought of respecting the Plantations" except continuing the Molasses Act, since "I conceive you want Information of several things from the Plantations, especially an 'Acc[oun]t what Duties are payable by an Act of Assembly.'" See further Royal Historical Manuscripts Commission Report (hereafter RHMCR.), *Knox Papers, Various Collections,* Governor Lyttelton to William Knox, July 22, 1764, 88–89. See also Huntington Library, Stowe Collection, Letterbook, "Copies of Letters that passed

dent of prior consultation with the Colonies in matters of imperial taxation would thus be established. It was not inconceivable that, in time, such a precedent could become as potent as that whereby the House of Commons in England had come to possess the power of the purse.

Unfortunately, Grenville allowed his position to become ambiguous. In his budget speech, he had stated that if the Colonists could suggest satisfactory alternatives to the Stamp Act, he would be glad to hear them.[26] The colonial agents immediately fastened upon this statement, and Grenville must have been chagrined, since it is clear that he had no expectation or desire that the Colonists would tax themselves for the imperial government. Certainly, they had never demonstrated in the past the spirit of co-operation necessary to carry through any common plan. When the colonial agents met with Grenville on May 17 and asked what propositions from the Colonies might be acceptable, Grenville, carefully refraining from repudiating his "offer," strongly stated his opinion that the Colonies would never co-operate in a scheme of self-taxation and recommended, as the most equitable and practicable means of a colonial contribution to the cost of their own defense, a stamp act passed with colonial consent.[27] His situation had indeed be-

between Mr. Whately, Secretary to the Treasury, and Mr. Temple, Surveyor General of the Customs in North America," Whately to Temple, June 8, 1764: "I shall be glad to hear what are the Sentiments of the Americans upon the New Taxes and what they think of a Stamp Duty, which was thought of but postponed to next Winter out of Regard to the Colonies to give them time to Consider of it. To Us it appears the most eligible of any, as being equal, extensive, not burthensome, likely to yield a considerable Revenue, and collected without a great number of officials." For an example of the home government's attempts to gain more information upon which to base the Stamp Act, see the Stowe Collection, Whately to Temple, August 14, 1764; and Add. MSS 36226, ff. 361–72. See also E. S. Morgan, "The Postponement of the Stamp Act," *William and Mary Quarterly*, Third Series, Vol. VII (1950), 353–92. Morgan's criticism of Grenville and his colleagues is unduly harsh.

[26] Cobbett and Wright, *Parliamentary History*, XV, 1426.

[27] Only two reports of the conference survive. One, written by Jasper Mauduit, agent for Massachusetts, and dated May 26, 1764, is printed in

come very awkward. What he must have seen initially as a highly satisfactory means of eliminating a constitutional anomaly—Parliament had no control over funds raised by requisitions—and of cultivating the goodwill of the Colonies by consulting with them had become a boomerang, laying him open to colonial charges of bad faith.

One result of this conference with the agents was to demonstrate to Grenville that his hope for an expression of colonial consent to the Stamp Act was a forlorn one. He stood pledged to the House, however, on the issue of an American revenue. There was no question of abandoning the plan. If the Colonies would not express their consent, then they would have to bow to an omnipotent Parliament. The question of the right of Parliament to tax the Colonies did not exist for Grenville. The Glorious Revolution had established the supremacy of Parliament; that Parliament itself, the guardian of the people's rights and the protector of the empire, might be thought tyrannical was a patent absurdity which needed no serious refutation.

Disappointed in his hope that the Stamp Act would be passed with American consent, Grenville took stock of his constitutional position. Long conversations with confidential friends such as Charles Jenkinson and Lord Mansfield, the eminent jurist, now followed. Indeed, his re-evaluation of the situation continued until July. Jenkinson then found it necessary to remind his chief that the summer was wearing on and that the time had come when definite steps for the introduction of the act had to be taken. Otherwise the ministry might have to bear the charge of neglect when Parliament reassembled in the autumn. On several occasions, Jenkinson forwarded memoranda to Grenville, wherein he argued powerfully in

Massachusetts Archives, XXII, 375. The other, by Charles Garth, agent for South Carolina, and dated June 5, is printed in the *English Historical Review*, Vol. LIV (1939), 646–48. Both are used extensively by Morgan, "Postponement of the Stamp Act," *William and Mary Quarterly*, Third Series, Vol. VII (1950), 353–92.

behalf of the expediency and justice of a stamp act and urged Grenville to order the drafting of a final bill.[28] Mansfield added his opinion that Parliament possessed the right to tax the Colonies. Moreover, any colony of a corporate or proprietary nature which claimed exemption from parliamentary taxation would have to base its contention upon the letters patent which had given it existence. Exemption for the royal colonies could be derived only from governors' commissions and instructions.[29]

It is when such arguments are compared with the American position that the essential conflict between Colonies and mother country comes to light. The views expressed by Mansfield and Jenkinson were legal and constitutionally unquestionable, but they failed to take into account the political evolution of the Colonies, a development not bound by statute books or formal parchments. There was love and affection for the mother country in the Colonies, but the sense of unity with Great Britain had already disappeared. British politicians presumed too much on a feeling which did not exist, refusing to recognize the unmistakable signs of a nascent American nationalism. The Colonies had already developed politically to the point where they considered self-government a right. They insisted upon investing their assemblies with the same sovereignty, within their individual borders, which the prototypic British Parliament possessed within the home islands. And they were determined to defend their stand upon the same grounds which British political thinkers had adduced in support of the Glorious Revolution.

It was not until shortly before the meeting of Parliament

[28] Add. MSS 38339, *passim*, and especially ff. 131–35, a paper of great value in demonstrating the wide gulf which had already developed between British and American views of the imperial relationship. It is summarized in C. R. Ritcheson, "Preparation of the Stamp Act," *William and Mary Quarterly*, Third Series, Vol. X, (1953), 543–59.

[29] Smith, *Grenville Papers*, II, 476–78, Mansfield to Grenville, December 24, 1764.

in autumn, 1764, that work on drafting the Stamp Act was resumed. Already grumblings had been heard from America. To the agents' notification of Grenville's plan, the Colonies returned answers differing in tone but agreeing in content. The Massachusetts Assembly warned that the goodwill and quiet of the Colonies would be endangered by a stamp act. Indeed, so far were they from taxing themselves for imperial purposes that they directed their agent to obtain a repeal of the Revenue Act of 1764. Their hint at united colonial action was unmistakable: "Measures will be taken, that you may be joined by all the other agents."[30] Grenville, sure of his constitutional position, was unperturbed.

Two months later, on December 6, 1764, Thomas Whately, using the sustained labors of his underlings as a basis, reported to a full meeting of the Treasury Board.[31] By-passing in one sentence the entire American argument, he declared that "a Stamp Act in the Colonies difers from those in England, only in the Rates with which the several Subjects of this Duty are to be charged, and in the mode of distributing the Stamps." Fully accepting the principle that stamp tax receipts should be applied solely to the cost of colonial defense, he further made a recommendation which was to be adopted in modified form in the final act. He proposed a graduated stamp duty on land grants in the Colonies, ranging from 6d. per 100 acres to 1/6d. for every grant of 320 acres. Certainly, the purpose of the tax was not to eliminate the westward movement. Whately admitted that the tax "does give some small check to the Settling of uncleared lands, which is directly contrary to the first Principles of Colonization," but, being a small duty, it would not

[30] Add. MSS 38202, f. 342, June 14, 1764, extracts.

[31] Add. MSS, 35910, ff. 310–23, copy. The administration of the act, Whately outlined as follows: The London Commissioners of the stamp duty would act as the administrative agency and would supply all stamps. Each colonial capital would have a head distributor who would possess authority to prosecute. Salaries would be a poundage of the amount collected. To insure smooth operation of the act, four traveling inspectors would be assigned to the Colonies.

hamper those who wanted grants of a reasonable size for the legitimate purpose of establishing new homes in the west. At the same time, it would give "some check" to the extravagant grants to speculators.

Whately's report was quickly approved by the Treasury Board, and during the remainder of the month, the final and formal act was drafted. Meantime, American reaction to the Revenue Act of 1764, while not violent, was annoying to the home government. There were colonial petitions asserting that Americans should not be taxed for revenue save by their own assemblies. This strengthened a growing conviction among British politicians that America's "absurdities" demanded firm action: The imperial Parliament should demonstrate in the most positive manner its right and authority to tax the Colonies.[32] In England, then, even before the Stamp Act had become law, a sentiment for "authoritarianism" had begun to form, and with it, the crisis which was to demonstrate how fragile were the ties binding mother country and Colonies.

As the time for parliamentary action approached, the colonial agents called upon Grenville once more in an attempt to "ward off the intended blow."[33] Again, Grenville asserted the absolute necessity of American financial aid to the mother country and his belief that this could best be accomplished by a stamp act. When the agents suggested that the old requisition system be employed, Grenville, to underscore the impracticability of that method, asked the agents if they could agree upon the proportions which each colony would pay. In conclusion, he vigorously denied any intention of undermining the power of the colonial assemblies: it was simply that the au-

[32]RHMCR. *Weston Papers*, 82, Edward Sedgwick to Edward Weston, February 14 and 28, 1765.

[33] Reports of the conference were written by Charles Garth and Jared Ingersoll. For that of the former, see *English Historical Review*, Vol. LIV (1939), 649. That of the latter is printed in the *Collections of the Connecticut Historical Society*, XVIII, 324-25. Both are used extensively by Morgan, "Postponement of the Stamp Act," *William and Mary Quarterly*, Third Series, Vol. X (1953).

thority of those assemblies did not reach to matters of common imperial defense.

On March 22, 1765, the Stamp Act passed the House of Commons without noticeable opposition. Pitt was ill, and the Newcastle Whigs did not oppose. The bill, scheduled to take effect on November 1, soon became law. By mid-April, Jenkinson was able to report to Grenville that he had devised a plan "for remitting the American Revenue" between the receiver general of the customs and those contracting to send the pay of the troops to North America. It would therefore be unnecessary to send American specie out of the Colonies. Henry McCulloh, too, was helping to put the final touches to the new plan by assisting the Board of Commissioners of the Stamp Office in London to proportion the stamps and to fix a security for them.[34]

In England, the framers of the act congratulated themselves on America's quiet reception of it. Early in May, Benjamin Hallowell, customs officer in Boston, had written an optimistic letter, and Jenkinson gleefully passed it on to Grenville, adding that it "shews that our Firmness here has got the better of the Obstinacy of the Colonies and that all there will end well." Grenville, however, cautiously sent word that he himself was not so certain that there would be no difficulty "in that part of America."[35] He was wise to wait. On May 29, the Virginia House of Burgesses in its famous Resolves expressed the American position of unconditional opposition to the Stamp Act which rode so roughshod over their doctrine of internal and external taxation.

When judged in the light of subsequent events, Grenville's decision to tax America "internally" was fatal. At the time, however, the equity and justice of it was generally conceded

---

[34] Add. MSS 38204, f. 166, John Brettely, secretary to the Board of the Stamp Commissioners, to Jenkinson, March 26, 1765.

[35] Add. MSS 38305, f. 11, June 19, 1765; printed in Jucker, *Jenkinson Papers*, 364–65. Add. MSS 38204, f. 285, Charles Lloyd, Grenville's secretary, to Jenkinson.

in England. Grenville had faced the tremendous problem of creating an orderly empire. The North American Colonies he proposed to tax to help provide for their own defense. Westward expansion under imperial supervision was to be allowed, the Indian rights being carefully and amicably extinguished beforehand. Nor was Canada neglected. A plan had been drawn which included Roman Catholic toleration. But by June, it was obvious that Grenville was falling. The Lord Chancellor, Northington, now intriguing against his former colleagues, curtly told Lord Sandwich, who had sent him the plan, that he could not "think this Plan for an established Roman Catholic Church in the Province of Quebec either approvable or practicable."[36]

Grenville's answer to the imperial problem had been comprehensive and in keeping with the British Constitution of his time. His attempt to find an American revenue, however, raised the question of the right of parliamentary taxation of the Colonies, a question which was increasingly to supplant the problem which Grenville had tried to solve.

The taxation of America for revenue represents one terminal of a process of change in British imperial thinking. Under the pressure of American resistance and revolution, British politicians eventually receded from the static and ultimately disastrous position of a proprietary empire consisting of a supreme center and subordinate parts. The belief in the unquestioned authority of Parliament to legislate for, and to tax, the Colonies was to give way, in the course of only thirteen years, to an offer of what amounted to "home rule" or "dominion status" for them. The true impact of the American problem on British politics must therefore be sought in this line of development.

Meantime, on the domestic political scene, the beginnings of coherent lines of "party" were in evidence. New groupings

[36] Hinchingbrooke Papers, Lord Northington to Lord Sandwich, June 9, 1765.

were emerging from the splinters of the Old Whig party. The alliance of Grenville, Bedford, the King, and their friends was becoming the seedbed of a new Tory party, although it was not to come to fruition for many decades.

The consolidation of the alliance was to be a hectic process. Bute had brought Grenville to power to be used as a tool in helping the King set himself at the head of the Old Whig system of patronage, although the King would have it that he was merely trying to resume those powers which the Old Whigs had snatched from the first two Georges. Both Bute and the King soon learned, however, that the tedious, boring lecturer was as much a Whig as Newcastle ever had been. He himself demanded the monopoly of patronage, stating that otherwise it would be impossible to control the House of Commons. By July, then, the King and Bute were attempting to displace Grenville. They were to fail disastrously.

When Egremont died in August, 1763, a ministerial reshuffle became necessary. The King and Bute seized this opportunity to make overtures to Pitt, and were answered with demands that the Grenville Ministry be completely overturned, that Pitt and the Newcastle Whigs—with whom he was temporarily in alliance—be given carte blanche, and that those responsible for the Peace of 1763 be absolutely proscribed. This last demand was especially unfortunate for the Opposition, since it threw the Duke of Bedford wholeheartedly into the arms of the ministry. He himself became lord president of the Council, while his friend Sandwich was promoted to the vacant secretaryship of state. Grenville, offended by Bute's and the King's intrigue, refused to continue in office unless the Scot should be removed from the King's presence. Hatred of Bute and all irresponsible advisers was in the future to furnish a strong ground for union between Bedford and Grenville.

In the reshuffle, the King's Friends received more offices. Lord Egmont took the Admiralty; Hillsborough became first lord of trade; and a few others were given minor places. The struggle for control of patronage now became a three-sided one between the King, Grenville, and Bedford. Quarrels became so warm that serious trouble appeared inevitable. A dramatic event was to force them into union.

On April 19, 1763, the King closed the spring session of Parliament with a speech in praise of the Treaty of Paris. Four days later, John Wilkes, a Member of Parliament, published his *North Briton*, No. 45, charging the ministers with putting a lying speech into the King's mouth, castigating the general inadequacy of the terms of peace, and condemning the promotion to high office of Scots and Jacobites. He ended his tirade with a declaration of the responsibility of the King to the people. It was a daring insult to the King and his ministers, and they, thinking it would be a popular point, decided to punish Wilkes. Lord Halifax immediately issued a general warrant under which forty-nine persons, Wilkes among them, were arrested. The affair from the ministerial side became a series of blunders, and Wilkes, cleverly utilizing all the engines of propaganda, quickly turned the contest into an attack of the prerogative of the Crown upon the privileges of Parliament.

The ministers' persecution of Wilkes culminated in his expulsion from the House of Commons in January, 1764, both Houses having pusillanimously voted that parliamentary privilege did not extend to writing or publishing seditious libels. The culprit had fled to France, but this did not prevent the Court of King's Bench declaring him to be an outlaw.

The significance of the Wilkes affair was that the harshness of the ministry served to make this reprobate the darling of the London mob, provided the Opposition with a promising issue, and set the ministry in opposition to the people. Much as the case embarrassed Grenville and his colleagues, however, it acted as a unifying factor within the cabinet. Petty squabbles over patronage ceased, or at least moderated, and the ministry, firmly supported by the King, turned a united front to the public and to the Opposition from whom they expected a formidable attack. A deeper meaning is to be attached to the Wilkes affair. Causing tumult and unrest on the domestic scene, it was to join with events in America to produce in British political circles a new conservatism. The King had come to loathe Grenville and Bedford, but eventually he was to find in a union of their friends with his own the safest harbor in the gathering storm.

Among the Opposition, Pitt had forgiven Newcastle's desertion of 1761 when their forces had joined to attack the budget in March, 1763. From the first, however, both Newcastle Whigs and Pitt saw the weakness of the alliance. A number of points were rankling with Pitt. The Newcastle Whigs' desire to diminish the military establishment, and their intimacy with the Duke of Cumberland, Pitt's old enemy, disturbed the Great Commoner. Further, as a result of Pontiac's rebellion, Pitt was turning his mind increasingly to America and was determined—if he came to power—to effect "the settlement of our colonies upon a proper foot with regard to themselves and their mother country."[37] He was uncertain and doubtful of Old Whig co-operation on this score. Several Old Whigs, particularly the younger group, were also dubious about the long duration of the alliance. Rockingham, for instance, reported himself as "flustered" when Pitt requested his presence in London to advise concerning the negotiations with the King in August.[38]

In such a state, the Wilkes affair should have been a godsend to the Opposition, affording an opportunity to unite firmly among themselves and with the public in support of parliamentary privilege and against general warrants. Unfortunately, it was not to be so; the Wilkes affair put a strain upon the Pitt-Newcastle alliance from which it never fully

[37] Quoted by Basil Williams, *The Life of William Pitt*, II, 160.

[38] RHMCR. *Savile-Foljambe Papers*, 144–45, Rockingham to Sir George Savile, August 28, 1763.

recovered. Initial unanimity was prevented since the Old Whig Charles Yorke, who preferred to hold his office rather than resign with his colleagues, still acted as attorney general. He had been consulted by Halifax before the general warrant had been issued, and had given a favorable opinion on its legality. This position Yorke now refused to abandon, although great pressure from Newcastle was to bring him soon to resign his post.

At the bottom of the friction between Pitt and Newcastle's group was the question of leadership, the Old Whigs feeling keenly Pitt's attempts to dictate to them. Failure to co-ordinate measures in the autumn session of 1763, when Pitt flew to the attack on the ministry's handling of the Wilkes affair, nearly led to the breakdown of the alliance then and there. In the succeeding session, Pitt was able to lead a united Opposition in an assault against general warrants, at one point cutting government majorities to ten and fourteen, but this was the high-water mark. His health failing under the great strain, Pitt retired to a sickbed. Some Old Whigs, notably Charles Townshend and Charles Yorke, promptly began to put out feelers to the government. Furthermore, during Pitt's absence, Grenville violently attacked his conduct and finance of the war. None rose to defend him. Pitt never forgave Newcastle for this second desertion, and the same session which saw a united Opposition almost overturning the ministry saw Pitt declare himself unconnected. In the future, the Old Whigs were to seek Pitt's advice and leadership in vain. Old Newcastle could only moan, "Let them say what they will, Mr. Grenville, I say, will have *champ libre.*"[39]

At the beginning of the New Year, however, both Grenville and Bedford found their positions extremely irksome. They feared the revival of the struggle over general warrants; the Attorney and Solicitor Generals had raised a minor crisis

---

[39] Earl of Albemarle (ed.), *Rockingham Memoirs*, I, 181–82, Newcastle to Rockingham, March 26, 1765.

GEORGE GRENVILLE

by allowing the order extending the 4½ per cent export duty to the Ceded Islands to pass under the Great Seal, and then raising doubts concerning the legality of the action.[40] Furthermore, Grenville was suspicious of his colleagues; and he was well aware of the King's cold dislike for him.

A new pitfall lay ahead. In February and March, 1765, the King suffered his first attack of insanity. Upon his recovery, he made known his desire that a Bill of Regency be prepared to insure the orderly carrying-on of government in case of another attack. Grenville, Halifax, and Sandwich, who took the lead in drawing the bill, were temperamentally incapable of exercising the great tact necessary in such a task. The King, already determined to rid himself of the ministers at the earliest possible moment, was hypercritical and took no pains to conceal his hostility. In May, therefore, after an apparently gratuitous insult to the King's mother who was excluded from the list of possible regents, George III authorized his uncle, Cumberland, to begin negotiations with Pitt.

Difficult months lay ahead for the young sovereign. Grenville's group—for he had accumulated one during his years in office, men such as William Knox, Thomas Whately, Lord Buckinghamshire, and Soame Jenyns—stood firmly united with the Bedfords. They had found their union in the Wilkes affair; it was confirmed by the weight of the royal displeasure. When Pitt refused to come into office, the King had no choice but to recall the old ministry upon their own terms. The humiliation for George III was too great to be borne, and although Grenville and Bedford had returned to office, there was no return of the royal confidence. The King was even more hostile toward the ministry than before. On June 12, the Duke of Bedford, having strongly remonstrated with the King, left London. Two days later, Grenville, too, retired to the country, and the King, rightly or wrongly, considered the ministry in

[40] Add. MSS 38191, ff. 81–82; printed in Jucker, *Jenkinson Papers*, 319–20, Grenville to Jenkinson, August 19, 1764.

a state of resignation. Once more he turned to Pitt, but it was only a gesture. Already he was writing of "those worthy Men, Ld. Rockingham, the Dukes of Grafton, Newcastle, and others," men who possessed "principles and therefore cannot approve of seeing the Crown dictated to by low men." Already he was hoping that they would "join amicably the few persons that have zealously stood by Me, and that the World will see that this Country is not at that low Ebb that no Administration can be formed without the Greenville family."[41]

On Wednesday, July 10, Grenville had his last audience of the King. Declaring that the new ministry would be "a total subversion of every act of the former," he warned the King that he was prepared to defend his measures in Parliament, especially since none of them had been undertaken without the King's approbation. Particularly was this true of "the regulations concerning the colonies." In that last interview, Grenville, with characteristic bluntness, advised George III "as he valued his own safety" not to allow anyone "to separate or draw the line between his British and American dominions" since the Colonies were "the richest jewel of his Crown." Should anyone try "to defeat the regulations laid down for the Colonies, by a slackness in the execution," Grenville would consider him "a criminal and the betrayer of his country."[42]

Grenville and his allies knew the chief point upon which their administration was to be arraigned. His last speech to the King indicated that for Grenville, America had become the touchstone of politics. There was no hesitation among the outgoing ministers concerning opposition as there had been with Newcastle. Halifax, Sandwich, and Grenville conferred at once, and their sentiment was stated by Sandwich when he declared to the Bedfordite Richard Rigby that the country "must

[41] Sir John Fortescue (ed.), *Correspondence of George III*, I, No. 88, the King to Cumberland.
[42] Smith, *Grenville Papers*, III, 215–16.

be governed by Combinations of People," a maxim of conduct out of office as well as in.[43]

Colonial reaction to the Stamp Act was forming. There had already been ominous indications. The American problem was about to enter British politics, dividing party from party, making old political divisions deeper, and cutting new ones just as deep.

[43] Hinchingbrooke Papers, Sandwich to Rigby, October 28, 1763.

CHAPTER TWO

THE YEAR OF THE
OLD WHIGS

THE American problem had assumed acute form during the ministry of George Grenville, whose vision of empire first brought that problem to a head. From his concept of a "supreme centre and subordinate parts," a retreat was now forced upon the government. The Old Whigs, who succeeded Grenville, were to seek to bring quiet by appeasing British merchant interests—interests which coincided for the moment with the colonial position. Their temporary success would not, however, represent a reversal of Grenville's basic maxim. Indeed, with the Declaratory Act, they were to give it official sanction in a very positive manner.

William Pitt refused to come to the aid of the King in his struggle to be free of his Grenville-Bedford captors. Fighting hard to maintain his independence, George III now turned unwillingly to the Old Whigs for deliverance: In July, 1765, the young, amiable, but ungifted Marquis of Rockingham led into office the inheritors of the Pelham "present system." Meanwhile the Old Whig group was in a process of transformation. Younger men who lacked experience in the art of government were assuming the lead, and old Newcastle found himself relegated to the position of a respected nuisance.

Both in point of number and of abilities the ministry was weak. Rockingham took the Treasury. The fickle and unsteady General Conway undertook to lead the House of Commons as secretary of state for the Northern Department. William

Dowdeswell, formerly of Tory connections but long since a mainstay of the Old Whigs, became chancellor of the exchequer. The great "Revolution families" were well represented, and Newcastle took office for the last time in his long career as lord privy seal. Lacking number and talent themselves, the Old Whigs were obliged to fill some vacancies with the King's Friends. Egmont took the Admiralty; Barrington became secretary at war. Moreover, Rockingham and his associates represented the King's necessity, not his wish, and it was generally supposed that their administration would be short lived. Sir Grey Cooper, for instance, refused to engage as secretary of the Treasury until he had secured a pension to commence when he should lose his place. And yet despite such gloom the Old Whigs were pleased because they had held together in the wilderness and had taken office as a party.

From the beginning it was evident that Pitt's attitude toward the new ministry would be decisive. A powerful Opposition was to be faced; and not much trust could be placed in the King's Friends. Outside support was thus imperative. Newcastle observed that "the world is running mad again about Mr. Pitt,"[1] and so the Old Whigs now made every effort to court his favor. Indeed, they had come into office with no set policy save that which Pitt would dictate. At a meeting on July 6, ministerial leaders decided "as far as It shall appear proper, and practicable To follow Mr. Pitt's plan" put forward in his recent interviews with the King.[2] The new administration in its construction was to be made "as palatable to Mr. Pitt, and as agreeable, as possible, to His Notions and Ideas." Since Pitt had intended the Duke of Grafton to serve

[1] Wentworth-Woodhouse, Rockingham Papers, Newcastle to Rockingham, July 12, 1765.

[2] Pitt's program included the formation of alliances with Prussia and Russia to contain the House of Bourbon; a parliamentary declaration against general warrants; a restitution of those removed from office because of their votes in Parliament, especially military officers; and a demonstration that Bute had no influence with the new administration by a removal of his chief friends from their places.

39

with him as secretary of state, this young and untalented nobleman was to be given that office and instructed "To keep up
His Correspondence with Mr. Pitt." He was to make certain
that Pitt knew the ministry was executing his own proposals.
Never before had men come into office with so weak a plan.
So eager was Newcastle to gain Pitt's support that, aware of
the latter's personal hostility toward him, he offered to resign
all claim to office, truly a great sacrifice for one who loved
so much the pomp, the circumstance, and power of office.[3]

As a further gesture toward the Great Commoner, his
friend Charles Pratt, the judge who had won his admiration
by an uncompromising stand against general warrants, was
made a peer and, as Lord Camden, called to the cabinet. A
second Pitt supporter, Thomas Nuthall, became solicitor to
the Treasury. Advances were made to other Pittites, particularly to Isaac Barré and Shelburne, but they held aloof, letting
it be known that they would regulate their conduct by the
measures of the ministry.

Formation of the new government lasted through July.
It was not until August 7 that the new Lord Camden could
report to Pitt that the ministry was "at last upon its legs." But
he wondered who would "steal fire from Heaven" and give it
animation.[4] Nursing a hope that Pitt would be their Prome-
theus, and sustained by fear of Grenville, the Old Whigs
waited for events to fix their course in Parliament.

By August, Anglo-American relations had reached a critical stage. In that month, the Virginia Resolves, an "alarm
Bell to the disaffected," were widely known in England. Serious rioting had broken out, especially in Boston, when the
names of the stamp distributors had been published. It was
also learned that Massachusetts had invited her sister colonies
to a general congress to consider the state of affairs arising
from the mother country's attempt to enforce the Stamp Act.

[3] Wentworth-Woodhouse, Rockingham Papers, minutes of July 6, 1765;
and also Newcastle to Albemarle, July 3, 1765.

It was with something like satisfaction that the Old Whigs viewed the storm now rising in America. Ever fearful of Grenville and the Opposition, they believed that these disorders would wholly discredit Grenville, and give color to their picture of him as a willful disrupter of the empire. "I don't imagine," wrote Rockingham to a Yorkshire friend, "Mr. G. Greenville's popularity is very high in your neighbourhood. The difficulties he has thrown upon trade by very inconsiderate regulations must affect any opinion in his favour among the mercantile gentlemen, and the notable confusion which he has raised in America, tho' it lays difficulties upon the present administration, yet so far it serves them, as it shows that he had neither prudence or foresight."[5] Under pressure, then, of convulsions in the Colonies, faced with an increasingly anti-American Opposition—which they longed to discredit—and still courting the favor of Pitt, Rockingham's administration now turned its attention perforce to colonial affairs.

Certainly, the Old Whigs could not be called "pro-American" at the outset. In September, they decided that the Virginia Resolves and the proceedings of the Massachusetts Assembly were "of too high a Nature" for the Privy Council and determined to lay the papers before Parliament itself. The action of Virginia they condemned as an "absolute Disavowal of the Right of the Parliament of Great Britain to impose Taxes upon the Colonies and a daring attack upon the Constitution of this Country." Such words might well have come from Grenville himself. In October, after Governor Bernard's report on the Boston riots, the Privy Council commanded that the governors, the Admiralty, and the secretary at war take all measures to maintain the honor and safety of the government. As it was admitted that the civil power might be inadequate, each governor was told he could apply to the com-

[4] Smith, *The Grenville Papers*, III, 77.
[5] RHMCR. *Lindley Wood Papers, Various Collections*, 183, to Lord Irwin.

manders-in-chief in America for military aid.[6] Thus there might have been a clash of arms; and the Revolution might have begun much earlier than it did.

Parliament would not meet until December. Meanwhile, the disorders in America grew more violent. Stamp distributors were intimidated and forced to resign; the stamps were impounded and destroyed. Radical organizations, the "Sons of Liberty," began to form throughout the Colonies. They had considerable success in inducing colonial merchants to give up British imports.[7] The absence of stamped paper rendered legal proceedings technically void, and many courts now closed. This in turn distressed British creditors who could no longer sue for the recovery of debts. In October, the Stamp Act Congress met at New York. However, the moderate tone of their resolutions and petitions proved that the radicals were not yet in command. Protesting their affection for the King and acknowledging "all due subordination" to Parliament, the Congress argued that the colonists possessed all the rights and exemptions of Englishmen: they could not be taxed but through their own assemblies. Great Britain's monopoly of her trade, it was asserted, was America's sufficient contribution to the expense of empire. Not yet, then, had the Colonies been driven to refuge in the laws of nature, although that doctrine had already had classic statement in America.[8] Still willing to submit to external taxes for the regulation of trade, they based their denial of Britain's right to tax them for revenue upon the British Constitution.

[6] Grant and Munro, *Acts of the Privy Council*, IV, 729–33.

[7] During the year of disturbance, American imports fell from £3,000,000 to half that amount. See E. Channing, *History of the United States*, III, 65, footnote. See also RHMCR. *Bathurst Papers*, 146–47, William Crawle to Lord Huntington, January 16, 1766, wherein Crawle quotes Lord Dartmouth as declaring in a House of Lords debate that "not less than 50,000 men in this kingdom were at this time ripe for rebellion for want of work, from the uneasy situation in the colonies."

[8] See James Otis, "The Rights of the British Colonies," and Daniel Dulaney, "Considerations," printed in extract in S. E. Morison, *Sources and Documents*, 4–9, and 24–32.

Despite these relatively mild words, the violence in America seemed to indicate impending revolution. The moderate John Dickinson wrote to Pitt from Philadelphia, warning him that the disorders were not to be taken lightly. The Revenue Act of 1764 had been "extremely disgusting and afflicting; though a high Veneration for the august Authority" which had imposed it had induced the Americans to accept it. The Stamp Act, however, had united them in a will to defend their invaded liberty. American dependence could be maintained only while affection for the mother country was unimpaired. The colonists would never regard the superintending of trade as a grievance; but the Stamp Act, an internal tax, must be repealed at once if their love were to continue.[9]

Governor Bernard, reporting from Boston, moaned that the home administration had failed to heed his advice of a year ago: wholesale reforms in the colonial governments were urgent and should have been made before "the Business of Finances." His warning was ominous. Defining the essence of the growing conflict, he stated, "In Britain the American Governments are considered as Corporations empowered to make by-Laws, existing only during the Pleasure of Parliament. . . . In America they claim . . . to be perfect States, not otherwise dependent upon Great Britain than by having the same King." The question was no longer "whether there shall be a Stamp Act or not; but whether America shall or shall not be Subject to the Legislature of Great Britain."[10] Colonial theorists were moving rapidly toward what can only be termed a "federal" concept of the imperial relation, wherein colonies were bound to Great Britain through the symbol of the Crown alone. Such a solution was, however, to remain in the realm of the impossible until the modern British party system had developed.

[9] Chatham Papers, 97, Dickinson to Pitt, December 21, 1765.
[10] Channing and Coolidge, *Barrington-Bernard Correspondence*, 93–102, Governor Bernard to Lord Barrington, November 23, 1765. For a confirmation of Bernard's assertion of the developing American view of the imperial relationship, see Jared Sparks (ed.), *Franklin's Works*, IV, 206–10.

Only then could a "commonwealth of nations" emerge, because the person of the sovereign had been removed from the center of domestic politics and had become a symbol in whom self-governing commonwealths could find their union. Just as British demands for an American revenue cut across the lines of internal political development in the Colonies, so did American assertions that they owed allegiance to the King and not to Parliament violate the sacred settlement of 1688.

In Great Britain it was generally perceived that a crisis in Anglo-American relations was at hand—and this at a time when the ministry was singularly weak and confused. Fearing hasty and ill-considered action, the King believed it to be "the most serious matter that ever came before Parliament."[11] The Grenville-Bedford group, convinced that the Old Whigs intended to repeal the Stamp Act, were intent on frustrating any such concession to "rebels." Even moderate Members to whom America had hitherto been but a name were alarmed at events and distrustful of Old Whig ability to cope with them. A new member of the government itself, the notorious Lord George Sackville—whose sins at Minden had been washed clean by the new King—was writing of America, "The Spirit that rages there is beyond conception. God only knows how it will end, for as yet I have heard no human reasoning that promises a happy issue to it."[12]

With America in flames, the weak Rockingham Ministry had now to face a domestic crisis which threatened its existence. As the opening of Parliament—in December—drew near, the Old Whigs, aware that Pitt's attitude could make or break them, were driven to measures of near desperation to gain his support. The Great Commoner was at Bath, however, and lashing out bitterly at Newcastle, he refused every overture. He was now increasingly loath to associate himself with any

[11] Albemarle, *Rockingham Memoirs*, I, 256–57, the King to General Conway, December 5, 1765.

[12] RHMCR. *Stopford-Sackville Papers*, I, 103, letter of December 23, 1765.

political group. It was not alone his animosity and suspicion of Newcastle. He had begun to recur to an earlier day when Walpole and the Pelhams had called down hell-fire upon "faction," and when Bolingbroke, taking them at their word, had called for a coalition of all persuasions in a truly national government around a "Patriot King." Already then, in 1765, Pitt, the supreme egotist, confident in his own great power, had begun to see himself the unifier of the nation, the extirpator of "faction." His persistent refusal to work with the Rockingham Ministry foreshadowed the "mosaic ministry" of 1766. In this attitude he was to find a solitary point of union with the King; but he was to make two cardinal errors when finally he was called upon to do what he had advocated. He was to underestimate the deep, dividing power of those principles which had entered politics since the accession of George III. Secondly, in his attempt to heal the divisions caused by Wilkes and America, he was to overestimate his own strength, political and physical. The turbulent sea from which, in years to come, the modern British party system would emerge was not so early to subside even at Pitt's command.

Pitt's aloofness shook the hopes of the Old Whigs, but it also disappointed the Opposition, who had hoped to draw him into alliance. They, too, failed to understand the growing importance of the American issue, which was solidifying the right wing of politics.[13] This process was soon to bring Pitt's brother-in-law and Grenville's brother, Lord Temple, into the conservative camp; but it was to drive Pitt to the left, separating him from them forever.

Grenville knew the course he must pursue at the opening of Parliament, and he exhorted Bedford to mobilize their friends for the event. Their working alliance intact, and believing that the ministry would push for a repeal of the Stamp

---

[13] Hinchingbrooke Papers, Sandwich to Augustus Hervey, August 11, 1765. See also Lord John Russell (ed.), *Bedford Correspondence*, III, 315–17, Sandwich to Bedford, August 26, 1765.

Act, Grenville and Bedford resolved to stun them by an early and violent onslaught. They had, however, misjudged the administration. The Old Whigs, preoccupied with gaining urgently needed support in Parliament, had actually reached no decision at all about the American crisis.

The question of their outside support grew ever more acute. Pitt had spurned their advances. Even unattached Members such as Lord North, half-brother of Dartmouth, president of the Board of Trade, would have naught of them. Furthermore, Paymaster Charles Townshend, miffed because he had not been made leader of the Commons, persistently declined to use his talents for their effective support. True, Sackville had accepted the office of vice treasurer of Ireland, a minor post. While he himself was pathetically pleased at "once more belonging to Court," even Newcastle was "very Doubtful" about the wisdom of his appointment. It would serve, he feared, further to alienate Pitt whose contempt for Sackville's behavior at the Battle of Minden was unabated. Furthermore, the King's Friends were ominously reserved.

In his necessity, Rockingham turned to the merchants of the country for that support which Pitt had refused him. Since the close of the Seven Years' War, there had been a steady increase in the political strength of those merchants with interests in the American and West Indian trade. In 1761, fifty or fifty-one merchants held seats in the Commons. At least ten of these had active American connections. About twenty-one or twenty-two, the "Jamaica cousinhood," had West Indian interests.[14] All were naturally concerned in questions relating to colonial trade. As long as the Laws of Trade and Navigation were enforced, all were eager to preserve friendly relations with the Colonies. Actually, they had more influence than the fifty-odd votes they commanded, for commercial considerations tempted Members from all larger urban constitu-

[14] Namier, *The Structure of Politics*, I, 61; *England in the Age of the American Revolution*, 277.

encies to vote with them.[15] What tended to dissipate this strength was that the aims of the American and the West Indian groups often diverged. Indeed, they sometimes came into violent conflict, as in the controversy over retention of Canada or the French Sugar Islands during negotiation of the Peace of Paris. Now, however, Rockingham found them united. Merchants trading to North America desired peaceable relations in order to restore trade and collect their debts. The West Indian group, fearing the effect of colonial nonimportation—and nonexportation of essential victual supplies—were equally desirous of placating the Americans.

The discontented merchants represented, then, Rockingham's best hope of survival. Parliament had ever shown itself solicitous for their welfare, and would now be apt to heed their complaints. By courting such support, however, the Old Whigs showed themselves determined to avoid the deep constitutional issues of the American problem. Fundamentally, they were to demonstrate that regarding Parliament's right to tax the Colonies, no great difference separated them from Grenville. Far more were they divided from Pitt, who was soon to deny the competence of Parliament to lay internal taxes.

As early as mid-November, the Lords of the Treasury had received memorials from mercantile and manufacturing centers throughout the kingdom: Bristol, Manchester, Liverpool, Lancaster, and many others. Rockingham and his colleagues were told that "the Export Trade of these Kingdoms has lately suffered a great and sudden Diminution and Stagnation." The American combinations against British trade were increasing their distress, and they begged for relief.[16]

To capitalize better on the distress of the merchants, Rockingham now began a series of conferences with their leaders in London. Prominent among them were Barlow Trecothick, William Beckford of Fonthill, and Stephen and Rose Fuller,

[15] Namier, *The Structure of Politics*, II, 80.
[16] Chatham Papers, 83. Treasury minutes.

all Members of Parliament possessing large interests in the American and West Indian trade. Rockingham's immediate object was to organize their discontent so that it might be brought more forcibly to bear upon Parliament as a whole. In so doing, he was to demonstrate a technique which the Old Whigs were to perfect in 1780, when a flood of petitions would threaten to engulf the North Ministry.

A committee of twenty-eight London merchants was quickly organized to agitate among their colleagues throughout the country. Leaving nothing to chance, Rockingham and Trecothick drafted an appeal from the committee addressed to merchants in all major ports and manufacturing towns. An open bid for their support, the letter declared, "The present State of the British Trade to North America, and the prospect of encreasing Embarrassments which threaten the Loss of our depending prosperity there as well as to annihilate the Trade itself have occasioned a general meeting to be called of the Merchants of this City concerned in that Branch of Business." Because the merchants of other cities must be suffering also, the London group asked their concurrence and assistance "in Support of a regular application to Parliament, or otherwise by a petition from your Body and all the Interest you can make with your Members [of Parliament] in your Neighbourhood. ... We desire to unite with you in a measure so essential to the best Interests of Great Britain ... it being our Opinion, that conclusive Arguments for granting every Ease or Advantage the North Americans can with propriety desire, may be fairly deduced from that principle only."[17] Rockingham thus made it clear that measures undertaken for the relief of British trade should not be viewed as concessions to the Americans.

Response to Rockingham's and Trecothick's letter was not

[17] Wentworth-Woodhouse, Rockingham Papers, December 6, 1765. Only Burke's endorsement calling the letter "the principal Instrument in the happy repeal of the Stamp Act" is printed in Albemarle, *Rockingham Memoirs*, I, 319.

long in coming, and revealed a genuine concern among commercial circles. Sir William Meredith, formerly a Tory, but baptized anew under the Old Whigs, wrote exultingly to a newcomer on the political stage, Edmund Burke: "I am just come from Manchester and am happy to tell you that Mr. Pitt was never more popular than Lord Rockingham and the present administration. T'is the same at Liverpool and all over this country."[18] The appeal to the merchants, however, had come too late to have any considerable effect before the opening of Parliament, but events were to play into the hands of the administration.

Although the ministry had formed no definite American policy before Parliament opened on December 17, the King in the speech from the throne referred to recent "matters of importance" in the Colonies. These, he said, demanded the serious attention of Parliament. New advices were expected daily, and of these Parliament would be at once informed. Battle lines were promptly drawn. Scarcely allowing the ministers to move their loyal address, Grenville lunged to the attack, indignant at so mild a reference to the "outrages" in America. For him, he declared, the colonial actions were rebellion, and he moved an amendment to the address calling them such. No serious test of strength was at hand, however. Grenville had given up his premeeting plan to stun the ministry by an initial defeat. Success would have depended upon the support of at least a large portion of the King's Friends. Many of them were to be with Grenville in the crucial vote on the repeal of the Stamp Act, but now, at the outset of the session, they refused to oppose the King's government. Grenville consequently withdrew his motion. It was significant, however, that two members of the government, Charles Townshend and Lord George Sackville, while speaking against Grenville's motion, had declared strongly in favor of the execution of the Stamp Act. The ministers could take some comfort from the uncom-

18 Wentworth-Woodhouse, Burke Papers, December 11, 1765.

promising stand which Pitt's friend George Cooke had taken against Grenville. Furthermore, Shelburne, in the House of Lords, had led the defense of the government, strongly combating the application of the term "rebels" to the Americans, and falling in with Rockingham's plan to consider the Stamp Act "in a commercial view."[19]

This pre-Christmas meeting of Parliament, though short, was important. The ministry had come through it unscathed, but the Opposition had shown "a great deal of factious ability." Bedford and Grenville had been aided by Temple, who had joined with them "on the principle of strongly asserting the rights of the English parliament over America."[20] Indeed, many Members had concluded that America would not be content to question the right of the mother country to lay internal taxes. She would also deny the supreme authority of Parliament in other spheres. Thus early arose a conviction that America aimed at independence. This was in turn to lead to measures which finally would drive the Americans themselves to embrace it.[21]

Reassured of Pitt's attitude, somewhat easier about the King's Friends, and awaiting the petitions of the merchants, Rockingham and his brother ministers set about the formation of a concrete American policy. Indeed, Newcastle and Sir George Savile had been urging such action since October. But it was only now that Rockingham called together the Old Whig leaders, Newcastle excepted, to discuss American measures. Conway, Dartmouth, Charles Yorke, Dowdeswell, Rock-

[19] Cobbett and Wright, *Parliamentary History*, XVI, 83–90, speech and debate.

[20] Chatham Papers, 2, Shelburne to Pitt, December 21, 1765; printed in W. S. Taylor and J. H. Pringle (eds.), *Chatham Correspondence*, II, 354–55. Shelburne feared that Parliament was becoming increasingly anti-American, and that America would not be quieted even by a repeal unless it was "accompanied with some circumstances of a firm Conduct, and some system immediately following such a concession."

[21] See RHMCR. *Weston Papers*, 399, Edward Sedgwick to Edward Weston, December 24, 1765, for an expression of this "all or nothing" attitude.

Marquis of Rockingham

ingham, and Egmont, the moderate King's Friend, met in the evening of December 27.

Yorke at once revealed himself a firm opponent of any concession to the Colonies. His family was traditionally Old Whig. His father, the first Lord Hardwicke, had been a mainstay in the Pelham "present system." Furthermore, to a man, they hated Pitt and feared his domination of their group. Imbued with the family traits of pride, ambition, hauteur, a legalistic mind, and a love of "firm" measures, Charles Yorke was determined to allow no "undignified" concessions. He now sought to seize control by bringing forward his own proposals. Probably, he favored an amendment to the Stamp Act, but his immediate concern was to "sell" Old Whig leaders a declaratory act which would affirm the unbounded power of Parliament. It should also, he said, be accompanied by addresses from both Houses assuring the King of their support of British sovereignty "to the Utmost Instant." The meeting now disintegrated into a wrangle between Yorke on the one hand and Conway and Egmont on the other. Consequently, no decision was reached. Yorke attributed the failure to a fear of offending Pitt and sarcastically wrote to Rockingham of his vexation with "the disjointed state of things for I know not what Reason, and with what expectation of a *Messiah*."[22]

Rockingham's first attempt to bring his cabinet to a decision on the Stamp Act had thus failed. Although he had accepted in principle Yorke's proposal of a declaratory act, the young Marquis seemed curiously unwilling to proceed further. Several days after the unsuccessful meeting, he was writing vaguely that "dignity must go hand in hand with Temper and Management"—which implied at least a partial retreat from the Stamp Act. Old Newcastle, understandably annoyed at being left out of the conclave, strongly urged on Rockingham

---

[22] Wentworth-Woodhouse, Rockingham Papers, Charles Yorke to Rockingham, December 30, 1765. See also Add. MSS 32973, ff. 3, 11, 25, referred to by D. A. Winstanley, *Personal and Party Government*, 256.

a positive course of action and lashed out at "the Idea of *Authority and Relief* going Hand in Hand." Far better, he believed, "to be Deficient in That which is only a Declaration in words, Than in the Other, in which depends the most material Interests of this Country, viz., The Recovery of our Trade and Commerce."[23] The old man was for outright repeal, but still Rockingham hesitated to commit himself until Pitt had given him his cue. To go against the Great Commoner's desires, Rockingham felt, would be fatal.

Pitt had coldly rebuffed all Old Whig attempts both to bring him into the ministry and to discover his American sentiments. Concerning the latter, a great part of Pitt's reticence arose from the fact that he himself had not reached a firm conclusion. To Shelburne's report on the parliamentary debates of December, Pitt had replied that those who argued for upholding the legislative and executive authority over America were in a strong position. The Grenville Ministry had been guilty of "preposterous and infatuated errors of policy" which force alone could make good. He had not yet, then, concluded that the Stamp Act, as such, was a violation of constitutional principles, although he would soon do so. It can be no coincidence that he was, at the time, in close and friendly communication with several proponents of the American view, particularly with Stephen Sayre, the radical American and future sheriff of London. Such correspondents supplied Pitt with information which must have influenced his thinking considerably.[24] In the meantime, Rockingham had no choice but to wait impatiently for the reconvening of Parliament when Pitt was expected to appear in London.

Parliament sat on January 14, 1766. It was soon apparent that the ministry had gained no new strength. Indeed, the

[23] Wentworth-Woodhouse, Rockingham Papers, Newcastle to Rockingham, January, 1766.

[24] Taylor and Pringle, *Chatham Correspondence*, II, 358–61, Pitt to Shelburne, December, 1765. See Chatham Papers, 55, for Pitt's correspondence with Sayre. Sayre to Pitt, January 27, 1766, is of special interest.

unrest of Grafton and Conway, increasingly eager to call Pitt to the leadership of the government, had served to weaken them. So dubious was their strength that the King would allow himself to hope only that they would last "till the arduous business of the American Colonys is over, then I can stand upon my own feet."[25] Their weakness was to be of little moment. They were to be dwarfed by a battle of giants. Pitt faced Grenville; both championed contradictory and mutually exclusive theories of empire. The ministry was hardly more than an onlooker.

The first attack came from Grenville's friend Robert Nugent, one day to rise upon the wealth of his successive wives to be Lord Clare. The honor and dignity of Parliament, he urged, required an execution of the Stamp Act "except the right was acknowledged, and the repeal solicited as a favour," for "a peppercorn in acknowledgment of the right [is] of more value, than millions without."

Pitt then rose and, in one of his greatest speeches, charged that every step of the Grenville Ministry in its American policy had been wrong. The difference between external and internal taxes was clear, and Britain had no right to levy those of the latter kind. The mother country was indeed sovereign and possessed supreme authority over America "in every circumstance of government and legislation whatsoever," but taxation was no part of the legislative power. It was a free gift of the people through their repesentatives. The House of Commons was in no way representative of the Colonies. So while Great Britain could bind the colonists' trade, she could not tax them for revenue. The great man had spoken. The ministers had their long awaited cue, and Conway hastened to espouse Pitt's thesis.

The rejoinder was to come from another quarter, and it was an able one. Grenville took the floor and, denying any distinction between internal and external taxes, asserted that

[25] Fortescue, *Correspondence of George III*, I, No. 186.

the power to tax was most assuredly a part of that supreme sovereignty of Parliament which Pitt admitted. Great Britain gave America protection; in return, the Colonies owed obedience. Pressing his attack home to Pitt, he charged that the tumults in America stemmed directly from "factions in this House."

Technically out of order, Pitt spoke a second time. In glowing phrases, he praised American resistance to the Stamp Act. The Americans were the champions of constitutional liberty. By submitting to the British trade monopoly, the colonists paid their share of the imperial expense. They may perhaps have acted imprudently, but "they have been wronged. They have been driven to madness by injustice." Concluding, he called for the Stamp Act to be repealed "absolutely, totally, and immediately," because it was "founded on an erroneous principle." At the same time, "let the sovereign authority of this country over the colonies be asserted in as strong terms as can be devised, and be made to extend to every point of legislation whatsoever. That we may bind their trade, confine their manufactures, and exercise every power whatsoever, except that of taking their money out of their pockets without their Consent."[26]

America had found her advocate. Although his victory was to be a transient one, Pitt's viewpoint contained the germ of a new imperial concept: the paradox of subordinate political units each possessing a sphere of autonomy which the supreme power of Parliament could not invade. With his unreasoning, instinctive genius, Pitt had risen above Grenville's legalistic constitutionalism. He was decades ahead of his time, and did not himself understand what he demanded. A necessary prerequisite to a "federalized" empire would be the development of the modern British party system and of a figurehead king in whom the components of the empire might find a common head.

[26] Cobbett and Wright, *Parliamentary History*, XVI, 103–108, debate.

Grenville had had his vision, too. He had proposed to create an empire within the framework of the eighteenth-century British Constitution. He had, however, gone at it tactlessly and ruthlessly, and he had failed to see that his attempt came too late, cutting across the whole political development of the Colonies. Yet Grenville's view of empire, with its supreme center and subordinate parts, solidly based on British political development, was finally to prevail in the rising domestic controversy. It was only natural that it should. It was just as natural that America should thereby be lost.

Pitt had asserted that he would be content with nothing less than a repeal of the Stamp Act. Secretary of State Conway, by his public agreement with Pitt, had committed the ministry to such a measure. Even so, all was not harmony within the ranks of the Old Whigs. Lord George Sackville, accepting Grenville's doctrine of the identity of internal and external taxation, had expressed admiration for his speech in Parliament. The Yorke family was openly adverse to repeal. Attorney General Charles Yorke would not accept the idea until a near-desperate Rockingham had assured him that a strong declaratory act would go with it, and that it would not seem a concession to the Colonies. Rather, Rockingham told him, the Stamp Act would be repealed because of "its own demerits and Inconveniences *felt here.*"[27]

Still Yorke was dissatisfied. When the Old Whig leaders met on the night of January 20, Conway presented his draft of resolutions upon which the declaratory act was to be based. Asserting the supreme authority of Parliament over the Colonies in all cases whatsoever, they went on to condemn the tumults in America. These were destructive of the just dependency of the Colonies upon the mother country. All governors were, therefore, to punish the authors of such riots and to insure the compensation of the victims. Yorke objected to the

[27] Add. MSS 35430, ff. 31–32, Rockingham to Yorke, quoted in part by Winstanley, *Personal and Party Government,* 262, n. 2.

mildness of the measures proposed in General Conway's resolves. Moreover, when they were sent to him for approval, he inserted specific references to Parliament's right to tax the Colonies. Rockingham, eager to avoid this constitutional quagmire, crossed out Yorke's harsh changes which were personally objectionable to him, and would be very goading to Pitt.[28]

Thus, the ministry at length agreed to a declaratory act and to repeal, but Rockingham had yet to face his greatest problem: how was he to achieve a parliamentary majority? He was assured of the support of Pitt's friends and of the merchant representation. But against him was the violent opposition of Grenville, Bedford, Temple, and their associates, whose strength in the Commons may conservatively be estimated at seventy-five votes.[29] They were alike contemptuous of the ministry, "our little masters," and of "those wretched merchants who living upon expedients . . . would adopt the same miserable plan for the Publick."[30] Moreover, most of the King's Friends were doubtful. Many were openly hostile to a repeal, while the King himself seemed strangely supine. In addition, Bute and his Scottish friends—with a maximum of forty-five seats in Commons—were beginning to reach an understanding with the leaders of the Opposition. The situation was thus extremely volatile. The idea of an amendment to the act, rather than a repeal, was gaining popularity among the Opposition, among unattached Members, and even among the ministry itself, where the Yorke family called loudly for such a solution. Nor were Pitt and his followers improving the temper of the House.

[28] Add. MSS 35430, ff. 37–38, Rockingham to Yorke, January 25, 1766; printed in Albemarle, *Rockingham Memoirs*, I, 287–88.

[29] Namier, *England in the Age of the American Revolution*, 247, estimates the Grenville-Bedford strength at not more than fifty in 1767; but the higher number for 1765, although a rough estimate, is justified, due to the tendency of group "fringes" to leave an unprofitable Opposition as favorable opportunities arose.

[30] RHMCR. *Lothian Papers*, 258, Lord Buckinghamshire to Robert Nugent, October, 1765.

On January 27, Pitt's friend George Cooke presented the petition of the Stamp Act Congress to the House of Commons. His action was much against the wishes of the ministry who feared it would merely inflame the situation. King's Friends joined Grenville in denouncing the Congress as a "dangerous federal union." And Pitt, whose tactlessness and violence now reached new heights, seized the opportunity to deliver his "second dissertation upon Government," as Sackville sneeringly called it. Demanding that the petition be received, Pitt declared that the Stamp Act had broken the original compact of government and that the Americans now had every right to resist. The conservative reaction was immediate. High words passed between Pitt and King's Friend Sir Fletcher Norton who called the Great Commoner a "trumpet of rebellion." Lord Hardwicke later declared that Pitt deserved the Tower; and he heatedly called for sending more troops to America to protect government from riot. Obviously, Pitt had merely angered those already against the repeal and alarmed moderates who had not yet decided.

Furthermore, Benjamin Franklin did nothing to calm the growing fear of American intentions. While examining the American papers in late January, the Commons called him in as agent for Pennsylvania. He readily admitted Britain's right to regulate colonial trade, but he resolutely denied any right to lay internal taxes—not even if the revenue were applied to the protection of the colonists. Concurring in Pitt's earlier argument, he declared that America paid her share of the common expense by submitting to the British trade monopoly. Besides there was not the least occasion for a British force in America. The colonists were "perfectly able to defend themselves." Franklin's final warning was unmistakable. Should Britain insist upon disregarding the difference between internal and external taxes, the colonists themselves might be driven to that position. Then, however, America's conclusion would be just opposite that of Britain's: she would refuse to pay *any* taxes levied by the home government.[31]

In such an atmosphere, panic began to stir among Rockingham and his friends. The King, preferring an amendment to the Stamp Act, refused to commit his Friends to a repeal despite Rockingham's remonstrances. Indeed, there was grave cause for concern. On a Scottish election petition presented against the wishes of the ministry on January 31, the government was saved by a margin of only nine votes. Joined against them in the division were Bute's friends, the Grenville group, the Bedfordites, and several placemen, including Lords Sackville and Strange. There were rumors that the King's Friends were planning to desert the ministry because it was pledged to a repeal, that Pitt was being called, and that the government was falling.

To Rockingham's anguished appeals for the support of the Friends, the King returned platitudes but not promises. Among the Old Whigs, however, there was a hardening core of wounded pride and a determination to take the plunge, come what might. On February 3, therefore, Conway moved the resolution embodying the Declaratory Act. Pitt, with Barré and Beckford, fought the motion tooth and nail, contending that Britain had no right to lay internal taxes on America. It was a forlorn stand, both Opposition and ministry vying with each other in answering Pitt's position. It is noteworthy that during this debate, a new Member of Parliament and an adherent of the ministry made his maiden speech, an argument for the supremacy of Parliament in all cases whatsoever. This man was Edmund Burke.

The House's acceptance of the Declaratory Act was, however, no test of strength for the ministry. (The conservative Opposition would scarcely combat so emphatic a statement of Parliament's right to tax the Colonies.) Indeed, the position of the government was gradually worsening. In the House of

[31] Sparks, *Franklin's Works*, IV, 161–200.

Lords, in debate on the Declaratory resolutions, the Old Whigs found themselves in a minority on two minor divisions, Bute's, Bedford's, and Grenville's followers having united against them with several of the King's Friends. These were relatively unimportant setbacks, but they showed Rockingham that his position had now become so precarious that immediate and effective royal support had become an absolute necessity. It was of ominous import that American affairs had pushed Bute into a union with his old enemies Bedford and Temple. The Scot must have been provided with ironic amusement in a scene which saw both Opposition and ministry competing in pouring out compliments upon the same man whom, a short time ago, they had so bitterly reviled as a "secret influence" and "minister behind the curtain."

In the Stamp Act crisis, it is possible to gauge the success of the King's project, adopted at the commencement of his reign, to recover what he considered his constitutional function as the center of British politics. In this highly critical period, it was generally believed that the King and his Friends had become the decisive factor. Courted by both sides, they were able to give victory to whomever they chose to support. The King desired an amendment of the Stamp Act rather than a repeal. Such a course, he believed, would be "more consistent with the honour of this Country and all the Americans would with any degree of Justice hope for."[32] For the ministry, however, amendment was impossible: they had declared publicly for repeal. Had the King so wished, he could have easily overturned the ministry by simply remaining silent. His Friends, following their own inclination, would have gone overwhelmingly against a repeal, and the ministry would have fallen. George III saw clearly, however, that the failure of the Old Whigs would restore the hated Grenville and Bedford to power. Understanding, therefore, that the issue had become either total

[32] Fortescue, *Correspondence of George III*, I, No. 247, memorandum by the King, February 10, 1766.

repeal or total enforcement, George acceded, in a limited manner, to Rockingham's demands for royal support. The minister was allowed to say that the King preferred repeal of the act to its enforcement. This statement, however equivocal, helped combat a belief that George was being forced to accept the repeal by his ministers.

Even with the King's lukewarm support—George had refused to crack the whip over his Friends by threatening a general dismissal from place of all those who went against the repeal—Rockingham very nearly resigned. The implication in the King's statement that he favored amendment was immediately seized upon by the Opposition. Seeking to open communication with the King through Bedford, they offered their services "in any possible way." George's reply, a cold rebuff, goes far to dispel the Old Whig legend that he intrigued against them and the repeal: "I do not think it constitutional for the Crown personally to interfere in Measures which it has thought proper to refer to the advice of Parliament."[33] It was evident, therefore, that the Opposition would not have royal support or that of the majority of the Friends in their fight against the ministry.

Rockingham's campaign for merchant support now began to pay dividends. Bristol, Liverpool, Manchester, Nottingham, Leeds, and many other commercial centers sent petitions through their merchant committees. They complained of the disastrous state of trade. Unemployment had become so widespread, and the volume of their business so curtailed that there was distress in all commercial districts in the kingdom. This catastrophe they laid to the Stamp Act. Glasgow merchants, for instance, demanded immediate repeal as the only measure which could give them relief and bring order to America. They themselves held £1,500,000 in debts in Virginia and Maryland

---

[33] *Ibid.*, No. 256, the King to the Duke of York, through whom Bedford made his offer, February 18, 1766; see also No. 253, Egmont to the King, February 17, 1766.

alone, a sum they could not collect until the pernicious act was repealed.[34] These were arguments which would appeal mightily not only to the fifty-odd merchants in Parliament and to the representatives of the large commercial cities but also to the independent and unattached Members.

A third development now served further to bolster the ministry. Grenville committed a political blunder which went far to save the government he was seeking to destroy. His course now should have been obvious. He should have pressed for an amendment of the act. The King's Friends, knowing their royal master's views, would have supported such a motion. So would have the unattached moderates. The ministry could not have retreated from repeal. Even with Pitt and the merchant interest solidly in support, it is doubtful that the government would have been saved. Lacking political finesse when principle was involved, however, and outraged by the intention to repeal, Grenville, on February 7, suddenly moved an address to the King asking unqualified enforcement of the Stamp Act. No special arrangements had been made for a solid attendance of the Opposition. The division was crucial. Grenville's surprising and signal defeat amazed the ministry as much as it did the Opposition. The House divided against the motion by a vote of 274–134, providing the ministry with a majority twice as large as their most sanguine expectations. With drooping ministerial spirits brightened by the much needed fillip, Sackville reported to a friend, "The conversation is that the ministry may now stand their ground."[35] Grenville's uncompromising tone had thus failed to draw to his support that considerable number of Members who would have voted for an amendment; and a good chance to overturn the ministry had gone glimmering.

Events had conspired in favor of Rockingham and his repeal. When the issue came to a vote at half-past one on the

[34] Wentworth-Woodhouse, Burke Papers.
[35] RHMCR. *Stopford-Sackville Papers*, I, 106–108.

morning of February 22, the ministry, strongly supported by Pitt and the merchants, carried the resolutions for repeal in a division of 275–167. Of the eighty representatives of the counties, chiefly country gentlemen and Old Tories who were the most independent element in Parliament, only twenty-nine voted against the government.[36] The merchants responded solidly to the petitions of the commercial cities; and representatives from the larger urban constituencies had felt the pressure also. Pitt's friends had increased the ministry's majority. And, finally, a large majority of King's Friends had joined to carry the measure through. In the House of Lords, they performed a similar service, Lord Egmont speaking powerfully for the ministry.

Pitt, basking in "the Sun of liberty," was jubilant. The thanks of the mercantile interests poured in upon the ministry and the Great Commoner for the assistance given to "almost expired" trade.[37] There were disquieting aspects, however. The minority in the House of Commons had consisted of Grenville and Bedford followers firmly united with those of Bute. The forty-five Scottish Members had gone overwhelmingly against the ministry. Some fifty-two voting with the Opposition had been placemen, including many King's Friends such as Barrington and Sackville; and forty-one Old Tories had joined the protest against the repeal.[38] So the tide of conservatism had begun to flow. Henceforward it was to become increasingly strong. Opinion was growing that America's "flame is too permanent to be accounted for from the fury of the mob." Charges of "unsettled pusillanimity" were levied more often at the ministry, while Pitt had been guilty of "violence tinctured with his foible, a passion for popular applause." The debates on repeal had convinced King's Friends and independents alike that Grenville offered the securest harbor in the rising storm.

[36] Namier, *The Structure of Politics*, I, 187–88.
[37] Chatham Papers, 48, merchants of Liverpool to Pitt, March 11, 1766.
[38] Keith Feiling, *The Second Tory Party*, Chap. VII.

The repeal had scarcely been carried before they began to feel that the measure had been "merely a temporary expedient which will embroil us more and more in the process of time."[39] Meantime, both the Declaratory Act and the repeal received royal assent on March 18. The King breathed a sigh of relief; and Benjamin Franklin celebrated by sending his patient wife fourteen yards of pompadour satin.

Having made its supreme effort, the ministry now went to pieces. Pitt retired to Bath in early May, and so withdrew the last hope of bringing him into the government. Grafton promptly resigned as secretary of state, and while the office was hawked about, the King prayed only that the Old Whigs might hold together until the end of the parliamentary session. Then he could act more independently in the formation of a new ministry.

In their short year in office, the Old Whigs had shattered Grenville's imperial vision which had been based on an American financial contribution. The corollary of the repeal of the Stamp Act was an abandonment of all plans to organize the west. Always doubtful of the wisdom of keeping Canada in preference to the West Indies Sugar Islands, the Old Whigs now showed themselves willing to treat the west as an immense Indian reservation, to make permanent the boundary provisions of the Proclamation of 1763—which Grenville had accepted only as a temporary measure—and to remand to the Colonies control of Indian affairs.

On October 18, 1765, the Privy Council, considering a Board of Trade report dealing with settlements upon the Ohio River contrary to the Proclamation, had ordered additional instructions for the Governors of Virginia and Pennsylvania. Such illegal settlements were to be evacuated at once, and appropriate measures must be taken to prevent the like in future.[40]

---

[39] RHMCR. *Gray Papers*, 298–99, Thomas Falconer to Thomas Gray, March 18 and 19, 1766.
[40] Grant and Munro, *Acts of the Privy Council*, IV, 729–30.

Convinced as the Old Whigs were that inland colonies would be too independent of the mother country, it is doubtful that harmonious relations with America could have been long preserved, even if the Rockingham government had not fallen. Eventual conflict with the rapidly growing numbers of American frontiersmen and land speculators would have been inevitable.

The ministry quickly dismissed, because of the cost, all thought of implementing Hillsborough's plan (1764) for imperial control of Indian affairs. They had, nonetheless, to face the problem presented by the ten thousand troops already in America. Since no satisfactory solution to the financial question had been reached, it was necessary to make some new arrangement concerning them.

In May, 1766, Barrington, the secretary at war, reported on the situation. Although the Rockingham Ministry fell before the report could be considered, it may be accepted as a statement of their view of the west. Barrington proposed to evacuate it. Calling for the abolition of forts, garrisons, and settlements in the Indian country, he declared that it was unlikely that Britain herself would ever be in a state of hostility with the Indians. Should the Colonies become embroiled by their own misconduct, "let them get themselves out of it ... or let them beg for military assistance, acknowledge their want of it, and pay its expense." New colonies would be confined to the Floridas, if the colonists were willing to erect them at their own expense. In any event, those already established offered room for expansion for "some ages."

The British troops in America, he urged, should be withdrawn from the western area and concentrated in East Florida, Canada, and Nova Scotia, leaving to the colonists the task of protecting the frontier. Troops so stationed could easily move to any point in North America where riot, tumult, or other contingency might require.[41] This report was a direct reversal of

[41] Fortescue, *Correspondence of George III*, I, No. 454; see C. W. Al-

Grenville's plan which had sought to transform the new conquests into valuable additions to the empire.

Time was now rapidly running out for the ministry, yet several other aspects of the American problem were treated before the Old Whigs fell. Truly commendable was their plan for Canada. Though never implemented, it foreshadowed the Quebec Act of 1774. In February, 1766, the Privy Council approved instructions to the governor of Canada which required him to grant to all Canadians, French and English alike, full and equal rights in courts of law, including the practice of law and jury service. A new and vigorous governor, General Sir Guy Carleton, who strongly favored a final settlement of Canadian affairs by Parliament, was appointed. Although the Old Whigs had neither time nor courage to carry out a parliamentary consideration of the state of the neglected province, they did indicate the course they would have pursued. Shortly before their fall, Attorney General Yorke and Solicitor General de Grey submitted to the Privy Council a report which suggested that French civil law be combined with the more humane English criminal law. Not daring to bring such a radical proposal before Parliament, the ministry decided to promulgate it through instructions to Carleton. Lord Chancellor Northington, the King's Friend, seized the chance, as he had done when Grenville was falling, to precipitate a cabinet crisis by violently opposing the plan. The King consequently called Pitt to settle a new administration.

Soon after the repeal had been carried, the united merchant support which had bolstered up Rockingham began to disappear. Rockingham was to learn upon what a shifting base of sand he had sought to build. In the closing months of their ministry, the Old Whigs had amended the Revenue Act of 1764, lowering the duty on molasses, British or foreign, from three pence a gallon to one penny. Bad feeling had immedi-

vord, *The Mississippi Valley in British Politics*, I, Chap. VIII, who dates the report May 10, 1766. A copy is in Chatham Papers, 97.

ately flared up between the American and the West Indian interests, and the alliance, born in common opposition to the Stamp Act, was so weakened that it became useless to Rockingham. The final and violent end of friendly co-operation came in April. The American merchants demanded a free port in the West Indies where the colonists might exchange surplus supplies and victuals for French and Spanish bullion. But British West Indians had to meet French and Spanish prices paid for American products; and a free port would facilitate the illicit purchase of foreign sugars which habitually undersold those of the English planters. When the free port plan gained Rockingham's support, the West Indian interest, led by William Beckford and Stephen and Rose Fuller, went into enraged opposition. Rockingham quickly moved to grant them comparable concessions, but the struggle had already exhausted the remaining energy of the ministry.[42]

Finally, it is important to note that while the duty on molasses was lowered, the act itself remained an act for revenue, indicating that, fundamentally, the Old Whig view of taxation did not differ from Grenville's.

In February, 1766, John Yorke complained to his brother Hardwicke that in Parliament "every point now turns immediately into something American."[43] With her resistance to the Stamp Act, America suddenly and unexpectedly presented herself as a problem of the first magnitude to British politicians. Having quieted her temporarily by repealing the Stamp Act, Rockingham had sought to walk the tightwire of commercial expediency between the views of Pitt and Grenville. He had sought to give the important question of right a mere academic answer, hoping to leave it actually in abeyance. But it had been raised on both sides of the Atlantic, and it would never be al-

---

[42] L. Stuart Sutherland, "Edmund Burke and the First Rockingham Ministry," *English Historical Review*, Vol. XLVII (January, 1932), 46–70.
[43] Add. MSS 35374, f. 286, February 14, 1766.

lowed to return to that comfortable obscurity whence it had sprung.

Pitt had sought a repeal on the ground of Parliament's incompetence to lay internal taxes, but far from adopting this view, the Old Whigs had brought forward the Declaratory Act. They had hoped that as a theoretical statement it would save the face of Parliament. In reality, it was the most explicit declaration and justification ever drawn up in support of Parliament's unbounded right to legislate for the Colonies. The repeal therefore represented no real departure from those traditions of eighteenth-century constitutionalism which formed the opinions of most parliamentarians. In the long run, the chief result of the repeal in England would be the alienation from America of a large body of moderate politicians, and their alliance with the conservatives. "I much fear," wrote Falconer to Gray, "the concessions to the Americans will have little effect. They did not complain of the weight of taxes, but of the power of taxing claimed by us."[44] In Great Britain, then, the repeal operated as an irritant and as a justification for later stringent measures against the "ungrateful" Colonies.

[44] RHMCR. *Gray Papers*, 299, May 11, 1766.

CHAPTER THREE

CHATHAM, FACTION, AND AMERICA

ITT came into office in July, 1766, with three major objects: to smash "faction," to bring the East India Company under government control, and to settle the American problem. These objects were not unconnected.

His persistent refusals to associate himself with the Old Whigs or with any other political group, his friendly references to Bute during the late session of Parliament, and his call for a union of parties into a truly national government—all these had made him acceptable to the King. George III, however, had already gathered about him a group of Friends who formed a "faction" very like those he wished to crush. George, it would seem, did not understand the dual role he was playing, as domestic party leader and as imperial monarch. Indeed, by accepting the former role he made himself incapable of the latter one. He could not now rise above domestic politics to be a symbol of union in a "federalized" commonwealth, and his failure spelled disruption to the first British Empire.

The Rockingham Ministry had seen the emergence of the King's Friends as a full-fledged party. Chatham's administration was to let them rise to power and then consolidate their position. This loosely-organized body, consisting of all who looked immediately to the King for political leadership, was the precursor of the modern civil service, the "subministers."[1]

[1] See Jucker, *Jenkinson Papers*, xiii–xv; Namier, *The Structure of Politics*, I, 47.

Charles Jenkinson and John Robinson, who was to achieve amazing power as North's secretary of the Treasury, were prototypes. Usually without private fortunes, the men who became King's Friends longed for permanence in place and freedom from the ebb and flood of political fortune. The King could offer them this security if they would but support his measures in Parliament. Servants of the same master, these men naturally gravitated toward one another.

By the turn of 1766, the King's Friends were meeting in true party fashion. At that time, a dissolution of the Rocking-ham Ministry had seemed likely. The Friends had accordingly gathered to map out their course of action. Their deliberations cast a flood of light on the hardening of party lines and on the position achieved by the King since his accession. Should the Rockingham government fall, they stated, "the End to be wished is that His Majesty should have the free choice of his own Servants and that He should not put the management of His Affairs unconditionally into the Hands of the Leaders of any party." In an analysis of existing political conditions, they listed four parties. The first was their own. It was composed of "those who have always hitherto acted upon the sole Principle of Attachement to the Crown." Further, they were "probably the most numerous Body," and lacked only a parliamentary leader to undertake the formation of a ministry. Bute was in-eligible because of his personal unpopularity. At any rate, his following, all but a few, were already counted among the King's Friends.[2] It was therefore necessary for the Friends to "be joined if it be possible to some one of the other Parties."[3]

[2] Romney Sedgwick (ed.), *Letters from George III to Lord Bute,* 255–58, Bute to the King, August, 1766. Bute complained that Chatham had disre-garded the former Bute supporters because of his belief that they continued to constitute a Bute "faction." He had told his group, however, "Look to the King, not to me, I want no men to attach themselves to me, 'tis to him alone you should pay regard."

[3] Add. MSS 38338, ff. 307–10, "Observations on the probable dissolu-tion of Lord Rockingham's [first] Administration at a Meeting of ——— [*sic*] King's Friends." Printed in Jucker, *Jenkinson Papers,* 404–408.

The three other parties were the Old Whigs, the Grenville-Bedford-Temple alliance, and the Pittites. The King's past experience ruled out the first two as possible allies. Pitt, however, presented no danger. His own strength was "merely ideal." His following rested "on no settled attachment and will be of no Importance if the Crown declares against them." Possessed of enormous personal prestige, he would yet be dependent upon the King's Friends for a majority. By declaring war against "faction," he had made himself acceptable to the King: George now felt, from Pitt's conduct during the past session, that he would work well with "those of my Servants who I have protected on every former change."[4] Pitt then was the obvious answer to their search for a parliamentary leader. George III, through clever appeals to patriotism and self-interest, had created just such a group as those he had called upon Pitt to combat. In effect, Pitt was to be set tilting at windmills. And the first of these would be the ramshackle structure of the Old Whigs which, almost miraculously, still functioned, albeit with many a creak and groan.

Pitt and the King in their initial conversations had agreed to accept the Rockingham Ministry as a basis whereon to build. From the first, however, Pitt showed such contempt for their "faction" that an open breach was not long to be postponed. The offer of the Treasury to Temple had been resented by the Old Whigs, and only Temple's refusal of it now prevented open hostilities.[5] Indignity after indignity was heaped upon them. Offices were filled without a word to them: Shelburne was made secretary of state for the Southern Department; Camden, lord chancellor; King's Friend Northington weathered yet another crisis and emerged as president of the Council; Egmont took the Admiralty, and Grafton the Treasury. Charles Townshend, at Grafton's express request, was forced

---

[4] Sedgwick, *Letters*, No. 339, the King to Bute, July 12, 1766.
[5] Add. MSS 35430, ff. 55–56, Rockingham to Charles Yorke, July 17, 1766.

to exchange the lucrative paymastership for the office of chancellor of the exchequer. Pitt himself took the privy seal and received the earldom of Chatham.

The new arrangement was thus an open affront to the Old Whigs. Conway, it is true, remained a secretary of state. Lord North, with Pelham family connections, was given Townshend's vacant post. A somewhat ungracious attempt was made to lay old Newcastle upon a "bed of roses" with a pension; but the veteran did not think he was "yet quite old enough to submit tamely to lie down on it, and be tuck'd up quietly."[6] Several other Old Whigs rested undisturbed in minor employment at various government boards. On the other hand, Pitt haughtily refused to place Dartmouth, erstwhile president of the Board of Trade, in a projected third secretaryship of state, that for America, although he had previously planned to create such a post. Dartmouth now resigned and was succeeded by King's Friend Hillsborough. Pitt offered the proud and ambitious Charles Yorke the honor of retaining his old office of attorney-general, but Yorke contemptuously declined. Dowdeswell was imperiously dismissed as chancellor of the exchequer to make room for Townshend. Rockingham immediately retaliated by refusing all personal communication with Pitt—now Earl of Chatham—and warmly asserted that only his friendship for Conway and Grafton kept him from calling for the resignation of all Old Whigs, even those in minor places.

Chatham's ministry as it now stood consisted of his own followers, the King's Friends, and the grumbling Old Whigs. This was a weak beginning. He was, moreover, faced with three dissatisfied factions: those of Bedford, Grenville and Temple, and Bute. Among his own people the Old Whigs were on the point of bolting, and several of the King's Friends, erstwhile followers of Bute—men like Charles Jenkinson,

---

[6] Add. MSS 35425, ff. 104–105, H. V. Jones to Hardwicke, July 26, 1766.

Thomas Whately, Sir Fletcher Norton, and Lord Darlington —had begun to resent his neglect for their interests.

Chatham, however, was moved by a higher consideration. He was preoccupied with the Old Whigs whom he thought the very embodiment of "faction." As long as they held office, that many more places were denied the King's Friends. Should they continue in place, however, and thus remain divided, some in office and some out, then a dissolution of the Old Whigs became a distinct possibility. Probably the King acquiesced in this reasoning. He was apparently willing to await the issue of the situation, gambling that in case of Old Whig resignations, the Bedfords, Chatham's choice as an ally among the hostile groups, would not come in. He could then bring in more of his Friends.

The conditions necessary for the success of Chatham's grandiose campaign were, however, not present. Group interests and loyalties had hardened too much, and after decades of vacuity, well-defined principles were re-entering politics. America and Wilkes had commenced to cut jagged lines across British political groupings.

Chatham took over the government intent on settling the affairs of America. He had fought passionately for the American cause during the two preceding sessions. That he was aware of the magnitude of the American problem and of the urgent need for its settlement is too evident. During the formation of his ministry, he had not only projected an American Department on a full parity with the older Departments of State but had contemplated taking its direction upon himself. However Temple's refusal of the Treasury had upset his outline of the new arrangement, and in the ensuing crisis, all idea of the new department had been dropped.[7] But just as Chatham had underestimated the strength of party divisions, he also failed to recognize the importance of the American issue as a divisive

[7] C. R. Ritcheson, "The Elder Pitt and an American Department," *American Historical Review*, Vol. LVII (January, 1952), 376–83.

force in British politics. He had wanted Temple at the Treasury, and Temple's opposition to the repeal of the Stamp Act had been notorious. Certain other elements in his cabinet possessed American views openly different from his own. In both cases—the campaign against party and the lack of attention to his colleagues' American sentiments—Chatham's attitude was a commentary on his monumental egoism which allowed him to believe that he would be able to impose his own ideas on the ministry and the nation. He had overestimated his own strength, political as well as physical.

When Temple had refused the Treasury in July, he had lashed out at the "new, virtuous, and patriotic administration." Consisting of Old Whigs and Chatham's friends, they were, he said, "all the most choice spirits who did in the last Session most eminently distinguish themselves in the sacrifice of the rights and honour of the whole Legislature and Kingdom of Great Britain."[8] America had thus united Temple and Grenville in firm alliance. Furthermore, certain of Bute's neglected followers, whom the Scot had willed the King while disclaiming his own party chieftainship, had already made approaches to Grenville. Sir Fletcher Norton and Lord Darlington were bade a cautious welcome. Grenville expressed his pleasure at their report that Bute had disavowed the new ministry. It was, Grenville told them, "certainly founded upon principles widely different from those which I am told he [Bute] laid down with such general approbation in the House of Lords last session."[9] The conservatism engendered by America's reaction to the Stamp Act was working rapidly now in the consolidation of the right wing of politics, and the process could not be stopped, even by a Chatham.

[8] Smith, *Grenville Papers*, III, 267–68, Temple to Grenville, July 18, 1766; 272–73, Temple to Gower.

[9] *Ibid.*, 273–77, Grenville to Thomas Whately, through whom the approaches were made, July 20, 1766. Chatham's only favor to Bute had been to restore his brother Mackenzie to the office of privy seal of Scotland, but the power of patronage had not been returned.

The American issue was of less immediate importance to the King's Friends and to the Bedfordites. The former group, whose American attitude at this point may be described as neutral, was now engaged in the practical struggle to achieve power. Without a definite American "plan," they were nonetheless confident that once they were in the saddle they could deal with the problem satisfactorily. "The Management of the American affairs," they admitted, "is certainly full of Difficulties but the House is so divided on that subject that whatever Sentiments are adopted, they will certainly find support from one side or another; and wherever the Crown casts its Influence there will be Success."[10] The King's Friends, then, had come to view themselves not merely as a separate political group but as the decisive one.

The Bedfords, too, were hungry for office and had hoped that Pitt would turn to them for support when forming his ministry.[11] In many ways, the Bedfords exhibited more signs of advanced party organization than any other group. Led by the Duke of Bedford, an honest, upright, conservative man of limited understanding, they worked together mightily to achieve one goal: office. That object being paramount, political principles were relative. Bedford himself was inclined to agree with Grenville in American affairs, but his friends, able talkers like Richard Rigby, Lord Weymouth and Lord Gower, could usually induce him to follow their lead. They themselves were capable of taking on any color that served their interest. So Bedford was soon reported as expressing himself in a friendly manner toward the new ministry: he would be perfectly satisfied, it seems, if he could but obtain office for a few of his friends.

In August, Egmont resigned the Admiralty. He had never liked Chatham, and he now declined to serve under him.

[10] Add. MSS 38399, ff. 307–10.
[11] Hinchingbrooke Papers, Sandwich to Augustus Hervey, July 15 and 23, 1766.

Chatham was at Bath, but Grafton, the titular head of government, immediately offered the vacant post to Bedford's relative Lord Gower. The Duke refused, averring his dislike of the measures pursued by many of the ministry during the last session—an obvious reference to the repeal of the Stamp Act—but it was clear that the offer had been merely insufficient. It would take more than this to tempt the Bedfords to break with Grenville.

The question of additional support for the ministry became a serious one before the meeting of Parliament, scheduled for November. Chatham, in August, had suffered a painful attack of gout—sinister portent of things to come—and had retired to Bath. While he was there, however, serious riots due to the grain shortage had occurred and had obliged him to hurry back to London. He and his ministry had then issued a proclamation prohibiting the export of grain. By doing so, they disregarded a law which allowed exportation of grain until a price higher than the prevailing one had been reached. Chatham had then returned to Bath. Grafton feared a strong attack from the Opposition for this exercise of the royal prerogative, and he longed for an accession of strength to meet it. By various half-hearted expedients he sought to quiet growing dissatisfaction. A Bute relative was made a Duke. One of Grenville's friends, Lord Buckinghamshire, was offered—but refused—the embassy to Madrid. Both Conway and Grafton suggested that the new Old Whig Edmund Burke be brought in. His oratorical skill would indeed have helped immeasurably, but Chatham, detesting all Old Whigs, would have none of him. His thoughts had returned to a Bedford accession. It would be a clever maneuver. That group possessed respectable strength, and they were the very center of opposition. Once they were drawn in, Rockingham and Grenville, diametrically opposed in American affairs, would find it exceedingly difficult, perhaps impossible, to unite. Furthermore, a new development was making a Chatham-Bedford *rapprochement* even more feasible: the disobedience of the New York Assembly was causing Chatham's own American views to stiffen.

Thus it occurred that Northington, representing the ministry, renewed the offers to Bedford while both men were at Bath. The Lord President called on the Duke on the nineteenth, expressed his desire to see Bedford in administration, and outlined Chatham's policy: to preserve the peace in Europe—an especially delicate point with the negotiator of the Treaty of Paris—to restore authority to government at home, and "to support the superiority of Great Britain over her colonies." A few days later, Chatham himself repeated the offer and elaborated upon his own plans. A chief point was that "measures for the proper subordination of America must be taken."

In a later interview, Chatham qualified this remark by declaring that he hoped he "was not understood to intend any violent measures toward the Americans at this time, unless absolutely necessary." It is apparent, however, that neither Chatham nor Bedford thought their American differences great enough to keep them apart. Bedford considered the openings so promising that he at once summoned his confidants, Weymouth, Gower, and Richard Rigby.

Chatham had promised the post office for Weymouth, an unspecified place for Rigby, and employment for Gower as master of the Horse. These, however, the Bedfords considered insufficient, and so negotiations failed. The first minister, though disappointed, parted with Bedford on "exceeding good terms," convinced that his party could be bought if more places were opened to them, and determined to create such vacancies as soon as he could.

Chatham had, in any case, driven a wedge between Bedford and Grenville. When Parliament opened on November 11, Bedford and his friends refused to join Grenville in opposing the loyal address. Next day, Bedford "went to the King's levee: was graciously received."[12] Meanwhile Chatham, now certain of an accession from the Bedfords, launched his most formidable attack upon the Old Whig "faction." Two days after the opening of Parliament, without previous warning, he demanded that one of them, Lord Edgecumbe, treasurer of the Household and possessor of several seats in Parliament, exchange his place for an inferior one in the Bedchamber. Deeply annoyed with Old Whig Edmund Burke and William Dowdeswell, who had spoken with Grenville for the necessity of a bill of indemnity to excuse those involved in the grain embargo, Chatham seemed determined to break Old Whig cohesion by a contemptuous display of his authority over them or else to drive them out, thereby creating the necessary vacancies for the Bedfords.

Old Whig leaders, Conway excepted, immediately consulted, and their decision was quickly made: mass resignation was necessary; "the Corps must be kept together." Portland, Bessborough, Scarborough, Morrison, Saunders, Keppel, and Meredith announced their withdrawal from the government. Only the fickle Conway remained, much to the disgust of his fellows, for he "doubted whether he would be justified in throwing the King's affairs into confusion."[13] Chatham's *coup de main* against faction was, in the end, an abysmal failure. The mass exit of the Old Whigs, binding its members in common adversity, saved that party from dissolution. They were to wander long in the wilderness, but they would live to fight another day.

Chatham had overreached himself, and he now saw his secondary object, an accession from the Bedfords, melt away. Immediately, the Bath offers had been renewed, but the Bed-

[12] Russell, *Bedford Correspondence*, III, 348 ff., Bedford's private journal. See also Smith, *Grenville Papers*, III, 337, Grenville to Temple, November 10, 1766.

[13] Wentworth-Woodhouse, Rockingham Papers, Dowdeswell to Rockingham, November 20, 1766; Hinchingbrooke Papers, Halifax to Sandwich, November 15, 1766; Albemarle, *Rockingham Memoirs*, II, 24, Hardwicke to Rockingham, November 20, 1766, 19–20, Rockingham to Scarborough, November 20, 1766.

fordites, realizing Chatham's exposed position, now proceeded to make the most of it. Their terms soared to shocking heights. Four more friends were to be provided for; three peerages were to be conferred; and the royal favor was to be manifested toward Sandwich. Thus, Chatham found himself faced with the same "evil" he had sought to extirpate. He had become a victim of his own highhanded ways. This painful situation might have been a demonstration to him that his campaign against faction was an attempt to sweep back the sea.

Both Chatham and the King denounced the Bedford's "extravagant proposals." But where were they to find the necessary support to replace that which Chatham had so haughtily tossed away? As soon as Rockingham's followers had resigned, Charles Jenkinson and Sir Fletcher Norton sent urgently to Bute's friend Sir James Lowther, begging him to urge Bute to hurry to London. Believing that the government was "drawing to a Conclusion," they represented the King as complaining of the apparent unwillingness of his Friends to come to his assistance. They warned Lowther that if immediate steps were not taken, the Friends would lose "an opportunity of the utmost Consequence."[14] Their worry was unnecessary. Chatham had no other recourse but the King's Friends. Robert Lord Nugent, whose connection with Grenville had always been amiable, became the first lord of trade. Sir Francis Dashwood, now Lord le Despencer, became a postmaster. Jenkinson went to the Admiralty Board. Hillsborough joined Le Despencer in the post office. The Duke of Ancaster, Lord Delaware, aged Sir Edward Hawke, Sir Percy Brett, and several others were called to minor offices. The first step toward the formation of the North Ministry had thus been taken. Those King's Friends now called into government in "subministerial" posts were to

[14] Add. MSS 38205, ff. 108–109, November 27, 1766; printed in Jucker, *Jenkinson Papers*, 437–38. See also Add. MSS 35430, ff. 61–62, Rockingham to Charles Yorke, November 27, 1766.

form a nucleus within the government around which the new conservatism could gather.

Prospects for the new arrangement were not too bad. Grenville had become suspicious of Bedford. Their co-operation with Rockingham was highly improbable. Bute had been made easy. Affairs in Parliament, however, were to create a dangerous point of union for the Opposition, while at the same time, Chatham's ministry was to be so weakened that it could not recover.

The Seven Years' War had delivered up to the East India Company much of the great subcontinent of India, and had seen the company established in the territories of Bengal, Orissa, and Bihar. From these lands, the company derived a revenue, exclusive of its profits as a trading concern, of over a million pounds sterling a year. Abuses and cruelties to the native population, the rise of the "moguls," whose immense fortunes flooded England, a knowledge that the company would not have made its great conquests without extensive assistance from the royal army and navy—all determined Chatham to bring East India Company affairs before Parliament. An even more important consideration, however, was the pressing need of government for some new source of revenue.

Chatham, for all of George Grenville's criticism of his financial abilities, appreciated as much as did his brother-in-law the need for more government income. The nation staggered under enormous debts incurred during the war, and new revenue was necessary to effect any general American settlement. Indeed, Chatham saw in a parliamentary inquiry into the company's affairs a necessary prelude to the formation of a comprehensive American plan.

As early as October, 1766, Chatham's attention had been focused on India as a possible source of revenue. His friend Beckford had pointed out to him the worsening financial condition of Great Britain and had asserted that the only alternative to taxing America was an East Indian revenue. Beckford

79

advised, "Unless you can procure a Revenue of a Million £ An[ually] without new Taxations, and oppressions on the people, there can [be] no salvation. . . . We must look to the East and not to the West."[15] An eastern revenue would bring relief to the suffering landowners and taxpayers of Great Britain and would finance the first expensive steps of empire building in the New World conquests. America would meanwhile be untaxed, and the distraught Colonies would enjoy a breathing spell. Then, in an atmosphere of peace and calm, the two countries could settle their differences and satisfactorily define their relationship.

Chatham's decision to inquire into the affairs of the East India Company was fully supported by the King.[16] Grafton therefore warned its representatives that steps would be taken to give the government the company's revenue.

The plan was, however, strongly opposed by Charles Townshend and General Conway, both members of the ministry. Townshend desired a ministerial negotiation with the company instead of a parliamentary inquiry. Conway, true to his Old Whig background, and believing that the principle of the sanctity of private property was involved, opposed any interference with the company whatsoever. Chatham, however, was insistent. He felt it was Parliament's duty to determine the company's right to the revenue—or lack of it. Moreover a successful ministerial-company negotiation, by giving the Crown control of a revenue independent of Parliament, would create a quite unconstitutional state of affairs.

The division in the cabinet soon became public knowledge, but Chatham was not one to brook opposition. On November 25, therefore, Beckford, at Chatham's prompting, moved in Commons to consider the East India Company's affairs. Succeeding here, he then demanded, on December 9, an account

[15] Chatham Papers, 19, William Beckford to Chatham, October 15, 1766.
[16] Fortescue, *Correspondence of George III*, I, No. 437, the King to Grafton, December 9, 1766.

of the company's revenue and expenditures, and an inspection of its charters and treaties. On this occasion, it was feared that Townshend would bolt, but he stood with the government on the division. The central core of the Old Whigs had, however, joined with Grenville, although they were able to divide only 56 against 140. The Bedfords had found it prudent not to attend.

The Christmas recess now intervened. The company adopted tactics designed to reduce the ministry to making such demands upon it as would be a tacit admission of its right to the revenue. Offers were made to Grafton early in February, Chatham having returned to Bath to recoup his energy. Grafton, refusing to commit himself and faced with a wrangling cabinet, wrote frantically to his chief, begging him to come to London with all haste.

Chatham's tragic eclipse had begun already. His illness was becoming serious. In reply to Grafton he wrote in characteristic high style, but with a disconcerting vagueness: "As for the reviving hopes of particular Factions, I confess they but little engage my Thoughts. My whole Mind is bent on acquiring such a Revenue, as must give Strength, Ease, and Lustre to the King's Reign." East Indian affairs were "the Transcendant Object," he declared, but it had not been his absence which had ruined the "Great Transaction." Rather, it had been "an unfortunate Original Difference of Opinion among the King's Servants."[17] These words, however grandiose, were devoid of help to the distracted Grafton. To Chatham's mind, slowly descending into utter depths of melancholia, the great game had been lost. He collapsed completely in March, and the inquiry dragged on until May, when Parliament took the indecisive step of limiting the company's dividend to 10 per cent. Chatham's plan had thus been stopped in its tracks. This event was to have a profound effect upon America. Together with a

[17] Taylor and Pringle, *Chatham Correspondence*, III, 199–201, Chatham to Grafton, February 9, 1767.

reduction of the land tax, which was to be forced upon the government, it was to make a second attempt to tax the Colonies inevitable.

The ministry's treatment of the East India Company affairs is important in a second way. It served to demonstrate the rigidity of the lines dividing Grenvillites and Old Whigs. The Bedfords, fearing to offend either Chatham or Grenville, remained inconspicuous throughout the whole affair. Beckford's first motion had brought Grenville and Rockingham into an embarrassed agreement concerning East Indian matters alone. Various attempts from the fringe element in both parties to develop a full-fledged alliance proved absolutely futile. Rockingham, admitting that his party's prospect appeared forlorn when "viewed through political glasses," had already reconciled himself to a sojourn in the wilderness. Old Whigs had come to believe that "every dictate of honour and principle" called for complete isolation from Grenville. They had gained their reputation and credit with the public because they had opposed Grenville when he was minister and had reversed his measures when they had come to power. Not only did Rockingham and his friends scorn friendship with Grenville, but they insisted upon holding aloof from the Bedfords as well, for any Old Whig approach, they felt, would give the Bedfords a chance to acquire merit with either Grenville or Chatham.[18]

Impractical as his attitude may have been in the political sense, and motivated as yet by no "platform" save a vague and idealistic love of principle, Rockingham's action does demonstrate the sharply emerging lines of party development. The Old Whigs had come a long way from the Pelham "present system," when Newcastle would have made a coalition with Lucifer to maintain or achieve power. Indeed, at this point, it

[18] Wentworth-Woodhouse, Rockingham Papers, Rockingham to Dowdeswell, January 8, 1767. Extracts are printed in Albemarle, *Rockingham Memoirs*, II, 31–32.

LORD CHATHAM

is obvious that the King and his Friends had become the heirs of the "present system," while the Rockingham Whigs had begun to tread the lonely path toward a new basis of power—the people.

The Old Whigs voted with Grenville again in March in opposing the printing of the East India papers. Government triumphed by a slender majority of thirty-three, Charles Townshend having stayed away to avoid openly opposing his cabinet colleagues. Co-operation between the two Opposition groups was by chance, however, not by plan. What America had put asunder, East India affairs could not permanently unite. On the other hand a division in Chatham's cabinet had appeared, and it was never to be healed—a fact of great importance in that cabinet's effort to deal with the American problem.

After the Stamp Act, America was to know but little peace under the British Crown. With the repeal, the colonists, against the sensible advice of Old Whigs, had revelled in their "victory" over Parliament. They had thus alienated a growing mass of conservative opinion in Great Britain. Chatham had hoped that with the Stamp Act abolished, quiet would return, so that he could chart a reorganization of the empire on "Revolution principles." Whether or not he would have succeeded, however, is a matter for speculation, because he was never to have a chance to try. He was to be forced to utilize his few remaining precious months of health in an attempt to settle a temporary but violent dispute in America, a matter which only served to demonstrate the urgent need for a fundamental readjustment of the empire.

In this task, Chatham was gravely handicapped by that division of his cabinet which had arisen from the East India affair. In American matters, moreover, his ministry represented the most diverse views. He himself, Camden, and Shelburne had fought for the repeal of the Stamp Act and against the Declaratory Act. Grafton and Conway had voted for both. Townshend had been for both the Stamp Act and its repeal.

Barrington, the Master of the Ordnance Lord Granby, and Northington had opposed the repeal and supported the Declaratory Act. With such a motley crew at his back, Chatham had now to face the disobedience of the New York Assembly. The troublesome question of Parliament's right of taxation in the Colonies was about to be resurrected.

During Grenville's ministry, the Mutiny Act had been extended to America at the express request of General Gage and other military leaders there. Under Rockingham it had been amended to prevent the quartering of troops in private houses. Americans were required, however, to put them in barracks, empty houses, or barns, and to supply any troops within their colony, or passing through it, with kitchen utensils, salt, vinegar, small beer, cider or rum, candles, and firewood.

As soon as the new act was known in America, the Massachusetts Assembly characteristically entered into a long disputation with the governor. The New Jersey Assembly also proved recalcitrant, refusing Governor William Franklin's request that they insert the words of the Mutiny Act into their bill—which only partially complied with that Act of Parliament. In a strong representation to Franklin, they condemned the Mutiny Act as an internal tax and more unfair than the old Stamp Act, inasmuch as troops were kept constantly in some colonies and not at all in others.[19]

It was the assembly of New York, however, which caused the greatest concern. As a major port of disembarkation and a military center, New York would have to accommodate far more troops than any of her sister colonies. In June, 1766, her assembly refused to comply with the act. A month later, that body agreed to supply the required articles, except salt, vinegar, and beverage, but for only about eleven hundred men. Moreover, they still refused to accept the Mutiny Act, which they too deemed an internal tax.

[19] Chatham Papers, 97, William Franklin to Shelburne, December 18, 1766, copy.

News of this conduct was widely known in Britain by early August. Chatham, Shelburne, and their colleagues at once conceded the necessity of New York's obeying the act. It is thus evident that Chatham regarded that colony's action as radically different from the Stamp Act disturbances. The Stamp Act, Chatham had maintained, was an internal tax, and so beyond the power of Parliament. The Mutiny Act, he believed, was no such thing. It was designed to care for His Majesty's armed forces—always a point of special concern with Chatham. And those forces were in America to protect the Colonies. Nonetheless, it is difficult to justify Chatham's logic here. Grenville had tried to raise a revenue to help pay the cost of a military force in America. Chatham now sought the same object—albeit on a smaller scale. Was there really any difference?

Chatham met his cabinet on August 5 to consider New York's disobedience. Camden, Northington, Lord Granby, Conway, and Shelburne were present. No serious alarm was felt. They all believed that a stern admonition would suffice. It was then quickly decided that Shelburne, whose office of secretary of state for the Southern Department gave him responsibility for colonial affairs, should write to Governor Sir Henry Moore. He should state that "as It is the Indispensible Duty of His Majesty's Subjects in America to obey the Acts of the Legislature of Great Britain, His Majesty expects and requires all due obedience to the same. And It cannot be doubted that the Province of New York after the Lenity of Great Britain so recently extended to North America will not hesitate duly to carry into Execution the Act of Parliament pass'd last Session for quartering His Majesty's Troops."[20]

Much ill feeling remained on either side of the Atlantic as a legacy of the Stamp Act disturbances. In America, the repeal was already being denounced as a mere commercial expedient. More and more attention was being focused on the ominous import of the Declaratory Act. The colonies had gen-

[20] *Ibid.*, minute of cabinet.

erally evaded or only partially complied with the mother country's order to compensate riot victims. Massachusetts had obeyed, but had added an Act of Indemnity for the participants, in flagrant violation of the royal prerogative of mercy. There were warnings that American "Demagogues" were "determined to bring all real power into the hands of the people."[21] Still Shelburne did not think the situation critical. In September, he wrote to Chatham, now again at Bath to combat his gout, calmly reporting that "at New York They have made difficulties about quarters—but It appears to me by the Letters that it's only the remains of the Storm, and wants a little good humour and Firmness to finish."[22] It must have been an unexpected and unpleasant surprise to Shelburne and his colleagues when, in spite of his stern letter, the New York Assembly staunchly reiterated their refusal to comply. To do so would "load them with Burthens they are incapable of supporting."[23] Sir Jeffrey Amherst, who was in New York at the time, also wrote to Shelburne warning that the assembly had no intention of retreating from their position: they feared an acceptance of the act would be but a precedent for some new attempt to tax them.

At no period in Shelburne's public life was he to appear to less advantage. One of the most mystifying characters of the eighteenth century, a man of undoubtedly great talent in public affairs, he was also one of the most despised men of his time. Suffering a deep-rooted sense of inferiority about his social and educational background, he sought psychological security in sly, hypocritical behavior. Unable to work on terms of equality with his colleagues, he gave his complete devotion to Chatham. Dependent upon his hero, he had only contempt for those who did not come up to Chatham's high standards.

[21] *Ibid.*, Governor Bernard to Shelburne, December 6, 1766.
[22] *Ibid.*, 56, September 20, 1766. Quoted by R. A. Humphreys, "Lord Shelburne and British Colonial Policy, 1766–1768," *English Historical Review*, Vol. L (April, 1935), 266.
[23] Chatham Papers, 97, address to the Governor, December 15, 1766.

Unfortunately, this included all his cabinet colleagues. When Chatham collapsed, therefore, Shelburne was set adrift upon a sea of his own fear and indecision. His confusion expressed itself partly in a cold silence toward his colleagues. He refused to believe that Chatham's illness would be of long duration. While it was Shelburne's job to find a plan for dealing with the New York Assembly, he maintained his aloofness even after it should have become obvious that Chatham was in no position to give direction to the cabinet. Shelburne's natural reticence, his reluctance to take any step without the most exhaustive researches, and his continued silence to the cabinet, resulted in his alienation from its other members. And so the initiative necessarily passed from his hands to those of one all too eager to employ it: Charles Townshend.

By the turn of the new year, 1767, Shelburne had begun to suspect that New York's disobedience would not be that simple matter he had previously imagined. In the same letter reporting the information from Amherst, he described the cabinet as in a "very weak state." Fearing that Grenville would brand New York's actions as rebellion, he begged Chatham to outline some proper mode of conduct.[24] Chatham, however, had already begun his descent into Inferno, and his answer—in tone much like that to Grafton on the East India Company— was specious, condemnatory, and quite unhelpful.

A few days later, Shelburne reported again to Chatham. He had had fresh word of New York's recalcitrance. Admitting that the act had many faults, he had directed Secretary at War Barrington to consider how it might better be adapted to colonial circumstances. Meantime, however, New York's obedience to the act as it stood was manifestly necessary. How that end might be obtained, he would not presume to suggest, for he looked to Chatham for guidance. "After a great deal

[24] *Ibid.*, 3; Taylor and Pringle, *Chatham Correspondence*, III, 182–88, February 1, 1767. Extracts are printed in Fitzmaurice, *Life of Shelburne*, I, 308–309, dated January 31, 1767.

of painful consideration on so disagreeable a Subject," he wrote, "I have nothing to submit to your Lordship, except what I took the Liberty to say to the King this morning, that I hop'd both He and Parliament would distinguish between *New York* and *America*."[25] Shelburne had conceded the necessity of parliamentary measures against that province.

Chatham's absence from London had by now nearly brought government to a standstill. Aware of the disastrous consequence of longer depriving the cabinet of his leadership, he girded himself for the grueling journey and set out on February 10. Unhappily, the effort proved too much, and he collapsed at Marlborough.

Meantime, events in America were forcing Shelburne willy-nilly toward a decision. On the sixteenth, he dispatched to Chatham a long and urgent letter. Some decisive action "as well on account of appearance here as effect there" was now so necessary that he had halted sailing of the American packet until Chatham's thoughts could be learned. Nor, although actual armed resistance in the Colonies was to be feared, had he laid the state of affairs before the cabinet, wishing first to learn his leader's wishes. He knew, however, that both the King and his own fellow ministers were "strong for enforcing," although nobody would commit himself to a definite course of action. Admitting the faults of the act, still the "infatuated conduct of the Assembly in refusing even present Obedience . . . precludes . . . all consideration of the Merits or Principles of it, by involving a far greater question." The act was then to be enforced. But how might this be done without creating a precedent which could be "turned to purposes of oppression"? The situation was in any case critical: "the public conviction goes so strongly to believing the dependence of the colonies at stake; and the opinion is so confirmed by their conduct since the repeal, which it must be expected will be both coloured and heightened by the

[25] Chatham Papers, 3; Taylor and Pringle, *Chatham Correspondence*, III, 191–93, February 6, 1767.

arts of their enemies, that, be the danger what it will, government appears called upon for some measure of vigour to support the authority of parliament and the coercive power of this country."

Under pressure from events in America and from a rapidly growing public conviction that the New York Assembly should be dealt with vigorously,[26] and fearful of the attacks of an anti-American Opposition, Shelburne had at last formulated a plan for Chatham's approval:

Governor Sir Henry Moore should be removed, partly for having transmitted the assembly's memorial against the Mutiny Act, and partly for certain irregularities in the granting of lands. As a successor, Shelburne suggested someone "of a Military Character, who might at the same time be entrusted with the Intentions of Government, and discretionary [power] to act with Force or Gentleness as circumstances might make necessary." (The idea of a military governor for a disobedient province did not, therefore, originate with Lord North.) Suggested now was Colonel John Burgoyne, or possibly General Monckton, "if his Mildness and Good Nature . . . is no objection." As for enforcing the act, Shelburne saw nothing to do but to let the governor billet in private houses if the assembly continued adamant.[27]

By this time, Chatham, quite beyond helping his troubled minister, could only reply that his shattered health prevented him entering "into any detail of things." He recommended merely that Shelburne and Grafton lay before Parliament both American and East Indian affairs.[28]

[26] On this point, see Chatham Papers, 3; Taylor and Pringle, *Chatham Correspondence*, III, 203, William Beckford to Chatham, February 12, 1767.

[27] Chatham Papers, 3, Shelburne to Chatham, February 16, 1767. Shelburne's plan has not been known hitherto. His letter is printed in a highly deleted form in Taylor and Pringle, *Chatham's Correspondence*, III, 206–11, the paragraphs in which the plan is outlined being omitted. Fitzmaurice, *Life of Shelburne*, I, 310–13, also deletes this very pertinent passage.

[28] Chatham Papers, 3; Taylor and Pringle, *Chatham Correspondence*, III, 214–15, Chatham to Shelburne and Grafton, February 17, 1767.

The cabinet was forced to meet without Chatham on March 12. All saw the intervention of Parliament as necessary to enforce the Mutiny Act. The provisions of an enforcing act were not, however, discussed at this time, and other matters now required all the attention of the cabinet for some weeks. There was a full cabinet on New York affairs on Friday, April 24.[29] Once again, Shelburne had an opportunity to act decisively, but as his alienation from his colleagues had meanwhile increased, he now suggested merely that the governor of New York be empowered to billet troops anywhere he saw fit—even in private houses—until New York should comply. His colleagues gave the idea no encouragement. Conway suggested a local extraordinary port duty, laid on the city of New York, which would be both a punishment and a source of revenue. This plan was vetoed, however, because it would have put a burden on British and West Indian trade to the colony. Anyway, it could have been easily subverted by smuggling.

It was Charles Townshend who now brought forward a proposal which was to serve as the basis for the measure finally adopted. He suggested a parliamentary address to the Crown asking that it assent to no laws whatever from the assembly of New York until that colony should obey the Mutiny Act. Shelburne wrote to Chatham of his dislike of the plan but weakly excused his failure to declare himself at the meeting by saying, "I did not care to dwell upon it." It was further suggested that the revenue of the colony be paid to the order of the governor. Thus royal officials could be paid no matter what retaliatory action the assembly might take. General approval greeted the proposal. However, Shelburne covered himself by writing Chatham, "I am far from satisfied with it."

Though Shelburne had refused to lay his own plan before

---

[29] For a report of the cabinet, see Chatham Papers, 56, minute of April 26, 1767. B. Tunstall, *William Pitt, Earl of Chatham*, 391, makes use of the letter, but misdates the meeting as April 26. Referred to by Humphreys, "Lord Shelburne and British Colonial Policy," *English Historical Review*, Vol. L (April, 1935), 257–77.

his colleagues, he did outline it for Chatham, now so ill that he could scarcely think, let alone direct affairs. The scheme was of so "reactionary" a nature that, had it been adopted, it would have given such a spur to colonial resentment and such aid to radicals that the Revolution would have been antedated by five years.

Since the Americans were generally questioning whether they were bound by Acts of Parliament, and since the cabinet had determined to enforce the Mutiny Act, Shelburne proposed that Parliament pass an act reciting the Declaratory Act—which he and Chatham had so bitterly opposed—and referring to the disobedience of New York as "an avow'd disregard of it." While pardon would be held out for past offenses, it should also be declared that from three months after the arrival of the new act, it would be high treason to refuse to obey or execute an Act of Parliament. Further, it would be misprision of treason for an American to write, preach or speak, publish or affirm that the King and Parliament did not possess power to bind the Colonies by their acts. Offenders would be tried either in America or Great Britain, and the act would be enforced by the military if necessary.[30]

It is most unlikely that the colonists, even in 1767, would have tolerated armed enforcement of the law, especially one openly based upon the detested Declaratory Act. At any rate, the plan was never presented to the cabinet. Townshend's suggestion was accepted, although it was to be embodied in an Act of Parliament, rather than in an address. On May 13, therefore, Townshend moved in the Commons for a bill forbidding the governor of New York to assent to any act of the assembly until the Mutiny Act should be obeyed. Parliament thus undertook to interfere in the internal polity of a colony. By doing so, it thought to demonstrate its authority to bind America in all cases whatsoever. Feeling against New York had begun to run high in British political circles. Nor was it improved when

[30] Chatham Papers, 56, Shelburne to Chatham, April 26, 1767.

the merchants of that colony chose to petition against the Revenue Act of 1764 and against certain other restrictions placed on their commerce by the Laws of Trade. The Old Whigs had established two free ports, in Jamaica and Dominica, but the New York merchants, some 240 in number, now asked for a whole system of free ports in America and the West Indies, warning that otherwise they would have to turn to manufacturing. Shelburne sharply rejected the petition and was sustained by Chatham, who wrote of the New Yorkers, "They are doing the work of their worst enemies themselves."[31] Both men thus stand revealed as good mercantilists, as good as Grenville or Rockingham. They had no intention of loosening the commercial bonds of the empire.

The disobedience of the Mutiny Act so soon after repeal of the Stamp Act, the bad grace with which riot victims had been compensated, the Bill of Indemnity passed in Massachusetts, and now this ill-timed petition "soured the minds of people here in general." Lord George Sackville—who had recently dropped his notorious surname and would hereafter be known as Lord George Germain—reported his own opinion that "the Colonys are growing worse and worse." Even men formerly inclined to defend, or at least to palliate, the American position were becoming critical. The Rockinghams, William Beckford, and even Lord Camden indicated publicly their growing dissatisfaction with the colonial attitude. Rumors circulated that Chatham himself "has changed his ideas about America, and means to act with vigour."[32] Such reports served to underline the rapidly growing opinion that the previous year's concession to America was unappreciated and that future attempts to placate her would be as futile.

In truth, however, save for that respect his name commanded, Chatham had ceased to exist as a political force. His

[31] *Ibid.*, 3, Shelburne to Chatham, February 1, 1767, and Chatham's answer, February 3, 1767; *Chatham Correspondence*, III, 182–90.
[32] RHMCR. *Stopford-Sackville Papers*, I, 119–20.

prolonged absence had reduced the cabinet to chaos. Grafton was too weak and too frightened of making his own decisions to exercise effective leadership. Shelburne had isolated himself from his colleagues. Conway was torn between his love of office and his obligation to his Old Whig friends. Camden was ineffectual without Chatham's leadership. Only Northington showed any degree of steadiness. And thus Charles Townshend, brilliant and erratic, found no real opposition from his colleagues.

Townshend had earlier been denied a place in the cabinet by Chatham himself. But with the great man absent, he had forced himself into its innermost council, and there was none to say him nay. Several points rankled in his breast. He had been forced to give up the lucrative paymastership and take the burdensome office of chancellor of the exchequer. He had been denied the lead of Commons and a seat in the cabinet. Furthermore, he soon found himself in fundamental disagreement with Chatham's East India Company policy. Of an irrepressible, spontaneous, and at times incorrigible nature, the youthful Townshend found in Chatham's absence from a "languid" ministry an occasion and an inspiration.

The opening debates of the first meeting of Parliament in January, 1767, saw him at his most irresponsible. His actions betrayed a complete absence of any concept of joint cabinet responsibility. For such a political idea—North was to enunciate it toward the end of his ministry—a necessary prerequisite would be well developed parties which could pledge their members to definite principles. Chatham's ministry was deliberately the antithesis of such an arrangement.

When the estimates for the military establishment in America were presented, the likely cost was found to be about £400,000, roughly equivalent to a shilling of the land tax. Grenville, insisting that the estimates be reduced by half, proposed that the remainder be borne by the Colonies and that a revenue be raised upon them for that purpose. Like a schoolboy on a lark, Townshend now rose declaring he would "assert his own opinions." Rejecting Grenville's suggestion, he nonetheless spoke warmly for America's bearing a part of the expense. Commending the Stamp Act ("only the heats which prevailed made it an improper time to press it"), he condemned "every word" of the doctrine of internal-external taxation. An astonished and delighted House then heard him pledge himself to find an American revenue nearly sufficient to cover all expenses there. "What he means," exclaimed Shelburne, "I do not conceive."[33]

Although Grenville's motion was defeated, Townshend's speech had reopened the whole question of taxing America. His own craving for attention and his desire to divert the House from its East India business now combined with the Members' irritation against the Colonies, their wish to assert the supremacy of Parliament once and for all, and with the nation's need for more revenue to make a new effort in this direction inevitable.

To oppose Townshend in his wild impetuosity should have been Shelburne's task. The Colonies were under Shelburne's care. He knew that Townshend had deliberately challenged the fundamental tenets of Chatham's policy and his own towards colonial taxation. However alone in the cabinet and distrusted by his colleagues, he cannot wholly be excused for the mildness and fatalism wherewith he accepted Townshend's action. Shelburne had been working for some time, methodically collecting information from every source, on his own plan for an imperial administration for the west. At this crucial time, when Townshend raised once more the fatal question of parliamentary right, Shelburne should have realized that the future of all British North America had been put to hazard. Perhaps he believed that Townshend's talk was merely talk,

---

[33] For an account of the debate, see RHMCR. *Lothian Papers*, 274–75, Grenville to Buckinghamshire, January 27, 1767; also Chatham Papers, 83, Shelburne's minutes.

but it was nonetheless incumbent upon him to act. Instead, he deliberately confined himself to his researches, never seriously attempting to combat Townshend's avowed intent which, if carried out, would make such painstaking efforts utterly futile.

An even more ominous situation now began to develop: one which would force Townshend to redeem his pledge of an American revenue. By mid-February, the ministry perceived they were to be faced with a combined Opposition attempt to reduce the land tax. The King testily ascribed this design to Grenville's "Hobby Horse, the reduction of expences," and to his "unbounded attachment to his own opinions and a desire of thwarting those of others." George III saw the Opposition's intent as mere false economy, writing somewhat naively to Conway that "the great acquisitions made by the Successful War must necessarily give rise to an encrease of expence in the Peace Establishment, which seems by them [the Opposition] unattended to."[34] Grenville was "attending to" it all too well.

Both King and ministry were as yet oblivious of their danger. Chatham's brother-in-law James Grenville sent urgently to the first minister—lying ill at Marlborough—warning that a move for reduction was imminent. The Opposition, he said, hard hit by the land tax, would be supported by the country members "in good number on the plea of the repeal of the Stamp Act."[35] It was not, however, until the very eve of the vote that a worried Grafton reported to his King the growing opposition to the ministry's four-shilling land tax. George III was bitter against Grenville. His conduct, the King wrote, was "as abundant in absurditys as in the affair of the Stamp Act; for there he first deprived the Americans by restraining their Trade, from the means of acquiring Wealth, and Taxed them;

[34] Fortescue, *Correspondence of George* III, I, No. 468, the King to General Conway, February 18, 1767. See also L. B. Namier, *Additions and Corrections to Sir John Fortescue's Edition of the Correspondence of George III*, 69.

[35] Chatham Papers, 35, James Grenville to Lady Chatham, February 23, 1767.

now he objects to the Public's availing itself of the only adequate means of restoring its Finances, I mean the taking such
part that shall be judged expedient, out of the Territorial Revenues now received contrary to their Charter by the [East
India] Company, and at the same time moves for a diminution
of the Land Tax."[36]

His august wrath was, however, in part, misdirected. Rumors early in February that Grenville intended to move a reduction of the land tax had brought the Old Whigs together
in party conclave. Grudging one iota of popularity to Grenville, they had decided to forestall him by undertaking the
motion themselves. Altogether, it was a foolish decision. Sir
George Savile, always full of common sense and good counsel,
had warned them to think gravely on a plan which would cut
the national income by £450,000. This would simply have to
be made up from some source.[37] The Old Whigs themselves
had helped to rule out the possibility of an East Indian revenue. What source remained—but America?

The debate began on February 25. From the first, Old
Whigs stood shoulder to shoulder with Grenville, the Bedfords, and the country gentlemen. Townshend opened by proposing the land tax at four shillings, pledging that should he
still be in office next year, he would move its reduction to three
shillings. Old Whig Dowdeswell countered by moving an
amendment immediately reducing the tax to the lower figure.
He was seconded by Sir Edmund Isham, a country gentleman and Member for Northamptonshire. The Old Tory Sir
Roger Newdigate, Member for Oxford University, declared
for the amendment. A Grenville supporter, affirming the connection between this motion and Townshend's pledge of an
American revenue, reminded him of his promise and by it justified the tax reduction.

[36] Fortescue, *Correspondence of George III*, I, No. 471, the King to
Grafton, February 24, 1767.

[37] Albemarle, *Rockingham Memoirs*, II, 37–39, Savile to Charles Yorke,
February 11, 1767.

Still, the administration did not believe itself in danger. And when the vote came, on February 27, their defeat by 188 to 206 surprised all parties. The country gentlemen had tipped the scales for the Opposition.

Although Sir George Savile thought the defeat of the ministry due solely to an approaching election and a desire to curry favor with landowning electors, yet it was a major catastrophe for the ministry—and for America. Coming as it did before they had got a revenue from the East India Company—Chatham's cherished plan for relieving his country's finances—the land tax reduction made imperative Townshend's early redemption of his pledge. Indeed, funds were so short that Grafton had to ask Chatham, quite against the usual practice, to pay some ninety thousand pounds which the first minister had held unaudited since his paymastership of the forces.

Chatham, shocked by news of the tax reduction, drove himself on to London, arriving on March 2, but once there was too ill to deal with either domestic or American matters. There was an abortive attempt to oust the captious Townshend by offering the exchequer to Lord North, but that noble lord refused because of the unclear political situation. Chatham, his strength and mind now failing rapidly, withdrew to his house on Hampstead Heath. From this time onward, he was no longer the effective head of an administration, but his colleagues and his King unfortunately refused to accept this fact for many months.

As chancellor of the exchequer, Townshend was directly faced with the nation's financial problem, a problem created by the delay in gaining a revenue from the East India Company and the unexpected reduction of the land tax. Nor was he long in bringing matters to a crisis. At the cabinet meeting on March 12, still smarting from the attempt to replace him, Townshend declared that if the estimates for the American extraordinaries were not reduced, he would resign. Well he knew that such action would overturn the ministry. To achieve the reductions, he could afford an ultimatum. British troops in America must be withdrawn from the frontier toward the larger cities. New port taxes must be laid upon America for revenue. Thus, to offset the decrease in national income and to pay even the reduced cost of the ten thousand troops in America, the colonists had to be taxed and the last remnant of Grenville's imperial scheme abandoned. Western forts, Indian trade, the disposition of troops, "in short the whole arrangement," must be reconsidered so as to cut expenses. American duties would do the rest. In effect, then, Townshend urged a western policy based on the principles set forth in Barrington's report of May, 1766.[38]

Plagued with an apparently insoluble domestic financial problem, Townshend was determined to force an American settlement upon the hesitating government and a slow-moving secretary of state. Shelburne, badgered by an insistent Townshend at home and beseiged with urgent calls for direction from royal officials in the Colonies, was at last obliged to act.

On March 30, therefore, he read a paper to the cabinet. Making no effort to combat Townshend's avowed intent to derive a revenue from America, he fixed his efforts on saving the west to the empire. He advised caution and begged his colleagues to be patient while he gathered the data whereon to base a western plan. The cost of his eventual plan, he thought, might be borne by a revenue from the quitrents and land-grant fees, augmented by a system of annual requisitions. Despite the cabinet's personal hostility towards him, Shelburne won his point, and his report was accepted.

Shelburne's victory, however, was a shadowy one; Townshend's the substantial one. Shelburne had asked for time to evolve his policy. There was no time. Time had run out at the reduction of the land tax. Townshend, on the other hand,

---

[38] Chatham Papers, 3; Taylor and Pringle, *Chatham Correspondence*, III, 231–32, Grafton to Chatham, March 13, 1767, 232–33, Shelburne to Chatham, March 13, 1767.

had presented a feasible, positive policy ready for immediate execution. Furthermore, it coincided with a general opinion among government and Opposition alike that "something must be done in support of the authority of the Mother Country." Townshend's taxes would produce a revenue, but more than that, they would be an exercise of British sovereignty—which most home politicians thought long overdue. When Townshend opened his budget on April 15, therefore, he "adopted most of Mr. Grenville's ideas, and spoke as freely of Administration as if he had not been in office"[39] To such an end had come Chatham's campaign against faction.

A full cabinet on American affairs, chiefly concerned with New York, was held on April 24. Shelburne, secure on the laurels of what he thought a long-range victory, made no effort to combat Townshend's American tax proposals or even to bring him to an explanation of them. The Chancellor of the Exchequer accordingly redeemed his promise on May 13, the day he moved for the bill suspending the New York Assembly. By his second and third bills, he proposed to establish a Board of Commissioners of the Customs in America, better to execute the Laws of Trade and to receive the revenue from the new duties, about forty thousand pounds annually. To avoid an American objection to internal taxes, these were to be port duties on tea, glass, paper, printer's colors, and red and white lead. To make smuggling unprofitable, the duty on tea was to be reduced from one shilling to three pence per pound. Coffee and cocoa imported from Great Britain were to be tax-free, but the drawback on china earthenware exported to America was to be withdrawn. The act would further empower the Superior Court in each province to grant general writs of assistance. These would allow officers of the customs to enter any house or shop by daylight to search for prohibited or smuggled goods. In his speech, Townshend scouted Shelburne's suggested use of

---

[39] RHMCR. *Stopford-Sackville Papers*, I, 121–23, letters of Lord George Germain.

a requisition system and affirmed that the time had come to assert British sovereignty by an Act of Parliament.

Townshend's plan, however, differed radically from Grenville's earlier one. The Stamp Act revenues were to have been applied solely to imperial defense. Now, Townshend proposed to create an American civil list whence governors, judges, and other royal officials would be paid. Such a provision cut violently across the lines of political evolution in America, where the power of the purse was as well understood and as jealously guarded by colonial assemblies as in the mother country by Parliament. The controversy between the Colonies and Great Britain was therefore to move to the highest constitutional level, even as Franklin had predicted in his testimony to the Commons during the Stamp Act crisis.

Opposition to Townshend's plan being weak and desultory, the resolutions were agreed to and reported on the 15th. At one stroke, then, America was taxed, an American Board of Customs set up, and the assembly of New York suspended—all this under a ministry which bore the name of one who had stood foremost in denying Parliament's right to tax the Colonies for revenue.

Townshend had sponsored the new taxation of America, but in doing so he had reflected the majority of opinion in Great Britain. Faced with an intolerable situation as chancellor of the exchequer, he simply put into legal form a deep-seated belief that Great Britain was entitled to financial help from her colonies. A minister more forceful than Shelburne might, by resolutely opposing his proposals, have driven Townshend from office. But at a moment when decisive action might have saved the first British Empire, he showed himself hesitant to stand forward. He failed to support those principles which he and his stricken chief had so long maintained. Here then he committed a cardinal error of statescraft and politics: he allowed the initiative to pass from his hands.

Grenville had aimed at creating an imperial system, partly

supported by funds from America. No similar grand motive influenced Townshend. He was indifferent to imperial plans, although his actions had the deepest imperial ramifications. The end product was as much a negation of Grenville's concept of empire as the Old Whig ministry had been. Grenville had seen the vision of an orderly and steadily expanding commonwealth; Townshend saw only an imperial budget. This much, however, Grenville, Townshend, and nearly all parliamentarians had in common: they believed America a proper object of imperial taxation and Parliament possessed of competent authority to tax her.[40]

[40] Franklin expressed the opinion that the anti-American sentiment in Britain was so great that it did not matter if Townshend was in or out of office. In all fairness to the Chancellor of the Exchequer, it must be remembered that he wished to allow colonial ships to sail directly from Spain and Portugal to the Colonies with wine, fruit, and oil. He was forced to drop this concession in the face of great opposition from British merchants. See Sparks, *Franklin's Works*, VII, 338–44.

CHAPTER FOUR

THE FALL OF THE CHATHAM SYSTEM

CHATHAM was gone, and without his leadership his government seemed on the verge of a breakup. Shelburne, considered a "secret enemy" by his colleagues, remained in office solely for Chatham's sake. Conway, under great pressure from his Old Whig friends, declared he would resign at the end of the session. Charles Townshend was flirting with the Old Whigs, and Northington announced that health obliged his retirement. Camden was helpless and ineffectual without his chief's support; and Grafton himself made it known that he would follow Conway out of the government.

The situation in Parliament was equally discouraging. On a division in the House of Lords in April, the government had been saved by a majority of only three. Evidently the Opposition was achieving a formidable measure of union.

The repeated appeals of the King and Grafton to the prostrate Chatham, urging him to chalk out a new ministerial arrangement, met with reiterated declarations of his incapacity to do so. Finally, on May 31, Grafton was allowed to see Chatham for a short time. He obtained however only a suggestion that he treat with the Bedfords or the Rockinghams, preferably the former. Grafton was, moreover, profoundly shocked at Chatham's condition; the more so as he realized that now his titular leadership of the ministry had become a real one. It is to the young Duke's credit that he rose to the challenge.

The King clung pathetically to a belief that if only Chatham would revive, all would go well. He was willing to gamble, as was the younger Pitt at a later date, on the chance of a sick man's recovery. Grafton knew all too well, however, that an accession of strength or, at least, the dispelling of the threat of a united Opposition was imperative. As soon, therefore, as the session ended, on July 2, Grafton, following the King's preference, not Chatham's, approached Rockingham about a coalition. The ensuing negotiations furnish an opportunity to appraise both the importance of the American problem as an issue in domestic politics and the development of lines of party division.

The three Whig "splinter groups" in Opposition, the Old Whigs, the Bedford group, and the Grenville-Temple supporters, possessed in reality only one common trait which might form a basis for union. This was a mistaken belief that the King's Friends belonged to Bute and that Bute himself was a secret adviser to the King. Bedford had shown a disposition to unite with the Rockinghams in order to extirpate Bute's supposed influence, that is, to pull down the ministry. Grenville, too, had expressed his desire to join in such an attack. And Newcastle was eager for a conjunction on this basis, for he was astute enough to see that an anti-Bute "platform" was the only foundation on which a united Opposition could stand.[1] Here then was a force working for Whig union and against those which were widening party divisions. How strong was the force? And what had happened to the American issue?

First, the inner council of the Old Whig party was split. The old corps, led by Newcastle, Albemarle, and Portland, looked nostalgically to the past when a united Whig party had held undisputed sway. They strongly desired an alliance with Bedford, and with Grenville, too, should that be possible. Control of the group had passed from their hands, however, and

---

[1] Wentworth-Woodhouse, Rockingham Papers, Newcastle to Rockingham, July 8, 1767.

now rested with the "boys," led by Rockingham, Burke, and Dowdeswell. Rockingham was not sanguine for an alliance built on so negative a ground as mere hatred of Bute. Indeed, he declared himself unwilling to treat the King's Friends harshly, and in fact he coveted their support should he come again to power. Underlying this reluctance to draw nearer to the other Opposition groups, however, was a consideration which the old corps could not be expected to understand. The "boys" feared that a Bedford alliance would draw them closer to Grenville whom they detested.[2] From the outset, then, this tendency toward union was not as strong as it looked.

Still, when Grafton approached Rockingham in July, the Marquis insisted that the Bedfords be included in the negotiations. Bedford, in turn, would not move without Temple and Grenville. The conversations which followed were two-sided, Rockingham holding talks with Grafton and the King on the one hand, and with Bedford, who was acting for Temple and Grenville, on the other.

On July 20, Bedford, Weymouth, and Rigby met Rockingham, Newcastle, and other Old Whig leaders at Newcastle House. Bedford immediately threw a bombshell by informing the Old Whigs that Grenville and Temple, besides certain other vague demands, required a declaration of intent "to assert and establish the rights of Great Britain over her colonies." Rockingham flew into a rage, denying that he and his friends had ever given ground for a suspicion that they intended giving up British sovereignty over the settlements. The Grenville demand he denounced as a trap for his own party and as a proof of the bad faith of theirs. The meeting would have ended then and there had not Bedford urged that the declaration be taken as a mere formula. Despite Rigby's warning that the Grenvilles would be satisfied with nothing but the words as

---

[2] Add. MSS 35430, ff. 834, Rockingham to Charles Yorke, July 18, 1767; Wentworth-Woodhouse, Rockingham Papers, William Dowdeswell to Rockingham, July 23 and 24, 1767.

Case= 7066654 5

ITD= 201163300000 20

Ref: 201163300000 20

Lightsey, Katie-UK-1 App D: Klohtsey

(803) 33...

@ tracking= 455147

UAB

UAB Undergraduate Admission
HUC 260
1530 3rd Ave, S Birmingham, AL 35294-1150
Undergrad Admit (205) 934-8221

Ref: 20110330000017

tracking: 22917

Payment Trans: SA0311033012154052022096

they stood, a compromise was eventually reached, whereby the phrase "maintain and support" was substituted for "assert and establish."

So it was not the American issue that ruined the Rockingham-Bedford negotiations. Rather it was an irreconcilable difference over General Conway. Despite this person's weak and fickle conduct—he had not resigned from Chatham's ministry with his friends—Rockingham insisted that in any new arrangement he have the lead of the House of Commons. The Bedfords demanded his exclusion, and the meetings then broke up. On July 23, therefore, Rockingham told the King he was unable to form a new administration.[3]

Newcastle and the old corps were thrown into despair, and the Duke wrote bitterly to Rockingham of the latter's misplaced loyalty. While Newcastle and Albemarle fervently advised him "for God's Sake my dear Lord·don't loose sight of the D. of Bedford," the "boys," particularly Burke, were congratulating him on his escape from the alliance and for refusing to enter office but "in corps."[4] America had not kept Rockingham apart from Bedford. Even old Newcastle saw that "as to the Declaration proposed by Mr. Grenville, relating to America, It was so whittled down by the Duke of Bedford, That It could not *finally* have created any Difficulty."[5] Rather, it was Rockingham's insistence—quixotic to the old corps— upon viewing his party as founded upon principle and a community of interest which took precedence over the love of office.

The American issue had, however, kept the Old Whigs irreconcilably apart from Grenville and Temple. Early in the negotiations, Grenville had informed Rigby that America was

[3] Russell, *The Bedford Correspondence*, III, 82–87.

[4] Wentworth-Woodhouse, Rockingham Papers, Newcastle to Rockingham, July 22, 1767, Albemarle to Rockingham, July 22, 1767; C. Williams, Earl Fitzwilliam, and Sir R. Bourke (eds.), *Burke Correspondence*, I, 132–37.

[5] Wentworth-Woodhouse, Rockingham Papers, Newcastle to Rockingham, July 22, 1767.

the great point. To other friends, he reiterated his intent never to retreat from his demand that Britain assert and establish her sovereignty over the Colonies.[6] Nor was he deceived when the negotiations failed. He knew well that Bedford and Rockingham had reached agreement about America, and that, consequently, his own connection with Bedford was weak indeed.

In September, Charles Townshend died, and was succeeded at the exchequer by the former paymaster Lord North. The whole political situation again became fluid, most of the Opposition expecting a renewal of offers from Grafton. Again, Newcastle and Albemarle preached to Rockingham the gospel of a Bedford alliance and the necessity for pulling down the *"Bute* Administration."[7] But Rockingham had taken his stand in July. Once more, now, he tried to explain himself to the old corps. He feared a Bedford alliance because the Old Whigs might thereby be pulled into alignment with Grenville and Temple, whose acid account of the July negotiations, now published, had fanned his hatred to new heights. His party, Rockingham stated, was eternally committed against joining a ministry in which Grenville might have a major part. The Old Whigs had won their honor and credit with the public by overturning Grenville's American plan. To admit him now as an ally would be the ruin of them, and a union with Bedford might well bring him in.[8] Rockingham's conception of "party" was thus taking on a surprisingly modern tone. While the old corps poured out a stream of advice, threats, and entreaties, he was writing to Dowdeswell of Newcastle's "hurries and Impatience and want of Steadiness to adhere strictly to . . . one of the Fundamental Principles on which we have acted."[9] Indeed, in the

---

[6] Smith, *The Grenville Papers*, IV, 48–52, Grenville to Suffolk, July 14, 1767; RHMCR, *Lothian Papers*, 277–78, Grenville to Buckinghamshire.

[7] Wentworth-Woodhouse, Rockingham Papers, Newcastle to Rockingham, September 11, 1767.

[8] *Ibid.*, Rockingham to Portland, September 15, 1767; Albemarle, *Rockingham Memoirs*, II, 57–59.

[9] Wentworth-Woodhouse, Rockingham Papers, September 14, 1767.

consolidation of the right wing of politics, the Old Whigs were in danger of being pulled to pieces. But by rejecting New-castle's advice and by adopting a standstill policy, Rockingham, though he doomed his party to tedious years out of office, saved it from dissolution. The failure of the negotiations in July and September, 1767, indicated that a reunion of the Old Whig party was a dream that was past. Henceforward, the modern party system was to develop without hindrance from a half-century-old myth.

For the Bedfords, the American issue, due to Grenville's insistence upon "the asserting and establishing the lawful authority of the King and Parliament of Great Britain over every part of our dominions in every part of the world,"[10] meant that a united Opposition was impossible. Motivated by no principle but love of office, they now turned their thoughts to a possible coalition with the Grafton Ministry. On December 11, Grafton learned from Weymouth that the Bedfords had "the greatest Desire . . . to make no Difficulties," and that their only condition for an alliance was the removal of Shelburne. Grafton eagerly began negotiations upon the basis of this offer.[11]

The point concerning Shelburne—now cordially disliked and distrusted by his colleagues—was, however, a rather delicate matter. He was Chatham's man. So how was his retreat to be achieved without offense to Chatham? The Earl might recover at some future date and demand a reckoning. With these considerations in mind, Grafton agreed to a shameful Bedfordite proposal that Shelburne's office, that of secretary of state for the Southern Department, be divided and that a new secretaryship of state for the Colonies be created. Such a humiliation, it was agreed, would force Shelburne to resign. The King too, loathing the Secretary, heartily concurred in the proposal.

[10] Russell, *The Bedford Correspondence*, III, 396–99, Grenville to Bedford, November 6, 1767.

[11] Fortescue, *Correspondence of George* III, I, No. 567, Grafton to the King, December 11, 1767.

The utility of a third secretary of state for the colonies had long been acknowledged. Both Rockingham and Chatham had thought seriously of such an arrangement. Grafton's decision now to create such an office was, however, one of pure political expediency and had nothing to do with improving the administration of the Colonies. It therefore came as a great disappointment to the King, Grafton, and the Bedfords when Shelburne, from his attachment to Chatham, reluctantly agreed to the division. Moreover, he chose to remain southern secretary, although Grafton, perhaps fearful of the Bedfords' American views, urged him to take the new office.

The Bedfords, however, would not allow the frustration of their plan to ruin so promising an opportunity for office. With the entire cabinet against him, Shelburne would scarcely be an important factor. The alliance was accordingly concluded. Observers then were convinced that American affairs had played a large part in the political "jobbing" which had produced it.[12] However, there is no evidence that any comprehensive American policy was insisted upon by either party, and the question was more likely set aside and left to the dictate of future events.

The consolidation in office of the conservative element in British politics had begun with Chatham's use of the King's Friends to replace the Rockinghams. A second great step in the process was the Bedford accession. In the coincident cabinet shuffle, Conway resigned his position as secretary of state for the Northern Department, but, retaining a seat in the cabinet, remained on friendly terms with the government. Bedfordites Weymouth and Gower became secretary of state and president of the Council respectively, old Northington retiring from the latter post. Sandwich was made a postmaster, and Rigby vice treasurer of Ireland with a promise of the paymaster's

[12] Smith, *Grenville Papers*, IV, 197–207, Whately to Grenville, December 25, 1767; 205, Lord Trevor to Grenville, December 29, 1767; 249–53, Lord Lyttelton to Temple, January 1, 1768.

office. King's Friend Hillsborough took the new office of secretary of state for the colonies. The original elements of Chatham's "mosaic," Camden, Shelburne, Grafton, Granby, and Hawke, still held a nominal majority in the cabinet, but unity and determination were on the side of the new members.

How would the incoming ministry handle the American issue? Franklin was pessimistic. Conway and Shelburne, whom he accounted friends to the Colonies, were no longer in a position to shield them from those who might counsel stern measures. This much was evident, however: some action about the Colonies was pressingly necessary. In December, it was known that America had not accepted the Townshend taxes quietly. Reports that Boston had adopted a nonimportation agreement put the newspapers "in full cry against America" and produced "a prodigious clamour."[13]

From the collapse of Chatham to the Bedfordite accession, Grafton and his government had seemed inert. Secretary at War Barrington had written his kinsman Bernard of the disgraceful confusion among the ministers. They feared, it seemed, to take any steps about America, lest Chatham, when he did emerge, would disapprove.[14] It was during these months, however, that Shelburne was working up a comprehensive policy for the American west. His slow and painful methods, his great personal unpopularity, and the division of his office were yet to render his efforts nugatory.

As soon as Shelburne had taken office, his mind had turned to the western problem, and he had begun to collect his information. In autumn, 1766, he had written to General Gage, the commander-in-chief in America, revealing the direction his plan was taking: "The forming an American fund to support the exigencies of government in the same manner as is done in Ireland, is what is so highly reasonable that it must take

[13] Sparks, *Franklin's Works*, VII, 371–73, Franklin to William Franklin, December 19, 1767.

[14] Channing and Coolidge, *Barrington-Bernard Correspondence*, 127–28, July 8, 1767.

place sooner or later." Shelburne's colonial ideas were none the less in harmony with Chatham's in that he felt Parliament had unlimited power within the Colonies to secure the British trade monopoly but none to levy taxes there for revenue. Where then did he propose to find that "American fund" which Grenville had sought to raise by a Stamp Act and Townshend by his port duties? Part of it would come from a diligent collection of the quitrents on both past and future land grants. In a paper read to the cabinet on March 30, however, he revealed that the fund would rest "chiefly on requisitions from the different provinces to be granted annually by their assemblies according to their respective abilities."[15]

This was the interim report which Shelburne had read to the cabinet during those weeks when Townshend was ramming through his taxes. In the intervening months, Shelburne had continued his work. It was thus not until September, 1767, that his final report was ready. In it, his basic hypotheses were that it was impossible to prevent westward expansion in North America and that to allow it would be to postpone colonial manufacturing. Further, the Colonies should be permitted to regulate Indian affairs because they were familiar with the problem. The imperial Indian establishment could then be abolished.

Two new colonies were to be formed, one at Detroit and the other in the Illinois country. Eight forts, manned by British troops, were to be maintained in the area. Thus betraying the influence of Franklin and Richard Jackson, the plan also stated that a fixed boundary line and a clarification of Indian rights were urgently necessary.

This plan was never implemented, although the Privy Council accepted the proposed boundary line, somewhat to the west of the older Proclamation Line, in January, 1768. Shel-

---

[15] Fitzmaurice, *Life of Shelburne*, 305–307, Shelburne to Gage, November 14, 1766; extracts of this letter and of Shelburne's paper of March 30, 1767, are printed in Alvord, *Mississippi Valley*, I, 282–83, 334.

burne was soon to lose control of American affairs; and Hillsborough, his successor, was to reject totally his proposal for a rapid settlement of the west. In any event, one doubts that the plan would have succeeded had it been adopted. It went quite against the grain of eighteenth-century British imperialism, and it was based financially on quitrents and requisitions which probably could not have been collected. A revival of the question of right would have followed.

Shelburne's plan held, however, the seeds of a concept of empire radically different from that then prevailing. It is not too much to say that the plan is one of Shelburne's best claims to greatness as a statesman. For the first time since Grenville, a scheme had been presented which envisaged the creation of a new imperial system and full utilization of the North American conquests. Grenville would have had a centralized empire minutely administered from Whitehall. His plan was in full accord with the eighteenth-century persuasion that a widespread empire had to have somewhere a center of supreme power. Shelburne, however, had now brought forward the idea of a decentralized empire. Had it been implemented, it would have spared Britain decades of bitter political controversy and the alienation of her colonial peoples everywhere. It would have been a tremendous step towards the modern Commonwealth of Nations. Shelburne believed that if the Colonies were given management of their own internal affairs, and if the westward movement should be allowed to develop naturally, colonial affection for the mother country would secure perpetual empire. His time, however, had run out. He was replaced by Hillsborough, and the uneasy calm of autumn gave way to mounting storms on either shore.

The new Board of Commissioners of the Customs appointed under Townshend's Act had held their first meeting in Boston on November 18, 1767. No overt indignity had been offered them, but the townspeople had left no doubt about their opinion of the proceedings. The board had immediately under-

taken a reorganization of the entire customs service. New officers were added and a better system of accounting adopted.
Further, a network of revenue cutters and royal naval vessels
was established. The molasses tax had been reduced to a penny.
This, with the increased efficiency of the new organization, cut
illicit trade until it became negligible..For the first time, the
entire system of trade and navigation laws, evolving since the
reign of Charles II, was put into efficient operation. American
merchants now suddenly found themselves bound and checked
on every side. Some drastic countermeasure was manifestly
necessary if American trade were to escape from strangula-
tion.[16] A great majority of American merchants therefore threw
themselves wholeheartedly into the nonimportation agreements. It was soon obvious, too, that the revolutionary apparatus developed during the Stamp Act crisis was very much
alive. Mob violence and intimidation again became the order
of the day in Boston. Bernard was so frightened that he refused
to ask for troops which the commissioners desired, so that he
might be able to swear that he had never called for them.
Nevertheless, his letters to England were but thinly disguised
appeals to the government to take the initiative and to send
the troops anyway.[17]

Obviously, the situation was rapidly worsening. In January,
1768, Bernard forwarded to Barrington a copy of the "Letters
of a Pennsylvania Farmer," written anonymously by John
Dickinson. The American readily admitted the right of Parliament to regulate trade. America was "as much dependent on

[16] See Channing, *History of the United States*, III, 87 ff. The new system
was a success in the immediate sense. In contrast to the small amounts collected before the Townshend Acts, thirty thousand pounds was collected annually between 1768 and 1774, at a cost of only thirteen thousand pounds a
year. Channing states, however, "The hardships of the regulations put an
end to existing modes of trade in many cases and the profits in foreign commerce dwindled to so low a figure that importers were far readier to sign
non-importation agreements in 1769 than they had been in 1766." (p. 90.)

[17] Channing and Coolidge, *Barrington-Bernard Correspondence*, 141–45.
See also 147–50, Bernard to Barrington, March 4, 1768.

Great Britain as a perfectly free people can be on another." The important point, however, was the disappearance of the confusion concerning internal and external taxes. Parliament, the Farmer declared, had no right to levy any taxes for revenue.[18] In British eyes, Dickinson's position was illogical and contradictory, besides being highly disrespectful to Parliament, but it cannot be doubted that Dickinson had presented the current American view.

In February, Bernard reported that the radicals in the assembly had gained control of it. They had then proceeded to expunge a previous adverse vote from their journal and had carried a resolution calling for petitions to the home government and a circular letter to the assemblies of the other North American Colonies. In such a letter, they would ask for cooperation and consultation in forming a program of "legal" resistance to the Townshend Acts. At the beginning of March, the distressed Governor could write only that the nonimportation agreements were gaining new supporters daily, and that it had been generally resolved in his province that the new duties would be disregarded until repealed.

Nor could Grafton take much comfort from the news, which arrived in April, that the New York Assembly had "complied" with the Mutiny Act. That body had indeed voted a sum of money to the Crown, but, bent upon minimum retreat, had refused to specify its use or otherwise acknowledge the act. This was at best a compromise which, in view of the increasingly violent disturbances at Boston, had barely the appearance of a government victory.

At that place, the commissioners had taken the step which Bernard had feared to take himself. Informing the home government that the revenue laws could not be enforced without assistance and that Boston was on the point of rising against them, they had sent to Commodore Hood at Halifax for warships. Hood had replied by sending them the fifty-gun "Rom-

[18] S. E. Morison, *Sources and Documents*, 34–54.

ney," but the Commissioners considered their situation so serious that they requested him to send an additional force.[19] This sense of danger was by no means confined to the commissioners. Indeed, all officers of the Crown and friends of government were in "a distressed State," and Bernard was in a fever to resign his burdensome office. Obviously, concerted and decisive measures were necessary if the cause of royal government were to be saved in Massachusetts, and probably in the other colonies as well. But Grafton did not act.

Affairs of empire had to await the result of a domestic political upheaval. On March 11, Parliament was dissolved, and a general election followed. It worked no radical change in the composition of the House, although 164 of its Members were elected for the first time, one of whom was Charles James Fox. The election was observed by Benjamin Franklin, and while it was in the main an average one, it served to point up his consciousness of American virtue and English corruption. In the critical days to come, a conviction in the Colonies that Old England, venal and degenerate, was unfit to rule an empire went far to render compromise impossible.

The election of 1768 was distinguished by the return from exile of that outlawed scapegrace John Wilkes. Having unsuccessfully sought pardon from both the Rockingham and Chatham Ministries, Wilkes now took the bull by the horns. He appeared suddenly in London, petitioned the King for pardon, and announced himself candidate for the city of London. Failing of that seat, he promptly stood for the radical county of Middlesex which on March 28 returned him at the head of the poll. Grafton's inclination was to pardon Wilkes and let him take his seat, so that his own character might sink him to a deserved obscurity. The King, however, remembering the *North Briton*, No. 45, vetoed such a solution. George III's obstinacy was to lead the government and Parliament into a

[19] Add. MSS 38340, ff. 309–10, memorial of the commissioners to the Lords of the Treasury, July 11, 1768.

Portraits courtesy New York Public Library

EARL OF SHELBURNE   DUKE OF GRAFTON

headlong collision with the radical element and to make them ridiculous in the eyes of the country.

Wilkes' imprisonment for seditious libel and blasphemy, and the ministry's refusal to release him—so that he might take his seat in the new Parliament on May 10—led directly to a nasty outbreak of riot and violence among the London mob. These formed the great mass of Wilkes' supporters. Troops actually clashed with rioters in St. George's Fields, but the "horrid massacre," far from restoring quiet, merely inflamed the situation. Many of the mob had been rendered desperate by unemployment, commercial depression, poor harvests, and high prices. Wilkes served as the focal point of their accumulated discontents.

Confronted with radicalism and tumult both at home and in the Colonies, the Grafton Ministry was at a loss which way to turn. The result was confusion and indecision at a moment when strength and diplomacy were needed on both "fronts." When the Lords of the Treasury, with Grafton presiding, met to consider the reports from the harassed Customs Commissioners of Boston, their only answer to the inflamed situation in America was to ask the American Secretary of State, Hillsborough, to send "most positive Instructions" to Bernard and to the other colonial governors, requiring them to aid the commissioners in the execution of their duty.[20] Such inanities were ill designed to encourage officials who felt their very lives in danger.

Hillsborough, however, sought to take more decisive action. The American Secretary, whose pomposity and determination to play the strong man could not conceal his want of talent, now wrote to Bernard in the King's name: he must order his assembly, on the pain of dissolution, to rescind their vote for the Circular Letter. Foolishly drawing in all the North American provinces, he told the other governors that they too must dissolve their assemblies should these be inclined to go

[20] *Ibid.*, ff. 314–19, Treasury minutes, January 26 to July 28, 1768.

along with Massachusetts. It was further implied that force, if needed, would not be lacking.

Before this order could reach America, however, yet more serious affrays had occurred over the seizure of John Hancock's sloop, "Liberty." The persons and property of the commissioners were assaulted by the Boston mob, and these unfortunate officials—all but one—together with their families, sought refuge first on the "Romney" and later at Castle William. Thence, they had appealed to Gage for troops and to Hood for more naval aid.[21]

Furthermore, Bernard was required to inform the home government at the end of June that despite the presence of two more armed schooners lately sent, the assembly had refused by a vote of ninety-two to seventeen, and "in a very offensive manner," to rescind their Circular Letter resolution. He consequently dissolved the Massachusetts Assembly on July 1. Henceforward, however, "ninety-two" was to form a rallying cry in Bernard's province similar to "forty-five" among Wilkes' admirers in Britain.

Indeed, attempts were going on to link up the radicalisms growing on either shore. A Committee of the Boston Sons of Liberty, for instance, wrote to the jailed but "Illustrious Patriot," acclaiming him a savior of the Constitution and sending him a monetary token of their esteem.[22]

In February, 1769, the House of Commons had declared Wilkes expelled the House, thereby seeking to invalidate his election for Middlesex. Then followed a scene without parallel in British political history, one that would have been ludicrous had not the constitutional implications been so serious. Twice was Wilkes re-elected by the voters of Middlesex, and twice more expelled the House. After a third contest, which saw Wilkes far ahead of his opponent, a Colonel Lut-

[21] *Ibid.*, f. 285, commissioners to Gage, June 15, 1768, copy.
[22] Add. MSS 30870, f. 45, signed by Benjamin Kent, Thomas Young, Benjamin Church, Jr., John Adams, and Joseph Warren.

trell, the House took the highhanded measure of declaring Luttrell duly elected. Radical ferment in the London area increased ominously with Wilkes again its focal point. From this time dates the rise of "The Society for Supporting the Bill of Rights," among whose founding members were the radical parson of Brentford, Horne Tooke, and several Members of Parliament. Three decades hence, radical ferment, engendered by the French Revolution, would find expression in similar organizations and would pose a serious problem to the home government. Now, however, fortunately for the ministry, the society did not long survive the blow of its hero's release from "martyrdom." When Wilkes had served his sentence and was freed, the society fell into the bitterest internal wrangling because Wilkes saw in it no other object but his personal welfare.[23] It was therefore incapable of seriously affecting the course of events, save by intensifying the conservative reaction now steadily growing as a result of the American disturbances.

American radicals, however, saw in the persecution of Wilkes and the disregard of the rights of the electors of Middlesex proof of their worst suspicions. For them it indicated that the ministry had openly abandoned any pretense of respect for constitutional government. Wilkes' letters to them confirmed their fears that the ministry was deep in a plot against all liberty and theirs in particular. Had Wilkes been less a charlatan, more diabolically clever, and less preoccupied with making money on his misfortunes, he might have played the role of a British Samuel Adams. He might have welded British radicalism into a potent political force, joining hands with that across the Atlantic. Crafty and shrewd Wilkes was, but he was no revolutionary. Lacking any motive but self-interest, he dallied with the American radicals, accepted their presents, laughed at their gullibility, fed them on hackneyed phrases, fanned the coals of their resentment against the home

[23] See Alexander Stephens, *Memoirs of John Horne Tooke*.

government, and encouraged them so long as he thought they might be of service to him.[24]

Grafton's position in the summer, 1768, was assuredly an unenviable one. Faced with riots at home and in the Colonies, and with a growing conservative demand that parliamentary supremacy be vindicated, he had also to reckon on the chance of Chatham's recovery. The fear of his master's disapproval of measures which might be adopted was a heavy burden for the young Duke, and he was fully resolved to avoid responsibility all he could. Hillsborough had written his stern letter; Bernard had dissolved the Massachusetts Assembly. The home government had ordered Gage to collect and make ready his troops at Halifax and to hold them there until Bernard should request them. These were steps forced by the weight of events upon a reluctant Grafton. Desperately, the Duke longed for the meeting of Parliament in the autumn, so that if necessity should require it, responsibility for American measures could be shifted from himself to that body. For instance, when Grafton's Treasury Board met on July 5 to consider the disastrous American situation, they did no more than send to the London Commissioners of the Customs asking how past obstructions had been dealt with. Not till more than two weeks later, on July 21, did they consider the "Liberty" riots. They then decided to lay the whole affair before the law officers of the Crown for an opinion on the legality of the Boston Commissioners' seizure of the vessel.

Such procrastination could not go on indefinitely in the face of repeated colonial insults to legal authority. And, at the end of the month, Grafton and his board wrote the Boston Commissioners that their "complaints" had been sent to Hillsborough to be laid before the King. Concern was expressed that they had been forced to retire to Castle William, but the Treasury Board had no doubt that they would soon return to

[24] For a sampling of Wilkes' correspondence with the Boston Sons of Liberty, see Add. MSS 30870, ff. 75–76, 135–36, and f. 166.

Boston and execute the revenue laws with "firmness and resolution." Only toward the end of this communication were the commissioners told that their urgent pleas had been heeded and that two regiments were bound for Boston to protect them.[25]

While Grafton dallied, British political opinion was solidifying. The desire was for some vindication of Parliament's supremacy over the Colonies. The new disorders in Massachusetts seemed to show that indulgence of the Colonies, as in the repeal of the Stamp Act, had been futile and that a settlement with the Americans was overdue. Grenville declared that a return to the requisition system or any effort to derive a revenue from quitrents would violate the Constitution. (The Crown would thereby derive an income independent of Parliament's control.)[26] This pronouncement summed up what had become accepted doctrine; and it was now adopted as an irrefutable answer to colonial demands for the abandonment of parliamentary taxation in favor of requisitions.

The conservative reaction was running strongly among the Old Whigs, too. Rockingham was as angry with "the dangerous madness of some in America, as at the passion and obstinacy of some at home." America's outbursts were "most dangerous and offensive," and, fearing the Colonists were impugning the Declaratory Act, he proclaimed his eternal support of that piece of Old Whig legislation.[27]

That country gentleman Thomas Falconer might consider Massachusetts' refusal to rescind her Circular Letter a "signal

[25] Add. MSS 38340, ff. 314–19.

[26] RHMCR. *Knox Papers, Various Collections*, 95–98, 101–102, Grenville to Knox, June 27, July 15, 28, October 9, 1768. See also Smith, *Grenville Papers*, IV, 316–19, Grenville to Thomas Pownall, July 17, 1768.

[27] Albemarle, *Rockingham Memoirs*, II, 78–81, Rockingham to Collector of the Boston Customs, Harrison, October 2, 1768; see also 76–77, Rockingham to Dowdeswell, August 11, 1768. Add. MSS 35374, ff. 350–53, John Yorke to Hardwicke, July 28, 1768; Wentworth-Woodhouse, Rockingham Papers, Sir George Savile to Rockingham, July 31, 1768.

for war,"[28] but he had even ruder shocks in store. Bernard had dissolved the Massachusetts Assembly, but he was powerless to prevent that unique New England institution, the town meeting. Before the arrival of the troops on October 1, such a conclave had resolved that the regiments could not be kept in the colony without the consent of the assembly. It was further recommended that the people procure arms on the pretext of an apprehended French invasion. Action was also taken for calling a "convention" in September, to be composed of delegates from the towns. Massachusetts was thus rapidly approaching a revolutionary state and was busily setting up an effective government independent of royal authority. In the autumn, a new assembly was elected to replace that which Bernard had dissolved. It was soon found, however, that it was as radical as the last had been. It promptly refused to provide barracks in the town of Boston, maintaining that quarters were available at Castle William. From such a point, its members knew, troops could not act effectively. A gloomier consideration for the mother country was the growing scope of the controversy. Within a few months' time, the assemblies of Virginia, Maryland, Georgia, North Carolina, and New York had been dissolved because they had exhibited too much inclination to follow the lead of Massachusetts.

By 1768, then, the great question of parliamentary right had obscured the home government's original purpose—the creation of a coherent imperial system. With near-anarchy in the eastern colonies, the west had become a secondary problem. Even so, the Board of Trade under Robert Nugent, now Lord Clare, presented a report on the west on March 7, 1768. Calling for a reduction in the imperial Indian establishment, a paring of expense to the minimum, and the control of Indian trade by each colony, the report went strongly against new inland settlements, thereby blasting the hopes of several colo-

---

[28] RHMCR. *Gray Papers,* 302–303, Falconer to Thomas Gray, September 19, 1768.

nial land companies. In the long run, however, the report was to have little influence except to alienate American speculators. Moreover, the westward movement had already assumed the character of a force of nature, and it was not now to be stopped by even the most solemn orders from the mother country. In the end, then, curtailment of imperial activity in the west would merely clear the way for a showdown between the Indians and the westerners.[29]

As summer turned into autumn, Grafton, still fighting to postpone a full-dress treatment of the American problem until Parliament should meet, had to face another unpleasant development on the domestic scene. The conservative elements in his ministry, the Bedfords and the King's Friends, were beginning to exert pressure against those farther to the left. The ministry now began to loose all pretext of existence under the name of Chatham. In August, Thomas Townshend, Chatham's friend, resigned from the Treasury Board. Demands by Sandwich for a place of greater power brought from Grafton the promise that Shelburne would soon be dismissed. Then followed a sordid intrigue which drove Chatham and Shelburne from office, both resigning in October.

Chatham's action came as an unpleasant surprise to Grafton, but the Opposition was elated. There were immediate attempts to unite the separate groups into an effective weapon against the ministry. These were, however, premature. Chatham was still ill and in retirement. Further, he had pleaded reasons of health as the ground for his resignation, an excuse not openly hostile to the ministry. Most of his friends therefore could be persuaded to remain in office. Furthermore, the Opposition, caught between the two millstones of radical disorders in America and in Britain, was in a declining state. Several of Grenville's friends were being drawn over to the Court. Lord Powis put his considerable Parliamentary interest at the dis-

[29] The report is printed in Morison, *Sources and Documents*, 62–73. See also his excellent introductory essay.

posal of the ministry. Rigby would soon capture Alexander Wedderburn. Sir Lawrence Dundas, the Scottish magnate who controlled several seats in Commons, let it be known he would not decline to support government. Far from overturning the ministry, then, Chatham's resignation merely pointed up the growing stability of a consolidating conservative bloc.

With the conservative tide running thus strong, Parliament met on November 8. Grafton, having now won his summer's battle to delay treatment of the American problem, was only too happy to turn that irksome task over to the representatives of the nation. Colonial affairs took precedence over all others. The two houses heard the King, in his speech from the throne, declare that a new "spirit of faction" was arising in North America. Actual violence had occurred in some colonies, and Boston seemed intent on throwing off her dependence altogether.[30] From the debates which followed it soon became obvious that Parliament would demand a new and sterner policy toward those Americans so presumptuous as to question Parliament's supremacy. It was equally apparent that the great majority of the ministry were also so inclined.

The Old Whigs immediately demanded a comprehensive parliamentary inquiry into the causes of the American disorders, but a week after the meeting of Parliament, Lord North, now chancellor of the exchequer and leader of the Commons, announced that the House's attention would be focused on Boston. Such a limitation was, of course, an attempt to localize the controversy and to isolate the captious town as much as possible. From the subsequent debates, two pertinent facts emerged. First, American violence had cut the ground from under Members who in the past had inclined to defend the colonists. Secondly, Parliament had firmly determined to vindicate the principle of its supremacy. When John Huske, American by birth and now a London merchant and Member

[30] Henry Cavendish, *Debates of the House of Commons*, I, 30–32, speech and debate.

of Parliament, tried to present a petition from the Pennsylvania Assembly against the Townshend taxes, the House resolutely refused to accept it because it contradicted the Declaratory Act.

The Boston papers were also being read in the House of Lords, and as the American Secretary, Hillsborough, was a member of that chamber, it was to be expected that the ministry's plans would first be presented there. Anti-American views were so prevalent among the peers that Rockingham sent urgently to his friend Dartmouth, asking him to hurry to London and lend his weight to the Old Whigs. Very soon after the meeting of Parliament, therefore, Grafton and his cabinet colleagues knew that any policy of stern American measures which they might choose to adopt would be supported by solid parliamentary majorities.

The inquiry in the Lords ended on December 15, and the ministry's American plan was then revealed in a series of resolutions moved by Hillsborough. Shelburne, seconded by the Old Whig Duke of Richmond, could put up only a token resistance. The Circular Letter of the Massachusetts Assembly was declared subversive of the Constitution, tending to create "repugnant combinations." The Council and civil magistrates of the province were charged with negligence in putting down riots. The resolutions of the town meeting of Boston were declared illegal. Summoning a convention manifested a design to become independent. The election of delegates to such a meeting was a "daring insult" to royal authority and "audacious usurpations of the powers of government."[31] Here, then, was Parliament's answer to American pretensions. To make it the more impressive, an address to the King, moved by Bedford, pledged the House's support to all measures designed to secure royal government and parliamentary supremacy in the Colonies. Having given the ministry a free hand, the address went on to call for the transportation of American traitors

[31] Cobbett and Wright, *Parliamentary History*, XVI, 477–80.

to England for trial—under an ancient Treason Law of Henry VIII. After the Christmas holidays, the Commons, by great majorities, voted their concurrence in the Lords' actions. Thus Hillsborough's plan had gained the united sanction of both Houses.

Harsh as the Americans might think this new policy, the prevailing opinion in parliamentary circles thought it moderate. Many thought it too much so. One who did was Secretary at War Barrington. The American Secretary, Hillsborough, was another. In reality, the adopted plan was merely a preamble to Hillsborough's intentions. There is evidence that the rump of Chatham's cabinet, Camden, Granby, and Conway, had a hand in frustrating a strong inclination within the ministry to adopt yet sterner measures.[32] The man chiefly responsible for vetoing Hillsborough's worst suggestions was, however, one whom the Americans would soon consider the very image of a tyrant. He was King George III.

Soon after the holiday recess, Hillsborough, adopting several suggestions from Barrington and Bernard, formulated and sent to the King new proposals for America. Intending to submit them at the next cabinet on American affairs, he desired first the royal approval. His plan recommended first that the Council of Massachusetts be appointed by the Crown and not elected as hitherto. Secondly, that any further vote or resolution of the assembly which denied or questioned Parliament's authority to bind the Colonies in all cases whatsoever should automatically cancel the charter. Thirdly, that four councilors of New York be removed for their radical sympathies. The

[32] Channing and Coolidge, *Barrington-Bernard Correspondence,* 182–83, Barrington to Bernard, January 2, 1769: "I wish there were a better prospect of such measures at home as will tend to preserve the Obedience of the Colonies, and such have been proposed; I can moreover assure you that they have been relish'd by the majority of the cabinet; but by some fatal catastrophe, two or three men there, with less ability, less credit, less authority, and less responsibility than the rest, have carry'd their point and produced that flimsey unavailing Address which has past the Lords."

governors of Georgia and South Carolina were to call their assemblies and lecture them on their duty to Parliament.

Two points in this plan had come from Barrington. First, the Townshend taxes should be repealed for Virginia and the West Indies, which had already made ample provisions for a civil establishment. They would be repealed for the other colonies as soon as these did the same. Finally, the Mutiny Act was to be altered to allow quartering of troops in public houses, or, if such were not available and if the colonists refused to provide barracks, in private houses.

Hillsborough told the King that the entire cabinet, except Camden and Conway, had approved the plan, although Grafton had had doubts about the alteration of the Massachusetts Council. The American Secretary was strong for this measure, however, declaring—with supreme and foolish optimism—that he was "almost convinced it will be generally approved at Home, and be popular in the Colony."[33]

Probably this inflammatory plan would have been adopted had it not been for the King. He approved the removal of the four New York councilors. But he considered Virginia's conduct in the spring so offensive as to make it improper to repeal the Townshend duties for that colony. He was willing to consider a repeal in 1770, however, should Virginia remain quiet and peaceful in the meantime. He further agreed that it might be necessary someday to vest appointment of the Massachusetts Council in the Crown if that province should persist in her unruly conduct. Until that time, however, such a step should be avoided, for "the altering Charters is at all times an odious measure." Never very confident in Hillsborough's ability, the King now directly opposed his suggestion that questioning the authority of Parliament work immediate forfeiture of Massachusetts' Charter. Such a procedure, the King felt, "seems cal-

[33] Fortescue, *Correspondence of George III*, II, No. 701, Hillsborough to the King, February 15, 1769.

culated to increase the unhappy feudes that subsist than to asswage them."[34]

While the King and the remnant of Chatham's cabinet could thus exercise a moderating influence upon Hillsborough and the Bedfordites, the Opposition was weak, divided, and ineffectual. It is interesting to note, however, the American issue was now bringing together a new group. Unfortunately for the colonial cause, it was always to remain on an informal basis and small in number, never breaking down previously existing interests. Nonetheless, it was a creative minority; and from some of its members arguments were heard which, had they been accepted by a Parliament all too determined to defend its total supremacy, might well have saved the first British Empire. First, there was the small Chatham contingent, led by his friends Barré, Thomas Townshend, and Frederick Montagu in Commons, and by Shelburne and Camden in the Lords. At the present conjunction, this group was usually joined by the Old Whigs Burke, Dowdeswell, Sir George Savile, and their friends. Both these parties were, however, preoccupied for the moment with defending their own past administrations and exculpating themselves from charges of having caused the American disorders. Barré, for instance, had found it necessary—at the beginning of the parliamentary inquiry into the Boston disturbance—to defend Chatham's view that taxation formed no part of the legislative power of Parliament. Similarly, when Burke and Dowdeswell had spoken against Hillsborough's American plan, it had soon become evident that Old Whig efforts were primarily bent toward a defense of the repeal of the Stamp Act.

A small group of Americans also sat in Parliament in those crucial years between 1763 and 1783. The group totalled only five Members, however, and never more than three held seats at any one time. One of these, Paul Wentworth, of New Hampshire, would become a staunch loyalist. Another, Henry Cru-

[34] *Ibid.*, No. 701 A, the King's memorandum, February, 1769.

ger, of New York, proved remarkably inept in presenting the American thesis to his colleagues. Two others, John Huske and Barlow Trecothick, did yeoman service, but, unfortunately, they died or left Parliament before the outbreak of hostilities.

More important than these was the "Jamaica cousinhood," consisting of some thirteen Members headed by William Beckford and Stephen and Rose Fuller. The West Indians had often offended the aims and aspirations of the North American merchants. In days to come, however, they would rally to the support of the American constitutional position.[35]

Finally, a small but important group—if two can constitute a group—opposed to the American measures were the former colonial governors Thomas Pownall and William Johnstone. Of the two, Pownall was the more capable. He had become famous as a colonial authority with the publication of his *Administration of the Colonies*. On April 19, 1769, Pownall moved for a repeal of the Townshend duties. In a very capable, if not brilliant, speech he displayed a deep understanding of the Anglo-American controversy and a fund of personal knowledge and experience with colonial affairs.[36] It may well be that Pownall's speech determined the ministry's decision in the following month to repeal the duties, except that on tea.

Pownall began by declaring that his motion was not an attack upon the administration and that he himself was associated with no party. The controversy, he said, was one in which only power could now operate. Both sides had taken up absolute and mutually exclusive positions. Compromise was therefore necessary. The taxes were, he believed, unjust in that they were for the purpose of creating a civil list independent of the control of the assemblies. At any rate, some colonies—Virginia and several of the West Indian governments—already pos-

---

[35] See Namier, *England in the Age of the American Revolution*, Chap. 4, and p. 278.

[36] Henry Cavendish, *Debates of the House of Commons*, I, 391–401.

sessed adequate civil lists. He then adduced a profound argument. Great Britain had an undoubted "right" to lay the Townshend duties, but to do so operated as a revocation of those rights and privileges the colonists had hitherto enjoyed. To tax America for revenue was contrary to the practice of Parliament. Unfortunately, the binding force of "parliamentary convention" was still far in the future. Yet it is significant that only a few months later, Hillsborough, in his private correspondence, stated views very similar to those here presented by Pownall. From the debates of the session, however, it was clear that the groups opposing the ministry's American measures were in a decided minority. Critical divisions, those on the presentation of American petitions or on Hillsborough's plan, stood at 70–133, 80–213, and 89–155.

Pownall had sensibly tried to destroy the strict legalism which, if persisted in by the home government, would make a headlong clash with the Colonies inevitable. He had also sought to remove America as a party issue. He would fail because the whole weight of domestic political development was against him; and America had become the strongest dividing principle in British politics since the Jacobite rebellion of 1745. Some months before, Franklin had already shrewdly noted that colonial affairs had become "one of the distinctions of party here." Burke, in supporting Pownall's motion, might lament that America was being "beat backwards and forwards, as the tennis ball of faction." Yet, in days to come, it would be the Old Whigs, and Burke in particular, who more than any other group would factiously spirit up America to resist a ministry they themselves could not overturn. Preoccupied with their own virtue, they sought to teach the Americans that only an Old Whig ministry could give them relief from the measures of an oppressive and tyrannical government. When, for instance, Rockingham learned of the Grafton Ministry's intention to repeal the Townshend taxes, he immediately wrote to a friend in Boston, urging the Americans to be quiet and that "tho' they might have no Reason to trust to Vague assurances from *this Administration,* yet it would be wise for them to act so, as might enable us to take some Steps in their behalf."[37] Lacking power and prestige at home, Old Whigs looked to the Colonies for the support they craved. They thought to be swept into office on the mounting waves of colonial dissatisfaction and disturbance. Old Whig attempts to make domestic political capital of the troubles of a distracted empire would grow to shocking heights in the years ahead. From that party, the colonists were to learn lessons of hate never to be forgotten.

The Old Whigs also courted extraparliamentary support at home. Decisively beaten in Parliament, they launched in the summer of 1769 a campaign to capture popular support by taking the Wilkes affair to the freeholders of the country. Working on the county and local level, Old Whig agents were indefatigable in their attempts to win petitions for the dissolution of Parliament. Furthermore, Grenville and Temple brought their support to the campaign; and when Chatham suddenly reappeared in July, he informed the King that he could not approve the ministry's measures concerning either Wilkes or America. It therefore seemed that a united Opposition was at last possible.

The Grenville-Old Whig working alliance was free of any American implications. Nor did Chatham's reconciliation with Grenville and Temple, in August, in itself touch the American question. Because of the grave constitutional issues then raised by the Wilkes affair, America had for the moment receded as the great dividing factor among Opposition groups. When, however, Rockingham sought to infuse the American issue into the campaign for petitions, calling it "aggravating circumstances," Grenvillite Whately gently, but firmly, rebuked him.[38] All knew that the alliance was but a temporary

[37] Wentworth-Woodhouse, Rockingham Papers, Rockingham to Dowdeswell, May 26, 1769.

[38] *Ibid.,* Rockingham to Crofts, his Yorkshire agent, July 11, 1769; Thomas Whately to Burke, August 30, 1769.

stratagem. The Old Whigs, in the very midst of it, could not overcome their deep suspicion of Grenville, while Burke's hatred for Chatham was almost pathological. They deliberately kept co-operation with Chatham and the Grenvilles at a minimum, therefore, because they were determined to monopolize the campaign and to capture support for themselves.

Although the joint Opposition campaign for petitions did not achieve its object—the dissolution of a Parliament corrupted by the expulsion of Wilkes and the consequent violation of the rights of the freeholders of Middlesex—yet it did profoundly stir the country and worry the ministry. At least fifteen counties, numerous cities, and many boroughs sent petitions. The government's strenuous efforts to get counterpetitions were successful only in the two universities, four counties, and three or four cities.

Furthermore, on the international scene, there was developing a crisis with Spain over the Falkland Islands. Rumors of war grew steadily stronger. Sir Edward Hawke, Chatham's friend and first lord of the Admiralty, caused considerable uneasiness by selling out his public stocks. There were fears for Gibraltar and Jamaica. There were reports that France had smuggled ten thousand troops to the West Indies. In addition, Ireland was in great unrest, with Lord Lieutenant Townshend barely able to cope with the unruly Parliament. At home, Grafton knew that Chatham's friends were on the point of resigning and that the ministry would have to bear the brunt of the great man's wrath at the opening of Parliament. In this troubled state of affairs, the "terrible shadow," Junius, in his letters to the London *Public Advertiser,* was adding his carefully distilled drops of venom to the steaming brew.

The direct result of all this was a desire on the part of the ministry to leave America alone. There could be indeed no retreat from the great principle of parliamentary supremacy, yet there was a clear disposition toward some peaceable solution of the knotty problem. Nor was such a wish confined to the ministry. Franklin reported to his colonial constituents that a spirit of moderation toward the Colonies was developing throughout the country. He pointed out that the petitions from Middlesex and London during the summer had listed "the unconstitutional taxes on America" as a grievance, and he assured them that if America would only persevere in her nonimportation scheme, repeal would be within her grasp.[39]

Chatham's return to the political scene had aroused among the British public almost a feeling of relief.[40] Suggestions were heard that British consuls in foreign ports be allowed to act as customs officers and empowered to clear American ships for their home ports after payment of legal duties. This would relieve Americans of lengthy and expensive trips to English ports to pay them. Further, there were those who counseled a return to the requisition plan; and Dartmouth had been given an outline of a new system of colonial government. Coming from an anonymous West Indian merchant, the proposal had included "a Lord Lieutenant and Parliament in America similar to that in Ireland." Dartmouth, declaring his own liking for the plan, sent it on to Rockingham for that leader's perusal.[41]

The new spirit of moderation was also conditioned by the considerable success of the colonial nonimportation agreements. In spite of government propaganda to the contrary, British trade was being seriously affected. In 1768, the value of goods exported to North America had been set at nearly £2,500,000. In 1769 it fell to £1,635,000.[42] Although this loss was being offset by the opening up of new channels of European trade and British merchants from this time onward were correspondingly reluctant to be drawn into a clamor on behalf of the

[39] Sparks, *Franklin's Works*, VII, 447–48, Franklin to James Bourdain.
[40] See RHMCR. *Weston Papers*, 416, Edward Sedgwick to Edward Weston, July 19, 1769.
[41] Wentworth-Woodhouse, Rockingham Papers, Dartmouth to Rockingham, October 21, 1769; see also Add. MSS 38341, f. 104.
[42] Add. MSS 38341, f. 119. The paper is in Jenkinson's hand.

Americans,[43] the decrease was nevertheless a problem of primary concern to the ministry.

In view of all these considerations, therefore, Grafton and his ministry decided in May, 1769, to repeal all the Townshend taxes except that on tea. Since British products were taxed, the arrangement was "uncommercial." Tea, not being of British manufacture, would continue to bear a tax and would thereby serve to uphold the principle of the Declaratory Act. Although no immediate action could be taken to repeal the taxes until Parliament should meet in the winter, it was hoped that the Americans would remain quiet so that the mother country might make her conciliatory step with dignity.

Thus the Colonies were at once informed of the ministry's intentions. When the new governor of Virginia, Lord Botetourt, went out to his post, he carried with him a circular letter from Hillsborough announcing in the King's name that the ministry had no intention of proposing any new taxes for America for purposes of revenue, and, indeed, that the Townshend taxes, except that on tea, would be repealed. At home, the American Secretary, speaking of the Colonies, let it be known he had "no apprehensions of everything doing well, if they be let alone by Parliament, and their affairs not intermixed with opposition points." Privately, he expressed sentiments similar to those of Pownall in his great speech at the preceding session. The proposed repeal, he said, was based on "principles of justice, that as the colonies are obliged to take our manufactures and cannot have others, we ought not to tax them." His correspondent William Knox declared himself agreed, adding, "I like the idea of letting the colonies alone."[44] Apparently, then, the time had come—if indeed it was ever to come—for a peaceable solution to the imperial problem. The mother

---

[43] Add. MSS 38577, ff. 9–10, Israel Mauduit to Thomas Hutchinson, November 4, 1769.

[44] Smith, *Grenville Papers*, IV, 479–81, Knox to Grenville, November 10, 1769.

country was frankly in a mood for compromise, and she would take the first step toward conciliation.

The American position had not, however, remained static. In November, William Strahan, busybody printer to the King and friend of Hillsborough, wrote to Franklin, probably at the American Secretary's suggestion, to ask his views on how a pacification of the Colonies might be accomplished without sacrifice to the honor, dignity, and supremacy of Parliament. In his answer, Franklin put forward a view which was already gaining wide acceptance in America: that the King governed the Colonies in a capacity independent of Parliament. It had been only with Cromwell that Parliament had usurped a sovereign power over the Colonies. Finally, Franklin affirmed that only a complete repeal of the Townshend taxes and a withdrawal of the troops from Boston could bring quiet to America.[45] Great Britain was to be forced to make periodic retreats from the position she took up in the spring of 1769. As often as she did so, however, American demands were to be at least one step ahead. A heartbreaking decade lay ahead for those who now struggled to preserve the empire.

Meantime, Chatham had declared war on a ministry which he felt had betrayed him. To make his assault more effective he was also resolved to form a strict union with Rockingham, employing to this end his friendships with his old admirals Keppel and Saunders.[46] Although Burke and the Yorkes continued to advise caution, it was soon clear that Rockingham and Chatham would stand together at the opening of Parliament.

The King began the new session on January 9, 1770, with his famous "horned cattle" speech. Besides giving a Wilkes wit occasion to suggest that the speech would have sounded

[45] Sparks, *Franklin's Works*, IV, 258–69, William Strahan to Franklin, November 21, 1769; Franklin to Strahan, November 29, 1769; VII, 475–79, Franklin to Samuel Cooper, June 8, 1770.

[46] Chatham Papers, 25, Calcraft to Chatham, November 22, 1769; 23, Sir Alexander Hood to Lord and Lady Chatham, December 3, 1769.

better sung to the tune of "Roast Beef of Olde England," the King called attention to the grave American situation. He asked Parliament to give it serious attention and admitted that his own efforts to restore obedience in North America had failed.

However the American question had now become a side issue with the Opposition. In the Commons, Old Whigs, City Radicals, and Chathamites excoriated the ministry for its violation of the rights of electors. In the Lords, Chatham blasted them with bombshell oratory. While expressing the hope that America would never return to tranquillity until the invasion of her liberty had been redressed, he made his primary concern the expulsion of Wilkes. His attack on this occasion brought Camden back to the fold, and there followed several minor resignations among his friends in the ministry.

On January 22, Chatham and Rockingham united again to assault what appeared to be a disintegrating ministry. Again, however, it was not America which provided Chatham's ammunition. "I need not look abroad for grievances," he proclaimed. "The grand capital mischief is fixed at home."

The debates of the session indicated that both Old Whigs and Chatham had begun to see confusion in America as but part of a wider and more unwholesome situation created by the steadily growing influence of the Crown. From this time dates Chatham's increasing preoccupation with the cause of Parliamentary reform. The joint assault against the irresistible consolidation of a new conservatism, called forth by Wilkes and America, was, however, the frenzied attack of an army near exhaustion. Failing to grasp the nature of this consolidation, Chatham and the Old Whigs could but attribute it to secret influence.

Chatham's nonpartisan illusion had been forever shattered. No longer was he the champion against party connection. In brilliant and glowing phrases he admitted that the necessity of party originated in nature itself: "There is a distinction between right and wrong—between Whig and Tory." Thus his merciless attack was an admission that he had formerly proceeded on the basis of a false principle—or at least one too ideal to be realized in his time. He could call for violence, could criticize the Old Whigs for their moderation, could bring down the stunned Grafton, but his attack had come too late.

The events following Grafton's resignation on January 28, 1770, indicated that government, after ten years of administrative chaos, had at last gained stability. There was no general overturn. North succeeded quietly. The King and his Friends had moved to center stage.

The North Ministry represents the final success of George III's long struggle to escape "capture" and to regain what he thought his rightful place in British politics. Henceforth, the government would be, in very truth, His Majesty's Government. The royal party leader had become in fact the chief executive. Unfortunately, he wore a crown, the touchy dignity of which would not, in the days to come, allow those compromises which less exalted politicians might have found so easy.

CHAPTER FIVE

PRELUDE TO CIVIL WAR

ORTH's quiet accession to power was possible because America and Wilkes had called into being a new conservatism supported not only by the King's Friends but by members of every other major group. Those means of corruption at the Crown's disposal did not create North's steady majorities. Rather they arose out of a frightened reaction against radicalism at home and abroad.

North became first lord of the Treasury and chancellor of the exchequer. The Great Seal was temporarily put into commission after the suspected suicide of Charles Yorke. Hillsborough remained as colonial secretary; and Lord Rochford, the veteran diplomatist, occupied the Northern Department of State. North's uncle Halifax came in; and Edward Thurlow buttressed the Bedford interest as attorney general. Among those who took minor office was Charles James Fox. This arrangement was the strongest and most stable the new reign had seen. It possessed a unique vigor and was quite determined to solve the ills of the empire.

North had been head of the ministry only a month when, on March 5, 1770, in accordance with the cabinet decision made before his elevation, he moved to repeal all of the Townshend taxes but that on tea. Refusing "to run after America

---

[1] In 1761, there were about 170 placemen; in 1774, about the same. See Feiling, *Second Tory Party*, Chap. 8.

in search of reconciliation," North made it clear to the Commons that the step was not undertaken because of American pressure. Nor was it to be interpreted as compromising the great principle of Parliament's supremacy and her right to tax America for revenue. The preamble of the act, providing for the creation of an American civil list, would remain, as would the tax on tea, which, North assured his listeners, could be brought to produce considerable sums.[2]

It is interesting to speculate upon the probable course of the Anglo-American conflict had there existed then the means of rapid communication available today. Time after time, irrevocable decisions were made during the "time gap" necessary to the transit of news from one country to the other. Had intelligence of North's motion on March 5 been known in Boston on the same day, would the clash between British troops and townspeople have occurred?

Be the answer what it may, this "bloody massacre" formed another step in the growing alienation of two kindred peoples and gave the Boston radicals grist for their propaganda mill. However, speedy action by Governor Hutchinson prevented a final crisis. Yielding a point for which the people had agitated ever since arrival of the troops, he quickly removed them from the city to Castle William. Such speedy compliance with a popular demand deprived the radicals of their chief grievance, and an uneasy quiet followed. The radicals continued to work for a system of Committees of Correspondence throughout the province.

Meantime, Franklin, in London, was claiming for the American cause "the body of Dissenters throughout England, with many others, not to mention Ireland and all the rest of Europe." It is significant that he did not mention either the merchants or any group in the Opposition. Indeed, from the American standpoint, an ominous change was occurring in Britain. The support of the American demands among the

[2] Cavendish, *Debates of the House of Commons*, I, 483–500, debate.

merchants and manufacturers, so helpful during the Stamp Act crisis, was no longer to be counted on. The merchants of London had with difficulty been brought to offer a weak petition against the Townshend taxes. Those of other cities now bluntly refused, asserting that they had enough trade without America, and that in any event, her nonimportation agreements would soon break down.

As for the Opposition, Americans had begun to feel that even should Rockingham or Chatham come to power, the situation would improve but little. Both men insisted upon the supremacy of Parliament, although they would not venture to exercise it in taxing the Colonies. In his speech on March 2, before proceeding to his main attack against secret influence, Chatham had uttered a somber warning that the Americans "must be subordinate. In all laws relating to trade and navigation especially, this is the mother country, they are children; they must obey and we prescribe."[3] In the early days of the new year, mutual consultation among Chatham, Camden, and Shelburne, Rockingham, Dartmouth, and Richmond, and Temple and Suffolk had been common. As the session wore on, however, Chatham's very violence on the threadbare issues of the Wilkes affair began to alienate the Old Whigs. Meanwhile the increasingly bad state of American affairs was turning the Grenville group toward the ministry.

By mid-February, Opposition numbers were dwindling rapidly. Sir Lawrence Dundas and his friends went over to Court. In March, the City Radicals led by Beckford and Trecothick, and those of Westminster, under the influence of Horne Tooke, were alienated permanently from the Old Whigs. As mayor, Beckford had presented a very strong remonstrance from the City to the King on the incapacitation of Wilkes. When he was called to explain his action by the Commons, the Old Whigs refused to come to his support. Total alienation resulted. Henceforward, the Old Whigs equally

[3] Viscount Mahon, *History of England*, V, Appendix, xli–xlii.

fearful of Chatham's violence and domination and of the City's radicalism, pursued an independent course. Their break both with Chatham and with the Radicals became irreparable when, in the summer of 1770, Burke published his "Thoughts on the Cause of the Present Discontents."

In this pamphlet the justification of party received classic statement. Lashing out bitterly at Chatham's "cant" of "not men, but measures," Burke called the Old Whigs to battle. The ideal he set up was that of a House of Commons responsible to the nation, and a ministry responsible to the House. It was an attempt to justify his own party's increasing inclination to look outside the doors of Parliament for its support. By deifying the constitutional arrangement which had existed, though but superficially, during the two previous Hanoverian reigns, he unconsciously projected the line of constitutional development several decades into the future. Prevailing constitutional doctrine in his own time was exactly what he said it was not: the freedom of the monarch to appoint his own ministers.

The chief weapon by which the Court had revived the power of the prerogative, he said, was "influence," wielded by a "junta" of persons holding "secondary, but efficient" posts in government and in the royal household, "so as on one hand to occupy all the avenues to the throne; and on the other to forward or frustrate the execution of any measure, according to their own interests." Burke was here describing the King's Friends. His observations were accurate, but his eagerness to present the Old Whig party as a spotless innocent, the victim of insidious and subterranean forces, led him too far in his interpretations. His *idée fixe* of a secret and wicked "Court system" was, however, at once seized upon by American radicals who saw in it a true account of domestic political conditions. Here then was their justification for resistance to measures carried out, it would seem, by a tyrannical ministry independent of constitutional checks.

Just as Burke's pamphlet was putting an end to united Opposition, the Grenvillites were about to make their peace with the Court. Grenville himself had become an old man since his wife's death a year before; and he now sought only retirement and quiet. In July, he sent William Knox his blessing upon that Grenvillite's accepting office as undersecretary of state for the colonies. In October he fell seriously ill, and his friends, fearful of his death, began to wonder "what part we are then to take?" What indeed could be the object of continued opposition? "I hope," exclaimed Lord George Germain in answer, "not to make Lord Chatham minister."[4]

Opposition was thus disintegrating rapidly. Chatham forsook the City Radicals, whose fight against press warrants had offended him. The City itself was soon to resound to the battle between Horne Tooke and Wilkes. This squalid struggle, together with the presence among the Radicals of such "crackpots" as Lord Buchan, ruined them with the public, and they never again could seriously affect the political balance of power.

Before Parliament could meet in the autumn, Beckford, Granby, and Grenville had died. Temple was so affected that he withdrew from politics, thus ending a career of sordid intrigue and self-aggrandizement. Beckford's death deprived Chatham of his chief contact with the City and removed one of the few men able to keep the City Radicals under a semblance of control.

The announcement in January, 1771, of a peaceful conclusion to the Falkland Islands dispute further weakened the Opposition cause. Chatham, intransigently attacking the convention with Spain, now saw his numbers melt away. Support simply could not be had for his thesis that a war would have been preferable to the compromise reached by the ministry. Chatham, gloomy and depressed, felt himself losing contact with affairs: "The Ministers are pretty much at their ease;

[4] RHMCR. *Stopford-Sackville Papers*, I, 131–32, letters of October 23, 25, 1770.

the *Public* is, I believe, a Scurvy Rascal, as I have long known it to be."[5] Thus discouraged and defeated on every hand, the leaders of Opposition went their separate ways. North and his ministry possessed the field.

Grenville's death made the defection of his friends to the Court a foregone conclusion. The Falkland Islands dispute had produced the resignation of Bedfordite Weymouth as secretary of state for the Southern Department. He had wished for war and felt himself overruled in his own office. The resulting shuffle gave the Grenvillites their opportunity, and they came over "en masse." Lord Suffolk, generally accepted as Grenville's successor, became lord privy seal, an office vacated by King's Friend Halifax who now became northern secretary of state. Bedfordite Sandwich took up at the Admiralty the place he was to hold so long. Grenvillite Wedderburn became solicitor general, and Thomas Whately a commissioner of trade. When, in June, Halifax died, Suffolk moved to the Northern Department, and Grafton, mortally offended at Chatham, took the vacant privy seal, although with a proviso that he be not of the cabinet. This accession of the Grenvillites was the last great step in that consolidation of the new conservatism which was preparing the advent of a new Tory party.

Now so well established in power that no Opposition could touch them, the North Ministry turned to the task of evolving a comprehensive American policy. Although all but one of the Townshend duties had been repealed, the past behavior of the Colonies suggested that the American problem would not be a transient one. That quality most lacking in the mother country's past efforts to deal with colonial outbursts had been firmness: the North Ministry now proposed to remedy this omission at the earliest possible moment. The American bluff was to be called.

[5] Chatham Papers, 4, Chatham to Lady Chatham, January 25, 1771. The quotation is deleted from the printed version. See Taylor and Pringle, *Chatham Correspondence*, IV, 86–88.

In January, 1770, when Lord Dunmore became governor of New York, his instructions clearly indicated an intent that he and other Crown officers of the province should have their salaries from a colonial revenue. In April, the Privy Council annulled an act of the South Carolina Assembly passed in the preceding year. It had provided for a present of £1,500 to a radical London organization, the Supporters of the Bill of Rights. Moreover the Privy Council forbade the assembly ever again to issue money in so illegal a manner and ordered the province attorney general to prosecute the treasurer.

These were but symptoms of the ministry's new firmness. In June, a committee of the Privy Council undertook to canvass the entire state of affairs in Massachusetts, the very center of American unrest. When Hillsborough laid before that body transcripts of earlier testimony and reports, the picture that emerged confirmed the belief that some fundamental readjustment of American affairs in general, and of those of Massachusetts in particular, was urgently needed. Maltreatment of customs officers, intimidation of royal officials, the appointment of committees to enforce the nonimportation agreements, riots, which, as Customs Officer John Robinson pointed out, could not "be properly called Riots as the Rioters appear to be under Discipline," all foreshadowed the dissolution of civil government. Testimony from Governor Bernard confirmed such fears. Since the Stamp Act, he told the investigators, an accepted doctrine in Massachusetts was that the colonists were not subject to parliamentary taxes. Ever since May, 1768, he had considered "all Government as at an end," for it was impossible to enforce laws against the will of the mob. Warning that his former province could produce forty thousand fighting men, all of them now armed by a law of the colony, he declared that the only cure of this unhealthy situation was a decisive intervention by Parliament.

In light of these disquieting facts, the Privy Council Committee concluded that despite a present calm in Massachusetts, further outbreaks were to be anticipated. Indeed, the proceedings of both the assembly and the town meetings demonstrated "an evident Disposition to support by force the unconstitutional Doctrines, which have been inculcated." The committee then made a series of recommendations, all soon to be adopted and implemented by the ministry. The rendezvous of the Royal Navy stationed in North America—hitherto at Halifax—should now be Boston harbor. Castle William should be put into a state of defense and fully garrisoned with regulars. More troops should be sent to America. Finally, as past disturbances demanded the "interposition of the Wisdom, and Authority of the Legislature," the King should recommend to Parliament a consideration of the state of Massachusetts.

The committee's report having been accepted, orders based upon it were issued on July 6 to the Admiralty, to the Ordnance, and to the secretary of war.[6] It was in keeping with the new policy when in January, 1771, Hillsborough refused to receive Franklin as agent for the Massachusetts Assembly, a post to which he had but recently been appointed. His Lordship maintained that Franklin could not legally represent the assembly because he had not been named agent by an act of that body duly concurred in by the council and the governor. The Privy Council, sustaining Hillsborough, in March issued instructions to Hutchinson forbidding his concurrence in the voting of a salary to any agent not appointed by an act of the assembly.[7]

The Falkland Islands crisis and the near war with Spain made it necessary however to postpone parliamentary intervention, and on May 15, 1771, Franklin reported to the Massachusetts Assembly that Parliament had been prorogued without taking notice of American affairs. The international situation thus brought a period of quiet to both sides of the Atlantic.

[6] Grant and Munro, *Acts of the Privy Council*, V, 247–65.

[7] Sparks, *Franklin's Works*, VII, 506–12, Franklin to Samuel Cooper, February 5, 1771. See also Grant and Munro, *Acts of the Privy Council*, V, 264.

In America there was a general feeling that a "pause in politics" had been reached; and it was hoped that the acquittal of Captain Prescott, commander of those troops involved in the "massacre," would make a good impression on the mother country. The nonimportation agreements were breaking down despite the tax on tea, and it was believed that "administration has a fair opportunity of adopting the mildest and most prudent measures respecting the colonies, without the appearance of being threatened or drove."[8]

Hillsborough seized this opportunity to attempt a solution of the western problem. Here, however, he was to be no more successful than his predecessors and would achieve, indeed, only his own overthrow and fall from office.

Hillsborough was in agreement with the report of the Board of Trade in 1768. That report had been a compromise, following neither Grenville's plan to imperialize the west, allowing orderly expansion, nor with Shelburne's more radical scheme for rapid and decentralized exploitation. It had deprecated new interior settlements and had assigned the management of Indian trade to the Colonies. The home government would maintain the boundary line.

In November, 1768, the Indian Superintendents, Johnson and Stuart, had concluded the Treaty of Fort Stanwix by which a boundary line had been settled and some Indian land had been ceded to the imperial government. Samuel Wharton, of Pennsylvania, present at the time as the representative of a group of merchant land speculators, had managed to obtain from the Indians a particular cession as compensation for those merchants who had suffered during Pontiac's Rebellion. Because this transaction had been unconfirmed by the imperial government, Wharton's associates had sent him to London to obtain the necessary ratification. There, failing in his intended mission, he became involved in a scheme to purchase from the government that area lawfully acquired by the treaty. Thanks

[8] Sparks, *Franklin's Works*, VII, 499–500, Samuel Cooper to Franklin, January 1, 1771.

to his friendship with Franklin, he soon met and managed to interest such highly placed politicians as Lords Gower, Rochford, Hertford, Temple, and many others. To the first petition of this new group, asking a grant of 2,500,000 acres, Hillsborough gave an encouraging answer but suggested they buy a larger tract, enough for a new colony.

In December, 1769, therefore, this group, enlarged and reorganized, emerged as the Grand Ohio or Walpole Company. They at once petitioned for a grant of 20,000,000 acres, offering £10,460 7s 3d., the exact amount paid by the imperial government at Fort Stanwix. Competing claims of other speculator groups—such as the Old Ohio Company and the Virginians, whose spokesman was George Washington—were quieted by the simple expedient of admitting them all to partnership in the new company.

Hillsborough's encouragement was strange in view of his long opposition to new inland colonies. In July, 1770, the American Secretary asked General Gage, then in America as commander-in-chief, for his personal views on the west. Gage's reply seems to have confirmed Hillsborough's own opinion. He was convinced that interior colonies would be disastrous, that the forts in the Indian country were of little value, and that the west could be adequately protected by troops stationed at the mouths of the avenues of commerce.

Hillsborough then proceeded to submit to the Privy Council a report which directly contradicted his encouragement of the Grand Ohio Company. (He was later to maintain that he had deliberately appeared favorable to the petition, believing that the magnitude of the request would of itself defeat it.) The report was accepted. Forts de Chartres and Pitt were ordered abandoned and the Ohio Valley sealed off. Only fur traders were to be admitted to the area. Here then was a willful shattering of the imperial vision.[9]

[9] RHMCR. *Dartmouth Papers*, II, 81, Hillsborough to Gage, December 4, 1771. See also Alvord, *Mississippi Valley*, II, Chap. 2.

Hillsborough now became the center of a political intrigue which amply repaid his two-faced conduct toward the Grand Ohio Company. The Bedford element in the cabinet, lead by Gower, sought nothing less than his overthrow and through him that of North. For while the new conservatism had driven many groups to take refuge with the Court, it had by no means wrought a complete amalgamation of interests.

When the Grand Ohio Company's petition was presented to Hillsborough, he promptly sent to the Privy Council an adverse report. On July 1, 1772, however, that body took the almost unprecedented action of rejecting the report and deciding in favor of the petitioners. Gower, as president of the Council, had engineered this maneuver. As North had asked him to delay bringing up the report, it was unmistakably an affront not only to Hillsborough but to the head of the ministry as well. Indeed North was so offended that he almost resigned, being dissuaded from that action only by the King himself. For Hillsborough, however, the humiliation was simply too great, and he resigned in August, salving his wounds with an English earldom.

The American seals North then offered to the Bedfordite Weymouth who refused them. Reasoning that he had done his duty by the Bedfords, he now gave the office to his half-brother, that erstwhile Old Whig the Earl of Dartmouth. Thereby North strengthened his own position in the cabinet. His ministry had successfully weathered its first storm of internal intrigue.

When the new session of Parliament had opened on January 21, 1772, Franklin had written home that he saw no disposition to "meddle" with American affairs, and that, indeed, he anticipated no such a desire for at least a year.[10] In Massachusetts, the response to Samuel Adams's and Joseph Warren's efforts to establish a network of Committees of Corre-

[10] Sparks, *Franklin's Works*, VII, 534–38, Franklin to William Franklin, January 30, 1772.

spondence throughout the province was apathetic. The nonimportation agreements were being dropped, although the tea tax had indeed created associations pledged to drink none of that beverage unless smuggled in tax-free. Nor did Hutchinson's announcement that he and other Crown officers would henceforth be paid from the colonial revenue rouse great excitement. Samuel Adams was, however, able to draw the Governor into an undignified debate with the assembly on the theory of government, an interesting dispute in that it showed a growing acceptance of the theory which Franklin had expressed to William Strahan: that the Colonies were bound to Britain only through the person of the King.

This suspicion-laden calm was shattered in America in the early hours of the morning of June 10, 1772. On the tenth— the same day that the King ended the parliamentary session in London thousands of miles away—a band of from 50 to 150 irate Rhode Islanders boarded the revenue cutter "Gaspée," aground not far from Providence, severely wounded the captain, and burned the vessel. Captain Dudingston, who had previously incurred the wrath of the Rhode Islanders by his overzealous enforcement of the Laws of Trade and Navigation, barely escaped with his life.

Here, then, was an open challenge to North's policy of firmness. Parliament was not in session, but the ministry acted at once. On July 30, Hillsborough laid before the cabinet an angry report from Admiral Montagu, the naval commander-in-chief in America. Although the opinion of the law officers was requested, Hillsborough was authorized to take certain immediate steps. The Governor of Rhode Island and the Admiral were to be ordered to discover the guilty parties and, under a recent act for securing the royal dockyards, send them to England for trial. Letters were at once dispatched to appropriate colonial officials, but on August 10, the law officers reported that American offenders could not be tried under this act although indictments might be had for treason. A few days later, Hillsborough resigned, and the direction of American affairs passed to Lord Dartmouth. Both the change and the adverse report of the law officers required a new approach to the problem. Meantime, public indignation mounted in Britain. Thurlow, the attorney general, considered the affair "five times the magnitude of the Stamp Act."[11] The King advised Secretary of State Rochford to moderate his attitude toward France whose *quai* at Dunkirk remained undemolished despite the Peace of 1763. "We must," said the King to North, "get the Colonies in order before we engage with our Neighbours."[12]

At the cabinet on August 20, a new plan was presented and adopted. Hillsborough's previous letters were cancelled. A commission would be issued to Governor Wanton of Rhode Island, to the admiralty judge at Boston, and to the chief justices of Massachusetts, New York, and New Jersey bidding them seek out the identity of the criminals. Once their identity was established, the civil magistrates of Rhode Island would be called upon to arrest them and deliver them to Admiral Montagu. General Gage would be ordered to furnish military assistance at need.[13] Six days later, the King duly approved the commission and a proclamation for apprehending the offenders.

It is difficult to believe that the ministry expected their plan to succeed. The Governor of Rhode Island, as an elected official, could hardly be expected to act with zeal under the commission. Further, the whole plan rested ultimately upon the civil magistrates of Rhode Island who would be asked to arrest their compatriots and turn them over to Montagu. That the commission proved a fiasco should have surprised no

[11] RHMCR. *Dartmouth Papers*, II, 91–92, John Pownall to Dartmouth, August 29, 1772.
[12] Fortescue, *Correspondence of George III*, II, No. 1102, the King to North, August 1, 1772.
[13] RHMCR. *Dartmouth Papers*, II, 88, minute of cabinet, August 20, 1772.

one. Two sessions, one in January and another in May, 1773, established only that no evidence of the identity of the mobsters could be found.

The colonists, not only in Rhode Island but throughout America, viewed the commission with "abhorrence." Chief Justice Smythe, of New Jersey, was convinced it would have required armed might to commit any of the offenders to Montagu's custody.[14] So probably the failure of the commission postponed the outbreak of hostilities in America. In England, however, it served to intensify the growing determination to bring the Colonies under effective control.

In the Colonies, the net result of the North Ministry's effort to vindicate law and order was three-fold. First, colonial unity was reaffirmed and strengthened. No longer could the ministry or Parliament delude themselves that Massachusetts was the sole disturber of the imperial peace. "If anything therefore be done by Parliament respecting America," Hutchinson wrote home in April, "it now seems necessary that it should be general and not confined to particular Colonies."[15] Secondly, the imperial government was further discredited. A royal commission had been made an object of ridicule, and American radicals were confirmed in their belief that royal government was too ineffectual to be feared. Finally, the commission lessened Dartmouth's initial popularity at a critical moment: when he was urgently needed as a bridge between the colonists and the ministry.

Lord Dartmouth was a sincere friend to the Colonies. Amiable, pious, and commonplace, the former Old Whig desperately wanted a peaceable settlement of the American problem. He found himself, however, surrounded by colleagues who disagreed with his American views, treated him as a well-meaning nonentity, and sought to engross American business

---

[14] Smythe is quoted by Channing, *History of the United States*, III, 127.
[15] RHMCR. *Dartmouth Papers*, I, 335, Hutchinson to John Pownall, April 19, 1773.

all they could.[16] Often circumventing these colleagues by seeking an accommodation outside the cabinet framework, Dartmouth would then encounter the stone wall of colonial hatred
for the ministry of which he was a member. Measures pursued
by the home government since the end of the war, and a constant confirmation of their view received from men like Wilkes
and Burke, had convinced most Americans that a wicked "Court
system" was plotting their enslavement. Indeed every new in-
cident in America had evoked an increasingly authoritarian reaction in the mother country. This, in turn, was then taken
as a further step in the ministerial design. Dartmouth found
himself involved in this tragic spiral.

It is impossible to say that Edmund Burke caused the colonists generally to harbor such thoughts and suspicions. There
is no doubt, however, that he had a hand in the formation of
New York's opinion of the North government. And as he
permitted the assembly of that province to circulate his letters
to them, he must also have had a part in the forming of American opinion at large. Burke had become colonial agent for the
New York Assembly at the turn of the decade. His violent and
passionate nature, his hatred of the King's Friends and the
North Ministry, his conviction that only the Old Whigs were
fit to govern an empire, and their discredited position which
he could but attribute to some dark influence, all led him to
seek among his American constituents that support so lacking
at home. When, for instance, in 1771, Hillsborough refused
to receive as colonial agent any person not duly appointed by
a full act of assembly, Burke immediately wrote, "This I consider in Effect, as destructive of one of the most necessary me-
diums of communication between the Colonies and the parent
Country. The provinces ought in my opinion to have a *direct*

[16] Bamber Gascoigne at the Board of Trade and Suffolk especially
constantly attempted to undermine Dartmouth. The Bedfords and Rochford
sided against him. Indeed, he had only one supporter in the cabinet, North,
and he was not always to be depended upon. See RHMCR. *Knox Papers,
Various Collections*, 110, John Pownall to Knox, July 23, 1773.

intercourse with Ministry and Parliament here, by some person who might be truly confidential with them who appoint him." Intervention of the governors in naming an agent "would totally frustrate" this end, and the agent would become a mere officer of the Crown. In short, the plan for Burke was so "ministerial" that if the government insisted upon carrying it into effect, he would, he declared, resign as agent. If the Colonies needed any encouragement to resist Hillsborough's new measure, Burke had given it. Only Hillsborough's fall prevented the development of a first-rate crisis.

In his reports to the assembly, Burke rarely confined himself to attacks upon the ministry's American policy. The Royal Marriage Bill, "little conformable to the Spirit of our Laws, and the genius of the English constitution," called forth a long tirade. To explain the weakness of his own party, he invoked time after time the bogey words, "Court Scheme," "all-prevailing influence," "well-formed and well-paid Bands of the Court," each designed to persuade the colonists that the Old Whigs, their only British friends, were fighting valiantly against ministerial werewolves.[17]

While Burke, unbeknownst to Dartmouth, added fuel to a fire soon to be grown beyond control, internal troubles had come to the Colonies. Hard times and depression, widely viewed as direct results of the ministerial American policy, were disrupting colonial life. Class war threatened, indeed in North Carolina actually broke out in the War of the Regulators. Never more than in these years just before the Revolution had frontiersmen and poor farmers been so hostile to eastern merchants and aristocrats who held them by the double bonds of debt and political domination.

In Massachusetts, which was especially hard hit by the de-

---

[17] Wentworth-Woodhouse, Burke Papers, Letterbook, Burke to the Committee of Correspondence of the New York Assembly, December 4, 1771; Burke to James Delancey, same date; Burke to the Committee, June 30, 1772; Burke to Delancey, August 20, 1772, December 31, 1772; Burke to Speaker Cruger, April 16, 1773.

pression, unrest took the form of a mounting discontent with the home government. The assembly sent two petitions and remonstrances against the decision to pay Crown officers from the American revenue. The old dispute between Hutchinson and his assembly flared again, and such contempt was expressed for parliamentary authority that Dartmouth told Franklin he saw no way to avoid bringing the affair before Parliament. The American Secretary's position had become very delicate. Fearing that Parliament's intervention would merely inflame the situation, he strongly opposed such a step. Yet, should he not lay the American papers before them, he risked being charged with criminal neglect and dereliction of duty.

In the summer of 1773, therefore, taking advantage of Parliament's absence, Dartmouth sought to stem the rising tide of ill-humor in Massachusetts by extracabinet means. Bypassing the usual chain of authority, he addressed himself directly to Thomas Cushing, the speaker of the assembly. Delighted colonial leaders saw in Dartmouth's action only an insult to Governor Hutchinson; but the American Secretary's real purpose was to establish contact with the malcontents and then use his personal prestige to procure some peaceable settlement. In his letter, Dartmouth expressed great concern at colonial unrest. Refusing to involve himself in a discussion of parliamentary right, he went straight to the heart of the dispute. Let such theories be what they might, he believed that the right to tax should be "suspended and lie dormant till some occasions should arise, if any such can be, in which the Expediency and Necessity of such Exercise should be obvious to every considerate Man in every Part of the Dominions of Great Britain." In contrast to his view, Dartmouth pointed to the "wild and extravagant Doctrines" put forward by the assembly in their disputes with the governor, terming them "a most serious (I had almost said, an insuperable) Bar" to the return of tranquillity. Only by their own actions, Dartmouth said, could that bar be removed. In return, he promised his aid and support in a general settlement of their complaints.

Such an attitude expressed by a secretary of state even two years earlier would probably have quieted America. Now, however, Cushing, while firmly denying that his assembly had rejected Parliament's supremacy, reminded Dartmouth that the Colonies were already laboring under an imperial revenue tax, and that only a repeal of it would bring peace.[18] Thus each side demanded a prior concession of the other, and concession itself would not come until too late.

Dartmouth's attempt at personal intervention consequently failed. Even before his letter had arrived in Massachusetts, events in that colony had blasted any hope there might have been for his success. The assembly had come into possession of Hutchinson's confidential letters to England and those of Lieutenant-Governor Oliver. Franklin had obtained the letters in London from an anonymous friend under certainly questionable circumstances. Both officials now stood revealed as favoring more rigorous measures by the home government, enforced by troops if necessary, in order to prevent colonial independence. The letters provided a fillip for the radical cause, and soon the whole colony was ablaze with indignation against two men whose confidence had been betrayed. The assembly, evading with sophistry Franklin's injunction that the letters not be published, immediately circulated copies throughout the colony and its neighbors. Soon, they had voted them as designed "to subvert the constitution and introduce arbitrary power," and a petition went to England asking the removal of both Hutchinson and Oliver, probably crossing paths with Dartmouth's letter to Cushing. Not only did Dartmouth's well-meaning attempt fail, then, but colonial radicalism got such a spur that

[18] B. F. Stevens, *Facsimilies of MSS in European Archives Relating to America*, No. 2025, Dartmouth to Cushing, draft; No. 2028, Cushing to Dartmouth, August 22, 1773.

Joseph Ward, writing from Boston in June, warned Dartmouth that "the System for a commonwealth in America seems by every appearance to be ripening fast."[19]

New events were to drive spiraling antagonisms to the breaking point. Once more, the history of the East India Company crossed that of the American Colonies. Chatham, during his ill-fated ministry, had hoped to derive a revenue from the company, thereby saving the Colonies from taxes. His collapse had brought failure to this plan, and Townshend, desperately needing funds, had substituted the Colonies for the company as more proper objects of imperial taxation. Subsequently, the government had arrived at an agreement with the company by which that body paid into the exchequer £400,000 a year. By then, of course, the Townshend taxes had been levied, and the controversy over right between the mother country and the Colonies had grown to such proportions that retreat was impossible.

Since their agreement with the government, however, the company had become increasingly embarrassed. Much of the parliamentary session which opened in November, 1772, had to be spent investigating the company and passing legislation to govern its operations. It was now brought directly under government control, but so critical were its finances that far from augmenting government revenue, it had to borrow a great sum to avoid total collapse.

Ironically, in view of what followed, Franklin sought to use the bad state of the company as an argument for the repeal of Townshend's tea tax, the "splinter in the wound." He pointed out to Dartmouth that the government had just lost a sizeable revenue from the company, while there had been numerous private bankruptcies because of the drastic fall in East India stock. The public credit itself had been shaken, and the failure of fifteen banking houses in Amsterdam had caused

[19] RHMCR. *Dartmouth Papers,* II, 158, Joseph Ward to Dartmouth, June 26, 1773.

what the King described as "a fresh stagnation of Credit." Yet in the company's warehouses lay four million pounds sterling in tea while the American market was being supplied by French, Dutch, Swedish, and Danish smugglers.[20] Should the tea tax be repealed, Franklin intimated, the whole American market would become available to the company.

This was a cogent argument. North was not unaware of the company's assets in tea, but he proposed to use them in quite a different manner from that Franklin had suggested. His policy of firmness forbade a repeal of the American tea tax. That would have to be maintained as a matter of principle. There remained however, a way in which he could relieve the company, maintain the principle, and, he thought, exploit the American market too. On April 27, 1773, therefore, North rose in the Commons and proposed that the company be allowed to export tea directly to British America. It should be free of duties payable in Britain, though still subject to the Townshend duty of three pence a pound in America. The price of the tea in the Colonies would then be substantially lower than that of the smuggled article.[21] Economic interest would induce the colonists to accept the taxed tea, thereby tacitly admitting Parliament's right to raise a revenue from them. The House accepted this plan and resolved that it take effect from May 10.

In America, the news of Parliament's boon to the company was a signal for renewed outbursts of violence. To American radicals, it was obviously a ministerial design to undermine the colonial determination to take no article taxed for revenue. Crown officials in Boston were soon warning the home government of a new "trumpery Spirit of independency" there springing up, with resistance to the landing of the tea fully to be

[20] Sparks, *Franklin's Works*, VIII, 28–31, Franklin to Cushing, January 5, 1773; see also Fortescue, *Correspondence of George III*, II, No. 1182, the King to North, January 1, 1773.

[21] Cobbett and Wright, *Parliamentary History*, XVII, 840–41.

expected.[22] Hutchinson reported in mid-November that conditions had become so chaotic, and the council so backward in putting down the new riots, that he despaired of restoring order. Indeed, riots in Boston, late in the month, drove the Customs Commissioners and five of the tea consignees to Castle William. On December 14, Hutchinson wrote that the radicals planned to prevent any landing of tea from the three tea ships which had just arrived.

Up and down the Atlantic seaboard, the tea had met with firm refusals. It had indeed been landed at Charleston but had been promptly stored, and was to be auctioned three years later for support of a rebel government. Philadelphia and New York had obliged reshipment of the tea to England. At Boston, however, Hutchinson felt that the time had come for a showdown with the radicals. Firmly believing that established government was at hazard, he now determined not to retreat an inch. Despite—or perhaps because of—ominous signs that a crisis greater than that of '65 was imminent, he refused to allow the ships to depart until they should discharge their cargo. Thus he forced the issue.

On December 17, therefore, it was his unhappy duty to report to Dartmouth that during the preceding night, a band of Boston "Indians" had boarded the tea vessels, had seized 340 chests of that article, and had thrown them into the harbor. Neither Admiral Montagu nor the temporary military commander, Colonel Leslie (Gage had returned to England), had been called upon for aid because the council had refused to sanction military intervention. Hutchinson was aghast. Here was a determination equal to his own. "At and near Boston," he wrote, "the people seem regardless of all consequences. I may not presume to propose measures. To enforce the duty appears beyond all comparison more difficult than I ever before imagined."[23]

[22] Stevens, *Facsimilies*, No. 2029, Benjamin Hallowell to John Pownall; see also Add. MSS 38207, f. 304, General Haldimand to Dartmouth, November 3, 1773, copy.

Thus a final crisis had come. Both sides were now committed to doctrines whence there was no retreat. To yield would be to forfeit all. Previously, Parliament had postponed a comprehensive treatment of the American problem. Now, however, a new chapter in Anglo-American relations was at hand—the era of parliamentary coercion.

"The popular current," Burke wrote to the New York Assembly soon after the Boston Tea Party, "both within doors and without, at present sets sharply against America." To make certain that the colonists should harbor no thoughts of a compromise, he added, "That you may not be deceived by any Idle or flattering report, be assured, that the Determination to enforce Obedience from the Colonies to Laws of Revenue, by the most powerful means, seems as firm as possible, and that the Ministry appears stronger than ever I have known them."[24]

Public opinion had in fact turned universally against the Bostonians. While Alderman Bull, radical Member and ardent admirer of Wilkes, might wish Boston cleared of British soldiers—"brutes that have too long been suffered to live there" —his voice was the exception.[25] The Opposition, weak and divided, was stunned. "The conduct of the Americans cannot be justified," wrote Rockingham to Burke, although he declared he would never sanction the use of force against the colonists.[26] Chatham himself branded the destruction of the tea as "certainly criminal." Moreover the King's own attitude had changed greatly. Receiving advice from General Gage, who had assured him that the Americans would be "lyons, whilst we are Lambs," and that four regiments of troops would quick-

[23] RHMCR. *Dartmouth Papers*, I, 342–44, Hutchinson to Dartmouth, December 17, 1773.

[24] Wentworth-Woodhouse, Burke Papers, Letterbook, Burke to the New York Assembly's Committee of Correspondence, April 6 and May 4, 1774.

[25] Add. MSS 30870, ff. 228–29, Bull to Wilkes, December 5, 1773.

[26] William, Fitzwilliam, and Bourke, *Burke's Correspondence*, I, 448–50, Rockingham to Burke, January 30, 1774.

ly bring Massachusetts to submission, the King now laid the blame for the renewed violence to "the fatal compliance in 1766." Believing that America had declared for independence, George was ready to endorse the use of force if necessary.[27]

Within the ministry, Dartmouth, hating the thought of military coercion as much as did his former chief Rockingham, soon found himself, in his plea for moderate measures, alone or supported only by a wavering North. The Bedfordites, erstwhile friends of Grenville, the King's Friends, and the King himself saw the Tea Party as utterly the last straw. Both Dartmouth and North, however, hoped to confine coercive measures to Boston. Both accepted the necessity of punishing that city, but beyond this they did not wish to go. They were nonetheless to be forced, by a cabinet solidly ranged against them, down a path for which neither had any inclination.

Of the four so-called Coercive Acts—a fifth, the Quebec Act, so regarded by the colonists may not be properly considered with the others—only the first derived from Dartmouth's American plan. Acting on a suggestion from his undersecretary, John Pownall, Dartmouth proposed to the cabinet on February 4 that both the Customs House and the assembly be moved from Boston until that city submit to Parliament's supremacy. Boston would cease to be the political and mercantile center of New England, and economic distress, he believed, would bring her to obedience. It should be noticed at this point that Dartmouth supposed—and it was a belief shared by all the cabinet even after the Coercive Acts had been broadened to include the whole of Massachusetts—that, for so patently criminal an act as the Tea Party, Boston would be condemned by the rest of the American settlements. No colony would intervene in behalf of the transgressor. So firm was this belief that the situation was not even seen to involve a calculated risk. Only Chatham, perhaps, was aware that colonial

[27] Fortescue, *Correspondence of George III*, III, No. 1379, the King to North, February 4, 1774.

resistance might become general. "The violence committed upon the tea-cargo is certainly criminal; nor would it be real kindness to the Americans to adopt their passions and wild pretensions," he wrote. Boston certainly owed reparation; but he feared, with reason, that Britain would lose her moral advantage if she sought by this opportunity to enforce her "general declared rights." Rather she ought to seek satisfaction merely for a specific wrong. Her demand for reparation and their refusal of that demand should, he believed, precede coercive measures.[28] An accumulated discontent and irritation against the Colonies, both in the cabinet and in Parliament, however, ruled out so wide a mode of action. The coercive measures were not, in fact, intended to win compensation for the East India Company: they were to punish "the last overt act of high treason, proceeding from over lenity and want of foresight." Great Britain would thus cross the Rubicon, and the colonists—not only those of Massachusetts but of all America—would know that the mother country could temporize no longer, and that the time for debate had passed.[29]

As soon as the cabinet had accepted Dartmouth's suggestion of a port bill for Boston, North and the American Secretary, aided by John Pownall, hoping to forestall harsher measures, quickly drew up the bill for introduction into Parliament. Until this time the two half-brothers had worked well together, but on February 25, North, suffering a chance defeat in the Commons on a relatively unimportant point, experienced one of those attacks of melancholia which were to become increasingly frequent during his ministry. So despondent was he that it was with the greatest difficulty that Suffolk, acting at the King's request, prevented his resignation. When, as soon became obvious, his colleagues demanded more stringent Ameri-

[28] Taylor and Pringle, *Chatham Correspondence*, IV, 336–38, Chatham to Shelburne, March 20, 1774.

[29] The quotations are from Mansfield's speech in the Lords during debate on the port act which was reported to Chatham by Shelburne. See Taylor and Pringle, *Chatham Correspondence*, IV, 339–41, Shelburne to Chatham, April 4, 1774.

can measures, he had neither the energy nor the courage to support Dartmouth. The temper of his colleagues had been demonstrated when on January 29, the Privy Council, under Gower, suddenly resumed consideration of the Massachusetts petition for removal of Hutchinson and Oliver. The hearing had been but an elaborately staged expression of imperial wrath, with Franklin as its target. Solicitor-General Wedderburn, by his splendid, malevolent, and venomous invective denouncing Franklin for his part in making public the Hutchinson-Oliver letters, had delighted thirty-five privy councilors and a large audience. The petition had then been contemptuously dismissed, and the next day, Franklin, who had resigned his agencies, was summarily turned out of his office as deputy postmaster for North America. The day's work had cost Britain much, however: she had made an implacable enemy.

It is impossible to gauge with precision Dartmouth's resistance to the subsequent Coercive Acts. Certainly, his task was not rendered easier by Boston's unrepentant belligerency. Far from seeking the forgiveness of Parliament, the people, on March 9, made a second raid upon a newly arrived tea ship and destroyed thirty more chests of that commodity. In any case, Dartmouth was brought to agree to the second act, that for regulating the government of Massachusetts. For that purpose, it was deemed necessary to alter the charter of the colony, long a favorite measure of that new baronet and old governor of Massachusetts Sir Francis Bernard, with whom North was in close communication at this time. Dartmouth wished to limit the changes to Hillsborough's old proposal of vesting the appointment of the council in the Crown. Probably at Bernard's suggestion, however, other "improvements" were incorporated in the act. North described it as designed "to take the executive power from the hands of the democratic part of government." The legislative power of the council and assembly would remain as they were. The governor would appoint magistrates, judges, sheriffs, and all civil officers except justices of the Supreme Court. Jurymen, no longer to be elected, would be summoned by the sheriffs. Town meetings were to be practically forbidden. Dartmouth, however, won a minor victory against a proposal that the tea rioters be tried for their crime in Great Britain.[30]

With the second measure, North had reached the limit of his own intentions. Serious tensions were now developing within his cabinet. Dartmouth and Suffolk, in violent disagreement on American measures, were at daggers drawn. The American Secretary told Shelburne of the great difficulties under which he labored but declared he was determined "to cover America from the present storm to the utmost of his power." Barré reported that North, too, was moderate. But extremely noticeable in parliamentary debate was "a more than disregard to Lord Dartmouth, and somewhat of the same sort towards Lord North" on the part of the other ministers.[31] It was apparent that the Bedfordites and Suffolk were trying to seize the initiative from the American Secretary.

The third Coercive Act had its origin in a cabinet meeting of March 30. It is significant that Bedfordite Sandwich, rather than Dartmouth, kept the minutes of the meeting. Sir Jeffrey Amherst and General Gage were examined. Under questioning, they declared that if British soldiers should be taken by the Bostonians during the suppression of a riot and after bloodshed and should then be tried by a local jury, they would have no fair chance for their lives. It was consequently decided that an act for the impartial administration of justice was indicated. Should British soldiers be charged with crimes committed in Massachusetts, they were to be tried in some court other than those of the province.[32]

[30] RHMCR. *Dartmouth Papers*, II, 198, cabinet minutes, February 16, 19, 1774. See also Fortescue, *Correspondence of George III*, III, No. 1416, the King to North, March 14, 1774.

[31] Taylor and Pringle, *Chatham Correspondence*, IV, 334 ff., Shelburne to Chatham, March 15, April 4, 1774.

[32] Hinchingbrooke Papers, Sandwich's cabinet minutes, March 30, 1774.

The Boston Port Bill received the royal signature on March 31, and Gage, now ordered back to Massachusetts as governor and captain general, was instructed to carry it with him and to put it into effect on June 1. The government would be transferred to Salem. Since the bill changing the charter had not yet become law, Gage was authorized to veto election of any member of the council. Concluding his instructions, Dartmouth made another bid to stave off the outbreak of hostilities: "Every care is to be taken to quiet the people by gentle means, the troops over whom the Governor has the command are not to be called out unless absolutely necessary."[33]

The fourth coercive measure was the Quartering Act, which improved upon the Military Act. It provided that where —as in Boston—barracks were not conveniently located, the province itself should provide accommodations. Should it refuse, the governor might seize unoccupied houses or barns, for which a reasonable compensation would be paid. The last of the acts became law in May.

It was with fear that Dartmouth viewed the future, and with pathetic eagerness that he sought a peaceful solution. In his correspondence with American friends, he argued that if only Massachusetts would submit, he was certain all grievances could be settled to colonial satisfaction.[34] For the colonists, however, Acts of Parliament spoke louder than one man's voice.

For the Opposition, the American problem had become difficult, indeed. They had heard North solemnly declare that at Boston, America and Britain were already considered separate and independent states, and that "we are no longer to dispute between legislation and taxation, we are to consider only whether or not we have any authority there."[35] Both Chathamites and Old Whigs were unwilling to identify them-

[33] RHMCR. *Dartmouth Papers*, I, 351–52, Dartmouth to Gage, April 9, 11, 1774.

[34] *Ibid.*, I, 354–55, Dartmouth to Joseph Reed, May 30, 1774, draft.

[35] Cobbett and Wright, *Parliamentary History*, XVII, 1159.

Courtesy Library of Congress

CHARLES TOWNSHEND

Courtesy New York Public Library

LORD NORTH

selves with Boston's cause, and felt it necessary rather to present apologies for measures pursued during their ministries. Shelburne, for instance, told Chatham in February that "the great object of my parliamentary conduct would be to prove, that if the King had continued his confidence in the sound part of his administration of 1767, the East Indies might have proved the salvation of this country, without injury to the Company, or to any individual; and that peace might have been preserved in Europe, and in America."[36] Both Shelburne and Barré subsequently supported the Boston Port Bill, in order, they said, the more effectively to counter future stringent measures. It was not, indeed, until the third coercive measure—that for the impartial administration of justice—that Barré raised his voice. He now warned the House that they were goading America into rebellion and that they were becoming the aggressors.[37] Chatham's own objections to the coercive system were made when, at the invitation of the ministry on May 27, he attended the debate on the Quartering Act. Still in a weakened condition, the sick man attacked the whole plan because it punished the innocent as well as "a few lawless depredators and their abettors."[38] He could do nothing, however, to stem the tide now running so strongly.

The Old Whigs, thwarted in their attempt to identify themselves with the public, had practically withdrawn from politics. On March 19, however, Burke presented his great apologia for his party in his speech on American taxation.[39]

Condemning the ministry for their but partial repeal of the Townshend taxes, Burke called for an honest and forthright repeal of the whole act. He then traced the rise of Amer-

[36] Taylor and Pringle, *Chatham Correspondence*, IV, 322–26, Shelburne to Chatham, February 3, 1774.

[37] Cobbett and Wright, *Parliamentary History*, XVII, 1205.

[38] *Ibid.*, 1356. Chatham was in constant communication at this time with Franklin; the radical American sheriffs of London, William Lee, brother of Arthur Lee, and Stephen Sayre; and with Samuel Wharton. See Chatham Papers, 48, 55, 66, *passim*.

[39] Cobbett and Wright, *Parliamentary History*, XVII, 1216 ff.

ican resistance from Grenville's administration forward. Internal taxes for revenue, he declared, were contrary to principles of commerce and political equity. For that reason his party had repealed the Stamp Act. So eager was he to justify the Old Whigs and to magnify their success in quieting the empire, that he denied Chatham's aid in winning the repeal.

The Townshend taxes had but revived the controversy, and now the only way to restore peace was to repeal those duties too. Striving with the paradox of the federal principle, stating it, but refusing to accept its implication—a limiting of Parliament's supremacy—Burke told his listeners that Parliament possessed two characters, one imperial, and the other local. In her relations with local assemblies, "she is never to intrude into the place of the others, whilst they are equal to the common ends of their institution." On the other hand, Great Britain, in her imperial character, superintended, guided, and controlled the inferior legislatures "as from the throne of heaven." Parliament had the power to say, if necessary, " 'Tax yourselves for the common supply, or parliament will do it for you.' " Her power of taxation, however, should be "an instrument of empire, and not . . . a means of supply." Requisitions, not internal taxes, were the constitutional mode of raising aids from America.

Involved in a basic contradiction of the federal principle, Burke sought to bury the inconvenient question of right. His speech did not touch the problem immediately at hand, nor did it attempt a defense of Boston. Furthermore, it did not offer a practical means for settling the troubles of the empire. Burke shut his eyes to the fact that Massachusetts had already proceeded beyond the question of taxation and had, at least in the opinion of most British politicians, actually denied the supremacy of Parliament.[40]

[40] See James Wilson, "Considerations on the Authority of Parliament," and John Adams, "Novanglus," extracts of both in Morison, *Sources and Documents*, 125–36. See also Thomas Jefferson, "Summary View." All appeared in 1774.

The colonists and the Old Whigs mistakenly accepted the Quebec Act as one of the coercive series. Yet the ministry had taken up the neglected affairs of Canada well before the Tea Party. In early December, North had suddenly called for, and William Knox had prepared, a précis of the affairs of the Province from the time of its first establishment.[41] A regulation of Canadian affairs, however, involved the whole of western policy.

Dartmouth's western views were almost identical with those of Shelburne. The new American Secretary firmly intended to create a new colony in the Ohio country and in March, 1773, actually offered the post of governor to a relative.[42] It would seem, therefore, that in view of the Privy Council's rejection of Hillsborough's earlier report against a grant to the Grand Ohio Company, and with a sympathetic Secretary presiding over colonial affairs, the Grand Ohio Company was upon the verge of success. Their grant, indeed, was ordered made out, but both the Attorney and Solicitor Generals, not usually on such terms of unanimity, joined to throw obstacles in its way, raising questions of law and procedure.

Dartmouth, however, supported by North and Mansfield, was determined to solve a problem which had been handed on to so many successive ministers. In the spring of 1773, he returned to Shelburne's idea of a regulation of the quitrents as a source of funds for developing the west. Consequently, the Privy Council received a report from the Board of Trade on June 3: lands on the Ohio were to be divided into lots of 100 to 1000 acres and were to be sold at auction, subject to a quitrent of a half-penny per acre. This proposal, had it come sooner, would probably have resulted in a final settlement of the vex-

[41] RHMCR. *Knox Papers, Various Collections*, 111, Pownall to Knox, December 3, 1773.

[42] RHMCR. *Dartmouth Papers*, I, 335, Dartmouth to Major Legge, March 17, 1773. The salary would have been £1,000 per annum, but Legge preferred to take the office of governor of Nova Scotia.

ing problem; now, however, it was too late.[43] Although the
report was accepted, and the Privy Council ordered additional
instructions to the governors based upon it, the net result was
merely an intensified resistance to the mother country. Virginia's claim to the Ohio territory had been ignored, driving
Jefferson to the radical assertion, in his "Summary View" of
1774, that vacant lands in America were not of the King's
domain. Governor Dunmore, who found his own speculative
schemes threatened, short-circuited the plan in that same year
by leading an army of Virginians into the back country, de-
feating the Indians, and wresting from them a new boundary,
the Ohio.

Dartmouth understood that any settlement of the western
problem must include Canada as well. Since he had come to
power, he had carried on a very full investigation of that province, consulting a wide variety of authorities. Among them
were Maurice Morgann, Shelburne's former undersecretary
and his confidential adviser on Canadian matters; Gage; Thurlow; Wedderburn; Hey and Maseres, the Canadian law officers; and many others. Even the Tea Party did not cause
Dartmouth to drop his grand design. The results of his researches are to be found in the Quebec Act.

This act sought primarily to remedy the faults of the
Proclamation of 1763. Bold and statesmanlike, it provided for
a military governor and council nominated by the Crown and
fully possessed of legislative power. Until the inhabitants of
Canada, the great majority of whom were French and without
experience in representative government, could be indoctrin-
ated in parliamentary processes, the blessings of a colonial assembly would have to be foregone. Furthermore, English
criminal and traditional French civil law were combined to
form a legal system more satisfactory and more humane.
Roman Catholics were given complete toleration and full legal
rights, including that of jury service. Tithes were legalized.

[43] See Alvord, *Mississippi Valley*, II, 237 ff.

The act was, then, a sincere attempt to right the wrongs inflicted upon a great body of alien people absorbed into the empire through conquest. No longer would a handful of English merchants and fur traders, constituting a "representative Assembly," rule a population who outnumbered them a hundredfold and yet were politically incapacitated.

The religious provisions greatly offended the ardently protestant seaboard colonies, but their chief outcry was raised because of the extension of the Canadian boundaries southward to include much of their own hinterland, the present states of Wisconsin, Michigan, Illinois, Indiana, and Ohio. The reason for such an extension was obvious. It was to bring that territory under the jurisdiction of some established government for purposes of law and order. It was a necessary step toward eventual settlement of the territory. The colonists, however, did not so regard it. Already on the brink of revolution, they saw in this act an insidious attempt to create a powerful French-Canadian and Indian threat on their frontiers. Such a belief was supported out of the words of various political figures in England. Lord Lyttelton had in debate delivered a philippic against the colonists and praised the Quebec Act for just such reasons. Burke, too, confirmed colonial apprehensions.

The Quebec Act so enraged him that his violent misinterpretation of ministerial policy reached new heights of fantasy. The act, he informed New York politicians, aimed at nothing less than to confine the Colonies' growth and so keep them weak and subordinate. He had fought the extension of Canada's boundary, but he had lost out to a ministry eager to extend prerogative over as much territory as possible.[44] Thus interpreted, the Quebec Act was of vast importance in swinging New York into line with the other colonies.

Burke apparently did not realize that his letters were inflaming a situation rapidly getting beyond control. One of the

[44] Wentworth-Woodhouse, Burke Papers, Letterbook, Burke to the New York Assembly Committee of Correspondence, August 2, 1774.

167

more curious misapprehensions of this time was a widespread conviction, especially apparent among the Old Whigs, that neither America nor Great Britain would proceed to the last resort. Sir George Savile predicted to Burke in September, 1774, that colonial affairs would not cause sufficient trouble to make the first session of the new Parliament one of great activity. Rockingham, confused and uncertain, thought America would soon grow quiet. Even Burke agreed that "the American and foreign affairs will not come to any crisis, sufficient to rouse the public from its present stupefaction."[45]

The Coercive Acts passed, Parliament was prorogued on June 22. The ministry had now to await America's reaction. There was abroad a general optimism. It was widely felt that since Britain had at last called the colonial bluff, the fractious Colonies would subside. Hutchinson, newly arrived from Boston, reported such would be the case and went on record with an opinion that Americans would never dare resist British troops. Rumors had it that her sister colonies had abandoned Massachusetts to her fate. Congratulations poured in upon the ministry for so happy a beginning of their American plan.

Soon, however, the news took a change for the worse. It became known that a general congress had been summoned in America. Gage reported from Boston that civil government was near an end, and that he despaired of a peaceable outcome unless the congress should recommend submission. In August, he published his list of "Mandamus Councillors." A meeting of delegates from the towns at once voted them unconstitutional, denied the supremacy of Parliament, and suggested a provincial congress to take charge of government. The new councilors, hunted out of their home towns by angry mobs, were forced to resign or to flee to Boston for protection. Gage, foreseeing an armed clash, did not think his troops sufficient

[45] *Ibid.*, Savile to Burke, September 13, 1774; William, Fitzwilliam, and Bourke, *Burke Correspondence*, I, 469–82, Burke to Rockingham, September 16, 1774.

to restore civil government until reinforcements should arrive.[46] A more sinister consideration for the ministry was the fact that the other colonies were rallying to the support of Massachusetts. Dartmouth pinned his rapidly declining hopes on the congress. Believing it illegal, he was nonetheless eager to use it in any way that might bring peace. He stood alone, however. Both sides had reached a point of no retreat: "The dye is now cast," the King told North; "the Colonies must either submit or triumph; I do not wish to come to severer measures but we must not retreat."[47]

To prepare for any contingency, the King determined upon an early dissolution of Parliament. North finally yielded despite misgivings about the government's unpreparedness, and against a background of a deepening Anglo-American crisis, the general election of 1774 proceeded. Although Gower wrote that affairs in America were "of a very alarming nature, and big with mischief to the two countries, for I am sure they may too properly be called two now,"[48] and although reports circulated with truth that American vessels at Southampton and Amsterdam were loading quantities of gunpowder and war stores, the American issue played a surprisingly small part in the general election. Burke came in at Bristol on a moderately pro-American "platform" based upon his concern for the welfare of the merchants of the kingdom. The electors in London, Westminster, the borough of Southwark, and the county of Middlesex—all radical strongholds—obliged candidates to sign a test which, among other things, bound them to work for the repeal of the Coercive Acts and for a reconciliation with America. The great majority of election contests were fought, however, along traditional lines of difference and were free

[46] RHMCR. *Dartmouth Papers*, I, 361–62, Gage to Dartmouth, September 2, 1774.
[47] Add. MSS 38208, f. 100, Israel Mauduit to Jenkinson, September 15, 1774. See also Fortescue, *Correspondence of George III*, III, No. 1508, the King to North, September 11, 1774.
[48] RHMCR. *Dartmouth Papers*, I, 364, Gower to Dartmouth, October 6, 1774.

of American implications. The colonists had counted on the general election for an overthrow of North and the adoption of a conciliatory policy, but the new Parliament represented an unqualified victory for the King, Lord North, and the latter's indefatigable secretary to the Treasury, John Robinson. The steady friends to government were calculated at 321, a more than comfortable majority. The contest produced no startling change or upheaval. David Hartley, a nephew of Lord Mansfield, came into Parliament in the Old Whig interest. Sheriff Stephen Sayre, although with Chatham's blessing, sought a seat unsuccessfully, and Lord Clare by declining the poll at Bristol inadvertently made room for Burke's colleague, "a hot Wilkite and American Patriot, Mr. Cruger."[49] It was, however, obvious that North and his ministry had retained a comfortable majority within Parliament and among the electors.

The meeting of the first Continental Congress in September, with delegates from all of the thirteen colonies but Georgia, indicated for Gage that he was up against a united resistance and made him painfully aware of his own helplessness. In September, he urged the hiring of Hanoverian and Hessian mercenaries, advising the home government that "these provinces must be first totally subdued before they will obey." Until Great Britain was actually prepared to crush resistance, he suggested a suspension of the Coercive Acts. For this seemingly pusillanimous suggestion, the King and a majority of the cabinet never forgave the hapless general. Even more disturbing to Gage, however, was the "considerable" number of desertions both from his small force and from the navy. Graves, the incompetent protégé of Sandwich, who had succeeded Montagu as naval commander-in-chief, joined with Gage in calling for reinforcements.[50]

---

[49] Add. MSS 35427, ff. 6, 8, 11–12, Hutchinson to Hardwicke, January 5, April 19, May 5, 29, 1775; Fortescue, *Correspondence of George III*, III, No. 1518, North to the King, September, 1774.

On October 3 the cabinet met to consider the dispatches from the two commanders. Rejecting Gage's diagnosis of affairs, they insisted upon believing that Massachusetts could be isolated. Indeed, this was a necessary premise to the success of their intended action. Should colonial resistance become general, it was admitted, Gage would "certainly want a much greater force than can well be spared here." Until future events should bear out his pessimistic forecast, however, it was decided to undertake no general mobilization of the country's military and naval power, although three ships of the line, with marine detachments amounting to some six hundred men, were to be sent to bolster both Gage and Graves. Underlying the cabinet's unwillingness to send greater reinforcements was the stark fact that no regiment could be spared from the home scene.[51]

Even at this early date there existed within the ministry a fundamental cleavage which was to become of great importance. From the first, Lord Sandwich, first lord of the Admiralty, and Barrington, secretary at war, were skeptical of sending large reinforcements to North America. Each saw France as potentially the main danger, and each wished to build up strength to counter any sudden attack from the House of Bourbon. United on this point, they nevertheless worked against each other, Sandwich preferring to send troops to North America while he husbanded British naval strength in European waters. Barrington, on the other hand, wished to make the struggle in America primarily a naval one and to avoid stripping Great Britain of her troops. Time after time, Barrington, who held no seat in the cabinet, advised withdrawing the troops from Massachusetts, "where at present they can

[50] RHMCR. *Dartmouth Papers,* II, 226, Gage to Hutchinson, September 17, 1774; Hinchingbrooke Papers, Lord Lisburne, a lord of the Admiralty, to Sandwich, October 1, 1774.

[51] RHMCR. *Dartmouth Papers,* I, 364, Rochford to Dartmouth, October 5, 1774, 228, cabinet minute, October 3, 1774; Hinchingbrooke Papers, George Jackson, a lord of the Admiralty, to Sandwich, October 8, 1774.

do no good, and without intentions, may do harm." Limited as he may have been in ability, he nonetheless recognized the North American continent for the quagmire it was and knew that British armies would be swallowed up in its immense expanses.

The conduct of Massachusetts, Barrington asserted to Dartmouth, merited military conquest, but he considered it highly doubtful that conquest could be achieved. Even should that happen, occupation would be a constant and ruinous expense, and attended with all the horrors of civil war. Let the troops be withdrawn from Boston, he pleaded, and stationed in Canada, Nova Scotia, and Florida. Then let a tight naval blockade be established on the coast, and within a few months the Colonies would consent "probably to submit to a certain degree; and in my humble opinion, the whole is then over, for with dignity we may make them concessions. I repeat it, our contest is merely a point of honour." Experience had proved that "we have not strength in that part of our dominions to levy such taxes, against an universal opinion prevailing there that we have no right to lay them. Besides, many among ourselves, though persuaded of the right, doubt at least the equity of such taxations; as Parliament is less acquainted with the state of the Colonies than of Great Britain, and as Members of neither House are to bear any part of the burthen they impose." When the Americans could be brought "to submit to a certain degree," then "if we are wise we shall for the future abstain from all ideas of internal taxation."[52] Barrington's sensible suggestions carried, however, too much an aspect of compromise. A point of honor was not to be dismissed so lightly. The supremacy of Parliament had to be vindicated. "The New Eng-

[52] Channing and Coolidge, *Barrington-Bernard Correspondence*, x–xi, Barrington to Dartmouth, November 12, 1774; RHMCR. *Dartmouth Papers*, II, 243, Barrington to Dartmouth, December 24, 1774. Knox and his fellow undersecretaries agreed with Barrington as to giving up the exercise of the right of taxation. See RHMCR. *Knox Papers, Various Collections*, 257–58, "Secrets of proceedings respecting America in the new Parliament."

land Governments are in a State of Rebellion," wrote the King; "blows must decide whether they are to be subject to this Country or Independent."[53]

Logic was nonetheless clearly on the side of Barrington. Great Britain was primarily a naval power: her rise to world power had been a brilliant illustration of that very fact. Why, then, was she to allow herself to slide into a land war which would mean her defeat and her disgrace? The answer is simple: her great naval strength was still not sufficient to meet at one time European and American commitments.

The blame for Britain's unreadiness at sea has traditionally been saddled upon North's first lord of the Admiralty, John, fourth Earl of Sandwich. His profligacy and his immoral private life have been allowed to blacken his name as a minister. His family life disrupted by a mad wife and a spendthrift son, he commonly sought diversion in the abbey at Medmenham. Hated by Wilkes because he had been elected a senior member in the Medmenham secret society before that worthy himself, Sandwich was set at target both by Wilkes and by his friend Churchill, whose brilliant satire helped to drag His Lordship's name through the mud of centuries. And yet, be Sandwich's private life as it may, and it was probably no worse than that of the average eighteenth-century nobleman, he never allowed such vagaries to interfere with his work as a minister of the Crown. One of the most experienced members of North's Ministry, and indifferent to slander, he preferred to devote his time and a very real talent to the progress of the King's affairs rather than to making what replies he could to these attacks against himself. Furthermore, he was ever watchful and solicitous for the welfare of the Royal Navy. The blame for Britain's naval unpreparedness must, then, rest upon Lord North and his royal master themselves.

During the first session of Parliament in 1772, North had

[53] Fortescue, *Correspondence of George III*, III, No. 1556–57, the King to North, November 18, 1774.

held out to the House a hope that £1,500,000 might be applied annually to the decrease of the public debt. Considering himself so committed, he then determined upon a reduction of the navy and discussed it, upon several occasions, with a resolute and resisting Sandwich. He stated his fear that the revenue for 1772 would fall by £400,000. This figure can be no accident. It was the sum which the East India Company was bound to pay annually into the exchequer. In 1772, however, with the company near bankruptcy, North knew that such payments could not be kept up. In short, if North were to pay £1,500,000 on the national debt that year, £600,000 would have to be found someplace, and he now proposed that a lion's share of that sum be withheld from the navy. This would mean decommissioning four of the twenty guardships, the very cornerstone of British naval might. Should that reduction not be sufficient, more decommissionings would have to follow. In words that are hard to credit, with the burning of the "Gaspée" fresh in all minds, and when within three years the mother country would be straining every nerve to put down colonial rebellion, North declared, "I do not recollect to have seen a more pacific appearance of affairs than there is."

Sandwich fought North's proposal with all the power and eloquence at his command. He pointed out to his chief that foreign affairs by no means wore so peaceable an aspect, and he called to aid his friend Secretary of State Rochford. North was, by such resolute opposition, indeed forced to give up his plan, but meantime, an increase in naval power was effectively vetoed. Sandwich felt lucky to hold on to what he had.[54]

Moreover the Admiralty Lord had to contend with other difficulties which rendered a solely naval war in America impossible. Britain's supply of seasoned wood, used in naval construction and repairs, had been exhausted during the late war. Thus unseasoned timber had to be used, and this caused many

[54] Hinchingbrooke Papers, North to Sandwich, September 5, 1772; Sandwich to North, September 10, 1772.

breakdowns and lengthy dry-docking.[55] Furthermore, North, desperately afraid of offending France, continued to block Sandwich's moves to increase the navy. In 1774, however, with reports that France was fitting out a fleet at Toulon, North began to take alarm. By that time the school of thought, formerly led by that minister himself, which so greatly deprecated any affront to France had gained a powerful supporter. The King himself warned North against measures likely to annoy the Bourbons, since "the conduct of our Colonies makes Peace very desirable."[56] Naval preparedness was therefore still allowed to slide. A "war of nerves" had started in Europe even before the outbreak of hostilities in America.

Faced with a full-scale rebellion, and with a call for reinforcements from his beleaguered commanders ringing in his ears, North now took a step imprudent to the point of folly. Bemused by his hope that there would yet be no general colonial war, and wishing to pay some of the national debt, he moved in the Commons (on December 12, 1774) for only 16,000 seamen in the following year, 4,000 less than in the previous year. As the East India fleet under Admiral Harland had been recalled, North convinced himself that this force, when augmented by the 16,000 sailors now requested, would be sufficient for any contingency. At this, even the Opposition was taken aback, Lord John Cavendish charging that it was a ministerial trick designed to surprise the House at some future date into "grants of a very improper and burdensome nature." At North's behest, Barrington moved for only 17,547 men for the army. Seven battalions and five companies of artillery, he revealed, were already in America, and three more battalions were ordered to join those at Boston. Ignoring information received, and speaking with almost unbelievable lack of foresight, North declared "the forces now demanded were suffi-

[55] Navy Record Society, LXIX, *Sandwich Papers*, I, Introduction and Chap. 1. See also R. G. Albion, *Forests and Sea Power*.

[56] Fortescue, *Correspondence of George III*, III, No. 1436, the King to North, April 3, 1774.

cient, unless from the conduct of the other colonies it should be judged necessary to extend the line with respect to them."[57] Despite the meeting of the Continental Congress, despite the petition from that body, and despite constant reports that the colonists were busily preparing for war, North apparently refused to believe that the cause of Massachusetts had become the cause of America. Yet it had been none other than he who had written the speech with which the King opened the new Parliament on November 29—a speech which had referred to "a most daring spirit of resistance and disobedience to the law" which still prevailed in Massachusetts. "These proceedings," the speech continued, "have been countenanced and encouraged in other of my colonies and unwarrantable attempts have been made to obstruct the commerce of this kingdom by unlawful combinations."[58] This speech clearly recognized that the conflict had now broadened far beyond Massachusetts. The reason North apparently refused to accept the facts was that he was considering a proposition to the Colonies of a conciliatory nature. He was therefore hesitant to plunge the country into an expensive mobilization.

The greatest obstacle to a conciliatory proposition at this time must have been the proceedings of the Continental Congress, news of which arrived in England early in December. The Congress had met in September. Its early sessions had been employed chiefly in a consideration of Joseph Galloway's Plan of Union. Cruelly torn between conflicting loyalties, Galloway fervently desired some compromise to settle the controversy. His plan, similar to the Albany Plan of 1754, although it also included a federative colonial council with a power to veto Acts of Parliament relating to the Colonies, might have been adopted had not ill-timed rumors of a British attack on Boston so strengthened the radicals that they gained control. The delegates then, on September 17, quickly adopted a series

[57] Cobbett and Wright, *Parliamentary History*, XVIII, 56.
[58] *Ibid.*, 33.

of resolutions denying obedience to the Acts of 1774 and recommending that public money be withheld from the provincial treasuries until government should be put on a constitutional basis, or until such time as Congress might direct. In mid-October had come the "Declaration of Rights," in which the Congress affirmed that since Americans could not from their circumstances be represented in Parliament, their own assemblies must and did hold the power of legislation within their own borders. Hitherto they had submitted in the common interest to the Laws of Trade and Navigation. They could not, however, accept that series of grievous laws running from the Revenue Act of 1764 to the Quebec Act. A few days later, Congress adopted an "Association" by which delegates bound their colonies in a strict nonimportation, nonexportation, and nonconsumption agreement. Local committees would enforce it. The petition to the King was adopted on October 26. Moderate and noble in expression, it was directed wholly against the ministers. To a King who had "the Signall distinction of reigning over freemen we apprehend the language of freemen cannot be displeasing. Your royal indignation, we hope will rather fall on those designing and dangerous men who daringly interposing themselves between your royal person and your faithful subjects" now make such a petition necessary. To British minds such sentiments meant open rebellion.

As soon as the transactions of the Congress became known in England, a cabinet was held. Rochford reported to Sandwich, who had been absent: "absurd as you are inclined to believe the Americans to be, [the proceedings of the Congress] exceed all Ideas of rebellion and even inconsistency." The inconsistency complained of was, of course, the anomaly of a petition to the King directed against those ministers whom the King himself had chosen, and who, moreover, commanded an overwhelming majority in Parliament.

Rochford was also plainly annoyed with Dartmouth who was becoming increasingly reluctant to form and direct coercive measures against all the North American colonies: "What surprises me," complained Rochford, "is that . . . Lord Dartmouth does not come with some plan to Cabinet. . . . I have been free enough to tell him to do it."[59] Still Dartmouth procrastinated, and so it fell to North to draw up such a plan. Dartmouth had, in fact, hit upon the idea of sending a royal commission to America to examine there on the spot the troubles and to negotiate a settlement. North liked the suggestion and on consultation found Mansfield in agreement. When he approached the King, however, George declared he was "not so fond of the sending Commissioners," for the colonists might take it as a sign of fear. Moreover, with the Bedfords and Suffolk watching his every move and with Dartmouth his only support, North was apprehensive that any suggestion smacking of compromise would be political suicide. Thus, to Dartmouth's great disappointment, he felt obliged to drop for the moment the plan for a conciliatory gesture.[60]

Dartmouth, foiled of his commission, now sought to lay the storm by extracabinet means. This attempt would demonstrate his own sincerity in seeking an amicable settlement with the Colonies and the irreconcilability of the antagonists' views. At Dartmouth's instigation, David Barclay, a Member with Old Whig connections, and Dr. John Fothergill, a well-known philanthropist, both Quakers and friends of Franklin, approached that American in December, 1774. Although they held no official powers and the Colonial Secretary never came out from behind the screen, daily reports of their conversations came to both Dartmouth and North.

Franklin, of course, possessed no authority save what his own considerable prestige in America and Britain might give him. Responding to a question by the two Quakers—how a

[59] Hinchingbrooke Papers, Rochford to Sandwich, December 10, 1774; also printed in Navy Record Society, LXIX, *Sandwich Papers*, I, 55–57.

[60] Fortescue, *Correspondence of George III*, III, No. 1563, the King to North, December 15, 1774; RHMCR. *Dartmouth Papers*, II, 251, North to Dartmouth, December, 1774.

peaceful settlement might be achieved—he brought forward certain proposals in a list of "Hints."[61]

1. All acts binding colonial trade should be reconsidered and then re-enacted by the colonial assemblies.

2. America should maintain her own military establishment, and there should be no requisitions during time of peace.

3. No British troops were to enter or to be quartered in any province, nor royal forts built within the Colonies without consent of the individual assemblies.

4. The tea duty, the Coercive Acts, and the Quebec Act were to be repealed, and Parliament should renounce internal legislation for America.

5. Colonial judges should hold office during good behavior. They and the governors should be paid by the assemblies.

6. In return, Franklin was willing to agree to reimbursement for the East India Company's losses at the hands of the Bostonians and to guarantee the British trade monopoly.

Such demands must have staggered both Dartmouth and North, for the talks were allowed to lapse. In February, 1775, however, Fothergill and Barclay resumed their conversations with Franklin. Meeting on the fourth, they presented him a list of counterproposals, which, they admitted, had come from certain ministers, obviously Dartmouth and North.[62]

1. The suggestion that Acts of Parliament should be re-enacted by the assemblies was completely unacceptable: it implied a deficiency in the power of Parliament. However, funds arising from the Acts of Trade might remain in the Colonies.

2. Customs officers would continue to be appointed from England.

[61] Sparks, *Franklin's Works*, V, 12–14; RHMCR. *Dartmouth Papers*, II, 264.
[62] Sparks, *Franklin's Works*, V, 56.

3. Castle William would be returned to Massachusetts, but the other "hint" concerning the troops and forts was inadmissible.

4. The Boston Port Act would be repealed. The Quebec Act would be amended by reducing the Canadian boundaries to their former limits.

5. The other Coercive Acts and especially that changing the charter of Massachusetts were absolutely necessary as "a standing example of the power of Parliament."

6. That Parliament should renounce the right of internal legislation for the Colonies was unthinkable.

Franklin found the counterproposals so unsatisfactory that he abruptly ended the conversations, declaring that "while Parliament claimed and exercised a power of altering our constitutions at pleasure, there could be no agreement." It was therefore with concern and regret that Fothergill reported to Dartmouth, on February 6, that Franklin and, through him, America had indicated an indisposition to peace and were not in a spirit of compromise.[63] Thus Dartmouth was again disappointed in his search for a peaceful settlement, and both parties continued to rush headlong toward war.

In the Opposition, Chatham and Rockingham clung to their separate ways. Both parties were in a weakened state, but the Old Whigs had gained a powerful supporter in Charles James Fox when he had been dismissed from government in February, 1774. The driving force within that party was still, however, Edmund Burke. Proclaiming that the new Parliament would be more responsive to Old Whig arguments and maintaining that public discontents with the ministry were mounting, Burke spurned Rockingham's suggestion of a secession from Parliament. Sounding a call to battle for the Old Whigs, he turned once more to the electors, particularly the

[63] *Ibid.*; RHMCR. *Dartmouth Papers,* II, 266, Fothergill to Dartmouth, February 6, 1775.

merchants, for support, dragging a reluctant Rockingham in his wake.

Before the new Parliament was many months old, however, Burke had perceived that the general election had by no means impaired the position of the ministry. More ominous for the Old Whigs, hoping against hope to repeat their performance of 1765, was a steady growth of anti-Americanism among the merchants. William Baker, Member for Hertfordshire and Burke's liaison with the London merchants, reported soon after the turn of 1774 that most of those trading to America had lately met in London and had shown themselves in chief part friends to the ministry's American system.[64] Although these London merchants were eventually brought to present a petition, Burke called it "cold and jejune." Even so, this mild document, setting forth the losses and dangers to British commerce likely to arise from any continuance of the American troubles, was a triumph for Baker.

Burke, disgusted with the London traders for their timidity, then turned to those of Bristol, taking the precaution of sending them a model petition. Adopted by the Society of Merchant Venturers of that city, it deplored the decrease of the American trade and, with it, that to Africa and the West Indies. Earlier saved from catastrophe by the repeal of the Stamp Act, but now threatened anew by the Townshend taxes in conjunction with the Coercive Acts, they prayed a return to "the former System of commercial Policy."[65]

In late January, petitions from Norwich, Glasgow, Birmingham, Dudley, Liverpool, Manchester, and Wolverhampton deplored the state of trade with America and asked redress. Yet, moderate in tone and few in number, these missives evidenced no very profound revulsion against American measures. It was soon obvious, even to Burke, that the Old

[64] Wentworth-Woodhouse, Burke Papers, Baker to Burke, December 26, 1774.

[65] *Ibid.*, Bristol petition.

Whigs were not again to ride to power on a wave of merchant discontent.

Nor was union with Chatham possible. Chatham, through his associations with Franklin, Sayre, and other Americans, was turning increasingly radical. Convinced that the proceedings of the Continental Congress offered a fair basis for restoring harmony, he attributed the revival of American troubles to the Old Whigs' Declaratory Act. Of this persuasion he curtly informed Rockingham, adding that "the *no* right to tax, and the *right* to restrain their trade, &c. was a most clear proposition." Indeed, he told the Marquis, he proposed to move in the Lords for a reconsideration of the Declaratory Act.[66] With a few sentences, then, Chatham had destroyed all hope of a united Opposition. Both parties could take a little comfort from the thought that probably, even if united, they could have done nothing to alter the course of events.

Both, however, were to try, though separately. The proceedings of the Continental Congress had obliged Dartmouth to lay the American papers before his House on January 19. The next day, Chatham made a previously much-advertised motion, the nature of which he had communicated to no one, save that it was to be about America. In the form of an address to the King, it called for the immediate removal of Gage and his soldiers from Boston. Proclaiming that America owed obedience only in a limited degree to the Laws of Trade and Navigation, he termed the recent colonial resistance as "necessary as it was just." The Americans were justified in defending "to the last extremity" their sole right to tax themselves. Indeed, to maintain this principle was "the common cause of the Whigs on the other side of the Atlantic as on this." England would eventually have to back down: let her do so now "while we can, not when we must."[67] To Lyttelton's charge that should

[66] Albemarle, *Rockingham Memoirs*, II, 261–64, Rockingham to Burke, January 8, 1775.
[67] Cobbett and Wright, *Parliamentary History*, XVIII, 150 ff. The notes for the speech are in Chatham Papers, 74.

America be indulged, she would at once proceed against the Laws of Trade and Navigation, Chatham replied that in such case he would be the first to advocate force. This statement he would have occasion to remember.

Chatham was undismayed by his overwhelming defeat—the vote was sixty-eight to eighteen against him—indeed, he said, he had only "knocked at the Minister's door." Moreover, when Dartmouth gave notice that American affairs would be taken up on February 2, Chatham determined to anticipate this move by offering a plan of his own. Working in great haste, but making no attempt to communicate with Rockingham until the very eve of his new motion, he proceeded to draft his Provisional Act for Reconciliation with America. Franklin was several times called in to help, but his influence on the bill, according to his own laconic testimony, was negligible.

On February 1, then, Chatham presented his plan "for settling the troubles in America, and for asserting the Supreme Legislative authority and superintending power of Great Britain over the Colonies."[68] Embodied in the Provisional Act, this plan was essentially as follows:

1. It opened with a declaration that the Colonies "have been, are, and of Right ought to be Dependent upon the Imperial Crown of Great Britain, and subordinate unto the British Parliament."

2. Parliament had full power to bind the Colonies "in all matters touching the General Weal of the whole Dominion of the Imperial Crown of Great Britain." Most especially did this apply to "an indubitable and indispensable Right to make and ordain Laws for regulating Navigation and Trade," for "the deep policy of such prudent Acts" contributed to the welfare of the Royal Navy.

3. The Colonies could not justly appeal to the Declaration

[68] Cobbett and Wright, *Parliamentary History*, XVIII, 198–205. Chatham's rough draft and notes for the bill are in Chatham Papers, 74.

of Right as an argument against keeping British troops in North America. That declaration, in forbidding a standing army save by consent of Parliament, applied only to Great Britain; the King's right to send forces to any British dominion was indisputable.

4. The Colonies might rest assured, however, that while the stationing of troops was a matter beyond their competence, such forces, though legally posted, could never lawfully be employed to violate or destroy the rights of the people.

5. No tax for revenue could ever be levied on a colony but by the consent of that province expressed in an act of its own assembly.

6. The meeting of the second Continental Congress scheduled for May, 1775, was to be declared legal, so that it might consider "the making due Recognition of the Supreme Authority and superintending Power of Parliament." A declaration to this effect was to be a necessary prelude to the meeting of that body.

7. The Congress was further to consider making a free grant of a perpetual revenue to the King, subject to the disposition of Parliament. Congress was to be authorized to assign quotas of the total sum to the various colonies participating in the meeting. Such a provision was not to be an act of redress but of "affection" for the mother country.

8. The powers of the Courts of Admiralty and Vice-Admiralty were to be retracted to their traditional limits; trial by jury in all civil cases was to be guaranteed; capital cases were to be tried in the vicinage of the crime, and the accused was to have a jury of his peers.

9. All the grievous Acts whereof Americans had made complaint, including the Revenue Act of 1764, the Coercive Acts, and the Quebec Act, were to be declared suspended, and, from whatever day the Congress made due recognition of the supreme legislative and superintending power of Parliament, were to stand repealed.

10. Judges were to be appointed by the Crown and were to hold salaries from it, but their tenure was to be for good behavior only.

11. Charters were to be declared inviolable.

Chatham had persuaded himself that his bill, unlikely to be adopted in its totality, would be accepted as a basis for negotiation. While it was going through changes and amendments, America would have time to signify her attitude, and in an easy atmosphere of "give and take," a peaceable settlement might be found. Even had the bill been accepted by Parliament, however, it would not have been well received in America. Many of the grievances listed by the Congress in their petition, Chatham accepted as valid. He was willing to guarantee to the Colonies a sole exercise of the right of internal legislation. On the other hand, many American complaints he rejected or ignored. He sternly condemned the colonial argument against maintaining troops in America, a cardinal complaint of the colonists. Further, the Congress would never have allowed its "affection" to be legislated by Parliament.

The Bill, moreover, offended Parliament more than it did the Americans. It demanded a renunciation of even a theoretical right to tax for revenue, although it sought to soften this action by holding out a permanent colonial grant to the Crown. As a practical means of settling the Anglo-American problem, Chatham's effort was a failure. The bill is important, however, because it demonstrated that a great British statesman understood—albeit intuitively—that the only way Britain could maintain and keep an empire was by accepting a new imperial structure. Such a new fabric would contain areas of local autonomy not to be infringed by the supreme power of an imperial Parliament. Unfortunately, those areas of local autonomy, as laid down by Chatham, were too large to be approved in Great Britain and too small to satisfy American leaders. Both at home and in the Colonies, then, the bill was received with coolness or disapprobation, the Lords declining it by a division of sixty-one to thirty-two.[69]

Meantime, Dartmouth had not given up hope of the ministry's adopting some conciliatory measure. When he had first heard Chatham's bill, he had been anxious to have it lie on the table, and had given up the idea only after his brother ministers had taken an uncompromising stand against it. He was still eager, too, to send a royal commission to the Colonies. Barclay was dispatched to talk once more with Franklin, and Dartmouth himself continued to press his cabinet colleagues for some step of a conciliatory nature.

North himself had undertaken to form the ministry's plan for dealing with what was recognized in all but form as a rebellion in New England, an obligation which Dartmouth apparently had abdicated. On February 2, therefore, North moved in the Commons for an address declaring New England in rebellion and asking his Majesty speedily to reduce that area to obedience. Despite fierce opposition from Fox, Burke, and Governor Johnstone, the crucial division stood at 296–106, and the Lords quickly concurred in this official recognition of rebellion. An augmentation of the forces requested in the King's answer on the tenth was quickly granted. North followed by moving for a bill to restrain the trade of New England and to exclude her people from the Newfoundland fisheries. Permission followed by an overwhelming majority.

Suddenly, in the midst of a violent debate on this harsh bill, North arose and moved his Conciliatory Proposition. Dartmouth's persistent efforts in this direction had triumphed at a cabinet meeting on January 21, when the resolution embodying North's proposition was adopted. Perhaps Dartmouth's unremitting insistence had worn down the Bedfordites and Suffolk into acquiesence; perhaps they saw it as a means of overturning North. Whatever their reasoning, the cabinet "agreed,

---

[69] RHMCR. *Stopford-Sackville Papers*, II, 1, Suffolk to Germain, June 15, 1775; Add. MSS 35427, f. 21, Hutchinson to Hardwicke, June 17, 1775.

that an address be proposed to the two Houses of Parliament to declare that if the Colonies will make sufficient and permanent provision for the support of the civil government and administration of Justice and for the defence and protection of the said Colonies, and in time of war contribute extraordinary supplies, in a reasonable proportion to what is raised by Great Britain, we will in that case desist from the exercise of the power of taxation, and that whenever a proposition of this kind shall be made by any of the Colonies we will enter into the consideration of proper laws for that purpose, and in the meantime to entreat his Majesty to take the most effectual methods to enforce due obedience to the laws and authority of the supreme legislature of Great Britain."[70] Dartmouth was apparently the only member of the cabinet who expected any good result of this proposition. North was not sanguine about it, though he hoped it would unite the nation at home since it was "precisely the plan which ought to be adopted by Great Britain; even if all America were subdued." The King, too, was not optimistic, but neither he nor North overlooked the possibility that the Conciliatory Proposition might prove a wedge which would destroy colonial unity.[71]

Having a day earlier notified the leading members of Opposition, North moved his resolution on February 20. In his speech, he maintained that every part of the empire was bound to pay its share for the common defense. If, however, America would undertake to raise its quota by self-taxation, he was certain Parliament would suspend the exercise of its own right. His resolution was mainly in accordance with the cabinet's previous decision, but it further provided that the net produce of trade regulations be carried to the account of each individual colony.

[70] RHMCR. *Dartmouth Papers*, II, 372–73, cabinet minute, January 21, 1775.
[71] Fortescue, *Correspondence of George III*, III, No. 1595, the King to North, February 15, 1775; No. 1599, North to the King, February 19, 1775.

North's position was not a comfortable one. The House was in the greatest confusion. Taunted by Fox and the Opposition, he was also threatened by a revolt among his own supporters. Franklin later declared he saw the Bedfords counting votes to see if they could overturn him. In the end, King's Friend Sir Gilbert Elliot rallied the ministerial ranks, and the proposition carried on February 27 in a division of 274–88. Dartmouth had won his point.

Again, however, an attempt to win a peaceful settlement was to fail. American claims against Parliament had already gone beyond the question of taxation, and the entire doctrine of parliamentary supremacy was now at issue. As with Chatham's Provisional Bill, the importance of the Conciliatory Proposition is to be found in its implications rather than in its surface content. It represented the first glimmering of a retreat from that absolute and uncompromising statement of the supreme power of Parliament laid down in the Declaratory Act. It recognized, after the fulfillment of certain conditions by those bodies, a sphere of authority reserved to colonial assemblies. Into this sphere Parliament would bind itself not to intrude. Despite the reservations and conditions laid down, which were indeed to result in the Americans' refusal of the offer, the proposition did represent the first appearance of a federal tendency in British imperial politics.

Unfortunately, more than a glimmering of federalism was needed to prevent a revolution in America. The principle had already been stated and accepted there. Had it, however, been equally received in Great Britain, it would have meant the end of the British Empire as then understood by British politicians. More concessions would have been needed, and the difficulty with which Dartmouth and North finally brought forward the Conciliatory Proposition showed that until the pressure of events became much greater, Great Britain had gone as far as she could go.

Meantime, in debates on the Restraining Act, the ministry was riding roughshod over the feeble opposition of Old Whigs and Chathamites. The bill, amended to include New Jersey, Pennsylvania, Maryland, Virginia, and South Carolina, all of whom had acceded to the nonimportation and nonexportation association, passed the Lords by a huge majority, seventy-three to twenty-one. The Old Whigs, however, were determined to present their own plan for America. They had been annoyed with Chatham who had seized the Opposition initiative with his Provisional Bill. Rockingham had been strongly advised by his friends to take countermeasures and especially to disclaim any thought of an American revenue, which Chatham's plan had promised.

On March 22, therefore, after he had sought full consultation with Chatham, Burke presented the Old Whig's Plan of Conciliation.[72] Announcing that "the proposition is peace," he called for a reconsideration of the Restraining Act, "that most infamous bill for famishing the four provinces of New England," which had been returned to the Commons for concurrence with a Lords' amendment.

Burke argued that by adopting North's Conciliatory Proposition, the "ransom by auction," Parliament had admitted that conciliation might come before American submission and that America's complaint about the exercise of the right of taxation was not unjustifiable. The proposal for peace should therefore come from the mother country. Refusing to innovate as Chatham and North had done, he insisted that in a great empire, occasional friction between the component parts was to be expected. Outlying districts necessarily possessed certain privileges, but the very exercise of them was an acknowledgement of the supreme power at the center. Recognizing and rejecting the new element which had entered British imperial thinking with Chatham and North, Burke declared, "I put my foot in the tracks of our forefathers; where I can neither wander nor stumble." With Georgian obstinacy holding firm to the De-

[72] Cobbett and Wright, *Parliamentary History*, XVIII, 495 ff.

claratory Act, he called for a return to the system before 1763. To achieve that end, he wished to establish the legal competence of colonial assemblies to support their own governments and to give public aids in time of war. Further, the Coercive Acts were to be repealed, and the powers of the Admiralty Courts restricted.

Burke's speech demonstrated again his immense talent for intensifying the thought around him, but of the three solutions to the American problem offered that session, his alone contained no hint of a federal principle. Looking nostalgically to the past, Burke sought once more to ignore the ugly question of right, a question which, once raised, had made a return to the old system as impossible as a return to childhood. To have avoided a breakup of the first British Empire would have demanded a genius who could cast in a new mold both the imperial and the domestic political scheme of things. It was an impossible task.

While the ministry, Chatham, and the Old Whigs sought parliamentary solutions to the American troubles, the City Radicals were carrying on an unceasing propaganda war outside of Parliament. A court of the Common Council voted a strong petition to the Lords against the Restraining Act. The Bill of Rights Society donated £500 for the New England sufferers. The Livery of London sent a remonstrance and petition against the American measures. William Lee, late sheriff of London and still a member of the corporation, was discovered in seditious attempts to dissuade the soldiers en route to America from serving against their American brothers.[73] Sixty-one Quakers, including John Fothergill, petitioned the King for a negotiated union with the Colonies. Burke, in his correspondence with the New York Assembly, was also doing his utmost to discredit North's Conciliatory Proposition, stating the pious wish that the ministers had been in earnest for a

[73] RHMCR. *Dartmouth Papers*, II, 280–81, Lee to Josiah Quincey, March 17, 1775. American letters were being intercepted regularly.

conciliation. As the New Yorkers had refused to elect delegates to the second Continental Congress, Burke pointedly told them, "I find that Ministry place their best hopes of dissolving the union of the Colonies and breaking the present Spirit of resistance, wholly in your Province."[74] When, however, Parliament refused to receive New York's petition and remonstrance, framed independently of the Congress, Burke's interpretation of ministerial policy was accepted, and the radical party quickly forced an election of delegates to the Congress. New York's accession made American union complete. On May 29 arrived the startling news of a clash at Lexington and Concord. "The horrid Tragedy is commenced,"[75] Sayre exclaimed to Chatham, and it was generally agreed that war had come.

In America, the colonists flew to arms. Denying that they intended independence or entertained "desires incompatible with the honour and dignity of the King and the welfare of the whole empire,"[76] they were determined to rid themselves of the unbounded supremacy of a Parliament which to them appeared as tyrannical as any Stuart monarch. In England, the ministry and a large majority in Parliament were resolved to defend that supremacy, which they had inherited from the Glorious Revolution and which they had long considered their only safeguard against royal absolutism.

[74] Wentworth-Woodhouse, Burke Papers, Letterbook, Burke to the New York Assembly Committee of Correspondence, and to James Delancey, both of March 14, 1775.

[75] Chatham Papers, 55, Sayre to Chatham, May 29, 1775.

[76] RHMCR. *Dartmouth Papers*, I, 377–78, Dr. Joseph Warren to the Selectmen of Boston, May 13, 1775, copy.

CHAPTER SIX

CIVIL WAR

T HE outbreak of hostilities in America took the British public by surprise. Their reaction was uncertain and slow to form. Only a few had expected the Americans to take up arms. But, for a moment, many hesitated to commit themselves to a civil war. John Wesley, leader of the Methodists, wrote to his coreligionist Dartmouth, "All my prejudices are against the Americans." Yet he could not avoid thinking "that an oppressed people asked for nothing more than their legal rights and that in the most modest and inoffensive manner which the nature of the thing would allow. But waiving this, waiving all considerations of right and wrong, I ask is it common sense to use force toward the Americans?"[1] The Dissenters, subject to varying degrees of legal disability in England, were the group most sympathetic to the American position; but politically disorganized and, for the most part, excluded from office, they had no way of bringing effective pressure to bear in the formation of official policy.

On the political scene, however, reaction was swift and vigorous. William Eden, Suffolk's undersecretary of state and an accomplished fisher in troubled waters, referred to the ministry as "tottering"; but Suffolk, henceforth a leader of the "war party," spurning all means but force, admonished him not to despond: "Now is the time for men of real Talent,

---

[1] RHMCR. *Dartmouth Papers*, I, 378–79, Wesley to Dartmouth, June 14, 1775.

Spirit, and Honour to appear gloriously." Already, as northern secretary, Suffolk was negotiating for twenty thousand Russian mercenaries. He would fail to buy their services, but at the time he believed they would "be charming visitors at New York and civilize that part of America wonderfully."[2] The King, too, favored quick, decisive measures, believing that "when once those rebels have felt a smart blow, they will submit." Charles Jenkinson, expressing an attitude now general among his colleagues, sharply told a friend—who had suggested sending peace commissioners—that the Americans had first to submit to the authority of Parliament. Only when they had thus earned their forgiveness would it be proper to tell them what terms they might have.

Immediately outside ministerial circles might be heard the same calls for prompt action to crush the rebellion. John Yorke feared only that the manufacturers might induce the government to adopt a conciliatory plan. Lord George Germain, soon to enter the ministry, was among the foremost in his demands for coercion; and out of the similarity of their American views, he struck up a confidential friendship with Suffolk. Hutchinson, still selling short the American fighting man and so engendering false optimism in official circles, warned that there could be no middle course between forcibly suppressing the rebellion and losing the Colonies.[3]

The situation of the Earl of Dartmouth, pious and a lover of peace, was tragic. Desperately he sought to delay the final plunge as long as possible. For the moment, he had North's co-operation. Both were hoping against hope that the second Continental Congress, which had met on May 10, might pro-

[2] Add. MSS 34412, f. 339; Stevens, *Facsimilies*, No. 851, Suffolk to Eden, June 20, 1775.

[3] Add. MSS 35375 ff. 145–46, John Yorke to Hardwicke, June 14, 1775. Add. MSS 35427, ff. 22–23, Hutchinson to Hardwicke, June 24, 1775. Hinchingbrooke Papers; Navy Record Society, LXIX, *Sandwich Papers*, I, 63, the King to Sandwich, July 1, 1775. Add. MSS 38306, f. 1, Letterbook, Jenkinson to Sir James Jay, July 17, 1775.

vide some ground for reconciliation. Nor, in their opinion, had the Conciliatory Proposition had its ultimate effect.[4] Sincerely desiring peace, they knew that the war party—Suffolk, Rochford, the Bedfords, and the rest of the King's Friends—expected vigorous action to defend Parliament's supremacy and to punish the colonists who had so boldly denied it. This group, as did Germain, believed that "it is come to that crisis which makes it necessary for Administration to adopt real offensive measures or to resign their offices and leave the conciliatory plan of meanness and submission to those who wish to be their successors upon such terms."[5]

North was not the man to resist such united demands for long, no matter what his personal views might have been. The news of the Battle of Bunker Hill was decisive. He capitulated to the war party, admitting that it was now necessary to treat the rebellion as a foreign war and the Americans as an alien foe.[6] Dartmouth, isolated in the cabinet, was soon reported to be declining cabinet meetings on American affairs and "letting it be understood in his own circle, that he is too old a *Whig* to approve of the Measures."[7] Pinning his hopes upon the Continental Congress, he struggled valiantly to delay the publication of the Proclamation of Rebellion until that body had been heard from. But the American Secretary had now to combat the wounded military pride of his colleagues. The Battle of Bunker Hill was accepted in London as a victory. Eden's laconic comment, however, indicated that it was such a one which gave no great cause for rejoicing: "If we have eight more such victories there will be nobody left to bring the news of them."[8] It was at once perceived that the fighting

[4] RHMCR. *Knox Papers, Various Collections,* 120–21, Dartmouth to Knox, August 6, 1775; 119, Dartmouth to Knox, July 3, 1775.
[5] RHMCR. *Stopford-Sackville Papers,* I, 135–36, Germain's letter of June 29, 1775.
[6] Fortescue, *Correspondence of George III,* III, No. 1682, North to the King, July 26, 1775.
[7] Add. MSS 35375, ff. 150–53, John Yorke to Hardwicke, July 29, 1775.

ability of the Americans had been underestimated; and the cabinet—except Dartmouth—agreed that "one decisive blow at land" was necessary. The government thus found itself committed to a land war.

Meantime, the Congress, immediately upon its assembling in May, had taken steps to organize colonial resistance, adopting the forces about Boston for its army and appointing Washington commander-in-chief. The moderate element, led by Dickinson and Jay, were able to carry one last petition to the King, the "Olive Branch." In it, the Congress stated that Anglo-American union had been broken by the ministry and its system of statutes and regulations pursued since 1763. They beseeched his Majesty to relieve America of her grievances and to direct some mode of reconciliation.

This petition, carried from America by Richard Penn, made a slow crossing, and it was not till August 21 that a copy reached Dartmouth's office. The Colonial Secretary, worn out with his struggle to delay publishing the Proclamation of Rebellion, had, moreover, gone to the country for a rest, so that he did not actually receive this document until the twenty-fourth. Appealing as it did to the King for aid against his own ministers, the Olive Branch could have had but slight effect, yet this delay was unfortunate; for the Proclamation of Rebellion was published on the twenty-third. The King and Suffolk had won. Dartmouth's last pitiful attempt to stave off war had failed.

Based on the declaration of 1745, the Proclamation of Rebellion called upon all good men to help suppress rebellion and to desist from any correspondence with the rebels. The nation thus stood committed to war, and there were immediate demonstrations that the people were rallying to the cause. In

[8] Add. MSS 34412, f. 340; Stevens, *Facsimilies*, No. 456, Eden to North, August, 1775. Howe referred to the battle as "most dreadful," and as attended with "fatal consequences"; 92 officers were killed or wounded, 160 rank and file killed, and 300 wounded. The rebels suffered 100 killed and 30 wounded. See Fortescue, *Correspondence of George III*, III, No. 1668.

September, Manchester, Lancaster, Liverpool, and Leicester, all strong manufacturing districts, presented loyal addresses. Bradford, Trowbridge, Milksham, and even Burke's Bristol joined in the cry. In October, the Irish House of Commons carried a resolution declaring their allegiance and loyalty to the Crown and expressing abhorrence of America's attempt to cast off her dependency. Affairs appeared in good train, then. A united nation, ignoring the arguments of Opposition, was firm in support of the ministry and looked for a speedy crushing of the rebellion. That events took no such course is due primarily to the fact that the head of the government was unfit to direct the struggle now beginning.

Frederick North, son of the Earl of Guilford and a courtesy lord, had shown no small ability as first lord of the Treasury. Of Old Whig background, he was of an amiable and conciliatory disposition, a master of parliamentary debate and procedure, and an excellent leader of the Commons. As head of a ministry and director of the course of empire, however, North was never able to establish an ascendency over his colleagues or to weld his cabinet into an effective whole. He had been called to his high office because George III saw in him those qualities he had hoped to find in Chatham in 1766. The two men could work together. For the first time the King found in the head of ministry not only one with whom he was to develop a deep personal attachment but also one who accepted him as an active political force. With North, the King's campaign to regain what he conceived to be his rightful place in British politics—as chief executive of the state, free of factions and parties trying to give him the law—was brought to a victorious conclusion. That he found in him, then, his ideal minister, is a symptom of his own mediocrity.

The fact that North had neither the strength of character nor the desire to "ape the Prime Minister"—as the King would some years later complain he did—spelled disaster for the empire, although it made him an agreeable working companion for George III. Constitutionally, the office of "Prime Minister" did not exist. This had not, however, prevented Walpole, Pelham, and Newcastle from establishing themselves as masters of the political field, or Pitt from exercising dictatorial power in a time of crisis. Inclined to vex himself and to fuss about trivialities, subject to periods of acute depression and melancholia, North was unable to rise to heights from which a comprehensive and statesmanlike view of the empire might have been possible. With no inkling of grand strategy, he had sought to solve a first-rate crisis with, at best, second-rate abilities. His personal tragedy was that he recognized his own lack of ability but did not possess the strength to refuse to serve when his sovereign called. Thus it was that he found himself driven into the leadership of a war naturally repugnant to him, and of whose outcome he was skeptical from the first.

North's pessimism in the summer of 1775 arose from several causes. He professed to fear that Opposition's attack in the coming session would be sustained and dangerous, and he was anxious about the reaction of the merchants to the Olive Branch. Furthermore, American propaganda was working its effect among the City Radicals, and the extent of seditious activity might well be great. A more fundamental reason for North's apprehension was his realization of his own inadequacies in dealing with a situation rapidly growing more complex. Immediate and grave decisions had to be made. General Burgoyne in America was violently impugning the abilities of his senior officer, Gage, and of Admiral Graves. William Howe and Henry Clinton, sent out to bolster Gage, were advising an evacuation of Boston for New York, while Burgoyne himself favored a withdrawal of the army from the Colonies altogether, leaving the Americans to fight among themselves.

Nor was the search for mercenaries proceeding with dispatch. By spring, 1776, an army of twenty thousand men had been promised the American commanders, and it had been assumed that Suffolk's negotiations with Russia would produce the required number of reinforcements. When the Czarina abruptly ended this hope—in a manner not devoid of humiliation to George III—North had to consider the extraordinary step of calling out the militia, although he admitted that "upon military matters I speak ignorantly, and therefore without effect."[9]

The manpower problem was somewhat relieved, though by no means solved, by a decision, illegal in the strict sense, to employ five regiments from the Irish establishment. The introduction of Hanoverian troops into Port Mahon and Gibraltar, although it deeply angered the Opposition, released additional contingents for American service. Yet despite these emergency measures, North's promise of an army of twenty thousand simply could not be fulfilled.

The state of the naval forces in American waters was equally deficient. There was growing a bitter criticism of the commander, Graves, for his supposed "delicacies" with the rebels. Incompetent as he was, however, it must be said that his force of twenty-seven ships, including only three ships of the line, frigates, sloops, and schooners, was much below the fifty vessels which were the estimated minimum for an effective naval force. Although reinforced with ten vessels in September and October, Graves' force remained well under the minimum.[10]

A third problem faced Lord North at home. His obvious hesitation to plunge into a war with the Colonies had caused much discontent among his cabinet colleagues. While North waited with growing and bitter disappointment for some salutary effect from the Conciliatory Proposition, the rest of the cabinet were pressing for extreme measures. Suffolk and Rochford were voluble in their demands. Germain, soon to join the

---

[9] Add. MSS 34412, ff. 343–44; Stevens, *Facsimilies*, No. 458, North to Eden, August 22, 1775.

[10] See Hinchingbrooke Papers; Navy Record Society, LXIX, *Sandwich Papers*, I, 66–67, Sandwich to Graves, July, 1775, 68–72, Sandwich to Graves, August, 1775, 64–66 and footnote, memorandum of Sir Hugh Palliser.

ministry, would agree with them. Gower, Thurlow, and their Bedford friends maintained an ominous silence, and North knew they were watching him narrowly, ready to overturn him at any false move. On the other hand, Dartmouth was sullen at cabinet. Barrington was openly opposing a land war and predicting gloomy consequences should his advice be ignored. Grafton, holding the privy seal but not one of the cabinet, was increasingly alienated by North's American measures. William Eden, already showing that amazing capacity for intrigue which he was to develop to so high a degree in the next decade, warned North that several of his ministers were "surly in their Language, sulky in their Conduct, and ill-disposed to your Administration."[11] North, then, sat at the center of an uneasy balance of power. Fully aware of his internal danger, he knew too that his colleagues, his King, and the nation at large expected vigorous action.

Events, however, now conspired to make him somewhat more secure. In response to pressure from the war party, Graves and Gage were recalled. And when Lord William Campbell, governor of South Carolina, suggested that two thousand men could subdue his province since the backsettlers were loyal, North eagerly adopted the idea. Without consulting with Secretary at War Barrington—an omission which caused that neglected minister's indignation to reach new heights—North recommended that the five Irish regiments, earlier destined for the army at Boston, should undertake a winter campaign against Charleston. The King quickly concurred and the war party was satisfied.

Secondly, when Parliament met on October 26, it soon became obvious that North's earlier fear of an effective Opposition attack had been chimerical. His ministry proved itself undisputed in control and backed by overwhelming majorities in both Houses.

[11] Stevens, *Facsimilies*, Nos. 853–54, Eden to North, September 13 and 17, 1775.

Furthermore, cabinet harmony was greatly increased when, early in the session, Grafton went over to the Opposition. His defection presented an ideal opportunity to provide a retreat for Dartmouth, now increasingly obnoxious to his colleagues and unhappy in his employment. The former American Secretary took the privy seal without a seat in the cabinet. Rochford was induced to retire. Bedfordite Weymouth became southern secretary. The fateful Lord George Germain, with his pathetic determination to redeem a soiled reputation by a brilliant military victory over the rebels, became secretary of state for the colonies. The team with which North would lose America had now been chosen.

Finally, any lingering doubt among the nation at large about the justice of stern measures was ended when in the autumn news arrived that the Americans had invaded Canada. No longer, in British minds, could the colonists maintain that they were merely repelling a wanton aggression. Rather, they had embarked upon a career of conquest. When North moved the land tax of 1776 to be four shillings, the country gentlemen supported it without a murmur.

Within the government there was a general optimism which transmitted itself to the nation. The ministry was firmly established at home. America's expedition against Canada was proving a fiasco, and the Congress, it was believed, was becoming unpopular with the colonists. Dartmouth's more vigorous successor was cheerfully predicting the end of the rebellion in one campaign and declaring that he would "establish his reputation as a minister by it."[12] The manpower problem appeared solved when in January, 1776, Britain received into her service some twenty-three thousand German mercenaries.

Feeling that he had proved himself to the war party, North turned his thought once more to an accommodation with America. Both he and Dartmouth had long favored sending

---

[12] RHMCR. *Carlisle Papers*, 306, George Selwyn to Carlisle, December 8, 1775; see also, 303, Gower to Carlisle, November 25, 1775.

royal commissioners to investigate the troubles on the spot and to negotiate a peaceable settlement. The idea had earlier been dropped in view of the opposition to the Conciliatory Proposition. In autumn, 1775, however, conditions had changed, and North, believing that commissioners could now be sent without the appearance of his being forced to the measure, determined to espouse the plan once more.

Indeed, steps had been taken even before the meeting of Parliament. By October 10, William Eden, to whom North had turned for assistance in forming the Peace Commission—much to the jealousy of John Pownall, undersecretary of state for America—had made sufficient progress to write to Lord George Germain. Germain was not yet in office, and North and Eden now offered him the commission. Eden explained that with the removal of Gage and Graves and with the prospect of a large force, both naval and military, an early end of the war seemed assured. North believed it might be hastened by giving a commissioner power to go to the Colonies to settle everything in dispute.

Eden continued that North had resolved never to bring forward such a plan until military and naval preparations were sufficient to show that he was not being compelled. That time had now arrived. The first minister had consulted his principal friends in both Houses and had assured them that the plan was not one of "wavering." Most of them had agreed in general with the projected commission, although, Eden admitted, a few had proved "rather rigid in their ideas" for uncompromising and forceful measures.

The commissioner would be empowered to supersede governors, to call assemblies, and to settle a form of taxation on easy terms in accordance with the Conciliatory Proposition. He would grant pardons, open ports, and make "corrections" in some of the colonial governments.[13]

[13] RHMCR. *Stopford-Sackville Papers*, II, 10–12, Eden to Germain, October 3 and 21, 1775.

Germain's refusal of the offer meant a temporary postponement of the plan. Meantime, a new question was raised. How
was an Act of Parliament embodying the commission to be
framed? Consulting with Lord Mansfield, who had long
favored sending commissioners, Eden concluded it would be
impossible to draw an act which would be for the purpose of
qualifying and diminishing the power of Parliament. They
then hit upon the idea of allowing the Crown to take the initiative in drawing up the commission. Parliament would simply
give approbation through a joint address. This point, though
it appears to be a minor one, was in reality of great importance. Deny it as they would, those engaged in forming the
commission knew that they were retreating from the concept
of absolute parliamentary supremacy. North, Eden, and Mansfield believed, moreover, that it was an act of necessity; and
the great lawyer openly expressed his fear that "neither our
Force nor the Exertion of it will be equal to the Magnitude
and Exigency of Affairs."[14]

The delay occasioned by Germain's refusal and the consultations with Mansfield caused Eden to be unprepared for
North to appoint a commissioner until February, 1776. A
short time before, Lord Howe, brother of Sir William, had
been named naval commander-in-chief in American waters.
As Howe had previously expressed his willingness to undertake a commission for restoring peace and had actually talked
of such a scheme with his friend Benjamin Franklin, Eden proposed that he now be appointed though joined with a civilian
colleague. Eden himself coveted the second post. Only Howe's
refusal to serve with Eden or with any one else prevented his
little intrigue from succeeding. Indeed, it was with great difficulty that Howe was finally induced to accept his own brother,
Sir William, as a fellow commissioner.[15]

[14] Add. MSS 34412, ff. 369–70, Eden to North, November, 1775.
[15] Add. MSS 34413, f. 17; Stevens, *Facsimilies*, No. 465, Germain
to Eden, February 18, 1776.

The beginnings of the Howe Peace Commission had thus not been auspicious. Worse was the settling of the powers of the commissioners. This brought North into a headlong conflict with the war party which nearly overturned his administration. The war party, while not objecting to a commission as such, were utterly determined to prevent even the shadow of a retreat from the principle of parliamentary supremacy. They believed—and North agreed with them—that indispensable conditions for peace were the laying down of arms by the rebels, the dissolution of Congress, and the restoration of legal governments. These acts North was prepared to accept as an adequate submission to Parliament's authority. The remainder of the cabinet, led by Germain who had but recently become American secretary, insisted however on a full and specific declaration of submission by the reconstituted colonial assemblies. Else there could be no treaty with the Americans. Germain, indeed, announced his intention of resigning if overruled on this point.

The Bedford group watched silently as battle lines were drawn, ready to seize any opportunity to strengthen their own position. The old Grenvillites Suffolk and Wedderburn openly assured Germain of their support. Suffolk wrote to the American Secretary, urging that he give up all thought of retiring even if North should succeed in vetoing his demand for colonial declarations of submission. Believing the point to be of little importance, Suffolk assured Germain, "If Lord North can ever insist upon anything derogatory to the authority of Parliament, I shall be against him. If he can mean to make a *paix plâtrée*, I shall be against him. If to get out of the war at any rate can be his object, he will find a very different intention mine."[16]

Wedderburn, too, wrote hastily to Germain, begging him not to resign, and his argument was more sinister. The imme-

[16] RHMCR. *Stopford-Sackville Papers*, II, 23–24, Suffolk to Germain, March 7 and 27, 1776.

diate effect of Germain's retreat, he contended, would be the abandonment of all coercive measures.[17] Thus encouraged, Germain stood fast for the declaration. North, as usual when forced with resolute opposition, was desperately seeking a compromise. However, he now found himself caught midway between two irreconcilable extremes—Germain on the one hand, and Dartmouth, supported by Germain's own undersecretary, William Knox, on the other.[18] Both of the latter were violently opposed to including any mention of Germain's declaration either in the commission or in the instructions to the commissioners. Avoiding a decision himself, North submitted the question to his cabinet. The result was a foregone conclusion, and John Pownall, who was drawing up the instructions, was directed to include the demand for a declaration.

Wrangling within the ministry had, however, by no means ended. Germain, fundamentally opposed to appeasement, as he regarded a negotiated settlement of the conflict, now insisted that the declaration of submission by the reconstituted assemblies should be previous to any treaty whatsoever with the Colonies. Infuriated at what he considered the hamstringing of the commission, Dartmouth declared he would "speak out" against Germain and resign his post. North, fearing to lose the only minister he could trust, announced that if Germain continued to press his point, he himself would retire. Germain countered with the statement that rather than permit North to resign he would do so himself. A breakup of at least a part of North's government thus appeared inevitable.

The showdown was to be in the cabinet meeting of March 18. In a last minute bid to stave off an open break with Germain—and probably his own overthrow as well—North proposed on the seventeenth that he and the American Secretary allow the venerable Mansfield to arbitrate their dispute. Mans-

---

[17] Ibid., 24–25, Alexander Wedderburn to Germain, March 7, 1776.

[18] RHMCR. Dartmouth Papers, II, 416, Knox to Dartmouth, March, 1776. See also RHMCR. Knox Papers, Various Collections, Knox's account, "The First Commissioners of the American Colonies."

field's proposal, accepted by both parties was a compromise: instead of the commissioners demanding the declaration, they were to await proposals from the Colonies. Any province, however, refusing to satisfy them on this point of submission was to be denied the King's peace; and no treaty would be begun with that colony until they had received further instructions.

This cabinet crisis over, a new one immediately took its place. Lord Howe, the commissioner designate, complained that the terms of the commission were too narrow, and began to demand discretionary power. As late as March 26, he declared that he would not accept the commission as it then stood. Germain reassured the Admiral upon most of his doubts, but Howe did not subside until he had offended the King and most of the ministers.[19]

These ill-natured bickerings prevented the commission and instructions from reaching final form until May. Precious months, during which America was steadily moving toward independence, had thus been wasted. In its final form, the commission stated that its purpose was to restore quiet on the basis of a mutual confidence and to induce submission to a lawful authority. To achieve these ends, the commissioners were instructed:

1. To proclaim free pardon for all, within certain time limits and excepting certain ringleaders.

2. To demand as a preliminary condition—before any colony should be declared at peace—a dissolution of all usurping revolutionary assemblies and of the Congress.

3. To demand that legitimate officers of government be allowed to resume their functions.

4. To require that armed forces acting under the Congress or under any revolutionary authority be disbanded and that colonial forts be delivered up to royal troops.

[19] RHMCR. *Stopford-Sackville Papers*, II, 25–27, Lord Howe to Germain, March 26 and April 1, 1776; see also 28–30, Alexander Wedderburn to Germain, April 24, 1776.

5. To summon legal assemblies, and upon their application, to relieve the provinces of restrictions upon their trade.

6. To declare a colony at peace, providing its application should indicate a true desire to return to duty.

7. To enter into treaty with those colonies so declared at peace.

8. To insist that loyalists be compensated, the damages to be adjudged by the Superior Court in each colony.

9. To implement North's Conciliatory Proposition. It was to be clearly understood, however, that monies raised under it were to be paid to a royal receiver, and Parliament was to be the last judge of the adequacy of the sum raised.

10. To leave to the treating province the mode of raising the money, although duties on the produce of British manufacturers or on colonial goods used by those manufacturers were not to be taxed.

11. To grant the tenure of judges during good behavior should that be requested.

12. To constitute colonial councils as separate and independent branches of the provincial legislatures.

13. To promise due examination by Parliament of American grievances, although any discussion of the Quebec Act was to be forbidden.

14. Any subject arising not covered by the instructions was to be referred to the home government, and all agreements were to be subject to its ratification.

Additional instructions covered the colonies of Rhode Island and Connecticut whose elective governorships had long been regarded as a grave weakness in the colonial system. Those provinces were to be required to repeal their laws restraining the subject's right of appeal to the Privy Council in civil cases. All laws impeaching the royal or parliamentary authority were to be abolished. Both colonies would have to accept royal government, or at least such alteration of their charters as would restrain the elected governor from entering office until royal approbation had been expressed. Until Rhode Island and Connecticut should agree to these demands, the commissioners were not to treat with them unless their refusal to do so should endanger a treaty with other colonies. In that case, both were to be declared at peace on the same terms as the rest.[20]

It is unlikely the American would have accepted such offers even before the outbreak of hostilities. After all the only major concession was a reaffirmation of North's Conciliatory Proposition, and this the Colonies had already contemptuously refused. The commission allowed of no colonial rights against the supreme power of Parliament and promised no more than a consideration of grievances after due submission had been made. The terms thus held out were those a victorious and reasonably benevolent mother country might have granted to discouraged and chastised rebels. As such, they were totally inadequate to achieve a restoration of peace.

In June, Lord Howe, arriving in America, proceeded to proclaim himself and his brother peace commissioners, and to call upon the rebels to return to their duty. No response came from the Congress, and the battle for New York followed. It was not, indeed, until September that a meeting was arranged between the commissioners and a committee of Congress. Meantime, the Declaration of Independence had been signed. At the conference on Staten Island, September 11, Lord Howe was careful not to admit the Congressional committee as a representation from a legal body. It was obvious from the first, moreover, that no agreement was possible, for neither party could nor would compromise on the great point of independence. The conferences broke off abruptly and, seeing the futility of looking to Congress for a solution, the commissioners had to content themselves with a declaration to all

[20] Add. MSS 34413, ff. 45–53, orders and instructions to the Commissioners, and additional instructions, May 6, 1776.

well-affected subjects, inviting conferences on the best means of restoring tranquillity. The feeble response to this invitation demonstrated the abject failure of the commission.

The period of optimism after the repulse of the Americans in Canada was not of long duration. Barrington rendered himself increasingly unpopular with the King and the ministers by his constant gloomy prognostications. Sandwich was profoundly disturbed by the steady arrival of news, from December, 1775, onward, that France and Spain were giving the rebels munitions and war stores and that France was stepping up her naval program. His efforts to keep pace with France were persistently blocked by both North and the King who were anxious at once to spare expense and to avoid offending France. On the other hand, out of Germain's bitter criticism of Sandwich for the lack of naval force in America was generated an ill will which in the troublesome times to come, was to assume the proportions of an open feud.[21]

How unfounded now seemed the fair hopes of autumn, 1775! Sir William Howe had evacuated Boston in March, 1776. It had been a tactical withdrawal, but the rebels had been elated at their first major success. Ministerial gloom increased in August when it was learned that the expedition against Charleston had miscarried due to a failure to co-ordinate measures with the western Carolina loyalists. Tension in the cabinet increased with the failure of the Howe Peace Commission.

Furthermore, in December, 1776, Franklin arrived in Paris

[21] Add. MSS 29475, f. 5, Germain to Eden, April 9, 1776. See also RHMCR. *Knox Papers, Various Collections*, 130–32, Germain to Knox, June 13, 15, 24, and July 1, 1777. Two points were at issue between the two ministers: the appointment of naval commanders which Germain tried to make a matter of joint cabinet decision; and Germain's insistence that Sandwich delegate authority to the West Indian governors to issue letters of marque. Sandwich violently resisted. Ships with letters of marque, because of the rich prizes they took, were constant temptations to sailors of the Royal Navy to desert. Furthermore, such privately owned ships were not over nice about their victims, and Sandwich feared embroilments with France and Spain. Germain was unsuccessful in his meddling, but not until the two ministers had become openly hostile.

as commissioner from the Congress. Other American agents, bent on securing aid from Britain's enemies, were soon busy throughout the continent. Industriously they spread the story that should Britain fail to recover the Colonies, she would recoup her losses by an attack on the foreign West Indies. This view Vergennes and the French government secretly accepted.[22] It soon became obvious that French naval preparations were increasing ominously. Sandwich, well aware of this steady build-up, was frantic. Though Lord Howe had demanded reinforcements, Sandwich steadfastly resisted his calls. He was trying to convince North and the King that vessels sent to the Colonies had to be replaced with newly commissioned ships in home waters. Both, however, rejected his pressing arguments. George III was particularly adamant. Convinced that the rebels would treat before winter, 1777, he wished to avoid what seemed an unnecessary expense. He believed, moreover, that "any farther demonstrations than absolute necessity requires would undoubtedly be highly imprudent as it would revive the jealousy of our Neighbours."[23]

Similarly, the King was offended with Germain's constant "harping" on his scheme to raise new corps of highlanders. These, George had learned from various military leaders, could not be available for service until 1778. By that time, he imagined, the rebellion would be crushed. Eager to avoid what seemed to be an enormous expense, wantonly incurred, the King directed North to "crush the plan in the Bud."[24] His ill-timed zeal for economy and his reluctance to offend France,

[22] Stevens, *Facsimilies*, No. 897. Vergennes read a secret paper to the French King in cabinet on August 31, 1776, in which this view was set forth. It referred to Britain's guardships as "an imposing scarecrow" and maintained that the American rebellion offered France a unique opportunity to attack her old enemy.

[23] Add. MSS 37833, f. 163, draft; Fortescue, *Correspondence of George III*, III, No. 1974, John Robinson to the King, March 14, 1777. See also Hinchingbrooke Papers; Navy Record Society, LXIX, *Sandwich Papers*, I, 159-62, Sandwich to Lord Howe, October 17, 1776.

[24] Add. MSS 37833, f. 165, 170, the King to John Robinson, March 14 and 15, 1777.

with North's willingness to accept his arguments rather than those of Sandwich and Germain, would be responsible for Britain's deplorably unready state in the coming war with France.

At first, it appeared that George III's optimism was not wholly unfounded. True, Howe had retired from Boston, and from his new base of operations, Halifax, he had reported that until the rebel armies should be defeated, there was not the least prospect of reaching an accommodation with America, or even of drawing a respectable number of loyalists to open support of the Crown.[25] (A final quietus had thus been put to Barrington's periodic and grumpy demands for a solely naval war.) Howe had then proceeded to deal hard blows to the rebel power in the summer of 1776. By the end of his campaign, the Peace Commission had failed, but New York had been wrested from Washington, and the American army driven across the Jersies into Pennsylvania. The King and the ministers were elated. Jubilantly, Germain confided to Eden, "It is clear that the Rebels will never face the King's Troops." To him Washington's withdrawal seemed proof that the rebellion was nearly finished. High in praise of Sir William Howe, only on one score did Germain criticize the General. The pardon which he and his brother had proclaimed for repentant rebels, he feared, might so depress the loyalists that they would hesitate to declare for the mother country.[26]

It was therefore with some reason that the King and his ministry looked to an early victory. Washington's pitiful and

[25] RHMCR. *Stopford-Sackville Papers*, II, 30–31, Sir William Howe to Germain, April 26, 1776.

[26] Add. MSS 34413, ff. 147–48, Germain to Eden, January 1, 1777. See also RHMCR. *Knox Papers, Various Collections*, 128, Germain to Knox, December 31, 1776, for more criticism of the commissioners. See, however, RHMCR. *Dartmouth Papers*, II, 431–32, Ambrose Serle to Dartmouth, January 1, 1777. Serle, serving with the British army in New York, was in charge of issuing pardons to repentant rebels. The proclamation had had the greatest effect, he wrote, with hundreds of pardons having been issued, the general sentiment in New York being that the rebellion was broken.

beaten army would dissolve under the hardships of a rigorous winter. The rebel governments, suffering from an inflated paper economy and from the ravages of war, would submit. Indeed, the American forces in their Pennsylvania retreat were in desperate circumstances. Had Howe plunged after them, instead of ending his campaign in December, he might well have ended the rebellion then and there. And yet Washington's force, however weakened, remained intact, a rallying point for the rebels. Their assemblies continued to function, and the control of the Congress was unshaken. John Yorke marvelled that "there is something which supports and keeps them together which the Ministers have not yet discovered."[27]

During the Christmas season, a time when all good professional soldiers should have been in winter quarters, that mysterious "something" carried Washington and his army across the Delaware for their amazing foray against the Hessians at Trenton. When in February news of this exploit arrived in Britain, it killed the hope that the rebel army would dissolve during the winter. Indeed, General Howe informed the ministers, this little success had so restored their morale that another campaign would be necessary.[28] To insure the end of the rebellion in 1777 he needed more troops, twenty thousand more.

This request was a signal for bitter outbursts on the part of the King and Germain against both Howe and his brother. George III well knew that such mammoth reinforcements were impracticable, and that, indeed, the General's requisition was fantastic. His shock betrayed itself in severe criticism of the Howe brothers for what he supposed to be their leniency toward the rebels. "Regaining their affection is an idle idea," he thought: the Americans could be defeated by that force already under the Howes' command if only the two command-

---

[27] Add. MSS 35375, ff. 185–86, Yorke to Hardwicke.

[28] RHMCR. *Stopford-Sackville Papers*, II, 53–55, Howe to Germain, December 31, 1776.

ers would exert themselves.[29] As Howe's exorbitant request had also angered Germain, the General ultimately got only twenty-five hundred more men. He then felt so restricted that he warned the home government to give up all hope of ending the rebellion in 1777.[30] Germain, however, was not dependent wholly on Howe's efforts.

General John Burgoyne, a Member of Parliament, earlier sent to Boston with Howe and Clinton, had returned to England in the winter of 1776–77, filled with his own thoughts on how to crush the rebellion. He immediately converted Germain to the idea of a descent with a British army from Canada. It was not actually a new idea. Howe's first plan had also been to isolate New England. He had proposed attacking Boston and simultaneously moving a column up the Hudson to Albany to join a force coming down from Canada. By the latter part of December, 1776, however, Howe had decided that the Canadian army could not reach Albany until September, 1777, at the earliest. Wishing to avoid a summer of inactivity, and believing Pennsylvania to be loyal at heart, he notified Germain that Philadelphia would be his prime target during the summer of 1777. Burgoyne and Germain, however, believing that Howe could take Philadelphia and then return to form a junction with the Canadian army at Albany by early autumn, continued work on their own plan. Their miscalculation was a fatal one, and they must bear the odium of it. North, who had broken his arm in September, 1776, and was recuperating from a persistent fever at his country place, had long been unable to meet the cabinet. Had he done so, he might have ex-

[29] Add. MSS 37833, f. 137, the King to John Robinson, March 5, 1777. Fortescue, *Correspondence of George III*, III, No. 2072, the King to North, October 28, 1777. Criticism of the Howes' supposed leniency was growing steadily. See Hinchingbrooke Papers, Sandwich to Lord Howe, March 10, 1777, urging the Admiral to more vigorous action against the Americans.

[30] RHMCR. *Stopford-Sackville Papers*, II, 56–57, Germain to Sir William Howe, January 14, 1777; 63–65, Howe to Germain, April 2, 1777.

ercised a co-ordinating influence in the formation of plans for this dual offensive.

Orders for the descent from Canada went out to General Sir Guy Carleton, governor of Canada, on March 26, about three weeks after Germain had sent Howe the royal assent for his expedition against Philadelphia. Giving way to characteristic spite—Carleton had testified against Germain at the latter's court martial after the Battle of Minden—the American Secretary induced the King to agree that the command of the expedition should be given, not to Carleton, the senior officer, but to Burgoyne. That General then proceeded to Canada, carrying orders minutely detailing the campaign he was about to undertake. Germain was taking no chances. Credit for crushing the rebellion was a prize he did not intend to give to another.

A tragedy of conflicting plans, ambiguous orders, and bad luck unfolded itself. Before he left New York in July, Howe received a letter from Burgoyne stating that his army was before Ticonderoga and was in full health and spirits. Thus made secure in a belief that Burgoyne was capable of fending for himself, Howe embarked for Philadelphia. Because of an extremely tedious passage—he arrived at the Head of Elk only on August 30—he was obliged to write Germain that co-operation with Burgoyne would now be impossible. He was disappointed too, he said, at the small number of loyalists who had come over to his standard. The situation was thought by no means critical, however. Early in August had come the comfortable report that Burgoyne's progress was without opposition and that Ticonderoga had fallen. The King and the ministry were in a fever of anticipation awaiting glorious news. On September 25, dispatches arrived from Burgoyne, and with them a cloud no bigger than a man's hand appeared on the horizon. His progress, the General wrote, had been as rapid as possible through the northern wilderness, but he had heard nothing from Howe. Of ten messengers sent to New York not one had returned.[31] Germain knew what Burgoyne did not: that the Canadian army would be disappointed of a junction with Howe's. Far from being alarmed, however, Germain merely reflected that it would be the greater honor for Burgoyne to reach Albany without assistance from New York.[32]

This general optimism grew on apace. William Knox predicted to his friend Governor Henry Ellis that an extraordinary *Gazette* would soon proclaim a great victory. William Eden was certain that the campaign then under way would see the end of the rebellion. Henry Dundas, the future Lord Melville, at his house in Ayrshire could scarcely wait for every post. John Robinson urged North to delay the opening of Parliament until the good news had arrived. There were, of course, some ominous undertones. "It has for many months been clear to me," Eden wrote North, "that if we cannot reduce the colonies by the force now employed under Howe and Burgoyne, we cannot send and support a force capable to reduce them." Dundas, too, though hoping for "some splendid business done this campaign," confided to Eden that if the present effort should not defeat the rebels, he would have "a very desperate opinion of the business." Old and ailing Henry Ellis replied to Knox's exuberant predictions with a quotation from Voltaire: "*le probable n'arrive presque jamais!*"[33] North, the King, the ministry, and the nation, however, confidently awaited good news.

Assuming that the conflict was practically over, North turned to the problem of the disposition of the "conquered" Colonies. Never fully trusting any cabinet colleague except

---

[31] Fortescue, *Correspondence of George III*, III, No. 2061, Germain to the King, September 25, 1777.

[32] RHMCR. *Knox Papers, Various Collections*, 139, Germain to Knox, September 29, 1777.

[33] *Ibid.*, 135, Ellis to Knox, August 13, 1777. Add. MSS 29475, ff. 11–12, Dundas to Eden, August 30, 1777. RHMCR. *Abergavenny Papers*, 17, Eden to North, August 25, 1777.

Dartmouth—and he was no longer in the cabinet—North found his confidants among the undersecretaries and subministers. Eden had been a moving force in the formation of the Peace Commission. North's own secretary to the Treasury, John Robinson, had been called upon to discharge the balance of the First Minister's duties during the latter's illness. Now it was to Charles Jenkinson, a lord of the Treasury, that he turned for advice, much to Eden's jealousy. North was frankly at a loss as to how to proceed, believing only that—whether any or all of the revolted provinces returned to their duty—Canada should henceforth be the main support of British authority in North America.[34] He was therefore anxious to receive suggestions for the future of the rebellious Colonies.

North conferred on several occasions with Jenkinson and with the latter's brother-in-law Cornwall, who was also a member of the Treasury Board. In June, 1777, just as he was about to depart for a vacation in France, Jenkinson wrote to North, summarizing the points raised in their conversations. His views are of interest because they represent those prevailing among British politicians. They serve to indicate that the American conflict had not as yet produced any radical change in British imperial thinking. Reaction to the American war was, as yet, primarily conservative. The vision of a new imperial relationship would be vouchsafed only when distress and defeat should prepare men for it.

Jenkinson contended that it was impossible ever to end the war by a negotiated treaty. While it had been wise to hold out such a prospect at the beginning of hostilities, nothing now could be done but "to state to the Americans in plain and explicit Terms, the Conditions on which alone you will allow them to resume a share in their own Government, and in the mean time to Govern them by Powers vested in the Crown." Jenkinson elaborated his analysis in a letter from Aix-la-Cha-

---

[34] RHMCR. *Abergavenny Papers*, 14–17, North to Carleton, August 3 and 26, 1777.

pelle in July. He then proposed that the Laws of Navigation should be tightened. The Colonies, he maintained, might be allowed to enjoy their own coasting trade, but all other trade should be carried on in ships belonging to subjects resident in England, Ireland, or in the colony producing that article of trade. Such a provision would serve to increase British naval strength and carrying trade. At the same time, it would restrain the growth of that branch of commerce in New England where, before the outbreak of hostilities, they had proved themselves formidable rivals to the mother country. Furthermore, such restrictions would diminish the colonial capacity for producing a naval force. The now existing American navy had already inflicted grievous losses on British shipping, and it should not be allowed to happen again.[35]

While Jenkinson indicated for the mother country the role of a stern parent, North was falling into melancholy. As the summer waned and September turned into October, the First Minister grew more apprehensive that the campaign would prove indecisive.[36] In early October, news of the capture of Philadelphia served to reassure the doubters, and for a time, London was tumultuous with joy. At the end of the month, however, Germain and the ministry learned of the affray at Bennington. The American Secretary immediately concluded that Burgoyne's campaign was "totally ruined"; but surely the General had withdrawn to Ticonderoga! Germain was seriously alarmed, however, at Burgoyne's apparent assumption that he possessed no discretionary authority, and that his orders were so positive that he had to press on to Albany at all costs.[37]

Parliament was to meet on November 18. Before that time, tension among the ministers had become almost unbearable. The drafting of the King's speech for the opening of the new

[35] Add. MSS 38306, f. 71, Letterbook, Jenkinson to North, June 26, 1777; ff. 72–74, Jenkinson to North, July 9, 1777.

[36] Add. MSS 34414, ff. 209–10, North to Eden, October 4, 1777.

[37] RHMCR. *Knox Papers, Various Collections*, 140, Germain to Knox, October 31, 1777.

session proved a difficult problem. On the ninth Eden sent North a sketch for the speech "on the Supposition of goodish News," and advised that, should such news not arrive before the eighteenth, the Parliament be prorogued for ten days. Eden had outlined a firm conciliatory message. More liberal than Jenkinson, he would have had the King promise the Americans that whenever they should return to their duty, they would be given proof of Parliament's benevolent care for them.[38] Both Eden and Jenkinson believed, however, in the supreme power of Parliament. They might agree to the puny qualification of it embodied in the Howe Peace Commission, but the time for a negotiated treaty was past. But what would be their attitude and that of the ministry in the face of new and catastrophic intelligence from Saratoga?

America, since the lingering death of Jacobitism, was the first fully developed "issue" in British politics. It was not to be a biding one, but the divisive force which it engendered was to remain, and new issues and principles springing from it would bring Britain to the threshold of her modern party system. The American problem in British politics had resulted in the consolidation of a new conservatism, the seedbed of a new Tory party. But it was also preparing, about the Old Whigs as a nucleus, the emergence of a new Whig party.

It would be a mistake to call the Opposition "pro-American," except in a very limited sense. Yet the Americans and the Opposition shared much common ground: a belief that King and ministers had somehow—mysteriously though corruptly—come to dominate the political scene free of any constitutional check. Both groups detected in the reign of George III an insidious attempt to re-create old Stuart despotism. The American reaction had been the formulation there of the concept of a federal empire. That solution, however, was viewed in the mother country as the very step which would render the Crown independent of Parliament. When, therefore, that solution

[38] Add. MSS 34414, ff. 337–39, Eden to North, November 9, 1777.

had been rejected by Britain, whose own political development rendered it impossible, the colonists proceeded to declare themselves independent. That same political development within the mother country, which saw the King as an active agent in British politics, meant for the Opposition—Old Whigs, Radicals, and Chathamites alike—that the American struggle was but one of several symptoms of a basic political maladjustment. In fact, however, the King and the North Ministry had merely placed themselves at the head of a system created by the Old Whigs themselves under the first two Georges. Those claiming descent from the Walpole and Pelham Whigs had, perforce, to find a new basis whereon to stand and to create myths to explain both their origin and their long exclusion from office. Both Old Whigs and Americans, the first because of their long sojourn in the wilderness, and the second because they could not reconcile their federal idea with the traditional concept of empire, were passing beyond the eighteenth-century framework.

During these years of the American war, a twofold impact upon the Opposition became evident. First, among their shattered and divided ranks were men for whom military defeat and national disgrace were not necessary prerequisites for glimpsing a new vision of empire. In their gradual acceptance of the Americans' federal idea, they were groping toward the only way by which Britain, as a free country, could build and keep an empire. Secondly, seeing the American issue in a broader context, the Old Whigs and those acting with them set themselves upon a path leading to an abridgement of the powers of the Crown and to parliamentary reform. Success would come to their descendants but not, indeed, until the nineteenth-century, long after the American Colonies had been irretrievably lost.

There is a subtle relationship between the American federal idea, the Opposition's growing acceptance of it, and the attack on the "overweening" influence of the Crown. The

Americans, Lord Mansfield had stated during debates on colonial petitions, sought, with their argument that the Colonies were bound to the mother country only through the person of the King, to reduce the monarch to a figurehead or "cipher." He was right. Before a federal empire—or a commonwealth of nations—would become possible, the King would have to retreat from a role of active participation in politics, would have to rise above the domestic scene where modern, well-organized parties in which he had no active part dominated. He would have to become a symbol wherein all portions of the empire might find union in equality. During the American war, and largely because of it, the Old Whigs and their friends began that domestic battle which would result in so salubrious an end.

The arrival, in June, 1775, of reports of the outbreak of hostilities caught the Opposition scattered throughout the kingdom, for Parliament was in recess. Chatham was so ill that Lady Chatham kept the news from him. Rockingham threw up his hands at the impotence of his own party, exclaiming that politics must be left "to take their own Time and their own Turns." Lord Edgcumbe, formerly an Old Whig, had already put his parliamentary seats at North's command, and most Old Whigs felt reluctant to engage against measures to put down open rebellion. Only the eccentric Duke of Manchester called for an immediate halt to the war, but his plan, whatever it may have been, was negatived by Rockingham. Even Burke was convinced that the Americans would have to suffer heavy blows.[39]

Burke, as so often before, was for action, and he became the driving force in his own party. War had begun, but Parliament had not yet committed itself. Again and again, he urged the necessity of an immediate consultation among Old Whig

[39] Chatham Papers, 10, Lady Chatham to William Pitt, July 16, 1775. Wentworth-Woodhouse, Burke Papers, Rockingham to Burke, June 23, 1775; Lord John Cavendish to Rockingham, August 2, 1775.

leaders: "I protest to God," he wrote to Rockingham, "I think that your reputation, your duty, and the duty and honour of us all . . . demand at this time one honest, hearty effort, in order to avert the heavy calamities that are impending." Should that last effort fail, Burke believed the Old Whigs would be justified in leaving the people and the ministry to their fate. But to that last effort they were clearly obligated. He was not so sanguine as to believe that his party could carry the nation against the war, but by factious conduct, he proposed to impede that war in every possible way. Acting under a set plan, the Old Whigs, he believed, could "clog a war in such a manner, as to make it not very easy to proceed."[40]

Rockingham expressed initial agreement with Burke, and in September wrote to his lieutenant that he would be in London for general consultations ten days or two weeks before the opening of Parliament. His plan at that moment was to resist the loyal address, and further, to induce all parts of the Opposition to join in a remonstrance to the King. In it they would warn him that the royal power could subvert the authority of Parliament, and that American measures were part of "a *System*, which somehow are thought more particularly patronized by his Majesty." Having thus placed themselves on record, the Old Whigs would then absent themselves from Parliament whenever American affairs were under discussion.[41]

Reassured by Rockingham that some plan would be adopted before the opening of Parliament, Burke turned to his own constituency, the city of Bristol. What he found was not encouraging. Formerly the most pro-American city of the kingdom, Bristol was now undergoing a profound change. Burke's colleague, the American Henry Cruger, had reacted to the outbreak of hostilities in a disconcerting manner, lashing out

[40] William, Fitzwilliam, and Bourke, *Burke Correspondence*, II, 33–34, Burke to Rockingham; 39–41, Burke to Rockingham, August 4, 1775; 46–57, Burke to Rockingham, August 23, 1775.
[41] Wentworth-Woodhouse, Burke Papers, Rockingham to Burke, September 11, 1775.

at his erstwhile fellow-countrymen for their violence and folly. After a canvass of the city, Burke estimated that only a fourth of the corporation was with the Old Whigs. Another fourth would act with them in a limited way. The other half were Tories, but they, too, were divided. The Bristol Quakers, a strong mercantile group, were still Burke's friends, but their London brothers had gone over to the Court. Furthermore, the Bristol merchants tended to view the present crisis as merely another alarm, and to feel that all would in the end be well. The rest of the merchants of the kingdom, upon whose support the Old Whigs had ridden to power in 1765, had already abandoned them. Considering America lost, they looked to the ministry for an indemnity. Government contracts had begun to overcome their initial opposition to war. This in conjunction with the great increase of northern European commerce made the American trade seem of secondary importance.

Burke nevertheless fell energetically to work. At his instigation, a secret committee of correspondence was created among his merchant supporters in Bristol. Although he at first predicted that this example would be followed in twenty or thirty other places—a number which was never achieved—his most sanguine opinion before he had been long at his task was that he and his party were strong enough in Bristol to prevent their enemies hurting them.[42]

A second and greater disappointment was in store for him. After a September meeting of several of his friends in Yorkshire, Rockingham informed Burke that he had changed his mind: he now believed that it would be futile to call a general meeting of Old Whigs before the opening of Parliament. "The generality of the people of England," the Marquis wrote, "are now led away by the misrepresentations and arts of the ministry, the court, and their abettors; so that the violent measures toward America are fairly adopted and countenanced by a ma-

---

[42] William, Fitzwilliam, and Bourke, *Burke Correspondence*, II, 57–66, Burke to Rockingham, September 14, 1775.

jority of individuals of all ranks, professions, or occupations, in this country." Opposition could do nothing to alter events, and Rockingham was convinced that only national disaster and disgrace could change the situation.[43]

Burke was nearly beside himself at what he considered a palpable rationalization and excuse for inactivity at this time of supreme crisis. Abandoned by Rockingham, he turned to the young Duke of Richmond. As that nobleman was possessed of large estates in Ireland, Burke suggested that he join other Old Whigs with Irish interests and induce the Irish Commons to express their disapprobation of the American war. They should also be persuaded to refuse extraordinary grants and supplies for troops to be used outside their kingdom, thereby helping to prevent the mother country's "enslaving all its dependencies." Should that be done, Burke was convinced, the ministry would hesitate to take "a contest with the whole empire upon their hands at once."[44] When Richmond failed to respond to this desperate plan, the disappointed Burke realized that his party, believing that only disaster would awaken the public, had overruled him.

A new snub awaited him. Despite their utmost efforts, his friends had been easily overwhelmed when Bristol adopted a loyal address to the King expressing their support of the government in its struggle with the American rebels.[45] In London, Burke and his party, working through the radical Members for the City—Oliver, Bull, Sawbridge, and Hayley—suffered an even greater rebuff.[46] Even before the meeting of

[43] Wentworth-Woodhouse, Burke Papers, Rockingham to Burke, September 24, 1775.
[44] William, Fitzwilliam, and Bourke, *Burke Correspondence*, II, 71–76, Burke to Richmond, September 26, 1775.
[45] Wentworth-Woodhouse, Burke Papers, Paul Farr to Burke, September 30, October 7 and 14, 1775; Richard Champion to Burke, September 26, 1775.
[46] *Ibid.*, Sir William Baker to Burke, October 4, 5, 1775. See also RHMCR. *Dartmouth Papers*, II, 392, William Molleson, a London merchant, to Dartmouth, October 11, 1775.

Parliament, then, it was obvious that the Old Whigs would have no chance of rallying the merchant interests of the kingdom to their support.

Old Whig contact with the London Radicals did nothing to improve their odor with the public. With the outbreak of hostilities, Wilkes and his group had become objects of great suspicion. It was known that large numbers of foreign officers and engineers, mostly French, were in London awaiting passage to America and that they were being received and aided by some of the Radicals.[47] An open appeal had been made by the revolutionary provincial congress of New York for support among this very group. By autumn, inflammatory and seditious fly sheets had begun to circulate. The ministry, who had been intercepting suspected correspondence for months, was, moreover, aware of attempts to debauch the soldiery.

Firm and decisive ministerial action against potential firebrands was to prevent any violent revolutionary or radical activity. Even the horrible Gordon Riots of 1780, having no direct connection with the American war, would be reactionary rather than radical in character. That radical parson of Brentford, Horne Tooke, upon his expulsion from the quarreling Society of the Supporters of the Bill of Rights, had formed the Society for Constitutional Information. In June, 1775, his group voted £100 "for the relief of the widows, and orphans, and aged parents, of our American fellow-subjects, murdered by the King's troops at Lexington and Concord." Rebellion had already been acknowledged by Parliament, and as soon as the Proclamation of Rebellion was made, Tooke was arrested and convicted of libel. In November, 1777, he was fined and sen-

[47] RHMCR. *Dartmouth Papers*, II, 349, John Pownall to Dartmouth, August 5, 1775. Pownall estimated that there were two hundred such officers in London at the time. For the extent of seditious activity among the Radicals, see RHMCR. *Dartmouth Papers*, II, 376, an anonymous officer of the East India Company to Dartmouth, September 9, 1775; 376–77, circular letter of Thomas Joel, September 4, 1775; Charles Simpson, Town Clerk of Litchfield, to Dartmouth, September 9, 1775; Sergeant John Osbaldeston to Dartmouth; see also 427–28.

tenced to a year in prison. It is noteworthy that his incarceration was unattended by that public clamor that had been raised at Wilke's imprisonment.

Radical ardor was further damped when, in autumn of 1775, a former sheriff of London, the American Stephen Sayre, was briefly committed to the Tower, charged on very flimsy evidence with plotting to seize the King's person at the opening of Parliament. Upon his release, he left the country and allied himself with his fellow Americans on the continent. Held in abhorrence by the great majority of men, the activity of the Radicals served to increase the nation's support of the ministry and to discredit all groups, however respectable, who opposed the American war.

Parliament met on October 26. As yet no effort had been made to secure Old Whig-Chathamite co-operation. Chatham was still sick, although reports of his recovery were circulating, and Burke grudgingly admitted that it would be wise to concert measures with him and with his friends. Even so, the first approach came from the Chathamites. On the twenty-eighth, Dr. Joseph Priestly, close friend and confidant of Shelburne, wrote to Savile seeking to present a comprehensive statement of Shelburne's views. The Earl, he said, was prepared to act with, or even under, Rockingham if only definite, distinct proposals were adopted. Not mincing words, he told Savile that the Americans would have more confidence in Shelburne than in Rockingham, whose Declaratory Act the colonists would never accept. It is clear, then, that in case a coalition of the two parties should achieve office, Shelburne counted on having the direction of American affairs.

Priestly was frankly despairing, however, of any chance to treat with the Americans. The chief interest of his letter lies in its indication that Shelburne was already looking beyond the American struggle. The war he saw as only one of several symptoms of a fundamental illness in the State. The object of future opposition, Shelburne believed, should be to achieve an abridgement of the power of the Crown, especially in respect to the disposal of revenue. Already, then, he was moving toward that "platform" of economy and reform which was to make possible his future coalition with the Old Whigs.[48]

Despite Savile's cautious reply, the debates of November indicated that substantial union had been achieved. Grafton's accession was a heartening sign, and when Burke was drawing up his bill for composing the troubles in America, he was in close communication with Camden, Shelburne, and other Chathamite leaders. No one indeed was so sanguine as to believe that North's ministry could be overturned. When, for instance, Richmond moved in the House of Lords in November that the Olive Branch afforded grounds for reconciliation with America, the combined Opposition could vote only thirty-two against eighty-six. They were, however, seeking to "go on the record." During the debates of October and November, their attitude toward the war was clearly delineated: America had been driven to resist because of Britain's unjust demand for a revenue. She did not aim at independence. The mother country had falsely assumed that she did and now sought to coerce her by force. Such an attempt was doomed to failure. Underlying their whole argument was the theme that the struggle must be brought to an immediate end: if it continued, France could not be expected to remain neutral. From an independent member of Opposition, former colonial Governor Johnstone, came a more creative analysis. In a brilliant speech he presented the first clear statement yet heard in Parliament of the principle of a federalistic empire. Johnstone maintained that it was ignorant to deny as the ministry did that two independent legislatures could not coexist within the same political community. A free government always contained many clashing jurisdictions: "The supremacy of the legislative authority of Great Britain! This I call unintelligible jargon; instead of running

[48] RHMCR. *Savile-Foljambe Papers*, 149, Priestly to Savile, October 28, 1775; 150, Savile to Priestly, October 29, 1775.

the different privileges belonging to the various parts of the empire into one common mass of power, gentlemen should consider that the very first principles of good government in this wide-extended dominion, consist in sub-dividing the empire into many parts, and giving to each individual an immediate interest, that the community to which he belongs should be well regulated."[49] His pronouncement indicated that a new idea was at work in imperial thinking, one which the government was eventually to accept under the harsh necessity of military defeat.

Johnstone, in his vision of a federal empire was far ahead of the rest of Opposition. Nonetheless, there were signs that the Old Whigs were feeling their way toward that solution. On November 16, Burke brought forward his bill for quieting America. Marking a fundamental change in Old Whig thinking and a limited acceptance of Johnstone's thesis, the bill signified Old Whig willingness to repudiate the right to tax America for revenue. Paradoxically, Burke proposed to achieve this object without actually repealing the Declaratory Act, for which his party had been responsible. He was still unwilling to admit that they had been wrong. Charles James Fox had earlier called for a repeal of all acts concerning America passed since 1763. In his own argument, however, Burke disagreed, maintaining that a repeal of the Declaratory Act would constitute a denial of the legislative power of Parliament, while a repeal of all the Acts of Trade since 1763 would destroy the whole system of British-American commerce. It is difficult to reconcile his attitude toward Fox's proposal with the new thesis enunciated in his bill: that sovereignty was an idea capable of great complexity and infinite modifications according to the temper of those governed and to the circumstances of the time. The power of taxation, although inherent in the supreme power of society taken as an aggregate, did not necessarily reside in any particular organ of that society. What he now pro-

[49] Cobbett and Wright, *Parliamentary History*, XVIII, 740–57.

EDMUND BURKE

posed was passage of a new act denying to Parliament the right to lay any tax upon America except for the regulation of commerce. Even in that case, the produce was to be remitted to the Colonies. A general congress was to be authorized whenever required by the colonists. The Coercive Acts would be repealed, and a general amnesty granted.[50]

Although the Old Whigs still clung to their Declaratory Act, believing that consistency demanded it, this proposal was a step forward for them. Once more, however, they found themselves on middle ground and satisfying no one but themselves. The ministry was hostile because of the proposed infringement of Parliament's supremacy. Governor Johnstone, on the other hand, attacked Burke's plan just as bitterly, branding it as only "part of a system." The Old Whigs knew their motion would be defeated—the House subsequently divided in favor of the previous question by 210 to 105—but they had gone on the record.

Despite the Opposition's positive achievement in pointing out the way to a federal empire, their attacks were clearly without influence in Parliament. Indeed, their numbers were steadily diminishing. In late November, on a rash motion of the City Radicals, they divided only 10 against 163. When, on December 1, North brought in his Prohibitory Bill, which forbade commerce with the rebels, the Opposition did not dare bring the debate to a division. A week later, when David Hartley moved to address the King asking an immediate cessation of military operations because of the colonial submission made in the Olive Branch, his motion was defeated by 21–123. Opposition could do no better in the Lords. Nothing apparently could alter the prevailing view that America must somehow be compelled to acknowledge the legislative supremacy of Parliament. Only after that would she be allowed to resume her privileges and rights.

Outside Parliament, Burke's campaign to build a network

[50] *Ibid.*, 963–92.

of local committees of correspondence and to win petitions against the ministry's American measures was meeting with no more success than Opposition had had in Parliament. Committees patterned after that of Bristol were set up in London and a few other places. The committee in Westbury, Wiltshire, sent Burke a petition deploring "the present unnatural and destructive contest with our American brethren."[51] But it was soon obvious that the movement had by no means achieved the magnitude necessary to exert any influence on Parliament. Indeed, public opinion in Bristol was running so strongly against Burke and his friends there that according to one of them, Paul Farr, "the stream runs too strong against us for us to stem it; if we can escape drowning, it is all we have to expect." With the Prohibitory Act, all pretense of merchant resistance even in Bristol collapsed. The merchants, perceiving that further attempts to halt the headlong rush to war were futile, now sought merely to salvage what they could from their American investments and to compensate themselves in other areas of trade.[52]

Their cause rejected by Parliament and public alike, their faith in the people and contact with them lost, the Old Whigs had now to pin their hopes on the defeat of British arms. The country was thus presented with the strange spectacle of a party claiming the name of patriot while desperately wishing her defeat and disgrace. "I look to the moment of the determination of the operations of the Campaign," wrote Rockingham to Burke. "Men's minds in this country are hung up, in the Suspense of Expectation; the End of the Campaign is the *Set-*

[51] William, Fitzwilliam, and Bourke, *Burke Correspondence*, II, 84–85, Rockingham to Burke, November 2, 1775. See also Wentworth-Woodhouse, Burke Papers, Lord Craven to Burke, November, 1775, concerning maneuvers in the city of Abingdon and the county of Berkshire; the Committee of Correspondence of Westbury, Wiltshire, to Burke, November 21, 1775.

[52] Wentworth-Woodhouse, Burke Papers, Paul Farr to Burke, October, 1775, and public letter from Nathaniel Wraxall, Paul Farr, Richard Champion, and others to Burke, December 12, 1775.

tling Day." When that day arrived, the people would look to the Old Whigs for leadership, for that party had incessantly warned them against the American war.[53]

In August, 1776, arrived the report that America had declared herself independent. While Chatham from his sickbed let it be known that he still abided by his Provisional Bill and would never agree to colonial independence, the Old Whigs vainly tried to ignore the American declaration. They still professed to believe that a negotiated peace was possible if only Britain would make the concessions outlined in Burke's bill. By October, it was known that Sir William Howe had been successful at New York. While Fox declared he was "far from being dismayed by the terrible news," Rockingham was despondent: the ministers were exultant, and "the Publick like a silly echo can only repeat the Sounds it hears . . . while the still voice of Reason is lost, as it were, in Vacuum."[54]

Parliament met on October 31, and although Old Whigs and Chathamites worked closely together, the number of their humiliating defeats continued growing. After a final attempt early in November when Lord John Cavendish moved to revise all laws wherein America thought herself aggrieved, the great majority of Old Whigs withdrew from Parliament. Fox was the most notable exception. Until future events should give them fresh ground whereon to make a stand, the Old Whigs knew that further opposition could only discredit them. "We are not only patriots *out of place,* but patriots out of the opinion *of the public,"* wrote Savile to Rockingham. The successes of British arms, he maintained, had converted ninety-nine in every hundred to the ministry's support.[55] When North brought in his bill suspending habeas corpus for those suspected of high treason in America and on the high seas, only Fox and the Chathamites Dunning and Barré were present to

[53] *Ibid.,* Rockingham to Burke, July 12, 1776.
[54] *Ibid.,* Rockingham to Burke, October 22, 1776.
[55] Albemarle, *Rockingham Memoirs,* II, 304–307, Savile to Rockingham, January 15, 1777.

resist it. In the House of Lords, only one peer—Lord Abingdon—signed a dissent against it.

Outside Parliament, after a winter of quiet, Burke once more took up the cudgel. In April, 1777, in his famous letter to the sheriffs of Bristol, he indicated that the Old Whigs were moving toward an acceptance of American independence. The ministers, he charged, had proceeded on a false premise: that the recovery of America depended upon her unconditional submission. Such was no longer to be expected. Nothing could now restore the old system. Justifying his party's opposition to the war, he asserted it was desirable for the Americans to believe there was "a formed American party" in England. Better for them to carry many points, "even some of them not quite reasonable," with the help of a British party than to be driven to seek foreign aid. Now agreeing with Fox, Burke called for a repeal of all acts concerning America passed since 1763. He believed the Americans would not then continue to insist upon independence. Even if they did, however, he preferred American independence without war to independence with it.[56]

In April, 1777, the King had to ask a grant of £600,000 so he could pay the arrears on the civil list. The Old Whigs, perceiving that their absence from Parliament had been attended with as little success as their presence, returned to assume a role they were to fill throughout the remainder of their existence: that of champions of economic reform as a means of abridging the overweening powers of the Crown. In both Houses, they now demanded particulars of the civil list. Failing to win their point, they charged that the debt had been incurred for the corrupt purpose of gaining unconstitutional influence. That influence had now become so strong, they declared, that any group could be called to lead government however independent of or contrary to the opinion and approbation of the electors.

At the end of the session, on May 30, Chatham appeared

[56] Edmund Burke, *Works*, III, 160 ff.

in the Lords to move for a cessation of hostilities.[57] It would be impossible, he solemnly warned, to conquer "the map of America." He scoffed at the ministry's "spring hopes and vernal promises" that the struggle would be won with the present campaign. Instead, he predicted, "at last will come your equinoctial disappointment." Adding his opinion that France would soon come openly to the aid of the Americans, he joined in full agreement with Burke's and Fox's earlier demands for a repeal of all American acts passed since 1763. However, with the defeat of Chatham's motion in a division of ninety to twenty-eight, Opposition once again lapsed into lethargy. All eyes—the ministry's and Opposition's alike—were now fixed upon the course of military operations. The former were confident of victory; the latter hoped desperately for defeat.

The summer of 1777 was indeed one of anxiety for both ministers and Opposition. As autumn came, and still no news from Howe or Burgoyne, Rockingham thought he detected "some dawn of Light breaking in upon the Minds of the Public," although he was convinced that if "what is called *good News*" should arrive from America, the public would suffer a "relapse" and again be hopeful.[58] The report of the capture of Philadelphia was as great a blow to the Old Whigs as was the loss of that city to the Americans. "The wild tumult of joy . . . in the minds of all sorts of people, indicates nothing right in their character and disposition," Burke told Rockingham. Governor Johnstone's brother William Pulteney, who had now thrown in his lot with the Old Whigs, expressed his agreement with Burke, Savile, and Portland that the victory made a settled plan for Opposition impossible. That would be practicable only after the country had suffered military disaster.[59]

---

[57] Cobbett and Wright, *Parliamentary History*, XIX, 316–51.

[58] Wentworth-Woodhouse, Burke Papers, Rockingham to Burke, October 20, 1777.

[59] William, Fitzwilliam, and Bourke, *Burke Correspondence*, II, 198–

Hope lay, perhaps, in the long delay of news from Burgoyne. In late November, a general meeting of the Opposition determined to move in both Houses a consideration of the state of the nation. Chatham had not been present, but Rockingham had sent to him asking his sentiments, and despite the usual verbiage, his answer was clear. Chatham was for "right forward" action, and he agreed that union was necessary.[60]

A few days later, on December 3, came the thunderbolt of Saratoga. Rockingham immediately penned a one-line note: "My dear Burke, My Heart is at Ease."[61] That military defeat which the Old Whigs had predicted, indeed had longed for, had come at last. They now had, they thought, a fair field on which to stand.

201, Burke to Rockingham, November 5, 1777. Wentworth-Woodhouse, Burke Papers, Pulteney to Burke, November 6, 1777.

[60] Albemarle, *Rockingham Memoirs*, II, 324–25, Chatham to Rockingham, November 27, 1777.

[61] Wentworth-Woodhouse, Burke Papers, Rockingham to Burke, December 3, 1777.

CHAPTER SEVEN

AGONY AND REVELATION

IN THE summer of 1777, days of golden hope, the North Ministry seemed the darling of good fortune. Burgoyne's expedition was proceeding well. Howe, at Brandywine, had administered a severe defeat to Washington. A dissolution of the rebel army seemed imminent. Philadelphia was captured. France, grown more conciliatory, had forced American privateers who had carried British captures into French ports to disgorge their prizes. The stocks had risen.

In such an atmosphere North searched for a means of ending the civil war. "I am very melancholy," he admitted to Eden; "my idea of American affairs is, that, if our success is as great as the most sanguine politician wishes or believes, the best use we can make of it is to get out of the dispute as soon as possible." Consulting with Eden on drafting the King's speech which would open the autumn session, he asked: "How shall we mention America? Shall we be very stout? or shall we take advantage of the flourishing state of our affairs to get out of this d——d war, and hold a moderate language?"[1] While Lord North thus debated with himself and with his friends, news was speeding across the Atlantic which would make all his doubts academic.

Early in the evening of December 2, Captain Moutray of the "Warwick" arrived from American waters carrying dispatches for Sandwich. At nine that same evening, the Admiralty Lord sent urgently to the King: Burgoyne with all his

[1] Add. MSS 34414, ff. 309–10, North to Eden, November 4, 1777.

army had surrendered to Gates at Saratoga some two months earlier. The shock was staggering. Next morning, Germain, agonized at the new development, wrote of the appalling news to Eden. Declaring he could think of nothing but America, he asked what Eden knew of North's reaction, whether the First Minister had slept, and, above all, if he had "thought of any Expedient for Extricating this Country out of its distress."[2] Secretary at War Barrington could not "write or talk about the dreadful catastrophe of Burgoyne's army, and I wish I could think of any other thing." The Duke of Marlborough, Eden's patron and a loyal supporter of the ministry, hoped "they will not think of sending more troops; for I suppose, they may as well think of subduing the moon, as America by force of arms."[3] While a troubled monarch tried to sooth his panic-stricken First Minister by calling the surrender a "misfortune . . . not without remedy," North knew that "some material change of system" was now indicated: peace, desirable before, was now imperative.[4] To achieve it, to salvage some part of the American connection, and to avoid a war with France, greater concessions must be made: greater than had hitherto been dreamed of in ministerial circles.

Burgoyne's surrender was followed by four major developments, much interrelated: a spate of "unofficial" negotiations with the American commissioners in Paris; the near-fall of the North Ministry; a concerted effort to change the mode of war in America; and the Carlisle Peace Commission.

Only two days after the catastrophic intelligence, Paul Wentworth, former colonial agent and now British secret agent, was dispatched to Paris there to seek out the American commissioners Franklin, Silas Deane and Arthur Lee. It was a measure of the influence Eden had achieved with North that

[2] *Ibid.*, f. 394, Germain to Eden, December 3, 1777.

[3] *Ibid.*, f. 517, Marlborough to Eden, December, 1777. RHMCR. *Lothian Papers*, 325, Barrington to Buckinghamshire, December, 1777.

[4] Fortescue, *Correspondence of George III*, III, No. 2094, the King to North, December 4, 1777; No. 2095, North to the King, December 4, 1777.

Wentworth worked under his immediate supervision in an area which appertained, strictly speaking, to the southern, not the northern, secretary of state. Behind Eden, however, stood North himself, fully supporting this attempt to achieve an accommodation through extracabinet and unofficial negotiations.

Before Wentworth departed for Paris, Eden wrote him a letter—to which North must have been privy—intended ultimately for perusal by the American commissioners. He admitted that Great Britain appeared far from her object, if that were reduction of the Colonies to obedience. He warned, however, that defeat and disgrace would but reanimate the nation should America persist in her demand for an unqualified independence. Nonetheless, "the Language, Sentiments and Expectations of the Country on the original pretensions of the War are certainly moderated." Should the Colonies desire "to revert to their old Connection on new grounds," he saw a good prospect for ending the war to the satisfaction of both sides. The Americans might insist that they already possessed a *de facto* independence. But surely they could not wish a final settlement which would leave them prey to anarchy and confusion. A "qualified controul" should rest somewhere; and surely—here Eden betrayed Britain's deep-seated fear of French intervention—the Americans could not wish it to rest in the hands of France, a nation wholly alien to the common blood, language, and constitution of Great Britain and America. If such were their sentiments, Eden urged the American commissioners to state frankly and fully what they considered acceptable grounds of an accommodation and the proper mode of negotiating it.

Eden then posed a list of questions to serve as a basis of negotiation with the commissioners:

1. Should Great Britain desist from taxing the colonists, would they bear the expense of their own governments?

235

2. Should colonial charters be restored intact, would the Colonists replace all property seized or confiscated, and the colonists pay their quitrents?

3. Should Great Britain consent to the Colonies undertaking their own military protection, would they bear that charge?

4. Should American ports be reopened and bounties revived, would the Americans place their trade on "some ground analogous to the Act of Navigation"? (It is significant that Eden made no mention of the Laws of Trade.)

5. Would both countries exchange mutual guarantees of possessions and restore common citizenship?

Eden professed to be cordially disposed, when he had the answers to these questions in his hands, "to turn such knowledge to the most immediate, the most benevolent, and the most important purposes."[5]

North and Eden, well aware of the probable reaction of France to the American victory over Burgoyne, knew they had reason to hurry. On December 6, the French King wrote *"Approuvé"* on Vergennes' paper expressing willingness to entertain propositions from the American commissioners looking toward an alliance. This was the same day Eden gave Wentworth his instructions, arranging to correspond with him in cypher through the British ambassador's messenger.

Wentworth left for Paris on December 10. He had close contacts with the commissioners, being a friend of the secretary, Edwards, and an acquaintance of Franklin's private secretary, the double-traitor Bancroft. Upon his arrival, Wentworth got in touch with Deane and arranged a meeting. On the fifteenth, they dined together, and had a long conversation, pledging themselves to secrecy and to "the Confidence of Private Gentlemen wishing well to both countries." Both were

[5] Stevens, *Facsimilies*, No. 483, Eden to Wentworth, December 5, 1777, draft.

Freemasons, and Wentworth asked the American to join him in building a "Temple of Peace and Concord." It soon appeared that Deane was jealous of Franklin and rather hostile to France, but, he assured the emissary, independence had struck such deep roots with the American people that they would never give it up.

The conference continued the next day. Deane, assuring Wentworth that America's prospects were growing better by the hour, put forward three propositions. The authority and conservatism with which he spoke would seem to indicate that he had conferred with his colleagues in the meantime. Deane now proposed: a cessation of all hostilities; an evacuation of the United States by British forces; and the appointment of British commissioners to treat with Congress for a basis of future Anglo-American relations. It was his opinion that "the Materials of the old House should be removed out of Sight, and the new Fabrick raised on new ground and foundations." Wentworth objected to this statement, asserting that some of the old material should be retained, namely, "the King's Authority and Rights." Should that be added to Deane's propositions, he thought peace might be obtainable.

All questions were now laid aside, however, to permit a discussion of the nature of a future union between the two countries. Deane thought it should be a commercial one, but refused to accept any system of Navigation Acts. Wentworth approached the question from another angle. Britain might lend America one million pounds at $7\frac{1}{2}$ per cent interest, and another three million pounds at 5 per cent so as to place her economy on a sound footing and to sink the enormous quantity of paper money issued to finance the war. Security would be furnished by farmers willing to mortgage their land in exchange for individual loans. The only condition to be imposed upon them would be the cultivation of one-fourth of an acre of an assigned commodity, the increase of which was to be sent to England. An agricultural officer in each colony would teach the inhabitants the cultivation of African and Asian products. A loan bank would be established in each province. Deane liked this variation of the mercantile theme, and another meeting was arranged.[6]

At this point, Franklin's secretary, Edward Bancroft, received a letter from London, unsigned, but obviously from a person of some authority, probably William Pulteney, a Member of Parliament and a brother of Governor Johnstone.[7] Independent of party affiliation although agreeing with the Old Whigs in American questions, Pulteney had asked Germain, as early as December 6, if he might go to Paris to ascertain Franklin's terms.[8] Because of great secrecy surrounding the North-Eden project, Germain was unaware that Wentworth had already been sent. Thus he did not reject Pulteney's idea, though he pointed out the difficulties it involved. Pulteney wrote again on the ninth, urging speed to forestall a Franco-American treaty, and saying he believed he could convert Franklin to terms short of independence.[9] We may assume then that Germain acquiesced, and that Bancroft's anonymous letter came from Pulteney.

The letter informed the secretary that the government intended, immediately after the recess, to make parliamentary offers designed to end the war. The author had been asked by a person of high rank to request of Bancroft some general intimation concerning terms which would be likely to satisfy the Congress and the American people. Peace, he hoped, would be obtained on "terms a little short of absolute Independency," terms which would save the honor of the Crown by leaving the King "a nominal sovereignty" and the exercise of "some small regal Prerogatives, particularly that of Putting America into a State of War and Peace with Great Britain."

[6] Add. MSS 34414, ff. 433–42, Wentworth to Eden, private dispatch, December 17, 1777.

[7] Stevens, *Facsimilies*, No. 1787, under date of December 19, 1777.

[8] RHMCR. *Stopford-Sackville Papers*, II, 81–82, Pulteney to Germain, December 6, 1777.

[9] *Ibid.*, II, 82–83.

Wentworth's mission and Pulteney's anonymous letter gave the American commissioners a strong hand. They could— and did—now play Britain against France. When Deane informed his colleagues of his conversations with Wentworth, the Americans at once notified the French Court urging that France take a decided part, since attractive offers were expected from Britain. It should have been obvious to Wentworth that the commissioners had no thought of an agreement short of independence. Though he suspected that he was being used, he was not sure. Inept at conveying his thoughts in writing, he produced rambling and verbose reports resulting chiefly in confusion at home: "I was above two hours reading Wentworth's dispatches last night," North told Eden. "I do not know what to think of them, and can not pretend to judge whether there is, or is not any wish of peace in 51 [code designation for Deane]."[10]

In Paris, the astute Franklin had now assumed direction of the interviews with Wentworth. Deane, pleading illness, had avoided another meeting, but the commission secretary, Edwards, had met him and had informed him on behalf of the commissioners that an acknowledgement of America's independence was a first requisite. Afterwards, an alliance would be possible. Edwards warned, however, that speed was of the utmost consequence. The ominous meaning of his statement— that a Franco-American alliance was in preparation—could not be misunderstood. Indeed, a subsequent meeting with Edwards on the twenty-seventh convinced Wentworth that France and Spain would, within six weeks, recognize American independence and attack Great Britain.[11]

Wentworth's intelligence in turn persuaded North that a Bourbon war was near. When he sought to urge this view upon the King, however, George III, obstinately and with great lack

[10] Add. MSS 34414, ff. 461–62, North to Eden, December 23, 1777.
[11] *Ibid.*, ff. 463–66, Wentworth to Eden, December 25, 1777; ff. 468–72, Wentworth to Eden, December 28, 1777.

of foresight, refused to see it. Wentworth, he said, was "an avowed stockjobber" trying to make a "killing." He would depress the public stocks and then capitalize on a restored market when the war rumors had proved unfounded. North, taking his cue from his royal master, thereupon allowed his initial anxiety to subside.

Meantime, the tempo of international intrigue increased. Thornton, an agent from the American commissioners, tried to arrange a meeting with North in London, but North refused to receive him, thereby probably missing firsthand and authentic information about the projected Franco-American treaties.[12] In Paris, Franklin met Wentworth, talked much at random, and remarked that Eden's letter was a "very interesting sensible letter—pity it did not come a little sooner." Obviously, Franklin and his colleagues had no serious thought that Wentworth, having no power to recognize American independence, could negotiate peace. On January 9, therefore, Edwards warned Wentworth for the last time that an acknowledgement of independence was a *sine qua non* and that it must come at once to forestall an American treaty with France. The substance of the projected agreement was actually communicated to the British agent.

Franklin himself sent word by the dull, but well-meaning Moravian James Hutton that recognition of independence was immediately necessary. David Hartley, too, was in touch with Franklin, begging him not to throw America into the arms of France, and recommending North's plan of peace. William Strahan, to whom Franklin had first made his "Hints," joined in the steady stream of English politicians who sought to persuade Franklin to make peace on the basis of the Conciliatory Acts. The fact that neither Franklin nor the other commissioners had power to negotiate with Britain did not discourage

<hr/>

[12] Add. MSS 34415, f. 24, copy, Samuel Wharton to M. Maisonville, January 2, 1778. Thornton was a friend of Wharton, and was concealed at the house of a relative of David Hartley during his stay in London.

the thought that should Franklin—with his immense prestige —be brought to agree to British propositions, Congress would accept them too. Even after the existence of the Franco-American treaties was known in Britain—they were signed in early February—unofficial efforts continued. In March, Pulteney went over to Paris (under the name of Williams), with full approbation of King and ministry, to try to draw Franklin into negotiations based on North's plan. In April, Hartley arrived and asked Franklin for an interview. Although Franklin saw his old friend, he kept his new ally Vergennes fully informed, and he steadfastly refused to become involved in unofficial negotiations.[13] The British approaches to the American commissioners, in their futility, clearly indicated that a Bourbon war was inevitable. That George III and Lord North failed to accept this betrays a shocking want of capacity. One fact North did comprehend, however: no treaty negotiations could begin with the American commissioners without a prior recognition of American independence. North and his colleagues therefore knew that the only course remaining was to make propositions directly to the Congress and the American people.

The attitude of the American commissioners was, however, only one of North's problems. In the hectic days following the receipt of the news of Burgoyne's surrender, the First Minister had to face an apparently inevitable collapse of his ministry. Eden, rising rapidly in influence with North—eventually the First Minister would unwittingly earn Eden's wrath and be reduced to begging abjectly that he remain in office—considered the administration as falling. Only a coalition, Eden believed, with at least one of the Opposition groups could save

---

[13] RHMCR. *Stopford-Sackville Papers*, II, 91–92, Hutton to Germain, January 25, 1778. Sparks, *Franklin's Works*, VIII, 237–38, Hartley to Franklin, February 20, 1778; 268–70, Franklin to Vergennes, April 24, 1778. Franklin also reported to Vergennes a conversation with Chapman, a Member of the Irish House of Commons who, Franklin supposed, had come from Shelburne. See also Stevens, *Facsimilies*, No. 1893, Strahan to Franklin, March 13, 1778.

it.[14] Within the cabinet, tensions approached the breaking point. Criticism of Germain was becoming bitter. Never able to work long in harmony with any military commander, Germain, convinced that Sir William Howe had sabotaged the Canadian army's offensive, was treating the General so coldly that Howe was demanding to be recalled. Germain had already resolved to throw Burgoyne to the wolves should that be necessary to save his own skin, and had determined to cover himself by a parliamentary inquiry into the surrender. When he raised the matter at a cabinet meeting, however, he found to his chagrin that his colleagues were divided—and evenly. Suffolk, Sandwich, and North supported him. Chancellor Bathurst, so offended with Germain that he was rapidly losing his habitual timidity, Dartmouth, and the two Bedfordites Gower and Weymouth were against him. In the face of such prodigious opposition to what he thought would be a matter of routine, Germain was forced to drop his proposal, although not without bitterness.[15]

Personal ambitions were further disrupting the ministry. Suffolk aspired to the Garter, an honor which the King resolutely denied him. Thurlow and Wedderburn, the law officers, earlier promised promotion by North, chose the present crisis to press their claims. North, unable to impose any effective control upon his squabbling colleagues, wrote despondingly to the King, "Let the resolutions taken by Administration be what they will, if a question is moved suddenly in both Houses at one time, it will always be very possible that the Ministers in the two Houses may think differently about it."[16] In the face of grave danger, both from France and from the coming Oppo-

[14] Hinchingbrooke Papers, Eden to Sandwich, December 27, 1777; printed in Navy Record Society, LXIX, *Sandwich Papers*, I, 314–15.

[15] RHMCR. *Stopford-Sackville Papers*, II, 88–90, Germain's memo; Fortescue, *Correspondence of George III*, III, No. 2126, North to the King, December 26, 1777.

[16] Fortescue, *Correspondence of George III*, IV, No. 2163, North to the King, January 14, 1778.

sition attack in Parliament, it was clear that a ministerial crisis was building up.

Early in February, Germain wrote to Howe that his resignation had been accepted and that Clinton would succeed him as commander-in-chief. The letter was so cold that Bathurst, whose reaction to Burgoyne's surrender had been to declare "for peace on any terms," curtly told Germain and Suffolk that he considered Howe's retirement as attended with "fatal consequences." He had then asked North to request the King's permission to withdraw his name from the list of his Majesty's confidential servants.[17] North, immediately concluding that his ministry had collapsed, told the King that he should think of a new ministerial arrangement, pointing out Chatham as the person in Opposition likely to be of most service to the King and least extravagant in his demands. Indeed, North revealed, approaches had already been made to Chatham. However the great man, lamenting in true Chathamesque style, feared that it was too late to save the country. He would undertake to form a government only with a direct mandate from the King and full power to re-form the whole ministry.[18]

The King, to whom Chatham's pronouncement conjured up visions of a sovereign in chains, determined then to prevent North's capitulation by inducing Bathurst to remain in office. Suffolk implored the Chancellor not further to embarrass the King's affairs, "which, God knows, are already sufficiently embarrassed." Germain himself offered him an humble apology and undertook to write to Howe again in a more friendly manner. The offended minister was thus placated, but while expressing esteem for most of his colleagues, he conspicuously excluded Germain.[19] And although both North and the King

[17] RHMCR. *Bathurst Papers*, 16–17. See also RHMCR. *Stopford-Sackville Papers*, II, 93, Bathurst to Germain and Suffolk, February 16, 1778; RHMCR. *Dartmouth Papers*, II, 457, Bathurst to Dartmouth, February 13, 1778.

[18] Fortescue, *Correspondence of George III*, IV, No. 2193, North to the King, February 16, 1778.

[19] RHMCR. *Bathurst Papers*, 17, Gower to Bathurst, February 18, 1778.

were hoping that the American Secretary would take the initiative and resign, he resentfully clung to office.

One danger, which North viewed with deadly fear, did not, however, materialize. The Opposition was never able to generate enough power to overturn him. As soon as news of Burgoyne's surrender had arrived, Rockingham had written to Chatham. The Marquis, Richmond, and Manchester had then called on Shelburne. Sawbridge, radical Member for London, conferred with Old Whig leaders, and it appeared that at least some of his fellows would make common cause with a united Opposition.

The storm soon broke about the ministers' heads. On December 5, David Hartley moved a series of resolutions against the further prosecution of the American war and asked "a perpetual federal alliance" with America, based on "a compact of trade."[20] In the debates that followed, the ministers argued that Burgoyne's defeat furnished only the more reason for continuing the war. The Old Whigs, in reply, gave indications that they were moving steadily toward accepting American independence as the only means of making peace with America and avoiding war with France. The great question in all minds was how would the country gentlemen react? It soon became evident that despite mutterings, they remained staunch in their support of the ministry. In point of numbers, the Opposition was forced to conclude, there had been no improvement in its condition. In the critical division of December 10, for instance, on the ministry's motion for an adjournment until January 20, which the combined Opposition had fought tooth and nail, they were able to vote only 68 against 155.

Events during the recess further demonstrated a public attachment to the ministry. A stream of loyal addresses poured in from Manchester, Liverpool, London, and several other cities. Widespread public subscriptions and private raising of

[20] See Cobbett and Wright, *Parliamentary History*, XIX, 549–60, for the debates at this time.

troops for the royal service indicated that the country had perceived the French menace however willfully blind might be the King and his First Minister. Burke had reverted to his favorite scheme of petitioning, only to find that his friend Paul Farr, although promising to do what he could in Bristol, was not at all hopeful. So great was the "langour or timidity or prudence or caution or what ever else you may please to call it of the Whigs in this City," said Farr, that the slightest effort would require more spirit than was apt to be found.[21]

Chatham was being widely mentioned as the probable leader in the approaching war with France. The nation appeared to be uniting in a patriotic fervor it had never known during the American war. At this critical moment, then, a sustained and united Opposition assault led by the popular Chatham might have brought down North's wavering ministry. Suddenly, however, Chatham blasted all such hopes. Late in January, he wrote to Rockingham that as the Old Whigs had apparently resolved to accept American independence, he could not possibly co-operate with them. Rockingham was aghast, answering that no matter what were their differing views on independence, the two parties could surely work together in demanding an inquiry into "the causes, mismanagements, distressed state, and impending ruin of this country." But the irascible old man, nearing the end of his long and eventful life, but still hoping to be called to form yet another ministry, now refused to be ruled by broader considerations. He would not be drawn into even limited co-operation with persons who differed with him so much on the fundamentals of an American settlement.[22] The Old Whigs would never forgive him. Their maledictions would follow him to his grave. Thus they had lost Chatham. They had also lost the City Radicals who

---

[21] Wentworth-Woodhouse, Burke Papers, Farr to Burke, January 31, 1778.

[22] Taylor and Pringle, *Chatham Correspondence*, IV, 489–91, Rockingham to Chatham, January 26, 1778; 492, Chatham to Rockingham, January 27, 1778.

had "betrayed" their allies shortly before the recess by bitterly attacking the Declaratory Act. They were alone once more.

Alone but not voiceless. The spring session saw them rise to new heights of invective and, in their hatred of the ministry, sink to grave depths of indiscretion. Striving to bring down North and his colleagues, to restore peace with America, and to avoid war with France, they publicly unmasked Britain's military weakness and naval unreadiness.[23] Early in February, young Richmond announced in the Lords that the current establishment of Britain, Ireland, Gibraltar, and Minorca amounted to five thousand troops less than was usual even in time of peace. A few days later, the Old Whig peers introduced testimony in the Upper House showing that 559 ships, valued at £1,800,634, had been lost in the war. Moreover, marine insurance had doubled. Such information could only confirm France in her opinion that the old enemy was ripe for defeat. The government was further belabored for employing Indians in the American conflict. All requests for funds, to meet whatever extraordinary expenditures, were opposed with great violence. When in February North introduced his Conciliatory Bills, the Old Whig attitude, after an initial acceptance, was one of carping criticism, while they claimed the credit for whatever good might be in them. When the Old Whig Admiral Keppel was named to command the home fleet, instead of acting with dispatch to meet the growing French menace, he felt obliged to make conditions. Demanding an audience of the King, he refused to take ships under his command except those he himself reported manned and ready—a vicious blow at Sandwich. When Governor Johnstone was given a naval command, the Old Whigs threw a score of taunts at the ministry.

Old Whig violence was now having one grave effect in that it had begun to raise doubts among the country gentlemen.

---

[23] See Cobbett and Wright, *Parliamentary History*, XIX, 614 ff., for debates.

When North opened his budget, on March 6, the House was truculent. There was a manifest air of revolt. Opposition was actually able, with the support of the rural gentry, to carry in committee a motion to tax by one-fourth the income of all placemen and pensioners, with a few exceptions, holding incomes above £200 a year. The move was defeated in the House in a very close division of 147 to 141. A motion by Fox to inquire into the defenseless state of the nation—as if that had not been done all too well by his colleagues in the Lords—was defeated by the previous question, but only after North had assured the Commons that "Versailles had checked her ardour" for war. This statement, patently untrue to the most casual observer, is a measure of the First Minister's desperation.

In direct contradiction to North's comfortable assurance to the House on the sixth, Secretary of State Weymouth received from the French ambassador, exactly one week later, a formal declaration that there now existed a commercial treaty between the French court and the Americans. Furthermore, the French King was determined to protect his trade. Such language made war inevitable. Four days afterwards, on March 17, North presented a royal message informing Parliament of the declaration. The immediate result was a decision by the Old Whigs to espouse, openly and formally, the cause of American independence. They were convinced that only by such action could a French war be avoided. This, in turn, brought them into open and violent conflict with the Chathamites.

Shelburne had already taken sharp issue with the Old Whigs. Addressing himself to the ministry, during debates in the Lords over the French ambassador's declaration, he told them that a French war was not now to be avoided. He had then called upon them to put their house in order, to "relieve the people of the burden of corruption," and to "drop scandalous exertion of undue influence." A more formal and dramatic break was to come on April 7, when Richmond moved in the Lords for an evacuation of America and an acknowledge‹ ment of that country's independence. It was a challenge which Chatham, sick as he was, could not let pass. Having dragged himself to the House for the last time, he directed his feeble, often incoherent, argument against a recognition of independence. The strain of the debate and its awful implication, the dismemberment of an empire which he, more than any man, had created, were too much for him. When he sought to rise a second time to answer Richmond, his weakened frame gave way; he swooned and was borne from the House a dying man.

Never again would he cross the Old Whigs; and it was with satisfaction that Burke, with malice rising from a thwarted soul, wrote to his friend Champion of Chatham's "apoplectick fit after he had spat his last Venom."[24] When the debate resumed, however—it had been adjourned until the eighth as a compliment to Chatham—Shelburne held the banner of his fallen chief. Declaring solidly against independence, he made a thinly disguised bid for coalition: "Combine and connect every party and description of men. Leave a way open for every man to enter, and every man will enter and co-operate in the support of government." To Richmond's demand to know how he would regain America without an acknowledgement of her independence, Shelburne was vague. Declaring he would "leave the Americans to themselves," he expressed a conviction that they would soon send commissioners to offer terms. A natural necessity would force them back into an alliance with Britain; and he refused to believe they could be so heedless of their own welfare as to continue long in close alliance with France.[25] The Chathamite pendulum had now swung as far to the left as it was to go. Although the division on Richmond's motion revealed a surprisingly wide acceptance of his view—the Old Whigs and their supporters dividing thirty-

[24] Wentworth-Woodhouse, Burke Papers, Burke to Champion, April 11, 1778. The printed version in William, Fitzwilliam, and Bourke, *Burke Correspondence*, II, 210–11, deletes this disgusting passage.

[25] Cobbett and Wright, *Parliamentary History*, XIX, 1031–58.

three to fifty—a united Opposition was nonetheless impossible.

In the Commons, too, Old Whigs moved for American independence. Fox spoke powerfully for it on April 10, and for the first time tied it to the cause of internal reform. Maintaining that should his motion pass, Britain would be spared a war with France, he charged that American dependence actually profited no one but the ministers and their hangers-on. For them it had a sinister significance: the power of the executive, growing for some years, already threatened the Constitution. A dependent America would give such advantage to the Crown that it would achieve what the Stuarts had never done: a perpetual control of the British Parliament.

Though Fox's motion failed, there were signs that Old Whig emphasis upon economic reform was drawing an increasing number of country gentlemen to their support. In April, one of them, Sir Philip Jennings Clerke, won leave, against the opposition of the ministry, to bring in a bill disabling contractors. North by the greatest effort was able to recover his position, but the primary fact could not be submerged. The country gentlemen, many of them Old Tories, had on two separate occasions—the Contractors' Bill and the tax on placemen's salaries—affirmed their independence of court control. Because of the high taxes and ill success in the American war, they were becoming restive under a King and ministry who, unconsciously, were laying the foundation of a new Tory party. The cry for reform and economy in government would, in the next few years, unite with the continuing misfortunes of the American war to cause the fall of the North Ministry.

Saratoga had not destroyed the ministry because the King was strong enough to prevent North's resignation; and the Opposition, caught between a rising tide of patriotism—produced by the approaching French war—and their own disunion, were too weak to force it.

The King was determined, at all events and at all costs, to retain North as first minister. Time and again, North pressed to resign; time and again, the King refused to allow it. He had no objection to North's making offers for a coalition to some Opposition group, but only with the specific understanding that any contemplated change would leave North at the head of the ministry.

North felt as the *coup de grâce* to his ministry the French Ambassador's declaration of March 13. Dismayed, and greatly fearing the effect of this development on raising the national loan, an integral part of his budget, he confessed to Eden that "the Ministry seems to be overturned."[26] The harassed First Minister immediately presented to the King the outline of a new ministry which Eden had drawn up for him. While it proposed that North should continue at the Treasury, that man, now declaring himself broken in mind and body, begged leave to resign. In general, Eden had envisaged a coalition with Shelburne, who would be a secretary of state, though not in charge of American affairs. Sir Joseph Yorke, ambassador at the Hague, would be Shelburne's colleague; and Amherst would be commander-in-chief. Shelburne's friends Dunning and Barré would become attorney general and secretary at war respectively, and Fox, treasurer of the navy. Germain would be retired at once—with a peerage—since, Eden maintained, the most pressing need of change was in the American Department which would be given to Yorke or possibly to Amherst. So urgent was the change that North declared to his royal master, "The present ministry cannot continue a fortnight."[27]

There followed the most pathetic episode in the history of the friendship between North and his sovereign. Desperately pressing to be allowed to resign for his country's welfare and his own health, North was kept in office against his will by a King fearing "capture." To achieve his purpose, George III

[26] Add. MSS 29475, f. 15, North to Eden, March 13, 1778.
[27] Add. MSS 34415, f. 1, Eden's outline of a new ministerial arrangement. See also Fortescue, *Correspondence of George III*, IV, No. 2219, North to the King, March 15, 1778.

used every appeal to his minister's loyalty, affection, and self-interest. The King believed that it required no more than an interior cabinet reshuffle, based on Thurlow's succeeding Bathurst as chancellor, to give the ministry the required stability. Therefore, he obstinately refused to see any leader of Opposition. Their demands of immediate access to the King and their threats of a complete sweep were altogether unacceptable. Fighting for his "system" and for his own position at the center of politics, the King, in rising hysteria, vehemently declared "no advantage to the country nor personal danger" could ever force him to call Opposition to his assistance. He would rather abdicate his crown than wear it with "the ignominy of possessing it under their shackles." Nor would he open the door to "a set of men who certainly would make me a slave for the remainder of my days." Rather than call Opposition, he would "see any form of Government introduced into this Island"; and "whilst any ten men in the kingdom will stand by me I will not give myself up into bondage."[28] Never was North's weakness and indecision more evident; never had his loyalty and love of the King been so severely tested. He would not, however, have had the moral strength to continue his campaign to be allowed to resign—in the face of such plain spoken sentiment—had he not been encouraged by William Eden. (The Undersecretary was counting strongly on replacing Yorke as ambassador at the Hague.) Sincere in his devotion to the King, bound to him by ties of affection—and there was also the £20,000 which the King had paid on North's personal debts—the First Minister gave way. The fatal collapse of Chatham in April, 1778, ended all thought of a coalition. All was to remain the same, and George III determined to ride out the storm with a first minister who had become the mere sum of the forces operating upon him.

North's agony thus continued. In April, the French Tou-

---

[28] Fortescue, *Correspondence of George III*, IV, Nos. 2221, 2224, 2226, 2230–32, all from the King to North.

lon fleet under D'Estaing sailed for an unknown destination, widely believed to be America. The cabinet was thrown into a paroxysm of anxiety. The Commons watched narrowly as the King and Sandwich repaired to Portsmouth to hurry a fleet under Byron in pursuit. While there, Sandwich received urgent reports from John Robinson in London of "more real ill humour" in Parliament than he had yet seen.[29] The ministry had been hard run on the Contractor's Bill, and new Irish bills holding out some small relief to Irish trade had upset country gentlemen and British manufacturers alike. Wedderburn, Barrington, and Germain were agitating for promotion or threatening to resign. Suffolk, in bad health, nearly died in June.

Feeling the confidence of the Commons slipping from him, and troubled by a factious cabinet, North told the King once more at the beginning of May that a new ministerial arrangement was indicated. With almost inexpressible pathos, he wrote of the violent parliamentary attacks against him because of delays in the sailing of Byron's fleet. He declared from his anguished heart that his personal disgrace was certain whether he remained in office or resigned. A more important matter, however, was "to prevent the ruin and disgrace of the Country," which would be the result of his continuing in the cabinet, "where I never could nor can decide between different opinions."[30] In the face of such confessions, it was a moral crime for the King to hold North in office, yet he did so because his system was at stake. Ever convinced that his was the right way, he extorted from his wretched Minister a promise to remain in place so long as the King desired.

Saratoga did not, then, mean the fall of North's administration because the King was strong enough—and weak enough —to prevent it. It did, however, make a French war inevitable; and it further implied the necessity of a basic change in the

[29] Navy Record Society, LXIX, *Sandwich Papers*, II, 44–45, Robinson to Sandwich, May 5, 1778.

[30] Fortescue, *Correspondence of George III*, IV, No. 2322, North to the King, May 1, 1778; No. 2329, North to the King.

mode of conducting war in America. Henceforth, that war was to be merged into the larger framework of a traditional Anglo-French struggle.

A most surprising change had meanwhile occurred in the thinking of Lord George Germain. Thoroughly deflated and on the defensive since Burgoyne's surrender, he declared it necessary to make the American war primarily a naval one: a few seacoast posts should be held by the army whose activity would be confined to attacks along the seaboard in support of naval operations. The King, too, believing that Wentworth's expedition had proved that America would not treat but on the basis of independence—and there was not, he maintained, "a Man either bold or mad enough to presume to treat for the Mother Country on such a basis"—also agreed that a change was needed. General Amherst, examined at a cabinet called to deliberate upon a new mode of war, added the weight of his authority. It was impossible, he said, to reduce the Colonies by land without thirty thousand more troops in America. Such a reinforcement was admittedly impossible. The American war had, therefore, to become a secondary consideration: future operations would be chiefly of a naval character.[31]

In very secret orders of March 8 Germain informed the new commander, Sir Henry Clinton, of the cabinet's decision: despite "the just ground there is to expect that the new Commission to negotiate will supersede the necessity of another campaign," he wrote, yet it was imperative there be no slackening of preparations for the new mode of war. If Washington could not be forced to a general action early in the present campaign, all idea of offensive inland operations must be abandoned. The troops that could be spared from the defense of posts already held were to attack American ports from New York to Nova Scotia and to destroy as much American shipping as possible.

[31] Add. MSS 34414, f. 394, Germain to Eden, December 3, 1777. RHMCR. *Stopford-Sackville Papers*, II, 84–85, Germain to Sir William Howe, December 11, 1777; 93–94, Germain to Sir William Howe, February 18, 1778.

Should it not be feasible to carry out this plan and still retain Philadelphia, that place was to be evacuated. Clinton would receive five thousand reinforcements, and with their aid attacks upon the southern provinces should be launched in the autumn. Should that plan prove successful, "the Northern Colonies might then be left to their own Feelings and distress to bring them back."[32] The idea of at least a partial loss of the rebel provinces had begun to operate in British thinking.

The decision that henceforth the American war should be mainly naval, made without regard to grim reality, rendered Sandwich's position well-nigh impossible. Early in December, he warned his colleagues that Britain possessed only forty-two ships of the line, and that the country could not hope to make necessary detachments to America and remain on a par with Bourbon in European waters. Sandwich and two members of the Admiralty Board, Lord Mulgrave and Sir Hugh Palliser, constantly pressed throughout December for permission to undertake emergency building and preparations. North, however, anxiously watching Wentworth in Paris, deep in the preparation of his Conciliatory Plan, and hoping vainly that the King would allow him to resign, let the precious weeks slip by with no decision taken. Again, at the beginning of March, Sandwich protested to North against the shocking delay in approving naval appropriations and told the cabinet that should war come with France, he would probably have to withdraw ten or twelve frigates from American waters. But, again, North, while expressing a general agreement, hesitated. He was too heavily engaged with the budget and the Conciliatory Plan to enter into details with Sandwich. It is plain that George III's insistence upon retaining him was having a most disastrous effect on Britain's preparation to meet the coming onslaught of France. It was not, indeed, until March 16, three days after the French ambassador's declaration, that the Ad-

[32] RHMCR. *Stopford-Sackville Papers*, II, 94–99, most secret orders of March 8, 1778.

miralty was allowed to order the Navy Board to put extra workmen in all naval yards where building, repairing, or fitting was under way. Nor were naval builders now to wait the regulation time for seasoning of wood.[33] Where all had before been hesitation, now all was haste.

As soon as France had recognized American independence, vessels of the young nation began to operate from the ports of her ally with new and unhindered freedom. American privateers, already active enough to cause alarm to the merchants, now doubled their effectiveness. There were severe inroads on British shipping; large coastal areas in England and Ireland were held under constant alarm by audacious attacks, which could not be prevented because of the lack of frigates. From various maritime parts of the kingdom came urgent requests for naval protection and adequate coastal defenses. The supply of seamen had become so critically low and the want of frigates so great, however, that Sandwich admitted to the Lord Lieutenant of Ireland, Lord Buckinghamshire, that means were simply not available to mount effectual measures against these privateers.[34]

A counterstroke was necessary. But where? An expedition against the French West Indies had been suggested in December. As Amherst fully approved the design, it was adopted by the cabinet on March 18. On the twenty-first, therefore, Germain dispatched to Clinton a new set of most secret orders —so secret that the Carlisle Peace Commissioners, still in England, were not informed of them.[35] The General was ordered

---

[33] Hinchingbrooke Papers, Sandwich to North, December 7, 1777; Sandwich's paper of December 8, 1777. Printed in Navy Record Society, LXIX, *Sandwich Papers*, I, 327–35; 363, the Admiralty's order to the Navy Board.

[34] Fortescue, *Correspondence of George III*, IV, No. 2391, the King to North, July 12, 1778. Hinchingbrooke Papers, North to Sandwich, May 10 and July 12, 1778. RHMCR. *Lothian Papers*, 330, Sandwich to Buckinghamshire, May 4, 1778.

[35] RHMCR. *Dartmouth Papers*, II, 461–62, most secret orders of March 21, 1778.

to detach five thousand troops immediately, to name a commander for them, and to embark this force for an attack against
St. Lucia. It was essential, the orders stated, that the scheme
be executed without delay. An additional three thousand men
should be dispatched to St. Augustine and Pensacola for the
defense of those ports. Philadelphia would be evacuated, and
Clinton would retire to New York to await the outcome of the
Carlisle Peace Commission. Should New York prove impossible to hold with his depleted army, he would evacuate the
port, leave enough troops with the garrison in Rhode Island
to hold that place, proceed to new headquarters at Halifax,
and send any surplus troops to General Haldimand in Canada.
This redisposition of Clinton's force of some fourteen thousand
troops was tantamount to official recognition that land conquest
of the Colonies was impossible.

Indeed, the St. Lucia expedition, and Sandwich's insistence
that Britain strengthen her naval force in European waters,
further meant an abandonment of even the idea of a large-scale
naval war against America. In consequence of a report to the
cabinet by Sandwich on March 15, thirty-three of the seventy
ships in American waters were recalled to England or were
ordered sent on the St. Lucia expedition.[36] A few days later,
Sandwich told his colleagues that a suspension of all naval and
military operations in America might become necessary.

The magnitude of the King's folly and of North's procrastination in the face of Sandwich's repeated warnings came
home fully to the cabinet when in April, D'Estaing took command of the Toulon fleet and sailed for America. Both King
and cabinet demanded that the French admiral be halted at
the Straits of Gibraltar, but a force adequate to stop him was
simply not available. Should Keppel's home fleet be sent out,
the English and Irish coasts would lie naked, and the Brest
fleet could then attack at will.[37]

[36] Hinchingbrooke Papers, Sandwich's paper of March 15, 1778, "State
of the Force in North America." Printed in Navy Record Society, LXIX,
Sandwich Papers, I, 362.

The situation was even blacker than first appears. Almost half of Lord Howe's fleet had been recalled from American waters or ordered sent to St. Lucia. Should D'Estaing's objective be in European waters, Howe's ships would be urgently needed at home. On the other hand, should the Frenchman be destined for America, as seemed more probable, the force there, even if Howe had not already sailed for home, would be inadequate to meet him. Moreover, D'Estaing's arrival in America would bear directly upon the plans for the British expedition against St. Lucia. But how? The blundering incompetencies of George III and Lord North had robbed Britain of the initiative.

Indeed, calamity seemed to stare the country in the face. Sandwich believed it impossible to carry on the war in America. Weymouth felt that peace was highly desirable. Germain expressed himself happy at no bad news from America, since he had long ago given up expectations of good news from that country. The King himself, although suspecting that Franklin in the Paris talks sought only to delay the departure of the Peace Commission, so desired to end the American war that he was willing to keep open the channel of intercourse with that "invidious man." Even George III had begun to think of the Colonies as "abandoned." Barrrington declared that there was no general in the country fit to direct the army in case of invasion. North himself believed an accommodation with America urgently necessary. If that could be achieved, Britain could avoid a French war, the expense of which, he predicted, would ruin her. As so often before, he warned his sovereign that peace with America and a change of ministry could alone save the country.[38] He was fervently hoping for the success of the Carlisle Peace Commission.

[37] Hinchingbrooke Papers, Sandwich's paper of April 6, 1778; printed in Fortescue, *Correspondence of George III*, IV, No. 2275.

[38] Navy Record Society, LXIX, *Sandwich Papers*, II, 292–94, Sandwich to Rear Admiral Gambier, commander at Halifax, April 13, 1778. Fortescue, *Correspondence of George III*, IV, No. 2246, North to the King, March 25,

The impact of the American problem on British imperial thinking reached its climax in this effort to end the war. North had thought tentatively of making peace even before the news of Saratoga had arrived. This surrender and the fear of French intervention were the prime movers behind the Peace Commission. Nonetheless, the Acts of Parliament creating it—there were no more hairsplitting questions about the propriety of acts for the admitted purpose of qualifying the powers of Parliament—the commission itself, and the instructions for it marked an acceptance by British political leaders of the federal principle in crude and unfinished form. Out of the stresses and the strains of the American war, a new concept of empire had emerged. Grenville's classic idea of a supreme center and subordinate parts had vanished.

The history of the Carlisle Peace Commission must begin with a letter from Eden to Lord North. On December 7, 1777, during a time of wildest confusion among ministerial circles, Eden sent North an analysis of the disastrous state of his government. He wrote "with the feelings of a man who has just seen some dreadfull Calamity or is this moment awakened from a feverish dream." He begged North to put aside his intention to resign, and to stand firm in the present crisis. He should, however, adopt a positive plan of action immediately or within three days at the most. Eden then outlined his own proposals. It would be wise, he thought, to desist from any internal operations in America. Should it be deemed necessary to hold any posts at all, they should be chosen from among New York, Long Island, Staten Island, perhaps Rhode Island, and those along the Canadian border. Halifax, New York, and St. Augustine should be strengthened, but Pennsylvania evacuated. The Howes should be recalled, their Peace Commission cancelled, and a purely naval war begun.

1778; No. 2247, North to the King; No. 2248, Weymouth to the King, March 25, 1778; No. 2251, the King to North, March 26, 1778. See also RHMCR. *Knox Papers, Various Collections,* 143, Germain to Knox, April 19, 1778.

WILLIAM EDEN (later Lord Auckland)

By far his most important point, however, was Eden's assertion that it was now highly expedient to bring into Parliament and before the public some plan for pacification. This should be done, he urged, immediately after the Christmas recess. The ministry could at that time lead an inquiry into the state of the nation, and "at a proper stage," produce a bill repealing every existing Act of Parliament touching America either by indulgence, restraint, or regulation. Commissioners should then be appointed to prepare the way for a new, comprehensive, and final act of legislation for the regulation of the Colonies.

That negotiation with the Colonies had become absolutely necessary should now be openly admitted. Eden well knew that by doing so North would open himself to severe criticism, and that his enemies would taunt him with his earlier declaration, at the time of his Conciliatory Proposition, that he would never agree to more drastic terms. To this, Eden advised, North should reply honestly and openly as he himself had answered Fox on that score: " 'I asked fifty guineas for my grey Horse last year, but He has since broken his Knees and I should be glad to get twenty.' "[39]

Thus stimulated, North roused himself from despair to begin a series of feverish conferences lasting through the Christmas recess. Eden, Jenkinson, Wentworth, the law officers Thurlow and Wedderburn—all subministers—North could not trust his cabinet colleagues—were consulted. Under the strain of formulating in great haste a pacific plan which would be acceptable to Parliament and to at least some of the colonists, North drove himself without pity. By late January, though near physical and mental collapse, he had at least a plan. It was to repeal the tea duty and the act regulating the charter of Massachusetts, and to create a commission to negotiate with the Colonies on every other point in dispute.[40]

[39] Add. MSS 34414, ff. 395–98, Eden to North, December 7, 1777.
[40] Fortescue, *Correspondence of George III*, IV, No. 2179, North to the King, January 29, 1778.

The King, while believing that a complete but temporary evacuation of the Colonies might become necessary—in order the more effectively to attack French and Spanish New World possessions should a Bourbon war break out—urged caution upon North in bringing forth a plan of conciliation. Germain, grumbling because he was not being consulted by North, strengthened the King's reticence,[41] but North, firmly supported by the undersecretaries and subministers, who agreed that a commission with the most extensive powers was necessary, could not be swerved from his path.[42]

To Eden, North assigned the task of perfecting the details of his plan; and, working immediately under the First Minister, Eden sketched out a draft of a conciliatory act. His close friend, Wedderburn, now completely won over to conciliation, also produced a draft bill.[43] On the basis of these two, Attorney General Thurlow drew up a third draft of a bill enabling the King to appoint commissioners. Meantime, North had begun to have qualms about an outright repeal of the tea duty and the Massachusetts Regulating Act. Eden, deciding that such unpleasant action was, after all, both needless and insufficient, then suggested a second bill renouncing completely the right of taxation. North accepting the suggestion, Eden, aided by John Hatsell, Clerk of the Commons and an expert on parliamentary procedure, drafted the bill. Stating that the right of taxation was given up "in the just and reasonable Expectation" that in return the Colonies would contribute to the cost of the common defense, the bill was sent to North on February 7, the day after the Franco-American treaties had been secretly signed in Paris.[44] While this event was unknown in London,

---

[41] *Ibid.*, No. 2182, the King to North, January 31, 1778.

[42] Stevens, *Facsimilies*, No. 344, William Fraser's report.

[43] *Ibid.*, No. 346, Eden's memorandum, "Measures for an Accommodation with America," January, 1778; No. 348, Eden's "Heads of Address on the American War."

[44] Add. MSS 34415, ff. 191–92; Stevens, *Facsimilies*, No. 355, Eden's paper on the Taxation Act. See also Add. MSS 34415, ff. 187–88; Stevens,

it was suspected that such an agreement was in the offing. It was thus with a sense of urgency that Eden, Wedderburn, and the King himself pressed North to get the bills quickly through Parliament.[45]

Throughout these proceedings, North had told his colleagues nothing of the plan. He had not so much as held a cabinet on the subject. Germain's conduct was becoming threatening, and having heard from some source that the tea duty and the Regulating Act were to be repealed, he took a heated protest to Eden. By that time, of course, North and Eden had decided in favor of renouncing taxation instead of repealing the two acts. Eden, in a friendly though somewhat patronizing vein, was therefore able to assure the American Secretary that the acts were not to be repealed since it was now proposed to give up the right completely. Mollified by Eden's letter and aware of the necessity for a treaty, Germain replied, "You go rather beyond my idea in putting so much Confidence in their [colonial] Generosity, but if that step will not revolt our friends, it is the most manly method of proceeding. The appointing Commissioners with the most ample powers must make part of the plan."[46] The most likely chief of intracabinet resistance to the Conciliatory Plan had thus been neutralized.

North presented the entire scheme at a full cabinet on February 11. He met with no opposition; and on the twelfth, stating that he "expected to be roasted," he brought his proposals before the Commons.[47] In his speech, long and comprehensive, although he labored under obvious and severe

Facsimilies, No. 360; Add. MSS 34415, ff. 110–11, Eden's draft of the Taxation Act.

[45] Add. MSS 34415, f. 133. Stevens, Facsimilies, No. 371, Wedderburn to Eden, February, 1778; No. 356, Wedderburn to Eden, February, 1778; No. 369, Eden to North, February 7, 1778. See also Fortescue, Correspondence of George III, IV, No. 2190, the King to North, February 9, 1778.

[46] RHMCR. Stopford-Sackville Papers, I, 139, Germain to General Irwin, February 3, 1778. Add. MSS 34415, f. 113; Stevens, Facsimilies, No. 370, Germain to Eden, February 10, 1778.

[47] Add. MSS 35375, ff. 204–205, John Yorke to Hardwicke. North's speech is in Cobbett and Wright, Parliamentary History, XIX, 762–67.

handicaps, he had not the courage to accept Eden's advice and make a frank plea of necessity. Rather, he sought to brazen it out, claiming even the virtue of consistency. Never had he thought an American revenue practicable or possible. He had merely inherited the tea duty which he had been unable to get rid of. All he had ever wished was a reasonable self-imposed American contribution to imperial expenses. Always disposed to peace, he had been shocked when the Coercive Acts had produced effects quite unintended. He was, therefore, prepared to give them up in the interest of a general settlement.

His earlier Conciliatory Proposition, he maintained, had been just. It had, however, been misrepresented by the radicals in America and by the Opposition at home. The Howe Commission had also been criticized because of its limited power. Both of those objections would now be met by new acts creating a commission with the most extensive powers, and by instructions to the commissioners to seek from the colonists a promise of voluntary contributions. This latter, however, was not to be a *sine qua non*. Should no such contributions be forthcoming, however, Americans were not to complain if in some future hour of need Britain refused her aid and assistance.

All acts grievous to America would be adjusted, North declared, but it would be better to leave this in the hands of the commissioners, for the Americans would consider every concession made in Parliament to be a part of the basis of the treaty. They would accordingly accumulate new claims. He then outlined the proposed powers of the commission, declaring that he had not offered his propositions earlier because he had always thought the moment of victory the time for concessions. On news of Saratoga, he had thought to raise more troops to prosecute the war but had then decided that, even after the greatest victory, the terms now presented were substantially those he would have offered. Denying, then, that the concessions were forced, and maintaining that Britain could at need carry on the war much longer, he offered this conciliatory plan to prevent further and useless bloodshed.

Melancholy silence greeted North's speech, and the debate was short. Fox declared the terms outlined "ample and satisfactory," indeed, the same as those in Burke's bill three years before. The country gentlemen appeared stunned. North, assaulted with a question originally raised by Fox, was forced to admit that very likely a Franco-American treaty had been signed. In deep gloom, therefore, the resolutions were agreed to without division, and leave was given to bring in the bills. In two days time, by a ship dispatched for that specific purpose, Germain forwarded copies of the bills to the commanders-in-chief in America.

While affairs went on in Parliament, Eden turned to selecting the commissioners. Probably he himself coveted a place on the commission from the first. He had hoped to succeed Sir Joseph Yorke as ambassador at the Hague, but had seen that scheme fail because of the King's obstinate refusal to treat with the Opposition. For the moment, however, he satisfied himself with coyly remarking to North that he had been mentioned as a likely commissioner by some of his friends, at the same time suggesting Governor Johnstone as a suitable candidate. Eden also undertook to approach Richard Jackson who at the time was solicitor to the Board of Trade. In doing so, he once more hinted that he himself might be on the commission. Jackson replied that while he was not hopeful, he would accept if named, for he truly believed that a continuation of the American war meant ruin to the empire. One stipulation he made, however: that the instructions be full and precise, a demand directly opposed to Eden's and Wedderburn's plan to make the powers as broad and as discretionary as possible.[48]

Eden's design to become a commissioner soon became obvious. On March 1, his superior, Suffolk, sent his blessings to

[48] Add. MSS 34415, ff. 151–52; Stevens, *Facsimilies*, No. 378, Jackson to Eden, February 28, 1778.

Eden's aspirations. Two days later, Eden drafted letters to Germain and Sandwich declaring his readiness to sacrifice himself in any service thought useful to the public.[49] He had both a talent and inclination to serve his country in a diplomatic post, but a stronger motive now urged him on to a place in the commission. To Wedderburn he confided that he was by no means happy to be going to America. Should he not do so, however, he foresaw "on the coolest reflection that I shall return very suddenly to the utmost obscurity; for I *know* that the present Government is not equal to its difficulties; and it will neither suit my Pride nor my Principles to struggle on with them from present Bad to certain worse."[50] Eden's expedition to America was thus to be a flight from fury, and a means of divorcing his own political fate from that of the North Ministry. Nor would he be content to be a mere member of the commission. He would be the "efficient Commissioner." His hand is seen constantly at work in arranging the commission to his own satisfaction, a task he had completed by early March. In a paper setting forth the desired qualifications for members of the commission, he had stated they should be Members of Parliament from both Houses, men of ability, and "particularly conversant" with the dispute and with Britain's commercial interests. They should be of conciliatory manners and untainted by opposition to "the honourable species of accomodation." At least one should be from the moderate part of Opposition.[51] As men thus qualified, he had selected the young Earl of Carlisle, the twenty-nine-year-old son-in-law of Gower; Richard Jackson; and himself. These three, with the

---

[49] Add. MSS 34415, ff. 235–37; Stevens, *Facsimilies*, No. 385, Eden to Sandwich and Germain, drafts. See also RHMCR. *Stopford-Sackville Papers*, II, 44, Eden to Germain. Further, Stevens, *Facsimilies*, No. 384, Suffolk to Eden, March 1, 1778.

[50] Stevens, *Facsimilies*, No. 386, Eden to Wedderburn, early March, 1778.

[51] Add. MSS 34415, f. 158; Stevens, *Facsimilies*, No. 374, Eden's paper setting forth the desired qualifications for the commissioners.

commanders-in-chief in America, would form the commission.

Even in the drafting of their instructions—Wedderburn was in charge of that task—Eden gave his "Hints." As points upon which he feared negotiations might break off, Eden named: independence; an American attempt to charge Britain with the expense of the war; an attempt to undermine the British right to regulate commerce; or an impeachment of the King's prerogative in naming military officers and governors.[52] Accepting Eden's ideas, Wedderburn was duly guided by them in his work.

Eden took a grandiose view of the role he was about to assume. At last, he felt himself rising from the lowly position of undersecretary of state. He would bear in his hands a part, and he intended it to be a major part, of the dignity and honor of the British nation. Pomp and panoply were necessary to this viceregal expedition. Captain Elliott of the "Trident," which would convey the commissioners to America, would have to have, Eden insisted, a commodore's pennant. The commissioners themselves would require full ambassadorial rank and salary. They would be privy councilors. Such was Eden's tacky pomposity that when Lord Cornwallis was ordered to repair to America at the earliest possible moment, and Lord Sandwich proposed to give him passage on the "Trident," his passion knew no bounds. Inducing Carlisle, a callow and inexperienced youth, to join him, Eden wrote a stinging complaint to Germain: Sandwich had used the commissioners badly; he had repeatedly assured them that the ship was to be reserved to the commissioners exclusively. This petty display of egotism was not rendered the more palatable by the fact that Eden had already demanded and received permission to take Mrs. Eden junketing with him to America. That lady, moreover, would occupy two cabins aboard the crowded ship, one for herself, and one for four female servants. With great justice, the King dryly remarked, "Parade is not the object of the mission,

[52] Stevens, *Facsimilies*, No. 379, Eden's "Hints."

but business."[53] George III, furthermore, resolutely refused to make the commissioners privy councilors. Sir Henry Clinton did not hold that rank. If the other commissioners were to have it, Clinton would come last in the commission instead of second, and the King refused to acquiesce in so unmerited a slight to a valiant commander.

Richard Jackson had never been wholly satisfied with the instructions since they were not, as he had wished, full and precise. For him, the declaration of the French ambassador on March 13 was decisive. At a stormy session on the night of March 29–30, he told Eden, Thurlow, and Wedderburn that it was "idle and ruinous" to go to war with France. To forestall such an event American independence must be recognized at once. Unless the commission had authority to do so, it would assuredly fail. He himself wanted no part of it.

Eden was shocked at Jackson's withdrawal. North clearly expected the commission to leave for America by April 12, and with the time for departure so near, Eden professed himself on the verge of resigning in disgust and despair. He desisted, however, only because he knew that should he throw up the commission, government would be "instantly and completely check-mated." Hurriedly, he and Wedderburn consulted about a successor for Jackson. Governor Johnstone, his brother Pulteney, and Andrew Stuart were suggested. Eden preferred Pulteney, but he was still in Paris vainly trying to draw Franklin into negotiation. Wedderburn, who thought Jackson's resignation good riddance, thereupon approached Johnstone. The Governor accepted, but this last minute crisis had proved depressing, although Eden could not help boasting to his brother Morton of the success of "my own private negociation."[54]

All seemed in good train when suddenly Johnstone, who

[53] Hinchingbrooke Papers, Eden to Sandwich, March 8, 1778. Fortescue, *Correspondence of George III*, IV, Nos. 2201, 2270.

[54] RHMCR. *Carlisle Papers*, 322, Eden's memorandum. See Stevens, *Facsimilies*, No. 427, Wedderburn to Eden; No. 416, Wedderburn to Eden; No. 432, Eden to Morton Eden, April 9, 1778.

had declared in Commons irrevocably against independence, developed personal scruples. He was much upset by accounts of a conversation in which North had declared his belief that the commission would fail and that only a recognition of independence would bring peace. Because of his respect for Chatham, Johnstone, and a few of his own friends, however—North was quoted as saying—he could not yet propose such a step.[55] Eden again grew furious, promising Johnstone to bring the First Minister to a firm stand against independence.

North presumably gave Eden satisfaction on this point, and after a final correction in the commission—Sir William Howe's name had been inserted instead of Clinton's—Germain sent the commissioners their instructions on April 12. They were ordered to embark at once for America.

British public reaction to the Conciliatory Plan was calm with no excesses of either optimism or pessimism. Thurlow, in a farewell letter to Eden, wrote that a more important mission had never been entrusted to any hands. Although he had entertained serious doubts, he now refused to view the commission as "Quixotism." Samuel Martin, a merchant of Whitehaven with interests in the American trade, told Sandwich that the offers would certainly be rejected by the Americans. Moreover this view had been supported by Franklin himself who, when David Hartley had sent him copies of the Conciliatory

---

[55] The conversation was between North and Temple, probably John Temple, formerly a member of the Customs Board at Boston. Temple had married an American and was then in England. North arranged to send him back to America at about the same time, but not on the same ship, as the commissioners. He was to "exert his utmost influence in assisting the commissioners now going out to bring about a reconciliation or reunion" between Britain and her Colonies. Probably Temple's primary task was to seek to corrupt American politicians. Temple and a Dr. Berkenhaut took passage to America a short time after the commissioners had sailed. There is evidence that the two men proceeded to Philadelphia, where presumably they contacted loyalists. There is no further report of Temple's expedition which was apparently unsuccessful. See Add. MSS 34415, f. 334; Stevens, *Facsimilies*, No. 424, a copy of Temple's note to North, and North's explanatory note. See also Stevens, *Facsimilies*, No. 426, Wedderburn to Eden.

Bills, had blasted them as "little arts and schemes for amusing and dividing us." The commission was also bitter news to the many American loyalists both at home and in refuge in England. North's plan they viewed as almost a death blow to their hopes of regaining their lost property. Indeed one former New York merchant took his own life on hearing of North's speech.[56] As the commissioners boarded the "Trident" at St. Helen's in the morning of April 16, Eden sat down to write a last letter to his brother Morton: "I am given to speculation upon most occasions, but in this it fails me totally: some cool-headed sensible men are very sanguine . . . ; others of the same description are equally positive that we shall totally fail. I only know that I am in neither extreme either of Confidence or Despondency."[57] Uncertain of the reception they would be accorded in America, the commissioners set forth into the unknown.

They would fail to restore peace to a shattered empire. To emphasize their failure, however, is to overlook a consideration of the greatest importance. They carried with them in embryo a new colonial system which indicated that British imperial thinking had gone—or been driven—far along the path to a modern commonwealth of nations. The Taxation Act had already renounced forever Grenville's touchstone of parliamentary supremacy, the right to tax for revenue. The tea tax was repealed. By their instructions, the commissioners, together or individually, could treat with Congress "as if it were a legal body," or indeed with any assembly or groups of individuals, civil or military.[58] They were to accept the claim of independence "during the time of Treaty, and for the pur-

[56] Stevens, *Facsimilies*, No. 356, Sir Grey Cooper to Eden, March 8, 1778, No. 394; Add. MSS 34415, f. 252, Thurlow to Eden, March 7, 1778. Hinchingbrooke Papers, Samuel Martin to Sandwich, March, 1778. For the loyalists' view, see Add. MSS 35427, ff. 136–37, Hutchinson to Hardwicke, August 3, 1778; Add. MSS 38210. ff. 60–61, Henry Cruger to Jenkinson, May 3, 1778, in which Cruger includes extracts of American loyalists' letters.

[57] Stevens, *Facsimilies*, No. 446, Eden to Morton Eden, April 16, 1778.

[58] RHMCR. *Carlisle Papers*, 322–33.

pose of Treaty," although such a document was to be referred to Parliament for its approbation. All acts concerning America passed since 1763 could be suspended. In the case of the Declaratory Act, it would be superseded by a mutual declaration, to be made at the conclusion of the treaty, of the respective rights of Britain and America.

More specific concessions were also to be made:

1. The mother country, without consent of the assemblies, would keep no standing army in the Colonies in time of peace.

2. The Colonies would maintain, at their own charge, their own military force, either regular or militia.

3. No charter would ever be changed save with the consent and at the request of the individual assembly.

4. The home government would assist in securing the debts of Congress, and in sinking those great quantities of depreciated paper currency issued by it. For this purpose, an American Bank was authorized.

5. Americans would be given preference in the most considerable colonial offices in the appointment of the Crown. Indeed, if the Americans asked it, all civil offices might be made elective.

6. If judges were to continue as royal appointees, and if independent provision should be made for them by the Colonies, they would hold office during good behavior and not, as hitherto, during pleasure.

7. Crown offices deemed unnecessary by the Americans would be suppressed.

8. Any future customs service would be composed of Americans.

9. Parliament was prepared to consider an American representation in the House of Commons.

10. Should the Americans insist, they might retain Congress as a permanent institution so long as it did not infringe the sovereignty of Parliament.

What was this new "sovereignty of Parliament"? First and foremost, Parliament was to retain a power to regulate the trade of the empire. Even on this fundamental point, however, America was to be indulged, although if she expanded her foreign trade, certain duties would be levied. Further, all articles not of British manufacture or not sent to America from Great Britain were to be taxed. Nor were the Americans to maintain ships of war unless employed and commissioned by the King. The command of American forts and fortifications would be vested in the governors, although such places would be garrisoned by American troops. Military forces maintained by the Colonies would be commanded in the King's name. Provincial officers would hold commissions from him. There would be no independent coinage. American debts to British merchants would be acknowledged. The loyalists would be restored to their estates, and all prisoners of war would be released.

Even at the conclusion of a treaty embodying these conditions and concessions, no formal revocation of the Declaration of Independence would be necessary, since a treaty would be sufficient to render it null and void. Full pardon, amnesty, and indemnity would be extended, and all other matters of controversy raised during the treaty period would be referred to the home government.

Secret and additional instructions were also given to the commissioners.[59] Should the Americans demand the recognition of their independence as a prerequisite to any treaty, their claim was not to be rejected, but referred home. In the meantime, a cessation of hostilities should be arranged. During the armistice, British troops would continue to occupy New York, Long and Staten Islands, Rhode Island, Connecticut and any other place where the inhabitants would receive them. During this period, the Restraining Act directed against colonial trade would be suspended. No trade, however, was to be

[59] RHMCR. *Stopford-Sackville Papers*, II, 105–106.

carried on between any part of the British dominions and the Colonies except that in British or Irish ships. Colonial ships and commodities would be deemed alien in all parts of the empire except at New York, Rhode Island, and Beaufort, in Port Royal Island. In those places, colonial ships would be allowed to enter without hindrance during the period of the armistice. All inhabitants of the Colonies were to have freedom of movement and disposal of property. American debts to British merchants could be repaid in paper money at a reasonable rate of exchange.

No hindrance was to be given either to British or American vessels, or to those of nations at peace with Great Britain going in or coming out of American ports during the cessation of hostilities. Ships of war and privateers were to be required to depart forthwith. Finally, Massachusetts would have to renounce all claims to the Kennebec River and to the territory north and east of its westernmost boundary.

On one other point, North gave his advice in a letter written to Eden on April 23. Warning him that America would try to get Canada as a fourteenth state, he asked him to exercise care in his negotiations that this should not happen. So long as Canada remained in British hands, he asserted, the Americans, with this constant threat upon their flank, would have a powerful incentive to remain on good terms with Britain. Alarmed at reports of an attempted sabotage of the "Trident" before she left port, he declared himself as most solicitous for the success of the commission: "God Grant that it may succeed and that you may in the course of the year give us the comfortable news of a peace with America upon honourable terms!"[60]

In great anxiety, British politicians awaited the results of this proposal embodying the ultimate concessions they could bring themselves to offer. Further military disaster would in-

[60] Add. MSS 34415, ff. 398–99. Stevens, *Facsimilies*, No. 447, North to Eden, April 23, 1778.

deed force them finally to recognize independence itself; and the empire would be shattered. But that does not detract from the fact that the Carlisle Peace Commission, by envisaging a new imperial relationship, was a bold and statesmanlike attempt to preserve it. Unfortunately for the empire, it came too late.

En route to America, Carlisle, Eden, and Johnstone occupied their time drafting an initial letter to the Congress. With them aboard the "Trident," besides Mrs. Eden and the unwelcome Lord Cornwallis, were Dr. Adam Fergurson, secretary to the commission, Carlisle's personal secretary Lewes, and Anthony Storer, a Member of Parliament and mutual friend without an official position. On May 27, the vessel overtook a British man-of-war, and the commissioners learned that both commanders-in-chief, Lord Howe and Sir Henry Clinton, were at Philadelphia. After due consultation, the commissioners ordered the "Trident" to change her destination from New York to the Pennsylvania capital, since immediate communication with Howe and Clinton was deemed necessary. It was an ill-fated decision. Germain's most secret orders of March 21, which called for the evacuation of Philadelphia and the attack on St. Lucia, had never been communicated to the commissioners. Although the need of secrecy is obvious, since there had been no formal declaration of war against France and an element of surprise in the assault on St. Lucia was of great importance, this omission was a blunder of major proportions. Failure to tell the commissioners of the proposed operation offered a perfect excuse for their subsequent failure; and North earned the vindictive spite of William Eden, whereby that harassed First Minister's last years in office were rendered a hell on earth.

The "Trident" arrived off Reeds Island at the mouth of the Delaware on June 5. There the commissioners were astounded to learn that an evacuation of Philadelphia had not only been ordered, but was actually about to be executed. They were more than thunderstruck when they met Sir Henry Clinton in Philadelphia on the seventh, and learned from him that the move had been ordered by dispatches from Germain bearing a date more than three weeks prior to their own departure from England. They had counted heavily upon the presence of a respectable British force as an inducement to the Congress to treat with them. This advantage the orders of the twenty-first had quite cast away, providing, as they did, not only for the abandonment of Philadelphia but also for the dismemberment of Clinton's army.

In Eden cold and calculating anger succeeded the first violent flare-up of rage. He would exonerate Suffolk and Carlisle's father-in-law, Gower, from complicity in the "deception" which had been practiced upon him. Neither minister had been present in cabinet when the orders had been adopted; indeed both had been ill for some time thereafter. As for the rest of the cabinet, "I consider the silence however of the other Ministers as a Species of Perfidy, which I shall resent no otherwise than by managing a delay in the intended Evacuation sufficient to enable us to state our Proposals fully to the Congress and to gain an Answer from them before this weak story becomes public: In the course of that delay there may be some fortunate Change of Men or Measures in England or of both." Should this "decided trial" at negotiation fail, he was determined to return to England and throw up the commission.[61]

Eden and his colleagues were convinced that the orders of March 21 had dissipated any chance of success they might have had, but a second unpleasant shock was in store for them. To reduce their chances even further, the commissioners learned that France had moved all too swiftly since the surrender at Saratoga. Simeon Deane, brother of Silas Deane, had arrived not long before them with the news of the Franco-American treaty. Indeed, Congress had already resolved against the Conciliatory Acts and in favor of the treaty. Furthermore when

[61] Stevens, *Facsimilies*, No. 496, Eden's minutes, June 5 and 8, 1778.

they approached him on the subject, Clinton resolutely refused to delay the evacuation of Philadelphia, stating that his orders left him no such discretionary power.

Already discouraged, then, but working in great haste, the commissioners—except Lord Howe who had declined acting because of his imminent departure for England—drew up and dispatched their first letter to President Henry Laurens and to the members of the Congress.[62] Included with it were copies of their commission and of the Conciliatory Acts. Their one wish, they wrote, was to "reestablish on the Basis of equal Freedom and mutual Safety the tranquillity of this once happy Empire." Further, they would concur in every just arrangement for a cessation of hostilities. They would agree to work for the restoration and freedom of trade. They were ready to promise the prohibition of any military forces in the states of North America without the consent of the Congress or of the individual assemblies. They were prepared to aid in the discharge of America's debt and in re-establishing the credit of her paper money. To perpetuate an Anglo-American union, they would propose a reciprocal deputation of agents, colonial representatives to sit in Parliament, and British agents to sit in the assemblies. In order to effect a general and mutually satisfactory settlement, they were eager to meet representatives from Congress. The commissioners wished, in short, to build such a system "so that the British states throughout North America acting with us in Peace and War under one Common Sovereign, may have the Irrevocable Enjoyment of every Privilege, that is short of a total Separation of Interests." The benevolent and conciliatory tone of their letter was somewhat marred by a reference to the "invidious Interposition" of France. That country, they charged, had made her treaty with America only after the Conciliatory Plan had become known. They now appealed strongly to ties of language, blood, and religion in an attempt to draw America away from the French

[62] *Ibid.*, No. 1104, June 9, 1778.

274

alliance. To gloss over the impending evacuation of Philadelphia, they wrote that their instructions, as well as their desire to remove themselves from the scene of war, might cause them to retire to New York. They were willing, however, to meet representatives of Congress whenever and wherever the Americans should wish.

Pouring out all their concessions at the beginning, they kept back nothing for negotiation. They had no alternative, however, because Philadelphia would soon be evacuated. After that, it was all too probable, the Americans would be so elated that they would admit of no terms but independence. Their chance for success was, at best, a small one, and it was without great hope that the commissioners dispatched their letter. Even before the Congress had answered, Carlisle, young and homesick, had begun to think their business practically finished.[63]

The evacuation of the Pennsylvania capital was set for June 18. Shortly before that time, Eden, seething with anger, penned the commissioners' first report to Germain. It was their united opinion, including the commanders-in-chief, Eden stated, that America could have been separated from her French alliance and reunited with Britain on the basis of the terms held out by the commission had vigorous military measures been pursued for one more campaign. As matters now stood, however, all was doubtful. Johnstone appended a violent postscript to Eden's report, denouncing the evacuation as a "fatal, ill concerted and Ill advised Retreat, highly dishonorable to his Majesty's Arms and most prejudicial to the Interest of his Dominions."[64]

On the eve of the withdrawal the commissioners again boarded the "Trident," and set sail for New York. Eden spent the voyage in composing a bitter letter to his friend Wedderburn. In it he interpreted the orders of March 21 as a total

[63] RHMCR. *Carlisle Papers*, 341, Carlisle to Lady Carlisle, June 14, 1778.

[64] Stevens, *Facsimilies*, No. 1107, Eden to Germain, with a postscript by Johnstone, June, 1778.

abdication of the idea of coercing the Americans. For years, he went on, he had been trusted with "the most sacred secrets of their unfortunate Government." The only one which had ever been kept from him was the one which had sacrificed his private happiness and public character. The ministers had deliberately connived to make the commission "a mixture of ridicule, Nullity and Embarrassements." No favorable response was to be expected from Congress. They had laid the basis for an appeal to the people, but this, too, would probably be unsuccessful, for the contraction of the war in America was tantamount to a recognition of independence. In great despondency, he wrote that it was "impossible to see even what I have seen of this magnificent Country and not to go nearly mad at the long Train of Misconduct and Mischances by which we have lost it."[65]

The commissioners felt most keenly for the loyalists of Philadelphia, more than four thousand of whom had taken an oath of allegiance during the British occupation. The evacuation now informed them, in effect, that Great Britain could not protect her friends from their implacable enemies. In fact, Clinton actually advised the loyalists who could not or would not flee the town to make what peace they could with the Congress. The French treaty and the withdrawal from Philadelphia were decisive, the commissioners believed, making impossible any counterrevolution. Had Britain only pursued vigorous measures for a short time, they moaned, she would have been able to retain "such a dominion though greatly, very greatly abridged," which would have been satisfactory in light of the misfortunes of the war.[66]

The commissioners arrived in New York on July 3. Awaiting them was Laurens' reply for the Congress then sitting at Yorktown. He wrote coldly that only an earnest desire to pre-

[65] *Ibid.*, No. 500, Eden to Wedderburn, June 18, 1778.
[66] RHMCR. *Carlisle Papers*, 344–48, Carlisle to Lady Carlisle, June 21, 1778.

vent further bloodshed could have induced the Congress to read the commissioners' letter which contained such insults to their ally, the French king, or to consider propositions so inconsistent with the honor of an independent nation. The Conciliatory Acts, the commission, and the commissioners' letter supposed them in a state of dependence which was inadmissible. Congress was, however, inclined to peace, and would discuss a treaty of peace and commerce with Great Britain as soon as the British King demonstrated his good faith either by an acknowledgement of independence or by the withdrawal of his fleet and army.[67]

News of the sharp action at Monmouth Courthouse in the Jersies on June 29, between Clinton's retiring force and Washington's army, lifted the spirits of the commissioners for a time. At first, it was thought that the British victory had been decisive, but in fact the extreme heat had prevented a pursuit of the rebels, and it soon became clear that their main force remained unbroken. On July 5, therefore, the commissioners wrote again to Germain stating that in view of the British evacuation and the French treaty, Congress could not be expected to treat upon reasonable terms. Further, as long as Washington kept the field, they could not expect any province to declare for the mother country. From the answer from Congress it was evident to them, at least, that only a "decided exertion" of royal arms would bring even a part of America to accept their offers. This being the case, they asked permission to return to England at their own discretion.[68]

The commissioners then proceeded to make their appeal to the public. Under a proclamation of July 9, they published all pertinent correspondence and called upon all Americans to form opinions independently of the Congress. On the eleventh, in a public letter to Laurens they asserted that as

[67] Stevens, *Facsimilies*, No. 1110, Laurens to the commissioners, June 17, 1778.

[68] *Ibid.*, No. 1116, the commissioners to Germain, July 7, 1778.

far as independence meant "the entire Privilege of the people of North America to dispose of their Property and to Govern themselves without any reference to Great Britain, beyond what is necessary to preserve that union of Force in which our mutual Safety and Advantage consists," they considered that they had already complied with the demand of Congress for a recognition of independence. A withdrawal of British forces was, however, impossible, since it was now necessary both to protect the loyalists and to counter the French intervention. Tactlessly, they proceeded to question the authority of Congress to enter into the French treaty since the Colonies had not yet ratified the Articles of Confederation.[69]

This second approach to the Congress met with even less success than the first. Congress promptly published a resolution that since the commissioners had not accepted either of the alternatives, they would make no answer to this new communication.

A new development now completed the checkmate of the commission. Admiral D'Estaing, who had left Toulon the middle of April, arrived off Philadelphia shortly after it had been abandoned by Clinton. Finding the British fleet gone to New York, he followed and proceeded to blockade that port with Howe caught inside the bar of the harbor with his inferior force. Howe, impatiently awaiting the arrival of Byron's fleet, was saved only by D'Estaing's undue caution and his fear that the draft of his large ships would not allow him to cross the bar.

The immediate result was to cause the commissioners to abandon all hope that even their appeal to the people could have any success. The French fleet had landed the French minister at Philadelphia, and the jubilation at this open recognition of American independence convinced the commissioners that all American affection for the mother country had died.[70]

[69] *Ibid.*, No. 1119.
[70] RHMCR. *Carlisle Papers*, 356–57, Carlisle to Lady Carlisle, July 21, 1778.

In the end, D'Estaing's expedition wrought no material damage to the British fleet. Although Byron's force had become separated on its Atlantic crossing, depriving Howe of needed reinforcements, Howe nonetheless engaged the Frenchman off Rhode Island in August and after an inconclusive encounter, sailed for England in late September. Byron arrived on October 1, made one attempt to find D'Estaing, but had his fleet again scattered by a storm.

Besides bolstering American morale the arrival of the French fleet and its maneuvers off the American coast had another important effect. It immobilized throughout the summer the British expedition against St. Lucia, permitting it to act neither in America nor in the West Indies. It is futile to speculate on what a strong British military force, acting under a vigorous leader, might have accomplished in America during this important summer. For Eden the arrival of the French fleet was a blessing in disguise. It had forced "a Pause in our Course to Destruction."[71] He now implored the home government to modify the orders of March 21 so that the St. Lucia task force could act in the North American theater. Neither Germain nor his colleagues, however, would allow an alteration of plans, continuing to demand that the expedition sail at the earliest possible moment. The ministers, conceding the dubiety of their cause in America, were now intent upon making France pay the price of her intervention. It thus occurred that, unable to sail while D'Estaing hovered off the coast, the St. Lucia expedition remained a dead weight all summer—an inexcusable waste.

By autumn, then, the commissioners knew that they had failed. Supplies in New York were running perilously low. The Cork supply fleet, long overdue, was feared taken by D'Estaing; if so, Clinton was determined to evacuate New

[71] Stevens, *Facsimilies*, No. 508; Add. MSS 34414, ff. 441–47, Eden's minutes, July 29, 1778.

York.[72] Scorned by the Congress and the assemblies, the commissioners found themselves no longer negotiators but suppliants. Having no thought of requesting powers to recognize independence, they had no hope of drawing the Congress into negotiations.

One other matter remained to be settled with the Congress. On his surrender at Saratoga, General Burgoyne had entered into a convention with the victorious General Gates: his army was to be sent home on promise that it would not be used again in the American war. Yet Burgoyne's soldiers—a force which would be of the utmost value in fighting the French in Europe —still languished in American prison camps. The commissioners determined therefore to make a remonstrance and requisition to Congress demanding compliance with the convention— the notorious breach of which was a stain on the honor of Congress. Even in this, however, the commissioners failed, Congress replying through its Secretary, with much heat and a discreditable evasion, that they made no answer to impertinent communications.

What remaining dignity the commission may have possessed was destroyed by Governor Johnstone who had already laid the commission open to ridicule by a well-meaning but undignified attempt to open a private correspondence with Laurens. The Governor now became involved in an attempt to corrupt Joseph Reed and Robert Morris, both members of Congress, hinting at honors and emoluments for those who would help to restore Anglo-American unity. The affair became

[72] Stevens, *Facsimilies*, No. 519, Eden to Wedderburn, September 6, 1778. The Cork supply fleet finally arrived when Clinton was down to five weeks' provisions. The handling of the fleet demonstrated the widespread mismanagement and inefficiency of the trans-Atlantic supply system. The fleet was ordered to sail from England by dispatches bearing the date of March 21, but the orders were not issued until two months later. Even then, however, the fleet was directed to proceed to Philadelphia, although that port had been evacuated by Germain's secret orders of March 21. The fleet actually anchored at the mouth of the Delaware and waited for three days for pilots when it was accidentally discovered that the city was in the hands of the Americans.

public, and Congress, expressing its high indignation, resolved to have no more communication with the hapless commissioner. Johnstone at once announced his withdrawal from the commission and soon returned to England. Both Carlisle and Eden were thus confirmed in their conviction that "lingering" in America could be attended only with bad consequences.[73] They discarded as futile an idea they were entertaining at the time— that of making one last appeal to Congress for a truce on the basis of *uti possidetis,* the question of reciprocal rights to lie dormant during that time.[74] On September 5, therefore, they informed Germain that the American demand for a recognition of independence or the withdrawal of British forces, and the public reception of the French minister by the Congress made further approaches impossible.[75]

Eden and Carlisle were, however, by no means convinced that the struggle in the former Colonies should be given up, although Lord Howe, before his departure for England, had expressed such an opinion. This view, Eden combatted with all his might. Every letter home, now, sought to persuade his superiors to retain North America as the center of war. An evacuation of America or a recognition of independence would not bring peace. American demands would then soar to possession of the entire continent. It was necessary to "beat them, or at least persevere in the defensive system."[76] D'Estaing, Eden and Carlisle believed, had failed materially to alter the local situation. On the other hand, the recent predatory raid led by General Grey on Bedford, Connecticut, had had a small but gratifying success. If such a plan were systematically adopt- ed—a plan of violence and destruction—there would still be

---

[73] RHMCR. *Carlisle Papers,* 360–61, Carlisle's minutes, August 21, 1778.

[74] *Ibid.,* 363–64, Carlisle's memorandum.

[75] Stevens, *Facsimilies,* No. 1144, Carlisle and Eden to Germain, September 5, 1778.

[76] *Ibid.,* No. 519, Eden to Wedderburn, September 6, 1778; No. 522, Eden to Wedderburn, September, 1778.

hope, not, perhaps, for a restoration of America to the empire, but for a larger British cause. French intervention, they reasoned, had fundamentally changed the nature of the American war. The question had ceased to be one of whether America could be coerced back into the empire, and had become one of whether she would become an accession of strength to an ancient enemy, an event which might well mean Britain's ruin.

Hitherto, reasons of humanity had forbidden a system based on a "mass of private calamities." But what might formerly have been inhuman and impolitic had now become absolutely necessary. Should America insist upon allying herself with Britain's strongest foe, it would be incumbent upon the erstwhile mother country to render her "as wretch'd and as miserable as we can." Now that America had refused Britain's most generous offer, she should be so reduced and exhausted that it would be long before France could benefit from her alliance.[77] It is to the credit of Clinton that he refused to lead such a war, and of the ministry that they refused to adopt it.

On October 3, the commissioners signed their last proclamation to the American people. In this final appeal, they announced that they would shortly leave America. They had held out the most honorable terms, but their offers had been rejected. It was, therefore, only fair to warn the Americans of the dreadful calamities that their obstinacy would bring upon them. Seeking to create a division between the people and Congress, they denied the right of Congress to reject their offers without referring them to the assemblies. It was equally "deceitful" for Congress to allude to "pretended foreign treaties" which had never been ratified by the people through their assemblies. The continuation of the war the commissioners laid solely at the door of the Congress.

They then made the assemblies the same offers which Congress had refused. All groups were invited to return to their duty. American soldiers were asked to give up the struggle

[77] *Ibid.*, No. 529; Add. MSS 34416, ff. 33–34, Carlisle's minute.

since no grievance remained, and to join in against the common and hereditary enemy, France. To the clergy went a warning against the danger of associating with papists. To those who persisted in demanding independence, however, it was solemnly declared that the "laws of self-preservation" would oblige Great Britain to use every means to make America's accession to France of as little value as possible. The proclamation was to continue in effect for forty days.

After this impotent gesture, the two disheartened commissioners turned their thoughts toward home. Their final acts in North America were to suspend the Prohibitory Act for the port of New York and to open it for limited shipping. Finally, they set up a procedure—which would be used only once, in the case ,of Georgia—whereby reconquered provinces could pass quickly from military occupation to civil government. On November 27, therefore, Carlisle and Eden embarked for England leaving behind them "an unsuccessful, embarrassing, and distressing Task."[78]

The Carlisle Commission had failed, and the first British Empire was dead. The dispatch of the commission represented the end of an historical process, which had begun with the first impact of the American problem on British politics. It had begun with the Peace of 1763 and with George Grenville whose concept of an empire in the classic sense, as "supreme center and subordinate parts," had first brought this problem into view. From this position the home government was soon forced to retreat. The Old Whigs under Rockingham had sought, by an appeasement of British merchant interests, which coincided for the moment with the colonial demand for a repeal of the Stamp Act, to bring quiet to the empire. They had succeeded but temporarily. Even so, their success was not really a reversal of Grenville's idea. Indeed, with their Declaratory Act, they gave his view of empire official sanction in the most

[78] Stevens, *Facsimilies*, No. 1213, Carlisle and Eden to Germain, November 15, 1778.

positive manner. With the disastrous Chatham Ministry following the Old Whigs, it seemed for a moment that the stream of imperial development would be diverted into more modern channels. Chatham and Shelburne denied the right of the British legislature to tax the Colonies for revenue. Had this view been implemented, the Colonies might well have been satisfied with this small abridgement of parliamentary supremacy. Unfortunately, the physical and mental collapse of Chatham allowed Townshend to bring forward a scheme even more offensive to the Americans than that of Grenville. That Townshend made his taxes of the "external" description carried no weight with the colonists. They were still taxes for a revenue wherewith a colonial civil list would be established. Having denied the validity of such taxes, they soon found themselves forced to extend that denial to trade regulations, and at last to parliamentary supremacy altogether.

North's Conciliatory Proposition, a step down from the high horse of unlimited parliamentary supremacy although it was thoroughly inadequate to the circumstances then existing in the Colonies, had set the government on the road to the Carlisle Peace Commission. Had a settlement been reached on the basis of the instructions to this body, a federal empire, albeit in crude and embryonic form, would have been created. Secure in their charters and holding a sole right of internal legislation, the Colonies would have enjoyed "home rule": they would have been, in effect, sovereign states within a sovereign union.

The offer, however, had come too late. The Americans, now committed to independence, had gained a powerful ally in France. A resurgence of hope, touched by desperation, drove the North Ministry onto the final scene of their tragedy. Clinton was reinforced. His armies conquered Savannah and Charleston; and for a time, Cornwallis threatened to roll up the American southern flank—for by then all hope or desire to retake New England had vanished.[79] In the end, however,

French intervention proved decisive. French troops and a superior French navy turned the scale and brought the final capitulation at Yorktown.

Why had the British government waited so long—too long indeed—to make the offers finally held out in the Carlisle Peace Commission? The answer must involve the King who had fought so desperately to regain a position lost by his two Hanoverian predecessors. His task had been simple because the Old Whigs had built up an elaborate machinery of patronage and political control. He had, then, only to displace them and to assume their old position. One fundamental reason for his easy victory lies in the splintered condition of the Whig party at the time of his accession. Another, however, was that American unrest created, strengthened, and made vocal a new conservatism—the origin of a new Tory party—centered around the King. A state of affairs in direct contradiction to the only permanent solution of the tangled problem of Anglo-American relations—the federal principle—was thus created. In the Carlisle Commission was a valiant effort, stimulated by defeat and by the fear of French intervention, to achieve a kind of federal settlement, but no real basis for its realization existed in the eighteenth century. It could only be achieved when the King should relinquish his central and active position in politics and assume a place impartial and above domestic affairs, a symbol of union in whom all members of the British Empire might find a common head. Only when the King had

[79] Add. MSS 38383, ff. 2–3, a paper by Charles Jenkinson, who was questioning the wisdom of continuing the war due to Britain's unhealthy economy. Jenkinson held that Britain should make a frontier of the Hudson River, abandoning New England completely. He justified his contention on thoroughly mercantilist grounds, since New England had always been a source of competition for the mother country. At any rate, Britain would have little difficulty in keeping an economic upper hand over New England, who would always buy British goods as long as they were cheap. Jenkinson's ideas had developed along an amazing path since the conversations with North in 1777. He had decided that tobacco, linens, and silks were the only articles worth monopolizing: "I bow with reverence to the Act of Navigation, but I pay very little respect to the Acts of Trade."

ceased to be a party manager was the road toward a commonwealth of nations discernible. Such a retreat would be forced upon George III by a cruel necessity, loss of his sanity. The full development of the modern British party system, begun in his reign, would prevent his successors from achieving the commanding position in politics which he had gained.

The federal principle would not be accepted by British empire builders for well on half a century, and its need would have to be underlined by another colonial revolt, this time in Canada. The day would come, however, when Great Britain, possessed of her modern party system, freed by the Industrial Revolution from the fear of an empire of competitors, and remembering her agony in the American Revolution, would turn to that idea. She would accept it as the only means whereby she, as a free nation, could build and keep an empire. When that day came she would find in her monarch no party manager but a beloved symbol of her imperial unity. It was the American experience which had first pointed the way to that solution.

NOTES ON SOURCES

CHAPTER I: *The American Problem and the Grenville Ministry*. Of primary importance are the Liverpool Papers, British Museum Additional Manuscripts (hereafter referred to as "Add. MSS") 38197–38470. The papers of Charles Jenkinson, later first Earl of Liverpool, constitute a rich collection little utilized by American or British historians. Successively political agent, associate of Lord Bute, secretary to the Treasury for Grenville, and member of the Treasury and Admiralty Boards, Jenkinson, the archetypal King's Friend, was in an excellent position to know the internal workings of the government. Of special value is the mass of "routine" material demonstrating the formation of the Grenville Ministry's plan to derive a revenue from America. Miss Nanette Jucker's excellent volume *The Jenkinson Papers* (London, 1949), while limited in scope, is a convenient introduction to the collection.

The Hardwicke Papers, Add. MSS 35360–35429, 35910–11, 36226, contain extremely valuable material relating to the drafting of the Stamp Act. As attorney general, Charles Yorke was constantly consulted on legal questions relating to the act.

The Hinchingbrooke (Sandwich) Papers are of minor importance, but serve to throw light on a veteran politician striving for office.

Grenville's papers in the Stowe Collection, now deposited in the Huntington Library, are generally disappointing.

Of the published sources, the most important is, of course, the *Grenville Papers* (ed. by W. J. Smith, 4 vols., London, 1852–53).

Manuscript sources were followed throughout this book whenever discrepancies between manuscripts and the published version of documents were found.

CHAPTER II: *The Year of the Old Whigs.* The papers of the Marquis of Rockingham and Edmund Burke, comprising the Wentworth-Woodhouse collection at the Public Library, Sheffield, have only recently been made available to the scholarly world. They are indispensable for a study of the two Old Whig ministries, and throw much light on the policy and tactics of the Opposition during the American war. Both the *Rockingham Memoirs* (ed. by Earl of Albemarle, 2 vols., London, 1852) and *Burke's Correspondence* (ed. by C. William, Earl Fitzwilliam, and Sir Richard Bourke, 4 vols., London, 1844) contain many inaccuracies, deletions and suppressions, and must be used with caution. The attempts of the editors to place their heroes in as favorable a light as possible are obvious.

Similarly, the *Chatham Correspondence* (ed. by W. S. Taylor and J. H. Pringle, 4 vols., London, 1838–40), while less open to such criticism, must be checked against the Chatham Papers, Public Record Office 30/8. Several unpublished letters to Pitt demonstrate the development of the American controversy. See, for instance, Chatham Papers, 97, for a letter from John Dickinson to Pitt; bundle 55 contains Pitt's correspondence with Stephen Sayre.

The Hardwicke Papers portray the stresses and strains, both internal and external, under which the Rockingham Ministry labored. The Liverpool Papers and the Hinchingbrooke Papers provide sources for a study of Opposition activities during the Old Whig Ministry. The published sources are voluminous. In addition to those mentioned above, *The Correspondence of George III* (ed. by Sir John Fortescue, 6 vols., Lon-

lon, 1927–28) is of great use, but it must be corrected by L. B. Namier, *Additions and Corrections* (Manchester, 1937).

CHAPTER III: *Chatham, Faction, and America.* The hundred volumes of Chatham Papers in the Public Record Office furnish the major source. The collection has yielded several "nuggets." Shelburne's plan for the disobedient assembly of New York, which he included in a letter to Chatham, has been suppressed both in the *Chatham Correspondence* and in Fitzmaurice's *Life of Shelburne* (2 vols., London, 1912). Of considerable interest, too, is Chatham's sketch for a new ministry which he composed during the formation of his government. The outline lists Chatham as holding a new office, the secretaryship of state for America. Although the scheme was dropped, the document underscores Chatham's determination to solve the American problem.

The Liverpool Papers are valuable in portraying the emergence of the King's Friends as a well-defined "party" grouping. (See particularly Add. MSS 38339, ff. 307–10; printed by Jucker.) Here, too, is graphic evidence of Chatham's failure to extirpate faction.

Accounts of his stormy relations with the Old Whigs are to be found in the Hardwicke Papers (particularly in Add. MSS 35430), and in the Wentworth-Woodhouse collection. Published sources, the *Grenville Papers* and the *Bedford Correspondence* (ed. by Lord John Russell, 3 vols., London, 1842–46) give good accounts of the remainder of the Opposition. The latter contains portions of Bedford's private journal which is of great use in tracing the growth of the Grenville-Bedford alienation. The Hinchingbrooke Papers indicate Bedfordite eagerness to win office under the Chatham Ministry even at the expense of the Grenville alliance.

CHAPTER IV. *The Fall of the Chatham System.* Evidence of Old Whig leadership of the successful move to reduce the land tax is to be found in the Wentworth-Woodhouse Papers. The vast number of Treasury Board minutes and the reports from the American Commissioners of the Customs in the Liverpool Papers show the growth of American resistance to the Townshend taxes, and the Grafton Ministry's confusion.

The correspondence of John Wilkes with committees of the American Sons of Liberty is to be found in the Wilkes Papers, Add. MSS 30865–30887. Evidence of the hardening conservative reaction to American resistance is seen not only in the Liverpool Papers but also in the Wentworth-Woodhouse Papers and the Hardwicke Papers. A growing acceptance of Grenville's idea that requisitions were unconstitutional means of raising revenue is to be seen in this latter collection.

The petitioning movement for the dissolution of a Parliament corrupted by the expulsion of Wilkes—and the failure of that movement to touch the American problem—is to be traced in the Wentworth-Woodhouse Papers, the *Grenville Papers,* and the *Burke Correspondence.*

CHAPTER V: *Prelude to Civil War.* The development of the American crisis and Dartmouth's futile attempts to solve it are best seen in the Liverpool Papers and in the *Royal Historical Manuscripts Commission Reports, Dartmouth Papers* (3 vols., London, 1887, 1895, 1896). North's unhappy position in his cabinet emerges from the Auckland Papers, Add. MSS 34412–34417, and Fortescue's *Correspondence of George III.* His plan to decrease the navy as a means of paring expenses, his refusal to allow an increase in British naval strength, and Sandwich's violent opposition to North's false sense of economy are to be found in the Hinchingbrooke Papers.

The Wilkes Papers portray the internal quarrels of the London Radicals; while Opposition affairs, the increasing gulf between Opposition and public, and the growing conservative reaction to American radicalism are best studied in the Hardwicke Papers, the Chatham Papers, and the Wentworth-Woodhouse Papers.

Burke's Letterbook in the Wentworth-Woodhouse collection includes his inflammatory letters to the New York Assembly and to politicians of that province.

CHAPTER VI: *Civil War*. The government's reaction to the outbreak of hostilities and the formation of its plans for crushing the rebellion are to be found in the Auckland Papers, the Liverpool Papers, the *Sandwich Papers*, and the Hardwicke Papers. Facsimilies of many important documents in the Auckland Papers are to be found in B. F. Stevens, *Facsimilies* (25 vols., London, 1889–98). Dartmouth's desperate attempts to arrive at a peaceable settlement of the dispute are seen in the *Dartmouth Papers*. The sources for the Howe Peace Commission—its formation and the bitter cabinet controversy concerning it—are the Auckland Papers, the *Dartmouth Papers*, the Royal Historical Manuscripts Commission Reports on the *Stopford-Sackville Papers* (2 vols., London, 1904, and Hereford, 1910), and the *Knox Papers, Various Collections*, VI (Dublin, 1909).

Sandwich's insistence on a naval build-up to counter French preparations, and North's and the King's refusal to allow such measures are seen in the Hinchingbrooke Papers and in Fortescue's *Correspondence of George III*, with some correspondence relating to this subject printed in the Navy Record Society publication, the *Sandwich Papers* (4 vols., London, 1932). Evidence of North's growing melancholy and the King's increasing dependence upon John Robinson to keep North in good spirits are to be found in the correspondence of John Robinson with George III, Add. MSS 37833–37835. The story of the collapse of Opposition's efforts to counter the ministerial American policy and of their hopes for the defeat of British arms is told in the Wentworth-Woodhouse Papers.

CHAPTER VII: *Agony and Revelation*. The most important source for reaction to Burgoyne's surrender and the formation of the Carlisle Peace Commission is the Auckland Papers. It is a measure of Eden's great influence with North that this source is also of primary importance in following the spate of "unofficial" British negotiations with the American commissioners in Paris. Sidelights on these interesting but futile attempts to stop the war are found in the *Stopford-Sackville Papers* and in *Franklin's Works* (ed. by J. Sparks, 10 vols., Chicago, 1882). North's pathetic struggle to be allowed to resign emerges from Fortescue's *Correspondence of George III*.

The gradual acceptance of the idea of at least a partial loss of the American Colonies is to be found in the Liverpool Papers. The two great sources for the functioning of the Carlisle Peace Commission are the Auckland Papers and the *Royal Historical Manuscripts Commission Reports, The Carlisle Papers* (London, 1897).

The account of the split between the Chathamites and the Old Whigs on the point of American independence is based on the Chatham Papers (especially bundles 54 and 56), the *Chatham Correspondence*, and the Wentworth-Woodhouse Papers.

BIBLIOGRAPHY

MANUSCRIPT SOURCES

Auckland Papers. British Museum Additional Manuscripts 29475, 34412–34417. Papers and correspondence of William Eden, first Lord Auckland, undersecretary of state and peace commissioner to America. They are especially valuable for the formation and functioning of the Howe and Carlisle Peace Commissions.

Chatham Papers. Public Record Office, 30/8. Bundles 1–100. The first four volumes are arranged more or less in accordance with the printed edition of the *Chatham Correspondence* (*q. v.*). In footnote references, the Arabic numeral refers to the bundle number in this collection.

Hardwicke Papers. British Museum Additional Manuscripts 35360–35430, 35511, 35910–11, 36226. The papers of Charles Yorke, attorney general, have yielded hitherto unsuspected information concerning the Stamp Act. The correspondence of the second Earl with his brother John and with Thomas Hutchinson portrays the growing conservative reaction to American radicalism.

Hinchingbrooke (Sandwich) Papers. The papers and correspondence of John, fourth Earl of Sandwich, preserved at his country seat, Hinchingbrooke, Huntingdonshire.

Liverpool Papers. British Museum Additional Manuscripts 38191, 38197–38470, 38577. The papers and correspondence of the Earls of Liverpool. The author has used only those belonging to Charles Jenkinson, later first Earl of Liverpool.

293

Newcastle Papers. British Museum Additional Manuscripts 32709, 32731, 32862, 32973, for an identification of Henry Mc-Culloh and his connection with the Stamp Act.

Robinson, John; his correspondence with George III. British Museum Additional Manuscripts 37833–37835.

Stowe Collection, Huntington Library, San Marino, California.

Wentworth-Woodhouse Papers. Public Library, Sheffield. The papers and correspondence of the Marquis of Rockingham and of Edmund Burke. The collection throws much light on the Old Whigs and their American views. Unfortunately, the papers are in great confusion and have not been adequately catalogued. It has been, therefore, impossible to make references to volumes and folio numbers. Many of the letters published in the *Rockingham Memoirs (q. v.)* are to be found in these papers.

Wilkes Papers. British Museum Additional Manuscripts 30865–30887. The papers and correspondence of John Wilkes. Valuable for ascertaining the connection between British and American radicalism.

FACSIMILIES

Stevens, B. F. *Facsimilies of MSS. in European Archives Relating to America, 1773–1783.* London. 1889–98. 25 vols. Stevens has drawn largely upon the Auckland Papers and the RHMCR. *Carlisle Papers (q. v.).* A limited edition of 200 copies of this monumental work was published and the photographic plates destroyed.

PERIODICALS

American Historical Review:

Andrews, C. M. "The American Revolution: An Interpretation." Vol. XXXI, No. 2 (January, 1926), 219–32.

————. "Anglo-French Commercial Rivalry." Vol. XX, No. 4 (July, 1915), 761–80.

————. "Colonial Commerce." Vol. XX, No. 1 (October, 1914), 43–63.

Basye, A. H. "The Secretary for the Colonies, 1768–1782." Vol. XXVIII, No. 1 (October, 1922), 13–23.

Becker, C. B. "Election of Delegates from New York to the Second Continental Congress." Vol. IX, No. 1 (October, 1903), 66–85.

―――. "Growth of Revolutionary Parties and Methods in New York Province, 1765–1774." Vol. VII, No. 1 (October, 1901), 56–76.

―――. "Horace Walpole's Memoirs of the Reign of George III." Parts I and II. Vol. XVI, No. 2 (January, 1911), 255–72.

Carter, C. E. "Observations of Superintendent John Stuart and Governor James Grant of East Florida on the Proposed Plan of 1764 for the Future Management of Indian Affairs." Vol. XX, No. 4 (July, 1915), 815–31.

―――. "The Significance of the Military Office in America, 1763–1775." Vol. XXVIII, No. 3 (April, 1923), 475–88.

Clark, J. "Responsibility for the Failure of the Burgoyne Campaign." Vol. XXXV, No. 3 (April, 1930), 542–59.

Clarke, M. D. "The Board of Trade at Work." Vol. XVII, No. 1 (October, 1911), 17–43.

Corwin, E. S. "The French Objective in the American Revolution." Vol. XXI, No. 1 (October, 1915), 33–61.

―――. "The Progress of Constitutional Theory Between the Declaration of Independence and the Meeting of the Philadelphia Convention." Vol. XXX, No. 3 (April, 1925), 511–36.

Davidson, P. G. "Whig Propagandists of the American Revolution." Vol. XXXIX, No. 3 (April, 1934), 442–53.

Doysié, A. "Journal of a French Traveler in the Colonies, 1765." Part I. Vol. XXVI, No. 4 (July, 1921), 726–47. The anonymous traveler heard Patrick Henry's famous speech and recorded the reaction of the people in Virginia to the Stamp Act: "Some of them mutter betwixt their teeth, let the worst Come to the worst we'l Call the french to Our succour." (p. 747.) Part II. Vol. XXVII, No. 1 (October, 1921), 70–89.

Farrand, M. "The Taxation on Tea, 1767–1773." Vol. III (1898), 266.

Gipson, L. H. "Connecticut Taxation and Parliamentary Aid Preceding the Revolutionary War." Vol. XXXVI, No. 4 (July, 1931), 721–39.

Guttridge, G. H. "Adam Smith on the American Revolution: An Unpublished Memorial." Vol. XXXVIII, No. 4 (July, 1933), 714–20.

———. "Lord George Germain in Office." Vol. XXXIII, No. 1 (October, 1927), 23–43.

Laprade, W. T. "The Stamp Act in British Politics." Vol. XXXV, No. 4 (July, 1930), 735–57.

Ogden, H. V. S. "The State of Nature and the Decline of Lockian Political Theory in England, 1760–1800." Vol. XLVI, No. 1 (October, 1940), 21–44.

Ritcheson, C. R. "The Elder Pitt and an American Department." Vol. LVII, No. 2 (January, 1952), 376–83.

Van Tyne, C. H. "Influence of the Clergy, and of Religious and Sectarian Forces, on the American Revolution." Vol. XIX, No. 1 (October, 1913), 44–64.

———. "Influences which Determined the French Government to make the Treaty with America, 1778." Vol. XXI, No. 3 (October, 1916), 528–41.

English Historical Review:

Carter, C. E. "The British Policy Toward the American Indians in the South." Vol. XXXIII, No. 129 (January, 1918), 37–56.

Davis, A. Mc. "The Employment of Indian Auxiliaries in the American War." Vol. II (1887), 709–28.

Egerton, H. E. "Lord George Germain and Sir William Howe." Vol. XXV (1910), 315–16.

Garth, Charles. Vol. LIV (1939), 646–49.

Hughes, E. "The English Stamp Duties, 1664–1764." Vol. LVI, No. CCXXII (April, 1941), 234–64.

Humphreys, R. A. "Lord Shelburne and British Colonial Policy, 1766–1768." Vol. L, No. CXCVIII (April, 1935), 257–77.

———. "Lord Shelburne and the Proclamation of 1763." Vol. XLIX, No. CXCIV (April, 1934), 241–64.

Imlach, G. M. "Earl Temple and the Ministry of 1765." Vol. XXX (1915), 317–21.

Namier, L. B. "Charles Garth and His Connexions." Part I. Vol. LIV, No. CCXV (July, 1939), 443–70; Part II. Vol. LIV, No. CCXVI (October, 1939) 632–52.

Sutherland, L. Stuart. "Edmund Burke and the First Rockingham Ministry." Vol. XLVII, No. CLXXXV (January, 1932), 46–72.

———. "Lord Shelburne and East India Company Politics, 1766–1769." Vol. XLIX, No. CXCV (July, 1934), 450–86.

Williams, B. "Chatham and the Representation of the Colonies in the Imperial Parliament." Vol. XXII (1907), 756–58.

Winstanley, D. A. "George III and his First Cabinet." Vol. XVII (1902), 678–91.

Parliamentary Affairs, the Journal of the Hansard Society:

Ritcheson, C. R. "The American Revolution: Its Influence on the Development of the British Empire." Vol. IV, No. 2 (Spring, 1951), 245–60.

William and Mary Quarterly:

Morgan, E. S. "The Postponement of the Stamp Act." Third Series, Vol. VII (1950), 353–92.

Ritcheson, C. R. "The Preparation of the Stamp Act." Third Series, Vol. X (1953), 543–59.

Sellers, Charles G., Jr. "Private Profits and British Colonial Policy: The Speculations of Henry McCulloh." Third Series, Vol. VIII (1951), 535–51.

PRINTED SOURCES AND CONTEMPORARY WORKS

Acts of the Privy Council (Colonial), George III, 1613–1783. Ed. by W. L. Grant and J. Munro. London, 1908–12. 6 vols.

Adams, John. *Works.* Boston, 1856. 10 vols.

Annual Register. London, 1760, etc.

Auckland Journal and Correspondence. By Eden's son, the Bishop of Bath and Wells. Ed. by G. Hogge. London, 1861–62. 4 vols. These volumes deal chiefly with a period later than that here treated, but are a convenient introduction to the study of the Auckland Papers.

Bedford Correspondence. Ed. by Lord John Russell. London, 1842–46. 3 vols.

Beloff, M. *The Debate on the American Revolution.* London, 1949. A collection of pamphlets, speeches, etc., in extract and with notes.

Bolingbroke's Miscellaneous Works. Edinburgh, 1768. 4 vols.

Burke's Correspondence. Ed. by C. William, Earl Fitzwilliam, and Sir Richard Bourke. London, 1844. 4 vols. Examination of the Wentworth-Woodhouse Papers has revealed many errors and unmarked deletions.

Burke's Works. London, 1826. 16 vols.

Calendar of New York Historical Manuscripts, (English). Ed. by E. B. O'Callaghan. Part II, 1664–1776. Albany (New York), 1866.

Cavendish, Henry. *Debates of the House of Commons, 1768–1771.* London, 1841–43. 2 vols.

———. *Debate on the Second Reading of the Quebec Act.* London, 1839.

Channing, E. and A. C. Coolidge (eds.). *Barrington-Bernard Correspondence, 1760–1770.* Cambridge (Mass.) and London, 1912.

Chatham Correspondence. Ed. by W. S. Taylor and J. H. Pringle. London, 1838–40. 4 vols. Examination of the Chatham Papers in the Public Record Office has revealed many errors and important and unmarked deletions, especially in the letters from Shelburne to Chatham at the time of the crisis occasioned by the disobedience of the assembly of New York.

Colonial History of New York, Documents. Albany (New York), 1856. 8 vols.

Documentary History of New York. Vol. III. Albany (New York), 1850. 4 vols.

Fitzmaurice, Lord. *Life of William Earl of Shelburne.* London, 1912. 2 vols.

Force, P. *American Archives, Fourth Series*. Ed. by M. St. C. Clarke. Washington, 1837–51. 6 vols.

Fortescue, Sir John. *Correspondence of George III*. London, 1927–28. 6 vols.

Franklin's Works. Ed. by J. Sparks. Chicago, 1882. 10 vols.

Grafton, Third Duke of. *Autobiography and Political Correspondence*. Ed. by Sir William Anson. London, 1898.

Grenville Papers. Ed. by W. J. Smith. London, 1852–53. 4 vols.

Guttridge, G. H. (ed.). *The American Correspondence of a Bristol Merchant, 1766–1776*. Berkeley, 1934.

Hutchinson, Thomas. *Diary and Letters*. Ed. by P. O. Hutchinson. London, 1883–86. 2 vols.

Jesse, J. H. *George Selwyn and His Contemporaries*. London, 1843–44. 4 vols.

———. *Memoirs of the Reign of George III*. London, 1867. 3 vols.

Jucker, N. S. *The Jenkinson Papers, 1760–1766*. London, 1949. Based on a study of the Liverpool Papers in the British Museum.

Knox, William. *Extra Official State Papers*. London, 1789.

Locke, J. *Of Civil Government and Toleration*. Ed. by Henry Morley. London, 1884.

Mahon, Viscount. *History of England from the Peace of Utrecht to the Peace of Versailles*. London, 1836–54. 7 vols.

Morison, S. E. *Sources and Documents Illustrating the American Revolution, 1764–1788*. Oxford, 1923. A convenient collection of contemporary documents, pamphlets, etc., printed in extract and with notes and an excellent introductory essay.

Parliamentary History. Ed. by Wm. Cobbett and J. Wright. Vols. XV–XXI. London, 1813–14. 36 vols.

Pickering, D. *Statutes at Large from the Magna Charta to . . . 1806*. Vols. XXV–XXXIII. Cambridge, 1763–1807. 46 vols.

Pownall, T. *The Administration of the Colonies*. Part I. London, 1764. 2nd ed. 1765. Part II. London, 1774.

Rockingham Memoirs. Ed. by the Earl of Albemarle. London, 1852. 2 vols.

Royal Historical Manuscripts Commission Reports:
  Abergavenny Papers. Report X. Appendix, Part VI. London,
    1885. The political correspondence of John Robinson.
  American MSS. in the Royal Institution of Great Britain.
    Vol. I. London, 1904. Vol. II. Dublin, 1906. Military
    affairs.
  Bathurst Papers. London, 1923. A few letters to and from
    North's Lord Chancellor, pp. 11–19.
  Carlisle Papers. Report XV. Appendix, Part VI. London,
    1897. Indispensable for a study of the Peace Commission
    of 1778.
  Dartmouth Papers. Vol. I. Report XI. Appendix, Part V.
    London, 1887. The letters from Hutchinson and Joseph
    Reed are especially interesting.
  ———. Vol. II. Report XIV. Appendix, Part X. London,
    1895. American papers. Indispensable.
  ———. Vol. III. Report XV. Appendix, Part I. London,
    1896.
  Denbigh Papers. Part V. London, 1911. Some letters of gen-
    eral interest during the early years of the reign of George
    III.
  Gray (Charles) Papers. The Round MSS. Report XIV. Ap-
    pendix, Part IX, London, 1895.
  Knox Papers. Various Collections, VI. Dublin, 1909.
  Lindley Wood Papers. Various Collections, VIII. Hereford,
    1913.
  Lothian Papers. London, 1905. Includes the papers of George
    Grenville's friend, the second Earl of Buckinghamshire.
  Savile-Foljambe Papers. Report XV. Appendix, Part V. Lon-
    don, 1897. Letters of Sir George Savile are calendared,
    pp. 141–60.
  Stopford-Sackville Papers. Vol. I. London, 1904. The papers
    of Lord George Germain.
  ———. Vol. II. Hereford, 1910.
  Townshend Papers. Report XI. Appendix, Part IV. London,
    1887. Includes many of Charles Townshend's letters.
  Weston Papers. MSS of C. F. Weston Underwood. Cal-
    endared in the report on the MSS of the Earl of Eglinton

and others. London, 1885. The *Weston Papers* are those of Edward Weston, long-time undersecretary of state under George II and George III.

Sandwich Papers. Publication of the Navy Record Society. Vol. LXIX. London, 1932. 4 vols. Based on the Hinchingbrooke Papers, but chiefly confined to Admiralty affairs and naval operations.

Sedgwick, Romney. *Letters from George III to Lord Bute, 1756–1766.* London, 1939. With a brilliant introductory essay.

Smith, Adam. *Wealth of Nations.* Ed. by E. Cannan. London, 1904. 2 vols.

Tucker, J. *The Humble Address and Earnest Appeal to those . . . fittest to decide whether a connection with, or a separation from the Colonies of America be most for the National Advantage.* London, 1775.

Van Doren, C. *Benjamin Franklin's Autobiographical Writings.* London, 1946.

Walpole, H. *Memoirs of the Reign of George III.* London, 1845. 4 vols.

————. *Correspondence wih George Montagu.* Ed. by W. S. Lewis and R. S. Brown. The Yale Edition of *Walpole's Correspondence.* Vol. X. New Haven, 1941. 16 vols.

Woodfall, H. S. *Junius.* London, 1772. 2 vols.

Wraxall, Sir N. W. *Memoirs.* London, 1884. 5 vols.

Yorke, P. C. *Life and Correspondence of Philip Yorke, Earl of Hardwicke.* Cambridge, 1913. 3 vols.

LATER WORKS

Albion, R. G. *Forests and Sea Power.* Cambridge (Mass.), 1926.

Alvord, C. W. *The Mississippi Valley in British Politics.* Cleveland, 1917. 2 vols. A definitive study of the colonial west.

Andrews, C. M. *The Colonial Background of the American Revolution.* New Haven, 1924.

Barrington, Shute. *Political Life of W. W. Viscount Barrington.* London, 1814.

Bayne-Powell, R. *Eighteenth Century London Life.* London, 1937.

Beer, G. L. *British Colonial Policy, 1754–1765.* New York, 1907. Reprinted, 1933.

———. *The Old Colonial System.* New York, 1933. 2 vols.

Bemis, S. F. *Diplomatic History of the United States.* 3rd ed. New York, 1950.

Butterfield, H. *George III, Lord North, and the People, 1779–1780.* London, 1949.

Cambridge History of the British Empire. Ed. by J. H. Rose, A. P. Newton, and E. A. Benians. Vol. I. *The Old Empire.* Cambridge, 1929. 8 vols.

Channing, E. *History of the United States.* Vol. III. New York, 1927. 6 vols.

Clark, D. M. *British Opinion and the American Revolution.* New Haven, 1930.

Coupland, R. *The Quebec Act.* Oxford, 1925.

———. *The American Revolution and the British Empire.* London, 1930.

Dictionary of National Biography. Ed. by Leslie Stephen and Sidney Lee. London, 1885–1901.

Egerton, H. E. *A Short History of British Colonial Policy, 1606–1909.* 12th ed. Revised by A. P. Newton. London, 1950.

Eyck, Erick. *Die Pitts und Die Fox.* Erlenbach-Zurich, 1946.

Feiling, K. G. *A History of the Tory Party, 1640–1715.* Oxford, 1924.

———. *A History of England.* London, 1950.

———. *The Second Tory Party, 1714–1832.* London, 1938.

Fitzgerald, P. *The Life and Times of John Wilkes.* London, 1888. 2 vols.

Greene, E. B. *The Provincial Governor.* Cambridge (Mass.), 1898.

Guttridge, G. H. *David Hartley, M. P., An Advocate of Conciliation, 1774–1783.* Berkeley, 1926.

Hotblack, K. *Chatham's Colonial Policy.* London, 1917.

Jones, T. *History of New York during the Revolutionary War.* Ed. by E. F. de Lancey. New York, 1879. 2 vols.

Keith, A. B. *Constitutional History of the First British Empire.* Oxford, 1930.

Labaree, L. W. *Royal Government in America*. New Haven, (Conn.), 1930.

———. *Royal Instructions to British Colonial Governors*. New York and London, 1935. 2 vols.

Macaulay, T. B. *Critical and Historical Essays*. Vol. II. 2nd ed. London, 1843. 3 vols.

McIlwain, C. A. *The American Revolution*. New York, 1923.

Magnus, Sir P. *Edmund Burke*. London, 1939.

Mantoux, P. *The Industrial Revolution in the Eighteenth Century*. 2nd ed. Revised and translated by M. Vernon. London, 1948.

Morgan, E. S. and H. M. *The Stamp Act Crisis*. Williamsburg, 1953. See the author's review in *William and Mary Quarterly*, Vol. X, Third Series (October, 1953), 633–35.

Namier, L. B. *Additions and Corrections to Sir John Fortescue's Edition of the Correspondence of George III*. Manchester, 1937.

———. *England in the Age of the American Revolution*. London, 1930.

———. *The Structure of Politics at the Accession of George III*. London, 1929. 2 vols.

Newman, B. *Edmund Burke*. London, 1927.

Osgood, H. L. *The American Colonies in the Eighteenth Century*. New York, 1924. 4 vols.

Petrie, Sir Charles. *The Four Georges*. 2nd ed. London, 1946.

Roseberry, Lord. *Chatham, His Early Life and Connections*. London, 1910.

Ruville, A. von. *William Pitt, Earl of Chatham*. Translated by H. G. Chaytor and Mary Morison. London and New York, 1931. 3 vols.

Schuyler, R. L. *Josiah Tucker*. New York, 1931.

———. *Parliament and the British Empire*. New York, 1929.

Stephans, A. *Memoirs of John Horne Tooke*. London, 1813. 2 vols.

Trevelyan, Sir G. O. *The American Revolution*. Part I. 2nd ed. London, 1899. Part II. Vol. II. London, 1903. Part III. London, 1907. 3 vols.

———. *George III and Charles Fox*. London, 1912 and 1914. 2 vols.

Tunstall, B. *William Pitt, Earl of Chatham*. London, 1938.

Van Tyne, C. H. *The Causes of the War of Independence.* Boston and New York, 1922.

———. *The Loyalists in the American Revolution.* New York, 1902.

Williams, B. *The Life of William Pitt, Earl of Chatham.* London, 1914. 2 vols.

———. *The Whig Supremacy, 1714–1760.* Oxford, 1939. Reprinted with corrections, 1949.

Winstanley, D. A. *Lord Chatham and the Whig Opposition.* Cambridge, 1912.

———. *Personal and Party Government.* Cambridge, 1910.

INDEX

tion, 128ff.; and North Ministry, 138f.; and Burke, 150, 163–64, 180–81; and opposition to war, 219–24; Burke's bill to quiet America, 226–27; tactics in Parliament, 229–30; and Pulteney, 238; for American independence, 244–49
"Olive Branch," petition: 195, 197, 225, 227
Oliver, lieutenant-governor of Massachusetts: letters published in colonies, 153; petition for removal of, 160
Osbaldeston, John: 223n.
Otis, James: 42n.

Palliser, Sir Hugh: 254
Penn, Richard: 195
Pennsylvania Assembly: 123
Pitt, William: *see* Chatham
Plan of Union, Joseph Galloway: 176
Pontiac: rebellion of, 13; results of, 15; and Pitt, 33; Treaty of Ft. Stanwix, 144
Portland, William, Duke of: 77, 103, 106n., 231
Powis, Herbert, Earl of: 121f.
Pownall, John: 148n., 149n., 156n., 165n., 201, 204, 223n.; and Dartmouth's American plan, 158f.
Pownall, Thomas: 119n., 132; moves to repeal Townshend duties, 127f.
Prescott, Captain: 144
Priestly, Dr. Joseph: 224

Proclamation of Rebellion: 194f., 223
Prohibitory Act: 22f.; suspended by Carlisle Peace Commission, 283
Provisional Act for Reconciliation with America (Chatham), 183–86, 188f.
Pulteney, William: 231; and Bancroft, 238–39, 241; and Carlisle Peace Commission, 266

Quartering Act, fourth Coercive Act: 162–63
Quebec Act, 1774: 65, 158, 165ff.; and Continental Congress, 177; and Franklin's "Hints," 179; to be amended, 180; and Chatham Provisional Act, 184; and Howe Peace Commission, 206
Quincey, Josiah: 190n.

Radicals, City: 190, 197, 227; and Old Whig opposition to American war, 222–23
Ramsden, Tom: 6n.
Reed, Joseph: 162n., 280
Regulating Act: 260f.
Restraining Act: 188–89, 190, 270
Revenue Act of 1764: 92; and Jenkinson research, 19; American reaction to, 27f.; amended, 65; and Continental Congress, 176; and Chatham Provisional Act, 184

318

QUEDA

Obras da autora publicadas pela Record

Tríptico

Fissura

Gênese

Destroçados

Queda

KARIN SLAUGHTER

QUEDA

Tradução de
Laura Folgueira

1ª edição

EDITORA RECORD
RIO DE JANEIRO • SÃO PAULO
2024

CIP-BRASIL. CATALOGAÇÃO NA PUBLICAÇÃO
SINDICATO NACIONAL DOS EDITORES DE LIVROS, RJ

S641q   Slaughter, Karin, 1971-
        Queda / Karin Slaughter ; tradução Laura Folgueira. 1. ed. - Rio de Janeiro :
    Record, 2024.
        Tradução de: Fallen
        ISBN 978-85-01-92006-5

        1. Ficção americana. I. Folgueira, Laura. II. Título.

24-88009   CDD: 813
                      CDU: 82-3(73)

Gabriela Faray Ferreira Lopes - Bibliotecária - CRB-7/6643

Título original:
FALLEN

Imagem no miolo: mão sangrenta (Adobe Stock/Julia)

Texto revisado segundo o Acordo Ortográfico da Língua Portuguesa de 1990.

Direitos exclusivos de publicação em língua portuguesa somente para o Brasil adquiridos pela
EDITORA RECORD LTDA.
Rua Argentina, 171 – Rio de Janeiro, RJ – 20921-380 – Tel.: (21) 2585-2000, que se reserva a propriedade literária desta tradução.

Impresso no Brasil

ISBN 978-85-01-92006-5

Seja um leitor preferencial Record.
Cadastre-se no site www.record.com.br e receba informações sobre nossos lançamentos e nossas promoções.

Atendimento e venda direta ao leitor:
sac@record.com.br

A todos os bibliotecários do mundo,
em nome de todas as crianças que vocês ajudaram
a se tornar escritoras.

SÁBADO

1

Faith Mitchell jogou o conteúdo de sua bolsa no banco do carona de seu Mini Cooper, tentando achar algo para comer. Exceto por um chiclete cheio de pelos e um amendoim de origem duvidosa, não tinha nada remotamente comestível. Ela pensou na caixa de barrinhas energéticas na despensa da cozinha e sua barriga fez um barulho que parecia uma dobradiça enferrujada rangendo ao abrir.

O seminário de informática de que ela havia participado naquela manhã deveria ter durado três horas, mas acabou se estendendo para quatro horas e meia graças ao babaca na primeira fila que não parava de fazer perguntas inúteis. O Georgia Bureau of Investigation treinava seus agentes com mais frequência do que qualquer outra agência da região. Estatísticas e dados sobre atividades criminosas eram martelados sem parar na cabeça deles. Precisavam estar atualizados sobre todas as últimas tecnologias. Tinham que se qualificar no estande de tiro duas vezes por ano. Faziam simulações de invasão e de atirador ativo tão intensas que, semanas depois, Faith ainda não conseguia ir ao banheiro no meio da noite sem conferir se havia sombras nas portas. Em geral, ela gostava do rigor da agência. Naquele dia, Faith só conseguia pensar em sua bebê de quatro meses e na promessa que fizera à própria mãe de voltar no máximo ao meio-dia.

Quando ela ligou o carro, o relógio do painel mostrava uma e dez da tarde. Faith xingou baixinho ao sair do estacionamento em frente à sede da Panthersville Road. Ela usou o Bluetooth para discar o número da mãe. Os alto-falantes do carro devolveram um silêncio estático. Faith desligou e tentou de novo. Desta vez, deu sinal de ocupado.

9

Faith tamborilou no volante ao ouvir o barulho. A mãe dela tinha caixa postal. *Todo mundo* tinha caixa postal. Faith não conseguia se lembrar da última vez que ouvira um sinal de ocupado no telefone. Quase tinha se esquecido do som. Provavelmente havia uma linha cruzada em algum lugar na operadora. Ela desligou e tentou o número pela terceira vez.

Ainda ocupado.

Faith ficou dirigindo só com uma das mãos enquanto verificava no BlackBerry se havia um e-mail da mãe. Antes de Evelyn Mitchell se aposentar, tinha sido policial por quase quatro décadas. Dava para dizer muita coisa sobre a polícia de Atlanta, mas não que eles eram desatualizados. Evelyn tinha celular na época em que eles pareciam mais uma bolsa pendurada no ombro. Ela aprendera a usar e-mail antes da filha. Fazia quase doze anos que tinha um BlackBerry.

Mas, naquele dia, não havia mandado mensagem.

Faith verificou sua caixa postal. Havia uma mensagem do consultório do dentista para ela marcar uma limpeza nos dentes, mas nada novo. Tentou o telefone fixo da própria casa, achando que talvez a mãe tivesse ido até lá buscar algo para a bebê. A casa de Faith ficava na mesma rua de Evelyn. Talvez as fraldas de Emma tivessem acabado. Ou a pequena precisasse de outra mamadeira. Faith escutou o telefone tocar em sua casa, depois ouviu sua própria voz atendendo e mandando deixar uma mensagem.

Ela desligou. Sem pensar, olhou para o banco de trás. A cadeirinha vazia de Emma estava lá. Ela viu a parte de cima do forro cor-de-rosa saindo do plástico.

— Idiota — sussurrou para si mesma.

Discou o número do celular da mãe. Segurou a respiração enquanto contava três toques. Caiu na caixa postal de Evelyn.

Faith teve que pigarrear antes de conseguir falar. Estava ciente de que sua voz tremia.

— Mãe, estou indo para casa. Você deve ter levado a Em para dar um passeio... — Faith olhou para o céu enquanto entrava na rodovia interestadual. Estava a uns vinte minutos de Atlanta e via nuvens brancas fofinhas enroladas como cachecóis nos pescoços magros dos

10

arranha-céus. — Me liga, tá? — disse Faith, com a preocupação cutucando um cantinho da sua mente.

Mercado. Posto de gasolina. Farmácia. A mãe tinha uma cadeirinha de carro idêntica à que estava no banco de trás do Mini de Faith. Provavelmente tinha ido resolver alguma coisa na rua. Faith estava mais de uma hora atrasada. Evelyn devia ter pegado a bebê e... deixado uma mensagem para Faith falando que ia sair. A mulher tinha ficado de prontidão no trabalho durante a maior parte da vida adulta. Não ia ao banheiro sem avisar a alguém. Faith e seu irmão mais velho, Zeke, faziam piada disso quando eram crianças. Sempre sabiam onde a mãe estava, mesmo quando não queriam. Especialmente quando não queriam.

Faith olhou para o celular na mão como se ele fosse capaz de dizer a ela o que estava acontecendo. Sabia que talvez estivesse se deixando surtar a troco de nada. O telefone fixo podia estar fora do gancho. A mãe dela só saberia disso se tentasse fazer uma ligação. O celular dela podia estar desligado, ou carregando, ou as duas coisas. O BlackBerry podia estar no carro, na bolsa ou em algum lugar onde ela não conseguisse escutar a vibração característica. Faith ficou alternando entre olhar para a estrada e para seu BlackBerry enquanto digitava um e-mail para a mãe. Falou as palavras em voz alta enquanto digitava:

— A-caminho. Desculpa-o-atraso. Me-liga.

Ela mandou o e-mail, em seguida jogou o celular no banco junto com os itens caídos da bolsa. Depois de um momento de hesitação, Faith colocou o chiclete na boca. Mascou enquanto dirigia, ignorando os fiapos de tecido da bolsa grudando na língua. Ligou o rádio, depois desligou. O trânsito afunilava conforme ela se aproximava da cidade. As nuvens se afastaram, deixando raios de sol forte passarem. O interior do carro começou a virar um forno.

A dez minutos de casa, os nervos de Faith ainda estavam à flor da pele e ela suava com o calor do carro. Abriu o teto solar para deixar um pouco de ar entrar. Provavelmente era só um caso simples de ansiedade de separação. Ela voltara a trabalhar havia pouco mais de dois meses, mas, toda manhã, quando deixava Emma na casa da avó, ainda sentia algo parecido com um derrame. A visão dela ficava borrada.

O coração chacoalhava dentro do peito. A cabeça zumbia como se um milhão de abelhas tivessem entrado em seus ouvidos. Ela ficava mais irritada do que o normal no trabalho, especialmente com seu parceiro, Will Trent, que ou tinha uma paciência de Jó, ou estava montando um álibi crível para quando ele finalmente surtasse e a estrangulasse.

Faith não conseguia lembrar se tinha sentido essa mesma ansiedade com Jeremy, seu filho, que já estava no primeiro ano da faculdade. Ela tinha dezoito anos quando entrou na Academia de Polícia. Jeremy, na época, estava com três. Ela tinha agarrado a ideia de entrar na força policial como se fosse o último colete salva-vidas do *Titanic*. Graças a uma decisão equivocada com duração de dois minutos, nos últimos assentos de um cinema, além do que previa ser uma vida inteira de um dedo podre para homens, Faith tinha ido direto da puberdade para a maternidade, sem nenhuma das paradas usuais no meio do caminho. Aos dezoito, ela se deleitava com a ideia de ter um salário estável para poder sair da casa dos pais e criar Jeremy como bem entendesse. Ir trabalhar todo dia parecia um passo em direção à independência. Deixá-lo na creche era um preço pequeno a se pagar.

Agora que Faith tinha trinta e quatro anos, com financiamento imobiliário, parcelas do carro e outro bebê para criar sozinha, o que mais queria era voltar para a casa da mãe, para Evelyn poder cuidar de tudo. Queria abrir a porta da geladeira e ver a comida que ela não precisava comprar. Queria ligar o ar-condicionado no verão sem se preocupar com a conta de luz. Queria dormir até meio-dia, depois ver TV o dia todo. Caramba, além disso, ela podia muito bem ressuscitar o pai, que tinha morrido onze anos antes, para ele poder fazer panquecas no café da manhã e falar como ela era linda.

Naquele momento, sem chance de nada daquilo acontecer. Evelyn parecia contente com o papel de babá na aposentadoria, mas Faith não tinha qualquer ilusão de que sua vida fosse ficar mais fácil. Sua própria aposentadoria ainda ia demorar quase vinte anos para chegar. O Mini tinha mais três anos de parcelas e perderia a garantia bem antes disso. Emma esperaria ter comida e roupas pelos próximos dezoito anos, se não mais. E não era igual a quando Jeremy era bebê e Faith podia vesti-lo com uma meia diferente da outra e roupas de segunda mão compradas em vendas de garagem. Ultimamente os bebês precisavam estar combinando. Precisavam de mamadeiras sem bisfenol e papinha de maçã com certificação orgânica feita por simpáticos produtores amish. Como Jeremy tinha entrado no curso de arquitetura da Georgia Tech, Faith teria que comprar livros e lavar as roupas dele por mais seis anos. E, mais preocupante, o filho tinha achado uma namorada séria. Uma namorada mais velha com um quadril todo curvilíneo e o relógio biológico já apitando. Faith podia ser avó antes dos trinta e cinco.

Um calor indesejado percorreu seu corpo enquanto ela tentava tirar esse último pensamento da cabeça. Dirigindo, ela conferiu o conteúdo da bolsa de novo. O chiclete não tinha adiantado nada. Sua barriga continuava roncando. Ela estendeu o braço e tateou dentro do porta-luvas. Nada. Podia parar em algum restaurante de fast-food e pelo menos comprar uma Coca-Cola, mas estava de uniforme — calça de brim cáqui e camiseta azul com as letras GBI estampadas em amarelo vivo nas costas. Aquela não era a melhor parte da cidade para se estar se você fosse da polícia. As pessoas tendiam a sair correndo, e aí você precisava persegui-las, o que não condizia muito com chegar em casa num horário decente. Além do mais, algo lhe dizia — urgia — para ir ver a mãe.

Faith pegou o celular e discou de novo os números de Evelyn. Fixo, celular, até o BlackBerry, que ela só usava para e-mail. Todos os três deram a mesma resposta negativa. Faith sentiu o estômago se embrulhar enquanto os piores cenários passavam por sua cabeça. Como policial de patrulha, ela já fora chamada para várias ocorrências em que uma criança chorando havia alertado os vizinhos de um problema sério. Mães que tinham escorregado na banheira. Pais que haviam acidentalmente se machucado ou tido uma parada cardíaca. Os bebês ficavam lá largados, aos prantos e impotentes, até alguém descobrir que tinha algo errado. Nada partia mais o coração do que um bebê chorando que ninguém conseguia acalmar.

Faith se repreendeu por pensar nessas imagens horríveis. Ela sempre foi ótima em imaginar o pior cenário, mesmo antes de virar policial. Evelyn provavelmente estava ótima. O horário da soneca de Emma era à uma e meia. A mãe de Faith provavelmente tinha desligado o telefone para que o toque não acordasse a bebê. Talvez tivesse encontrado uma vizinha ao sair para olhar a caixa de correio ou ido até a casa ao lado para ajudar a idosa Sra. Levy a tirar o lixo.

Mesmo assim, as mãos de Faith escorregaram no volante enquanto ela virava no Boulevard. Ela estava suando apesar do clima ameno de março. Não podia ser só por causa da bebê, nem da mãe, nem da namorada absurdamente fértil de Jeremy. Faith tinha sido diagnosticada com diabetes havia menos de um ano. Media a glicemia religiosamente, comia as coisas certas, garantia que sempre tivesse lanchinhos à mão. Mas naquele dia, não. Isso provavelmente explicava por que tinha dado uma pirada. Ela só precisava comer alguma coisa. De preferência com a mãe e a filha à vista.

Faith conferiu de novo o porta-luvas para ter certeza de que estava mesmo vazio. Tinha uma vaga lembrança de ter dado a última barrinha energética para Will no dia anterior, enquanto esperavam em frente ao tribunal. Era isso ou vê-lo engolir um pãozinho doce da máquina de comida. Ele tinha reclamado do gosto, mas, mesmo assim, comeu a barrinha toda. E, agora, ela estava pagando por isso.

Ela ultrapassou um sinal amarelo, acelerando o máximo que ousava numa via parcialmente residencial. A estrada se estreitava na Ponce de Leon. Faith passou por uma fileira de restaurantes de fast-food e um hortifruti orgânico. Fez a marcação do velocímetro subir, acelerando nas curvas e mais curvas que contornavam o Piedmont Park. O flash de uma câmera de trânsito rebateu em seu retrovisor quando ela passou por mais um sinal amarelo. Ela pisou no freio por causa de um pedestre desorientado. Mais dois supermercados passaram num borrão, e aí veio o último sinal que, graças a Deus, estava verde.

Evelyn ainda morava na mesma casa em que Faith e o irmão mais velho tinham sido criados. A casa térrea em estilo rancho ficava numa região de Atlanta chamada Sherwood Forest, aninhada entre Ansley Park, um dos bairros mais ricos da cidade, e a rodovia interestadual 85, que oferecia o ruído constante de trânsito, dependendo de para onde o vento soprava. O vento estava soprando normal naquele dia e, quando Faith abriu a janela para deixar entrar mais ar fresco, ouviu o zumbido familiar que tinha marcado quase todos os dias de sua infância.

Tendo sido a vida inteira residente de Sherwood Forest, Faith tinha um ódio profundo dos homens que haviam planejado o bairro. A subdivisão havia sido desenvolvida depois da Segunda Guerra Mundial, as casas de tijolo em estilo rancho, ocupadas por soldados que retornavam e aproveitavam os empréstimos da Associação de Veteranos. Os planejadores das ruas tinham adotado descaradamente o tema de Robin Hood. Depois de virar à esquerda na Lionel, Faith cruzou a Frei Tuck, dobrou à direita na Robin Hood, passou pela bifurcação da Donzela Marian e deu uma olhada na entrada de sua própria casa na esquina da Doncaster com a Barnesdale antes de finalmente parar na casa da mãe, na rua João Pequeno.

O Chevrolet Malibu bege de Evelyn estava parado de ré na garagem. Isso, pelo menos, era normal. Faith nunca vira a mãe parar de frente numa vaga. Hábitos de seu tempo de policial. Você sempre tinha que deixar o carro pronto para sair na hora que recebesse um chamado.

Faith não tinha tempo de refletir sobre as rotinas da mãe. Ela subiu a pista de acesso à garagem e estacionou o Mini de frente para o Malibu. Quando se levantou, suas pernas doíam. Todos os músculos de seu corpo tinham ficado sob tensão nos últimos vinte minutos. Ela ouvia uma música alta vindo da casa. Heavy metal, não os Beatles de sempre da mãe. Faith colocou a mão no capô do Malibu enquanto ia para a porta da cozinha. O motor estava frio. Talvez Evelyn estivesse no banho enquanto Faith tentava ligar. Talvez não tenha olhado o e-mail nem o celular. Talvez tivesse se cortado. Tinha uma marca de mão ensanguentada na porta.

Faith olhou mais uma vez.

A marca de sangue era de uma mão esquerda. Estava uns quarenta e cinco centímetros acima da maçaneta. A porta tinha sido fechada, mas não tinha travado. Um feixe de luz solar passava pelo batente, provavelmente vindo da janela acima da pia da cozinha.

Faith ainda não conseguia processar o que estava vendo. Ela levantou a própria mão para comparar com a marca, uma criança pressionando os dedos junto aos da mãe. A mão de Evelyn era menor. Dedos mais esguios. A ponta de seu dedo anelar não havia tocado a porta. Havia um coágulo de sangue onde ela deveria estar.

15

De repente, a música parou no meio da batida. No silêncio, Faith ouviu um gorgolejar conhecido, uma preparação que anunciava a chegada de um berro. O som ecoou na garagem, de modo que, por um momento, Faith achou que estivesse vindo da sua própria boca. Aí veio de novo e ela se virou, sabendo que era Emma.

Quase todas as outras casas em Sherwood Forest tinham sido demolidas ou reformadas, mas a dos Mitchell era basicamente a mesma de quando havia sido construída. A planta era simples: três quartos, uma sala de estar, uma sala de jantar e uma cozinha com uma porta que dava para a garagem aberta. Bill Mitchell, pai de Faith, tinha construído um quarto de ferramentas do lado oposto da garagem. Era uma construção robusta — o pai dela nunca fazia nada pela metade — com uma porta de metal que trancava com ferrolho e um vidro de segurança na única janela. Faith tinha dez anos quando percebeu que a construção era reforçada demais para algo tão simples quanto armazenar ferramentas. Com a ternura que só um irmão mais velho consegue ter, Zeke tinha explicado o verdadeiro propósito daquele quarto:

— É onde a mamãe guarda a arma dela, estúpida.

Faith passou correndo pelo carro e tentou abrir a porta do quarto de ferramentas. Estava trancada. Ela olhou pela janela. Os arames de metal no vidro de segurança formavam uma teia de aranha em frente a seus olhos. Ela via a mesa de jardinagem e sacos de terra empilhados embaixo de forma organizada. As ferramentas estavam penduradas nos ganchos corretos. O equipamento para cuidar do gramado estava guardado direitinho no seu lugar. Um cofre de metal preto com cadeado de senha estava pregado no chão embaixo da mesa. A porta estava aberta. O revólver Smith and Wesson de cabo de cerejeira não estava ali dentro. Nem o pacote de munição que costumava ficar ao lado.

Ouviu o gorgolejar de novo, desta vez mais alto. Uma pilha de cobertores no chão se movia para cima e para baixo, pulsando como as batidas de um coração. Evelyn os usava para cobrir as plantas durante geadas inesperadas. Em geral, ficavam dobrados na prateleira de cima, mas, agora, estavam embolados no canto ao lado do cofre. Faith viu um tufo cor-de-rosa saindo por trás dos cobertores cinza, depois a curva de um encosto de cabeça de plástico que só podia ser a cadeirinha de Emma. O cobertor se mexeu de novo. Um pezinho minúsculo chutou; uma meia amarela de algodão macio com acabamento de renda branca no tornozelo. Em seguida, um punho pequeno e rosado deu um soquinho. Ela viu, então, o rosto de Emma.

Emma sorriu para Faith, o lábio superior formando quase um triângulo. Ela gorgolejou de novo, desta vez de alegria.

— Ah, meu Deus.

Faith puxou inutilmente a porta trancada. Suas mãos tremiam enquanto ela tateava o topo do batente, tentando achar a chave. Caiu uma chuva de poeira. A ponta afiada de uma farpa entrou no dedo dela. Faith olhou de novo pela janela. Emma juntou as palmas das mãos, confortada pela visão da mãe, apesar de Faith estar o mais perto de um ataque de pânico que já estivera na vida. Aquele quarto era quente. Estava calor demais do lado de fora. Emma podia superaquecer. Podia desidratar. Podia morrer.

Apavorada, Faith ficou de quatro, achando que a chave tinha caído, possivelmente deslizado por baixo da porta. Ela viu que a parte de baixo da cadeirinha de Emma estava amassada onde fora enfiada entre o cofre e a parede. Escondida embaixo dos cobertores. Bloqueada pelo cofre.

Protegida pelo cofre.

Faith parou. Seus pulmões travaram no meio da respiração. Seu maxilar estava tenso como se tivesse sido fechado com um arame. Devagar, ela se sentou. Havia gotas de sangue no chão de concreto à sua frente. Seus olhos seguiram o rastro que ia até a porta da cozinha. Até a marca de mão ensanguentada.

Emma estava trancada no quarto de ferramentas. A arma de Evelyn tinha sumido. Havia um rastro de sangue indo até a casa.

Faith se levantou, de frente para a porta destrancada da cozinha. O único som era sua própria respiração difícil.

Quem tinha desligado a música?

Faith correu de volta ao carro. Pegou a Glock de baixo do banco do motorista. Conferiu o pente e prendeu o coldre na lateral do corpo. Seu celular continuava no banco da frente. Faith o pegou antes de abrir o porta-malas. Tinha sido investigadora do esquadrão de homicídios de Atlanta antes de virar agente especial do estado. Seus dedos digitaram a linha de emergência não listada que ela conhecia de cor. Ela não deu tempo para a atendente falar. Recitou seu antigo número de distintivo, sua unidade e o endereço da mãe.

Faith fez uma pausa antes de dizer:

— Código trinta. — As palavras quase a fizeram engasgar. Código trinta. Ela nunca tinha usado essa frase na vida. Significava que um policial precisava de assistência urgente. Significava que um colega estava correndo sério perigo, possivelmente morto. — Minha filha está trancada no quarto de ferramentas do lado de fora da casa. Tem sangue no concreto e uma marca de mão ensanguentada na porta da cozinha. Acho que minha mãe está dentro da casa. Ouvi uma música, mas desligaram. Ela é policial aposentada. Acho que está... — Faith sentiu um bolo na garganta. — Socorro. Por favor. Preciso de ajuda.

— Código trinta entendido — respondeu a atendente, com um tom incisivo e tenso. — Fique do lado de fora e espere reforços. Não entre na casa, repito, não entre na casa.

— Entendido.

Faith desligou e jogou o celular no banco de trás. Girou a chave na fechadura que mantinha sua espingarda presa ao porta-malas do carro.

A GBI dava pelo menos duas armas para cada policial. A Glock modelo 23 era uma pistola semiautomática de calibre .40 que continha treze balas no pente e uma na câmara. A Remington 870 tinha quatro cargas de chumbo grosso no tubo. A espingarda de Faith tinha seis cargas extras na sela lateral que ficava presa na frente da coronha. Cada carga continha oito chumbos. Cada chumbo tinha mais ou menos o tamanho de uma bala calibre .38.

Cada puxada de gatilho da Glock disparava uma bala. Cada puxada da Remington disparava oito.

A política da agência determinava que todos os agentes deviam manter uma munição na câmara da Glock, dando-lhes catorze no total. Não tinha a trava de segurança externa convencional na arma.

Agentes tinham autorização legal para usar força letal se achassem que a própria vida ou a vida de outra pessoa estivesse em risco. Você só puxava o gatilho se quisesse atirar e só atirava com a intenção de matar.

A espingarda era outra história com o mesmo fim. A trava de segurança ficava atrás do gatilho, um sistema de ferrolhos duplos que precisava de um músculo ágil para ser movido. Não mantinha munição na câmara. Você queria que todo mundo ouvisse aquela munição encaixando, sendo preparada para o tiro. Faith já tinha visto marmanjos caírem de joelhos com aquele som.

Ela olhou de novo para a casa ao soltar a trava de segurança. A cortina da janela da frente tremulou. Uma sombra passou correndo pelo corredor. Faith bombeou a espingarda com uma mão só enquanto caminhava na direção da garagem. A ação produziu um som satisfatório de *tá-tum* que ecoou pelo concreto. Em um único movimento fluido, apoiou a coronha no ombro e alinhou o cano à frente. Ela chutou a porta, segurando firme a arma enquanto gritava:

— Polícia!

A palavra retumbou pela casa como um trovão. Veio de um lugar profundo e sombrio no âmago de Faith que ela ignorava a maior parte do tempo por medo de ligar algo que nunca pudesse ser desligado.

— Saia com as mãos para cima!

Ninguém saiu. Ela ouviu um barulho vindo de algum lugar nos fundos da casa. Sua visão ficou mais aguçada quando ela entrou na cozinha. Sangue na bancada. Uma faca de pão. Mais sangue no piso. Gavetas e armários abertos. O telefone na parede estava pendurado como uma corda de forca. O BlackBerry e o celular de Evelyn estavam estilhaçados no chão. Faith manteve a espingarda à sua frente, o dedo descansando bem ao lado do gatilho para ela não cometer nenhum erro.

Ela devia estar pensando na mãe ou em Emma, mas só passavam as seguintes palavras pela sua cabeça: *pessoas e portas*. Ao verificar uma casa, essas eram as maiores ameaças à sua segurança. Você tinha que saber onde estavam as pessoas — não importava se eram do bem ou não — e precisava saber o que poderia atacar você em cada porta.

Faith se virou para o lado, apontando a espingarda para a área de serviço. Viu um homem deitado de bruços com a cara no chão. Cabelo preto. A pele parecia uma cera amarela. Estava abraçando o próprio corpo, como uma criança quando brinca de girar. Sem arma na mão ou perto dele. A parte de trás da cabeça era uma maçaroca ensanguentada. Havia massa encefálica salpicada na máquina de lavar. Ela viu o buraco feito pela bala na parede ao sair do crânio dele.

Faith se virou de volta para a cozinha. Havia uma passagem para a sala de jantar. Ela se agachou e girou.

Vazia.

A planta da casa lhe veio à mente como um diagrama. Sala de estar à esquerda. Hall de entrada grande e aberto à direita. Corredor à frente. Banheiro no fim. Dois quartos à direita. Um quarto à esquerda — o da mãe dela. Dentro, havia um banheiro minúsculo e uma porta levando ao pátio dos fundos. A porta do quarto de Evelyn era a única que estava fechada no corredor.

Faith começou a ir na direção da porta fechada, mas parou.

Pessoas e portas.

Em sua mente, viu as palavras gravadas em pedra: *Não prossiga em direção à sua ameaça até ter certeza de que não há perigo atrás.*

Faith se abaixou ao virar à esquerda e entrar na sala de estar. Examinou as paredes, inspecionou a porta deslizante de vidro que levava ao quintal dos fundos. O vidro estava estilhaçado. Uma brisa balançava as cortinas. O cômodo tinha sido saqueado. Alguém estava procurando alguma coisa. Gavetas estavam quebradas. Almofadas, estripadas. De sua posição estratégica, Faith conseguia ver, do outro lado do sofá, que os pés da poltrona *bergère* estavam sem os protetores. Ela ficou girando a cabeça para um lado e para o outro, entre a sala e o corredor, até ter certeza de que podia seguir.

A primeira porta era seu antigo quarto. Alguém tinha revistado lá também. As gavetas da velha escrivaninha de Faith estavam muito abertas, parecendo línguas de fora. Seu colchão estava rasgado ao meio. O berço de Emma, destroçado. O cobertor dela havia sido partido em dois. O móbile que ficara pendurado acima da cabeça dela todos os meses de sua vida tinha sido moído no carpete como um monte de terra. Faith engoliu a raiva fervente que se acendeu dentro dela. Forçou-se a continuar.

Rapidamente, conferiu os armários e debaixo da cama. Fez o mesmo no quarto de Zeke, que tinha sido transformado no escritório de sua mãe. Havia papéis espalhados pelo chão. As gavetas da escrivaninha tinham sido jogadas contra a parede. Ela verificou o banheiro. A cortina do chuveiro estava recolhida. O armário de roupas de cama e banho, escancarado. Toalhas e lençóis caídos no chão.

Faith estava parada à esquerda da porta do quarto da mãe quando ouviu a primeira sirene. Era distante, mas clara. Ela devia esperar o reforço.

Faith chutou a porta e se virou, abaixando-se. Seu dedo foi para o gatilho. Havia dois homens ao pé da cama. Um estava ajoelhado. Ele era hispânico e vestia só uma calça jeans. A pele de seu peito tinha lacerações, como se ele tivesse sido chicoteado com arame farpado. O suor brilhava em cada parte de seu corpo. Hematomas vermelhos e roxos pontuavam suas costelas. Ele tinha tatuagens em ambos os braços e no torso, a maior delas no peito: uma estrela do Texas verde e vermelha com uma cascavel enrolada. Era membro da Los Texicanos, uma facção criminosa mexicana que controlava o tráfico de drogas em Atlanta havia vinte anos.

O segundo homem era asiático. Sem tatuagens. Camisa havaiana de um vermelho forte e calça de sarja marrom. Ele estava de pé com o Texicano à sua frente, segurando uma arma na cabeça do homem. Uma Smith and Wesson de cinco tiros com cabo de cerejeira. O revólver da mãe dela.

Faith manteve a espingarda apontada para o peito do asiático. O metal frio e duro parecia uma extensão de seu próprio corpo. A adrenalina fazia o coração dela pulsar num frenesi. Cada músculo de seu corpo queria puxar o gatilho.

Ela articulou bem as palavras, com dureza:

— Cadê minha mãe?

Ele falou com um sotaque fanhoso do Sul.

— Se atirar em mim, vai pegar nele.

Ele tinha razão. Faith estava parada no corredor, a menos de dois metros. Os homens estavam próximos demais um do outro. Mesmo que desse um tiro na cabeça, corria o risco de um projétil se desviar e atingir — e possivelmente matar — o refém. Mesmo assim, ela manteve o dedo no gatilho, a espingarda estável.

— Me diga onde ela está.

Ele pressionou o cano ainda mais na cabeça do homem.

— Solte a arma.

As sirenes estavam ficando mais altas. Estavam vindo da Zona 5, da região de Peachtree, ali no mesmo bairro. Faith falou:

— Está ouvindo? — Ela mapeou o caminho deles por Nottingham, calculando que as viaturas chegariam em menos de um minuto. — Diga onde está a minha mãe, senão juro por Deus que vou matar você antes de eles chegarem na porta.

Ele sorriu outra vez, apertando a arma com mais força.

— Você sabe por que estamos aqui. É só entregar que a gente solta ela.

Faith não sabia de que diabos ele estava falando. A mãe dela era uma viúva de sessenta e três anos. A coisa mais valiosa da casa era o terreno sob os pés deles.

Ele entendeu, pelo silêncio, que ela estava hesitante.

— Você quer mesmo perder a mamãe por causa do *chico* aqui?

Faith fingiu entender.

— É simples assim? Você vai fazer a troca?

Ele deu de ombros.

— É o único jeito de nós dois sairmos daqui.

— Conversa fiada.

— Não. É uma troca justa. — As sirenes ficaram mais altas. Pneus chiaram na rua. — Anda, vaca. Tique-taque. Negócio fechado ou não?

Ele estava mentindo. Já tinha matado uma pessoa. Estava ameaçando outra. Assim que descobrisse que Faith estava blefando, a única coisa que ia dar a ela era uma bala no peito.

— Fechado — concordou ela, usando a mão esquerda para jogar a espingarda à sua frente.

O instrutor de armas de fogo no estande de tiro usava um cronômetro que contava cada décimo de segundo, e era por isso que Faith sabia que levava exatamente oito décimos de segundo para tirar a

Glock do coldre lateral com a mão direita. Enquanto o asiático estava distraído pela espingarda caindo aos pés dele, ela fez exatamente isso, puxando a Glock, enganchando o dedo no gatilho e atirando na cabeça do homem.

Os braços dele se levantaram. A arma caiu. Ele estava morto antes de bater no chão.

A porta da frente se abriu soltando farpas. Faith virou na direção do hall assim que uma equipe de operações especiais com equipamento tático completo encheu a casa. E então ela se virou de volta para o quarto e percebeu que o mexicano tinha desaparecido.

A porta do pátio estava aberta. Faith saiu correndo enquanto o mexicano pulava o alambrado. A Smith and Wesson estava na mão dele. As netas da Sra. Johnson estavam brincando no quintal e gritaram quando viram o homem armado indo em sua direção. Ele estava a seis metros. Quatro. Levantou a arma na direção das garotas e disparou um tiro acima da cabeça delas. Reboco de parede voou no chão. Elas estavam assustadas demais para continuar gritando, se mexer, se salvar. Faith parou na cerca, alinhou sua Glock e apertou o gatilho.

O homem deu um solavanco como se um fio tivesse sido puxado em seu peito. Ele ficou de pé por pelo menos um segundo, aí seus joelhos cederam e ele caiu de costas no chão. Faith pulou a cerca e correu até lá. Enfiou o salto alto no pulso dele até a mão do homem soltar a arma da mãe dela. As garotas voltaram a gritar. A Sra. Johnson saiu na varanda e as pegou como se fossem filhotinhos de pato. Olhou para Faith enquanto fechava a porta e seu olhar era de choque, horrorizado. Ela costumava correr atrás de Zeke e Faith com a mangueira do jardim quando eram pequenos. A mulher se sentia segura ali.

Faith colocou a Glock no coldre e o revólver de Evelyn na parte de trás da calça. Agarrou o mexicano pelo ombro.

— Cadê minha mãe? — exigiu saber. — O que fizeram com ela?

Ele abriu a boca, o sangue escorrendo por baixo das coroas prateadas dos dentes. Estava sorrindo. O filho da puta estava sorrindo.

— Cadê ela? — Faith pressionou a mão no peito ferido dele, sentindo suas costelas quebradas se moverem sob seus dedos. Ele gritou

23

de dor e ela apertou mais forte, esmagando um osso contra o outro.

— Cadê ela?

— Agente! — Um policial jovem se apoiou com uma das mãos e pulou a cerca. Ele chegou perto e sacou a arma, apontando na direção do chão. — Afaste-se do homem detido.

Faith se aproximou ainda mais do mexicano. Sentia o calor dele irradiando da pele.

— Me diga onde ela está.

Ele tentou engolir. Não estava mais sentindo a dor. Suas pupilas estavam do tamanho de moedas de dez centavos. Suas pálpebras se agitaram. O canto de seu lábio tremeu.

— Me diga onde ela está. — A voz dela ficava mais desesperada a cada palavra. — Ah, meu Deus, só, por favor, me diga onde ela está!

A respiração dele tinha um som pegajoso, como se os pulmões estivessem atados por fita adesiva. Ele mexeu os lábios e sussurrou algo que ela não conseguiu distinguir.

— Quê? — Faith colocou o ouvido tão perto da boca dele que sentia o cuspe saindo. — Me diga — sussurrou. — Por favor, me diga.

— *Almeja.*

— Quê? — repetiu Faith. — O que você falou?

Ele abriu a boca. Em vez de palavras, saiu uma poça de sangue.

— O que você falou? — gritou ela. — Me diga o que você falou!

— Agente! — o policial gritou outra vez.

— Não! — Ela apertou as palmas no peito do mexicano, tentando forçar o coração dele a voltar a bater. Faith fechou a mão em punho e golpeou o mais forte que conseguia, surrando o homem, tentando fazê-lo ressuscitar à força. — Me diga! — berrou. — Me diga logo!

— Agente!

Ela sentiu as mãos em torno de sua cintura. O policial praticamente a levantou no ar.

— Me solte!

Faith enfiou o cotovelo para trás com tanta força que ele a soltou como se fosse uma pedra. Ela foi tropeçando pela grama, engatinhando até a testemunha. O refém. O assassino. A única pessoa que sobrava capaz de dizer o que raios tinha acontecido com a mãe dela.

Ela colocou as mãos no rosto do mexicano e olhou para seus olhos sem vida.

— Por favor, me diga — implorou, embora soubesse que tinha chegado tarde demais. — Por favor.

— Faith? — O investigador Leo Donnelly, seu ex-parceiro na polícia de Atlanta, estava parado do outro lado da cerca, sem fôlego. Ele estava com as duas mãos no topo do alambrado. O vento tinha aberto o paletó de seu terno marrom barato. — Emma está bem. O chaveiro está chegando. — As palavras dele saíam grossas e lentas, como melaço sendo jogado numa peneira. — Venha, garota. Emma precisa da mãe.

Faith olhou atrás dele. Policiais por todo lado. Uniformes azul-escuros virando um borrão enquanto eles revistavam a casa, vasculhavam o quintal. Pelas janelas, ela acompanhou o progresso da equipe tática de cômodo em cômodo, armas apontadas, vozes gritando "Limpo" quando não encontravam nada. O som de várias sirenes tomava o ambiente. Viaturas policiais. Ambulâncias. Um caminhão de bombeiro.

O chamado tinha sido enviado. Código trinta. Policial precisa de assistência urgente. Três homens mortos baleados. A bebê dela, trancada num quarto de ferramentas. A mãe, desaparecida.

Faith se sentou sobre os calcanhares, colocou a cabeça nas mãos trêmulas e tentou não chorar.

2

— Aí, ele me disse que estava trocando o óleo do carro e estava quente na garagem, então ele tirou a calça...

— Aham — Sara Linton conseguiu dizer, tentando fingir interesse enquanto mal comia a salada.

— E eu falei: "Olha, cara, eu sou médico. Não estou aqui para julgar ninguém. Pode ser sincero sobre..."

Sara observou a boca de Dale Dugan se mexer, a voz dele felizmente se mesclando com o ruído da pizzaria na hora do almoço. Música suave tocando. Gente rindo. Pratos deslizando pela cozinha. A história dele não era muito instigante, nem nova. Sara era pediatra-chefe do pronto-socorro do Grady Hospital, em Atlanta. Antes disso, tivera seu próprio consultório por doze anos, trabalhando esse tempo todo como legista do condado em uma cidade universitária pequena, mas movimentada. Não havia utensílio, ferramenta, produto de uso doméstico ou estatueta de vidro que ela não tivesse visto enfiado dentro de um corpo humano em algum momento.

Dale ainda não tinha terminado:

— Aí veio a enfermeira com a radiografia.

— Ih — disse ela, tentando injetar um pouco de curiosidade no tom.

Dale sorriu para ela. Tinha um pouco de queijo enfiado entre os incisivos central e lateral dele. Sara tentou não julgar. Dale Dugan era um homem bacana. Não era bonito, mas era passável, com o tipo de feição que muitas mulheres acham atraentes depois que ficam sabendo que ele se formou em medicina. Sara não era tão fácil assim de impressionar. E estava morta de fome, porque a amiga que tinha marcado aquele encontro às cegas ridículo para ela a aconselhou a pedir uma salada, não uma pizza, porque causaria uma impressão melhor.

— Aí, quando eu levanto a radiografia, o que eu vejo...

Chave soquete, pensou ela logo antes de ele finalmente chegar à conclusão da história.

— Uma chave soquete! Dá para acreditar?

— Não! — Ela forçou uma risada que parecia mais o barulho de um brinquedo de dar corda.

— E mesmo assim ele continuou dizendo que tinha escorregado.

Ela fez *tsc* com a língua.

— Que queda, hein.

— Né?

Ele sorriu de novo para ela antes de dar uma bela mordida na pizza.

Sara mastigou um pouco da alface. O relógio digital acima da cabeça de Dale mostrava 2:12 e alguns segundos. Os números em LED vermelho eram um lembrete doloroso de que ela podia estar em casa vendo basquete e dobrando a montanha de roupa no sofá. Sara tinha criado um jogo de não olhar o relógio, vendo por quanto tempo conseguia se conter antes de seu autocontrole desmoronar e ela voltar a olhar os segundos passarem borrados. Três minutos e vinte e dois segundos era seu recorde. Ela deu mais uma garfada na salada, jurando vencê-la.

— Então — disse Dale. — Você estudou na Emory.

Ela fez que sim.

— E você na Duke?

Previsivelmente, ele começou uma longa descrição de suas conquistas acadêmicas, incluindo artigos publicados em periódicos e o fato de ter sido o principal palestrante em vários congressos. De novo, Sara fingiu prestar atenção, se obrigando a não olhar o relógio, mastigando alface na velocidade de uma vaca no pasto para Dale não se sentir obrigado a fazer uma pergunta.

Não era o primeiro encontro às cegas de Sara, nem, infelizmente, o menos tedioso. O problema naquele dia tinha começado nos primeiros seis minutos, que Sara tinha marcado no relógio. Eles haviam passado rápido demais pelas preliminares antes de o pedido ser anunciado.

27

Dale era divorciado, sem filhos, se dava bem com a ex-mulher e jogava basquete amador no hospital no tempo livre. Sara era de uma cidade pequena no sul da Geórgia. Tinha dois galgos e um gato que tinha escolhido morar com os pais dela. O marido tinha sido assassinado quatro anos e meio antes.

Em geral, essa última parte deixava a pessoa sem saber o que falar, mas Dale tinha passado direto, como se fosse um detalhe. De início, Sara lhe dera pontos por não perguntar mais sobre o assunto, depois decidiu que ele era egocêntrico demais para isso, e depois se repreendeu por ser tão dura com o cara.

— O que seu marido fazia?

Ele a pegou com a boca cheia de alface. Ela mastigou, engoliu e então disse:

— Ele era policial. Chefe da polícia do condado.

— Que diferente. — A expressão dela deve ter sido esquisita, porque ele completou: — Quero dizer, porque ele não é médico. Não era médico. Nem colarinho-branco, acho.

— Colarinho-branco? — Ela escutou o tom acusador na própria voz, mas não conseguiu parar. — Meu pai é encanador. Eu e minha irmã trabalhamos com ele por...

— Ei, ei. — Ele levantou as mãos, rendendo-se. — Não foi minha intenção. Quero dizer, é nobre trabalhar com as mãos, né?

Sara não sabia que tipo de medicina o Dr. Dale praticava, mas ela mesma tendia a usar as mãos todos os dias.

Sem perceber, a voz dele assumiu um tom solene.

— Tenho muito respeito por policiais. E combatentes. Soldados, quero dizer. — Nervoso, ele limpou a boca com o guardanapo. — É um trabalho perigoso. Foi assim que ele morreu?

Ela fez que sim, olhando o relógio. Três minutos e dezenove segundos. Tinha perdido o recorde por pouco.

Ele tirou o celular do bolso e olhou para a tela.

— Desculpe. Estou de plantão. Queria confirmar se tem sinal aqui.

Pelo menos ele não fingiu que o telefone estava tocando no mudo, embora Sara tivesse certeza de que isso iria acontecer.

— Me desculpe por estar tão na defensiva. É difícil falar desse assunto.

— Lamento muito pela sua perda. — O tom dele tinha uma cadência ensaiada que Sara reconhecia do pronto-socorro. — Deve ter sido difícil.

Ela mordeu a ponta da língua. Sara não conseguia pensar numa forma educada de responder e, quando pensou em mudar de assunto e falar do clima, tinha passado tanto tempo que a conversa parecia ainda mais desconfortável. Finalmente, ela disse:

— Bom, enfim. Que tal a gente...

— Licença — interrompeu ele. — Preciso ir ao banheiro.

Ele se levantou tão rápido que a cadeira quase caiu. Sara o viu partir quase correndo para os fundos. Talvez fosse a imaginação dela, mas Sara achou tê-lo visto hesitar em frente à saída de emergência.

— Idiota.

Ela soltou o garfo no prato de salada.

Sara olhou de novo o relógio. Eram duas e quinze. Se um dia Dale voltasse do banheiro, ela poderia acabar com aquilo às duas e meia. Sara tinha vindo a pé de casa, então não teria aquele silêncio prolongado e desconfortável enquanto Dale a levava de volta. A conta já tinha sido paga logo depois de fazerem o pedido no caixa. Ela levaria quinze minutos para chegar em casa, bem a tempo de trocar o vestido por uma calça de moletom antes de o jogo começar. Sara sentiu a barriga roncando. Talvez pudesse fingir que tinha ido embora e depois dar meia-volta para pedir uma pizza.

Mais um minuto se passou no relógio. Sara olhou o estacionamento. O carro de Dale continuava lá, supondo que fosse o Lexus verde com a placa que dizia DRDALE. Ela não sabia se estava decepcionada ou aliviada.

Mais trinta segundos se passaram no relógio. O corredor que levava aos banheiros continuou vazio por outros vinte e três. Uma senhora de idade em um andador veio andando centímetro por centímetro. Não havia ninguém atrás dela.

Sara apoiou a cabeça com a mão. Dale não era um cara ruim. Ele era estável, relativamente saudável, tinha um bom emprego, a maior

29

parte do cabelo e, exceto pelo queijo no meio dos dentes, aparentava ter boa higiene. E, mesmo assim, tudo isso não era suficiente. Sara estava começando a achar que ela era o problema. Estava se tornando o Sr. Darcy de Atlanta. Depois que alguém caía no conceito dela, não voltava mais. Era mais fácil desempacar um burro que mudar a opinião de Sara.

Ela devia se esforçar mais nesse sentido. Não tinha mais vinte e cinco anos, e os quarenta estavam bufando pesado no seu cangote. Com um metro e oitenta, o número de candidatos já era limitado. Seu cabelo castanho-avermelhado e a pele clara não eram do gosto de todos. Ela trabalhava muito. Não conseguia cozinhar nem se a própria vida dependesse disso. Aparentemente, tinha perdido a capacidade de jogar conversa fora, e a mera menção a seu marido morto era capaz de fazê-la ter um chilique.

Talvez seus parâmetros fossem altos demais. O casamento dela não tinha sido perfeito, mas era bom para caramba. Ela amara o marido mais do que a própria vida. Perdê-lo quase a tinha matado. Mas já fazia quase cinco anos que Jeffrey havia falecido e, sendo sincera, Sara se sentia solitária. Sentia saudade da companhia de um homem. Sentia saudade da forma como a cabeça deles funcionava e as coisas surpreendentemente fofas que eles eram capazes de dizer. Sentia saudade da sensação áspera da pele deles. Sentia falta das outras coisas também. Infelizmente, a última vez que um homem tinha feito seus olhos revirarem era porque ela estava lutando contra o tédio, não se contorcendo de êxtase.

Sara precisava enfrentar o fato de que era extremamente, terrivelmente, abissalmente ruim nisso de começar relacionamentos. Não tinha tido muito tempo para praticar. Desde a puberdade, Sara fora monogâmica em série. O primeiro namorado tinha sido um *crush* do ensino médio e eles haviam ficado juntos até a faculdade, depois ela namorara um colega até terminar o curso de medicina; em seguida, conhecera Jeffrey e nunca mais teve interesse em qualquer outro homem. Exceto por uma transa desastrosa três anos antes, não houve ninguém desde então. Ela só conseguia pensar em um homem que tinha chegado mesmo que remotamente perto de acender uma faísca, mas ele era casado. Pior, era um policial casado.

Ainda pior, estava parado no caixa a menos de três metros dela.

Will Trent estava usando shorts de corrida preto e camisa preta de manga comprida, dando uma bela visão de seus ombros largos. O cabelo cor de areia estava mais comprido do que alguns meses atrás, quando Sara o vira pela última vez. Na época, ele estava trabalhando num caso que envolvia uma das antigas pacientes dela na clínica pediátrica de sua cidade natal. Sara tinha se metido tanto no assunto que Will não tivera escolha a não ser permitir que ela ajudasse na investigação. Eles tinham compartilhado algo que parecia um flerte e aí, quando o caso foi encerrado, ele voltou para casa e para a esposa.

Will era extremamente observador. Devia ter notado Sara sentada à mesa quando entrou. Ainda assim, ficou de costas para ela, olhando um anúncio no quadro de avisos na parede. Ela não precisava do relógio para contar os segundos enquanto esperava que ele a notasse.

Ele voltou a atenção a outro anúncio.

Sara puxou a presilha que segurava o cabelo e deixou os cachos caírem ombro abaixo. Levantou-se e foi até ele.

Ela sabia algumas coisas sobre Will Trent. Ele era alto, tinha pelo menos um e noventa, um corpo esguio de corredor e as pernas mais lindas que ela já vira num homem. A mãe havia sido morta quando ele tinha menos de um ano. Ele tinha crescido num orfanato e não foi adotado. Era agente especial da GBI. Era um dos homens mais inteligentes que ela já conhecera e era tão disléxico que, pelo que ela notava, tinha o nível de leitura de um aluno de segunda série.

Ela parou ombro a ombro com ele, olhando o anúncio que tinha chamado a atenção de Will.

— Parece interessante.

Ele fez uma péssima atuação de surpresa ao vê-la.

— Dra. Linton. Eu estava só... — Ele rasgou uma das tirinhas de informação do anúncio. — Andei pensando em comprar uma moto.

Ela olhou de relance o anúncio, que tinha um desenho detalhado de uma Harley Davidson embaixo de um cabeçalho convidando novos membros.

— Não acho que o grupo Sapatonas Motorizadas seja para você.

Ele deu um sorriso torto. Tinha passado a vida inteira tentando esconder a deficiência e, embora Sara tivesse descoberto, ele ainda detestava admitir que tinha um problema.

— É um ótimo jeito de conhecer mulheres.

— Você está querendo conhecer mulheres?

Sara foi lembrada de mais uma das características de Will: ele tinha um dom incrível de ficar calado quando não sabia o que dizer. Isso gerava aqueles momentos desconfortáveis que faziam a vida amorosa de Sara parecer francamente exuberante.

Por sorte, chamaram o pedido de Will. Sara ficou afastada enquanto ele pegava a caixa de pizza com a atendente tatuada e cheia de piercing. A jovem deu a Will algo que só podia ser descrito como um olhar elogioso. Ele pareceu nem perceber, enquanto olhava a pizza para garantir que o pedido estava certo.

— Bem. — Ele usou o polegar para girar a aliança no dedo. — Acho melhor eu ir.

— Tudo bem.

Ele não se mexeu. Sara também não. Um cachorro começou a latir lá fora, os ganidos agudos entraram pela janela. Sara sabia que havia um poste e uma tigela de água ao lado da porta para quem levasse o animal de estimação ao restaurante. Também sabia que Will tinha uma cachorrinha chamada Betty cuja responsabilidade de cuidar e alimentar era, em grande parte, dele.

O latido se intensificou. Will continuou sem fazer menção de ir embora.

Ela falou:

— Parece muito um chihuahua.

Ele escutou com atenção, depois concordou com a cabeça.

— Acho que você tem razão.

— Ah, aí está você. — Dale finalmente tinha voltado do banheiro.
— Olha, recebi uma ligação do hospital... — Ele levantou os olhos para Will. — Oi.

Sara fez as apresentações.

— Dale Dugan, este é Will Trent.

Will fez um gesto de cabeça tenso. Dale devolveu.

O cachorro continuou latindo, um gritinho penetrante e desesperado. Sara percebeu, pela expressão de Will, que ele estava disposto a morrer antes de reconhecer o bicho como dele.

Ela encontrou alguma misericórdia no coração.

— Dale, eu sei que você precisa ir ao hospital. Muito obrigada pelo almoço.

— Imagina. — Ele se inclinou e a beijou bem nos lábios. — Eu te ligo.

— Ótimo — ela conseguiu dizer, resistindo à vontade de limpar a boca. Ficou vendo os dois homens trocarem mais um aceno de cabeça tenso que a fez se sentir como o único poste em um parque para cachorros.

Os ganidos de Betty se intensificaram enquanto Dale atravessava o estacionamento. Will murmurou algo que não deu para ouvir antes de empurrar a porta. Ele desamarrou a coleira e pegou a cachorrinha com uma só mão, mantendo a caixa de pizza estável na outra. O latido parou na mesma hora. Betty aconchegou a cabeça no peito dele e pôs a língua para fora.

Sara fez carinho na cabeça da cachorra. Pontos recém-feitos cruzavam as costas estreitas dela.

— O que houve?

O maxilar de Will ainda estava apertado.

— Ela se meteu numa briga com um Jack Russell Terrier.

— Sério?

A não ser que o Jack Russell tivesse uma tesoura no lugar da pata, não tinha como as marcas terem sido feitas por outro cachorro.

Ele indicou Betty.

— Melhor levá-la para casa.

Sara nunca tinha ido à casa de Will, mas sabia em que rua ele morava.

— Você não vai para a direita? — Ela esclareceu: — Por aqui?

Will não respondeu. Pareceu estar avaliando se podia mentir e se safar.

Ela pressionou:

— Você não mora numa travessa da Linwood?

— A sua casa é para o outro lado.

— Eu posso cortar pelo parque.

Ela começou a caminhar, sem dar escolha a ele. Ficaram em silêncio enquanto desciam a Ponce de Leon. O barulho do trânsito estava alto o suficiente para preencher o vazio, mas nem as fumaças dos carros eram capazes de encobrir o fato de que estavam no meio de um dia maravilhoso de primavera. Casais andavam pela rua de mãos dadas. Mães empurravam carrinhos de bebê. Pessoas praticando corrida atravessavam quatro pistas de tráfego. As nuvens que cobriam o céu naquela manhã tinham migrado para leste, expondo um céu azul-claro. Havia uma brisa contínua no ar. Sara juntou as mãos atrás das costas e baixou a cabeça para a calçada quebrada. Três raízes empurravam o concreto como dedos retorcidos de um pé idoso.

Ela olhou Will de canto de olho. O sol fazia brotar suor da testa dele. Havia duas cicatrizes em seu rosto, embora Sara não tivesse ideia de qual fosse a causa. O lábio superior dele tinha sido aberto em algum momento, depois costurado muito mal, dando uma certa crueza à sua boca. A outra cicatriz seguia a linha da mandíbula esquerda e entrava pelo colarinho. Quando o conhecera, ela havia tomado as cicatrizes como sinais de travessuras de infância, mas, conhecendo sua história, sabendo que ele tinha sido criado aos cuidados do Estado, Sara agora supunha que tivesse algo mais sombrio por trás das lesões.

Will a olhou, e ela desviou o olhar. Ele disse:

— Dale parece um cara legal.

— Parece mesmo.

— Médico, pelo jeito.

— Isso.

— Pareceu beijar bem.

Ela sorriu.

Will mudou Betty de posição no braço para segurá-la melhor.

— Pelo jeito, você está saindo com ele.

— Hoje foi nosso primeiro encontro.

— Vocês pareceram mais amigáveis do que isso.

Sara parou de andar.

— Como vai sua esposa, Will?

A resposta dele demorou. Seu olhar recaiu em algum ponto acima do ombro dela.

— Não a vejo faz quatro meses.

Sara teve uma sensação esquisita de traição. A esposa tinha ido embora e Will não havia ligado para ela.

— Vocês estão separados?

Ele deu um passo para o lado, para uma pessoa que estava correndo poder passar.

— Não.

— Ela está desaparecida?

— Não exatamente.

Um ônibus metropolitano parou com um solavanco no meio-fio, o motor reverberando um rugido demorado. Sara tinha conhecido Angie Trent quase um ano antes. Sua aparência mediterrânea e corpo curvilíneo eram exatamente o tipo de coisa em que as mães pensavam quando alertavam os filhos sobre mulheres vulgares.

O ônibus se afastou. Sara perguntou:

— E onde ela está?

Will soltou uma expiração longa.

— Ela me deixa com bastante frequência. É o que ela faz. Vai embora e depois volta. E aí fica um pouco e aí vai embora de novo.

— Para onde ela vai?

— Não faço ideia.

— Você nunca perguntou?

— Não.

Sara nem fingiu entender.

— Por que não?

Ele olhou a rua, observando o trânsito passar.

— É complicado.

Sara estendeu a mão e a pousou no braço dele.

— Me explique.

Ele ficou olhando para ela, parecendo ridículo com a cachorrinha minúscula numa mão e uma caixa de pizza na outra.

Sara estreitou o espaço entre eles, movendo a mão para o ombro de Will. Conseguiu sentir a musculatura rígida por baixo da camisa, o calor da pele dele. À luz forte do sol, os olhos pareciam absurdamente azuis. Ele tinha cílios delicados, loiros e macios. Havia um ponto em seu maxilar com barba por fazer, que ele parecia ter esquecido de raspar. Ela era alguns centímetros mais baixa. Ficou na ponta dos pés para olhá-lo nos olhos.

Sara pediu:

— Fale comigo.

Ele continuou em silêncio, observando todo o rosto dela e se demorando na boca, antes de voltar a olhá-la nos olhos.

Finalmente, ele disse:

— Eu gosto do seu cabelo solto.

Sara perdeu a oportunidade de responder porque uma SUV preta surgiu, dando uma freada brusca no meio da rua. O carro deslizou uns seis metros e aí deu ré num solavanco, cantando pneu. O cheiro de borracha queimada impregnou o ar. A SUV parou bem na frente deles. A janela foi abaixada.

A chefe de Will, Amanda Wagner, gritou:

— Entre!

Os dois estavam muito chocados para se mover. Buzinas soaram. Motoristas estavam com punhos em riste. Sara tinha a impressão de ter sido jogada no meio de um filme de ação.

— Agora! — ordenou Amanda.

— Você pode... — Will começou, mas Sara já estava pegando Betty e a caixa de pizza. Ele enfiou a mão na meia e entregou a chave da casa dele. — Ela precisa ficar trancada no primeiro quarto para não...

— Will!

O tom de Amanda não deixava espaço para hesitação. Sara pegou a chave. O metal estava quente pelo contato com o corpo dele.

— Vá.

Will não precisava ouvir duas vezes. Ele pulou no carro, com o pé deslizando pela rua enquanto Amanda se afastava do meio-fio. Mais buzinas soaram. Um sedã de quatro portas derrapou. Sara viu uma adolescente no banco traseiro. As mãos da garota estavam pressionadas contra a janela. Sua boca, aberta de terror. Outro carro estava vindo atrás, acelerando, mas desviou no último segundo. Sara fez contato visual com a jovem, e então o sedã se endireitou e saiu.

Betty estava tremendo, e Sara não estava muito melhor. Ela tentou acalmar a cachorrinha enquanto caminhava na direção da rua de Will, abraçando-a firme, pressionando os lábios na cabeça dela. O coração das duas batia loucamente. Sara não tinha certeza do que estava tornando tudo aquilo pior — pensar no que poderia ter acontecido entre ela e Will ou no acidente grave que Amanda Wagner quase causou.

Ela ia ter que ver o noticiário ao chegar em casa para descobrir o que estava acontecendo. Com certeza, aonde quer que Will estivesse indo, as vans de emissoras iriam atrás. Amanda era vice-diretora da GBI. Ela não andava por aí procurando seus agentes por capricho. Sara imaginou que Faith, a parceira de Will, provavelmente estaria correndo que nem doida para a cena do crime também.

Ela tinha esquecido de perguntar o número da casa dele, mas, por sorte, a coleira de Betty tinha uma plaquinha com os detalhes. Mesmo sem isso, ela identificou facilmente o Porsche preto de Will parado numa entrada de veículos mais para o fim da rua. Era um modelo antigo que tinha sido inteiramente restaurado. Will provavelmente o havia lavado naquele dia. Os pneus estavam brilhando e a imagem dela se refletiu no meio do capô quando ela passou.

Sara sorriu para a casa dele, que nunca tinha visto. Ele morava numa casa térrea de tijolo vermelho com uma garagem anexa. A porta de entrada era pintada de preto, com o batente amarelo-manteiga. O gramado era bem-cuidado, com os limites bem aparados e os arbustos esculpidos. No jardim da frente, um canteiro de flores circundava a árvore-da-seda. Sara se perguntou se Angie Trent tinha dedo verde. Amor-perfeito era uma planta resistente, mas precisava ser regada. Pelo jeito, a Sra. Trent não era do tipo que ficava lá por muito tempo para fazer isso. Sara não sabia bem o que achava dessa situação, nem se entendia. Mesmo assim, escutou a voz irritante da mãe no fundo da mente: *Uma esposa ausente ainda é uma esposa.*

Betty começou a se contorcer enquanto Sara subia a entrada de carros. Ela a segurou mais forte. Era tudo de que ela precisava para piorar o dia — perder a cachorrinha da esposa do homem que ela desejara beijar no meio da rua.

Sara balançou a cabeça enquanto subia os degraus da frente. Não tinha nada que ficar pensando em Will daquele jeito. Devia ficar feliz por Amanda Wagner ter interrompido os dois. No início do casamento, Jeffrey tinha traído Sara. Aquilo havia quase os dilacerado, e reconstruir a relação exigira anos de muito esforço. Para o bem ou para o mal, Will tinha feito sua escolha. E, além do mais, não era um romance casual. Ele tinha sido criado com Angie. Os dois haviam se conhecido no lar de acolhimento quando eram crianças. Tinham quase vinte e cinco anos de história juntos. Sara não tinha nada que se meter entre eles. Ela não ia fazer outra mulher sentir a mesma dor que ela sentira, não importava quão deprimentes fossem suas outras opções.

A chave deslizou fácil na fechadura. Uma brisa fria a recebeu enquanto ela atravessava a porta. Ela colocou Betty no chão e tirou a coleira. Livre, a cachorrinha foi direto para os fundos da casa.

Sara não conseguiu controlar a curiosidade enquanto olhava os primeiros cômodos. O gosto de Will definitivamente era mais masculino. Se a esposa tinha contribuído para a decoração, não parecia. O lugar de honra no meio da sala de jantar era de uma máquina de pinball, logo abaixo de um lustre de vidro. Will obviamente estava trabalhando na máquina — as entranhas eletrônicas estavam dispostas de forma organizada ao lado de uma caixa de ferramentas aberta no chão. O cheiro de óleo do equipamento impregnava o ar.

O sofá da sala de estar era de camurça sintética marrom-escura, com um pufe grande combinando. As paredes eram de um bege discreto. Uma elegante poltrona reclinável preta estava virada para uma televisão de plasma de cinquenta polegadas com várias caixinhas eletrônicas empilhadas abaixo de maneira organizada. Tudo parecia estar no lugar certo. Não tinha poeira nem bagunça, nada de roupa lavada empilhada que nem o Everest no sofá. Obviamente, Will era um dono de casa melhor do que Sara. Mas até aí, quase todo mundo era.

A escrivaninha dele ficava no canto da sala principal, perto do corredor. De cromo e metal. Ela passou o dedo pelas hastes dos óculos de leitura dele. Havia papéis empilhados com cuidado em torno de um laptop e uma impressora. Um pacote de marcadores de texto descansava em cima de uma pilha de pastas coloridas. Havia pequenos escaninhos de metal com elásticos e clipes de papel separados por cor e tamanho.

Sara já tinha visto essa configuração. Will sabia ler, mas não com facilidade e com certeza não com rapidez. Ele usava os marcadores e clipes coloridos como pistas para ajudá-lo a achar o que estava procurando sem ter que realmente procurar no texto de uma página ou pasta. Era um truque bem bacana que ele provavelmente tinha inventado bem cedo na vida. Sara não tinha dúvidas de que ele era uma daquelas crianças que se sentava no fundão da sala e decorava tudo o que a professora dizia, mas não conseguia — ou não queria — escrever nada no dia da prova.

Ela levou a caixa de pizza para a cozinha, que tinha sido reformada com os mesmos tons de marrom vívidos e profundos do resto da casa. Ao contrário da cozinha de Sara, as bancadas de granito estavam limpas e organizadas, os únicos itens à mostra eram uma cafeteira e uma televisão. Da mesma forma, a geladeira estava vazia, exceto por uma garrafa de leite e um pacote de potinhos de pudim da marca Jell-O. Sara deslizou a caixa para a prateleira de cima e voltou para dar uma olhada em Betty. Achou o primeiro quarto. As luzes do teto estavam apagadas, mas Will tinha deixado acesa a luminária de piso atrás de outra poltrona reclinável de couro. Ao lado da poltrona, havia uma caminha de cachorro em formato de *chaise longue*. No canto, tinha um pote de água e um pouco de ração. Havia outra TV fixada na parede, com uma esteira ergométrica dobrável abaixo dela.

O quarto era escuro, as paredes pintadas de um marrom profundo que combinava com o da sala. Ela acendeu a luz do teto. Surpreendentemente, havia estantes de livros pelas paredes. Sara passou o dedo pelos títulos, reconhecendo clássicos misturados a um punhado de textos feministas que costumavam ser recomendados a jovens sérias no primeiro ano de faculdade. Todas as lombadas estavam quebradas, bem manuseadas. Nunca tinha ocorrido a ela que Will teria uma biblioteca em casa. Com a dislexia dele, ler um romance grosso seria uma tarefa de Sísifo. Os audiolivros faziam mais sentido. Sara se ajoelhou e olhou as caixas de CD empilhadas ao lado de um aparelho Bose que parecia caro. Os gostos de Will certamente eram mais de um intelectual que os dela — muitas obras históricas e de não ficção que Sara normalmente sugeriria para insones. Ela pressionou um adesivo que estava descolando e leu as palavras "Propriedade da Rede de Bibliotecas do Condado de Fulton".

O *clac-clac* de unhas anunciou Betty no corredor. Sara corou, se sentindo pega no pulo. Ela se levantou para pegar a cachorra, mas Betty saiu correndo com uma velocidade surpreendente. Sara a seguiu até depois do banheiro, entrando no segundo quarto. O quarto de Will.

A cama estava arrumada, com um cobertor azul-escuro em cima dos lençóis combinando. Só tinha um travesseiro apoiado na parede onde devia ficar a cabeceira. Uma mesinha de cabeceira. Um abajur.

Ao contrário do resto da casa, havia naquele quarto uma sensação de utilitarismo. Sara não queria pensar muito no porquê do seu alívio ao perceber a ausência de um cenário romântico. As paredes eram brancas, sem quadros. O relógio e a carteira de Will estavam em cima da cômoda, ao lado de mais uma televisão. Uma calça jeans e uma camisa estavam dispostas no banco ao pé da cama. Havia um par de meias pretas dobradas. As botas dele estavam debaixo do banco. Sara pegou a camisa. Algodão. Manga comprida. Preta, como a que Will estava usando mais cedo.

A cachorrinha pulou na cama, puxou o travesseiro para baixo e se acomodou como um pássaro no ninho.

Sara dobrou a camisa e a colocou de volta ao lado da calça jeans. Aquilo estava beirando o comportamento de um *stalker*. Pelo menos ela não tinha cheirado a camisa nem fuçado dentro das gavetas dele. Ela pegou Betty no colo, pensando que era melhor trancar a cachorrinha no primeiro quarto e sair de lá logo. Estava fazendo exatamente isso quando o telefone começou a tocar. A secretária eletrônica atendeu. Ela escutou a voz de Will lá no quarto.

— Sara? Se estiver aí, por favor, atenda.

Ela voltou ao quarto dele e atendeu o telefone.

— Eu estava indo embora.

A voz dele estava tensa. Ela ouvia um bebê chorando no fundo, gente gritando.

— Preciso que você venha agora para cá. Para a casa de Faith. Da mãe dela. É importante.

Sara sentiu uma onda de adrenalina aguçando seus sentidos.

— Ela está bem?

— Não — respondeu ele sem rodeios. — Posso dar o endereço?

Sem pensar, ela abriu a gaveta da mesa de cabeceira, supondo que ia achar um pedaço de papel e uma caneta. Em vez disso, viu uma revista do tipo que seu pai guardava no fundo da caixa de ferramentas na garagem.

— Sara?

A gaveta não queria fechar.

— Me deixe pegar alguma coisa para escrever. Espere aí. — Will parecia ser a única pessoa dos Estados Unidos que não tinha telefone sem fio. Sara deixou o aparelho em cima da cama, achou caneta e papel na escrivaninha dele e voltou. — Pronto.

Will esperou alguém parar de berrar. Manteve a voz baixa ao dar o endereço a Sara.

— Fica em Sherwood Forest, logo depois de Ansley. Você conhece?

Ansley ficava só a cinco minutos.

— Consigo descobrir.

— Pegue meu carro. A chave está num gancho ao lado da porta dos fundos, na cozinha. Você sabe dirigir carro manual?

— Sei.

— O pessoal de reportagem já está aqui. Vá no primeiro policial que você encontrar, diga que veio a meu pedido e eles vão trazer você aqui atrás. Não fale com mais ninguém. Tudo bem?

— Tudo bem.

Ela desligou e empurrou a gaveta da mesa de cabeceira com as duas mãos até fechar. Betty tinha voltado ao travesseiro. Sara a pegou de novo. Começou a ir embora, mas então pensou melhor. Will estava de shorts da última vez que ela o viu. Ele provavelmente ia querer a calça jeans. Ela colocou o relógio e a carteira dele no bolso de trás.

Não dava para saber onde ele guardava a arma, mas Sara não ia ficar fuçando as coisas dele mais do que já tinha fuçado.

— Posso ajudar?

Sara sentiu uma onda de horror queimando o corpo. Angie Trent estava apoiada na porta do quarto com a palma da mão descansando casualmente no batente. Seu cabelo escuro encaracolado caía em cascata pelos ombros. A maquiagem estava perfeita. As unhas estavam perfeitas. A saia justa e a blusa reveladora a colocariam facilmente na capa da revista na gaveta de Will.

— E-eu... — Sara não gaguejava desde os doze anos.

— A gente já se conheceu, né? Você trabalha no hospital.

— Sim. — Sara se afastou da cama. — Will foi chamado para uma emergência. Ele me pediu para trazer sua cachorra...

— Minha cachorra?

Sara sentiu as vibrações de um rosnado começando no peito de Betty. Angie contorceu a boca, cheia de desgosto.

— O que aconteceu com esse bicho?

— Ela foi... — Sara se sentia uma tonta ali parada. Enfiou a calça jeans de Will embaixo do braço. — Vou deixá-la no outro quarto e ir embora.

— Aham.

Angie estava bloqueando a porta. Não teve pressa em deixar Sara passar, depois a seguiu até o quarto, viu-a colocar Betty na caminha e fechar a porta.

Sara começou a sair pela porta da frente, mas aí lembrou que precisava da chave de Will. Ela se esforçou para não deixar a voz tremer.

— Ele me falou para ir com o carro dele.

Angie cruzou os braços. Seu dedo anelar estava nu, mas havia uma aliança prateada no dedão.

— Claro que falou.

Sara voltou à cozinha. Seu rosto estava tão vermelho que ela suava. Ao lado da mesa, havia uma mala de mão de lona que não estava lá antes. A chave do carro de Will estava pendurada num gancho ao lado da porta dos fundos, como ele tinha dito. Ela pegou a chave e voltou à entrada, ciente de que Angie estava parada no corredor observando todos os seus movimentos. Sara caminhou o mais rápido que conseguia para a porta da frente, com o coração na boca, mas Angie Trent não ia facilitar para ela.

— Há quanto tempo você está trepando com ele?

Sara balançou a cabeça. Aquilo não podia estar acontecendo.

— Eu perguntei há quanto tempo você está trepando com o meu marido.

Sara ficou olhando a porta, envergonhada demais para encará-la.

— Isso é um mal-entendido. Eu juro.

— Eu achei você na *minha* casa, no *meu* quarto, que eu divido com o meu marido. Qual é sua explicação? Estou doida para ouvir.

— Eu disse para você, eu...

— Você curte policiais? É isso?

Sara sentiu o coração pular.

— Seu marido morto era policial, não era? Você sente alguma emoção com isso, por acaso? — Angie deu uma risada irônica. — Ele nunca vai me abandonar, querida. Melhor você achar outro pau para brincar.

Sara não conseguia responder. A situação era horrível demais para qualquer palavra. Ela tateou a porta, procurando a maçaneta.

— Ele se cortou por mim. Ele contou isso para você?

Ela obrigou a mão a ficar estável para conseguir abrir a porta.

— Preciso ir agora. Desculpe.

— Eu fiquei olhando enquanto ele enfiava a lâmina no braço.

A mão de Sara não se mexia. Sua mente tentou em vão processar o que ela estava escutando.

— Eu nunca vi tanto sangue na vida. — Angie fez uma pausa. — Você podia pelo menos olhar para mim enquanto eu falo com você.

Sara não queria, mas se obrigou a se virar.

O tom de Angie era passivo, mas o ódio em seus olhos tornava difícil encará-la.

— Eu fiquei abraçada com ele o tempo todo. Ele contou isso para você? Ele contou como eu fiquei abraçada com ele?

Sara ainda não conseguia encontrar a voz.

Angie levantou o braço esquerdo, mostrando a pele nua. Com uma lentidão excruciante, ela passou o indicador direito do pulso até o cotovelo.

— Dizem que a navalha cortou tão fundo que chegou a raspar o osso. — Ela sorriu, como se fosse uma memória feliz. — Ele fez isso por *mim*, vagabunda. Você acha que ele faria isso por você?

Agora que Sara olhava para ela, não conseguia parar. Alguns segundos se passaram. Ela pensou no relógio lá no restaurante, nos segundos virando borrões. Finalmente, pigarreou, incerta de que conseguiria falar.

— É no outro braço.

— Quê?

— A cicatriz — disse ela, curtindo a expressão de surpresa de Angie Trent. — É no outro braço.

As mãos de Sara suavam tanto que ela mal conseguiu girar a maçaneta. Encolheu-se enquanto saía apressada, pensando que Angie viria correndo atrás ou, pior, exporia a mentira dela.

A verdade era que Sara nunca tinha visto cicatriz no braço de Will, porque nunca tinha visto o braço dele à mostra. Ele sempre usava camisa de manga comprida. Nunca arregaçava as mangas nem desabotoava os punhos. Ela havia chutado com base no que sabia. Will era canhoto. Se tentasse se matar enquanto a esposa odiosa o encorajava, ia cortar o braço direito, não o esquerdo.

3

Will cutucou o colarinho da camisa. O veículo de comando móvel estava escaldante, com tanta gente engravatada e uniformizada que quase não dava para respirar. O barulho era igualmente insuportável. Telefones tocando. BlackBerries apitando. Monitores de computador passavam transmissões ao vivo das três emissoras locais de notícia. Acima de toda a cacofonia, havia Amanda Wagner, que estava gritando fazia já quinze minutos com os três comandantes de zona que estavam no local do crime. O chefe da polícia de Atlanta estava a caminho. O diretor da GBI também. A competição entre as jurisdições para ver quem mijava mais longe só ia piorar.

Enquanto isso, ninguém estava trabalhando de verdade no caso.

Will abriu a porta com um empurrão. A luz do sol atravessou a escuridão lá dentro. Amanda parou de gritar por uns segundos, depois continuou, quando Will fechou a porta. Ele respirou fundo o ar fresco, analisando a cena do crime do alto dos degraus metálicos. Em vez da atividade rápida de sempre que se seguia a um crime chocante, estava todo mundo por ali esperando ordens. Os investigadores estavam sentados em seus carros à paisana checando e-mails. Seis viaturas bloqueavam os dois lados da rua. Vizinhos olhavam tudo de suas varandas, embasbacados. A van da unidade de perícia criminal da polícia de Atlanta estava lá. A van da unidade de perícia criminal da GBI estava lá. O caminhão de bombeiros continuava parado atravessado na frente da casa dos Mitchell. Os paramédicos estavam fumando no para-choque traseiro da ambulância. Vários oficiais uniformizados se recostavam em veículos de emergência, jogando conversa fora, fingindo não se importar com o que estava rolando no centro de comando.

Apesar disso, todos olharam feio para Will enquanto ele descia para a rua. Carrancas por todo lado. Braços cruzados. Um xingamento murmurado. Alguém cuspiu na calçada.

Will não tinha muitos amigos na polícia de Atlanta. O som de lâminas cortando o ar ressoou. Will olhou para cima. Dois helicópteros de reportagem pairavam logo acima da cena do crime. Não ficariam sozinhos por muito tempo. A cada dez minutos, passava um MD 500 da SWAT. No nariz do helicóptero, que parecia um mosquito, havia uma câmera infravermelha, que conseguia enxergar através de florestas densas e telhados, identificando corpos de sangue quente, direcionando os investigadores para os suspeitos. Era um equipamento incrível, mas completamente inútil na área residencial, onde, a todo momento, tinha milhares de pessoas andando sem cometer crime nenhum. No máximo, iam acabar identificando as formas vermelhas brilhantes de gente sentada no sofá assistindo à televisão, que, por sua vez, estava mostrando o helicóptero da SWAT pairando acima delas.

Will procurou Sara na multidão, desejando que ela chegasse. Se estivesse pensando direito quando Amanda parou na rua, teria falado para Sara vir junto. Devia ter antecipado que Faith precisaria de ajuda. Ela era parceira dele. Will devia cuidar dela, protegê-la. Agora talvez fosse tarde demais.

Ele não tinha certeza de como Amanda ficara sabendo dos tiroteios tão rápido, mas chegaram na cena do crime quinze minutos depois de a última bala ser disparada. O chaveiro estava terminando de abrir a porta do quarto de ferramentas quando o carro deles chegou ao local. Faith tinha ficado andando para lá e para cá como um animal enjaulado enquanto esperava a filha ser libertada e continuou fazendo isso bem depois de estar com Emma nos braços. Assim que viu Will, Faith começou a tagarelar, falando da vizinha de trás, a Sra. Johnson, do irmão dela, Zeke, do quarto de ferramentas que o pai tinha construído quando ela era pequena e de mais um milhão de coisas que não faziam sentido nenhum do jeito que ela estava ordenando as ideias.

No início, Will achou que Faith estava em choque, mas gente em choque não fica andando por aí cacarejando que nem uma lunática.

A pressão das pessoas cai tão rápido que, em geral, elas não conseguem ficar de pé. Elas ofegam que nem cachorro. Ficam olhando sem expressão para o nada. Falam devagar, e não tão rápido que mal dá para entender. Tinha mais alguma coisa acontecendo, mas Will não sabia se era algum colapso mental, ou a diabetes de Faith, ou o quê.

Para piorar tudo, naquele momento, havia vinte policiais em volta que sabiam exatamente o que esperar de uma pessoa quando algo horrível acontecia. Faith não se encaixava nesse perfil. Não estava chorando. Não estava tremendo. Não estava brava. Estava só maluca, completamente fora de si. Nada que ela falava tinha sentido algum. Ela não conseguia contar a eles o que tinha acontecido. Não conseguia detalhar o ocorrido passo a passo e explicar a carnificina. Ela estava pior do que inútil, porque as respostas de todas as perguntas estavam trancadas em sua cabeça.

Foi quando um dos policiais murmurou algo sobre ela estar alcoolizada. Em seguida, alguém se voluntariou para pegar o bafômetro no carro.

Rapidamente, Amanda interveio. Arrastou Faith pelo jardim da frente, bateu na porta da vizinha — não a Sra. Johnson, que estava com um morto no quintal, mas uma velha chamada Sra. Levy — e praticamente ordenou que a senhora cedesse a Faith um lugar para se recompor.

Àquela altura, o centro de comando móvel tinha chegado. Amanda foi direto para a traseira do veículo e começou a exigir que o caso fosse imediatamente entregue à GBI. Sabia que não ia ganhar a briga territorial com os comandantes de zona. Por lei, a GBI não podia simplesmente cair de paraquedas e assumir um caso. O legista local, o Ministério Público ou o chefe de polícia, em geral, eram quem poderia pedir ajuda ao estado, e, via de regra, isso só acontecia quando eles não conseguiam montar um caso sozinhos ou não queriam gastar dinheiro ou equipe indo atrás de suspeitos. A única pessoa capaz de arrancar esse caso de Atlanta era o governador, e qualquer político do estado diria que irritar a capital era péssima ideia. A tática de berros de Amanda era só performance. Ela não gritava quando ficava brava. Sua voz ficava grave, parecendo um estrondo, e era preciso ficar de orelha

47

em pé para escutar os insultos que voavam de sua boca. Ela estava tentando ganhar tempo para eles. Tentando ganhar tempo para Faith.

Aos olhos da polícia de Atlanta, Faith não era mais uma policial. Ela era uma testemunha. Uma suspeita. Um alvo de investigação, e eles queriam falar com ela sobre os homens que ela havia matado e por que a mãe dela tinha sido sequestrada. Os policiais não eram um bando de caipiras. Eram uma das melhores forças armadas do país. Se não fosse Amanda berrando com eles, já teriam enfiado Faith na delegacia e a estariam interrogando como se ela fosse um terrorista em Guantánamo.

Will não podia culpá-los. Sherwood Forest não era o tipo de bairro em que se esperava encontrar um tiroteio no meio de uma linda tarde de sábado. Ansley Park ficava a dois passos de distância. Se estendessem um pouco o perímetro, encontrariam ali uns oitenta por cento da renda de imóveis da cidade — casas multimilionárias com quadras de tênis e suítes para *au pairs*. Gente rica não deixava coisas ruins acontecerem sem colocar a culpa em alguém. Haveria retaliação. Se Amanda não conseguisse achar um jeito de evitar isso, essa pessoa provavelmente acabaria sendo Faith. E Will não tinha a menor ideia do que fazer.

O detetive Leo Donnelly se aproximou, arrastando os pés pelo asfalto. Estava com um cigarro pendurado na boca. A fumaça subiu serpenteando até seus olhos. Ele piscou para afastá-la.

— Eu ia odiar ouvir essa vaca na cama.

Estava falando de Amanda. Ela continuava gritando, embora fosse difícil discernir suas palavras com a porta fechada.

Leo continuou:

— Sei lá. Pode ser que valha a pena. As velhas viram tigres no rala e rola.

Will suprimiu um tremor, não porque Amanda tinha sessenta e tantos anos, mas porque Leo estava claramente considerando aquela possibilidade.

— Ela sabe que não vai ganhar, né?

Will se apoiou numa das viaturas. Leo tinha sido parceiro de Faith por seis anos, mas era ela quem fazia o trabalho pesado. Aos quarenta e oito, Leo não era, de forma alguma, velho, mas tinha envelhecido enquanto policial. A pele dele estava amarelada por causa do fígado sobrecarregado. Ele tinha vencido um câncer de próstata, mas o tratamento havia cobrado seu preço. Era um cara ok, mas preguiçoso, o que seria perfeitamente aceitável se você fosse vendedor de carros usados, mas incrivelmente perigoso se você fosse policial. Faith se considerava sortuda de ter se afastado daquele homem.

Leo falou:

— Não vejo uma cagada astronômica dessas desde a última vez que trabalhei num caso com você.

Will analisou a cena: o zumbido do gerador do centro de comando se misturando com o chiado metálico vindo das televisões da van. Os policiais parados com a mão descansando no cinto. Os bombeiros jogando conversa fora uns com os outros. A ausência total e completa de atividade. Ele decidiu que devia falar com Leo.

— Ah, é?

— Qual é o nome do seu perito...? Charlie? — Leo assentiu para si mesmo. — Ele deu um jeito de entrar na casa usando a lábia.

O agente especial Charlie Reed era chefe da unidade de perícia criminal da GBI e faria qualquer coisa para entrar na cena de um crime.

— Ele é bom no que faz.

— Vários de nós somos. — Leo se recostou numa viatura a alguns metros de Will. Ele soprou ruidosamente pela boca. — Nunca soube que Faith era de beber.

— Ela não é.

— Comprimidos?

Will lançou a ele o olhar mais feio que conseguiu.

— Você sabe que eu preciso falar com ela.

Will não conseguiu evitar o escárnio na voz:

— Você está encarregado do caso?

— Tente não parecer tão confiante.

Will nem gastou saliva. O tempo de holofote de Leo duraria pouco. Assim que o chefe da polícia de Atlanta chegasse ao local, ia chutar Leo para escanteio e reunir sua própria equipe. Leo teria sorte se o deixassem servir café

— Sério — disse Leo. — Faith está bem?

— Está ótima.

Ele deu uma última tragada no cigarro e o jogou no chão.

— A vizinha surtou. Quase viu as netas morrerem baleadas.

Will tentou manter a expressão neutra. Sabia um pouco do que tinha acontecido ali, mas não muito. Os caras da equipe tática tinham se entediado depois de ficar lá parados por cinco minutos sem nada para quebrar. Os detalhes da cena do crime vazaram como um cano enferrujado. Dois corpos na casa. Um no quintal da vizinha. Duas armas com Faith — a Glock dela e uma Smith and Wesson. A escopeta dela no chão do quarto. Will havia parado de escutar ao ouvir um policial que acabava de chegar ao local dizendo que tinha visto Faith com os próprios olhos e ela estava loucona.

De sua parte, Will só sabia de duas coisas: não fazia ideia do que tinha acontecido naquela casa e Faith tinha feito a coisa certa.

Leo pigarreou e cuspiu uma bolota de catarro no asfalto.

— Então, a vovó Johnson falou que escutou uns gritos no quintal. Olhou pela janela da cozinha e viu o atirador, um cara mexicano, mirando nas netas dela. Ele deu um disparo, atingiu uns tijolos da casa. Faith correu até a cerca e matou o cara. Salvou as menininhas.

Will sentiu um pouco do peso sair do peito.

— Que sorte delas Faith estar lá.

— Que sorte de Faith a vizinha ser uma boa testemunha.

Will começou a enfiar as mãos nos bolsos, lembrando, tarde demais, que ainda estava de shorts de corrida.

Leo deu uma risadinha.

— Eu gosto desses uniformes novos. A ideia é você ser o policial do Village People?

Will cruzou os braços na frente do peito.

— Los Texicanos — falou Leo. — O cara no quintal. É um integrante deles, tem tatuagem no peito todo e nos braços.

— E os outros dois?

— Asiáticos. Os dois. Não faço ideia se são de alguma facção. Não parecem ser. Não se vestem como tal. Corpos limpos, sem tatuagem.

— Leo demorou acendendo mais um cigarro. Soltou um fluxo contínuo de fumaça antes de continuar. — O Scott Shepherd ali... — Ele apontou com a cabeça para um jovem musculoso vestindo equipamento tático. — ...disse que estava com a equipe armada em frente à casa esperando reforços. Escutaram uma arma disparando. Uma possível ocorrência com refém, certo? Uma policial lá dentro, duas, se contar Evelyn. Perigo iminente. Então, arrombaram a porta. — Leo deu mais um trago no cigarro. — Scott vê Faith parada no corredor, pés afastados, Glock à frente. Ela vê Scott, não fala nada, só sai correndo para dentro do quarto. Eles vão atrás dela e encontram um cara morto no carpete. — Leo tocou a testa com os dedos. — Ela o atingiu bem aqui no meio.

— Deve ter tido um bom motivo.

— Bem que eu queria saber qual. Ele não estava armado.

— O outro cara estava. Aquele que correu para o quintal e ameaçou atirar nas crianças.

— Tem razão. Estava mesmo.

— Digitais?

— Estamos procurando.

Will apostaria a própria casa que encontrariam dois conjuntos de digitais — um do asiático e um do mexicano.

— Onde vocês acharam o terceiro cara?

— Área de serviço. Bala na cabeça. O tiro foi feio, arrancou metade do crânio. Tiramos uma trinta e oito do fundo da parede.

A Glock de Faith era calibre .40.

— A Smith and Wesson aceita trinta e oito?

— Aham. — Leo se afastou do carro. — Nada da mãe ainda. Temos equipes procurando. Ela cuidava do esquadrão de narcóticos, mas aposto que você já sabia disso, Ratatouille.

Will fez força para não travar o maxilar. Praticamente o único talento de Leo era saber provocar. Aquele era o motivo dos olhares feios e expressões hostis dos companheiros de uniforme de Will. Todos os policiais ali sabiam que Will Trent era o motivo de Evelyn Mitchell ter sido forçada a se aposentar. Um dos trabalhos mais odiosos que ele tivera na GBI havia sido investigar policiais corruptos. Quatro anos antes, ele tinha construído um caso sólido contra o esquadrão de narcóticos de Evelyn. Seis investigadores tinham sido presos por desviar dinheiro de apreensão de drogas e aceitar suborno para fazer vista grossa, mas a capitã Mitchell tinha saído incólume, com a aposentadoria e a maior parte da reputação intactas.

Leo disse:

— Fale para a garota que posso dar mais dez minutos para ela, no máximo. Depois disso, ela precisa colocar a cabeça no lugar e começar a falar comigo. — Ele se inclinou para perto. — Ouvi a ligação para a central. Disseram para ela não entrar na casa. Ela precisa esclarecer muito bem por que diabos entrou mesmo assim.

Leo começou a se afastar, mas Will perguntou:

— Como estava a voz dela?

Ele se virou.

— Na ligação para a central. Como estava a voz dela?

De modo nada surpreendente, Leo não tinha considerado a questão. Fez isso então e logo começou a assentir.

— Talvez meio assustada, mas lúcida. Calma. No controle.

Will também assentiu.

— É bem a cara de Faith.

Leo abriu um sorriso, mas Will não conseguia saber se ele estava aliviado ou só fazendo seu papel recorrente de sabichão.

— Falei sério sobre os shorts, cara. — Leo deu um tapinha no braço dele. — Você devia tentar fazer essas pernas bonitas aparecerem na TV.

Leo acenou para os repórteres parados junto à fita amarela. Eles foram para a frente num movimento único, achando que ele fosse dar uma entrevista. Houve um resmungo coletivo quando ele se afastou. Os policiais que cuidavam da barreira empurraram todos para trás, só porque tinham esse poder. Will sabia que eles não davam a mínima para controle de multidão. Não paravam de olhar para o centro de comando, como se esperassem um anúncio vindo de cima. Os policiais estavam tão ansiosos quanto os repórteres para descobrir o que tinha acontecido. Talvez mais.

A capitã Evelyn Mitchell tinha servido à polícia de Atlanta por trinta e nove anos. Tinha subido por mérito próprio, abrindo caminho desde o secretariado, avançando para leitura de parquímetro e, finalmente, recebendo uma vinte e dois e um distintivo que não era de plástico. Fazia parte do grupo conhecido como as pioneiras: as primeiras mulheres a dirigir sozinhas, as primeiras detetives. Evelyn foi a primeira tenente mulher da polícia de Atlanta, depois a primeira capitã. Independentemente dos motivos para a aposentadoria, ela tinha mais medalhas e condecorações do que todos os policiais ali juntos.

Fazia muito tempo que Will tinha aprendido que policiais eram cegamente leais. Também tinha aprendido que havia uma hierarquia distinta naquela lealdade. Era como uma pirâmide, com todos os policiais do mundo na base e seu parceiro no topo. Faith tinha trabalhado na polícia de Atlanta desde o começo, mas passado para a GBI havia dois anos, virando parceira de Will, que não era exatamente o mais popular da turma. Leo talvez ainda estivesse meio do lado de Faith, mas, no que dizia respeito aos membros gerais da polícia de Atlanta, ela tinha perdido seu lugar na pirâmide. Especialmente porque o primeiro policial a chegar na cena do crime, um novato ávido, tinha sido levado às pressas para uma cirurgia de emergência depois de Faith lhe dar uma cotovelada que fizera os testículos dele subirem para o cérebro.

Will viu um borrão amarelo quando a fita foi levantada. Sara tinha prendido bem o cabelo atrás da cabeça. O vestido de linho que estava usando parecia amarrotado. Ela trazia uma calça jeans dobrada embaixo do braço. De início, Will achou que ela parecia confusa, mas, quanto mais perto chegava, mais ele achava que ela estava aborrecida, talvez até brava. Seus olhos estavam vermelhos nos cantos. As bochechas, coradas.

Ela entregou a calça jeans para ele.

— Por que você precisa de mim aqui?

Ele colocou a mão no cotovelo dela e a afastou dos repórteres.

— Por causa de Faith.

Ela cruzou os braços, mantendo alguma distância entre eles.

— Se ela precisa de cuidados médicos, é melhor levá-la para o hospital.

— Não podemos. — Will tentou não dar muita atenção à frieza na voz dela. — Ela está na casa da vizinha. Não temos muito tempo.

— Ouvi no rádio o que aconteceu.

— A gente acha que tem relação com drogas. Não conte a ninguém.

— Ele parou de andar. Esperou que ela o olhasse. — Faith não está normal. Está confusa, não fala nada com nada. Eles querem conversar com ela, mas... — Ele não sabia o que dizer. Amanda tinha mandado Will chamar Sara. Sabia que a mulher tinha sido casada com um policial e supunha que a lealdade não havia morrido com o homem. — Isto pode ser muito ruim para Faith. Ela matou dois caras. A mãe dela foi sequestrada. Vão considerá-la suspeita por vários motivos.

— A reação dela foi desproporcional?

— Havia reféns. As crianças vizinhas estavam na linha de fogo. — Will não deu todos os detalhes. — Ela atirou na cabeça de um homem e nas costas de outro.

— As crianças estão bem?

— Estão, mas...

As portas dos fundos do centro de comando se abriram com um baque. O chefe de polícia Mike Geary, comandante da zona de Ansley e Sherwood Forest, desceu pulando os degraus. Estava de uniforme completo, um poliéster azul-escuro e áspero, apertado demais na barriga saliente. Ele piscou para o sol, uma ruga funda marcando a testa bronzeada. Como a maioria da velha guarda, mantinha o cabelo grisalho cortado em estilo militar. Geary colocou o chapéu e se virou para estender a mão para Amanda. No entanto, ele se deteve pouco antes de tocá-la e baixou a própria mão antes que ela a pudesse segurar.

— Trent — latiu o comandante. — Quero falar com a sua parceira agora mesmo. Vá buscá-la. Vamos levá-la para a delegacia.

Will olhou para Amanda, que tentava descer as escadas instáveis de salto alto. Ela balançou a cabeça uma vez. Não podia fazer mais nada.

Para surpresa dele, foi Sara quem os salvou.

— Preciso examiná-la primeiro.

Geary não gostou da resistência.

— E quem é você, hein?

— Sou médica traumatologista do pronto-socorro do Grady. — Sara foi esperta evitando o próprio nome. — Estou aqui para avaliar a agente Mitchell, para que qualquer depoimento que ela der seja válido. — Ela inclinou a cabeça para o lado. — Com certeza sua política não é tomar depoimentos sob coação.

Geary bufou pelo nariz.

— Ela não está sendo coagida.

Sara levantou uma sobrancelha.

— É sua posição oficial? Porque eu detestaria ter que depor dizendo que você conduziu um interrogatório coercitivo contra recomendação médica.

A confusão nublou a raiva de Geary. Médicos em geral estavam mais do que dispostos a ajudar a polícia, mas tinham o poder de acabar com qualquer oitiva se achassem que ia prejudicar o paciente. Mesmo assim, Geary tentou:

— De que tipo de tratamento médico ela precisa?

Sara não cedeu.

— Só posso dizer depois que a examinar. Ela pode estar em choque. Pode estar machucada. Pode precisar de internação. Talvez seja melhor eu a transferir para o hospital agora mesmo e começar os exames.

Sara se virou para chamar os paramédicos.

— Espere. — Geary sibilou um xingamento e disse a Amanda: — Suas táticas de enrolação de merda são notáveis, vice-diretora.

O sorriso dela era falsamente doce e leve.

— É sempre bom ter algum reconhecimento.

Geary anunciou:

— Quero que o sangue dela seja coletado e levado para um laboratório independente para um exame toxicológico completo. Dá para fazer isso, doutora?

Sara assentiu.

— Claro.

Will colocou a mão no braço de Sara e a conduziu para a casa da vizinha. Assim que alcançaram uma distância em que não podiam mais ser ouvidos, ele disse:

— Obrigado.

De novo, ela se afastou dele enquanto subiam pela entrada da casa. Quando chegaram à varanda, Sara estava vários metros à frente, mas a distância entre eles parecia um abismo. Não era a mesma Sara de meia hora antes. Talvez por estar na cena de um crime, embora Will já a tivesse visto em outras cenas de crime. Sara tinha sido legista. Não estava nem um pouco fora de sua zona de conforto. Ele não sabia o que fazer com relação àquela mudança. Tinha passado a vida toda analisando o humor das pessoas, mas ler aquela mulher em particular estava além de suas habilidades.

A porta se abriu, e a Sra. Levy os olhou de trás dos seus óculos grossos. Estava usando um vestido simples, amarelo, com a gola puída. Tinha um avental branco, com filhotes de ganso na barra, envolvendo sua cintura fina. Seus calcanhares ficavam para fora dos chinelos felpudos, também amarelos, combinando com o vestido. Ela tinha mais de oitenta anos, mas sua mente era aguçada e ela claramente gostava de Faith.

— Essa é a médica? Me disseram para só deixar entrar uma médica. Sara respondeu:

— Sim, senhora. Eu sou a médica.

— Ah, mas como você é linda! Entre. Que dia mais maluco. — A Sra. Levy deu um passo para o lado, abrindo bem a porta para poderem entrar no vestíbulo. — Já recebi mais visitas nesta tarde do que no ano todo.

A sala ficava alguns degraus abaixo e tinha provavelmente os mesmos móveis de quando a Sra. Levy comprara a casa. O carpete de lã que revestia todo o piso era amarelo-alaranjado e tinha os pelos amassados, rentes ao chão. O sofá seccional de almofadas fixas tinha cor de mostarda. A única coisa atualizada na decoração era uma poltrona reclinável que parecia do tipo que tinha alavanca mecânica para ser mais fácil de sentar e levantar. A única iluminação da sala vinha do console de televisão com luz bruxuleante. Faith estava jogada no sofá segurando Emma perto do ombro. A capacidade de falar tinha se esvaído dela. Aparentemente, sua alma fora junto. Era mais isso que Will estava esperando ao ficar sabendo que Faith estava envolvida num tiroteio. Ela tendia a ficar quieta quando estava muito aborrecida. Mas aquilo ali também não estava muito normal.

Ela estava quieta demais.

— Faith? — disse ele. — A Dra. Linton está aqui.

Ela ficou olhando a televisão muda, sem responder. Em alguns sentidos, Faith parecia pior do que antes. Seus lábios estavam tão brancos quanto a pele, que brilhava de suor. O cabelo loiro estava emaranhado na cabeça. A respiração, superficial. Emma balbuciou, mas Faith não pareceu notar.

Sara acendeu a luz do teto antes de se ajoelhar na frente dela.

— Faith? Pode olhar para mim?

Os olhos de Faith continuavam na televisão. Will aproveitou o momento para colocar a calça jeans por cima dos shorts. Sentiu um volume no bolso de trás e puxou a carteira e o relógio.

— Faith? — A voz de Sara ficou mais alta e firme. — Olhe para mim.

Devagar, ela olhou para Sara.

— Quer deixar Emma um pouco comigo?

Ela enrolou as palavras:

— Elatá dumino.

Sara pôs as mãos na cintura de Emma. Com delicadeza, levantou a bebê do ombro de Faith.

— Veja só. Ela está tão grande. — Sara fez um exame superficial, olhando os olhos de Emma, checando os dedos das mãos e dos pés, a gengiva. — Acho que está um pouco desidratada.

A Sra. Levy ofereceu:

— Preparei uma mamadeira, mas ela não me deixou dar.

— Pode ir buscar agora? — Sara fez sinal para Will se aproximar. Ele pegou Emma. A bebê era surpreendentemente pesada. Ele a colocou no ombro. A cabeça dela caiu em seu pescoço como um saco de farinha molhada. — Faith? — Sara falava de forma sucinta, como quem tenta atrair a atenção de uma pessoa idosa. — Como está se sentindo?

— Levei no médico.

— Você levou Emma? — Sara segurou o rosto de Faith. — O que o médico disse?

— Não sei.

— Você consegue olhar para mim?

A boca de Faith se moveu como se ela estivesse mascando chiclete.

— Que dia é hoje, meu bem? Você sabe me dizer que dia da semana é?

Ela retraiu a cabeça.

— Não.

— Não tem problema. — Sara pressionou a pálpebra de Faith para abri-la. — Quando você comeu pela última vez?

Ela não respondeu. A Sra. Levy voltou com a mamadeira. Entregou a Will, que aninhou Emma no braço para ela poder tomá-la.

— Faith? Quando você comeu pela última vez?

Faith tentou afastar Sara. Quando não funcionou, ela a empurrou mais forte.

Sara continuou falando, segurando as mãos de Faith.

— Foi hoje de manhã? Você tomou café da manhã?

— Vaimbora.

Sara se virou para a Sra. Levy.

— Você não é diabética, é?

— Não, querida, mas meu marido era. Morreu faz quase vinte anos, que Deus o tenha.

Sara falou para Will:

— Ela está tendo uma crise de hipoglicemia. Cadê a bolsa dela?

A Sra. Levy informou:

— Não estava junto quando a trouxeram para cá. Talvez tenha ficado no carro.

De novo, Sara se dirigiu a Will:

— Ela deve ter um kit de emergência na bolsa. É de plástico. Vem escrito "glucagon". — Ela acrescentou, lembrando-se de dar mais detalhes: — É comprido, mais ou menos do tamanho de um estojo de lápis. Vermelho ou laranja vivos. Pegue para mim agora, por favor.

Will levou a bebê junto, correndo para a porta da frente e pelo jardim. Os lotes em Sherwood Forest eram maiores que a maioria, mas alguns eram compridos e estreitos, não largos. Da garagem da Sra. Levy, Will enxergava dentro do banheiro de Evelyn Mitchell. Ele viu um homem parado no longo corredor. Will se perguntou, não pela primeira vez, como a senhora não tinha escutado o tiroteio na casa ao lado. Não seria a primeira testemunha a não querer se envolver, mas Will ficava surpreso com sua relutância.

Só quando estava a alguns metros do Mini lhe ocorreu que o carro de Faith fazia parte da cena do crime. Havia dois policiais parados do outro lado do carro, mais quatro na garagem. Will passou os olhos pelo interior. Viu o estojo de plástico que Sara havia mencionado, misturado com vários itens femininos no banco do carona.

Ele disse aos policiais:

— Preciso pegar uma coisa no carro.

— Que bosta, hein — devolveu um deles.

Will indicou Emma, que estava mamando como se tivesse feito uma trilha de quinze quilômetros.

— Ela precisa de uma coisa para acalmar os dentinhos. Estão nascendo.

Os policiais o olharam. Will considerou se tinha falado besteira. Ele havia trocado um bom numero de fraldas no lar de acolhimento, mas não fazia ideia de quando os dentes dos bebês nasciam. Emma tinha quatro meses. Seu alimento vinha todo de Faith ou de uma mamadeira. Até onde ele sabia, ela não precisava mastigar nada.

— Sério, cara. — Will levantou Emma para verem o rostinho cor--de-rosa dela. — É uma bebezinha.

— Tá — um deles cedeu. Ele contornou o carro e abriu a porta. — Cadê?

— É essa coisa vermelha de plástico. Parece um estojo de lápis.

O policial não pareceu estranhar. Pegou o kit e entregou a Will.

— Ela está bem?

— Só estava com sede.

— Estou falando de Faith, babaca.

Will tentou pegar o kit, mas o homem não soltava. Ele repetiu a pergunta.

— Faith vai ficar bem?

Will percebeu que tinha mais coisa ali.

— Vai. Vai ficar ótima.

— Diga a ela que Brad mandou dızer que vamos achar a mãe dela.

Ele soltou o kit e bateu a porta.

Will não deu tempo para o homem mudar de ideia. Voltou correndo para a casa, tentando não sacudir a bebê. A Sra. Levy ainda estava de sentinela na porta. Abriu antes de Will bater.

A cena lá dentro tinha mudado. Faith estava deitada no sofá. Sara estava segurando a parte de trás da cabeça dela, fazendo-a beber de uma lata de refrigerante.

Sara imediatamente começou a falar com Will.

— Você devia ter chamado os médicos desde o começo — repreendeu ela. — A glicemia dela está baixa demais. Ela está em estupor e diaforética. O coração está acelerado. Não é brincadeira.

Ela pegou o kit e o abriu com um *pop*. Lá dentro, havia uma seringa cheia de um líquido transparente e um frasco de pó branco que era muito parecido com cocaína. Sara limpou a agulha com uma bola de algodão e um pouco de álcool que obviamente tinha conseguido com a Sra. Levy. Ela falou enquanto inseria a seringa no frasco e puxava o líquido:

— Estou supondo que ela não come desde o café da manhã. A adrenalina do confronto na casa deve ter causado um pico de glicemia, mas fez com que a queda também fosse mais forte. Considerando o que aconteceu, fico surpresa por ela não ter entrado em coma.

As palavras atingiram Will com o devido peso. Não importava o que Amanda tinha dito, ele devia ter puxado um paramédico para lá meia hora atrás. Estava preocupado com a carreira de Faith quando devia estar preocupado com a vida dela.

— Ela vai ficar bem?

Sara chacoalhou o frasco, misturando os conteúdos antes de puxá-los de novo com a seringa.

— Já, já vamos saber.

Ela levantou a blusa de Faith e passou álcool numa parte da barriga. Will viu a agulha entrar, o êmbolo deslizando pelo cilindro de plástico enquanto o líquido era injetado.

Sara perguntou:

— Está preocupado por acharem que ela estava debilitada quando atirou naqueles dois homens?

Ele não respondeu.

— A piora dela provavelmente foi súbita. Ela deve ter começado a falar enrolado. Provavelmente parecia bêbada ou drogada. — Sara limpou o kit, colocando tudo de volta no lugar. — Diga para eles olharem os fatos. Ela atirou na cabeça de um homem e nas costas de outro, provavelmente à distância, com duas espectadoras inocentes ao alcance da mira. Se estivesse debilitada, não tinha como acertar os dois tiros.

Will olhou de relance para a Sra. Levy, que provavelmente não devia estar ouvindo aquela conversa. Ela afastou as preocupações dele com um gesto de mão.

— Ah, não se preocupe comigo, querido. Hoje em dia, não me lembro de muita coisa. — Ela estendeu os braços para pegar Emma. — Que tal me deixarem cuidar dessa pequetita?

Com cuidado, ele transferiu a bebê à Sra. Levy. A velha saiu na direção dos fundos da casa. Seus chinelos faziam um som de batida nos calcanhares secos.

Will questionou Sara:

— E a diabetes? Podem dizer que foi isso?

O tom dela era profissional.

— Como ela estava agindo quando você chegou?

— Ela parecia... — Ele balançou a cabeça, pensando que nunca mais queria ver Faith tão mal. — Parecia que tinha enlouquecido.

— Você acha que uma pessoa mentalmente ou quimicamente alterada poderia ter matado dois homens com um único tiro em cada um? — Sara colocou a mão no ombro de Faith. Seu tom se suavizou. — Faith, pode se sentar, por favor?

Devagar, Faith se moveu para se endireitar. Parecia grogue, como se tivesse acabado de acordar de uma longa soneca, mas a cor estava voltando. Ela colocou as mãos na cabeça e fez uma careta.

Sara disse a ela:

— Você vai ter dor de cabeça por um tempo. Tome o máximo de água que conseguir. Precisamos do seu medidor para ver como você está.

— Está na minha bolsa.

61

— Vou tentar pegar um de uma das ambulâncias. — Ela pegou uma garrafa de água da mesa de centro e desrosqueou a tampa. — Agora, é água. Chega de refrigerante.

Sara saiu sem olhar para Will. Suas costas pareciam uma parede de gelo. Ele não sabia o que fazer com aquilo, então, ignorou, sentando-se na mesa de centro na frente de Faith.

Ela tomou um longo gole de água antes de falar com ele.

— Minha cabeça está me matando. — O choque do que tinha acontecido voltou a ela como um raio. — Cadê minha mãe? — Ela tentou se levantar, mas Will a manteve sentada. — Cadê ela?

— Estão procurando.

— As menininhas...

— Estão bem. Por favor, só fique aqui um segundo, tá?

Ela olhou ao redor, e um pouco da loucura voltou.

— Cadê Emma?

— Está com a Sra. Levy. Está dormindo. Liguei para Jeremy na escola...

A boca de Faith se abriu. Ele via a vida voltando a ela aos borbotões.

— Como você contou para ele?

— Eu falei com Victor. Ele ainda é reitor dos alunos. Eu sabia que você não ia querer que eu mandasse um policial na sala de Jeremy.

— Victor. — Faith apertou os lábios. Ela tinha namorado Victor Martinez por um tempo, mas eles haviam terminado fazia quase um ano. — Por favor, diga que você não mencionou Emma.

Will não lembrava exatamente o que tinha falado para Victor, mas chutou que Faith ainda não conseguira contar ao cara que ele tinha uma filha.

— Desculpe.

— Deixe pra lá. — Ela soltou a garrafa de água, e suas mãos trêmulas derramaram um pouco no carpete. — O que mais?

— Estamos tentando encontrar seu irmão. — O Dr. Zeke Mitchell era cirurgião da Aeronáutica e ocupava um posto em algum lugar da Alemanha. — Amanda falou com um amigo na Base Aérea da Reserva de Dobbins. Estão resolvendo umas burocracias.

— Meu celular... — Ela pareceu se dar conta de onde o tinha deixado. — Minha mãe tem o número dele ao lado do telefone da cozinha.

— Eu pego assim que a gente terminar — prometeu Will. — Me conte o que aconteceu.

Ela respirou, tremendo. Ele viu o sofrimento dela por saber o que tinha feito.

— Eu matei duas pessoas.

Will segurou as mãos dela. A pele estava fria e pegajosa. Ela tinha um leve tremor, mas ele não achava que era por causa da taxa de glicose.

— Você salvou duas menininhas, Faith.

— O homem no quarto... — Ela parou. — Não entendo o que aconteceu.

— Você está confusa de novo? Quer que eu chame a Dra. Linton?

— Não. — Ela balançou a cabeça por tanto tempo que ele achou que talvez fosse melhor buscar Sara, sim. — Ela não é ruim, Will. Minha mãe não é uma policial corrupta.

— A gente não precisa falar de...

— Precisa, sim — insistiu Faith. — E, mesmo que ela fosse, coisa que não é, ela está aposentada faz cinco anos. Não está mais no emprego. Não vai aos bailes beneficentes nem aos eventos. Não fala com ninguém daquela vida antiga. Ela joga baralho às sextas com umas senhoras do bairro. Vai à igreja toda quarta e todo domingo. Cuida de Emma enquanto eu trabalho. O carro dela tem cinco anos. Ela acabou de pagar a última parcela da hipoteca da casa. Não está metida em nada. Não tem motivo para alguém achar que...

Os lábios dela começaram a tremer. Lágrimas ameaçaram cair.

Will começou a listar as coisas concretas que podia apontar.

— Tem um centro de comando móvel lá fora. Todas as vias estão sendo monitoradas. A foto de Evelyn está em todas as emissoras. Todas as viaturas patrulhando a região metropolitana têm a foto dela. Estamos acionando todos os informantes para ver se sabem de alguma coisa. Eles grampearam e rastrearam todos os telefones de vocês caso alguém exija resgate. Amanda deu um chilique, mas eles colocaram um dos investigadores deles na sua casa para monitorar todas as correspondências e ligações. Jeremy está na sua casa. Puseram um homem à paisana com ele. Você também vai ter um.

63

Faith já tinha trabalhado em casos de sequestros.

— Você acha mesmo que vai ter resgate?

— É possível.

— Eles eram Texicanos. Estavam procurando alguma coisa. Foi por isso que a levaram.

Will perguntou:

— O que eles estavam procurando?

— Não sei. A casa estava revirada. O asiático disse que trocava minha mãe pelo que estavam procurando.

— O asiático disse que trocava?

— Isso, ele estava apontando uma arma para o Texicano... o do quintal.

— Espere aí. — Eles estavam fazendo aquilo do jeito errado. — Me ajude aqui, Faith. Você tem que tratar sua memória como uma cena do crime. Comece do começo. Você tinha aquele treinamento presencial hoje de manhã, né? De informática?

Ela começou a fazer que sim com a cabeça.

— Eu me atrasei quase duas horas para voltar para casa.

Ela detalhou cada passo de sua manhã até ali, como tinha tentado ligar para a mãe, como tinha escutado música na casa ao sair do carro. Faith só tinha percebido que havia algo de errado quando a música parou. Will deixou que ela contasse toda a história — a casa destruída, o homem morto que ela tinha encontrado e os dois que ela mesma matou.

Quando ela terminou, ele repassou tudo mentalmente, visualizando Faith parada na garagem ao lado do quarto de ferramentas, voltando ao carro. Apesar dos problemas médicos recentes, a memória dela parecia claríssima naquele momento. Ela havia ligado para a central e depois pegado a arma. Will sentiu esse detalhe incomodando no fundo de sua mente. Faith sabia que Will estava em casa naquele dia. Eles tinham falado disso no dia anterior à tarde. Ela estava reclamando de ter que ir fazer o treinamento de informática e ele dissera a ela que ia lavar o carro e cuidar do jardim. Will morava a pouco mais de três quilômetros e meio de onde estavam sentados. Poderia ter chegado em menos de cinco minutos.

Mas Faith não tinha ligado para ele.

— O que foi? — perguntou ela. — Esqueci alguma coisa?

Ele pigarreou.

— Que música estava tocando quando você chegou?

— Do AC/DC — disse ela. — "Back in Black."

Esse detalhe parecia estranho.

— É o que sua mãe costuma ouvir?

Ela fez que não com a cabeça. Obviamente ainda estava em choque, a cabeça girando com o que tinha acontecido.

Ele segurou os braços dela, tentando fazer com que ela se concentrasse.

— Pense bem. — Ele esperou que ela o olhasse. — Tem dois homens mortos na casa. Os dois são asiáticos. O cara do quintal é mexicano. Los Texicanos.

Ela se concentrou.

— O asiático no quarto... estava usando uma camisa havaiana espalhafatosa. Ele parecia ser do sul. — Ela estava falando do sotaque dele. — Ele estava apontando uma arma para o Texicano. Estava ameaçando matar o cara.

— Ele disse mais alguma coisa?

— Eu atirei nele.

O lábio dela voltou a tremer.

Will nunca tinha visto Faith chorar e não queria ver naquele momento.

— O cara de camisa havaiana estava apontando uma arma para a cabeça de outra pessoa — lembrou ele. — O Texicano já tinha levado uma surra, possivelmente sido torturado. Você estava temendo pela vida dele. Foi por isso que puxou o gatilho.

Ela concordou com a cabeça, mas ele via a dúvida surgindo em seus olhos. Ele disse:

— Depois que o Camisa Havaiana caiu, o Texicano saiu correndo para o quintal, certo?

— Certo.

— E você correu atrás dele, ele apontou a arma para aquelas meninas e disparou, então, você atirou nele também, certo?

— Sim.

— Você estava protegendo o refém no quarto e estava protegendo as duas meninas no quintal da sua vizinha. Certo?

— Sim — confirmou ela, com a voz mais forte. — Estava.

Ela estava voltando a ser ela mesma. Will se permitiu sentir um pouco de alívio. Ele soltou as mãos dela.

— Você se lembra da diretiva, Faith. Força letal é autorizada quando a sua vida ou a vida de outra pessoa está em risco. Você fez seu trabalho hoje. Só precisa articular o que estava pensando. Tinha gente em perigo. Atiramos para acabar imediatamente com a ameaça. Não para machucar.

— Eu sei.

— Por que você não esperou os reforços?

Ela não respondeu.

— A atendente falou para você esperar lá fora. Você não esperou.

Faith continuou sem responder.

Will sentou-se mais para trás na mesa, com as mãos entre os joelhos. Talvez ela não confiasse nele. Nunca tinham falado abertamente da investigação dele contra a mãe dela, mas ele sabia que Faith supunha que eram os investigadores do esquadrão que tinham feito merda, não a capitã no comando. Por mais esperta que fosse, ainda era ingênua em relação à política do trabalho. Will tinha notado em todos os casos de corrupção em que trabalhou que as cabeças que tendiam a rolar nesse ramo eram as que não tinham estrelas douradas no colarinho. Faith tinha uma posição baixa demais na cadeia alimentar para esse tipo de proteção.

Ele disse:

— Você deve ter ouvido algo lá dentro. Um grito? Um tiro?

— Não.

— Você viu alguma coisa?

— Vi a cortina se mexer, mas foi depois...

— Ótimo, isso é ótimo. — Ele se inclinou de novo para a frente. — Você viu alguém lá dentro. Achou que sua mãe pudesse estar lá. Sentiu um perigo iminente à vida dela e entrou para proteger o local.

— Will...

— Preste atenção, Faith. Eu fiz essas mesmas perguntas a vários policiais e sei qual é a resposta. Você está prestando atenção?

Ela fez que sim.

— Você viu alguém dentro da casa. Achou que sua mãe pudesse estar correndo sério perigo...

— Eu vi sangue na garagem. Na porta. Uma marca de mão ensanguentada na porta.

— Exato. Ótimo. Isso lhe dá motivo para entrar. Tinha alguém gravemente ferido. A vida da pessoa estava em risco. O resto aconteceu porque você foi incitada a agir em uma situação na qual era justificado usar força letal.

Ela balançou a cabeça.

— Por que você está me treinando? Você odeia quando os policiais mentem para proteger uns aos outros.

— Não estou mentindo por você. Estou tentando garantir que você não perca o emprego.

— Estou cagando para o meu emprego. Só quero minha mãe de volta.

— Então, diga o que a gente acabou de falar. Você não vai ser útil para ninguém dentro de uma cela.

Ele viu o choque nos olhos de Faith. Por mais que as coisas estivessem ruins naquele momento, nunca lhe tinha ocorrido que podiam piorar.

Houve uma batida alta na porta. Will começou a se levantar, mas a Sra. Levy chegou primeiro. Ela veio requebrando pelo corredor, balançando os braços. Ele imaginou que ela tivesse colocado Emma numa das camas e torceu para ela ter se lembrado de empilhar uns travesseiros ao redor.

Geary foi o primeiro a entrar, depois Amanda, depois uns homens mais velhos, um negro, um branco. Ambos tinham sobrancelhas grossas, rosto bem barbeado e vários broches e fitas no peito, daqueles que vinham de uma carreira gloriosa atrás de uma escrivaninha. Estavam ali como adereços para Geary parecer importante. Se ele fosse jogador de futebol, eles seriam chamados de "parças". Como ele era comandante de zona, eram chamados de equipe de apoio.

67

— Senhora — murmurou Geary para a Sra. Levy, tirando o chapéu.

Os funcionários imitaram, colocando o chapéu debaixo do braço, assim como o chefe. Geary caminhou na direção de Faith, mas a senhora os interrompeu.

— Querem um chá, ou talvez uns biscoitos?

Geary se irritou:

— Estamos no meio de uma investigação, não de um chá da tarde.

A Sra. Levy não se abalou.

— Está bem, então. Por favor, fiquem à vontade.

Ela deu uma piscadela a Will antes de dar meia-volta e seguir pelo corredor.

Geary disse:

— Levante-se, agente Mitchell.

Will sentiu um aperto no estômago quando Faith se levantou. Não havia mais nada do tremor anterior, embora a blusa estivesse para fora da calça e o cabelo continuasse desgrenhado. Ela disse:

— Estou pronta para dar depoimento se...

Amanda interrompeu:

— Seu advogado e um representante do sindicato estão esperando na delegacia.

Geary fez uma careta. Obviamente não estava nem aí para a representação legal de Faith.

— Agente Mitchell, você tinha ordens de esperar reforço. Não sei como se fazem as coisas na GBI, mas os homens da minha divisão seguem ordens.

Faith olhou para Amanda, mas disse a Geary com tranquilidade:

— Tinha sangue na porta da cozinha. Eu vi uma pessoa dentro da casa. A Smith and Wesson da minha mãe tinha sumido. Eu temi que houvesse uma ameaça iminente à vida dela, então entrei na casa para garantir sua segurança.

Ela não teria dito melhor nem se Will tivesse dado um roteiro.

Geary perguntou:

— E o homem na área de serviço?

— Estava morto quando entrei na casa.

— O do quarto?

— Estava com o revólver da minha mãe apontado para a cabeça de outro homem. Eu estava protegendo a vida do refém.

— E o homem no quintal?

— O refém. Ele pegou o revólver depois que eu atirei no primeiro homem. A porta da frente foi arrombada e minha atenção foi desviada. Ele correu para o quintal com a arma e atirou na direção de duas meninas. Eu atirei, fiz isso para salvar a vida delas.

Geary olhou para os adereços condecorados enquanto decidia o que fazer. Os dois homens também pareciam incertos, mas prontos para concordar com o chefe sem questionar. Will sentiu o corpo tensionar, porque era ali que as coisas iam bem ou mal. Talvez uma lealdade predominante a Evelyn Mitchell tivesse convencido o homem a adotar uma abordagem mais branda. Ele disse a Faith.

— Um dos meus homens vai levar você para a delegacia. Pode tirar um momento para se recompor, se precisar.

Ele começou a pôr o chapéu, mas Amanda o interrompeu.

— Mike. Acho que preciso lembrá-lo de uma coisa. — Ela deu o mesmo sorriso doce de antes. — Os casos relacionados a tráfico de drogas no estado são da competência da GBI.

— Você está me dizendo que achou evidências de que tinha narcóticos envolvidos nesses disparos?

— Não estou dizendo nada, estou?

Ele a encarou enquanto punha o chapéu.

— Não pense que eu não vou descobrir por que você está me fazendo perder tempo.

— Parece um uso maravilhoso dos seus recursos.

Geary saiu batendo o pé, com os lacaios correndo atrás. Lá fora, Sara estava subindo os degraus da varanda. Rapidamente, colocou as mãos atrás das costas para esconder o monitor de glicemia que tinha pegado emprestado.

— Dra. Linton. — Geary tirou de novo o chapéu. Os homens imitaram o gesto. — Perdão por não ter reconhecido seu nome antes. — Will supôs que fosse por Sara não ter se apresentado. Obviamente, outra pessoa tinha contado a ele. — Eu conheci seu marido. Era um bom policial. Um bom homem.

Sara continuou com as mãos atrás das costas, girando o monitor de plástico. Will reconheceu o olhar que ela deu aos homens — ela não queria conversar. Para Geary, conseguiu dizer, seca:

— Obrigada.

— Por favor, entre em contato comigo se eu puder ajudá-la com qualquer coisa.

Ela assentiu. Geary colocou o chapéu e o gesto foi imitado como uma ola em um jogo de futebol.

Faith falou assim que a porta foi fechada:

— O Texicano no quintal me falou uma coisa antes de morrer. — Sua boca se moveu enquanto ela tentava lembrar o que tinha ouvido. — "Alma" ou "al-may".

— *Almeja?* — perguntou Amanda, falando com um sotaque estrangeiro.

Faith fez que sim.

— Isso. Você sabe o que significa?

Sara abriu a boca para falar, mas, antes de conseguir pronunciar uma palavra, Amanda explicou:

— É uma gíria em espanhol para "dinheiro". Literalmente, quer dizer "marisco". Acha que estavam atrás de dinheiro?

Faith fez que não e deu de ombros ao mesmo tempo.

— Sei lá. Não disseram isso em momento nenhum. Quer dizer, faz sentido. Los Texicanos é sinônimo de drogas. Drogas são um sinônimo de dinheiro. Minha mãe trabalhava no esquadrão de narcóticos. Talvez achem que ela...

Faith olhou de relance para Will. Ele praticamente conseguia ler a mente dela. Depois da investigação que ele conduzira, muita gente achava que Evelyn Mitchell era exatamente o tipo de policial que tinha pilhas de dinheiro em casa.

Sara aproveitou o silêncio.

— É melhor eu ir. — Ela entregou o monitor de glicemia a Faith. — Você precisa seguir seu cronograma religiosamente. O estresse vai dificultar. Ligue para a sua médica para falar da dosagem, dos ajustes que precisa fazer, em quais sinais precisa ficar de olho. Ainda está se consultando com a Dra. Wallace? — Faith confirmou com a cabeça. — Vou ligar para o consultório dela no caminho de casa e contar o que aconteceu, mas você precisa falar com ela assim que possível. É um momento estressante, mas você tem que manter a rotina. Entendido?

— Obrigada.

Faith nunca se sentiu à vontade com gratidão, mas essa fala foi a mais sincera que Will já tinha ouvido sair de sua boca.

Ele perguntou a Sara:

— Você vai fazer o exame toxicológico para Geary?

Ela dirigiu as palavras a Amanda:

— Faith trabalha para você, não para a polícia de Atlanta. Eles precisam de mandado para tirar o sangue dela e imagino que você não queira esse trabalho.

Amanda perguntou:

— Hipoteticamente, o que esse exame veria?

— Que ela não estava intoxicada nem com seu estado comprometido por nenhuma das substâncias que eles testarem. Quer que eu faça a coleta?

— Não, Dra. Linton. Mas agradeço pela ajuda.

Ela saiu sem falar mais nada, sem um olhar sequer na direção de Will. Amanda sugeriu:

— Por que não vai lá ver a viúva alegre?

Will achou que ela estava falando de Sara, mas então seu raciocínio interveio. Ele caminhou até os fundos da casa atrás da Sra. Levy, mas não antes de ver Amanda puxando Faith num abraço apertado. O gesto era chocante vindo de uma mulher cujos instintos maternais eram mais parecidos com os de um dingo comedor de bebês.

Will sabia que Faith e Amanda tinham um passado conjunto do qual nenhuma das duas falava e que não assumiam. Enquanto Evelyn Mitchell abria caminho para as mulheres na polícia de Atlanta, Amanda Wagner estava fazendo o mesmo na GBI. Eram contemporâneas, mais ou menos da mesma idade, com a mesma postura durona. Também eram amigas de uma vida inteira — Amanda tinha até namorado o cunhado de Evelyn, tio de Faith —, um detalhe que Amanda deixou de mencionar a Will ao escalá-lo para investigar o esquadrão de narcóticos liderado pela velha amiga.

Ele encontrou a Sra. Levy no quarto dos fundos, que parecia ter sido transformado num cômodo genérico para tudo o que a velha curtia.

Tinha uma estação de *scrapbooking*, algo que Will só reconhecia porque tinha trabalhado num tiroteio num bairro de classe média nos arredores da cidade, onde uma jovem mãe tinha sido assassinada enquanto colava fotografias cortadas em zigue-zague numa cartolina colorida. Havia um par de patins de quatro rodas. Uma raquete de tênis estava apoiada num canto. Vários tipos de câmeras estavam dispostas no sofá-cama. Algumas eram digitais, mas a maioria era do tipo antigo que usava filme. Ele adivinhou, pela luz vermelha em cima da porta do closet, que ela revelava as próprias fotografias.

A Sra. Levy estava sentada numa cadeira de balanço de madeira ao lado da janela, com Emma no colo. A bebê estava embrulhada no avental dela como se fosse um cobertor. Os pequenos gansos estavam de ponta-cabeça na barra. Os olhos de Emma estavam fechados e ela sugava ferozmente a mamadeira na boca. O barulho lembrou Will da bebê dos *Simpsons*.

— Não quer se sentar? — ofereceu a velha. — Emma já parece estar se recuperando bem.

Will se sentou no sofá-cama, com cuidado para não mexer nas câmeras.

— Que bom que por acaso você tinha uma mamadeira para ela.

— Não é? — Ela sorriu olhando a bebê. — Com tanta animação, a coitadinha perdeu a soneca.

— Você tem um berço para ela também?

Ela deu uma risadinha rouca.

— Imagino que você já tenha olhado no meu quarto.

Ele não tinha sido tão ousado, mas entendeu aquilo como uma abertura.

— Com que frequência você cuida dela?

— Em geral, só algumas vezes por semana.

— Mas ultimamente?

Ela piscou para ele.

— Você é espertinho.

Ele era mais sortudo que esperto. Tinha achado estranho a Sra. Levy por acaso ter uma mamadeira ali quando Emma precisava. Ele perguntou:

— O que Evelyn anda fazendo?

— Eu pareço mal-educada de ficar me metendo na vida dos outros?

— Como posso responder isso sem insultá-la?

Ela riu, mas até que cedeu com facilidade:

— Evelyn não me contou nada, mas acho que ela estava com um namoradinho.

— Há quanto tempo?

— Três ou quatro meses? — Ela parecia estar fazendo uma pergunta a si mesma. Assentiu com a cabeça enquanto respondia. — Foi logo depois de Emma nascer. Eles começaram devagar, uma vez por semana ou a cada quinze dias, mas eu diria que ficou mais frequente nos últimos dez dias. Parei de usar calendário quando me aposentei, mas Eve me pediu para olhar Emma três manhãs seguidas na semana passada.

— Era sempre de manhã?

— Em geral, por volta das onze até umas duas da tarde.

Três horas parecia tempo suficiente para um encontro.

— Faith sabia dele?

A Sra. Levy fez que não.

— Tenho certeza que Eve não queria que os filhos soubessem. Eles amavam tanto o pai. E ela também, entenda, mas já faz dez anos, pelo menos. É muito tempo para ficar sem companhia.

Will chutou que ela estivesse falando por experiência própria.

— Você disse que seu marido morreu há vinte anos.

— É, mas eu não gostava muito do Sr. Levy, nem ele de mim. — Ela usou o polegar para fazer carinho na bochecha de Emma. — Evelyn amava Bill. Tiveram uns obstáculos, mas é diferente quando a gente ama. A pessoa vai embora e sua vida racha no meio. Leva um tempão para consertar.

Will se permitiu pensar em Sara só por um segundo. A verdade era que ele nunca parava de pensar nela. Ela era como a tarja de notícias que ficava passando na parte inferior da televisão enquanto a vida dele, a reportagem principal, era transmitida.

— Você sabe o nome do homem?

— Ah, não, querido. Nunca perguntei. Mas ele dirigia um belo Cadillac CTS-V. O sedã, não o modelo cupê. Todo preto, com a grade da frente de aço inoxidável. Um V8 bem gutural. Dava para ouvir a quarteirões de distância.

Por um momento, Will ficou surpreso demais para responder.

— Você gosta de carros?

— Ah, nem um pouco, mas pesquisei na internet porque queria saber quanto tinha custado.

Will esperou.

— Imagino que uns setenta e cinco mil dólares — confidenciou a velha. — O Sr. Levy e eu compramos esta casa por menos da metade disso.

— Evelyn chegou a falar o nome dele?

— Nunca confessou nada. Apesar do que os homens gostam de achar, as mulheres não ficam falando de vocês o tempo todo.

Will se permitiu um sorriso.

— Como ele era?

— Bem, era careca — disse ela, como se fosse de se esperar. — Meio pançudo. Usava calça jeans na maior parte do tempo. A camisa vivia amarrotada e ele usava as mangas arregaçadas, o que me deixava perplexa, porque Evelyn sempre gostou de homem bem-vestido.

— Quantos anos você acha que ele tem?

— Sem o cabelo, difícil saber. Eu diria que a idade de Evelyn, mais ou menos.

— Uns sessenta e poucos anos.

— Ah. — Ela pareceu surpresa. — Achei que Evelyn estivesse na casa dos quarenta, mas acho que faz sentido, já que Faith tem trinta e poucos anos. E o bebê não é mais bebê, né? — Ela abaixou a voz como se tivesse medo de que alguém ouvisse. — Acho que já está fazendo vinte anos, mas não é o tipo de gravidez que a gente esquece. Quando ela começou a ter barriga, foi meio que um escândalo. Uma pena o jeito como as pessoas se comportaram. Todo mundo já se divertiu de vez em quando, mas, como eu disse para Evelyn na época, uma mulher corre mais rápido com a saia levantada do que um homem com a calça arriada.

Will não tinha considerado o dilema adolescente de Faith para além de achar incomum ela ter ficado com a criança, mas provavelmente havia abalado o bairro o fato de ter uma garota de catorze anos grávida naquele meio mais abastado. Atualmente era quase lugar-comum, mas, na época, uma menina na situação de Faith em geral era, de repente, convocada para longe, para cuidar de uma tia frágil até então desconhecida, ou passava pelo que se chamava eufemisticamente de apendicectomia. Algumas menos sortudas acabavam no lar de acolhimento com jovens como Will.

Ele perguntou:

— Então, o homem do carro caro tem uns sessenta e poucos anos?

Ela fez que sim.

— Você viu demonstração de afeto entre os dois?

— Não, mas Evelyn sempre foi discreta. Entrava no carro com ele e ia embora.

— Sem beijo na bochecha?

— Pelo menos, eu nunca vi. Mas, olha, eu nunca nem conheci o homem. Evelyn deixava Emma aqui, voltava para casa e esperava.

Will absorveu aquilo.

— Ele alguma vez entrou na casa?

— Não que eu tenha percebido. Acho que hoje as pessoas fazem as coisas de outro jeito. Na minha época, o homem batia na porta e escoltava você até o carro. Não tinha isso de parar e buzinar.

— Era isso que ele fazia? Buzinava?

— Não, filho, foi só modo de dizer. Acho que Eve devia ficar olhando pela janela, porque sempre saía assim que ele parava.

— Você sabe para onde eles iam?

— Não, mas, como falei, em geral ficavam fora por umas três horas, então eu imaginava que tivessem ido ver um filme ou almoçar.

Eram muitos filmes, então.

— O homem apareceu hoje?

— Não, e também não vi ninguém na rua. Nem carro, nem nada. Só fiquei sabendo que tinha acontecido alguma coisa quando ouvi as sirenes. Aí escutei os tiros, lógico, um e depois outro alguns minutos mais tarde. Eu sei como é um som de tiro. O Sr. Levy era caçador. Na época, todos os policiais eram. Ele me obrigava a ir junto, para cozinhar para eles. — Ela revirou os olhos. — Que falastrão chato ele era. Que Deus o tenha.

— Ele tinha sorte de ter você.

— E eu tenho sorte de ele não estar mais aqui. — Ela se levantou da cadeira de balanço com dificuldade, mantendo a bebê estável no colo. A mamadeira estava vazia. Ela a colocou na mesa e ofereceu Emma a Will. — Segure-a um segundinho, sim?

Ele apoiou Emma no ombro e deu tapinhas nas costas dela, que soltou um arroto excepcionalmente satisfatório.

A Sra. Levy estreitou os olhos.

— Você tem familiaridade com bebês.

Will não ia começar a contar sua história de vida.

— É que é fácil conversar com eles.

Ela descansou a mão no braço dele antes de ir ao closet. Will tinha razão. Havia uma câmara escura montada no pequeno espaço. Ele parou na porta, com cuidado para não bloquear a luz enquanto ela folheava uma pilha de fotos cinco por sete. As mãos dela tremiam de leve, mas ela parecia firme de pé.

Ela explicou:

— O Sr. Levy nunca deu muita bola para os meus hobbies, mas um dia foi chamado numa cena de crime e perguntaram se alguém conhecia um fotógrafo. Pagavam vinte e cinco dólares só para tirar fotos! O maldito não ia negar isso. Então, me ligou e mandou levar minha câmera. Quando eu não desmaiei com aquele caos, porque era um incidente com espingarda, disseram que eu podia fotografar outras vezes. — Ela acenou com a cabeça para a cama. — Aquela Brownie Six-16 ajudou a manter este teto sobre a nossa cabeça.

Ele sabia que ela estava falando da câmera caixote. Parecia gasta, mas muito amada.

— Depois, passei a trabalhar na vigilância. O Sr. Levy já tinha bebido até perder o emprego e, claro, eu sou mulher, então levou um tempo para entenderem que eu não estava lá para flertar e transar com eles.

Will sentiu o rosto começando a corar.

— Foi na polícia de Atlanta?

— Cinquenta e oito anos! — Ela parecia tão surpresa quanto Will por ter durado tanto. — Eu posso até ser só pele e osso hoje, mas teve uma época que Geary e os puxa-sacos dele teriam batido continência para mim em vez de me desprezar que nem um fiapinho nas calças brilhantes deles. — Ela estava passando por mais uma pilha de fotos cinco por sete. Will viu imagens em preto e branco de pássaros e vários animais de estimação, todas tiradas de um ponto de vista que implicava estarem sendo espionados, não admirados. — Esse carinha aí anda cavando no meu canteiro de flores.

Ela mostrou a Will uma foto de um gato cinza e branco com terra no focinho. A luz na impressão preto e branco era dura. Só faltava uma placa na frente do peito com o nome e número de presidiário do bicho.

— Aqui. — Finalmente, ela achou o que estava procurando. — É este. O namoradinho de Evelyn.

Will olhou por cima do ombro encurvado dela. A foto era granulada, obviamente tirada de trás de persianas que cobriam a janela da frente. A lente havia empurrado ripas finas e achatadas de plástico para abrir espaço. Um homem alto, mais velho, se apoiava num Cadillac preto, com as palmas das mãos no capô e antebraços virados para fora. O carro estava estacionado na rua, com os pneus da frente direcionados para o meio-fio. Will estacionava do mesmo jeito. Atlanta era uma cidade de ladeiras, instalada no piemonte das montanhas Apalaches. Quem dirigia carro de câmbio manual sempre apoiava as rodas no meio-fio para o carro não sair rolando.

— O que foi? — Faith estava parada na porta. Will passou a bebê para ela, mas ela parecia mais preocupada com a foto. — Você viu alguma coisa?

— Eu estava mostrando o Snippers para ele.

A Sra. Levy, de algum jeito, tinha feito um truque de mágica. A foto do homem tinha sumido e, no lugar, estava o gato escavador de canteiro de flores.

Emma se mexeu no colo de Faith, claramente percebendo o humor perturbado da mãe. Faith deu vários beijinhos rápidos na bochecha dela e fez caretas até a bebê sorrir. Will sabia que Faith estava encenando. Seus olhos estavam cheios de lágrimas. Ela abraçou forte a menina.

A Sra. Levy falou:

— Evelyn é dura na queda. Ela não vai se entregar.

Faith balançou a bebê para a frente e para trás, como as mães fazem automaticamente.

— Você não ouviu nada?

— Ah, minha querida, você sabe que, se eu tivesse ouvido qualquer coisinha, teria ido lá com meu trabuco. — Will reconheceu a gíria para o revólver de calibre largo. — Eve vai sair bem dessa. Ela sempre cai de pé. Pode apostar nisso.

— É que... — A voz de Faith falhou. — Se eu tivesse chegado antes ou... — Ela balançou a cabeça. — Por que isso aconteceu? Você sabe que minha mãe não está metida em nada errado. Por que alguém a levaria?

— Às vezes, não tem motivo nenhum para as pessoas fazerem coisas idiotas. — A velha deu de ombros, girando-os de leve. — Só sei que você vai se acabar se continuar por esse caminho de: e se eu tivesse feito isso ou se eu tivesse feito aquilo. — Ela pressionou o dorso dos dedos na bochecha de Faith. — Confie que o Senhor vai cuidar dela. "Não se apoie no seu próprio entendimento."

Faith assentiu, solene, embora Will nunca tivesse ouvido falar que ela era religiosa.

— Obrigada.

Os saltos de Amanda soaram pelo corredor acarpetado.

— Não consigo mais enrolar — disse ela a Faith. — Tem uma viatura lá fora esperando para levar você para a delegacia. Tente ficar calada e fazer o que seu advogado mandar.

— O mínimo que eu posso fazer é cuidar da bebê — ofereceu a Sra. Levy. — Não precisa levá-la para aquela delegacia imunda, e Jeremy não vai nem saber por onde se enfia a fralda.

Faith obviamente queria aceitar a oferta, mas alertou:

— Não sei quanto tempo vou demorar.

— Você sabe que eu sou noturna. Não tem problema.

— Obrigada.

Faith entregou com relutância a bebê para a senhora. Ela passou a mão nos cabelos castanhos fininhos de Emma e beijou o topo da cabeça dela. Seus lábios ficaram ali alguns segundos mais, depois ela saiu sem falar nada.

Assim que a porta da frente se fechou, Amanda foi direto ao ponto.

— Que foi?

A Sra. Levy puxou a foto de algum lugar debaixo do avental.

— Evelyn tinha um visitante frequente — explicou Will.

A Sra. Levy tinha boa memória: o homem era careca. A calça jeans era larga. A camisa estava amarrotada, as mangas, arregaçadas. Ela não havia mencionado um detalhe bem mais importante, o fato de ele ser hispânico. A tatuagem no braço estava borrada na imagem, mas Will reconheceu facilmente o símbolo no antebraço que o identificava como membro da facção Los Texicanos.

Amanda dobrou a foto no meio antes de enfiar no bolso do paletó. Perguntou à Sra. Levy:

— Os policiais já falaram com você?

— Com certeza vão acabar chegando nas velhinhas.

— Imagino que você vá cooperar como sempre.

Ela sorriu.

— Não sei o que é que tenho para dizer a eles, mas já vou deixar uns biscoitos assados caso eles passem aqui.

Amanda deu uma risadinha.

— Cuidado, Roz.

Ela fez um sinal para Will segui-la enquanto saía do quarto.

Will pôs a mão na carteira e puxou um de seus cartões para a Sra. Levy.

— Todos os meus números estão aqui. Me ligue se lembrar de qualquer coisa ou se precisar de ajuda com a bebê.

— Obrigada, meu filho.

A voz dela tinha perdido um pouco da gentileza de velhinha, mas mesmo assim ela pôs o cartão no avental.

Amanda já estava no meio do corredor quando Will a alcançou. Ela não falou nada da foto, nem da condição de Faith, nem da disputa de território que tivera com Geary. Em vez disso, começou a dar ordens:

— Preciso que você revise todos os documentos arquivados da sua investigação. — Ela não precisava especificar qual investigação. — Passe um pente fino em todos os depoimentos de testemunhas, todos os relatórios de informantes confidenciais, todas as declarações de delatores presos. Não me importa se for coisa pequena. Quero saber.

Amanda parou. Will sabia que ela estava pensando nos problemas dele com a leitura.

Ele manteve a voz estável.

— Não vai ser um problema.

— Seja adulto, Will. Se precisar de ajuda, fale agora para eu poder resolver.

— Quer que eu comece já? As caixas estão na minha casa.

— Não. Temos uma coisa para resolver antes. — Ela parou no hall de entrada, com as mãos na cintura. Era uma mulher magra, e Will vivia esquecendo o quanto ela era baixa até a ver esticando o pescoço para olhá-lo. — Consegui arrancar umas informações enquanto Geary dava o chilique dele. O Texicano no quintal fez o favor de se identificar como Ricardo, segundo a tatuagem enorme nas costas dele. Ainda não temos uma identificação completa. Tem vinte e poucos anos, mais ou menos um e setenta e cinco, uns setenta e cinco quilos. O asiático no quarto tem cerca de quarenta anos de idade, um pouco mais baixo e magro que o amigo hispânico. Eu chutaria que ele não é daqui. Deve ter sido trazido só para isso.

Will lembrou:

— Faith disse que ele tinha um sotaque do sul.

— Isso deve ajudar a reduzir as opções.

— E também estava usando uma camisa havaiana chamativa. Não é muito coisa de gângster.

— Vamos acrescentar isso à lista de crimes dele. — Ela olhou pelo corredor, depois de novo para Will. — Agora, o asiático na área de serviço também tem uma história estranha, que sabemos graças à carteira que ele trazia no bolso traseiro. Hironobu Kwon, dezenove anos. É calouro na Georgia State. Também é filho de uma professora de escola local, Miriam Kwon.

— Não é membro da facção?

— Pelo que estamos vendo, não. A polícia de Atlanta pegou a mamãe Kwon antes de conseguirmos chegar até ela. Vamos ter que encontrar a mulher amanhã de manhã para ver o que ela sabe. — Ela apontou para Will. — Mas com cautela. Ainda não estamos oficialmente no caso. Somos só nós dois até eu achar um jeito de entrar.

Ele falou:

— Faith parece achar que os Texicanos estavam procurando alguma coisa. — Will tentou analisar a expressão de Amanda. Em geral, ficava entre divertida e irritada, mas, naquele momento, estava completamente neutra. — Ricardo foi espancado. Não estava procurando nada exceto salvar a própria vida. Devíamos falar primeiro com os asiáticos.

— Parece bem lógico.

— Isso aponta para um problema maior — continuou ele. — Os Texicanos, eu entendo, mas o que os asiáticos iam querer com a Evelyn? Qual a jogada deles?

— É a pergunta de um milhão de dólares.

Ele detalhou mais:

— Evelyn cuidava do esquadrão de narcóticos. Los Texicanos controlam o tráfico em Atlanta. Já fazem isso há vinte anos.

— Sem dúvida fazem.

Will sentiu a pontada familiar da cabeça batendo numa muralha de tijolos. Era a mesma sensação que Amanda sempre causava nele quando tinha informação que não ia compartilhar. Por algum motivo, desta vez era pior, porque ela não estava só ferrando com a cabeça dele, estava acobertando a velha amiga.

Ele tentou:

— Você falou que o cara de camisa havaiana provavelmente foi trazido para "isso". O que é "isso"? Sequestro? Encontrar o que quer que Evelyn tivesse em casa?

— Não acho que ninguém vá achar o que está procurando hoje. — Ela pausou para deixá-lo entender o que ela queria dizer. — Charlie está ajudando os policiais locais com a cena do crime, mas eles não são tão suscetíveis ao charme dele quanto eu gostaria. Ele está com acesso bem limitado e está sendo supervisionado de perto. Dizem que vão compartilhar os resultados de laboratório. Não confio muito no ML deles.

O médico-legista de Fulton.

— Ele apareceu?

— Ainda está investigando aquele incêndio num apartamento em People's Town. — Cortes de orçamento tinham arrasado o Instituto

81

Médico-Legal. Se havia mais de um crime sério acontecendo dentro dos limites da cidade, em geral significava que os investigadores iam ter que esperar sentados. — Eu adoraria colocar Pete nisso.

Ela estava se referindo ao médico-legista da GBI. Will perguntou:

— Ele não pode dar uns telefonemas?

— Improvável — admitiu ela. — Pete não está exatamente cheio de amigos. Você sabe como ele é esquisito. Perto dele, você parece normal. E Sara?

— Ela não vai falar nada.

— Disso eu sei, Will. Eu vi a dancinha de vocês lá na rua. Estou perguntando se você acha que ela conhece alguém no IML.

Will deu de ombros.

— Pergunte a ela — ordenou Amanda.

Will duvidava que Sara fosse gostar de receber essa ligação, mas, mesmo assim, assentiu, concordando.

— E os extratos de cartão e registros telefônicos de Evelyn?

— Pedi para puxarem.

— Ela tem GPS no carro? Ou nos telefones?

Ela não deu resposta sobre isso.

— Vamos passar por alguns canais alternativos. Como falei, não vai ser muito às claras.

— Mas o que você falou para Geary está certo. Casos relacionados a tráfico de drogas são de nossa competência.

— Só porque Evelyn cuidava da divisão de narcóticos não quer dizer que isso tenha relação com o tráfico. Pelo que coletei, não acharam indícios de drogas na casa nem em nenhum dos mortos.

— E Ricardo, o Texicano morto, da facção criminosa Los Texicanos, ligada ao tráfico de drogas?

— Uma coincidência estranha.

— E o Texicano vivinho da silva que também é ligado ao tráfico de drogas e dirige um Cadillac preto no qual Evelyn Mitchell entra tranquilamente para passear?

Ela fingiu surpresa.

— Você acha que ele é um membro?

— Eu vi a tatuagem na foto. Evelyn está saindo há pelo menos quatro meses com um Texicano. — Will tentou moderar o tom. — Ele é mais velho. Deve ter um cargo mais alto na organização. A Sra. Levy diz que as visitas aumentaram nos últimos dez dias. Eles têm ido a algum lugar juntos no carro dele, em geral saindo às onze e voltando às duas.

De novo, Amanda ignorou o argumento dele e colocou o seu:

— Você prendeu seis investigadores do esquadrão da Evelyn. Dois saíram em condicional ano passado por bom comportamento. Ambos foram transferidos para fora do estado: um para a Califórnia, o outro para o Tennessee, que é onde estavam nesta tarde quando Evelyn foi levada. Dois estão na prisão de segurança média estadual de Valdosta, a quatro anos de serem soltos e sem bom comportamento à vista. Um está morto: overdose, que é um belo exemplo de carma. E o último está esperando para bater cartão na D&C.

A Prisão de Diagnóstico e Classificação da Geórgia. Pena de morte.

Will perguntou, relutante:

— Quem ele matou?

— Um guarda e um detento. Estrangulou um estuprador condenado com uma toalha, o que não foi nenhuma perda, mas aí espancou o guarda até a morte com as próprias mãos. Alegou legítima defesa.

— Contra o guarda?

— Você parece a acusação do caso dele.

Will tentou de novo.

— E Evelyn?

— O que tem ela?

— Eu a investiguei também.

— É verdade.

— A gente vai continuar varrendo esse assunto para baixo do tapete?

— Varrendo? Dá um tempo, Will, isto aqui é uma *faxina* completa.

Ela abriu a porta da frente. A luz do sol cortou a escuridão da casa como uma lâmina.

Amanda colocou os óculos de sol enquanto atravessavam o jardim em direção à cena do crime. Dois policiais à paisana estavam indo para a casa da Sra. Levy. Ambos olharam Will com raiva e deram um aceno de cabeça breve a Amanda.

Ela murmurou a Will, como se ela própria não tivesse causado o atraso:

— Já estava na hora de irem.

Ele esperou até os homens começarem a bater na porta.

— Pelo jeito, você conhece a Sra. Levy da sua época na polícia de Atlanta, né?

— Na GBI. Eu a investiguei pelo assassinato do marido. — **Amanda** pareceu curtir a expressão horrorizada de Will. — Nunca consegui provar, mas tenho certeza que ela envenenou o homem.

— Biscoitos? — ele chutou.

— Era minha teoria. — Um sorriso de satisfação curvou os lábios de Amanda enquanto ela pisava com cuidado na grama. — Roz é uma velha ardilosa. Viu mais cenas de crime do que todos nós juntos e tenho certeza de que fez anotações o tempo todo. Eu não confiaria em metade do que ela falou para você. Lembre-se: o Diabo pode citar as Escrituras quando isso lhe convém.

Amanda não estava errada, ou pelo menos Shakespeare não estava. Mesmo assim, Will a lembrou:

— Foi a Sra. Levy que me contou que o Texicano estava visitando Evelyn. Ela tirou a foto dele.

— Tirou mesmo, não foi?

Will sentiu a pergunta atingi-lo como um tapa na nuca. Considerando que o talento artístico da Sra. Levy se prestava mais a fotos nada lisonjeiras de bichos de estimação como se fossem presidiários, parecia estranho ela por acaso ter à mão uma foto do Texicano parado ao lado do Cadillac preto. Era uma velhinha inteligente. Estava espionando por um motivo.

— A gente devia voltar e falar com ela.

— Você acha mesmo que ela vai dizer alguma coisa útil?

Silenciosamente, Will concordou. A Sra. Levy parecia gostar de joguinhos e, com Evelyn desaparecida, eles não tinham tempo para brincar com isso.

— Evelyn sabe que ela matou o marido?

— Lógico que sabe.

— E mesmo assim deixa Emma com ela?

Eles tinham chegado ao Mini de Faith. Amanda colocou as mãos em concha no vidro e espiou lá dentro.

— Ela matou um alcoólatra abusivo de sessenta e quatro anos, não um bebê de quatro meses.

Will imaginou que, em algum lugar do mundo, esse tipo de lógica fizesse sentido.

Amanda foi na direção da casa. Charlie Reed estava na garagem falando com um monte de outros técnicos da unidade de perícia criminal. Alguns estavam fumando. Um estava apoiado num Malibu marrom estacionado de ré na frente do Mini de Faith. Todos estavam vestidos com macacão de segurança branco Tyvek que os fazia parecer marshmallows sujos de tamanhos variados. O bigode antiquado de Charlie era a única coisa que o distinguia dos homens barbeados. Ele viu Amanda e se afastou do grupo.

Ela disse:

— Conte-me tudo, Charlie.

Charlie virou-se para trás para olhar um homem de pele marrom, corpulento, cuja constituição esquisita fazia o macacão Tyvek ficar apertado em todas as áreas críticas. O homem deu um último trago no cigarro e o entregou a um dos colegas. Ele se apresentou a Amanda com um sotaque britânico bem articulado:

— Dra. Wagner, eu sou o Dr. Ahbidi Mittal.

Ela indicou Will.

— Este é o Dr. Trent, meu colega.

Will apertou a mão do homem, tentando não fazer uma careta pelo fato de Amanda mencionar com tanta tranquilidade um diploma que ambos sabiam que ele obtivera de uma faculdade online duvidosa.

Mittal ofereceu:

— Como cortesia, estou disposto a apresentar para vocês a cena do crime.

Amanda deu um olhar cortante para Charlie, como se ele tivesse culpa.

— Obrigado — disse Will, porque sabia que ninguém mais iria agradecer.

Mittal entregou um par de sapatilhas descartáveis para cada um colocar nos pés. Amanda agarrou o braço de Will para se equilibrar enquanto tirava os saltos e cobria os pés, que estavam com meia-calça. Will teve que ficar pulando sozinho num pé só. Mesmo sem sapato, os pés dele eram grandes demais, e ele acabou parecendo a Sra. Levy com os calcanhares para fora dos chinelos.

— Vamos começar por aqui?

Mittal não esperou que eles aceitassem o convite. Conduziu-os, passando por trás do Malibu, e entrou na casa pela porta aberta da cozinha. Instintivamente, Will abaixou a cabeça ao andar pelo cômodo de pé-direito baixo. Charlie esbarrou nele e murmurou um pedido de desculpas. A cozinha era pequena para quatro pessoas, tinha formato de ferradura, com a extremidade aberta dando para a área de serviço. Will percebeu o odor característico de ferro oxidado que o sangue exalava ao coagular.

Faith tinha razão — os invasores estavam procurando algo. A casa estava uma zona. Talheres e gavetas estavam espalhados pelo chão. Havia buracos abertos nas paredes. Um celular e um BlackBerry que parecia mais antigo estavam esmagados no chão. O telefone da parede tinha sido arrancado do gancho. Exceto pelo pó preto para revelar impressões digitais e os marcadores de plástico amarelo usados pela equipe forense, nada do que Faith tinha declarado ter visto ao entrar na casa havia sido alterado. Até o cadáver continuava na área de serviço. Faith devia ter ficado apavorada, sem saber o que a esperava em cada canto, morta de medo de a mãe estar machucada — ou coisa pior.

Will devia ter estado lá. Devia ser o tipo de parceiro em que Faith confiasse para chamar em qualquer situação.

Mittal falou:

— Ainda não escrevi meu relatório, mas estou disposto a compartilhar minha teoria atual.

Amanda fez um círculo com a mão, apressando as coisas.

— Me diga o que você tem.

O tom de ordem fez Mittal apertar os lábios.

— Imagıno que a capitã Mitchell estivesse fazendo almoço quando o crime se iniciou.

Havia sacos de frios na bancada ao lado de uma faca e uma tábua onde Evelyn estava visivelmente cortando tomates. Havia um saco vazio de pão de forma amassado na pia. Os pães na torradeira tinham pulado muito tempo atrás. Quatro fatias. Evelyn provavelmente sabia que Faith ia precisar comer quando chegasse em casa.

Era uma cena relativamente normal, até agradável, exceto pelo fato de cada item da bancada estar com respingos ou manchas de sangue. A torradeira, os pães, a tábua. Mais sangue tinha pingado no chão, formando poças nos azulejos. Dois pares de pegadas vermelhas de sapato cruzavam o chão de porcelana branca, um par de pés pequenos, um de pés grandes; tinha acontecido uma briga.

Mittal continuou:

— A capitã Mitchell se assustou com um barulho, possivelmente a porta de vidro quebrando, o que provavelmente a fez cortar o dedo com a faca que estava usando para fatiar os tomates.

Amanda notou:

— É muito sangue para um acidente de cozinha.

Mittal obviamente não queria opiniões. Ele fez mais uma pausa antes de continuar:

— A bebê, Emma, devia estar ali. — Ele apontou para o espaço na bancada ao lado da geladeira, na frente da área em que Evelyn estava preparando o almoço. — Achamos uma gotinha de sangue na bancada ali. — Ele apontou para o ponto ao lado de um modelo antigo de tocador de CD. — Tem um rastro de sangue indo e vindo do quarto de ferramentas, então, muito provavelmente a capitã Mitchell estava sangrando ao sair da cozinha. A marca da mão dela na porta reforça essa tese.

Amanda assentiu.

— Ela escuta um barulho, então esconde a bebê para que fique em segurança, depois volta com sua Smith and Wesson.

As palavras de Charlie saíram apressadas, como se ele não conseguisse mais segurar a língua.

— Ela deve ter envolvido o corte com papel-toalha, mas o sangue vazou rápido. Tem sangue na porta da cozinha e no cabo de madeira da Smith and Wesson.

Will perguntou:

— E a cadeirinha do carro?

— Está limpa. Ela deve ter carregado com a outra mão. Temos um rastro de sangue indo e voltando pela garagem, o trajeto que ela fez com Emma até o quarto de ferramentas. É sangue de Evelyn. A equipe do Ahbidi já examinou o tipo sanguíneo, então, podemos meio que montar o quebra-cabeça a partir disso. — Ele levantou os olhos para Mittal. — Foi mal, Ahbi. Espero não estar invadindo seu território.

Mittal fez um gesto expansivo com as mãos, indicando que Charlie devia continuar.

Will sabia que essa parte do trabalho era a favorita de Charlie. Ele andou com gingado até a porta aberta e colocou as mãos juntas perto do rosto como se estivesse segurando um revólver.

— Evelyn volta para a casa. Ela se vira, vê o bandido número um esperando na área de serviço e atira na cabeça dele. A força do impacto fez o cara girar que nem um cata-vento. O que a gente vê na parte de trás da cabeça dele é o buraco de saída da bala. — Charlie se virou, levantando de novo as mãos numa pose clássica de *As Panteras*, que era o melhor jeito de levar um tiro no peito. — Aí, vem o bandido número dois, provavelmente dali. — Ele apontou para a passagem entre a cozinha e a sala de jantar. — Eles começam a lutar. Evelyn perde a arma. Está vendo ali?

Will seguiu o dedo que ele apontava para um marcador plástico no chão. Depois de Charlie o sugestionar com aquela ideia, ele via o desenho fraco e ensanguentado de um revólver.

— Evelyn pega a faca na bancada. O sangue dela está no cabo, mas não na lâmina.

Amanda interrompeu:

— O sangue dela não é o único na faca?

— Não. Segundo a ficha de Evelyn, ela é O positivo. Temos B negativo na lâmina e aqui perto da geladeira.

Mittal acrescentou:

— É um respingo passivo. Não teve artéria comprometida, senão haveria um padrão de spray. Todas as amostras foram enviadas ao laboratório para análise de DNA. Imagino que os resultados demorem uma semana.

Um sorriso se insinuou nos lábios de Amanda enquanto ela olhava o sangue.

— Boa garota, Eve. — Havia um som de triunfo em sua voz. — Algum dos caras mortos era B negativo?

Charlie olhou outra vez para Mittal. O homem assentiu, concordando.

— O asiático de camisa feia era O positivo, que é um sangue relativamente comum em vários grupos étnicos. É o tipo de Evelyn. É o meu. O outro, o cara que estamos chamando de Ricardo por causa da tatuagem, era B negativo, mas veja isto: ele não tem ferimentos a faca. Quer dizer, em algum momento, ele sangrou. Obviamente foi torturado. Mas o sangue que estamos vendo aqui está num volume maior do que qualquer coisa...

Amanda interrompeu:

— Então, temos alguém por aí com um ferimento a faca cujo tipo sanguíneo é B negativo. Isso é raro?

— Menos de dois por cento da população caucasiana dos Estados Unidos é B negativo — informou Charlie. — Entre os asiáticos, é um quarto disso, e corresponde a mais ou menos um por cento dos hispânicos. Resumindo, é um tipo sanguíneo muito raro, o que torna provável que nosso Ricardo B negativo seja parente de sangue de nosso B negativo sumido e ferido.

— Então, temos um homem ferido solto, tipo sanguíneo B negativo.

Desta vez, para variar, Charlie estava à frente dela:

— Eu já coloquei um alerta em todos os hospitais num raio de cento e sessenta quilômetros para ferimento a faca em qualquer um: homem, mulher, branco, negro, laranja. Já descartamos três acidentes domésticos só na última meia hora. Tem mais gente sendo esfaqueada do que eu imaginava.

Mittal aguardou ter certeza de que Charlie havia terminado antes de apontar o sangue lambuzado no chão.

— Essas pegadas de sapato são condizentes com uma luta entre uma mulher pequena e um homem de tamanho mediano, provavelmente de uns setenta quilos. Dá para ver pela variação de claro a escuro nas pegadas que teve uma rolagem medial do pé, ou supinação.

Amanda interrompeu a aula:

— Vamos voltar para o ferimento a faca. Estamos falando de algo fatal?

Mittal deu de ombros.

— O IML teria que fazer essa avaliação. Como falei antes, não tem spray de sangue nas paredes nem no teto, então conseguimos afirmar que nenhuma das artérias foi atingida. Esse respingo pode ser talvez resultado de um ferimento na cabeça, em que se encontraria uma boa quantidade de sangue, mas com danos mínimos. — Ele olhou para Charlie. — Concorda?

Charlie fez que sim, mas completou:

— Uma perfuração intestinal pode sangrar assim. Não sei quanto tempo uma pessoa duraria com isso. Se der para confiar nos filmes, não muito. Se fosse um pulmão perfurado, ele teria uma hora, no máximo, antes de sufocar. Não tem absolutamente nenhum spray arterial, então, é um ferimento que está vazando. Não discordo do Dr. Mittal sobre a possibilidade de ser um ferimento na cabeça... — Ele deu de ombros e discordou mesmo assim. — A lâmina estava coberta de sangue da ponta ao punho, o que pode indicar que a faca foi enfiada fundo no corpo. — Ele viu Mittal franzir a testa e voltou atrás. — Mas também pode ser que a vítima tenha pegado a faca, cortado a mão e coberto a lâmina de sangue. — Ele mostrou a mão com a palma para cima. — Nesse caso, temos por aí um B negativo também com um ferimento na mão.

Amanda nunca abraçava as ambiguidades da ciência criminal. Ela tentou resumir em termos absolutos:

— Então, criminoso B negativo luta com Evelyn. Aí, suponho, chega o segundo homem, o asiático de camisa havaiana, que depois acabou morto no quarto. Eles conseguiram dominar Evelyn e tirar a arma dela. Em seguida, um terceiro homem, Ricardo, que em algum momento era refém, virou atirador e aí, graças à ação rápida da agente Mitchell, virou um cadáver antes de conseguir ferir alguém. — Ela se virou para Will. — Eu aposto que Ricardo está envolvido em tudo isso, com ou sem tortura. Ele fingiu ser refém para tentar usar isso contra Faith.

Mittal pareceu desconfortável com o tom conclusivo.

— É uma interpretação.

Charlie tentou acalmar as coisas.

— Sempre tem chance de...

Houve um som similar à queda de uma cachoeira tropical. Mittal abriu o zíper do macacão e tateou o bolso da calça. Puxou o celular e disse, antes de voltar à garagem:

— Com licença.

Amanda se virou para Charlie:

— Vamos direto ao ponto.

— Eles não estão me dando acesso completo, mas não tem motivo para eu discordar do que Ahbi falou até agora.

— E?

— Não quero parecer racista — começou Charlie —, mas não é comum ver mexicanos e asiáticos trabalhando juntos. Especialmente Los Texicanos.

— Os mais jovens não são tão apegados a esse tipo de coisa — propôs Will, perguntando-se se dava para chamar isso de progresso.

Amanda não levou nenhum dos dois comentários em consideração.

— O que mais?

— A lista ao lado do telefone. — Charlie apontou para um pedaço de papel amarelo com um monte de números e nomes. — Tomei a liberdade de ligar para Zeke. Deixei uma mensagem pedindo para ele entrar em contato com você.

Amanda olhou o relógio no pulso.

— E o resto da casa? A equipe forense achou alguma coisa?

— Não que tenham me dito. Ahbi não está sendo explicitamente grosso, mas também não está se esforçando para falar voluntariamente. — Charlie fez uma pausa antes de completar: — Parece óbvio que fosse lá o que os bandidos estivessem procurando não foi achado, senão teriam ido embora no minuto em que Faith chegou.

— E estaríamos planejando o velório de Evelyn. — Amanda não se deteve nisso. — O que quer que estivessem procurando... você chutaria que o item misterioso tem que tamanho?

— Não dá para saber — admitiu Charlie. — Obviamente, estavam olhando em todo lugar: gavetas, armários, almofadas. Acho que foram ficando mais irados conforme andavam pela casa e começaram a destruir mais do que procurar. Rasgaram as camas, quebraram os brinquedos de bebê. Tem muita fúria aqui.

— Havia quantas pessoas fazendo busca?

— Desculpe, Dra. Wagner. — Mittal estava de volta. Guardou o celular no bolso, mas deixou o macacão branco aberto. — Era o médico-legista. Está atrasado porque descobriram mais um corpo no incêndio do apartamento. Qual era sua pergunta?

Charlie respondeu por ela, talvez sentindo que o tom de Amanda podia fazer todo mundo ser expulso da casa.

— Ela estava perguntando quantas pessoas você acha que estavam fazendo uma busca aqui.

Mittal assentiu com a cabeça.

— Um bom palpite é de três a quatro homens.

Will viu a expressão de desgosto de Amanda. Tinham de ser mais de três, senão, todos os suspeitos estavam mortos e Evelyn Mitchell havia sequestrado a si mesma.

Mittal continuou:

— Eles não usaram luvas. Talvez tenham achado que a capitã Mitchell ia se entregar sem lutar. — Amanda soltou uma risada pelo nariz e Mittal fez mais uma de suas pausas patenteadas. — Tem digitais na maioria das superfícies, o que, claro, vamos compartilhar com a GBI.

Charlie falou:

— Já liguei para o laboratório. Vão vir dois técnicos para digitalizar tudo e colocar na base de dados. Daí, é só questão de tempo para sabermos se são fichados.

Amanda indicou a cozinha:

— Quando Evelyn foi neutralizada, eles devem ter começado a busca aqui. Estavam olhando gavetas, então, é algo que caberia nelas. — Ela olhou para Charlie, depois para Mittal. — Algum rastro de pneu? Pegadas?

— Nada importante.

Mittal a levou até a janela da cozinha e começou a apontar coisas no quintal que tinham sido verificadas. Will analisou os CDs quebrados no chão. Beatles. Sinatra. Nada de AC/DC. O aparelho de som era de plástico branco, manchado de pó preto de digitais. Will usou a unha do polegar para apertar o botão de ejetar. A bandeja estava vazia.

A voz de Amanda se voltou para ele.

— Onde eles prenderam Evelyn enquanto estavam arrasando a casa?

Mittal começou a ir na direção da sala. Will ficou na retaguarda enquanto Charlie e Amanda seguiam o doutor pelo caminho de destroços. A disposição era similar à casa da Sra. Levy, exceto pela sala de estar mais baixa. Na frente do sofá e de uma poltrona *bergère*, havia uma parede repleta de prateleiras de livros e uma pequena televisão de plasma com uma rachadura no meio do tamanho de um pé. A maioria dos livros estavam jogados pelo chão. O sofá e as poltronas tinham sido estripados, as molduras, quebradas. Havia um aparelho de som na prateleira ao lado da TV, do tipo antigo que tocava discos, mas os alto-falantes estavam estourados e o braço tinha sido arrancado do prato. Uma pequena pilha de discos de vinil tinha claramente sido pisoteada.

Havia uma cadeira estilo Thonet de madeira curvada apoiada na parede, a única coisa no cômodo que parecia ter permanecido intacta. O assento era de palha. As pernas estavam arranhadas. Mittal apontou para partes onde o verniz tinha sido arrancado.

— Parece que usaram fita adesiva. Achei cola onde deviam estar os pés da capitã Mitchell. — Ele levantou a cadeira e a afastou da parede. Um marcador plástico com um número tinha sido colocado ao lado de uma mancha escura. — Podemos deduzir, pelas gotas de sangue no carpete, que as mãos da capitã Mitchell estavam para baixo. O corte no dedo dela ainda estava sangrando, mas não de forma significativa. Talvez meu colega tenha razão de supor que ela o envolveu com papel-toalha.

Amanda se debruçou para olhar a mancha de sangue, mas Will estava mais interessado na cadeira. As mãos de Evelyn tinham sido amarradas atrás das costas. Ele usou o pé para inclinar a cadeira à frente e poder ver a parte de baixo do assento de palha. Havia uma marcação, uma flecha, desenhada com sangue.

Will olhou pela sala, tentando descobrir para o que a flecha apontava. O sofá diretamente à frente da cadeira estava estripado, bem como a poltrona ao lado. O piso de madeira excluía a possibilidade de se esconder algo debaixo de um carpete. Será que Evelyn estava apontando para algo no quintal?

Ele escutou um chiado, um som de ar passando entre dentes. Will levantou os olhos e viu Amanda lhe dando um olhar tão abrasador que ele derrubou a cadeira de volta no lugar sem o cérebro perceber o que seu pé estava fazendo. Ela balançou de leve a cabeça, indicando que ele devia ficar calado sobre a descoberta. Will olhou Charlie de relance. Todos tinham visto a flecha embaixo da cadeira, enquanto Mittal, sem perceber nada, fazia altas divagações sobre a eficácia do rastreamento de impressões digitais em superfícies porosas versus não porosas.

Charlie abriu a boca para falar, mas Amanda falou por cima:

— Dr. Mittal, na sua opinião, a porta de vidro foi quebrada com um objeto encontrado, como uma pedra ou um enfeite de jardim? — Ela olhou Charlie de soslaio, e Will pensou que, se ela fosse capaz de atirar laser com os olhos, teria grudado a boca do homem. — Estou só querendo saber o quanto o ataque foi planejado. Eles trouxeram algo para quebrar o vidro? Cercaram a casa? Se sim, conheciam a planta de antemão?

Mittal franziu a testa, porque eram perguntas que nenhum deles conseguia responder.

— Dra. Wagner, esses cenários não podem ser avaliados em nível forense.

— Bem, vamos só jogar algumas hipóteses e ver se colam. Será que usaram um tijolo para quebrar o vidro?

Charlie começou a balançar a cabeça. Will reconheceu o conflito interno. Gostassem ou não, a cena do crime era de Mittal e havia evidência embaixo da cadeira — possivelmente, evidência importante — que o cara não vira. Charlie obviamente estava dividido. Como na maioria dos casos que envolviam Amanda, havia a coisa certa a se fazer e o que ela mandava fazer. Cada decisão tinha sua própria consequência.

Mittal estava balançando a cabeça também, mas só porque Amanda não estava falando nada com nada.

— Dra. Wagner, já examinamos cada centímetro desta cena do crime e estou lhe falando que não achamos nenhum outro item importante além do que já detalhei.

Will sabia sem dúvida alguma que não tinham examinado cada centímetro. E perguntou:

— Alguém olhou o Malibu?

Isso distraiu Charlie de seu dilema. Ele franziu o cenho. Will tinha cometido o mesmo erro com o Mini de Faith. Toda a violência havia acontecido dentro da casa, mas ainda assim os carros faziam parte da cena do crime.

Amanda foi a primeira a se mexer. Já tinha saído para a garagem e aberto a porta do Malibu antes de qualquer um pensar em questionar o que ela estava fazendo.

Mittal falou:

— Por favor, ainda não analisamos...

Ela deu um olhar fulminante:

— Você pensou em olhar o porta-malas?

O silêncio chocado dele foi resposta suficiente. Amanda abriu o porta-malas. Will estava parado do lado de dentro da porta da cozinha, o que lhe dava uma visão elevada da cena. Havia várias sacolas plásticas de supermercado no porta-malas, com o conteúdo amassado pelo cadáver em cima. Como na cozinha, tudo estava coberto de sangue — ensopando a caixa de cereal, pingando na embalagem dos pães de hambúrguer. O homem morto era grande. Seu corpo estava quase completamente dobrado no meio para poder caber no espaço. Um corte fundo na cabeça careca mostrava osso estilhaçado e pedaços de cérebro. A calça jeans estava amarrotada. As mangas da camisa, arregaçadas. Havia uma tatuagem de Los Texicanos no antebraço.

O namoradinho de Evelyn.

4

A Prisão de Diagnóstico e Classificação da Geórgia ficava em Jackson, a mais ou menos uma hora ao sul de Atlanta. O caminho em geral era uma reta pela I-75, mas no Autódromo de Atlanta estava tendo alguma exposição que fez o trânsito parar. Sem se deixar abalar, Amanda ficava entrando e saindo do acostamento, virando o volante aos solavancos rápidos para ultrapassar grupos de carros lentos. Os pneus da SUV faziam um som arranhado ao passarem pelas tachas colocadas no chão para impedir que os motoristas saíssem da pista. Entre o barulho e a vibração, Will se viu lutando contra uma onda inesperada de enjoo.

Finalmente, ultrapassaram a pior parte do trânsito. Na saída da estrada, Amanda deu uma última entrada no acostamento, depois voltou a SUV para a pista. Os pneus pularam. O chassi tremeu. Will abriu a janela para o ar fresco ajudar a acalmar o estômago. O vento bateu na cara dele com tanta força que ele sentiu a pele esticar.

Amanda apertou o botão para subir a janela de novo, dando a ele o olhar que reservava para gente idiota e crianças. Estavam indo a mais de cento e sessenta por hora. Will tinha sorte de não ter sido sugado para fora da janela.

Ela soltou um longo suspiro, voltando o olhar para a estrada. Uma das mãos descansava no colo, enquanto a outra segurava firmemente o volante. Ela estava usando o tailleur de sempre: uma saia azul-vivo e um blazer combinando com uma blusa clara por baixo. Os saltos eram exatamente da mesma cor do conjunto. As unhas estavam curtas, mas feitas. O cabelo era o capacete de sempre, cheio de fios grisalhos. Na maior parte do tempo, Amanda parecia ter mais energia que todos os homens de sua equipe. Naquele momento, porém, parecia cansada, e Will via as rugas de preocupação mais pronunciadas em torno dos olhos dela.

Ela disse:

— Fale sobre Spivey.

Will tentou ligar o cérebro de volta no velho caso contra a equipe da capitã Evelyn Mitchell. Boyd Spivey era o antigo investigador-chefe do esquadrão de narcóticos, atualmente tentando ganhar tempo no corredor da morte. Will só tinha conversado com o homem uma vez antes de os advogados mandarem Spivey ficar de boca fechada.

— Não acho difícil acreditar que ele matou alguém com os próprios punhos. Era um cara grande, mais alto do que eu, com uns vinte quilos a mais, tudo de músculo.

— Rato de academia?

— Acho que os anabolizantes deram uma boa ajuda.

— E como ele ficou com isso?

— O cara ficou incontrolavelmente irado — lembrou Will. — Ele não é tão esperto quanto acha, mas eu não consegui arrancar uma confissão, então, de repente eu também não sou.

— Mesmo assim, você o colocou na prisão.

— Ele se colocou na prisão sozinho. A casa dele na cidade estava quitada. A casa no lago estava quitada. Todos os três filhos estudavam em uma escola particular. A esposa trabalhava só dez horas por semana e dirigia uma Mercedes top de linha. A amante tinha uma BMW. Ele deixava o Porsche 911 novinho estacionado na entrada da casa dela.

— Os homens e seus carros — murmurou ela. — Ele não me parece muito esperto, não.

— Não achava que ninguém fosse questionar.

— Em geral, não questionam.

— Spivey era bom em ficar de boca fechada.

— Se bem me lembro, todos eram.

Ela tinha razão. Num caso de corrupção, a estratégia básica era achar o membro mais fraco e convencê-lo a entregar os outros conspiradores em troca de uma pena mais branda. Os seis investigadores do esquadrão de narcóticos de Evelyn Mitchell tinham se provado imunes a essa estratégia. Nenhum deles queria entregar o outro e todos insistiam rotineiramente que a capitã Mitchell não tinha nada a ver com os supostos crimes. Fizeram de tudo para proteger a chefe. Era ao mesmo tempo admirável e incrivelmente frustrante.

Will falou:

— Spivey trabalhou no esquadrão de Evelyn por doze anos, que é mais tempo que todos os outros.

— Ela confiava nele.

— Sim — concordou Will. — Farinha do mesmo saco.

Amanda lhe lançou um olhar penetrante.

— Cuidado.

Will sentiu o maxilar se apertando tanto que o osso doeu. Não entendia como ignorar a parte mais importante do caso ia ajudar a chegar a algum lugar. Amanda sabia tão bem quanto Will que a amiga dela era culpada até o último fio de cabelo. Evelyn não vivia de maneira extravagante, mas, como Spivey, tinha sido estúpida à sua própria maneira.

O pai de Faith era corretor de seguros, bem de classe média, com o tipo de dívida normal que todo mundo tinha: financiamento de carro, de imóvel, cartões de crédito. Mas, durante a investigação, Will havia achado uma conta bancária aberta no nome de Bill Mitchell em outro estado. Na época, fazia seis anos que o homem estava morto. Apesar de o saldo da conta sempre pairar em torno de dez mil dólares, o extrato mostrava depósitos mensais desde a morte dele, totalizando quase sessenta mil. Era claramente uma conta fantasma, o tipo de coisa que os promotores chamam de prova irrefutável. Com Bill morto, Evelyn era a única signatária. O dinheiro era sacado e depositado com o cartão dela numa agência do banco em Atlanta. Não era o marido morto quem estava mantendo as atividades bem separadas e os depósitos logo abaixo do limite que chamaria a atenção da Secretaria de Segurança.

Até onde Will sabia, Evelyn Mitchell nunca tinha sido questionada sobre aquela conta. Ele imaginava que seria mencionada durante o julgamento dela, mas o julgamento nunca aconteceu. Houve uma coletiva de imprensa anunciando sua aposentadoria e fim de papo.

Até aquele momento.

Amanda abaixou o quebra-sol para bloquear os raios. Havia alguns canhotos amarelos presos na parte interna do quebra-sol que pareciam ser de uma lavanderia. O sol não estava ajudando em nada. Amanda não parecia mais cansada. Parecia abatida.

Ela disse:

— Tem alguma coisa incomodando você.

Ele resistiu a pronunciar o maior "dã" já vocalizado na história do universo.

— Não isso — disse ela, como se conseguisse ler a mente dele. — Faith não ligou para você pedindo ajuda porque ela sabia que não ia agir de maneira correta.

Will olhou pela janela.

— Você a teria obrigado a esperar reforços.

Ele odiava o alívio que as palavras dela traziam.

— Ela sempre foi cabeça-dura.

Ele sentiu a necessidade de dizer:

— Ela não fez nada de errado.

— Esse é meu garoto.

Will viu as árvores da rodovia se misturarem, virando um mar de verde.

— Você acha que vai ter resgate?

— Espero que sim.

Os dois sabiam que um resgate indicava um refém vivo, ou, pelo menos, daria a oportunidade de exigirem prova de vida.

Ele disse:

— Isso parece pessoal.

— Em que sentido?

Ele balançou a cabeça.

— O jeito como a casa foi destruída. Tem uma diferença entre alguém com raiva e furioso.

— Duvido que a velhota tenha ficado sentada quietinha enquanto eles faziam a busca.

— Provavelmente, não. — Evelyn Mitchell não era nenhuma Amanda Wagner, mas Will conseguia facilmente imaginá-la provocando os homens que estavam destruindo a casa. Ninguém se tornava uma das primeiras capitãs da polícia de Atlanta sendo fofa. — Eles obviamente estavam procurando dinheiro.

— Por que você acha isso?

— Mariscos: a última palavra que Ricardo disse para Faith antes de morrer. Você falou que é gíria para dinheiro. Então, estavam procurando dinheiro.

— Na gaveta de talheres?

Outro bom argumento. Dinheiro era bom, mas volumoso. Um montante que valesse sequestrar uma ex-capitã da polícia de Atlanta encheria várias gavetas de talheres.

Ele disse:

— A flecha estava apontando para o quintal.

— Que flecha?

Will suprimiu um gemido. Em geral, ela não dava tanto na cara.

— A flecha desenhada com o sangue de Evelyn embaixo da cadeira em que ela foi presa. Eu sei que você viu. Você chiou para mim que nem um compressor de ar.

— Você precisa melhorar suas metáforas. — Ela ficou em silêncio por um momento, provavelmente considerando a rota mais tortuosa para levá-lo a lugar nenhum. — Você acha que Evelyn enterrou um tesouro no quintal?

Ele tinha que admitir que era improvável, especialmente considerando que o quintal dos Mitchell ficava à vista de todos os outros vizinhos, a maioria dos quais eram aposentados com tempo de sobra para xeretar. Além do mais, Will não conseguia imaginar a mãe de Faith com uma pá e uma lanterna no meio da noite. Não que ela pudesse simplesmente colocar aquilo no banco.

— Um cofre de segurança bancário — tentou Will. — Podiam estar procurando uma chave.

— Para ter acesso, Evelyn teria que ir ao banco e assinar. Eles iam comparar a assinatura dela e pedir identidade. Nosso sequestrador devia saber que a foto dela estaria em todas as emissoras de televisão no minuto em que ela fosse levada.

Silenciosamente, Will concordou. Além do mais, valia a mesma regra. Uma quantia grande de dinheiro ocupava muito espaço. Diamantes e ouro eram mais para filmes de Hollywood. Na vida real, joias roubadas valiam frações ínfimas do valor original.

Ela perguntou:

— E a cena do crime? Acha que Charlie acertou?

Will assumiu uma posição de defesa.

— Mittal foi quem falou mais.

— Tá, você já tirou o cu de Charlie da reta. Agora, responda minha pergunta.

— O Texicano no porta-malas do Malibu, o namoradinho de Evelyn. Ele nega toda a teoria.

Ela concordou com a cabeça.

— Ele não foi esfaqueado. Morreu com um tiro na cabeça, além do mais, é B positivo. Isso ainda nos deixa com nosso B negativo por aí com um ferimento feio.

— Não é disso que estou falando.

Will resistiu à vontade de completar: "E você sabe." Amanda não estava só o deixando de mãos atadas. Ela o estava vendando e empurrando para a beira de um abismo. A recusa dela em falar do passado sórdido de Evelyn Mitchell ou mesmo mencionar o assunto não ia ajudar Faith e com certeza não ia ajudar a recuperar a mãe dela inteira. Evelyn tinha trabalhado no esquadrão de narcóticos. Obviamente estava em contato quase diário com um chefão da Los Texicanos, a facção que dominava o tráfico de drogas dentro e fora de Atlanta. Eles deviam estar na cidade falando com as unidades da facção e juntando as peças das últimas semanas da rotina de Evelyn, não numa missão inútil de visitar um cara que não tinha nada a perder e um histórico de silêncio persistente.

— Ande, Dr. Trent — repreendeu Amanda. — Não me obrigue a tomar medidas drásticas.

Will deixou seu ego atrapalhar por mais uns segundos antes de dizer:

— O namoradinho de Evelyn. A carteira dele tinha sumido. Ele não tinha identidade nem dinheiro. A única coisa nos bolsos era a chave do Malibu de Evelyn. Ela deve ter entregado a ele.

— Prossiga.

— Ela estava fazendo almoço para dois. Tinha quatro fatias de pão na torradeira. Faith estava atrasada. Evelyn não sabia a que horas ela ia voltar, mas devia supor que Faith ligaria quando estivesse a caminho. Tinha compras no porta-malas do Malibu. A nota fiscal diz que Evelyn usou o cartão de débito no Kroger às 12h02. O homem estava trazendo as compras enquanto ela preparava o almoço.

Amanda sorriu.

— Eu vivo esquecendo como você é inteligente, mas aí acontece um negócio desses e eu lembro por que o contratei.

Will ignorou o elogio sarcástico.

— Então, Evelyn está fazendo almoço. Começa a se perguntar onde está o namoradinho. Ela sai e encontra o corpo dele no porta-malas. Pega Emma e a esconde no quarto de ferramentas. Se ela tivesse pegado Emma depois de cortar a mão, como o Dr. Mittal falou, teria sangue em algum lugar da cadeirinha. Evelyn é forte, mas não é o Hércules. A cadeirinha, mesmo sem um bebê, é bem pesada. Ela não ia conseguir levantar um negócio daqueles da bancada só com uma das mãos, pelo menos não com segurança. Ia ter que apoiar a parte de baixo com a mão livre. Emma é pequena, mas é pesadinha.

Amanda completou:

— Evelyn passou um tempo no quarto de ferramentas. Pegou os cobertores. Não tem sangue neles. Ela digitou a senha do cofre. Não tem sangue nos botões dos números. O chão está limpo. Ela começou a sangrar depois de trancar a porta.

— Não sou especialista em machucados de cozinha, mas em geral você não corta o dedo anelar quando está fatiando alguma coisa. Costuma ser o polegar ou o indicador.

— Outra boa observação. — Amanda conferiu o retrovisor e mudou de faixa. — Certo, o que ela fez depois?

— Como você disse. Evelyn esconde a bebê, depois pega a arma no cofre, volta para a casa e atira em Kwon, que está esperando na área de serviço para fazer uma emboscada. Em seguida, ela domina um segundo homem, provavelmente nosso tipo sanguíneo B negativo misterioso. A arma de Evelyn é derrubada da mão dela durante a luta. Ela esfaqueia o B negativo, mas tem um terceiro cara, o Sr. Camisa

Havaiana. Ele pega a arma de Evelyn no chão e para a briga. Pergunta a ela onde está o que eles estão procurando. Ela manda os homens irem para o inferno. É presa com fita adesiva na cadeira enquanto eles revistam a casa.

— Parece plausível.

Parecia confuso. Havia tantos bandidos que Will estava tendo dificuldade de acompanhar. Dois asiáticos, um ou possivelmente dois hispânicos, talvez um terceiro de origem étnica desconhecida, uma casa sendo revistada atrás de sabe lá Deus o quê, e uma ex-policial de sessenta e três anos desaparecida com seus próprios segredos.

E tinha ainda a grande pergunta, que Will sabia que não devia fazer: por que Evelyn não tinha pedido socorro? Pela contagem de Will, ela tivera pelo menos duas oportunidades de fazer uma ligação ou correr atrás de ajuda: ao ouvir o barulho e depois de atirar em Hironobu Kwon na área de serviço. E, mesmo assim, tinha ficado ali.

— O que você está pensando?

Will sabia que não devia responder sinceramente.

— Estou me perguntando como eles tiraram Evelyn da casa sem ninguém ver.

Amanda o lembrou:

— Você está partindo do pressuposto de que Roz Levy está falando a verdade.

— Você acha que ela está envolvida?

— Acho que ela é uma vaca velha e ardilosa que se recusaria a mijar em você se seu cabelo estivesse pegando fogo.

Will achou que o veneno no tom dela vinha de experiência própria.

Amanda continuou:

— Isso não foi feito no calor do momento. Foi planejado. Eles não entraram ali de qualquer jeito. Tinha um carro em algum lugar, talvez uma van. Tem um beco de atalho que dá na rua João Pequeno. Eles sairiam pelos fundos para o quintal de Evelyn. Seguindo a linha da cerca entre os vizinhos, você chega em dois minutos.

— Quantos homens você acha que tinha?

— Temos três na cena. Mais o B negativo ferido e pelo menos um homem fisicamente apto. Não tem como Evelyn ter ido a um segundo local sem lutar. Ela preferiria arriscar levar um tiro primeiro. Tinha que ter alguém lá forte o suficiente para amarrá-la ou dominá-la.

Will não acrescentou que podiam, com a mesma facilidade, tê-la machucado ou matado e removido o corpo.

— Vamos ter certeza quando conseguirmos as digitais. Todos devem ter encostado em alguma coisa.

Abruptamente, Amanda mudou de assunto:

— Você e Faith já falaram do seu caso contra a mãe dela?

— Não muito. Nunca contei a ela da conta bancária, não tem por quê. Ela supõe que eu estava errado. Muita gente supõe isso. Meu caso nunca foi a tribunal. Evelyn se aposentou com todos os benefícios intactos. Não é difícil tirar essa conclusão.

Ela assentiu como se estivesse aprovando.

— O homem no porta-malas, que você chama de namoradinho de Evelyn. Vamos falar dele.

— Se ele estava trazendo compras, quer dizer que eram íntimos.

— Com certeza é possível.

Will pensou no cara. Tinha levado um tiro na nuca. A carteira e a identidade não eram as únicas coisas que não estavam com ele. Ele não tinha celular. Não tinha o relógio dourado grosso que estava usando na foto tirada pela Sra. Levy. As roupas dele eram discretas — tênis Nike com palmilhas ortopédicas Dr. Scholl's, calça jeans da J. Crews e uma camisa da Banana Republic que tinha custado bem caro, e ele nem se dera ao trabalho de passar. O cavanhaque do queixo tinha um punhado de pelos brancos. Os fios de cabelo raspados na cabeça brilhante indicavam que ele estava mais escondendo a alopecia androgenética do que fazendo uma escolha ousada de estilo. Exceto pela estrela dos Texicanos no antebraço, ele poderia ser um corretor de valores na crise da meia-idade.

Amanda disse:

— Falei com a divisão de narcóticos. Houve algumas reclamações dos asiáticos tentando assumir o tráfico de cocaína, que está em disputa desde a queda da BMF.

A Black Mafia Family. Eles controlavam as vendas de coca desde Atlanta até Los Angeles, com Detroit no meio.

— É muito dinheiro. A Family faturava centenas de milhões de dólares por ano.

— Os Texicanos estavam mandando em tudo. Sempre foram fornecedores, não distribuidores. É um jeito inteligente de fazer o negócio. É por isso que sobreviveram por todos esses anos. Apesar do que Charlie pensa sobre raça, eles não querem nem saber se o traficante é preto, marrom ou roxo, desde que o dinheiro seja verde.

Will nunca tinha trabalhado num caso importante de tráfico de drogas.

— Não sei muito da organização.

— Os Texicanos começaram ainda em meados dos anos 1960, na Penitenciária de Atlanta. A distribuição demográfica na época era quase o contrário do que é hoje: setenta por cento de brancos, trinta por cento de negros. O crack mudou isso do dia para a noite. Foi mais rápido do que a manobra de usar ônibus para integração racial depois da segregação. Ainda tinha um punhado de mexicanos no lugar, e eles se uniram para não terem a garganta cortada. Você sabe como funciona.

Will fez que sim com a cabeça. Praticamente todas as facções criminosas dos Estados Unidos tinham começado com um grupo de minoria, fosse irlandesa, judia, italiana ou outra, unindo-se em busca de sobrevivência. Em geral, levava uns anos para começarem a fazer coisas piores do que faziam com eles.

— Como é a estrutura?

— Bem solta. Ninguém vai fazer um organograma que nem o da MS-13.

Ela estava se referindo àquela que era muitas vezes considerada a facção mais perigosa do mundo. A estrutura organizacional deles era comparável à do exército, e sua lealdade, tão feroz que ninguém nunca conseguiu se infiltrar.

Amanda explicou:

— Nos primeiros anos, os Texicanos estavam na primeira página do jornal todo dia, às vezes nas duas edições. Tiroteios na rua, heroína, maconha, apostas, prostituição, roubo. O cartão de visita deles era marcar crianças. Eles não iam atrás só da pessoa que os tinha contrariado. Iam atrás de uma filha, um filho, uma sobrinha, um sobrinho. Abriam a cara da criança, um risco horizontal na testa e depois uma linha vertical do nariz ao queixo.

Sem pensar, Will levou a mão à cicatriz do maxilar.

— Teve um momento durante a investigação dos assassinatos das crianças de Atlanta em que os Texicanos estavam no topo da nossa lista. Foi bem no início, no outono de 1979. Eu era praticamente assistente do oficial sênior que ligava Fulton, Cobb e Clayton. Evelyn estava na força-tarefa de Atlanta, basicamente pegando café até a hora de falar com os pais, e depois ficava tudo nas costas dela. O consenso geral era de que os Texicanos estavam tentando mandar uma mensagem mais ampla à clientela. Parece ridículo agora, mas, na época, estávamos torcendo para serem eles. — Ela ligou o pisca-alerta e mudou de faixa. — Você tinha uns quatro anos na época, então, não vai lembrar, mas foi uma época muito tensa. Toda a região metropolitana estava aterrorizada.

— Parece mesmo — falou ele, surpreso por ela saber sua idade.

— Não foi muito depois dos assassinatos das crianças que um dos Texicanos mais importantes foi morto durante uma briga interna. Eles são bem fechados. Nunca descobrimos o que aconteceu nem quem assumiu, mas sabemos que o cara novo era bem mais voltado a negócios. Nada mais de violência a troco de nada. Ele priorizava o negócio, tirando o componente mais arriscado. O lema dele era manter o pó circulando e as ruas sem sangue. Quando passaram a atuar secretamente, ficamos satisfeitos em ignorá-los.

— Quem é o líder agora?

— Ignatio Ortiz é o único nome que temos. É o rosto da facção. Tem mais dois, mas são muitíssimo discretos e os três nunca são vistos juntos no mesmo lugar. Antes que você pergunte, Ortiz está na Prisão Estadual de Phillips cumprindo o terceiro ano de sete sem condicional por tentativa de homicídio.

— Tentativa?

Não parecia muito uma coisa de gângster.

— Voltou para casa e achou a esposa na cama com o irmão dele. Diz a lenda que ele errou de propósito.

Will supunha que Ortiz não tinha dificuldade de administrar os negócios da cadeia.

— Vale a pena falar com ele?

— Mesmo que tivéssemos como justificar isso, ele não se sentaria com a gente sem o advogado, que ia insistir que o cliente dele é só um empresário comum que deixou sua paixão sair de controle.

— Ele já foi preso antes?

— Algumas vezes quando mais novo, mas nada sério.

— Então, a facção continua voando baixo.

— Eles saem do bueiro de vez em quando para educar a molecada mais nova. Lembra do assassinato do Dia dos Pais em Buckhead no ano passado?

— O cara que teve a garganta cortada na frente dos filhos?

Ela fez que sim.

— Há trinta anos, eles teriam matado as crianças também. Dá para dizer que ficaram moles com o tempo.

— Eu não chamaria isso de mole.

— Dentro das cadeias, os Texicanos são conhecidos como cortadores de garganta.

— O homem no porta-malas ocupa um lugar alto na hierarquia.

— Por que diz isso?

— Ele só tem uma tatuagem.

Membros jovens das facções criminosas costumavam usar o corpo como tela para ilustrar a vida, tatuando lágrimas sob os olhos para cada assassinato, fechando os cotovelos e ombros com teias de aranha para mostrar que tinham cumprido pena. As tatuagens eram sempre feitas com tinta azul tirada de canetas esferográficas, o que eles chamam de "tinta de gaiola", e sempre contavam uma história. A não ser que a história fosse tão ruim que não precisasse ser contada.

Will falou:

— Um corpo limpo quer dizer dinheiro, poder, controle. O homem é mais velho, provavelmente com sessenta e poucos anos. Isso o coloca no topo dos Texicanos. A idade dele é seu distintivo de honra. Não é o tipo de vida que garante longevidade.

— Ninguém envelhece sendo burro.

— Ninguém envelhece sendo de uma facção.

— Só podemos torcer para a polícia de Atlanta compartilhar a identidade desse homem com a gente quando conseguirem descobrir.

Will a olhou de soslaio. Ela continuava olhando para a estrada. Ele tinha uma suspeita incômoda de que Amanda já sabia quem era o homem e exatamente qual o papel dele na hierarquia dos Texicanos. Tinha alguma coisa no jeito como ela dobrou a foto da Sra. Levy e a colocou no bolso que lhe dava quase certeza de Amanda ter passado alguma mensagem em código para a velha não contar a história a ninguém.

Ele perguntou:

— Você ouve AC/DC?

— Eu tenho cara de quem ouve AC/DC?

— É uma banda de metal. — Ele não contou que tinham criado um dos álbuns mais vendidos da história da música. — Tem uma música chamada "Back in Black". Estava tocando quando Faith chegou. Olhei todos os CDs da casa. Evelyn não tinha nada da banda na coleção dela e o aparelho de som estava vazio quando ejetei a bandeja.

— Essa música fala do quê?

— Bem, do óbvio. De voltar. De usar preto. Foi gravada depois que o cantor original do grupo morreu de overdose de drogas e álcool.

— Sempre é triste quando alguém morre de um clichê.

Will pensou na letra, que por acaso ele sabia de cor.

— Fala de ressurreição. Transformação. Voltar de um lugar ruim e falar para as pessoas que talvez o tenham subestimado ou ridicularizado que ele não vai aceitar mais isso. Tipo, agora ele é maneiro. Está usando preto. É um fodão. Está pronto para enfrentar os outros. — De repente, Will percebeu por que tinha gastado o disco de tanto ouvir quando era adolescente. — Ou algo do tipo. — Ele engoliu em seco. — Pode significar outras coisas.

— Hum.

Foi só o que ela respondeu.

Ele batucou com os dedos no descanso de braço.

— Como você conheceu Evelyn?

— A gente fez escola de negras juntas.

Will quase engasgou sozinho.

Ela riu da reação dele ao que devia ser uma piada bem antiga.

— Era como chamavam na idade da pedra: Escola de Trânsito de Mulheres Negras. As mulheres eram treinadas separadas dos homens. Nosso trabalho era conferir parquímetros e dar multas para carros estacionados ilegalmente. Às vezes, tínhamos permissão de falar com prostitutas, mas só se os meninos permitissem, e em geral tinha alguma piada grosseira no meio. Evelyn e eu éramos as únicas duas brancas num grupo de trinta que se formaram naquele ano. — Havia um sorriso de ternura nos lábios dela. — Estávamos prontas para mudar o mundo.

Will sabia que não devia dizer o que estava pensando, que Amanda era bem mais velha do que parecia.

Ela obviamente adivinhou os pensamentos dele.

— Dá um tempo, Will. Eu entrei em 1973. A Atlanta que você conhece hoje foi conquistada por mulheres daquelas classes. Policiais negros não tinham nem permissão de prender brancos até 1962. Eles nem tinham uma delegacia. Precisavam ficar na YMCA da rua Butler até alguém ter a ideia de chamá-los. E era pior ainda se você fosse mulher: duas falhas só, com a terceira ameaçando cortar sua cabeça. — A voz dela assumiu um tom solene. — Todo dia era uma luta para fazer o certo sendo que tudo ao seu redor era errado.

— Parece que você e Evelyn passaram por uma prova de fogo.

— Você não faz ideia.

— Então me conte.

Ela riu de novo, mas, desta vez, com a falta de jeito dele.

— Você está tentando me interrogar, Dr. Trent?

— Estou querendo entender por que você não está falando do fato de Evelyn ter uma relação pessoal e íntima com um Texicano das antigas que acabou assassinado no porta-malas do carro dela.

Ela ficou olhando para a estrada à frente.

— Parece estranho mesmo, né?

— Como podemos trabalhar neste caso se não vamos pelo menos admitir o que aconteceu? — Ela não respondeu. — Vai ficar entre nós, tudo bem? Ninguém mais precisa saber. Ela é sua amiga. Eu entendo isso. Eu mesmo passei muito tempo com ela. Parece uma pessoa bem bacana e obviamente ama Faith.

— Em algum lugar aí vem um "mas".

— Ela estava aceitando dinheiro que nem o resto da equipe. Deve ter conhecido os Texicanos de...

Amanda o interrompeu.

— Falando em Texicanos, vamos voltar a Ricardo.

Will fechou o punho, querendo socar alguma coisa.

Amanda o deixou sofrer um pouco em silêncio.

— Eu conheço você há muito tempo, Will. Preciso que confie em mim em relação a algumas coisas.

— E eu tenho escolha?

— Na verdade, não, mas estou dando a você uma chance de me devolver todo o benefício da dúvida que lhe dei ao longo dos anos.

A vontade dele era dizer a ela exatamente onde enfiar o benefício, mas Will nunca tinha sido o tipo de homem que falava a primeira coisa que vinha à cabeça.

— Você está me colocando em rédea curta.

— É um jeito de interpretar a situação. — Ela pausou por um momento. — Já lhe ocorreu que eu posso estar protegendo você?

Ele coçou de novo a lateral do maxilar, sentindo a cicatriz que tinha sido um corte na pele anos antes. Will em geral evitava introspecção, mas até um cego podia ver que ele tinha relações estranhamente disfuncionais com todas as mulheres de sua vida. Faith era como uma irmã mais velha mandona. Amanda era a pior mãe que ele nunca tivera. Angie era uma mescla das duas coisas, o que era perturbador por motivos óbvios. Sabiam ser rígidas e controladoras, e Angie, especialmente, sabia ser cruel, mas Will jamais tinha pensado que qualquer uma delas lhe desejava mal. E Amanda tinha razão em pelo menos uma coisa: sempre havia protegido Will, mesmo nas raras ocasiões em que isso punha o emprego dela em risco.

Ele disse:

— Precisamos ligar para as concessionárias que vendem Cadillac na região metropolitana. O homem não estava dirigindo um Honda. É um carro caro. Provavelmente há poucos Cadillacs como aquele rodando. Acho que tem câmbio manual. É raro num quatro portas.

Para sua surpresa, ela falou:

— Boa ideia. Faça isso.

Will enfiou a mão no bolso, lembrando tarde demais que estava sem o celular. E sem a arma e o distintivo. E, aliás, sem o carro.

Amanda jogou seu telefone para ele enquanto pegava a saída da estrada sem nem encostar no freio.

— O que está rolando entre você e Sara Linton?

Ele abriu o celular dela.

— Somos amigos.

— Trabalhei num caso com o marido dela faz uns anos.

— Que bacana.

— Você vai ter que se esforçar para ocupar o lugar do cara, amigo.

Will discou o número do serviço de auxílio à lista telefônica e pediu o telefone da concessionária Cadillac mais próxima de Atlanta.

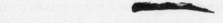

Enquanto seguia Amanda pelo corredor que levava à câmara da morte, Will teve que admitir, mesmo que só para si, que odiava visitar prisões — não só a D&C, mas qualquer uma. Ele conseguia lidar com a ameaça constante de violência que fazia qualquer instituição de detentos parecer uma panela em ebulição esquecida no fogo. Conseguia lidar com o barulho, a sujeira, os olhares vazios. O que ele não aguentava era a sensação de impotência que vinha com o confinamento.

Os presidiários traficavam drogas e faziam outros esquemas, mas, no fim das contas, não tinham poder sobre as coisas básicas que os tornavam seres humanos. Não podiam tomar banho quando queriam. Não podiam ir ao banheiro sem plateia. Podiam passar por revista corporal ou íntima a qualquer momento. Não podiam dar uma caminhada nem pegar um livro na biblioteca sem permissão. Suas celas eram constantemente revistadas para ver se havia contrabando, que podia ser qualquer coisa, desde revistas sobre carros a um rolo de fio dental. Eles comiam no horário determinado por outra pessoa. A luz era apagada e acesa no tempo de outra pessoa. De longe, a pior parte era o quanto viviam sendo manuseados — tinham os braços torcidos atrás das costas, levavam batidas na cabeça durante a contagem, eram empurrados à frente ou puxados para trás. Nada pertencia a eles, nem seus próprios corpos.

Era como o pior lar temporário da Terra, só que com mais grades.

A D&C era a maior prisão da Geórgia e, entre outras coisas, servia como um dos principais centros de processamento para todos os detentos que entravam no sistema penal do estado. Havia oito blocos de celas com beliches individuais e duplas, além de mais oito dormitórios que abrigavam o excedente. Como parte da admissão, todos os presidiários estaduais eram sujeitos a um exame médico geral, avaliação psiquiátrica, testes comportamentais e uma avaliação do nível **de ameaça** para que fosse feita uma classificação de segurança que determinava se deviam estar numa instituição de segurança mínima, média ou máxima.

Se tivessem sorte, esse processo de diagnóstico e classificação levava cerca de seis semanas até serem designados a outra prisão ou movidos para unidades permanentes na D&C. Até então, os detentos viviam em isolamento por vinte e três horas, o que significava que, exceto por uma hora do dia, ficavam confinados nas celas. Cigarro, café e refrigerantes eram proibidos. Podiam comprar só um jornal por semana. Livros não eram permitidos, nem a Bíblia. Não havia TV. Nem rádio. Nem celular. Tinha um pátio, mas os detentos só podiam sair três dias por semana, e isso se o clima estivesse bom e pelo tempo que sobrasse em sua uma hora livre por dia. Só residentes de longo prazo tinham permissão de receber visitantes e isso era feito numa sala dividida por uma tela de metal, em que era necessário gritar para ser ouvido por cima das vozes dos outros visitantes. Sem toques. Sem abraços. Sem qualquer contato.

Segurança máxima.

Havia um motivo para as taxas de suicídio em prisões serem três vezes mais altas do que fora. Era desolador pensar nas condições de vida deles, até ler algumas das fichas. Estupro de menor. Sodomia qualificada com taco de beisebol. Violência doméstica. Sequestro. Agressão. Tiro. Espancamento. Mutilação. Esfaqueamento. Ferimentos com objetos cortantes. Queimadura infligida com água fervente.

Mas os criminosos ruins de verdade estavam no corredor da morte. Tinham sido acusados de assassinatos tão odiosos que a única forma de o Estado conseguir lidar com eles era executá-los. Eram segregados do resto da população. A vida deles era até mais limitada do que a dos presidiários em processo de admissão. Confinamento total. Isolamento total. Nenhuma hora por dia no sol. Nenhuma refeição compartilhada. Nada de ultrapassar as grades de ferro que os prendia

112

à cela, exceto uma vez por semana, para tomar banho. Podiam passar dias sem ouvir a voz de outro homem. Podiam passar anos sem sentir o toque de outra pessoa.

Era ali que Boyd Spivey estava vivendo. Era onde o outrora condecorado investigador morava enquanto esperava para morrer.

Will sentiu os ombros se encolherem quando o portão que levava às celas do corredor da morte se fechou atrás dele. A prisão tinha sido projetada com corredores amplos e abertos, onde um homem correndo podia ser facilmente derrubado com um rifle a cem metros de distância. Os cantos eram em ângulos retos de noventa graus, que desencorajavam deliberadamente a vadiagem. O pé-direito era alto, para reter o calor constante de tantos corpos suando. Tudo era telado ou gradeado — janelas, portas, luzes do teto, interruptores.

Apesar do clima da primavera, a temperatura lá dentro chegava perto dos trinta graus. Will instantaneamente se arrependeu dos shorts de corrida de alta absorção por baixo do jeans pesado, que claramente não deviam ser usados juntos. Amanda, como sempre, parecia em casa, sem se importar com as grades de aparência gordurosa ou com os botões de pânico que cobriam as paredes a cada três metros. Os detentos permanentes da D&C eram classificados como criminosos violentos. Vários deles não tinham nada a perder e tinham tudo a ganhar se envolvendo em atos deliberados de violência. Tirar a vida de uma vice-diretora da GBI seria motivo de orgulho para qualquer homem. Will não sabia o que achavam de policiais que derrubavam outros policiais, mas não imaginava que houvesse muita distinção para detentos que procuravam elevar seu status.

Por esse motivo, eles foram escoltados por dois guardas aproximadamente do tamanho de geladeiras industriais. Um caminhava à frente de Amanda e outro, atrás de Will, fazendo-o se sentir quase delicado. Ninguém tinha permissão de trazer arma para a prisão, mas cada guarda tinha um leque de armamentos no cinto: spray de pimenta, cassetetes de aço e, o pior de tudo, um molho de chaves que balançava e parecia anunciar, a cada passo, que a única forma de sair daquele lugar era através de trinta portas trancadas.

Eles viraram em um corredor e acharam um homem de terno cinza parado na frente de mais uma porta trancada. Como em todas as outras portas do lugar, havia um botão de pânico grande e vermelho ao lado do batente.

Amanda estendeu a mão.

— Diretor Peck, obrigada por marcar esta visita de última hora.

— Sempre fico feliz em ajudar, vice-diretora. — Ele tinha uma voz rouca de velho que combinava perfeitamente com seu rosto cansado, de um tom marrom-escuro avermelhado, e a cabeleira grisalha penteada para trás. — Você sabe que só precisa ligar.

— Seria demais eu pedir uma lista impressa de todos os visitantes que Spivey recebeu desde que entrou no sistema penitenciário?

Peck obviamente achava que era demais, mas fingiu bem.

— Spivey esteve em quatro instituições diferentes. Vou ter que dar uns telefonemas.

— Muito obrigada por se dispor a esse trabalho. — Ela indicou Will. — Este é o agente Trent. Ele vai precisar ficar em uma sala de observação, tem um passado meio complicado com o detento.

— Tudo bem. Preciso avisar que demos o prazo da execução do Sr. Spivey na semana passada. Vai ser no dia primeiro de setembro.

— Ele sabe?

Peck fez que sim, sério, e Will percebeu que ele não gostava dessa parte do trabalho.

— Minha política é dar aos detentos o máximo de informação que conseguimos assim que podemos. A notícia afetou bastante o Sr. Spivey. Eles em geral ficam bem dóceis durante essa época, mas não se deixe enganar sendo complacente. Se, em qualquer momento, você sentir uma ameaça, levante e saia imediatamente da sala. Não toque nele. Evite ficar perto demais. Para sua segurança, você vai ser monitorada pelas câmeras e um dos meus homens vai ficar em frente à porta o tempo todo. Só lembre que esses homens são rápidos e não têm absolutamente nada a perder.

— Então vou precisar ser mais rápida. — Ela piscou para ele como se aquilo fosse uma festa de faculdade em que havia o risco de os meninos fazerem arruaça. — Estou pronta, quando você quiser.

Will foi levado para a sala de observação por uma porta. O espaço era pequeno e sem janelas, o tipo de escritório de prisão que podia fa-

114

cilmente se passar por armário de depósito. Havia três monitores lado a lado numa mesa de metal, cada um mostrando um ângulo diferente de Boyd Spivey na sala adjacente. Ele estava algemado numa cadeira que sem dúvida tinha sido aparafusada ao chão.

Quatro anos antes, Spivey não era exatamente bonito, mas tinha um gingado de policial que compensava seus pontos fracos. Tinha reputação de fazer pegadinhas, mas ser um bom policial — o cara que você ia querer ao seu lado quando as coisas fossem de mal a pior. A ficha dele era cheia de menções honrosas. Mesmo depois de aceitar um acordo para se declarar culpado em troca de menos tempo de pena, havia homens na delegacia dele que se recusavam a acreditar que Spivey era corrupto.

Agora, tudo no homem gritava "condenado". Ele tinha a aparência dura de um granito polido. A pele era cheia de marcas e inchada. Um rabo de cavalo comprido e desleixado caía pelas costas. Tatuagens de cadeia decoravam os antebraços e subiam pelo pescoço. Os pulsos grossos estavam presos a uma barra de cromo soldada no centro da mesa. As pernas estavam cruzadas na altura dos tornozelos. As correntes presas aos ferros das pernas estavam esticadas numa linha reta. Will chutaria que Boyd passava os dias malhando na cela. O uniforme laranja-vivo estava estourando nos braços excessivamente musculosos e peito largo.

Will considerou se o peso extra era uma coisa boa ou ruim no que dizia respeito à execução iminente. Depois de vários percalços grotescos com a cadeira elétrica, incluindo um homem cujo peito tinha pegado fogo, a Geórgia enfim havia recebido uma ordem do Supremo Tribunal para aposentar a Velha Faísca. Agora, em vez de terem a cabeça raspada, algodão enfiado no corpo e serem fritos até ficarem crocantes, os condenados eram amarrados a uma mesa e recebiam uma série de drogas que interrompia a respiração, o coração e, por fim, a vida. Boyd Spivey provavelmente receberia uma dose maior que quase todos os outros. Seria preciso uma combinação poderosa de drogas para derrubar um homem tão grande.

Uma tosse chiada soou pelos alto-falantes minúsculos na mesa. Na sala ao lado, Will via Boyd olhando direto para Amanda, apoiada na parede, apesar de ter uma cadeira vazia junto à mesa na frente dele.

O tom da voz de Boyd era surpreendentemente agudo para um homem do tamanho dele.

— Está com medo de se sentar na minha frente?

Will nunca tinha visto Amanda demonstrar medo, e aquele momento não era exceção.

— Não quero ser grossa, Boyd, mas você está cheirando muito mal.

Ele abaixou os olhos para a mesa.

— Eles só me deixam tomar banho uma vez por semana.

A voz dela tinha uma cadência de provocação.

— Ah, isso é cruel e desumano.

Will olhou para a câmera que estava dando zoom no rosto de Boyd. Havia um sorriso nos lábios dele.

Os saltos altos de Amanda ecoaram na sala de concreto enquanto ela andava até a cadeira. As pernas de metal arranharam o chão. Ela se sentou, cruzando as pernas delicadamente e descansando as mãos no colo.

Boyd permitiu que seus olhos se demorassem nela.

— Você está bonita, Mandy.

— Andei ocupada.

— Com o quê?

— Você ficou sabendo de Evelyn.

— A gente não tem TV aqui.

Ela riu.

— Você deve ter ficado sabendo que eu vinha antes de mim mesma. Este lugar poderia desbancar a CNN.

Ele deu de ombros, como se não pudesse fazer nada quanto a isso, e perguntou:

— Faith está bem?

— Excelente.

— Fiquei sabendo que ela acertou os dois caras na mosca.

Acertar na mosca se referia ao círculo central num alvo de papel, o tiro da morte.

Amanda disse a ele:

— Um foi na cabeça.

— Ui. — Ele fingiu se encolher. — E Emma, como está?

— Dando trabalho. Pena que não tenho uma foto para você. Deixei a bolsa no carro.

— Os pedófilos iam roubar.

— Que falta de decoro deplorável.

Ele sorriu mostrando os dentes. Estavam lascados e quebrados, o tipo de lembrança que se recebia em brigas com golpe baixo.

— Lembro o dia que a Faith recebeu o distintivo dourado. — Ele se recostou na cadeira, as correntes se arrastando na mesa. — Eve estava com um sorriso tão brilhante que parecia uma lanterna Maglite.

— Acho que todos estávamos — admitiu Amanda, e Will absorveu a informação de que sua chefe conhecia Boyd Spivey bem melhor do que ela tinha dado a entender no carro. — Como você anda, Boyd? Eles estão te tratando bem?

— Até que sim. — Ele voltou a sorrir, e então parou. — Desculpe pelos meus dentes. Não vi sentido em arrumar.

— Não é pior que o cheiro.

Ele deu um olhar tímido.

— Faz tempo que eu não ouço uma voz de mulher.

— Odeio admitir, mas essa foi a coisa mais bonita que um homem me falou este ano.

Ele riu.

— Tempos difíceis para nós dois, pelo jeito.

Amanda deixou o momento se estender por mais uns segundos. Ele disse:

— Acho melhor falarmos do motivo por você estar aqui.

— Podemos fazer o que você quiser.

O tom dela deixava implícito que ela podia conversar o dia todo com ele, mas Boyd entendeu a mensagem.

Ele perguntou:

— Quem a levou?

— A gente acha que foi um grupo de asiáticos.

Ele franziu a testa. Apesar do macacão laranja e do lugar infernal que ele tinha como casa, uma parte de Boyd Spivey ainda era policial.

— Os amarelos não têm força na cidade. Os hispânicos andam aliciando de novo os negros para cumprirem as ordens deles.

117

— Os hispânicos estão envolvidos nisso, mas não sei bem como.

Ele fez que sim com a cabeça, indicando que estava absorvendo tudo, mas não sabia o que achar.

— Hispânicos não gostam de sujar as mãos.

— A merda sempre vem de baixo para cima.

— Eles mandaram algum sinal? — Prova de vida. Amanda fez que não. — O que querem em troca dela?

— Me diga você.

Ele ficou em silêncio.

Ela falou:

— Nós dois sabemos que Evelyn era limpa, mas pode ser alguma retaliação?

Ele olhou rapidamente para a câmera, depois baixou os olhos para as mãos.

— Não consigo imaginar isso. Ela estava protegida. Independentemente do que acontecesse, não havia um homem da equipe que não desse a vida por ela até hoje. Não se dá as costas para a família.

Will sempre achara que Evelyn era protegida dos dois lados da lei. Ouvir isso sendo validado não era consolo.

Amanda disse ao homem:

— Você sabe que Chuck Finn e Demarcus Alexander já saíram?

Ele fez que sim com a cabeça.

— Chuck ficou lá no Sul. Demarcus foi para Los Angeles, onde mora a família da mãe.

Amanda já devia saber a resposta, mas perguntou a ele:

— Não estão se metendo em confusão?

— Chuck está fissurado em açúcar e pedra. — Ou seja, ele injetava heroína e, em seguida, fumava crack. — O cara vai acabar de volta na gaiola se não morrer na rua primeiro.

— Ele já emputeceu alguém?

— Não que eu tenha ficado sabendo. Chuck é sacizeiro, Mandy. Seria capaz de foder a própria mãe pela sobra de uma colher.

— E Demarcus?

— Está tão limpo quanto dá para ficar com uma ficha criminal nas costas.

— Ouvi falar que ele está tentando conseguir uma licença para trabalhar como eletricista.

— Que bom para ele. — Boyd parecia sinceramente contente. — Você falou com Hump e Hop?

Ele estava se referindo a Ben Humphrey e Adam Hopkins, colegas detetives cumprindo pena na Prisão Estadual de Valdosta.

Amanda pesou as palavras.

— Eu deveria falar com eles?

— Valeria tentar, mas duvido que ainda estejam por dentro. Eles têm mais quatro anos. Estão se mantendo limpos e não acho que vão ser muito sinceros com você, considerando seu papel no encarceramento deles. — Ele deu de ombros. — Já eu não tenho mais nada a perder.

— Ouvi dizer que recebeu sua data.

— Primeiro de setembro. — Um silêncio pesado se instalou na sala, como se o ar que ainda existia ali tivesse sido sugado. Boyd pigarreou. Seu pomo de adão subiu e desceu. — Isso dá uma perspectiva diferente sobre as coisas.

Amanda se inclinou à frente.

— Tipo o quê?

— Tipo não ver meus filhos crescerem. Nunca ter a chance de segurar meus netos no colo. — Ele engoliu em seco de novo. — Eu amava estar na rua perseguindo os bandidos. Outro dia, tive um sonho. A gente estava na van de operação. Evelyn tinha colocado aquela música idiota, lembra qual era?

— "Would I Lie to You"?

— Annie Lennox. Coração gelado. Ainda conseguia ouvir quando acordei. A cabeça latejando, apesar de eu não ouvir música há o quê, quatro anos? — Ele balançou a cabeça, triste. — É tipo uma droga, né? Você estoura aquela porta, tira todo o lixo, aí acorda no dia seguinte e repete. — Ele abriu os braços o máximo que conseguiu com as correntes. — E eles pagavam a gente para fazer aquilo? Fala sério. A gente que devia estar pagando.

Ela concordou com a cabeça, mas Will estava pensando no fato de que eles tinham conseguido se pagar de diversas outras formas.

Boyd falou:

— Era para eu ser um homem de bem. Mas este lugar... — Ele olhou para a sala. — Obscurece a alma.

— Se você ficasse limpo, já teria saído.

Ele olhou sem expressão para a parede atrás dela.

— Eles me gravaram... indo atrás daqueles caras. — Não tinha humor no sorriso que chegou aos lábios dele, só escuridão e pesar. — Coloquei na cabeça que foi diferente, mas eles passaram no meu julgamento. O vídeo não mente, né?

— É.

Ele pigarreou duas vezes antes de conseguir falar.

— Tinha um homem espancando o guarda com os punhos, enrolando uma toalha ao redor do pescoço do cara. Os olhos brilhando, um show de horrores. Gritando que nem uma porra de um bicho. Fiquei pensando na minha época nas ruas. Todos os bandidos que prendi, todos os homens que eu achava que eram monstros, e aí eu olho aquele cara no vídeo, aquele monstro matando o guarda, e percebo que sou eu. — A voz dele era quase um sussurro. — Era eu espancando o homem. Era eu matando dois caras... por causa do quê? E foi quando percebi: eu virei tudo o que combati todos aqueles anos. — Ele fungou. Tinha lágrimas nos olhos. — A gente vira o que mais odeia.

— Às vezes.

Will não conseguia saber se Boyd estava com pena dos homens que havia matado ou dele mesmo. Provavelmente uma combinação dos dois. Todo mundo sabia que ia morrer alguma hora, mas Boyd Spivey tinha a data e o horário exatos. Ele sabia o método. Sabia quando faria a última refeição, cagaria pela última vez, faria a última oração. E, depois, iriam buscá-lo e ele precisaria se levantar e caminhar com os próprios pés até o lugar em que ia deitar a cabeça pela última vez.

Boyd precisou pigarrear de novo antes de conseguir falar.

— Fiquei sabendo que os amarelos estão invadindo a área da rodovia. Você devia conversar com Ling-Ling lá no Camboja. — Will não reconheceu o nome da pessoa, mas sabia que Camboja era o termo usado para descrever o trecho da rodovia Buford que ficava dentro das fronteiras da cidade de Chamblee. Era uma meca de imigrantes

120

asiáticos e latinos. — Você não pode ir direto até os amarelos. Não sem convite. Diga para Ling-Ling que Spivey falou para deixar baixo.

— Ou seja: não contar para ninguém. — Se cuide. Me parece que esse negócio está saindo do controle.

— Mais alguma coisa?

Will viu a boca de Boyd se mover, mas não conseguiu distinguir as palavras. Perguntou ao guarda:

— Você entendeu o que ele falou?

— Não faço ideia. Pareceu "amém" ou algo do tipo.

Will observou a reação de Amanda. Ela estava assentindo com a cabeça.

— É isso. — O tom de Boyd indicava que tinham terminado. Seus olhos seguiram Amanda enquanto ela se levantava da cadeira. Ele perguntou: — Sabe do que eu sinto mais saudade?

— Do quê?

— De me levantar quando uma mulher entra na sala.

— Você sempre foi educado.

Ele sorriu, mostrando os dentes destruídos.

— Se cuide, Mandy. Leve Evelyn de volta para os bebês dela.

Ela contornou a mesa e parou a alguns passos do presidiário. Will sentiu um embrulho no estômago. O guarda ao seu lado ficou tenso. Não tinha motivo para preocupação. Amanda colocou a mão na bochecha de Boyd e saiu da sala.

— Meu Deus do céu — sussurrou o guarda. — Que filha da puta maluca.

— Segure a onda aí — alertou Will.

Amanda podia ser uma filha da puta maluca, mas era a filha da puta maluca *dele*. Ele abriu a porta e a encontrou no corredor. As câmeras não estavam focadas no rosto dela, mas Will via então que ela tinha suado dentro da sala minúscula sem ar. Ou talvez Boyd tivesse provocado aquela reação nela.

Os dois guardas tinham voltado à posição, cada um parado de um lado de Amanda e de Will. Por cima do ombro dela, ele viu Boyd sendo levado de cabeça baixa pelo corredor, com correntes nas mãos e nos pés. Só tinha um guarda com ele, um homenzinho cuja mão mal conseguia se fechar no braço do detento.

Amanda se virou para observar Boyd até ele desaparecer dobrando o corredor. Ela disse:

— É esse tipo de cara que me dá vontade de trazer de volta a Velha Faísca.

Os guardas deram fortes gargalhadas que ecoaram pelo corredor. Amanda tinha pegado bem leve com Spivey e precisava mostrar que era só uma farsa. A forma como ela agiu na salinha tinha sido bem convincente. Will fora momentaneamente enganado, embora da única vez que ele tinha escutado Amanda falando sobre pena de morte, a reação dela tinha sido dizer que o único problema que tinha com isso era que não matavam os presos rápido o suficiente.

— Senhora? — chamou um dos guardas, indicando o portão no fim do corredor.

— Obrigada. — Amanda foi atrás dele em direção à saída. Olhou para o próprio relógio, dizendo a Will: — São quase quatro horas. Com sorte, temos pelo menos uma hora e meia até voltar a Atlanta. Valdosta fica duas horas e meia ao sul daqui, mas, com trânsito, vão ser quase quatro. Nunca vamos chegar a tempo de uma visita. Consigo mexer uns pauzinhos, mas não conheço o novo diretor e, mesmo que conhecesse, duvido que ele seria tolo o bastante de arrancar dois homens da segurança máxima a essa hora da noite.

Prisões dependiam de rotina, e qualquer coisa que mudasse essa rotina trazia o risco de desencadear violência.

Will perguntou:

— Ainda quer que eu reveja meus documentos arquivados da investigação?

— Lógico. — Ela falou como se nunca tivesse sido colocado em questão o fato de que iam falar da investigação que levou à aposentadoria forçada de Evelyn Mitchell. — Me encontre no escritório amanhã às cinco da manhã. Vamos falar do caso a caminho de Valdosta. São umas três horas para ir e três para voltar. Não deve levar mais de meia hora para falar com Ben e meia hora com Adam, se é que eles vão falar. Com isso, conseguimos voltar para a cidade no máximo até meio-dia para falar com Miriam Kwon.

Will tinha quase se esquecido do garoto morto na área de serviço. O que ele lembrava com clareza era que Amanda tinha passado por cima do fato de que conhecia Boyd Spivey bem o suficiente para ele chamá-la de Mandy. Will só podia supor que Ben Humphrey e Adam Hopkins tinham a mesma intimidade, o que significava que, mais uma vez, Amanda tinha seu próprio caso dentro do caso.

Ela disse:

— Vou dar uns telefonemas para o departamento de liberdade condicional em Memphis e Los Angeles para falar com Chuck Finn e Demarcus Alexander. Só podemos mandar a eles uma mensagem dizendo que Evelyn está correndo perigo e que, se estiverem dispostos a falar, nós estamos dispostos a ouvir.

— Todos eles eram muito leais a Evelyn.

Ela parou no portão, esperando o guarda achar a chave.

— Eram, sim.

— Quem é Ling-Ling?

— Já vamos chegar aí.

Will abriu a boca para falar, mas o ambiente foi invadido por um alarme estridente. As luzes de emergência se acenderam. Um dos guardas agarrou Will pelo braço. O instinto o dominou e Will se afastou dele com um movimento brusco. Amanda obviamente tinha tido uma reação similar, mas não parou por aí. Correu pelo corredor, os saltos batendo contra o piso de azulejo. Will foi atrás dela. Ele dobrou a esquina e quase bateu nas costas de Amanda, que parou de repente.

Amanda não falou. Não ofegou nem gritou. Só agarrou o braço dele, enfiando as unhas através do algodão fino da camisa.

Boyd Spivey estava morto no fim do corredor. Sua cabeça estava virada num ângulo que não era natural. O guarda ao seu lado estava sangrando com um corte grande na garganta. Will foi até o homem. Caiu de joelhos e pressionou as mãos no ferimento, tentando estancar o fluxo. Era tarde demais. O sangue estava formando uma poça no corredor, como uma auréola torta. Os olhos do homem encontraram os de Will e se encheram de pânico, depois se encheram de absolutamente nada.

5

Aproximando-se da casa, Faith desacelerou o Mini. Passava das oito da noite. Durante as últimas seis horas, ela havia relatado sem parar o que tinha acontecido na casa da mãe, repetindo a mesma coisa várias vezes enquanto o advogado dela, o representante do sindicato, três policiais de Atlanta e um agente especial da GBI faziam perguntas, tomavam notas e basicamente a faziam se sentir uma criminosa. Em algum nível, fazia sentido acreditar que Faith estava envolvida no que quer que tivesse levado sua mãe a ser sequestrada. Evelyn tinha sido policial. Faith era policial. Evelyn tinha atirado e matado um homem. Faith tinha atirado em dois — duas possíveis testemunhas — a sangue-frio. Evelyn estava desaparecida. Se Faith estivesse do outro lado da mesa, interrogando, talvez fizesse as mesmas perguntas.

Ela tinha algum inimigo? Já havia aceitado suborno? Já tinha sido abordada para fazer algo ilegal? Já tinha aceitado dinheiro ou presentes para fazer alguma vista grossa?

Mas Faith não estava do outro lado da mesa e, independentemente do quanto quebrasse a cabeça, não conseguia pensar em nenhum motivo para alguém querer levar a mãe dela. A pior parte de estar presa na sala de interrogatório era que cada minuto que passava lembrava a Faith que cinco policiais fisicamente aptos estavam desperdiçando tempo num cômodo claustrofóbico, sendo que podiam estar todos lá fora procurando sua mãe.

Quem faria uma coisa dessas? Evelyn tinha inimigos? O que eles estavam procurando?

Faith estava tão sem ideias naquele momento quanto no início do interrogatório.

Ela parou o carro no meio-fio na frente de casa. Todas as luzes estavam acesas, coisa que ela jamais havia permitido a vida inteira. A casa parecia uma decoração de Natal. Uma decoração de Natal caríssima. Havia quatro carros parados na entrada. Ela reconheceu o Impala velho que Jeremy tinha comprado de Evelyn após a avó adquirir o Malibu, mas as duas caminhonetes e o Corvette preto eram novidades para ela.

— Shhh... — ela acalmou Emma, que estava ficando agitada depois de o carro ter parado.

Desafiando todas as leis e o bom senso, Faith tinha colocado Emma no banco da frente ao seu lado. O trajeto da casa da Sra. Levy até lá levava só alguns minutos, mas não foi a preguiça, e sim a carência que fez Faith querer manter a filha perto. Ela pegou Emma no colo e a abraçou forte. O batimento cardíaco da bebê era um *staccato* calmante no peito de Faith. A respiração dela era suave e familiar, como lenços sendo puxados de uma caixa.

Faith queria sua mãe. Queria colocar a cabeça no ombro de Evelyn e sentir as mãos fortes e magras dela lhe dando tapinhas em suas costas enquanto sussurrava que ia ficar tudo bem. Queria que a mãe pegasse no pé de Jeremy por causa do cabelo comprido e balançasse Emma apoiada no joelho. Acima de tudo, queria conversar com a mãe sobre como o dia tinha sido horrível, ouvir o conselho dela sobre confiar ou não no representante do sindicato que dizia que ela não precisava de advogado, ou no advogado que dizia que o representante era próximo demais da polícia de Atlanta.

— Meu Deus — falou, com a voz fraca, no pescoço de Emma.

Faith precisava da mãe.

Lágrimas encheram seus olhos e, desta vez, ela não tentou impedi-las. Ela estava sozinha pela primeira vez desde que tinha botado o pé dentro da casa da mãe horas antes. Ela queria perder o controle. *Precisava* perder o controle. Mas Jeremy também queria a mãe. Precisava que Faith fosse forte. Seu filho precisava acreditar quando ela dissesse que ia fazer o que fosse necessário para trazer a avó dele de volta a salvo.

A julgar pelos carros, tinha pelo menos três policiais esperando lá dentro com o filho dela. Jeremy estava chorando quando ela ligara da delegacia — confuso, preocupado, aterrorizado pela avó e pela mãe também. A advertência de Amanda veio à mente de Faith. Parada na sala da Sra. Levy, Faith tinha ficado surpresa com o abraço de Amanda, mas não com suas palavras, cochichadas baixinho em alerta:

— Você tem dois minutos para se recompor. Se esses homens virem você chorar, a única coisa que você vai ser para eles durante o resto da sua carreira é uma mulher inútil.

Às vezes, Faith achava que Amanda estava lutando uma batalha que fora travada muito tempo atrás, mas de vez em quando percebia que a chefe tinha razão. Faith usou o dorso da mão para secar os olhos. Abriu a porta do carro e colocou a bolsa no ombro livre. Emma mudou de posição, sobressaltada com o ar frio. Faith puxou o cobertor dela para cima e pressionou os lábios no topo da cabeça da bebê. A pele dela estava quente. Os cabelinhos finos fizeram cócegas nos lábios de Faith enquanto ela subia o caminho de entrada da casa.

Ela pensou em tudo o que precisava fazer antes de poder ir dormir. A casa precisaria ser arrumada, independentemente das circunstâncias. Emma precisava ser colocada na cama. Jeremy precisaria de algum conforto e, provavelmente, jantar. Em algum momento, ela teria que falar com o irmão, Zeke. Se havia alguma benevolência no mundo, ele estaria em algum lugar no meio do Atlântico, num avião, voltando da Alemanha, para que ela não tivesse que conversar com ele naquele dia. O relacionamento dos dois nunca havia sido bom. Felizmente, Amanda tinha se encarregado de dar os telefonemas, senão, Faith teria gastado a maior parte da tarde berrando com Zeke em vez de falando com a polícia. Faith sentiu um mínimo de alívio ao subir as escadas da varanda. Só a ameaça de ter que conversar com o irmão era capaz de tornar convidativa a maneira como ela passara as últimas seis horas. Ela pôs a mão na maçaneta bem quando a porta se abriu.

— Onde diabos você estava?

Faith ficou boquiaberta, olhando o irmão.

— Como você...

— O que aconteceu, Faith? O que você fez?

— Como...

Faith se sentia incapaz de formar uma frase completa.

— Cara, relaxa. — Jeremy empurrou o tio para o lado e pegou Emma do colo de Faith. — Você está bem, mãe?

— Estou — respondeu ela, mas sua atenção estava em Zeke. — Você veio da Alemanha?

Jeremy informou:

— Ele está morando na Flórida agora. — Jeremy puxou Faith para dentro da casa. — Você comeu? Posso fazer alguma coisa.

— Sim... quer dizer, não. Estou bem. — Ela parou de se preocupar com Zeke por um segundo e se concentrou no filho. — Você está bem?

Ele fez que sim, mas ela viu que ele estava se fazendo de forte.

Faith tentou puxá-lo mais para perto, mas ele não se mexeu, provavelmente porque Zeke estava observando cada movimento. Ela disse a Jeremy:

— Quero que você durma aqui na minha casa hoje.

Ele deu de ombros. *Sem grilo.*

— Claro.

— Vamos trazê-la de volta, Jaybird. Eu prometo.

Jeremy baixou os olhos para Emma, que se agitava nos braços dele. "Jaybird" era o apelido de Evelyn para ele, até que um dia toda a escola de ensino fundamental ouviu e começou a zoar o menino a ponto de ele cair no choro. Ele falou:

— A tia Mandy me disse a mesma coisa quando ligou. Que vai trazer a vovó de volta.

— Bem, você sabe. A tia Mandy não mente.

Ele tentou transformar aquilo em piada.

— Eu odiaria ser um daqueles caras quando forem encontrados por ela.

Faith pôs a mão na bochecha de Jeremy. Estava com a barba por fazer, algo com que ela jamais se acostumaria. Seu menino agora era mais alto do que ela, mas Faith sabia que ele não era tão forte.

— A vovó é durona. Você sabe que ela é boa de briga. E sabe que ela vai fazer o que precisar para voltar para você. Para a gente.

Zeke fez um som de desgosto e Faith lhe deu um olhar fulminante por cima do ombro de Jeremy. Ele falou:

127

— Victor quer que você ligue para ele. Você se lembra de Victor, né?

Victor Martinez era a última pessoa do mundo com quem ela queria falar naquele momento. Ela disse a Jeremy:

— Coloque Emma na cama para mim, pode ser? E apague algumas dessas luzes. A gente não é sócio da Georgia Power e eles não precisam do meu salário todo.

— Você parece o vovô.

— Anda.

Jeremy olhou para Zeke de canto de olho, relutante em sair. Ele sempre teve o instinto de proteger Faith.

— Agora — ela mandou, empurrando-o delicadamente na direção das escadas.

Pelo menos Zeke teve a decência de esperar Jeremy se afastar o suficiente para não conseguir ouvir. Ele cruzou os braços, inflando o corpo que já era de um tamanho considerável.

— Em que merda você enfiou a nossa mãe?

— Bom ver você também.

Ela o empurrou e caminhou pelo corredor até a cozinha. Apesar do que tinha dito a Jeremy, Faith não havia comido nada de substancial desde as duas da tarde e sentia aquela enxaqueca latejante e onda de náusea que sinalizavam que havia alguma coisa errada.

— Se acontecer alguma coisa com a mamãe...

— E aí, Zeke? — Faith girou para encará-lo. Ele sempre foi um valentão e, como com todos de sua laia, o único jeito de fazê-lo parar era enfrentá-lo. — O que você vai fazer comigo? Jogar minhas bonecas fora? Torcer meu braço?

— Eu não...

— Eu passei as últimas seis horas sendo interrogada por um bando de babacas que acham que eu fiz minha mãe ser sequestrada e depois me embrenhei numa fúria assassina. Não preciso ouvir essa merda do babaca do meu irmão.

Ela deu as costas a ele e caminhou para a cozinha. Havia um jovem ruivo sentado à mesa dela. Ele estava sem casaco. Uma Smith and Wesson M&P estava pendurada em seu coldre de ombro, como uma língua preta. As faixas estavam apertadas em torno do peito, embolando a

128

camiseta. Ele estava folheando o catálogo da Lands' End que tinha chegado no dia anterior pelo correio, fingindo que não tinha acabado de ouvir Faith gritar a plenos pulmões. Levantou-se quando ela entrou.

— Agente Mitchell, Derrick Connor, da força-tarefa de negociação de sequestros da polícia de Atlanta.

— Obrigada por estar aqui. — Ela esperava parecer sincera. — Imagino que não tenham ligado ainda.

— Não, senhora.

— Alguma novidade?

— Não, mas a senhora vai ser a primeira a saber.

Faith duvidava bem seriamente disso. O ruivinho não estava lá só para ouvir telefonemas. Até os mandachuvas decidirem outra coisa, Faith estava com uma nuvem carregada pairando acima da cabeça.

— Tem algum outro policial aqui?

— O detetive Taylor. Ele está verificando o perímetro. Posso ir buscá-lo se a senhora...

— Eu só queria um pouco de privacidade, por favor.

— Sim, senhora. Se precisar de mim, vou estar logo aqui fora.

Connor deu um aceno de cabeça a Zeke antes de sair pela porta de correr de vidro.

Faith gemeu ao sentar-se à mesa, sentindo que estava de pé havia horas, apesar de ter passado a maior parte do dia sentada. Zeke ainda estava de braços cruzados e bloqueando a porta como se achasse que ela talvez fosse tentar fugir.

Ela perguntou:

— Você continua na Aeronáutica?

— Fui transferido para a base de Eglin há quatro meses.

Mais ou menos quando Emma nasceu.

— Na Flórida?

— Até onde eu sei, sim. — As perguntas dela estavam obviamente piorando a raiva dele. — Estou no meio de um serviço de duas semanas no hospital de veteranos em Clairmont. Que bom que por acaso eu estava na cidade, senão Jeremy teria ficado o dia todo sozinho.

Faith ficou olhando o irmão. Zeke Mitchell sempre parecia estar em posição de sentido. Mesmo aos dez anos, ele agia como um major

129

da Aeronáutica, ou seja, provavelmente tinha nascido com uma barra enorme de aço enfiada no cu para ser tão chato.

Ela perguntou:

— A mamãe sabe que você voltou para o país?

— Claro que sabe. A gente ia jantar amanhã à noite.

— E você não pensou em me contar?

— Eu não queria drama.

Sentando de novo na cadeira, Faith soltou um longo suspiro. Lá estava — a palavra definidora do relacionamento deles. Faith tinha ficado grávida e causado *drama* no último ano do ensino médio de Zeke. O *drama* dela o forçou a abandonar a escola mais cedo e entregar dez anos de vida aos militares. Houve mais *drama* quando ela decidiu ficar com Jeremy e uma cacetada de *drama* quando ela chorou descontroladamente no velório do pai.

— Eu andei vendo as notícias — disse ele, como se fosse uma acusação.

Usando as mãos para se apoiar, Faith se levantou da mesa.

— Então sabe que eu matei dois homens hoje.

— Onde você estava?

As mãos dela tremiam ao abrir o armário e pegar uma barrinha energética. Ela disse como se não fosse nada — tinha matado dois homens naquele dia. Durante o interrogatório, Faith havia notado que, quanto mais falava do assunto, mais anestesiada ficava à realidade do ato, de modo que pronunciar aquilo naquele momento só a deixou entorpecida.

Zeke repetiu:

— Eu te fiz uma pergunta, Faith. Onde você estava quando a mamãe precisou de você?

— Onde *você* estava? — Ela jogou a barrinha na mesa. Estava ficando zonza outra vez. Era melhor testar a glicemia antes de comer alguma coisa. — Eu estava num seminário de treinamento.

— Você estava atrasada.

Ela supôs que ele estivesse chutando.

— Não estava.

— Eu falei com a mamãe hoje de manhã.

Faith sentiu os sentidos ficando mais aguçados.

— A que horas? Você contou para a polícia?

— Lógico que eu contei para a polícia. Conversei com ela por volta de meio-dia.

Faith tinha chegado à casa da mãe menos de duas horas depois.

— Ela parecia bem? O que ela disse?

— Disse que você estava atrasada de novo, Faith, como sempre. É assim que as coisas são. O mundo tem que se ajustar à sua agenda.

— Pai do céu — sussurrou ela.

Ela não conseguia lidar com aquilo naquele momento. Ela estava suspensa do trabalho sabia Deus até quando. A mãe podia estar morta. O filho estava arrasado e ela não conseguia tirar o irmão da sua frente por tempo suficiente para recuperar o fôlego. Para piorar o estresse, parecia que sua cabeça estava presa num torno. Ela procurou dentro da bolsa um kit para teste de glicemia. Entrar em coma, embora parecesse uma perspectiva atraente no momento, não ia ajudar em nada.

Faith depositou o kit na mesa. Odiava ser observada quando testava o sangue, mas Zeke não parecia disposto a lhe dar privacidade. Faith trocou a agulha da caneta e desembrulhou um lenço antisséptico. Zeke a observava com olhos de águia. Ele era médico. Ela quase conseguia ouvir o cérebro dele catalogando a forma errada como ela estava fazendo as coisas.

Faith espremeu uma gota de sangue na tira. O número apareceu. Ela mostrou o LED a Zeke, sabendo que ele ia perguntar.

Ele falou:

— Quando foi sua última refeição?

— Comi uns biscoitos salgados de queijo na delegacia.

— Não é suficiente.

Ela se levantou e abriu a geladeira.

— Eu sei.

— Está alta. Deve ser o estresse.

— Eu sei disso também.

— Quanto estava sua hemoglobina glicada da última vez?

— Seis ponto um.

Ele se sentou à mesa.

— Não é ruim.

— Não — concordou ela, pegando a insulina na porta da geladeira.

Na verdade, era só um pouquinho acima da meta dela, o que era bom para caramba, considerando que Faith tinha acabado de dar à luz.

— Você acredita mesmo no que falou? — Ele parou, e ela viu que tinha sido difícil para ele fazer a pergunta. — Acha mesmo que vamos trazê-la de volta?

Faith voltou a se sentar.

— Não sei.

— Ela estava machucada?

Faith balançou a cabeça e deu de ombros ao mesmo tempo. A polícia se recusava a contar qualquer coisa para ela.

O peito dele subiu e desceu.

— Por que alguém a levaria? Você... — Para variar, ele tentou ser sensível. — Você está metida em alguma coisa?

— Por que você é tão babaca o tempo todo? — Ela não esperava uma resposta. — A mamãe liderou um esquadrão de narcóticos por quinze anos, Zeke. Ela fez inimigos. Fazia parte do trabalho. E você sabe da investigação. Sabe por que ela se aposentou.

— Já faz quatro anos.

— Esse tipo de coisa não tem limite de tempo. Talvez alguém tenha decidido que quer alguma coisa dela.

— Tipo o quê? Dinheiro? Ela não tem. Eu tenho acesso a todas as contas dela. Ela recebe a aposentadoria da prefeitura, um pouco da pensão do papai e só. Nem recebe tudo da previdência social ainda.

— Com certeza está relacionado a algum caso. — Faith puxou a insulina com a seringa. — A equipe toda dela foi presa. Muitos criminosos ficaram putos de ver os policiais que eles tinham comprado serem tirados do jogo.

— Você acha que os caras da mamãe estão envolvidos nisso?

Faith fez que não. Eles sempre tinham chamado a equipe de Evelyn de "os caras da mamãe", principalmente porque, assim, era mais fácil se manterem informados sobre eles.

— Não faço ideia de quem está envolvido nem por quê.

— Você está pesquisando todos os casos antigos deles e entrevistando os meliantes?

132

— "Meliantes"? Sério, de onde você tirou essa? — Faith levantou a blusa só o suficiente para enfiar a agulha na barriga. Não houve uma onda imediata, o medicamento não funcionava assim. Apesar disso, Faith fechou os olhos, querendo que a náusea passasse. — Eu estou suspensa, Zeke. Pegaram meu distintivo, minha arma e me mandaram para casa. Me diga o que você quer que eu faça.

Ele cruzou as mãos na mesa e ficou olhando os polegares.

— Você consegue dar uns telefonemas? Falar com algumas fontes? Sei lá, Faith. Você é policial há vinte anos. Cobre uns favores de alguém.

— Quinze anos, e não tem ninguém para cobrar. Eu matei dois homens hoje. Você não viu o jeito como aquele policial estava me olhando? Eles acham que eu estou envolvida nisso. Ninguém vai me fazer favor nenhum.

Ele mexeu o maxilar de um lado para o outro. Estava acostumado a ser obedecido.

— A mamãe ainda tem amigos.

— E provavelmente estão todos cagando de medo de que esse rolo que a fez ser sequestrada caia na cabeça deles.

Ele não gostou disso. Abaixou o queixo e encostou-o no peito.

— Tá. Então não tem nada que você possa fazer. Estamos desamparados. E a mamãe também.

— Amanda não vai aceitar isso quieta.

Zeke soltou uma risada de descrença pelo nariz. Ele nunca tinha gostado de Amanda. Uma coisa era a irmã mais nova tentar mandar nele, mas ele não ia aceitar aquilo de alguém que não era família de sangue. Era uma reação estranha, considerando que Zeke, Faith e Jeremy tinham sido criados chamando-a de tia Mandy, um apelido carinhoso que Faith tinha quase certeza que, se usasse atualmente, a faria ser demitida. Ainda assim, sempre tinham considerado Amanda como parte da família. Era tão próxima de Evelyn que, às vezes, parecia uma mãe substituta.

Mas ela ainda era sua chefe e ainda estava com o pé bem na nuca de Faith, como fazia com todo mundo que trabalhava para ela. Ou que entrava em contato com ela. Ou que sorria para ela na rua.

Faith abriu a barrinha e deu uma mordida grande. O único som na cozinha era sua mastigação. Ela queria fechar os olhos, mas tinha medo das imagens que veria. A mãe amarrada e amordaçada. Os olhos vermelhos de Jeremy. A forma como aqueles policiais a tinham olhado naquele dia, como se o fedor do envolvimento dela fosse insuportável.

Zeke pigarreou. Ela achava que a hostilidade havia passado, mas a postura dele indicava que não. Se havia uma coisa constante em sua vida, era a sensação de superioridade moral de Zeke.

Ela tentou acabar logo com aquilo.

— Que foi?

— Aquele tal de Victor pareceu surpreso ao ouvir falar de Emma. Quis saber a idade dela, quando tinha nascido.

Ela engasgou, tentando engolir.

— Victor veio aqui? Aqui em casa?

— Você não estava, Faith. Alguém tinha que ficar com seu filho até eu chegar.

A lista de xingamentos que veio à mente de Faith provavelmente era pior do que qualquer coisa que Zeke já tinha ouvido enquanto costurava soldados em Ramstein.

Ele continuou:

— Jeremy mostrou uma foto dela para ele.

Faith tentou engolir de novo. Parecia que a garganta estava cheia de pregos enferrujados.

— Emma tem a cor da pele dele.

— De Jeremy?

— É um padrão seu, por acaso? Você curte ser mãe solteira?

— Putz, não contaram quando você voltou que o presidente não é mais o Ronald Reagan?

— Caramba, Faith. Fala sério, pelo menos uma vez. O cara tem direito de saber que é pai.

— Victor não tem interesse em ser pai, pode acreditar.

O homem não era capaz nem de pegar as meias sujas do chão ou se lembrar de abaixar a tampa do vaso sanitário. Só Deus sabia o que ele seria capaz de esquecer cuidando de uma bebê.

Zeke repetiu:

— Ele tem direito de saber.

— Então, agora ele sabe.

— Tudo bem, Faith. Se *você* está feliz.

Qualquer ser humano normal teria saído andando vitorioso depois dessa cutucada, mas Zeke Mitchell nunca se retirava de uma briga. Ele só ficou lá sentado, olhando para ela, desafiando-a a subir o tom. Faith voltou ao seu antigo comportamento. Se ele ia agir como se tivesse dez anos, ela também ia. Ignorou a presença dele, folheando o catálogo da Lands' End, rasgando a página que mostrava a cueca de que Jeremy gostava para poder comprá-la para ele depois.

Ela foi até a página das camisas térmicas, e Zeke inclinou a cadeira para trás, olhando pela janela.

Essa tensão entre eles não era novidade. Zeke amava bater na tecla do egoísmo de Faith. Como sempre, ela aceitou a desaprovação dele como parte de sua punição. Ele tinha bons motivos para odiá-la. Não dava para voltar atrás no episódio de um garoto de dezoito anos descobrindo que a irmã de catorze estava grávida. Especialmente quando Jeremy ficou mais velho e ela viu como era a adolescência para os meninos — não era nada do mar de rosas que ela imaginava quando era uma menina adolescente —, Faith se sentia culpada pelo que fizera com o irmão.

Por mais difícil que tivesse sido para o pai dela, que fora convidado a se retirar do grupo de estudos bíblicos dos homens, e para a mãe, ostracizada por quase todas as mulheres do bairro, Zeke tinha suportado um inferno particular por causa da gravidez inesperada de Faith. Ele voltava para casa pelo menos uma vez por semana com o nariz sangrando ou o olho roxo. Quando perguntavam o motivo, ele se recusava a falar. Fazia cara feia para Faith à mesa de jantar. Dava olhares de nojo se ela passasse em frente ao quarto dele. Zeke a odiava pelo que ela tinha feito com a família, mas fazia um inferno na vida de quem falasse uma palavra contra ela.

Não que ela se lembrasse de muita coisa daquela época. Mesmo naquele momento, era um grande borrão infeliz de uma chorosa autocomiseração. Era difícil acreditar que tanta coisa havia mudado em vinte anos, mas Atlanta, ou pelo menos a parte em que Faith vivia, na época parecia uma cidade de interior. As pessoas ainda estavam na onda de valores conservadores das eras Reagan e Bush. Faith era uma adolescente egoísta e mimada quando aquilo aconteceu. Só conseguia enxergar o quanto a própria vida era infeliz. A gravidez tinha sido resultado de sua primeira — e, na época, ela jurou que última — relação sexual. Os pais do pai do bebê imediatamente se mudaram com ele para outro estado. Não teve festa de aniversário quando ela fez quinze anos. Seus amigos a abandonaram. O pai de Jeremy nunca escreveu nem telefonou. Ela precisava ir a médicos que a cutucavam e sondavam. Ela vivia cansada e mal-humorada, e tinha hemorroidas e dores nas costas, e tudo doía sempre que ela se mexia.

O pai de Faith passava muito tempo fora, de repente tendo viagens a trabalho que antes não faziam parte de suas obrigações. A igreja era o centro da vida dele, mas esse centro foi abruptamente arrancado quando o pastor lhe informou que ele não tinha autoridade moral para ser diácono. A mãe tinha tirado uma licença do trabalho para ficar com ela — Evelyn nunca dissera se havia sido de forma voluntária ou forçada.

Faith lembrava que ela e a mãe ficavam presas em casa todo dia, comendo um monte de besteira que as deixava gordas e vendo novelas que as faziam chorar. De sua parte, Evelyn suportara a vergonha de Faith como uma ermitã. Só saía de casa se fosse obrigada. Acordava toda segunda de manhã cedíssimo para ir ao mercado do outro lado da cidade, para não encontrar ninguém que conhecia. Recusava-se a se sentar no quintal com Faith mesmo quando o ar-condicionado quebrara e a sala virara uma estufa. O único exercício que fazia era uma caminhada pelo bairro, mas só tarde da noite ou de manhã cedo, antes de o sol nascer.

A vizinha ao lado, a Sra. Levy, deixava biscoitos na porta delas, mas nunca entrava. Ocasionalmente, alguém deixava folhetos religiosos na caixa de correio e Evelyn os queimava na lareira. A única visitante durante todo esse tempo era Amanda, que não tinha a opção de sumir do calendário social daquela que era praticamente sua cunhada. Ficava sentada na cozinha com Evelyn conversando numa voz baixa que Faith não conseguia escutar. Depois de Amanda ir embora, Evelyn entrava no banheiro e chorava.

Não foi surpresa quando um dia Zeke voltou da escola não com o lábio estourado, mas com uma cópia de seu alistamento. Faltavam cinco meses para a formatura. Seu serviço no ROTC, o corpo de treinamento de reservas, e as notas no vestibular tinham garantido a ele uma bolsa integral na Rutgers. Mas ele fez uma prova para tirar um diploma de equivalência e entrou no programa pré-medicina praticamente um ano antes do esperado.

Jeremy tinha oito anos quando conheceu o tio. Ele e Zeke tinham ficado se rondando como gatos, até um jogo de basquete melhorar as coisas. Mesmo assim, Faith conhecia o filho e reconhecia a reticência dele em relação a um homem que ele sentia que não tratava sua mãe bem. Infelizmente, ele tivera muitas oportunidades ao longo dos anos para ruminar aquele sentimento em particular.

Zeke voltou a cadeira que estava inclinada para o chão, mas continuou sem olhar para ela.

Faith mastigou devagar a barrinha, forçando-se a comer apesar da náusea que tomava seu estômago. Ela olhou a porta de correr e viu a mesa da cozinha e a postura de Zeke, ereta como uma tábua, refletidas. Atrás do vidro, havia um brilho vermelho. Um dos investigadores estava fumando.

O telefone tocou e os dois deram um pulo. Faith saiu correndo para atender o sem fio bem quando os investigadores voltaram do quintal.

— Nenhuma notícia — Will disse a ela. — Só queria saber como estão as coisas.

Faith acenou para dispensar os policiais. Levou o telefone para a sala de estar e perguntou:

— Onde você está?

— Acabei de chegar em casa. Tinha um trailer derrapado na 675. Levou três horas para tirarem da estrada.

— Por que você estava lá?

— Fui na D&C.

Faith sentiu o estômago revirar.

Will não se deu ao trabalho de jogar conversa fora. Contou a ela sobre a visita à prisão e o assassinato de Boyd Spivey. Faith levou a

137

mão ao peito. Quando era mais nova, Boyd era convidado frequente em jantares de família e churrascos no quintal. Tinha ensinado Jeremy a andar de bicicleta. E, mais tarde, paquerado Faith tão abertamente que Bill Mitchell sugerira que o cara achasse outro jeito de passar os fins de semana.

— Eles sabem quem foi?

— A câmera de segurança por acaso estava quebrada só naquela seção. Fizeram um *lockdown* no lugar. Todas as celas estão sendo revistadas. O diretor não está muito esperançoso de acharem grande coisa.

— Teve ajuda externa.

Um guarda provavelmente havia sido subornado. Nenhum detento teria tempo de desativar uma câmera montada dentro de um corredor de prisão.

— Estão conversando com a equipe, mas os advogados já estão no local. Esses caras não são suspeitos comuns.

— Amanda está bem? — Faith balançou a cabeça com a idiotice. — Claro que ela está bem.

— Ela conseguiu o que queria. Temos uma entrada possível no caso da sua mãe por causa disso.

A GBI tinha jurisdição sobre todas as investigações de homicídio dentro de prisões estaduais.

— Acho que é uma boa notícia.

Will ficou quieto. Não queria perguntar se ela estava bem, porque obviamente sabia a resposta. Faith pensou no jeito como ele tinha segurado as mãos dela à tarde, fazendo-a prestar atenção enquanto ele explicava o que ela devia falar. A sensibilidade dele tinha sido inesperada, e ela precisou morder o interior da bochecha, com força suficiente para tirar sangue, só para não cair no choro.

Will falou:

— Sabia que eu nunca vi Amanda ir ao banheiro? — Ele parou por um momento. — Não pessoalmente, quero dizer, mas, quando saímos da prisão, ela parou no posto de gasolina e entrou. Nunca a vi fazer uma pausa assim. Você já?

Faith estava acostumada com as digressões esquisitas de Will.

— Não, também não.

Amanda frequentava aqueles jantares e churrascos familiares com Boyd Spivey. Brincava com ele do jeito típico dos policiais — questionando a masculinidade dele, elogiando quando ele era promovido na polícia, apesar da falta de capacidades mentais. Ela não era completamente feita de pedra. Devia ter se abalado por ver Boyd morrer.

Will comentou:

— Foi muito perturbador.

— Imagino.

Faith pensou em Amanda no posto, entrando na cabine, fechando a porta e se permitindo dois minutos para lamentar por um homem que em algum momento tinha sido importante para ela. E, então, provavelmente tinha conferido a maquiagem, arrumado o cabelo e devolvido a chave para o atendente do posto, perguntando se mantinham a porta trancada para evitar que alguém fosse limpar.

Will falou:

— Ela provavelmente acha que urinar é uma fraqueza.

— A maioria das pessoas acha. — Faith se recostou no sofá. Ele tinha dado a ela o melhor presente que ela poderia receber naquele momento: um pouco de distração. — Obrigada.

— Pelo quê?

— Por ter estado lá hoje. Por chamar Sara. Por me dizer o que... — Ela lembrou que o telefone estava grampeado. — Por me dizer que ia ficar tudo bem.

Ele pigarreou. Houve um silêncio curto. Ele era horrível nesse tipo de coisa, quase tão ruim quanto ela.

— Você pensou no que eles estavam procurando?

— Não consigo pensar em outra coisa. — Ela ouviu a porta da geladeira abrir e fechar. Zeke provavelmente estava fazendo uma lista de comidas que ela não devia ter em casa. — E qual é o próximo passo?

Ele hesitou.

— Me diga.

— Amanda e eu vamos a Valdosta amanhã cedo.

Prisão Estadual de Valdosta. Ben Humphrey e Adam Hopkins. Estavam falando com todo mundo da antiga equipe da mãe dela. Faith devia ter esperado isso, mas a notícia da morte de Boyd a havia tirado do prumo. Ela devia saber que Will ia reabrir o caso.

Faith disse:

— É melhor eu manter a linha desocupada, caso alguém ligue.

— Tudo bem.

Ela desligou, porque não tinha mais o que dizer. Ele ainda achava que a mãe dela era culpada. Mesmo depois de trabalhar com Faith por quase dois anos, ver que ela fazia as coisas direito porque tinha sido criada pela mãe para ser esse tipo de policial, Will ainda achava que Evelyn Mitchell era corrupta.

Zeke estava pairando na porta.

— Quem era?

— Do trabalho. — Ela se levantou do sofá. — Meu parceiro.

— O babaca que tentou prender a mamãe?

— O próprio.

— Ainda não sei como você consegue trabalhar com esse escroto.

— Eu falei com a mamãe antes.

— Mas não falou comigo.

— Eu devia ter mandado o pedido para a Alemanha ou para a Flórida?

Ele a olhou fixamente.

Faith não ia se explicar ao irmão. Tinha sido Amanda quem pedira para ela fazer dupla com Will, e Evelyn dissera para Faith fazer o que fosse melhor para a carreira dela. Não precisava nem comentar que não era má ideia sair da polícia de Atlanta, onde a aposentadoria precoce de Evelyn era considerada ou uma vantagem, ou um crime, a depender de quem estivesse opinando.

— A mamãe chegou a conversar com você sobre a investigação?

— Não é melhor você perguntar ao seu parceiro sobre isso?

— Estou perguntando para você — irritou-se Faith. Evelyn tinha se recusado a discutir o caso contra ela e não só porque Faith podia ser chamada como testemunha em potencial. — Se ela falou alguma coisa, mesmo que parecesse um pouco estranha, mas que você não tenha ligado na época...

— A mamãe não conversa de trabalho comigo. Isso é coisa sua.

A voz dele tinha o mesmo tom de acusação, como se Faith tivesse o poder de encontrar a mãe e estivesse simplesmente escolhendo não exercê-lo. Ela olhou o relógio na parede. Eram quase nove, tarde demais para aquilo.

— Vou dormir. Mando Jeremy descer com uns lençóis. O sofá é bem confortável.

Ele assentiu, e Faith se despediu com uma continência. Ela já estava no meio da escada quando ele falou.

— Ele é um menino bacana. — Faith se virou. — Jeremy. É um menino bacana.

Ela sorriu.

— É, sim.

Ela estava quase no topo da escada quando veio o ataque.

— A mamãe fez um bom trabalho.

Faith continuou subindo, se recusando a morder a isca. Ela foi ver como estava a bebê. Emma estalou os lábios quando Faith se debruçou para beijar a testa dela. Estava naquele sono profundo e abençoado que só os bebês conhecem. Faith conferiu se a babá eletrônica estava ligada. Passou a mão pelo bracinho de Emma, deixando os dedos minúsculos da bebê segurarem um dela, antes de sair.

No quarto ao lado, a cama de Jeremy estava vazia. Faith se demorou na porta. Ela não tinha mexido no quarto dele, mesmo considerando que seria bom ter um escritório. Os pôsteres dele continuavam pendurados na parede — um Mustang GT com uma loira de biquíni debruçada no capô, outro com uma morena seminua deitada em cima de um Camaro, um terceiro e um quarto mostrando carros conceituais com a modelo peituda onipresente. Faith ainda se lembrava de um dia ter voltado 'o trabalho e achado os pôsteres dele da série "Pontes do Sudeste dos Estados Unidos" substituídos por essas pérolas. Jeremy ainda achava que tinha sido esperto de enganá-la e fazê-la achar que a puberdade tinha trazido um interesse repentino por automóveis.

— Estou aqui.

Faith o encontrou no quarto dela. Jeremy estava deitado de barriga para baixo, com a cabeça virada para o pé da cama, pés para cima, iPhone na mão. O som da TV estava mudo, mas as legendas estavam ligadas.

Ela perguntou:

— Está tudo bem?

Ele inclinou o iPhone que estava segurando, obviamente jogando.

— Está.

Faith se lembrou da namorada fértil. Estranho ela não estar ali. Os dois viviam grudados.

— Cadê Kimberly?

— A gente deu um tempo — disse ele, e ela quase soluçou de alívio.
— Escutei você e Zeke gritando.

— Tem uma primeira vez para tudo.

Ele inclinou o celular para o outro lado.

Ela disse:

— Estou querendo um desses. — Ele entendeu a dica e colocou o aparelho no bolso. — Sei que você escutou o telefone tocar. Era Will. Ele está trabalhando com a tia Amanda.

Ele olhou para a TV.

— Que bom.

Faith começou a desamarrar os tênis dele. Numa lógica típica de adolescente, ele achava que manter os pés para cima impediria a sujeira de cair.

— Me conte o que aconteceu quando Zeke chegou.

— O cara estava sendo um babaca.

— Me conte como se eu fosse sua mãe.

Ela o viu ficar levemente corado no brilho da TV.

— Victor ficou comigo. Eu falei que não precisava, mas ele disse que queria, então...

Faith desamarrou o outro tênis dele.

— Você mostrou uma foto de Emma?

Ele continuou olhando a TV. Jeremy adorava Victor — provavelmente mais do que Faith, o que só era parte do problema.

Ela disse:

— Não tem problema.

— Zeke foi meio escroto... quer dizer, grosso... com ele.

— Em que sentido?

— Só meio que estufando o peito e provocando.

Só sendo Zeke.

— Não aconteceu nada, né?

— Não, Victor não é desses.

Faith imagınou. Victor Martinez trabalhava num escritório, lia o *Wall Street Journal* todos os dias, usava ternos sob medida e lavava as mãos dezesseis vezes por dia. Era tão passional quanto uma parede. A sına de Faith era só conseguir se apaixonar pelo tipo de homem que usava regata e socava a cara do irmão dela.

Ela tirou o sapato de Jeremy e fez uma careta ao ver o estado da meia.

— Os dedos ficam para dentro, universitário.

Ela fez uma anotação mental de comprar maıs meıas para ele quando fosse fazer o pedido das cuecas. A calça jeans dele também parecia meio puída. Lá se iam os trezentos dólares que ela tinha na conta corrente. Graças a Deus ela tinha sido suspensa com o salário intacto. Faith ia ter que usar a poupança só para impedir que o filho parecesse um mendigo.

Jeremy se virou de barriga para cima para olhá-la.

— Mostrei a ele a foto de Emma na Páscoa.

Ela engoliu em seco. Victor era um cara inteligente, mas não precisava ser gênio para fazer a conta. Mesmo sem isso, Faith era loira e de pele clara. Emma tinha a pele escura e os olhos castanhos do pai.

— Aquela com orelhas de coelho?

Ele fez que sim.

— É muito boa. — Faith via a culpa brotando nele como água transbordando de um copo. — Está tudo bem, Jay. Alguma hora ele ia descobrir.

— Então, por que você não contou?

Porque Faith era a mescla perfeita de emocionalmente atrofiada e controladora, que era algo que Jeremy descobriria quando a futura esposa gritasse isso na cara dele. Por ora, Faith disse:

— Não vou conversar com você sobre isso.

Ele se sentou para olhá-la.

— A vovó gosta do Will.

Faith imaginou que ele tivesse escutado a conversa dela com Zeke.

— Ela falou isso para você?

Ele fez que sim.

— Ela disse que ele era um cara legal. Que tratava ela de um jeito justo e que teve que fazer um trabalho difícil, mas não foi cruel.

Faith não sabia se a mãe estava tranquilizando as preocupações de Jeremy ou revelando sua verdadeira opinião. Conhecendo a mãe, devia ser uma mistura dos dois.

— Ela chegou a conversar com você sobre o motivo de ela ter se aposentado?

Ele puxou um fio solto na colcha.

— Ela disse que era a chefe, então, era culpa dela não notar o que estava rolando.

Aquilo era mais do que ela tinha dito a Faith.

— Mais alguma coisa?

Ele fez que não.

— Que bom que Will está ajudando a tia Amanda. Ela não consegue fazer tudo sozinha. E ele é muito inteligente.

Faith pegou a mão dele e a segurou até Jeremy olhar para ela. A televisão era a única luz do quarto. Dava um brilho esverdeado ao rosto dele.

— Eu sei que você está preocupado com a vovó e sei que não tem nada que eu possa fazer para melhorar as coisas para você.

— Obrigado.

Ele estava sendo sincero. Jeremy sempre gostava de honestidade.

Ela o puxou da cama e o abraçou. Os ombros dele eram magros. Ele era desengonçado, ainda sem o porte do homem que se tornaria, apesar de comer o próprio peso em macarrão com queijo todos os dias.

O filho permitiu que ela o abraçasse por mais tempo que o normal. Ela deu um beijo na cabeça dele.

— Vai ficar tudo bem.

— É o que a vovó sempre fala.

— E ela sempre está certa.

Faith o apertou mais forte.

— Mãe, você está me sufocando.

Relutante, ela o soltou.

— Pega uns lençóis para o tio Zeke. Ele vai dormir no sofá.

Jeremy deslizou os pés de novo para dentro dos tênis.

— Ele sempre foi assim?

Faith não se fez de desentendida.

— Quando éramos pequenos, toda vez que ele precisava peidar, entrava correndo no meu quarto e mandava ver.

Jeremy começou a rir.

— E, aí, ele dizia que, se eu contasse, ele ia comer um monte de feijão e queijo, me segurar e fazer na minha cara da próxima vez.

Isso o fez cair na gargalhada. Ele se debruçou, segurando a barriga, e zurrou que nem um burro.

— E ele fez isso?

Faith fez que sim, o que o levou a rir ainda mais. Ela deixou que ele curtisse a humilhação dela mais um pouco antes de o cutucar no ombro.

— Hora de dormir.

Ele secou as lágrimas dos olhos.

— Cara, preciso fazer isso com Horner.

Horner era o garoto que dividia o quarto com ele. Faith duvidava que alguém fosse notar mais um cheiro tóxico no dormitório estudantil.

— Pegue um travesseiro do armário para Zeke.

Ela o empurrou para fora do quarto. Ele continuou rindo enquanto andava pelo corredor. Era um pequeno preço a se pagar para ver a preocupação desaparecer momentaneamente do rosto do filho.

Faith puxou o edredom da cama. A sujeira dos tênis de Jeremy tinha sujado o lençol. Ela estava cansada demais para trocar. Estava cansada demais para pôr a camisola ou até escovar os dentes. Tirou os sapatos e subiu na cama com o mesmo uniforme da GBI que estava usando desde as cinco da manhã.

Havia silêncio na casa. Seu corpo estava tão tenso que ela sentia como se estivesse deitada numa tábua. Ouvia o ressonar de Emma pela babá eletrônica. Faith olhou o teto. Tinha se esquecido de desligar a televisão. As luzes do filme de ação a que Jeremy estava assistindo pareciam as de um estrobo.

Boyd Spivey estava morto. Parecia algo impossível de conceber. Ele era um cara enorme, cheio de vida, o tipo de policial que se imagina morrendo numa explosão gloriosa. Era o exato oposto do parceiro. Chuck Finn era sisudo, cheio de previsões sombrias e morria de medo de levar um tiro no cumprimento do dever. Sua defesa durante a investigação era a única que Faith achara crível naquela confusão toda. Chuck alegara estar só seguindo ordens. Para quem o conhecia, parecia completamente plausível. O investigador Finn era um seguidor por excelência, que era o tipo exato de personalidade que homens como Boyd Spivey sabiam explorar.

Mas Faith não queria pensar em Boyd, Chuck, nem em qualquer outro da equipe da mãe naquele momento. A investigação tinha consumido seis meses da vida dela. Seis meses de noites sem dormir. Seis meses preocupada de a mãe infartar, ou acabar na cadeia, ou as duas coisas.

Faith se obrigou a fechar os olhos. Queria pensar em épocas boas com a mãe, lembrar algum momento de gentileza ou o prazer da companhia dela. Em vez disso, o que ela viu foi o homem no quarto de Evelyn, o buraco preto no meio da testa onde Faith havia atirado. As mãos dele haviam se levantado num movimento brusco. O refém ficara olhando Faith sem acreditar. Boquiaberto. Ela vira o aparelho prateado nos dentes e o fato de que a língua tinha um piercing prateado combinando.

Almeja, ele tinha dito.

Dinheiro.

Faith ouviu as tábuas do chão do corredor rangerem.

— Jeremy?

Ela se apoiou no cotovelo e acendeu o abajur. Ele deu um olhar tímido.

— Desculpa, eu sei que você está cansada.

— Quer que eu leve os lençóis para Zeke?

— Não, não é isso. — Ele tirou o iPhone do bolso. — Apareceu uma coisa no meu Facebook.

— Achei que você tivesse parado de usar isso quando obriguei você a me aceitar como amiga. — Faith nunca foi o tipo de mãe que confiava completamente no filho. Seus próprios pais tinham confiado nela e veja só no que deu. — O que foi?

Ele moveu os polegares pela tela enquanto falava.

— Eu fiquei entediado. Quer dizer, não entediado, mas não tinha nada para fazer, aí...

— Está tudo bem, amor. — Ela se sentou na cama. — O que foi?

— Muita gente andou postando coisas. Acho que ficaram sabendo da vovó pela televisão.

— Que legal — disse Faith, embora achasse meio macabro e, para emprestar uma palavra do irmão, *dramático*. — O que estão falando?

— Principalmente que estão pensando em mim e coisas do tipo. Mas tem isso aqui.

Ele virou o telefone e entregou para ela.

Faith leu a mensagem em voz alta:

— "Ei, Jaybird, espero que você esteja bem. Com certeza alguém vai apontar o dedo para os culpados. Só lembre o que sua avó sempre dizia: mantenha a boca fechada e os olhos abertos."

Faith olhou o nome do usuário.

— GoodKnight92. É alguém que estudou com você na Grady?

O mascote da escola de Jeremy era um *knight*, um cavaleiro, e ele tinha nascido em 1992.

Ele deu de ombros.

— Nunca ouvi falar.

Faith notou que o post tinha entrado às 14h32 da tarde, menos de uma hora depois de Evelyn ser sequestrada. Ela tentou não parecer preocupada ao perguntar:

— Quando ele adicionou você?

— Hoje, mas muita gente fez isso. Meio que todo mundo brotou do nada.

Ela entregou o aparelho para ele.

— O que o perfil dele diz?

— Só que ele mora em Atlanta e trabalha com distribuição.

Ele clicou na tela e mostrou a Faith.

Os olhos dela estavam tão cansados que era difícil focar. Faith segurou o telefone perto do rosto para conseguir ler o que dizia. Não tinha mais nada, nem foto. Jeremy era o único amigo de GoodKnight. Ela sentiu sua intuição policial lhe dizendo que tinha alguma coisa errada, mas devolveu o telefone como se não fosse nada.

— Com certeza é alguém que estudou com você na Morningside. Eles provocavam tanto você por causa do apelido que a vovó usava, Jaybird, que você me implorou para trocar de escola.

— Mas é estranho... né?

Ela não ia deixá-lo ficar preocupado.

— A maioria dos seus amigos são estranhos.

Ele se recusava a ser tranquilizado.

— Como ele sabe que a vovó sempre fala isso?

— É um ditado bem comum — respondeu Faith. — Boca fechada, olhos abertos. Eu tinha um instrutor na Academia que praticamente tatuou isso na testa. — Ela forçou a voz a ficar leve. — Vamos. Não é nada. Deve ser um filho de policial. Você sabe a regra. Quando acontece alguma coisa, todo mundo é família.

Isso finalmente pareceu tranquilizá-lo. Jeremy tinha sido arrastado a uma boa quantidade de hospitais e casas de estranhos quando um policial era ferido ou morto. Ele guardou o celular de volta no bolso.

Ela perguntou:

— Certeza que você está bem?

Ele fez que sim.

— Pode dormir aqui, se quiser.

— Seria esquisito, mãe.

— Me acorde se precisar de alguma coisa.

Faith voltou a se deitar, colocando a mão por baixo do travesseiro. Seus dedos tocaram em algo molhado. Familiar. Jeremy percebeu imediatamente a mudança.

— O que foi?

A respiração de Faith estava presa no peito. Ela não confiava que fosse conseguir falar.

— Mãe?

— Cansada — ela conseguiu dizer. — Só estou cansada. — Seus pulmões doíam, querendo oxigênio. Ela sentiu suor pelo corpo todo.

— Pegue os lençóis antes que Zeke suba aqui.

— Você está...

— Foi um dia longo, Jeremy. Preciso dormir.

Ele continuava relutante.

— Tudo bem.

— Pode fechar minha porta?

Ela não tinha certeza de que conseguiria se mover mesmo que quisesse.

Jeremy olhou preocupado mais uma vez enquanto puxava a porta. Faith escutou o clique da fechadura, depois os pés dele pisando de leve enquanto ele ia pelo corredor até a área de serviço. Foi só quando ouviu o terceiro degrau lá embaixo ranger que Faith se permitiu puxar a mão de baixo do travesseiro.

Ela abriu o punho fechado. A dor aguda do medo recuou e, naquele momento, Faith só sentia uma fúria cega.

A mensagem no iPhone de Jeremy. A escola dele. O ano de nascimento.

Mantenha a boca fechada e os olhos abertos.

O filho dela tinha deitado na cama com os pés a centímetros do que ela havia encontrado.

Com certeza alguém vai apontar o dedo para os culpados.

As palavras só fizeram sentido quando Faith segurou o dedo decepado da mãe.

6

S ara Linton não era estranha à autodepreciação. Sentira vergonha ao ser pega pelo pai roubando um chocolate da caixinha da honestidade da igreja. Tinha se sentido humilhada ao descobrir a traição do marido. Tinha se sentido culpada ao mentir para a irmã sobre gostar do cunhado. Tinha ficado constrangida quando a mãe dissera que ela era alta demais para usar calça cápri. Mas ela nunca havia se sentido vulgar, e saber que não era melhor do que uma participante de reality show a atingira no âmago.

Mesmo naquele momento, horas depois, o rosto de Sara continuava ardendo ao pensar no confronto com Angie Trent. Ela só se lembrava de uma vez na vida uma mulher ter falado com ela do mesmo jeito que Angie. A mãe de Jeffrey ficava cruel quando bebia, e Sara a pegara numa noite péssima. A única diferença naquele caso era que Angie tinha absolutamente todo o direito de rotular Sara de puta.

Jezabel, teria dito a mãe de Sara.

Não que Sara fosse contar algo disso à mãe.

Ela pôs a TV no mudo, porque o som a estava irritando. Tinha tentado ler. Tinha tentado fazer faxina no apartamento. Tinha cortado as unhas dos cachorros. Tinha lavado a louça e dobrado as roupas, que estavam tão amarrotadas de ficarem empilhadas no sofá que ela precisaria passá-las para que coubessem nas gavetas.

Duas vezes, ela tinha ido na direção do elevador para levar o carro de Will de volta para a casa dele. Duas vezes, tinha desistido. O problema era a chave dele. Ela não podia deixá-la no carro e de jeito nenhum ia bater na porta da frente e entregá-la a Angie. Deixá-la na caixa de correio não era uma opção. O bairro de Will não era perigoso, mas ele morava no meio de uma grande metrópole. O carro sumiria no tempo que Sara levasse para voltar a pé para casa.

Então, ela só ficou arrumando coisa para fazer, o tempo todo temendo a chegada de Will como se fosse um canal no dente. O que ela diria quando ele enfim chegasse para pegar o carro? As palavras não vinham, embora Sara tivesse ensaiado silenciosamente vários discursos sobre honra e moralidade. A voz em sua cabeça tinha assumido a cadência de um pregador da igreja batista. Era tudo tão sórdido. Não estava certo. Sara não ia ser uma amante barata. Não ia roubar o marido de ninguém, mesmo que ele estivesse dando sopa. Nem ia entrar numa briga de mulheres com Angie Trent. Acima de tudo, não ia se meter no meio da relação bizarramente disfuncional dos dois.

Que tipo de monstro se gabava do marido tentando se matar? Aquilo fazia o estômago de Sara se revirar. E ainda tinha o problema principal: a que fundo do poço Will tinha chegado para acreditar que cortar o braço com uma lâmina era a única solução? O quanto ele estava obcecado por Angie para fazer uma coisa tão terrível? E o quão doente era Angie para abraçá-lo enquanto ele fazia isso?

Essas questões eram mais adequadas para um psiquiatra. A infância de Will obviamente não tinha sido nenhum mar de rosas. Só isso já podia causar alguns danos. A dislexia dele era um problema, mas não parecia paralisar sua vida. Ele tinha suas excentricidades, mas eram adoráveis, não desconcertantes. Será que ele tinha lidado com suas tendências suicidas ou só era bom em escondê-las? Se tinha superado esse período da vida, por que continuava com aquela mulher horrorosa?

E, já que Sara tinha decidido que não ia acontecer nada entre eles, por que continuava gastando tempo pensando nessas coisas?

Ele nem fazia o tipo dela. Will não era nada parecido com Jeffrey. Não tinha nada da autoconfiança inacreditável do marido dela à mostra. Apesar de sua altura, Will não era um homem intimidador. Jeffrey tinha sido jogador de futebol americano. Sabia como liderar um time. Will era um bicho do mato, satisfeito de se misturar no plano de fundo e fazer seu trabalho sob a sombra de Amanda. Não queria glória nem reconhecimento. Não que Jeffrey tivesse sido um louco por atenção, mas era incrivelmente seguro sobre quem era e o que queria. As mulheres suspiravam em sua presença. Ele sabia como fazer praticamente tudo do jeito certo, que era um dos muitos motivos para Sara ter mandado a própria razão às favas e se casado com ele. Duas vezes.

Talvez ela não estivesse mesmo interessada em Will Trent. Talvez Angie Trent estivesse parcialmente certa. Sara tinha gostado de ser casada com um policial, mas não pelos motivos pervertidos sugeridos por Angie. A característica típica das forças de segurança de ser tudo preto no branco atraíam Sara num nível mais profundo. Tinha sido criada pelos pais para ajudar pessoas, e um policial ajudava mais que qualquer um. Também havia uma parte do cérebro dela que gostava dos aspectos de quebra-cabeça de uma investigação criminal. Ela amava falar com Jeffrey sobre os casos dele. Sentia-se útil trabalhando no necrotério como legista do condado, encontrando pistas, dando a ele informações que ela sabia que ajudariam em seu trabalho.

Sara gemeu. Como se ser médica não fosse útil. Talvez Angie Trent tivesse razão sobre a perversão. Daqui a pouco, Sara ia começar a imaginar Will de uniforme.

Ela tirou os dois galgos do colo para poder ficar de pé. Billy bocejou. Bob rolou de barriga para cima para ficar mais confortável. Ela olhou o apartamento em volta e foi tomada por uma inquietação. Sentia-se oprimida pelo desejo de mudar alguma coisa — qualquer coisa — para se sentir mais no controle da própria vida.

Começou pelos sofás, colocando-os num ângulo em relação à televisão, enquanto os cachorros olhavam para o chão que passava por baixo deles. A mesa de centro era grande demais para o novo arranjo, então, ela mudou tudo outra vez, só para descobrir que também não funcionava. Quando terminou de enrolar o tapete e botar tudo de volta no lugar original, só com a força do muque, estava suando.

Havia poeira no porta-retratos que ficava acima do aparador. Sara pegou o lustra-móveis e voltou a tirar a poeira. Havia muita superfície para limpar. O prédio em que ela morava era antes uma fábrica de processamento de leite. Paredes de tijolo vermelho sustentavam um teto de seis metros de altura. Todos os dispositivos mecânicos ficavam expostos. As portas internas eram de madeira desgastada com ferragens de porta de celeiro. Era o tipo de loft industrial que se esperaria encontrar em Nova York, apesar de Sara ter pagado consideravelmente menos do que os dez milhões de dólares que um lugar assim custaria em Manhattan.

Ninguém achava que o espaço era adequado para ela, que era o que tinha atraído Sara para começo de conversa. Quando se mudara para Atlanta, ela desejava algo completamente diferente do bangalô aconchegante que tinha em sua cidade natal. Ultimamente, andava pensando que havia exagerado. O conceito aberto parecia quase inóspito. A cozinha, com tudo de aço inoxidável e bancadas de granito preto, tinha sido muito cara e era totalmente inútil para alguém como Sara, conhecida por queimar sopa. Todos os móveis eram modernos demais. A mesa da sala de jantar, esculpida em uma peça única de madeira e com espaço para doze pessoas, era um luxo ridículo, considerando que ela só usava para organizar correspondência e apoiar a caixa de pizza enquanto pagava o motoboy.

Sara guardou o lustra-móveis. O problema não era a poeira. Ela devia se mudar. Devia encontrar uma casa pequena em um dos bairros mais tranquilos de Atlanta e se livrar dos sofás de couro baixo e das mesas de centro de vidro. Devia ter sofás fofinhos e poltronas amplas em que desse para se aconchegar e ler. Devia ter uma cozinha com uma pia de fazenda e uma vista alegre do quintal pelas janelas bem largas.

Devia morar num lugar parecido com a casa de Will.

A televisão chamou a atenção dela. O logo do noticiário da noite subiu na tela. Um repórter sério estava na frente da Prisão de Diagnóstico e Classificação da Geórgia. A maioria das pessoas inteiradas no assunto se referia a ela como D&C, completamente ciente de que era o corredor da morte da Geórgia. Sara tinha visto mais cedo a reportagem sobre os dois homens assassinados e pensado a mesma coisa que pensou naquele momento: eis mais um motivo para não se envolver com Will Trent.

Ele estava trabalhando no caso de Evelyn Mitchell. Provavelmente não tinha passado nem perto daquela prisão naquele dia, mas, no minuto em que Sara viu a matéria sobre um policial assassinado, seu coração quase saiu pela boca. Mesmo depois de darem tanto o nome do homem quanto o do detento morto, o coração dela se recusava a se acalmar. Graças a Jeffrey, Sara sabia como era quando o telefone tocava inesperadamente no meio da noite. Ela lembrava como cada matéria, cada pedacinho de fofoca, fazia algo dentro dela se apertar de medo de ele sair para mais um caso, arriscar a própria vida. Era uma forma de transtorno de estresse pós-traumático. Só quando o marido se foi que Sara percebeu que tinha vivido todos aqueles anos com medo.

O interfone tocou. Billy deu um rosnado meio sem vontade, mas nenhum dos dois cachorros saiu do sofá. Sara apertou o botão de viva-voz.

— Sim?

Will disse:

— Oi, desculpe, eu...

Ela abriu o portão para ele subir. Pegou a chave dele na bancada da cozinha e já abriu a porta da frente. Não ia convidá-lo para entrar. Não ia deixá-lo pedir desculpas pelo que Angie tinha dito, porque Angie Trent tinha todo o direito de falar o que achava e, além do mais, tinha usado alguns ótimos argumentos. Sara ia só dizer a Will que foi ótimo conhecê-lo e desejar boa sorte para resolver as coisas com a esposa.

Se um dia ele chegasse. O elevador estava demorando. Ela viu no painel digital a cabine descendo do quarto andar até o lobby. Levou mais uma eternidade para os números começarem a subir. Ela os cochichou em voz alta, "três, quatro, cinco", e aí finalmente soou o *plim* do sexto.

As portas se abriram. Will espiou de trás de uma pirâmide de duas caixas de papelão cheias de pastas, uma embalagem de isopor e uma sacola do Krispy Kreme. Os galgos, que só pareciam notar Sara quando era hora do jantar, saíram correndo para recebê-lo no corredor.

Sara murmurou um xingamento.

— Desculpe pelo horário.

Ele virou o corpo para Bob não o derrubar.

Sara agarrou os dois cachorros pelo pescoço, mantendo a porta aberta com o pé para Will poder entrar. Ele deslizou as caixas para a mesa de jantar dela e imediatamente começou a fazer carinho nos

154

galgos. Eles o lamberam como se fosse um velho amigo, balançando o rabo e raspando o piso de madeira com as unhas. A determinação de Sara, que apenas alguns segundos antes estava tão forte, começou a ruir.

Will levantou a cabeça e olhou para ela.

— Você estava dormindo?

Ela tinha colocado uma roupa apropriada para seu humor, uma calça de moletom antiga e uma camisa de futebol americano do Grant County Rebels. O cabelo estava preso com tanta firmeza que sentia os fios repuxando a pele da nuca.

— Aqui, sua chave.

— Obrigado. — Will espanou o pelo de cachorro do peito. Continuava usando a mesma camisa preta da tarde. — Opa! — Ele segurou Bob, que estava tentando pegar os donuts do Krispy Kreme.

— Isso é sangue?

Havia uma mancha escura e seca na manga direita da camisa dele. Instintivamente, Sara pôs a mão no braço dele.

Will deu um passo para trás.

— Não é nada. — Ele puxou o punho da camisa para baixo. — Teve um incidente hoje na prisão.

Sara teve aquela sensação familiar de aperto no peito.

— Você estava lá.

— Não pude fazer nada para ajudar o cara. Será que você... — Ele não completou. — O médico da equipe disse que foi um ferimento mortal. Tinha muito sangue. — Ele fechou a mão ao redor do pulso. — Eu devia ter trocado de camisa quando cheguei em casa, mas tenho muito trabalho e minha casa no momento está meio de ponta-cabeça.

Ele tinha passado em casa. Sem motivo, Sara se permitiu pensar por um momento que ele não tinha visto a esposa.

— A gente deveria conversar sobre o que aconteceu.

— Ah... — Ele pareceu não entender de propósito. — Não tem muito a dizer. Ele está morto. Não era um cara exatamente bacana, mas com certeza vai ser difícil para a família.

Sara ficou olhando para ele. Não havia malícia em seu rosto. Talvez Angie não tivesse contado sobre o confronto. Ou talvez tivesse, e Will estivesse se esforçando para ignorar. De todo modo, ele estava

155

escondendo algo. Mas, de repente, depois de passar as últimas horas entrando em frenesi, Sara não estava nem aí. Não queria falar do assunto. Não queria analisar. Sua única certeza era que não queria que ele fosse embora.

Ela perguntou:

— O que tem nas caixas?

Ele pareceu notar a mudança na atitude dela, mas escolheu ignorar.

— Documentos de uma antiga investigação. Talvez tenha alguma coisa a ver com o desaparecimento de Evelyn.

— Não um sequestro?

O sorriso dele indicou que tinha sido pego no pulo.

— Só preciso saber tudo o que está nestas pastas até as cinco da manhã.

— Precisa de ajuda?

— Não. — Ele se virou para levantar as caixas. — Obrigado por levar Betty para casa por mim.

— Ser disléxico não é uma falha de caráter.

Will deixou as caixas na mesa e se virou. Ele não respondeu de imediato. Só a olhou de um jeito que fez Sara desejar ter tomado banho. Enfim, ele disse:

— Acho que eu gostava mais quando você estava brava comigo.

Sara não respondeu.

— É Angie, né? É por isso que você está chateada?

Os níveis variáveis de subterfúgio eram novidade para ela.

— Pareceu que estávamos ignorando isso.

— Quer continuar nesse caminho?

Sara deu de ombros. Ela não sabia o que queria. O certo seria dizer a ele que o flerte inocente dos dois tinha acabado. Ela deveria abrir a porta e obrigá-lo a ir embora. Deveria ligar para o Dr. Dale bem cedo na manhã seguinte e convidá-lo para sair de novo. Deveria esquecer o Will e deixar o tempo apagá-lo da memória.

Mas o problema não era a memória dela. Era o aperto no peito quando pensava nele correndo perigo. Era aquela sensação de alívio quando ele entrava pela porta. Era a felicidade que sentia só de estar perto dele.

Ele falou:

156

— Angie e eu não estamos juntos, *juntos mesmo*, há mais de um ano. — Will fez uma pausa, como se para deixar que ela absorvesse a informação. — Desde que eu conheci você.

Sara só conseguiu falar:

— Ah.

— E, então, quando a mãe dela morreu, há alguns meses, a gente se viu por umas duas horas e ela foi embora. Não apareceu nem no velório.

Ele fez uma pausa de novo, aquilo obviamente era difícil.

— É complicado explicar nosso relacionamento. Pelo menos sem me fazer parecer um pobre coitado e otário.

— Você não me deve explicação.

Ele pôs as mãos nos bolsos e apoiou o corpo na mesa. A luz do teto iluminou a cicatriz irregular na boca dele. A pele era rosada, uma linha fina que ia do meio do lábio superior ao nariz. Sara não conseguia nem calcular o tempo que tinha gastado se perguntando como seria a sensação daquela cicatriz tocando sua boca.

Tempo demais.

Will pigarreou. Olhou para o chão, depois levantou a cabeça de novo para ela.

— Você sabe onde eu cresci. Como eu cresci.

Ela fez que sim com a cabeça. O Lar de Crianças de Atlanta tinha fechado havia muitos anos, mas o prédio abandonado ficava a menos de oito quilômetros de onde eles estavam.

— As crianças iam embora o tempo todo. Estavam tentando colocar mais de nós em lares temporários. Acho que assim é mais barato. — Ele deu de ombros, como se fosse de se esperar. — Para as crianças mais velhas, não costumava dar certo. Duravam talvez algumas semanas, às vezes, dias. Voltavam diferentes. Acho que você consegue imaginar o motivo.

Sara balançou a cabeça. Não queria imaginar.

— Não tinha exatamente uma fila longa de gente querendo acolher um menino de oito anos que não conseguia ser aprovado na terceira série. Mas Angie era menina, e bonita, e inteligente, então era enviada para muitas casas. — Mais uma vez, ele deu de ombros. — Acho que me acostumei a esperar que ela voltasse, e acho que me acostumei a não perguntar o que acontecia enquanto ela não estava. — Ele desencostou da mesa e pegou as caixas. — Então, é isso. Um pobre coitado e otário.

— Não. Will...

Ele parou na frente da porta, com as caixas à frente como uma armadura.

— Amanda queria que eu perguntasse se você conhece alguém no IML de Fulton.

O cérebro de Sara levou um tempo para trocar de marcha.

— Provavelmente. Fiz uma parte do meu treinamento lá quando comecei.

Ele mudou o peso das caixas para o outro braço.

— É um pedido de Amanda, não meu. Ela quer que você faça algumas ligações. Não é sua obrigação, mas...

— O que ela quer saber?

— Qualquer coisa que aparecer nas autópsias. Eles não vão compartilhar com a gente. Querem ficar com o caso.

Ele estava virado para a porta, esperando. Ela olhou para o pescoço dele, para os pelos finos na nuca.

— Tudo bem.

— Você tem o telefone de Amanda. É só ligar para ela se aparecer algo. Ou se não aparecer. Ela é impaciente.

Ele ficou esperando que ela abrisse a porta.

Sara passou a maior parte do dia querendo que ele saísse da vida dela, mas, no momento em que ele estava indo, não conseguia suportar.

— Amanda estava errada.

Ele se virou para ela.

— O que ela disse hoje. Amanda estava errada.

Ele fingiu ficar chocado.

— Acho que nunca ouvi ninguém falar isso em voz alta antes.

— *Almeja*. A última palavra do homem que estava morrendo. — Ela explicou: — A tradução literal, "mariscos", está certa, mas não é gíria para "dinheiro". Pelo menos, não do jeito que eu ouvi ser usada.

— É gíria para o quê?

158

Ela odiava a palavra, mas disse mesmo assim:

— "Vagabunda."

Ele franziu a testa.

— Como você sabe disso?

— Eu trabalho num hospital público grande. Desde que comecei, não passa uma semana sem alguém me chamar de alguma variação dessa palavra.

Will colocou as caixas de volta na mesa.

— Quem chamou você disso?

Ela balançou a cabeça. Ele parecia pronto para enfrentar todo o rol de pacientes dela.

— A questão é que o cara estava chamando Faith dessa palavra. Não estava falando de dinheiro.

Will cruzou os braços. Obviamente estava irritado.

— Ricardo — anunciou ele. — O cara no quintal que atirou naquelas menininhas, o nome dele era Ricardo. — Sara manteve o contato visual. Will continuou falando. — Hironobu Kwon era o cara morto na área de serviço. Não sabemos nada do asiático mais velho, só que gostava de camisas havaianas e falava com um sotaque arrastado do sul. E teve mais alguém que se feriu, provavelmente numa briga de faca com Evelyn. Você deve ver o alerta no hospital quando voltar ao trabalho. Tipo sanguíneo B negativo, possivelmente hispânico, ferimento de faca no abdome, possivelmente ferimento na mão.

— Que belo elenco de personagens.

— Pode acreditar, não é fácil de entender, e nem tenho certeza de que qualquer um deles é o motivo real de tudo isso estar acontecendo.

— Como assim?

— Parece pessoal, como se tivesse mais alguma coisa em jogo. Ninguém fica esperando quatro anos para roubar alguém. Tem que ser por algo mais do que dinheiro.

— Dizem que é a raiz de todo mal. — O marido de Sara sempre adorava motivações financeiras. Na experiência dela, ele tendia a estar certo. — Esse cara ferido no abdome... é membro de uma facção?

Will fez que sim.

— Em geral eles têm seus próprios médicos. E não são ruins, vi o trabalho de alguns no pronto-socorro. Mas um ferimento na barriga é algo que exige um tratamento bem sofisticado. Talvez precise de sangue, e B negativo é difícil de achar. Também precisariam de um ambiente estéril para operar, remédios que não dá para simplesmente comprar na farmácia local. Só existiriam numa farmácia hospitalar.

— Pode me dar uma lista? Posso adicionar ao alerta.

— Claro.

Ela foi à cozinha achar um bloco e uma caneta. Ele ficou ao lado da mesa de jantar.

— Quanto tempo alguém consegue viver com um ferimento a faca na barriga? Havia muito sangue no local.

— Depende. Horas, talvez dias. A triagem pode ganhar algum tempo, mas qualquer coisa perto de uma semana seria um milagre.

— Você se importa de eu jantar enquanto você faz isso? — Ele abriu a caixa de isopor. Ela viu dois cachorros-quentes de sessenta centímetros cada, lotados de chili. Ele cheirou, depois franziu a testa. — Pelo jeito, o cara do posto de gasolina ia jogar fora por um bom motivo.

Mesmo assim, ele pegou um dos cachorros-quentes.

— Não ouse.

— Provavelmente está ok.

— Sente aí.

Ela pegou uma frigideira no armário e achou uma caixa de ovos dentro da geladeira. Will se sentou no bar em frente ao *cooktop* de aço inoxidável. A caixa de isopor estava na bancada ao lado dele. Bob deu uma cutucadinha com o nariz, depois se afastou.

Ela perguntou:

— Isso era mesmo seu jantar, dois cachorros-quentes e um donut do Krispy Kreme?

— Quatro donuts.

— Como está seu colesterol?

— Deve estar branco, que nem eles mostram nos comerciais de remédio.

— Muito engraçado. — Ela embrulhou a caixa de isopor com papel-alumínio e jogou no lixo. — Por que você acha que a mãe de Faith não foi sequestrada?

— Na verdade, não foi isso que eu disse. Só acho que muita coisa não está se encaixando. — Ele viu Sara quebrar os ovos dentro de uma tigela. — Não acho que ela tenha ido embora por vontade própria. Não faria isso com a família. Mas acho que talvez ela conheça os sequestradores. Tipo, que eles tinham uma relação profissional anterior.

— Como?

Ele ficou de pé e caminhou até a mesa de jantar, onde pegou um punhado de pastas amarelas de uma das caixas. Agarrou a sacola de donuts antes de voltar a se sentar no bar da cozinha.

— Boyd Spivey — disse ele, abrindo a primeira pasta e mostrando a ela a foto de identificação criminal do homem.

Sara reconheceu o rosto e o nome do noticiário.

— É o homem que foi morto hoje na prisão.

Will fez que sim e abriu a próxima pasta.

— Ben Humphrey.

— Outro policial?

— Aham. — Ele abriu mais uma pasta. Havia uma estrela amarela colada dentro. — Este é Adam Hopkins. Era parceiro de Humphrey. — Outra pasta, essa com uma estrela roxa. — Este é Chuck Finn, parceiro de Spivey, e este cara... — Ele se atrapalhou para abrir a última pasta. Estrela verde. — É Demarcus Alexander.

Ele tinha esquecido um. Will voltou à mesa e achou mais uma pasta amarela. Esse tinha uma estrela preta, que pareceu profética quando ele anunciou:

— Lloyd Crittenden. Morreu de overdose de drogas faz três anos.

— Todos policiais?

Will confirmou com a cabeça enquanto enfiava meio donut na boca.

Sara colocou os ovos na frigideira.

— Qual é a relação que não estou vendo?

— A chefe deles era Evelyn Mitchell.

Sara quase derrubou os ovos.

— A mãe de Faith? — Ela voltou às fotos, analisando o rosto dos homens. Todos tinham a mesma inclinação arrogante do queixo, como se o problema deles fosse só uma bobagenzinha. Ela passou os olhos pelo relatório de prisão de Spivey, tentando decifrar o texto com erros

161

de digitação. — Roubo durante a averiguação de um crime. — Ela abriu a página e leu os detalhes. — Spivey deu uma ordem permanente para a equipe remover dez por cento de cada apreensão de drogas envolvendo dinheiro vivo no valor de mais de dois mil dólares.

— Ia se acumulando.

— Até quanto?

— Pelo que a contabilidade conseguiu estimar, ao longo de doze anos, roubaram cerca de seis milhões de dólares.

Ela deu um assovio baixo.

— É um pouco menos de um milhão para cada um, sem impostos. Ou pelo menos era. Com certeza o Tio Sam foi atrás deles no primeiro dia de prisão.

Até dinheiro roubado era renda tributável. A maioria dos detentos recebia o aviso da Receita Federal na primeira semana da sentença.

Sara leu a primeira página do relatório de prisão, parando num nome familiar.

— Você era o investigador principal.

— Não é minha parte favorita do trabalho.

Ele enfiou o resto do donut na boca.

Sara baixou os olhos para a pasta, fingindo continuar lendo. Os erros de digitação não tinham sido um sinal de alerta. Todo relatório policial que ela já lera era lotado de erros de gramática e ortografia. Como a maioria dos disléxicos, Will considerava sacrossanta a verificação ortográfica. Ele havia substituído palavras que não estavam fazendo sentido no contexto, depois assinado no fim da página. Sara analisou a assinatura dele. Era pouco mais que um rabisco inclinado em relação à linha preta.

Will a observava de perto. Ela percebeu que precisava fazer uma pergunta.

— O que desencadeou a investigação?

— A GBI recebeu uma denúncia anônima.

— Por que Evelyn não foi acusada?

— A promotoria se recusou a levar o processo adiante. Ela teve permissão para se aposentar com o salário integral. Chamaram de aposentadoria precoce, mas ela já tinha passado dos trinta anos obrigatórios. Não estava trabalhando por dinheiro. Pelo menos, não pelo dinheiro que recebia da prefeitura.

Sara usou uma espátula para mexer os ovos. Will comeu mais um donut em duas mordidas. O açúcar em pó caiu na bancada de granito preto.

Ela disse:

— Posso fazer uma pergunta?

— Claro.

— Como Faith trabalha com você depois de você ter investigado a mãe dela?

— Ela acha que eu estou equivocado. — Bob tinha voltado. Ele pôs o focinho na bancada e Will começou a fazer carinho na cabeça dele. — Eu sei que ela consultou a mãe primeiro, mas nunca conversamos além disso.

Sara não teria acreditado em mais ninguém que lhe dissesse a mesma coisa, mas conseguia imaginar facilmente como aquilo funcionava. Faith não era de ficar falando sobre seus sentimentos e Will era tão digno que era difícil lhe atribuir segundas intenções vingativas.

— Como Evelyn é?

— Das antigas.

— Que nem Amanda?

— Não exatamente. — Ele pegou mais um donut da sacola. — Quer dizer, é durona, mas não tão intensa.

Sara entendeu o que ele queria dizer. Aquela geração não tivera muitas formas de se provar aos colegas homens. Amanda tinha tomado o caminho da agressividade com um gosto evidente.

— Elas subiram juntas na carreira — contou Will. — Fizeram juntas a Academia, depois trabalharam em forças-tarefas conjuntas na polícia e na GBI. Ainda são boas amigas. Acho que Amanda namorou o irmão, ou o cunhado, de Evelyn.

Sara não conseguia pensar num conflito de interesse mais óbvio.

— E Amanda era sua superior quando você estava investigando Evelyn?

— Era.

Ele botou mais um donut para dentro.

— Você sabia disso na época?

Ele fez que não, mantendo o donut na parte interna da bochecha, como um esquilo com uma noz, para poder perguntar:

— Você sabe que o fogão não está ligado, né?

— Merda.

Isso explicava por que os ovos continuavam líquidos. Ela pressionou o botão até subir a chama.

Ele limpou a boca com o dorso da mão.

— Eu também gosto de deixar os ovos descansando por um tempo. Dá um toque meio amadeirado.

— Isso é *E. coli.* — Ela conferiu a torradeira, perguntando-se por que o pão não tinha subido. Devia ser porque não tinha nada dentro. Will sorriu quando ela pegou um pacote de dentro do armário. — Não sou muito boa cozinheira.

— Quer que eu assuma o posto?

— Quero que você me conte sobre Evelyn.

Ele se recostou na cadeira.

— Eu gostei dela quando a gente se conheceu. Sei que, nessas circunstâncias, parece estranho. Acho que seria de se esperar que eu a odiasse, mas não dá para ver as coisas dessa forma. Trabalhamos para o governo. Às vezes, as investigações começam pelos motivos errados e você se vê na posição contrária a alguém que foi preso por falar algo errado ou irritar o político errado. — Enquanto falava, ele juntava o pó de açúcar num montinho. — Evelyn era muito educada. Respeitosa. Até aquele momento, a ficha dela era impecável. Ela me tratou como se eu estivesse fazendo meu trabalho, não como se eu fosse um pedófilo, que é o que em geral acontece.

— Talvez ela soubesse que nunca ia ser processada.

— Acho que estava preocupada, mas principalmente com a filha. Ela se esforçou muito para manter Faith longe da coisa toda. Eu só a conheci depois que Amanda nos colocou juntos.

— Pelo menos, ela é uma boa mãe.

— É uma mulher de classe. Mas também é inteligente, forte, durona. Eu não apostaria contra ela nesta situação.

Sara tinha esquecido os ovos. Usou a espátula para raspá-los do fundo da frigideira.

Will disse:

— Evelyn foi presa com fita adesiva numa cadeira enquanto revistavam a casa dela. Achei uma ponta de flecha desenhada embaixo do assento. Ela desenhou com o próprio sangue.

— Para onde estava apontando?

— Para dentro da sala. Para o sofá. Para o quintal. — Ele deu de ombros. — Vai saber. Não achamos nada.

Sara pensou naquilo.

— Só a ponta de uma flecha? Só isso?

Ele espalhou de novo o açúcar e desenhou o formato.

Sara analisou o símbolo, avaliando silenciosamente como proceder. Enfim, decidiu que sua única opção era dizer a verdade.

— Para mim, parece um V. A letra V.

Ele ficou quieto de um jeito que mudou o clima do cômodo. Ela achou que ele fosse mudar de assunto ou fazer uma piada, mas ele disse:

— Não era perfeito. Estava meio manchado em cima.

— Assim? — Ela desenhou outra linha. — Tipo a letra A?

Ele ficou olhando a figura.

— Acho que Amanda não estava fingindo quando falou que não sabia do que eu estava falando.

— Ela também viu?

Ele varreu o açúcar para a palma da mão e jogou na sacola com o último donut.

— Aham.

Sara colocou o prato de ovos na frente dele. A torradeira subiu. O pão estava quase preto.

— Ah, não — murmurou ela. — Me desculpe. Não precisa comer. Quer que eu pegue os cachorros-quentes do lixo?

Ele pegou a torrada queimada da mão dela e pôs no prato. O barulho foi de um tijolo sendo arrastado no concreto.

— Um pouco de manteiga seria bom.

Ela tinha margarina. Ele enfiou a faca no pote e a encheu de margarina, depois passou no pão até ele ficar mole o suficiente para se dobrar. Os ovos estavam mais para castanhos do que amarelos, mas mesmo assim ele começou a comê-los.

Sara lhe disse:

— O nome "Amanda" começa com A. *Almeja* começa com A. E agora talvez Evelyn tenha desenhado um A embaixo da cadeira.

Ele soltou o garfo. O prato estava limpo.

Ela continuou:

— *Almeja* tem o som parecido com "Amanda". Mesmo número de sílabas. Mesmas primeira e última letras.

Ele não teria percebido a aliteração. A maioria dos disléxicos não conseguiam rimar duas palavras nem com uma arma apontada para a cabeça.

Ele afastou o prato.

— Amanda não está me contando tudo. Não quer nem admitir que o caso de corrupção tem alguma coisa a ver com a situação de Evelyn.

— Mas ela mandou você revisar todos os documentos da sua investigação.

— Ou ela precisa de informação, ou está me mantendo ocupado. Ela sabe que vou levar a noite toda.

— Não se eu ajudar você.

Ele pegou o prato e foi até a pia.

— Quer que eu lave isso antes de ir?

— Quero que você me fale da cena do crime.

Ele passou uma água no prato, depois começou a lavar as mãos.

— Essa é a torneira fria — disse Sara e, então, como era inútil falar que, por ser canhota, ela tinha trocado a torneira de água quente para o lado direito, ela se debruçou e ajustou a temperatura para ele.

Will abriu a mão para ela poder jogar um pouco de detergente na palma dele.

— Por que você está com cheiro de lustra-móvel de limão?

— Por que você me deixou acreditar que Betty era da sua mulher? Ele fez espuma com o detergente.

— Alguns mistérios nunca vão ser resolvidos.

Ela sorriu.

— Me fale da cena do crime.

Will contou a ela o que tinham achado: as cadeiras viradas e os brinquedos de bebê quebrados. Passou para a história da Sra. Levy e do namoradinho de Evelyn, a teoria de Mittal sobre o rastro de sangue e a teoria divergente do próprio Will. Quando chegou à parte em que tinham achado o homem no porta-malas, Sara tinha conseguido fazê-lo sentar à mesa da sala.

Ela perguntou:

— Você acha que Boyd Spivey foi assassinado por ter conversado com Amanda?

— É possível, mas improvável. — Ele explicou: — Pense na linha do tempo. Amanda ligou para o diretor duas horas antes de chegarmos na prisão. O médico de lá disse que usaram uma faca serrilhada. Não é algo que se faz com escova de dente. A câmera foi desativada no dia anterior, o que indica que foi planejado com pelo menos vinte e quatro horas de antecedência.

— Então, foi coordenado. Evelyn foi levada. Boyd foi morto algumas horas depois. Os outros homens da equipe dela estão seguros?

— É uma ótima pergunta. — Ele puxou o celular do bolso. — Você se importa se eu fizer umas ligações?

— Não, fique à vontade.

Ela se levantou da mesa para dar um pouco de privacidade a ele. A frigideira ainda estava quente, então, ela passou água gelada. Os ovos estavam grudados no metal. Ela cutucou a meleca com a unha do polegar antes de desistir e enfiar a frigideira na prateleira superior da lava-louças.

Sara abriu de novo a pasta de Boyd Spivey. Will tinha usado uma estrela cor-de-rosa para identificá-lo, talvez como piada. O homem tinha cara de policial corrupto. O rosto em formato de lua indicava uso de anabolizantes. Mal dava para discernir as pupilas em seus olhos apertados. A altura e o peso dele eram de um jogador de futebol americano da linha de defesa.

Ela passou os olhos pelos detalhes da prisão de Spivey enquanto meio que escutava Will falando com alguém na Prisão Estadual de Valdosta. Eles discutiam se deveriam ou não colocar Ben Humphrey e Adam Hopkins na solitária e concordaram que seria melhor só aumentar o monitoramento dos dois.

A ligação seguinte de Will foi mais complicada. Sara supôs que ele estivesse conversando com alguém na sede da GBI sobre localizar os dois homens remanescentes usando os oficiais de condicional deles.

Ela abriu a pasta de Spivey e achou a ficha de RH dele atrás do relatório de prisão. Sara leu os detalhes da vida profissional do homem. Spivey tinha entrado para a Academia logo depois de sair do ensino médio. Tinha feito aulas noturnas na Georgia State para conseguir um bacharelado em ciência criminal. Tinha três filhos e uma esposa que trabalhava como secretária no consulado holandês nos arredores da cidade.

A promoção de Spivey para a equipe de Evelyn fora uma conquista. O esquadrão de narcóticos estava entre os de mais alto nível do país. Tinham todas as melhores armas e instalações, e vários criminosos importantes na área de Atlanta para fazer com que recebessem muitas menções honrosas e bastante tempo de exposição na imprensa, o que Spivey, em particular, parecia adorar. Will tinha coletado recortes de jornal sobre as apreensões mais notáveis da equipe. Spivey estava no centro de todas as matérias, embora a líder fosse Evelyn. Uma foto mostrava Spivey de barba feita e com fitas suficientes no peito para decorar a bicicleta de uma menininha.

E, mesmo assim, não tinha sido o suficiente.

— Ei.

Sara levantou os olhos da leitura. Will tinha terminado as ligações.

— Me desculpe por isso. Queria garantir a segurança deles.

— Não tem problema. — Sara nem ia fingir que não tinha escutado. — Você não ligou para Amanda.

— Não, não liguei.

— Me passe mais umas pastas para eu ler.

— Não precisa mesmo fazer isso.

— Eu quero.

Sara já não estava sendo gentil nem tentando passar mais tempo na companhia dele. Ela queria saber o que havia feito um homem como Boyd Spivey virar um canalha daqueles.

Will a olhou por tempo suficiente para fazê-la pensar que ele ia dizer não. Então, ele abriu uma das caixas. Havia um walkman antigo enfiado no meio de uma pilha de fitas cassete. Nenhuma tinha rótulo, a não ser que os adesivos de estrelas coloridas contassem. Will explicou:

— São gravações de todas as entrevistas que fiz com cada suspeito. Nenhum deles disse nada de mais no começo, mas todos acabaram fazendo acordos para reduzir o tempo de prisão.

— Eles se delataram?

— De jeito nenhum. Tinham informações sobre alguns vereadores locais. Ganharam algum poder de barganha com o promotor.

Sara não conseguia fingir surpresa com os problemas de drogas dos políticos.

— Quanto eles conseguiram na barganha?

— O suficiente para falarem, não o suficiente para entregarem os peixes grandes. — Ele abriu a caixa seguinte e começou a puxar pastas. Como todo o resto, estavam organizadas por cor. Ele entregou primeiro as verdes. — Depoimentos de testemunhas para a promotoria. — Empilhou as vermelhas, que estavam em menor quantidade. — Testemunhas da defesa. — Tirou as azuis. — Operações de valores altos em espécie: qualquer coisa acima de dois mil dólares era apreendida.

Sara começou a trabalhar, lendo com cuidado a ficha seguinte de RH. Ben Humphrey tinha sido o mesmo tipo de policial que Boyd Spivey: robusto, bom no que fazia, faminto por imprensa e, no fim, completamente corrupto. O mesmo valia para Adam Hopkins e Demarcus Alexander, ambos elogiados pela coragem em um tiroteio durante um roubo a banco, ambos tendo pagado em dinheiro pela casa de veraneio na Flórida. Lloyd Crittenden havia ganhado seu distintivo depois de capotar seis vezes com a viatura durante uma perseguição a um homem que havia atirado em um bar sórdido com uma escopeta de cano curto. Também tinha a boca suja. Ele tinha duas advertências por insubordinação, mas as avaliações anuais de Evelyn eram todas elogiosas.

O único ponto fora da curva era Chuck Finn, que parecia mais inteligente que os colegas. Finn estava no processo de conclusão do doutorado em arte italiana renascentista quando foi pego. Seu estilo de vida não era luxuoso como o dos outros. Ele usou os ganhos ilegais para investir na própria educação e viajar pelo mundo. Deve ter complementado a equipe de maneiras mais sutis. Evelyn Mitchell obviamente tinha escolhido a dedo cada um dos homens. Alguns eram líderes. Outros, como Chuck Finn, eram claramente seguidores. Todos se encaixavam no mesmo perfil geral: ambiciosos com reputação no departamento de fazer o que tinha que ser feito. Três eram brancos. Dois eram negros. Um era descendente de indígenas cherokees. Todos tinham aberto mão de tudo puramente por dinheiro.

Will virou a fita no walkman. Ele estava sentado de olhos fechados, com fones no ouvido. Sara escutava as rodas do tocador de fita girando com um pequeno rangido.

A pilha seguinte de pastas detalhava todas as apreensões de valores em espécie feitas pela equipe, e presumidamente desviadas, ao longo dos anos. Sara achava que seriam as pastas mais difíceis, mas acabaram não tendo nada de mais. Pela natureza do tráfico de drogas, a maioria dos homens detidos já estavam mortos ou encarcerados quando a equipe de Evelyn foi pega. Só alguns continuavam na rua, mas obviamente na ativa. Sara reconheceu alguns dos nomes do noticiário noturno. Dois pareciam promissores, cada um por seu próprio motivo. Ela separou as pastas para Will.

Sara olhou a hora. Passava bastante da meia-noite e ela tinha plantão cedo na manhã seguinte. Bem nessa hora, sua mandíbula abriu em um bocejo tão grande que o maxilar dela estalou. Ela olhou de soslaio para garantir que Will não tivesse visto. Ainda havia uma grande pilha de pastas à sua frente. Ela só tinha visto metade, mas não conseguiria parar nem se quisesse. Era como tentar encaixar todas as pistas de um livro de suspense. Os mocinhos eram tão corruptos quanto os vilões. Os vilões pareciam entender que os meios ilícitos eram só uma forma de fazer negócios. Ambos provavelmente tinham uma longa lista de justificativas para suas ações.

Ela começou a pilha seguinte. Os seis homens da equipe de Evelyn nunca tinham ido a julgamento, mas deviam ter chegado perto disso quando os acordos foram feitos. A lista de testemunhas potenciais da promotoria tinha sido altamente filtrada, mas não mais do que a lista de testemunhas a favor dos réus. Os nomes seriam familiares a Will, mas, mesmo assim, Sara leu atentamente cada pasta. Depois de uma boa hora comparando depoimentos, ela se permitiu passar para a última pasta, que tinha guardado como recompensa por não desistir.

A foto de identificação criminal de Evelyn mostrava uma mulher magra com uma expressão indecifrável. Devia ter se sentido humilhada por ser fichada e processada depois de passar tanto tempo do outro lado. Nada em sua expressão entregava isso. A boca estava fechada numa linha fina. Os olhos encaravam o nada à frente. O cabelo era loiro, como o de Faith, com fios grisalhos nas têmporas. Olhos azuis, sessenta e poucos quilos, um e setenta e cinco — um pouco mais alta do que a filha.

Sua carreira tinha sido daquelas que ganhavam prêmios do Clube de Mulheres local por pioneirismo, que a capitã Mitchell recebeu duas vezes. Sua promoção a investigadora foi precedida por uma negociação de sequestro que resultou na libertação de duas crianças e na morte de um pedófilo abusador em série. Sua patente de tenente veio quase dez anos depois de ela passar na prova com a nota mais alta já registrada. A de capitã foi resultado de um processo por discriminação de gênero aberto na Comissão de Oportunidades Igualitárias de Emprego.

Evelyn tinha subido do jeito mais difícil, trabalhando por um tempo nas ruas. Tinha dois diplomas, um da Georgia Tech, ambos com menção honrosa. Era mãe, avó, viúva. Seus filhos eram o que Sara chamava de servidores — uma da comunidade, o outro do país. O marido tivera um emprego estável e digno como corretor de seguros. Em muitos sentidos, ela lembrava a Sara sua própria mãe. Cathy Linton não era mulher de carregar armas, mas era determinada a fazer o que acreditava ser certo para si e para sua família.

Mas ela jamais teria aceitado suborno. Cathy era uma honesta incurável, o tipo de pessoa que dava meia-volta e dirigia oitenta quilômetros de volta até uma armadilha turística na Flórida porque tinham lhe dado troco a mais. Talvez isso explicasse por que Faith conseguia trabalhar com Will. Se alguém tivesse dito a Sara que a mãe havia roubado quase um milhão de dólares, ela teria dado risada na cara da pessoa. Era digno de conto de fadas. Faith não achava só que ele estava errado sobre a mãe dela. Achava que ele estava fora da realidade.

Will trocou a fita.

Ela fez sinal para ele tirar o fone.

— Não faz sentido.

— O quê?

— Você disse que cada membro da equipe lucrou pouco menos de um milhão de dólares. Você encontrou sessenta mil, no máximo, numa conta aberta em outro estado no nome de Bill Mitchell. Evelyn não dirige um Porsche. Não tem amante. Faith e o irmão não estudaram em escolas particulares, e nas férias ela só viajava para Jekyll Island com o neto.

— Depois de hoje, faz sentido — lembrou ele. — Quem levou Evelyn quer esse dinheiro.

— Não acho, não.

A maioria dos policiais defendia suas teorias como defenderia os próprios filhos. Will só perguntou:

— Por quê?

— Intuição. Instinto. Só não acho que seja isso.

— Faith não sabe da conta bancária.

— Não vou contar para ela.

Ele arrumou a própria postura na cadeira, juntando as mãos.

— Andei escutando minhas primeiras entrevistas com Evelyn. Ela fala principalmente do marido.

— Bill, né? Era corretor de seguros.

— Ele morreu alguns anos antes de o caso contra Evelyn ser aberto. — Sara se preparou para uma pergunta sobre ser viúva, mas Will seguiu por outro caminho. — No ano anterior à morte de Bill, ele foi processado pela família de um titular de apólice por ter uma cobertura negada. Disseram que Bill havia preenchido a documentação de forma errada. Era um pai de três filhos que tinha um problema cardíaco raro. A seguradora negou o tratamento.

Aquilo não era novidade para Sara:

— Disseram que era uma doença preexistente.

— Só que não era, pelo menos não diagnosticada. A família contratou um advogado, mas era tarde demais. O cara acabou morrendo porque um item foi marcado errado num formulário. Três dias depois, a viúva recebeu uma carta da seguradora pelo correio, dizendo que Bill

Mitchell, o corretor original, havia cometido um erro nos formulários e que o tratamento do marido dela estava aprovado.

— Que horror.

— Bill ficou abalado. Era um homem muito cuidadoso. Sua reputação era importante para ele, importante para seu trabalho. Ganhou uma úlcera de tanto se preocupar com isso.

Não era tecnicamente assim que as úlceras funcionavam, mas ela disse:

— E aí?

— Ele acabou sendo inocentado. Acharam os formulários originais. A seguradora é que tinha errado, não Bill. Alguém que inseria os dados tinha clicado na caixinha errada. Não era prevaricação, era só incompetência. — Will fez um gesto com a mão para deixar aquilo de lado. — Enfim, o que Evelyn falou foi que Bill nunca superou essa história. Ela ficava ensandecida porque ele se recusava a deixar aquilo para lá. Eles discutiam. Ela achava que ele estava só com pena de si mesmo. Acusou o marido de ser paranoico. Ele disse que estava sendo tratado de um jeito diferente pelos colegas de trabalho. Muita gente achava que a empresa tinha levado a culpa e que o erro era de Bill.

Sara não comprou aquilo.

— Uma seguradora levando a culpa?

— As pessoas têm cada ideia — comentou Will. — Enfim, Bill achou que aquilo anulava todo o bem que ele tinha feito ao longo dos anos. Evelyn disse que, quando veio o câncer, como Bill morreu de câncer pancreático três meses depois do diagnóstico, ela achava que parte do motivo de ele não conseguir lutar contra a doença era aquela culpa que não saía da cabeça dele. E ela nunca perdoou o marido por isso, por não lutar contra o câncer. Ele meio que só aceitou e esperou a morte.

Não era fácil vencer um câncer pancreático. As chances de sobrevivência a longo prazo eram de menos de cinco por cento.

— Um estresse assim pode mesmo impactar o sistema imunológico.

— Evelyn estava preocupada de que a mesma coisa fosse acontecer com ela.

— Que ela fosse ter câncer?

173

— Não. Que a investigação fosse arruinar a vida dela, mesmo que ela fosse inocentada. Que a desconfiança ia ficar pairando para sempre sobre ela. Disse que, em todos aqueles anos desde a morte do marido, ela nunca tinha desejado mais do que naquele dia que ele estivesse vivo, para poder falar que finalmente o entendia.

Sara considerou o peso dessa afirmação.

— Parece algo que uma pessoa inocente diria.

— Parece, sim.

— Quer dizer que você está se afastando da sua conclusão original?

— Muito gentil da sua parte colocar sua pergunta de um jeito tão diplomático. — Ele sorriu. — Não sei. Meu caso foi arquivado antes de eu conseguir finalizá-lo de um jeito satisfatório. Evelyn assinou os documentos e se aposentou. Amanda nem me falou que a investigação tinha se encerrado. Escutei numa manhã no noticiário: policial condecorada se aposenta para passar mais tempo com a família.

— Você acha que ela se safou.

— Eu fico sempre voltando ao seguinte: ela era responsável por uma equipe que roubou um montão de dinheiro. Ou ela fez vista grossa, ou não era tão boa quanto parecia no papel. — Will ficou cutucando a emenda de plástico de uma das fitas cassete. — E ainda tem a conta bancária. Pode não parecer muito se comparado a milhões, mas sessenta mil é um belo trocado. E está no nome do marido, não no dela. Por que não mudar agora que ele morreu? Por que ainda manter a conta em segredo?

— Todos ótimos argumentos.

Ele ficou quieto por um momento, o único som na sala era o polegar dele cutucando a emenda de plástico.

— Faith não me ligou quando tudo aconteceu. Eu não estava com o celular, então não teria adiantado nada, mas ela não me ligou. — Ele fez uma pausa. — Achei que talvez ela não confiasse em mim porque a mãe dela estava envolvida na situação.

— Duvido que ela tenha pensado nisso. Você sabe como o cérebro dá branco quando acontece uma coisa dessas. Chegou a perguntar para ela?

— Ela tem mais com o que se preocupar do que ficar me consolando. — Ele deu uma risadinha autodepreciativa. — Talvez eu devesse escrever no meu diário. — Ele começou a guardar tudo nas caixas. — Enfim, vou deixar você dormir. Achou alguma coisa que eu deva saber?

Sara puxou as duas pastas que havia separado.

— Talvez valha a pena dar uma olhada nesses caras. Estavam nas apreensões de valores em espécie. Um deles também estava na lista de testemunhas de defesa de Spivey. Eu separei esse porque ele tem um histórico de realizar sequestro como forma de chantagear gangues rivais.

Will abriu a pasta de cima.

Sara forneceu o nome:

— Ignatio Ortiz.

Will soltou um gemido.

— Está na Prisão Estadual de Phillips por tentativa de homicídio.

— Então não vai ser difícil de encontrar.

— Ele é líder dos Texicanos.

Sara estava familiarizada com a facção. Tinha atendido uma boa quantidade de jovens envolvidos com a organização. Poucos saíam inteiros do pronto-socorro.

Will continuou:

— Se Ortiz estiver envolvido nisso, nunca vai falar com a gente. Se não estiver, aí que nunca vai falar mesmo. Seja qual for o caso, dirigir até aquela prisão seriam três ou quatro horas do nosso dia a troco de nada.

— Ele ia ser chamado como testemunha pela defesa de Spivey.

— Boyd tinha uma quantidade surpreendente de bandidos dispostos a testemunhar dizendo que o cara não tinha encostado na grana deles. Tinha todo um rol de criminosos querendo defender a equipe de Evelyn.

— Você conseguiu alguma coisa com Boyd na prisão?

Will franziu a testa.

— Foi Amanda quem o entrevistou. Conversaram usando algum tipo de código. Uma coisa que eu entendi foi que Boyd falou que os asiáticos estavam tentando tirar os mexicanos do fornecimento.

— Los Texicanos — falou Sara.

— Amanda me disse que o método preferido deles é cortar a garganta.

Sara colocou a mão no pescoço, tentando não estremecer.

— Você acha que Evelyn continuava fazendo negócios com aqueles traficantes?

Ele fechou a pasta de Ortiz.

— Não vejo como. Ela não tem nada de interessante sem o distintivo. E não consigo imaginá-la como chefona do crime, a não ser que ela seja uma sociopata. Vovozinha de dia, traficante de noite.

— Você disse que Ortiz está preso por tentativa de homicídio. Quem ele tentou matar?

— O irmão. Encontrou o cara na cama com a esposa.

— Talvez este seja o irmão. — Sara abriu a pasta seguinte. — Hector Ortiz. Teoricamente não é bandido, mas entrou na lista de testemunhas da defesa. Eu o separei por ter o mesmo sobrenome de Ignatio.

Will soltou a foto de identificação criminal da pasta para olhá-la mais de perto.

— Seu instinto está dizendo que Evelyn é inocente?

Sara olhou o relógio. Precisava estar no trabalho em cinco horas.

— Meu instinto já foi dormir. O que foi?

Ele levantou a foto de Hector Ortiz. O homem era careca com um cavanhaque grisalho. A camisa estava amarrotada. Ele estava com o braço levantado, mostrando uma tatuagem à câmera: uma estrela do Texas verde e vermelha com uma cascavel enrolada nela.

Will falou:

— Este é o namoradinho de Evelyn.

DOMINGO

7

Os tapas tinham virado socos horas atrás. Ou dias atrás? Evelyn não tinha certeza. Estava vendada, sentada na escuridão total. Algo pingava — se torneira, esgoto ou sangue, ela não sabia. O corpo dela estava tão tomado de dor que mesmo quando ela fechava bem os olhos e tentava bloquear cada músculo que gritava, cada osso quebrado, não havia nada que parecesse intacto.

Ela soltou uma risada ofegante. O sangue esguichou da boca. O dedo cortado. Parecia não haver um osso que não estivesse quebrado, um pedaço de carne sem hematoma.

Eles tinham começado pelos pés, batendo nas solas com um cano de aço galvanizado. Era uma forma de tortura que aparentemente tinham visto em um filme, o que Evelyn sabia porque um deles havia dito enquanto explicava como fazer:

— O cara estava balançando para trás mais alto, tipo assim.

Não dava nem para nomear a sensação que Evelyn sentiu como dor. Era uma queimação na pele que a corrente sanguínea espalhava pelo corpo todo como se fosse fogo.

Como a maioria das mulheres, era o estupro o que mais a aterrorizava, mas ela sabia que havia perigos muito piores. No crime de estupro, pelo menos existia uma lógica animalesca. Esses homens não estavam sentindo prazer em machucá-la. Sua recompensa vinha das comemorações dos amigos. Estavam tentando impressionar uns aos outros, num jogo de quem era mais homem, vendo quem conseguia fazê-la gritar mais alto. E Evelyn *gritava*. Gritava tão alto que tinha certeza que suas cordas vocais iam estourar. Gritava de dor. Gritava de terror. Gritava de raiva, fúria, luto. Gritava principalmente porque essas emoções concorrentes pareciam lava quente subindo pela garganta.

Em um dado momento, eles tinham começado uma discussão sobre onde ficava o nervo vago. Três deles se revezaram socando-a nas costas até que, como crianças batendo numa bexiga cheia de doces, um deles acertou em cheio. Eles riram descontroladamente enquanto Evelyn tinha espasmos como se tivesse sido eletrocutada. A sensação era de terror primitivo. Ela nunca na vida havia se sentido tão perto da morte. Tinha se urinado. Tinha gritado na escuridão até não sair mais som nenhum da boca.

Em seguida, eles quebraram a perna dela. Não fora uma fratura de um golpe só, e sim o resultado de um cano de metal pesado batendo sem parar contra a perna até haver o estalo retumbante de um único osso se partindo em dois.

Um deles apertou a parte quebrada com a mão, com o hálito pútrido em sua orelha.

— Foi isso que aquela filha da puta fez com Ricardo.

Aquela filha da puta era a menina dela. Eles não tinham como saber quanto as palavras haviam dado esperança a Evelyn. Ela tinha sido nocauteada e arrastada para fora da cena do crime, pouco depois de o carro de Faith ter parado na entrada. Evelyn acordara na traseira de uma van. O barulho do motor rugia nos ouvidos dela, mas ela tinha ouvido dois tiros claros, o segundo uns bons quarenta segundos depois do primeiro.

Mas, naquele momento, Evelyn sabia a resposta da única pergunta que a impedia de simplesmente desistir. Faith estava viva. Tinha fugido. Depois disso, todo horror que faziam com ela era irrelevante. Ela pensou em Emma nos braços da filha e em Jeremy junto da mãe. Zeke devia estar lá. Ele tinha muita raiva, mas sempre cuidara da irmã. A polícia de Atlanta os cercaria como um manto. Will Trent daria a vida para proteger Faith. Amanda moveria céus e terra atrás de justiça.

— *Almeja...* — A voz de Evelyn era rouca no espaço fechado.

Ela só podia pedir que os filhos estivessem a salvo. Ninguém conseguiria salvá-la daquilo. Não havia promessa de salvação. Amanda não tinha como conversar com ela até aquela dor passar. Bill Mitchell não viria resgatá-la montado num cavalo branco.

Ela tinha sido tão idiota. Um erro tantos anos antes. Um erro terrível e idiota.

Evelyn cuspiu um dente quebrado. O último molar direito. Sentiu o nervo exposto reagindo ao ar frio. Tentou cobrir o ponto com a língua enquanto respirava pela boca. Precisava manter as vias aéreas desobstruídas. O nariz dela estava quebrado. Se ela parasse de respirar ou desmaiasse com sangue na garganta, iria engasgar e morrer. Seria um alívio bem-vindo, mas pensar na morte ainda a aterrorizava. Evelyn sempre foi uma lutadora. Sua natureza era fincar os pés quanto mais a empurravam. E, apesar disso, ela se sentia começando a ceder — não pela dor, mas pela exaustão. Percebia a determinação se esvaindo como água por uma peneira. Se ela se entregasse, talvez eles conseguissem o que queriam. Talvez sua boca se movesse, a voz funcionasse, apesar da mente pedindo que ela ficasse em silêncio.

E depois?

Eles precisariam matá-la. Ela sabia quem eram, apesar de estarem de máscara e ela, vendada. Conhecia a voz deles. Os nomes. O cheiro. Sabia o que estavam planejando, o que já tinham feito.

Hector.

Ela o encontrara no porta-malas do seu carro. Mesmo com silenciador, não existe tiro que não faça barulho. Evelyn tinha ouvido aquilo duas vezes na vida e instantaneamente reconhecera o assovio do ar passando por um cilindro de metal.

Pelo menos, ela havia protegido Emma. Pelo menos, garantira que a filha de sua filha estivesse segura.

Faith.

Mães não deviam ter filhos favoritos, mas Zeke era a escolha óbvia. Era decidido. Inteligente. Capaz. Leal. Era o primogênito, um menininho tímido que se agarrava à saia de Evelyn quando estranhos visitavam a casa deles. Uma criança que se sentava ao lado da mãe enquanto ela fazia o jantar e que amava ir ao mercado para ajudá-la a carregar as sacolas. Com o peito pequenino estufado, os braços lotados e os dentes mostrando um sorriso orgulhoso e feliz.

Mas era de Faith que Evelyn se sentia mais próxima. Faith, que cometera tantos erros. Faith, que Evelyn sempre conseguia perdoar porque, cada vez que olhava para a filha, via um lampejo de si mesma.

O tempo que as duas passaram juntas. Presas em casa. Aqueles meses de confinamento forçado. Exílio forçado. Infelicidade forçada.

Bill nunca havia entendido, mas era porque não fazia parte de sua natureza entender erros. Ele fora o primeiro a notar a barriga dela inchada. Fora o primeiro a confrontar a filha. Por nove longos meses, ele fora estoico e moralista, de repente fazendo Evelyn compreender de quem Zeke puxava essas tendências. Durante o momento mais difícil, ele praticamente tinha desaparecido da vida delas. Mesmo depois de tudo terminar e Jeremy iluminar a vida deles, como o sol finalmente brilhando após uma tempestade de verão, Bill nunca mais voltou a ser como antes.

Mas, bem, Evelyn também não era como antes. Nem ninguém. Faith estava ocupada descobrindo como criar um filho; Zeke, que só queria a atenção de Evelyn desde bebê, tinha se afastado o máximo que podia dela sem ir embora do planeta. O menininho dela, perdido. O coração dela, dividido em dois.

Ela não suportava mais pensar naquilo.

Evelyn endireitou a coluna, tentando tirar pressão do diafragma. Não podia continuar daquele jeito. Estava desmoronando. Aqueles jovens com seus videogames e fantasias de filmes tinham uma reserva ilimitada de ideias à disposição. Só Deus sabia a que recorreriam em seguida. Não teriam dificuldade de encontrar drogas. Barbitúricos. Etanol. Escopolamina. Tiopental sódico. Qualquer um desses podia agir como soro da verdade. Qualquer um desses podia arrancar a informação de sua boca.

Só a passagem terrivelmente lenta do tempo era capaz de fazê-la falar. A agonia incessante. A lista implacável de acusações. Eles eram tão raivosos, tão hostis.

Tão bárbaros.

Ela ia morrer. Evelyn soube, no minuto que acordara na van, que a morte era o único fim. No início, achou que seria a morte deles pelas suas mãos. Logo depois percebeu que seria o contrário. A única coisa que ela controlava era a própria boca. Em meio a tudo aquilo, nem uma única vez ela havia implorado para pararem. Não havia pedido que tivessem compaixão. Não lhes dera o poder de saber que tinham se infiltrado tão profundamente na cabeça dela que cada pensamento vinha com uma sombra se esgueirando por trás.

E se ela contasse a verdade?

Evelyn passara tantos anos escondendo o segredo que até pensar em desabafar lhe trazia algo parecido com paz. Aqueles homens eram seus torturadores, não seus confessores, mas ela não estava em posição de se preocupar com tais subterfúgios. Talvez a morte a absolvesse de seus pecados. Talvez houvesse um momento de alívio quando, pela primeira vez em muito tempo, Evelyn sentisse o peso da mentira enfim saindo de seus ombros.

Não. Nunca acreditariam nela. Ela teria que contar uma mentira. A verdade era decepcionante demais. Comum demais.

Teria que ser uma mentira crível, algo tão convincente que eles a matassem sem esperar confirmação. Esses homens eram criminosos insensíveis, mas não experientes. Não tinham paciência de manter ali uma mulher que os desafiara por tanto tempo. Iam ver o assassinato dela como prova final de sua masculinidade.

Seu único ressentimento seria não estar lá quando eles percebessem que tinham sido enganados. Torcia para que a escutassem do inferno rindo deles pelo resto da vidinha infeliz e patética que teriam.

Então ela riu, só para escutar o som, o desespero.

A porta se abriu. Um facho de luz entrou por baixo da venda. Ela escutou homens murmurando. Estavam falando de outra série de TV, outro filme, com uma nova técnica que queriam testar.

Evelyn respirou fundo, apesar de suas costelas quebradas espetarem os pulmões a cada inspiração. Tentou fazer o coração se acalmar. Rezou pedindo forças ao Deus com quem parara de falar no dia da morte do marido.

O que tinha hálito pútrido disse:

— Pronta para falar, vagabunda?

Evelyn se preparou. Não podia parecer que estava se entregando fácil demais. Ela teria que permitir que a espancassem, fazê-los pensar que enfim tinham vencido. Não era a primeira vez que ela deixava um homem pensar que tinha controle total sobre ela, mas com certeza seria a última.

Ele apertou a perna quebrada dela.

— Pronta para sentir dor?

Daria certo. Tinha que dar certo. Evelyn faria sua parte, e sua morte terminaria tudo, lavaria seus pecados. Faith jamais descobriria. Zeke nunca saberia. Seus filhos e netos estariam seguros.

Seguros exceto por uma coisa.

Evelyn fechou os olhos e mandou uma mensagem silenciosa a Roz Levy, rezando para a velha ficar de boca fechada.

8

Faith estava de olhos fechados, mas não conseguia dormir. Não queria dormir. A noite tinha passado lentamente, se arrastando como a foice da Morte sendo raspada no chão. Por horas, ela ouviu cada ranger e gemido da casa, esforçando-se para escutar qualquer movimento lá embaixo que indicasse que Zeke enfim tinha acordado.

O dedo da mãe estava escondido numa caixa de Band-Aids quase vazia no armário de remédios de Faith. Estava dentro de um saco Ziploc que ela encontrara numa mala velha. Faith ficara na dúvida se devia ou não colocar no gelo, mas pensar em preservar o dedo da mãe fazia a bile subir pela garganta. Além do mais, na noite anterior ela não quisera descer e enfrentar Zeke, nem os investigadores sentados à mesa da cozinha, nem o filho, que com certeza se juntaria a todos eles se ouvisse que a mãe tinha acordado. Faith sabia que, se os visse, começaria a chorar e, se começasse a chorar, rapidamente descobririam o motivo.

Mantenha a boca fechada e os olhos abertos.

Era exatamente o que ela estava fazendo, apesar de seu lado policial estar gritando que seguir as ordens de um sequestrador era um erro gravíssimo. Nunca se podia dar vantagem a eles. Nunca se devia ceder a um pedido deles sem ganhar algo em troca. Faith tinha ensinado essas estratégias básicas dezenas de vezes a várias famílias. Agora, via que era completamente diferente quando a pessoa amada em perigo era parente seu. Se os sequestradores de Evelyn tivessem mandado Faith se banhar em gasolina e acender um fósforo, ela teria obedecido. Não existia razão possível frente à possibilidade muito real de talvez nunca mais ver a mãe.

Ainda assim, seu lado policial queria detalhes. Dava para fazer testes para determinar se Evelyn estava viva ou não quando o dedo fora removido. Outros testes podiam provar definitivamente se a digital pertencia a Evelyn. Parecia um dedo de mulher, mas Faith nunca tinha passado muito tempo analisando a mão da mãe. Não tinha aliança de casamento; Evelyn parara de usá-la havia alguns anos. Era uma daquelas coisas que, de início, Faith não tinha notado. Ou talvez a mãe só mentisse bem. Ela tinha rido quando Faith perguntara sobre a mão sem aliança, dizendo:

— Ah, eu tirei faz séculos.

Será que a mãe dela era mentirosa? Essa era a pergunta central. Faith mentia o tempo todo para Jeremy, mas eram coisas sobre as quais toda mãe devia mentir para os filhos: sua vida amorosa, o que estava acontecendo no trabalho, como ela estava cuidando da saúde. Evelyn tinha mentido sobre Zeke ser transferido de volta para os Estados Unidos. Mas era para manter a paz e provavelmente evitar que a desaprovação de Zeke obscurecesse a ocasião feliz do nascimento de Emma.

Esse tipo de mentira não contava. Eram mentiras de proteção, não mentiras malignas que apodreciam como uma farpa debaixo da pele. Será que Evelyn tinha mentido para Faith em algo importante? Evelyn estava escondendo alguma coisa maior, algo que ia além do óbvio. A casa dela mostrava isso. As circunstâncias de seu sequestro entregavam tudo. Ela estava em posse de algo que homens muito ruins queriam. Havia alguma relação com drogas. Pelo menos uma facção estava envolvida. A mãe dela tinha trabalhado com narcóticos. Será que tinha passado esse tempo todo sentada num monte de dinheiro? Havia um cofre secreto escondido em algum lugar? Será que Faith e Zeke descobririam, na leitura do testamento de Evelyn, que a mãe na verdade era rica?

Não, não era possível. Evelyn devia saber que os filhos devolveriam qualquer dinheiro ilícito, independentemente do quanto facilitasse a vida deles. Hipotecas. Parcelas de carro. Empréstimos estudantis. Nada disso sumiria. Nem Zeke, nem Faith jamais aceitariam dinheiro sujo. Evelyn os criara para não fazer isso.

E ela criara Faith para ser uma policial melhor do que alguém que passa a noite toda sem levantar a bunda da cama, esperando o sol nascer.

Se Evelyn estivesse ali naquele momento, o que ia querer que Faith fizesse? A resposta óbvia era ligar para Amanda. As duas sempre foram próximas. "Farinha do mesmo saco", dizia com frequência Bill Mitchell, e não de um jeito elogioso. Mesmo após o tio de Faith, Kenny, ter decidido fazer papel de trouxa indo atrás de mulheres mais novas nas praias do sul da Flórida, Evelyn havia deixado claro que preferia Amanda a Kenny Mitchell na mesa de Natal da família. As duas tinham uma linguagem própria, como soldados voltando da guerra.

Ligar naquele momento para Amanda, porém, estava fora de questão. Ela viria correndo como um elefante numa loja de cristal. A casa de Faith seria revirada de ponta-cabeça. Uma equipe da SWAT seria destacada. Os sequestradores dariam uma única olhada naquela demonstração de força e decidiriam que era mais fácil meter uma bala na cabeça da vítima do que negociar com uma mulher obcecada por vingança. Porque era exatamente assim que Amanda agiria. Ela nunca fazia nada discretamente. Sempre era tudo ou nada.

Will era bom em entrar com delicadeza. Tinha aperfeiçoado a técnica. E era parceiro dela. Ela *devia* ligar para ele, ou pelo menos mandar notícias. Mas o que diria? "Preciso da sua ajuda, mas não pode contar para Amanda e talvez a gente acabe agindo fora da lei, mas, por favor, não faça perguntas." Era algo insustentável. No dia anterior, ele já tinha feito vista grossa para as regras por ela, mas ela não podia pedir que ele as quebrasse. Will era a pessoa em quem ela mais confiaria para protegê-la, mas às vezes ele tinha um senso irritante de certo e errado. Parte dela tinha medo que ele lhe negasse ajuda. Uma parte ainda maior dela tinha medo de acabar enfiando-o no tipo de problema do qual ele nunca conseguiria sair. Uma coisa era Faith jogar a própria carreira pela janela. Mas ela não podia pedir que Will fizesse o mesmo.

Ela apoiou a cabeça nas mãos. Mesmo que quisesse falar com ele, os telefones estavam grampeados para o caso de haver pedido de resgate. O e-mail dela era uma conta da GBI, que muito provavelmente estava sendo monitorada. Deviam estar escutando as ligações do celular dela também.

E isso era só da parte dos mocinhos. Vai saber o que os sequestradores de Evelyn tinham conseguido fazer. Eles sabiam o apelido de Jeremy, o ano de seu nascimento, a escola em que havia estudado. Tinham mandado uma advertência pelo Facebook dele. Talvez também tivessem grampeado a casa. Dava para comprar aparelhos com qualidade de espionagem pela internet. A não ser que Faith começasse a remover espelhos de interruptores e desmontar telefones, não dava para saber se tinha alguém ouvindo ou não. E, no minuto em que ela começasse a demonstrar paranoia perto da família, eles saberiam que tinha alguma coisa errada. Isso sem falar nos detetives da polícia de Atlanta, que observavam cada movimento dela.

Finalmente, ela escutou a descarga lá debaixo. Alguns segundos depois, a porta da frente se abriu e fechou. Zeke provavelmente ia correr, ou talvez os investigadores tivessem decidido tomar um ar fresco no quintal da frente, em vez de nos fundos.

As panturrilhas de Faith vibraram de dor quando ela pôs os pés no chão. Ela estava em posição fetal havia tanto tempo que o corpo estava duro. Exceto pelo momento em que foi dar uma olhada em Emma, ela não ousara andar pela casa na noite anterior, por medo de Zeke subir para perguntar o que diabos ela estava fazendo. A casa era velha, as tábuas do piso rangiam, e o irmão tinha sono leve.

Ela começou pela cômoda de roupas, abrindo com cuidado cada uma, conferindo lingeries, camisetas e pijamas para ver se algo tinha sido mexido. Nada parecia fora do lugar. Então, ela foi até o armário. As roupas de trabalho consistiam basicamente em terninhos pretos com elástico nas calças para ela não precisar se preocupar com conseguir ou não abotoá-las de manhã. Suas roupas de maternidade estavam numa caixa na prateleira mais baixa. Faith arrastou uma cadeira até ali para verificar se continuava fechada com durex. A pilha de calças jeans azuis lá dentro parecia intocada. Ainda assim, ela conferiu todos os bolsos, depois voltou aos terninhos e fez o mesmo.

Nada.

Faith subiu de novo na cadeira e ficou na ponta dos pés para alcançar a prateleira mais alta, onde tinha guardado a caixa de lembranças da infância de Jeremy. Quase caiu na cabeça dela. Ela a pegou no último segundo, prendendo a respiração por medo de fazer muito barulho. Sentou-se no chão com a caixa entre as pernas. O papelão estava aberto. O durex tinha sido arrancado meses atrás. Quando ela estava grávida de Emma, Faith ficou obcecada por rever as lembranças de infância de Jeremy. Que bom que ela morava sozinha, senão alguém teria questionado seriamente sua estabilidade mental. Só de ver a escultura em bronze dos sapatinhos dele e as botinhas de tricô já começava um chororô. Os boletins de Jeremy. Seus trabalhos de escola. Cartões de Dia das Mães que ele tinha desenhado com giz de cera. Cartões de Dia dos Namorados que ele havia recortado com a tesourinha sem ponta.

Os olhos dela arderam ao abrir a caixa.

Uma mecha de cabelo de Jeremy estava em cima do boletim de seu último ano do ensino médio. O laço azul parecia diferente. Ela o levantou na direção da luz. O tempo havia desbotado a seda em azul-claro, dando às dobras um tom esquálido. O cabelo havia escurecido e ficado castanho-dourado. Algo parecia estranho. Ela não sabia se o laço tinha ou não sido refeito ou se havia se desamarrado na caixa. Também não conseguia lembrar se ela havia empilhado os boletins do primeiro ano do fundamental ao último ano do ensino médio ou o contrário. Parecia contraintuitivo o último estar no topo, especialmente com a mecha de cabelo em cima. Ou talvez ela só estivesse se convencendo a surtar quando não havia nada de errado.

Faith levantou a pilha de boletins e olhou embaixo. Os trabalhos continuavam lá. Ela viu os sapatinhos de bronze, as botinhas, os cartões comemorativos de cartolina que ele tinha feito na escola.

Tudo parecia estar lá, mas ela não conseguia afastar a sensação de que alguém tinha mexido na caixa. Será que tinham revirado as coisas de Jeremy? Tinham visto os corações que ele havia desenhado numa foto do Sr. Billingham, o primeiro cachorro dele? Tinham remexido os boletins e dado risada porque a professora Thompson, do quarto ano, o chamara de anjinho?

Faith fechou a caixa. Ela a levantou bem alto e a deslizou para a prateleira. Quando enfiou a cadeira de volta no lugar, estava tremendo de fúria só de pensar nas mãos pegajosas de um estranho nas coisas do seu menino.

Ela foi para o quarto de Emma em seguida. A bebê em geral não dormia a noite toda, mas o dia anterior tinha sido incomumente longo e tumultuado. Ela continuava adormecida quando Faith foi olhar o berço. A garganta dela fazia um ruído com a respiração. Faith colocou uma mão no peito da filha. O coração de Emma parecia um pássaro preso sob a palma de Faith. Em silêncio, ela olhou o armário, a caixa pequena de brinquedos, as fraldas e o estoque de alimentos.

Nada.

Jeremy continuava dormindo, mas mesmo assim Faith entrou no quarto dele. Pegou as roupas do chão para fingir que tinha motivo para estar ali. Parte dela só queria ficar ali parada, olhando para ele. O filho estava no que ela chamava de pose de John Travolta, de barriga para baixo, pé direito pendurado para fora da cama, braço esquerdo esticado acima da cabeça. As escápulas magras se projetavam como asinhas de frango. O cabelo dele cobria a maior parte do rosto. Tinha uma mancha de saliva no travesseiro. Ele ainda dormia de boca aberta.

O quarto dele estava impecável no dia anterior, mas a mera presença dele havia mudado tudo. Papéis cobriam a mesa. A mochila estava aberta no chão, com itens caindo para fora. Cabos de vários equipamentos de informática estavam esticados pelo carpete. O laptop, que ela havia economizado por seis meses para conseguir comprar, estava aberto e de lado, como um livro descartado. Faith usou o pé para endireitá-lo antes de sair do quarto. Depois, entrou mais uma vez, mas só para cobrir o ombro dele com o lençol, para que não sentisse frio.

Faith jogou as roupas de Jeremy em cima da máquina de lavar e desceu. O detetive Connor estava sentado na cadeira de sempre na mesa da cozinha. A camisa era diferente da do dia anterior e o coldre de ombro não estava tão apertado no peito. O cabelo ruivo estava desgrenhado, provavelmente de dormir com a cabeça na mesa. Ela tinha começado a pensar nele como "Ruivo" e tinha medo de abrir a boca e o apelido escapar.

Ele disse:

— Bom dia, agente Mitchell.

— Meu irmão foi correr?

Ele fez que sim.

— O detetive Taylor foi comprar café da manhã. Espero que goste de McDonald's.

Pensar em comida foi suficiente para Faith ficar enjoada outra vez, mas ela respondeu:

— Obrigada.

Metade do conteúdo da geladeira tinha desaparecido, embora provavelmente fosse por causa de Jeremy e Zeke, já que os dois comiam como garotos de dezoito anos. Ela pegou o suco de laranja. A embalagem estava vazia. Nem o filho, nem o irmão gostavam de suco de laranja.

Ela perguntou ao Ruivo:

— Vocês tomaram suco?

— Não, senhora.

Faith sacudiu a embalagem. Continuava vazia. Ela não achava que o Ruivo fosse mentir sobre uma coisa dessas. Tinha oferecido qualquer coisa da cozinha aos dois detetives. A julgar pelo estoque reduzido de refrigerantes Diet Rite, eles tinham aceitado a oferta.

O telefone tocou. Faith verificou a hora no relógio do fogão. Eram exatamente sete da manhã.

— Deve ser minha chefe — explicou ela ao Ruivo.

Mesmo assim, ele esperou até ela atender o telefone.

Amanda falou:

— Nenhuma notícia.

Faith fez um sinal dispensando o detetive.

— Onde você está?

Ela não respondeu à pergunta.

— Como Jeremy está?

— Bem, na medida do possível.

Faith não falou mais. Conferiu se o Ruivo estava na sala e então abriu a gaveta de talheres. As colheres estavam viradas na direção errada, com a parte plana do cabo para a direita, não para a esquerda. Os garfos estavam de ponta-cabeça. Os dentes apontavam para a frente da gaveta, em vez de para trás. Faith piscou, sem ter certeza do que estava vendo.

Amanda continuou:

— Você ficou sabendo de Boyd?

— Will me contou ontem à noite. Sinto muito. Eu sei que ele fez coisas ruins, mas ele era...

Amanda não a obrigou a terminar a frase.

— Era, mesmo.

Faith abriu a gaveta de tralhas. Todas as canetas tinham sumido. Ela guardava todas juntas com um elástico vermelho, no canto direito ao fundo. Ela as procurou entre os cupons, tesouras e chaves soltas não identificadas. Nada das canetas.

— Você sabia que Zeke estava no país?

— Sua mãe estava tentando proteger você.

Faith abriu a outra gaveta de tralhas.

— Pelo jeito, ela tentou me proteger de várias coisas.

Ela colocou a mão no fundo e achou as canetas. Com um elástico amarelo. Será que ela o havia trocado? Faith tinha uma vaga memória de o elástico ter estourado fazia um tempo, mas podia jurar por tudo o que era mais sagrado que tinha usado o elástico vermelho do maço de brócolis que havia comprado no mercado no mesmo dia.

— Faith? — O tom de Amanda estava tenso. — O que você tem? Aconteceu alguma coisa?

— Está tudo bem. É que... — Ela tentou pensar numa desculpa. Ia mesmo fazer aquilo: estava decidida a não contar a Amanda que os sequestradores tinham entrado em contato com ela. Que tinham deixado algo pertencente a Evelyn embaixo de seu travesseiro. Que sabiam coisas de mais sobre Jeremy. Que tinham mexido nos talheres dela. — Está cedo. Não dormi bem ontem à noite.

— Você precisa se cuidar. Comer direito. Dormir o máximo possível. Tomar muita água. Eu sei que é difícil, mas você tem que manter as forças.

192

Faith sentiu a raiva chegando. Não sabia se estava falando no momento com a chefe ou com a tia Mandy, mas qualquer uma das duas podia muito bem ir à merda.

— Eu sei me cuidar.

— Fico muito feliz de você achar isso, mas, pelo que estou vendo, não é o caso.

— Ela fez alguma coisa, Mandy? Minha mãe está nessa situação porque...

— Você precisa que eu vá até sua casa?

— Você não está em Valdosta?

Amanda ficou em silêncio. Faith obviamente tinha passado dos limites. Ou talvez fosse só a chefe sendo esperta o bastante para lembrar que a conversa estava sendo gravada. Naquele momento, Faith não estava nem aí. Ficou olhando o elástico amarelo e se perguntando se estaria enlouquecendo. Sua glicemia devia estar baixa. A visão de Faith estava ligeiramente borrada. Sua boca estava seca. Ela abriu a geladeira de novo e pegou a embalagem de suco de laranja. Continuava vazia.

Amanda falou:

— Pense na sua mãe. Ela ia querer que você fosse forte.

Se ao menos ela soubesse que Faith estava prestes a surtar por causa de um elástico amarelo. Ela murmurou:

— Eu estou bem.

— Vamos trazê-la de volta e vamos garantir que o responsável pague pelo que nos fez passar. Pode apostar nisso.

Faith abriu a boca para dizer que não estava nem aí para vingança, mas Amanda já tinha desligado.

Ela jogou a embalagem de suco no lixo. Havia um saco de doces de emergência no armário. Faith o pegou e um monte de balas Jolly Ranchers caíram no chão. Ela olhou o saco. O fundo estava rasgado.

O Ruivo tinha voltado. Ele se abaixou para ajudá-la a recolher as balas.

— Tudo bem?

— Sim.

Faith jogou um punhado de balas na bancada e saiu da cozinha. Acendeu a luz da sala, mas não aconteceu nada. Faith pressionou o interruptor para baixo e para cima. Ainda nada. Ela mexeu na lâmpada da luminária. Uma volta fez a luz se acender. Ela fez o mesmo com a lâmpada da outra luminária. Sentiu o calor arder nos dedos quando a luz se acendeu.

Faith se jogou na poltrona. Seu humor ficava subindo e descendo, como as escalas de um piano. Ela sabia que precisava comer alguma coisa, testar a glicose no sangue e fazer os ajustes necessários. Seu cérebro só funcionaria direito quando ela estivesse estável. Mas, agora que estava sentada, ela não tinha forças para se mexer.

O sofá ficava à sua frente. Zeke tinha dobrado os lençóis num quadrado perfeito e os colocado em cima do travesseiro. Ela viu a mancha vermelha na almofada bege do assento, onde Jeremy havia derramado Kool-Aid quinze anos antes. Sabia que, se virasse aquela almofada, encontraria uma mancha azul de um picolé que ele tinha derrubado dois anos depois. Se ela virasse a almofada do assento em que estava, veria o rasgo feito pela chuteira de futebol dele. O tapete no chão estava desgastado de tanto os dois irem e voltarem da cozinha. As paredes tinham sido pintadas pelos dois com uma tinta acrílica durante o recesso de primavera de Jeremy no ano anterior.

Faith considerou a possibilidade bem real de estar enlouquecendo. Jeremy era velho demais para aquele tipo de jogo, e Zeke nunca tinha sido de fazer guerra psicológica. Ele preferiria espancá-la até a morte do que desrosquear umas lâmpadas. Além do mais, nenhum dos dois estava em clima de pegadinha. Não podia ser só a glicemia de Faith. As canetas, os talheres, as lâmpadas — eram coisas pequenas que só Faith notaria. O tipo de coisa que faria qualquer um pensar que você estava maluca se contasse a alguém.

Ela levantou o olhar para o teto, depois o baixou até as prateleiras instaladas na parede atrás do sofá. Bill Mitchell tinha sido colecionador de itens brega. Tinha saleiro e pimenteiro de meninas dançando hula, trazidos do Havaí. Tinha óculos no formato do monte Rushmore, uma coroa da estátua da Liberdade de espuma e um conjunto de colheres esmaltadas de prata mostrando alguns dos cenários mais notáveis do Grand Canyon. Sua coleção mais estimada eram os globos de neve. A cada viagem de carro, cada voo, cada vez que saía de casa, Bill Mitchell procurava um globo de neve para marcar a ocasião.

Quando o pai morreu, ninguém na família questionou: aquilo tudo ia para Faith. Na infância, ela amava sacudir os globos e ver a neve cair. Ordem se transformando em caos. Era algo que Faith compartilhava com o pai. Permitindo-se um raro luxo, ela mandou construir prateleiras sob medida para os globos e deixou Jeremy com tanto medo de quebrar algum que, durante um mês inteiro, ele fez o trajeto mais longo para a cozinha, só para não esbarrar sem querer nas prateleiras.

Sentada na sala naquela manhã, Faith olhou para as prateleiras e viu que todos os trinta e seis globos tinham sido virados de frente para a parede.

9

Sara se perguntou se era uma peculiaridade do Sul as crianças ficarem doentes na meia hora que havia entre as aulas dominicais e a missa. A maioria de seus primeiros pacientes naquela manhã tinha ficado doente naquele período específico de tempo. Dores de barriga, dores de ouvido, mal-estar generalizado — nada que pudesse ser diagnosticado por um exame de sangue ou uma radiografia, mas que era facilmente curado com um conjunto de livros de colorir ou um desenho animado na televisão.

Perto das dez da manhã, os problemas ficaram mais sérios. Os casos se sucediam rapidamente e eram do tipo que Sara odiava, porque podiam ser evitados. Uma criança tinha comido veneno de rato que havia encontrado debaixo do armário da cozinha. Outra tinha ficado com queimadura de terceiro grau por tocar numa panela no fogo. Havia um adolescente que ela tinha precisado internar à força na ala de isolamento porque o primeiro contato com maconha o levara a um surto psicótico. Depois, uma menina de dezessete anos tinha chegado com a cabeça aberta. Aparentemente, ainda estava bêbada ao voltar de carro para casa de manhã e acabou enfiando o carro num ônibus de viagem estacionado. A menina ainda estava em cirurgia, mas Sara chutava que, mesmo que conseguissem controlar o inchaço no cérebro, ela jamais seria a mesma.

Às onze, Sara queria voltar para a cama e recomeçar o dia.

Trabalhar num hospital era uma negociação constante. O trabalho sugava da sua vida tudo o que você permitisse. Sara tinha concordado em trabalhar no Grady sabendo dessa verdade, abraçando-a, porque não queria ter vida depois da morte do marido. No último ano, ela estava dando menos plantões no pronto-socorro. Ter horários regulares era difícil, mas Sara travava essa batalha todos os dias.

Era na verdade uma forma de autopreservação. Todo médico carregava um cemitério dentro de si. Os pacientes que ela podia ajudar — a menininha em quem fizera lavagem estomacal, o bebê cujos dedos queimados ela salvara — eram desvios momentâneos. Eram os pacientes perdidos de que Sara mais se lembrava. O garoto que havia sucumbido lenta e dolorosamente à leucemia. A criança de nove anos que tinha levado dezesseis horas para morrer por envenenamento por anticongelante. A de onze que havia quebrado o pescoço mergulhando de cabeça numa piscina. Todos ainda estavam dentro dela, lembretes constantes de que, não importava o quanto ela trabalhasse, às vezes — muitas vezes —, não era suficiente.

Sara se sentou no sofá da sala de descanso médico. Tinha prontuários para ver, mas precisava de um minuto sozinha. Ela havia dormido menos de quatro horas à noite. Will não era o motivo central para seu cérebro se recusar a se desligar. Ela não parava de pensar em Evelyn Mitchell e seu bando corrupto. A dúvida sobre aquela mulher ser culpada ou não pesava em sua mente. As palavras de Will ficavam voltando: ou Evelyn Mitchell era uma chefe ruim, ou era uma policial corrupta. Não havia meio-termo.

E provavelmente era por isso que Sara não tinha achado tempo de manhã para ligar e ver como Faith Mitchell estava. Tecnicamente, Faith era paciente de Delia Wallace, mas Sara sentia uma estranha responsabilidade pela parceira de Will. Aquilo mexia com ela, assim como Will, que parecia estar presente em todos os pensamentos que ela tinha ultimamente.

Todo o aborrecimento. Nada do prazer.

Nan, uma das estagiárias de enfermagem, se jogou no sofá ao lado de Sara. Enquanto falava, mexia no BlackBerry.

— Quero saber tudo do seu encontro maravilhoso.

Sara forçou um sorriso. Naquela manhã, quando chegara ao hospital, havia um buquê de flores enormes esperando na sala de descanso. Pelo jeito, Dale Dugan havia comprado todo o estoque de mosquitinhos e cravos cor-de-rosa da cidade. Todo mundo do pronto-socorro tinha comentado com Sara antes mesmo de ela conseguir colocar o jaleco. Todos pareciam envolvidos com o romance da viúva apaixonada.

Sara disse à garota:

— Ele é muito legal.

— Ele também acha você legal. — Nan deu um sorriso malicioso enquanto digitava um e-mail. — Encontrei com ele no laboratório. Ele é supermaneiro.

Sara viu os polegares da menina se mexendo e se sentiu com trezentos anos. Não conseguia lembrar se um dia tinha sido tão jovem. Também não conseguia imaginar Dale Dugan se sentando e fofocando com essa jovem enfermeira risonha.

Nan finalmente tirou os olhos do aparelho.

— Ele disse que você é fascinante, que se divertiram muito e que vocês deram um beijo muito bom.

— Você está trocando e-mails com ele?

— Não. — Ela revirou os olhos. — Ele disse isso no laboratório.

— Que ótimo — Sara conseguiu dizer.

Ela não sabia como lidar com Dale, que ou estava iludido, ou era um mentiroso patológico. No fim, ia ter que falar com ele. Só as flores já eram péssimo sinal. Ela teria que arrancar rápido o Band-Aid. Mesmo assim, não conseguia deixar de se perguntar por que o homem que ela queria não estava disponível e o homem que estava disponível ela não queria. Assim continuava sua busca de transformar sua vida numa novela.

Nan voltou a digitar:

— O que quer que eu diga para ele que você falou?

— Eu não falei nada.

— Mas poderia.

— Hum... — Sara se levantou do sofá. Era bem mais fácil quando dava para só colocar um bilhete no armário de alguém. — Melhor eu ir almoçar enquanto as coisas estão tranquilas.

Em vez de ir em direção à lanchonete, Sara virou à esquerda, para os elevadores. Quase foi atropelada por uma maca voando pelo corredor. Facada. A faca continuava no peito do paciente. Paramédicos gritavam os sinais vitais. Médicos davam ordens. Sara apertou o botão de descer e esperou as portas do elevador se abrirem.

O hospital tinha sido fundado nos anos 1980 e havia funcionado em quatro localidades diferentes antes de achar sua casa final na Jesse Hill Jr. Drive. Administração ruim constante, corrupção e pura incompetência significavam que, a qualquer momento de sua célebre história, o hospital estava prestes a falir. O prédio em formato de U tinha sido expandido, remodelado, derrubado e reformado tantas vezes que Sara tinha certeza de que ninguém mais conseguia contar. O terreno ao redor era uma ladeira que descia até a Georgia State, universidade que compartilhava o estacionamento com o hospital. As vagas de ambulância do pronto-socorro davam para a rodovia interestadual, no que se chamava Curva Grady, e ocupavam um andar inteiro acima da entrada principal que dava para a rua. Durante a época de Jim Crow, o hospital se chamava Gradys, porque as alas para brancos ficavam de um lado, com vista para a cidade, e as de pessoas negras ficavam de outro, com vista para o nada.

Margaret Mitchell tinha sido levada às pressas para aquele hospital, após ser atropelada por um motorista bêbado na Peachtree Street, e morrido cinco dias depois. Vítimas da explosão a bomba no Centennial Olympic Park tinham sido tratadas ali. O Grady ainda era o único centro de trauma nível 1 da região. Vítimas com os ferimentos mais graves, com risco de vida, vinham de avião para receber tratamento, o que significava que o Instituto Médico-Legal do condado de Fulton tinha um posto secundário ali para processar as entradas no necrotério. A qualquer momento haveria dois ou três corpos esperando transporte. Na época que Sara aceitou o emprego como legista do condado de Grant, estudou no Instituto Médico-Legal na Pryor Street, no centro. Eles viviam com falta de pessoal. Ela passara muitas horas de almoço levando corpos às pressas até o Grady.

As portas do elevador se abriram. George, um dos seguranças, desceu. A corpulência dele preenchia o corredor. Ele tinha sido jogador de futebol americano até um tornozelo deslocado o convencer a procurar uma carreira diferente.

— Dra. Linton.

Ele segurou as portas para ela.

— George.

Ele deu uma piscadinha e ela sorriu.

Já havia um casal jovem ali dentro. Eles ficaram juntinhos enquanto o elevador descia um andar. Trabalhar num hospital também tinha disto: para onde você ia, encontrava alguém que estava tendo um dos piores dias de sua vida. Talvez fosse essa a mudança de que Sara precisava — não vender o apartamento e se mudar para um bangalô aconchegante, mas voltar a uma clínica particular, onde a única emergência do dia era decidir qual representante farmacêutico ia pagar o almoço.

Dois andares abaixo, no subsolo, a temperatura era mais baixa. Sara fechou o jaleco enquanto passava pelo departamento de registros. Ao contrário da época em que ela fazia residência no Grady, não era mais necessário ficar na fila para pegar prontuários. Tudo era automatizado, as informações de um paciente estavam nos tablets que funcionavam com a rede interna do hospital. Radiografias ficavam nos monitores maiores dentro dos quartos, e todos os medicamentos eram codificados nas pulseiras do paciente. Sendo o único hospital com fundos públicos que sobrava em Atlanta, o Grady estava constantemente à beira da falência, mas pelo menos tentava sair com estilo.

Sara parou na frente das portas duplas grossas que separavam o necrotério do resto do hospital. Acenou o crachá na frente do leitor. Houve um som repentino da pressão do ar mudando quando as portas de aço isoladas se abriram.

O atendente pareceu surpreso ao encontrar Sara em seu espaço. Ele era o mais próximo de um gótico que dava para ser enquanto se usava um uniforme hospitalar azul. Tudo nele anunciava que era descolado demais para aquele trabalho. Seu cabelo preto tingido estava preso num rabo de cavalo. Os óculos pareciam ter pertencido a John Lennon. O delineador era algo saído de um filme de Cleópatra. Para Sara, a barriga saliente e o bigode de Fu Manchu o deixavam parecido com Spike, irmão do Snoopy.

— Você está perdida?

— Júnior — ela leu no crachá dele. Era jovem, provavelmente da idade de Nan. — Queria saber se tem alguém do IML de Fulton por aqui.

— Larry. Está fazendo um carregamento lá atrás. Algum problema?

— Não, só queria a mente dele emprestada.

— Boa sorte, mande um postal quando encontrar.

Um homem hispânico magrelo saiu da sala dos fundos. O uniforme hospitalar parecia um roupão nele. Tinha mais ou menos a idade de Júnior, ou seja, provavelmente usava fraldas até poucas semanas atrás.

— Muito engraçado, *jefe*. — Ele deu um soquinho no braço de Júnior. — Do que precisa, doutora?

Aquilo não estava indo como o planejado.

— Nada. Desculpem pelo incômodo.

Ela começou a se virar, mas Júnior a interrompeu.

— Você é a namorada nova do Dale, né? Ele falou que você era uma ruiva alta.

Sara mordeu o lábio. Por que é que Dale andava com aquela molecada de dez anos?

O rosto de Júnior se abriu num sorriso.

— Dra. Linton, suponho.

Se não fosse o crachá pendurado no jaleco, ela teria mentido. Isso e o nome bordado no bolso. E o fato de ser a única médica ruiva do hospital.

Larry ofereceu:

— Vai ser um prazer ajudar a gata do Dale.

— Ô, se vai — opinou Júnior.

Sara botou um sorriso na cara.

— Como vocês dois conheceram Dale?

— Basquete, cara. — Larry fingiu fazer uma cesta. — Qual a natureza da sua emergência?

— Não é uma emergência — disse ela, antes de perceber que ele só estava fazendo graça. — Eu tinha uma pergunta sobre o tiroteio de ontem.

— Qual?

Desta vez, não era piada. Perguntar sobre um tiroteio em Atlanta era como perguntar sobre o bêbado num jogo de futebol americano.

— Em Sherwood Forest. Aquele com uma policial.

Larry fez que sim com a cabeça.

— Caceta, foi uma doideira. O cara estava cheio de H na barriga.

— Heroína?

—Embaladas em pequenos balões. O tiro estourou todas que nem...

— Ele perguntou ao Júnior: — Porra, cara, como é aquele negócio que tem açúcar dentro?

— DipnLik?

— Não.

— É de chocolate?

— Não, cara, tipo no canudo de papel.

Sara sugeriu:

— Pixie Stix?

— É, isso aí. O cara morreu numa onda épica.

Sara esperou os dois darem soquinhos de cumprimento.

— Isso foi o asiático?

— Não, o porto-riquenho. Ricardo — falou ele, vibrando os Rs com um sotaque estrangeiro.

— Achei que ele fosse mexicano.

— Sério, você acha que todos nós temos a mesma cara?

Sara não sabia como responder.

Larry riu.

— Tudo bem. Estou só pegando no seu pé. Sim, ele é porto-riquenho, que nem minha mãe.

— Conseguiram o sobrenome dele?

— Não. Mas ele tinha o nome Neta tatuado na mão. — Ele apontou para a junção entre o polegar e o indicador. — É um coração com um N no meio.

— Neta?

Sara nunca tinha escutado aquele nome antes.

— Uma facção porto-riquenha. Os doidões querem se separar dos Estados Unidos. Minha mãe estava toda metida nessa merda quando fomos embora. Toda "precisamos sair do comando de opressores colonialistas". Aí, ela chega aqui e fica toda: "Preciso arrumar uma dessas TVs de plasma grandonas que nem da sua tia Freda." Papo reto.

Outro soquinho com Júnior.

— Tem certeza de que é um símbolo de facção, esse N dentro de um coração?

— É um deles. Todo mundo que entra tem que levar mais gente.

— Que nem as Wiccas — comentou Júnior.

— Exato. Vários deles saem ou partem para outra. O tal Ricardo não deve ser importante. Não tem os dedos. — Larry levantou de novo a mão, desta vez com o indicador cruzado na frente do dedo médio. — Em geral é assim, com a bandeira de Porto Rico enrolada no pulso. Eles só querem saber de independência. Pelo menos é o que dizem.

Sara se lembrou do que Will dissera.

— Achei que Ricardo tivesse a tatuagem dos Texicanos no peito, não?

— É, como eu falei, vários deles saem ou partem para outra. O irmão deve ter partido para algo melhor. A Neta não tem influência aqui que nem os Texicanos. — Ele assobiou entre os dentes. — Puta negócio assustador, cara. Esses Texicanos não brincam.

— O IML sabe de tudo isso?

— Mandaram as fotos para a unidade de facções. Neta é a principal organização de Porto Rico. Vai estar na Bíblia.

A Bíblia das Facções era o livro usado por policiais para rastrear sinais e movimentos das facções criminosas.

— Identificaram algo sobre o asiático? Sobre as outras vítimas?

— Um era estudante. Algum gênio da matemática. Ganhou vários prêmios, uma porra assim.

Sara se lembrou da foto de Hironobu Kwon no noticiário.

— Achei que ele estudasse na Georgia State.

A State não era uma faculdade ruim, mas um prodígio da matemática acabaria na Georgia Tech.

— Só sei disso. Estão fazendo a perícia no outro cara agora. Aquele incêndio no apartamento atrasou a gente pra caramba. Seis corpos. — Ele balançou a cabeça. — Dois cachorros. Cara, odeio quando tem cachorros.

Júnior falou:

— Pode crer, cara.

— Obrigada — disse Sara. — Obrigada aos dois.

Júnior bateu com a lateral do punho no peito.

— Seja legal com meu parceiro Dale.

Sara saiu antes de ter mais soquinhos. Ela enfiou a mão no bolso, tentando achar o celular enquanto andava pelo corredor. A maioria dos funcionários carregava tantos aparelhos eletrônicos que provavelmente todos iam morrer de envenenamento por radiação. Ela tinha um BlackBerry em que recebia relatórios de laboratório e comunicados do hospital, além do iPhone de uso pessoal. O celular do hospital era um flip que antes pertencia a alguém com mãos muito pegajosas. Dois bipes ficavam presos no bolso do jaleco, um para o pronto-socorro e um para a ala pediátrica. Seu celular pessoal era fino e em geral o último que ela encontrava, que foi o que aconteceu naquele momento.

Ela foi passando os contatos na agenda, parou um pouco no número de Amanda Wagner e depois passou para Will Trent. O telefone dele tocou duas vezes antes de ele atender.

— Trent.

Ao ouvir a voz dele, Sara ficou inexplicavelmente sem palavras. No silêncio, ela conseguiu ouvir o vento soprando e o som de crianças brincando.

Ele disse:

— Alô?

— Oi, Will... desculpe. — Ela pigarreou. — Estou ligando porque falei com alguém do IML. Como você pediu. — Ela sentiu o rosto ficando vermelho. — Como Amanda pediu.

Ele murmurou algo, provavelmente para Amanda.

— O que você descobriu?

— A vítima dos Texicanos, Ricardo. Ainda sem sobrenome, mas provavelmente era porto-riquenho. — Ela esperou enquanto ele transmitia a informação a Amanda. Ela fez a mesma pergunta que Sara fizera. Sara respondeu: — Ele tinha uma tatuagem de facção, da Neta, que fica em Porto Rico, na mão. O homem que falou comigo disse que provavelmente Ricardo mudou a afiliação quando veio para Atlanta. — De novo, ela esperou que ele contasse a Amanda. — Ele também tinha um monte de heroína na barriga.

— Heroína? — A voz dele ficou aguda com a surpresa. — Quanto?

— Não sei bem. O homem que falou comigo disse que o pó estava dentro de pequenos balões. Quando Faith atirou nele, a heroína foi liberada. Só isso já teria matado o cara.

Will repetiu aquilo a Amanda, depois voltou à linha.

— Amanda está agradecendo por você ter apurado isso.

— Lamento não ter mais informação.

— O que você conseguiu está ótimo. — Ele esclareceu: — Quer dizer, obrigado, Dra. Linton. Todas essas informações são muito úteis.

Ela sabia que ele não podia falar na frente de Amanda, mas não queria desligar ainda.

— Como as coisas estão andando por aí?

— A ida à prisão não deu em nada. Estamos na frente da casa de Hironobu Kwon agora. Ele morava com a mãe em Grant Park. — Ele estava a menos de quinze minutos do Grady. — O vizinho disse que a mãe dele deve voltar já, já. Acho que ela deve estar organizando o velório e essas coisas. Ela mora em frente ao zoológico. A gente teve que estacionar a mais ou menos um quilômetro e meio do local. Eu tive, pelo menos. Amanda me fez deixá-la aqui em frente. — Enfim, ele parou para respirar. — Como você está?

Sara sorriu. Ele parecia querer continuar no telefone tanto quanto ela.

— Você conseguiu dormir alguma coisa ontem à noite?

— Não muito. E você?

Ela tentou pensar em algo sedutor para responder, mas acabou com:

— Não muito.

A voz de Amanda estava abafada demais para entender, mas Sara pegou o tom. Will disse:

— Então, a gente se fala mais tarde. Obrigado de novo, Dra. Linton.

Sara se sentiu tola ao desligar. Talvez devesse voltar à sala de descanso e fofocar com Nan.

Ou talvez devesse falar com Dale Dugan e acabar logo com aquilo, antes de os dois passarem ainda mais vergonha. Sara pegou o BlackBerry do hospital e procurou o e-mail de Dale, depois começou a inserir o contato no seu iPhone. Ia pedir para ele a encontrar na lanchonete para poderem conversar sobre esse assunto. Ou talvez sugerisse o estacionamento. Ela não queria causar mais fofocas do que as que já estavam circulando.

Lá na frente, o elevador fez *plim* e ela viu Dale. Estava rindo com uma das enfermeiras. Júnior devia ter dito que ela estava ali embaixo.

Sara perdeu a coragem. Abriu a primeira porta que encontrou, que por acaso era do departamento de registros médicos. Duas mulheres mais velhas com permanentes combinando, bem arrumados, estavam atrás de mesas com pilhas de prontuários. Digitavam furiosamente nos teclados dos computadores e mal levantaram os olhos para Sara.

Virando a página no prontuário aberto ao lado, uma delas perguntou:

— Posso ajudar?

Sara ficou lá parada, por um momento sem saber o que fazer. Percebeu que, em algum lugar bem lá no fundo, estava pensando no departamento de registros desde que entrara no elevador. Jogou o iPhone de volta no bolso do jaleco.

— O que foi, meu bem? — perguntou a mulher.

As duas a encaravam naquele momento.

Sara levantou o crachá do hospital.

— Preciso de um prontuário antigo de mil novecentos e... — Ela fez o cálculo rapidamente de cabeça. — Setenta e seis, talvez?

A mulher entregou a ela um bloco e uma caneta.

— Me dê o nome. Isso vai facilitar.

Sara soube, mesmo enquanto escrevia o nome de Will, que o que estava fazendo era errado, e não só porque estava violando leis federais de privacidade e arriscando uma demissão sumária. Will tinha estado no Lar de Crianças de Atlanta desde bebê. Não devia ter médico de família cuidando dele. Todas as suas necessidades médicas teriam sido resolvidas no Grady. Toda a infância dele estava armazenada ali, e Sara estava usando seu crachá do hospital para ter acesso a isso.

— Sem nome do meio? — perguntou a mulher.

Sara fez que não. Não confiava em si mesma para falar nada.

— Me dê um minuto. Não vai estar no computador, senão você conseguiria puxar no seu tablet. A gente mal pôs os pés nos anos 1970.

A mulher se levantou da cadeira e entrou pela porta indicada como "Sala de Arquivo" antes que Sara pudesse interrompê-la.

A outra voltou a digitar, com as unhas vermelhas compridas fazendo um som de gato correndo por um piso de azulejo. Sara olhou os próprios sapatos, manchados, só Deus sabe com o quê, depois dos casos da manhã. Mentalmente, ela repassou os possíveis culpados, mas, por mais que tentasse, não conseguia deixar de sentir que o que estava fazendo era absolutamente e sem nenhuma dúvida a coisa mais antiética que já tinha feito na vida toda. Além do mais, era uma traição completa da confiança de Will.

E ela não podia fazer aquilo. Não ia fazer.

Não era assim que Sara agia. Em geral, ela era uma pessoa bem direta. Se quisesse saber sobre a tentativa de suicídio de Will ou algum detalhe sobre a infância dele, devia perguntar a ele, não agir pelas suas costas e olhar seu prontuário médico.

A mulher tinha voltado.

— Nenhum William, mas achei um Wilbur. — Ela estava com uma pasta embaixo do braço. — De 1975.

Sara tinha usado prontuários de papel durante a maior parte da carreira. Aos dezoito anos, a maioria das crianças saudáveis tinha um de umas vinte páginas. O prontuário de uma criança doente podia ter lá por cinquenta. O de Will tinha quase três centímetros de grossura. Um elástico se desfazendo unia folhas de papel branco e amarelo desbotado.

— Sem nome do meio — disse a mulher. — Com certeza em algum momento ele teve, mas várias dessas crianças não recebiam um acompanhamento adequado naquela época.

A colega dela comentou:

— Ellis Island e Tuskegee, tudo misturado.

Sara estendeu a mão para a pasta, e então se deteve. Sua mão ficou pairando no ar.

— Você está bem, querida? — A mulher olhou para sua colega atrás, depois se voltou para Sara. — Precisa se sentar?

Sara abaixou a mão.

— Acho que, na verdade, não preciso disso. Desculpe por desperdiçar seu tempo.

— Certeza?

Sara fez que sim. Não conseguia se lembrar da última vez que tinha se sentido tão mal. Nem seu encontro com Angie Trent tinha gerado tanta culpa.

— Me desculpe mesmo.

— Não precisa pedir desculpas. Foi bom levantar.

Ela começou a guardar a pasta debaixo do braço, mas o elástico estourou e os papéis saíram voando pelo chão.

Automaticamente, Sara se abaixou para ajudar. Juntou as páginas, obrigando-se a não ler as palavras. Havia resultados de exames, impressos em matriz de pontos, resmas de anotações de prontuário e o que parecia um antigo boletim de ocorrência da polícia de Atlanta. Ela borrou a visão, rezando para não identificar uma palavra ou frase.

— Veja só.

Sara levantou os olhos. Era uma reação natural. A mulher segurava uma Polaroid desbotada. A foto era um close da boca da criança. Havia uma pequena régua prateada ao lado de uma laceração da largura do filtro labial, o sulco do meio entre o topo do lábio e o nariz. O ferimento não vinha de uma queda ou batida. O impacto tinha sido significativo o bastante para abrir a pele ao meio, revelando os dentes. Pontos pretos grossos uniam a ferida. A pele estava inchada e irritada. Sara estava mais acostumada a ver esse tipo de ponto desleixado num necrotério, não no rosto de uma criança.

— Aposto que ele estava naquele estudo de poli-sei-lá-das-quantas — comentou a mulher, mostrando a foto à amiga.

— Ácido poliglicólico. — Ela explicou a Sara: — O Grady liderou um estudo sobre diferentes tipos de suturas absorvíveis que estavam criando na Tech. Pelo jeito, ele foi uma das crianças que tiveram reação alérgica. Tadinho. — Ela voltou a digitar. — Mas acho ainda melhor do que grudar um monte de sanguessugas nele.

A outra perguntou a Sara:

— Você está bem, anjo?

Sara teve vontade de vomitar. Endireitou-se e saiu da sala. Só parou de andar depois que subiu correndo dois lances de escada e chegou lá fora, ao ar fresco.

Ela ficou andando de lá para cá em frente à porta fechada. Suas emoções iam de raiva para vergonha como uma bola de Pinball. Ele era tão pequeno. Tinha sido internado para um tratamento e passado por um experimento, como um animal. Provavelmente ainda não fazia ideia do que haviam feito. E, por Deus, como Sara queria também não saber, mas era bem feito para ela, por ter sido enxerida. Ela nunca devia ter pedido o prontuário dele. Mas ela o tinha feito e agora não conseguia tirar aquela imagem da cabeça — a boca linda dele unida de qualquer jeito com uma sutura que não atendia nem aos padrões básicos para ser aprovada pelo governo.

A Polaroid desbotada ia ficar gravada a fogo em sua memória até o dia de sua morte. Era exatamente o que ela merecia.

— Ei, você.

Ela se virou. Havia uma jovem parada atrás dela. Era terrivelmente magra. Seu cabelo loiro oleoso batia na cintura. Ela coçou as marcas recentes de agulha nos braços.

— Você é médica?

Sara ficou na defensiva. Os drogados viviam ao redor do hospital. Alguns podiam ser violentos.

— Se você precisa de atendimento, é melhor entrar.

— Não sou eu. Tem um cara ali. — Ela apontou para a caçamba de lixo num canto atrás do hospital. Mesmo à luz do dia, a área ficava escura pela sombra que a fachada alta do prédio fazia. — Ele passou a noite toda lá. Acho que está morto.

Sara moderou o tom.

— Vamos entrar e conversar sobre isso.

Os olhos da menina brilharam de ódio.

— Olha só, eu tô tentando ajudar. Não precisa ficar toda se achando.

— Eu não...

— Tomara que ele te passe aids, sua puta.

Ela saiu mancando e murmurando mais insultos.

— Nossa — ofegou Sara, perguntando-se como o dia podia piorar.

Como tinha saudade da educação das pessoas de bem do interior, onde até os drogados a chamavam de "senhora". Ela começou a retornar para o hospital, mas parou. A menina podia estar falando a verdade.

Sara caminhou até a caçamba, sem se aproximar demais, para o caso de o cúmplice da garota estar escondido lá dentro. O lixo não tinha sido levado no fim de semana. Caixas e sacolas plásticas saíam do contêiner de metal e sujavam o chão. Sara se aproximou. Havia alguém deitado embaixo de uma sacola de plástico azul. Ela viu a mão. Um corte fundo na palma. Trabalhar no Grady a deixara hipercautelosa. Ainda podia ser uma armadilha. Em vez de ir até o corpo, ela se virou e correu na direção da área das ambulâncias para pedir ajuda.

Havia três paramédicos parados lá, batendo papo. Ela os levou até os fundos do prédio e eles a seguiram com uma maca. Sara afastou o lixo. O homem estava respirando, mas inconsciente. Seus olhos estavam fechados. A pele marrom estava com uma aparência amarelada de cera. A camiseta estava ensopada de sangue, obviamente vindo de um ferimento perfurante no baixo-ventre. Sara pressionou os dedos na carótida e viu uma tatuagem familiar no pescoço: uma estrela do Texas com uma cascavel ao redor.

O B negativo desaparecido de Will.

— Vamos — disse um dos paramédicos.

Sara correu ao lado da maca enquanto entravam com o homem no hospital. Escutou os médicos tirarem os sinais vitais ao mesmo tempo em que ela puxava a gaze da barriga dele. A entrada do ferimento era fina, provavelmente feita com uma faca de cozinha. A borda era irregular por causa da serra. Havia pouco sangue novo, indicando um sangramento fechado. A barriga estava distendida e o odor característico de pele apodrecendo indicava que ela não conseguiria fazer muito por ele no pronto-socorro.

Um homem alto de terno escuro correu ao lado dela. Ele perguntou:

— Ele vai sobreviver?

Sara procurou George. O segurança não estava em lugar nenhum.

— O senhor precisa se afastar.

— Doutora... — Ele levantou a carteira. Ela viu o flash do distintivo dourado. — Eu sou policial. Ele vai sobreviver?

— Não sei — disse ela, pressionando a gaze de volta no lugar. E então, como o paciente talvez estivesse ouvindo, ela respondeu: — Talvez.

O policial ficou para trás. Ela olhou para o corredor, mas ele havia sumido.

A equipe de trauma agiu de imediato, cortando as roupas do homem, tirando sangue, conectando fios para ligá-lo a várias máquinas.

Uma bandeja cirúrgica foi disposta. Pacotes de instrumentos foram abertos. O carrinho de emergência apareceu.

Sara pediu dois acessos venosos de alto fluxo para administrar fluidos. Confirmou que as vias aéreas estavam liberadas, a respiração estava ok e a circulação, tão boa quanto se podia esperar. Notou o ritmo diminuir consideravelmente conforme as pessoas começavam a perceber com o que estavam lidando. A equipe foi rareando. No fim, ela estava só com uma enfermeira.

— Sem carteira — disse a enfermeira. — Nada nos bolsos, só fiapo.

— Senhor? — tentou Sara, abrindo os olhos do homem.

As pupilas estavam fixas e dilatadas. Ela examinou a cabeça, para ver se havia ferimento, pressionando delicadamente os dedos num padrão em sentido horário pelo couro cabeludo. No osso occipital, sentiu uma fratura com fragmentação penetrante no crânio. Olhou a luva. Não havia sangue fresco do ferimento.

A enfermeira fechou a cortina para dar um pouco de privacidade ao homem.

— Radiografia? Tomografia de abdome?

Sara estava tecnicamente fazendo o trabalho do plantonista. Pediu:

— Pode chamar o Krakauer?

A enfermeira saiu, e Sara fez um exame mais completo, embora soubesse que Krakauer ia dar uma única olhada nos sinais vitais e concordar com ela. Não tinha emergência nenhuma. O paciente não sobreviveria à anestesia geral e provavelmente nem aos ferimentos. Só podiam enchê-lo de antibióticos e esperar que o tempo decidisse seu destino.

A cortina foi aberta. Um jovem olhou lá dentro. Estava de barba feita, com uma jaqueta esportiva preta e um boné preto puxado bem para baixo.

— Você não pode entrar aqui — disse ela. — Se estiver procurando o...

Ele deu um soco tão forte no peito de Sara que ela caiu no chão. O ombro dela bateu numa das bandejas. Instrumentos de metal causaram um estrondo ao seu redor — bisturis, pinças hemostáticas, tesouras. O jovem apontou uma arma para a cabeça do paciente e atirou duas vezes.

Sara ouviu gritos. Eram dela. O som saía de sua própria boca. O homem apontou a arma para a cabeça de Sara, e ela parou. Ele foi em sua direção. Ela tateou cegamente atrás de algo para se proteger. Sua mão se fechou em um dos bisturis.

Ele estava perto, quase em cima dela. Pretendia atirar nela ou ir embora? Sara não lhe deu tempo para decidir. Atacou, cortando o interior da coxa dele. O homem gemeu e soltou a arma. A ferida era funda. O sangue jorrou da artéria femoral. Ele caiu apoiado em um joelho. Os dois viram a arma ao mesmo tempo. Ela a chutou para longe. Ele, por sua vez, foi para cima de Sara, agarrando a mão dela que segurava o bisturi. Ela tentou puxar o braço para trás, mas ele segurou seus pulsos com mais força. O pânico a dominou quando ela percebeu o que ele estava fazendo. A lâmina estava indo na direção de seu pescoço. Ela usou as duas mãos, tentando empurrá-lo enquanto ele aproximava cada vez mais a lâmina.

— Por favor... não...

Ele estava em cima dela, pressionando-a no chão com o peso do corpo. Ela olhou seus olhos verdes. A parte branca estava cruzada com linhas vermelhas que pareciam um mapa rodoviário. A boca era uma linha reta. O corpo dele tremia tanto que ela sentia na própria coluna.

— Solte isso! — George, o segurança, ficou parado com a arma apontada à frente. — Agora, filho da puta!

Sara sentiu o homem apertar mais forte. As mãos deles tremiam de empurrar em direções opostas.

— Solte agora!

— Por favor — Sara implorou.

Seus músculos não conseguiriam aguentar muito mais. As mãos dela começaram a enfraquecer.

Sem aviso, a pressão parou. Sara viu o bisturi fazer um movimento para cima e a lâmina cortar a pele do homem. Ele manteve a mão firme em torno da dela enquanto enfiava várias vezes o bisturi na própria garganta.

10

Will tinha passado tanto tempo preso no carro com Amanda que estava preocupado de desenvolver síndrome de Estocolmo. Já estava se sentindo enfraquecido, especialmente depois de Miriam Kown, mãe de Hironobu Kown, cuspir na cara de Amanda.

Em defesa da Sra. Kwon, Amanda não tinha sido exatamente delicada com a mulher. Os dois tinham praticamente emboscado a mulher no jardim de entrada da própria casa. Ela obviamente tinha acabado de resolver questões relativas ao velório do filho. Estava com panfletos cheios de cruzes espremidos nas mãos ao se aproximar de casa. A rua dela estava cheia de carros. Ela precisara estacionar meio longe. Parecia exausta e sem forças, como qualquer mãe pareceria depois de escolher o caixão em que o único filho seria enterrado.

Depois de murmurar as condolências obrigatórias em nome da GBI, Amanda tinha ido direto na jugular. Pela reação da Sra. Kown, Will entendeu que a mulher não estava esperando que o nome do filho morto fosse manchado daquele jeito, apesar das circunstâncias nefastas de sua morte. A tradição das emissoras de notícias de Atlanta era que todo jovem morto com menos de vinte e cinco anos fosse celebrado como estudante exemplar até que provassem o contrário. Segundo sua ficha criminal, esse estudante exemplar em especial tinha sido fã de oxicodona. Hironobu Kwon tinha sido preso duas vezes por vender a droga. Só seu potencial acadêmico o havia salvado de um bom tempo na cadeia. O juiz o mandara para uma clínica de reabilitação três meses atrás. Pelo jeito, não tinha dado muito certo.

Will olhou o horário no celular. A mudança recente para o horário de verão tinha colocado os números em formato militar, de vinte e

213

quatro horas. Ele não conseguia de jeito nenhum descobrir como voltar o relógio ao horário de doze em doze. Felizmente, era meio-dia e meia, então ele não precisava ficar fazendo conta nos dedos que nem um macaquinho.

Não que ele não tivesse bastante tempo para equações matemáticas. Apesar de terem percorrido quase oitocentos quilômetros naquela manhã, eles não tinham resultado nenhum para apresentar. Evelyn Mitchell continuava desaparecida. Estavam prestes a se completar vinte e quatro horas desde o sequestro. Os cadáveres estavam se empilhando e a única pista que Will e Amanda haviam recebido até ali tinha vindo da boca de um presidiário do corredor da morte que fora assassinado antes de o Estado conseguir matá-lo.

A ida até a Prisão Estadual de Valdosta podia muito bem nem ter acontecido. Os ex-detetives do esquadrão de narcóticos Adam Hopkins e Ben Humphrey tinham ficado encarando Amanda como se ela fosse invisível. Will já esperava aquilo. Anos antes, tinham se recusado a falar com ele, que aparecera na porta de cada um. Lloyd Crittenden estava morto. Demarcus Alexander e Chuck Finn provavelmente estavam igualmente fora de alcance. Os dois ex-detetives haviam ido embora de Atlanta assim que foram soltos da prisão. Will falara com os oficiais de condicional de ambos na noite anterior. Alexander estava na Costa Oeste tentando reconstruir a vida. Finn estava no Tennessee, se afundando na desgraça do vício em drogas.

— Heroína — falou Will.

Amanda se virou e olhou para ele como se tivesse esquecido que ele estava no carro. Estavam indo para o norte na rodovia interestadual 85, atrás de outro criminoso que muito provavelmente se recusaria a falar com eles.

Ele explicou:

— Boyd Spivey falou que Chuck Finn estava viciado em heroína. Segundo Sara, Ricardo estava carregado de heroína.

— É uma conexão bem tênue.

— Então, aqui vai mais uma: oxicodona em geral leva a vício em heroína.

— Está forçando bem a barra. Não dá para jogar uma pedra hoje em dia sem atingir um viciado em heroína. — Ela suspirou. — Quem me dera ter mais pedras.

Will batucou com os dedos na perna. Estava segurando uma informação a manhã inteira, torcendo para pegar Amanda desprevenida e arrancar a verdade. Aquele momento parecia tão bom quanto qualquer outro.

— O namoradinho de Evelyn era Hector Ortiz.

Ela levantou o canto da boca.

— Ah, é?

— É irmão de Ignatio Ortiz, apesar de eu estar percebendo, pela sua expressão, que isso não é muita novidade.

— Primo de Ortiz — corrigiu ela. — Essas observações são cortesia da Dra. Linton?

Will sentiu os dentes começando a se pressionar.

— Você já sabia quem ele era.

— Quer passar os próximos dez minutos discutindo seus sentimentos ou quer fazer seu trabalho?

Ele queria passar os próximos dez minutos esganando Amanda, mas decidiu guardar isso para si.

— O que Evelyn estava fazendo metida com o primo do cara que controla toda a cocaína que entra e sai do sudeste dos Estados Unidos?

— Hector na verdade era vendedor de carro. — Ela o olhou. Tinha algo parecido com humor em seus olhos. — Ele vendia Cadillacs.

Isso explicava por que o nome do cara não tinha surgido na busca por veículo feita por Will. Ele estava dirigindo um carro de concessionária.

— Hector tinha uma tatuagem dos Texicanos no braço.

— Todo mundo comete erros na juventude.

Will tentou ainda:

— E a letra *A* que Evelyn desenhou embaixo da cadeira?

— Achei que a gente estava chamando de flecha, não?

— *Almeja* parece com "Amanda".

— Parece um pouco mesmo, né?

— É gíria para "vagabunda".

Ela riu.

— Ora, ora, Will, você está me chamando de vagabunda?

Se ela soubesse quantas vezes ele tinha se sentido tentado a fazer isso...

— Acho que eu devia recompensá-lo por um bom trabalho de investigação. — Amanda puxou uma folha de papel dobrada do quebra-sol e entregou a Will. — As ligações de Evelyn das últimas quatro semanas.

Ele passou os olhos pelas duas páginas.

— Ela andou telefonando muito para Chattanooga.

Amanda lhe lançou um olhar curioso. Will a encarou de volta, sério. Ele sabia ler, só não rápido e com certeza não com alguém o observando. A sucursal do leste do Tennessee Bureau of Investigation ficava em Chattanooga. Quando trabalhava no norte da Geórgia, ele ligava constantemente para coordenar casos envolvendo metanfetaminas. O código de área 423 aparecia pelo menos doze vezes nos registros telefônicos de Evelyn.

Ele perguntou:

— Tem alguma coisa que você queira me contar?

Ela ficou em silêncio, o que era uma novidade.

Will puxou o celular para ligar para o número.

— Deixe de ser tonto. É a Healing Winds, uma clínica de reabilitação.

— Por que ela estava ligando para lá?

— Eu tive a mesma dúvida. — Ela deu seta e trocou de faixa. — Eles não têm permissão de dar informações dos pacientes.

Will comparou as datas com os números. Evelyn só tinha começado a ligar para a clínica nos últimos dez dias, mesmo período em que a Sra. Levy disse que as visitas de Hector Ortiz a Evelyn aumentaram.

Will comentou:

— Chuck Finn mora no Tennessee.

— Ele mora em Memphis. Fica a cinco horas de carro da Healing Winds em Chattanooga.

— Ele tinha um vício sério em drogas. — Will esperou que ela respondesse. Quando não aconteceu, ele continuou: — Os caras ficam

216

limpos e às vezes querem desabafar. Talvez Evelyn tivesse medo de ele começar a falar.

— Que teoria interessante.

— Ou talvez Chuck tenha precisado limpar a mente para perceber que Evelyn continuava sentada na parte dela do dinheiro. — Ele insistiu: — É difícil achar trabalho com uma ficha criminal que nem a de Chuck. Ele foi expulso da polícia. Passou muito tempo na prisão. Precisa lutar contra o vício. Mesmo estando limpo, ninguém ia se esforçar para contratar o cara. Não com a economia do jeito que está.

Amanda deu mais uma pequena dose de informação:

— Havia oito conjuntos de digitais na casa de Evelyn, excluindo as dela e de Hector. Identificaram três. Um conjunto era de Hironobu Kwon, outro era de Ricardo, a mula de heroína, e outro pertencia ao nosso fã de camisa havaiana. O nome dele é Benny Choo. É um capanga de quarenta e dois anos dos Yellow Rebels.

— Yellow Rebels?

— É uma facção asiática. Não me pergunte de onde tiraram esse nome. Imagino que tenham muito orgulho de ser caipiras. A maioria tem.

— Ling-Ling — chutou Will. Era quem eles iam visitar. — Spivey disse que você devia falar com Ling-Ling.

— Julia Ling.

Will ficou surpreso.

— Uma mulher?

— É, uma mulher. Minha nossa, como o mundo mudou. — Amanda olhou no retrovisor e voou para a faixa ao lado. — O apelido vem da impressão, que agora já se mostrou errada, de que ela não é muito esperta. O irmão dela gosta de rimas. Ele dizia "dling-dling" para representar um sino tocando na cabeça dela. Virou "Ling-Ling".

Will não entendeu nada do que ela estava falando.

— Faz sentido.

— A senhora Ling é a chefe da Yellow Rebels aqui fora. O irmão dela, Roger, ainda controla as coisas de dentro da prisão, mas ela cuida do dia a dia. Se a Yellow está tentando controlar os hispânicos, isso está sendo feito pelo Roger por meio da Ling-Ling.

— Por que ele foi preso?

— Pegou prisão perpétua por estupro e homicídio de duas adolescentes. De dezesseis e catorze anos. Elas estavam se prostituindo em nome dele. Ele não achava que estavam trazendo dinheiro suficiente, então, estrangulou as duas com uma coleira de cachorro. Mas não antes de as estuprar e rasgar os seios delas com os dentes.

Will sentiu um tremor subindo pela espinha.

— Por que ele não está no corredor da morte?

— Fez um acordo. O Estado estava preocupado de ele alegar insanidade; e, cá entre nós, não seria absurdo, porque o homem é completamente maluco. Não foi a primeira vez que Roger foi pego com carne humana na boca.

O tremor fez os ombros dele se encolherem.

— E as vítimas?

— As duas eram meninas que tinham fugido de casa e caído nas drogas e na prostituição. As famílias delas acreditavam mais em castigo divino do que em olho por olho.

Will estava familiarizado com o conceito.

— Elas provavelmente tinham motivo para fugir.

— As jovens costumam ter mesmo.

— A irmã de Roger ainda o apoia?

Ela lhe lançou um olhar significativo.

— Não se engane, Will. Julia é cheia de lábia, mas é capaz de cortar sua garganta e não perder um minuto de sono. Essa gente não é flor que se cheire. Temos que seguir vários procedimentos. Você precisa demonstrar o máximo de respeito.

Will repetiu as palavras de Boyd:

— "Você não pode ir direto até os amarelos sem convite."

— Sua memória é incrível.

Will conferiu o número da saída seguinte. Estavam indo em direção à rodovia Buford. Camboja.

— Talvez Boyd só estivesse certo em parte. Heroína é bem mais viciante que cocaína. Se a Yellow Rebels inundar o mercado com heroína barata, a Los Texicanos vai perder a base de clientes de cocaína. Isso aponta para uma luta por poder, mas não explica por que dois asiáticos e um Texicano estavam na casa de Evelyn Mitchell procurando alguma coisa. — Will parou. Ela o tinha desviado outra vez do caminho. — Hironobu Kwon e Benny Choo. Qual o sobrenome de Ricardo?

Ela sorriu.

— Excelente. — Ela ofereceu a informação como mais uma recompensa: — Ricardo Ortiz. É o filho mais novo de Ignatio Ortiz.

Will tinha entrevistado assassinos a sangue-frio mais comunicativos que ela.

— E estava sendo mula de heroína.

— Estava.

— Você vai me dizer se alguns desses caras estão conectados ou preciso descobrir sozinho?

— Ricardo Ortiz foi para o reformatório duas vezes, mas nunca cruzou com Hironobu Kwon lá dentro. Nenhum dos dois tem conexões visíveis com Benny Choo e, como falei, Hector Ortiz era um simples vendedor de carros. — Ela ultrapassou um caminhão de entregas, cortando um Hyundai no processo. — Pode acreditar, se eu visse uma conexão entre qualquer um desses homens, estaríamos trabalhando nela.

— Com exceção de Choo, são todos jovens, com vinte e poucos anos.

Will tentou pensar em onde poderiam ter se conhecido. Reuniões do AA. Casas noturnas. Quadras de basquete. Igreja, quem sabe. Miriam Kwon usava uma cruz dourada no pescoço. Ricardo Ortiz tinha uma cruz tatuada no braço. Não seria a coisa mais estranha que já aconteceu.

Amanda disse:

— Olha o número para o qual Evelyn ligou um dia antes de ser levada. Às três e dois da tarde.

Will passou o dedo embaixo da primeira coluna, achando o horário. Moveu-o na horizontal. O número tinha um código de área de Atlanta.

— Eu deveria reconhecer isso?

— Eu ficaria surpresa se reconhecesse. É o número da delegacia de Hartsfield. — Hartsfield-Jackson, aeroporto de Atlanta. — Vanessa

Livingston é a comandante. É uma velha amiga de muitos anos. Ela foi parceira de Evelyn depois que eu saí da polícia de Atlanta.

Will esperou, antes de perguntar:

— E?

— Evelyn pediu para ela procurar um nome nos manifestos de passageiros.

— Ricardo Ortiz — chutou Will.

— Você deve ter dormido bem ontem à noite.

Ele tinha ficado acordado até as três da manhã escutando o resto das gravações, aparentemente sem motivo nenhum exceto descobrir coisas que Amanda já sabia.

— De onde Ricardo estava vindo?

— Da Suécia.

Will franziu a testa. Não estava esperando aquilo.

Amanda saiu para a rampa da I-285.

— Noventa por cento de toda a heroína do mundo vem do Afeganistão. O imposto que a gente paga está funcionando. — Ela desacelerou para fazer a curva no entroncamento. — O grosso do fornecimento europeu passa pelo Irã, subindo para a Turquia e pontos mais ao norte.

— Como a Suécia.

— Como a Suécia. — Ela acelerou de novo enquanto entravam na pista de alta velocidade. — Ricardo ficou três dias lá. Depois pegou um voo de Gotemburgo até Amsterdã, depois direto para Atlanta.

— Cheio de heroína.

— Cheio de heroína.

Will esfregou o maxilar, pensando no que tinha acontecido com o homem.

— Alguém espancou o cara. Ele estava cheio de balões. Talvez não tenha conseguido evacuar.

— Seria uma pergunta para o legista.

Will tinha suposto que ela recebera todas essas informações do IML.

— Você não perguntou para ele?

— Eles gentilmente me prometeram o relatório completo até o fim do expediente de hoje. Por que você acha que eu mandei você pedir para Sara falar com eles? — Ela completou: — E como vai essa situação, aliás? Suponho, pela sua boa noite de sono, que sem muito progresso.

Estavam chegando na saída da rodovia Buford. A U.S. Route 23 ia de Jacksonville, Flórida, a Mackinaw City, Michigan. O trecho da Geórgia tinha cerca de seiscentos e quarenta quilômetros, e a parte que passava por Chamblee, Norcross e Doraville era uma das mais racialmente diversas da região, se não do país. Não era exatamente um bairro — parecia mais uma série de centros comerciais desolados, prédios residenciais frágeis e postos de gasolina que ofereciam rodas caras e empréstimos rápidos usando seu carro como garantia. O que faltava em termos de comunidade era compensado com o comércio rudimentar.

Will tinha quase certeza de que Camboja era um termo pejorativo, mas o nome para a área tinha pegado, apesar do esforço do condado de DeKalb de chamá-la de Corredor Internacional. Havia gente de muitos povos diferentes, de portugueses a hmongs. Ao contrário da maioria das áreas urbanas, não parecia haver uma linha clara de segregação entre as comunidades. Consequentemente, dava para encontrar um restaurante mexicano ao lado de um de sushi, e o mercado de orgânicos era o tipo de caldeirão em que as pessoas pensavam quando imaginavam os Estados Unidos.

Aquela faixa era bem mais próxima da terra das oportunidades do que as ondas cor de âmbar de plantações de grãos no interior. As pessoas podiam chegar lá com pouco mais do que alguma ética profissional e mesmo assim construir uma vida estável de classe média. Desde que Will se lembrava, a população demográfica vivia em constante fluxo. Os brancos reclamaram quando os negros chegaram. Os negros reclamaram quando os hispânicos chegaram. Os hispânicos reclamaram quando os asiáticos chegaram. Um dia, todos estariam resmungando do influxo de brancos. A corrida de rato do sonho americano.

Amanda entrou na faixa do meio, que servia como pista de retorno para os dois lados da rodovia. Will viu um monte de placas empilhadas uma em cima da outra, como um jogo de Jenga. Alguns caracteres eram irreconhecíveis, parecendo mais obras de arte do que letras.

— Estou com um carro no endereço comercial de Ling-Ling a manhã inteira. Ela não recebeu nenhuma visita. — Amanda pisou no acelerador e por pouco não bateu em uma minivan ao fazer a curva. Buzinas soaram, mas ela falou por cima do barulho. — Dei alguns telefonemas ontem. Roger foi transferido para a Coastal há três meses. Ele tinha ficado seis meses no Augusta, mas os remédios o estabilizaram, então ele voltou para o confinamento. — O Augusta Medical Hospital fornecia serviços temporários de saúde mental nível 4 para detentos. — O primeiro dia do Roger na Coastal acabou com um incidente feio envolvendo uma barra de sabão embrulhada numa meia. Aparentemente, ele não está feliz com a nova acomodação.

— Você vai oferecer de transferir o cara?

— Se chegarmos a isso.

— Vai usar o nome de Boyd?

— Talvez não seja uma boa ideia.

— O que você acha que vamos conseguir com Roger? — Mentalmente, Will deu um tapa na testa. — Você acha que ele está por trás do sequestro de Evelyn.

— Ele pode ser clinicamente louco, mas nunca seria idiota de fazer uma coisa dessas. — Ela deu um olhar sério para Will. — Roger é extremamente inteligente. Pense em um jogo de xadrez, não de dama. Ele não tem nada a ganhar levando Evelyn. Toda a organização dele seria afetada.

— Certo, então, você acha que Roger sabe quem está envolvido?

— Se você quer saber de um crime, pergunte para um criminoso. — O celular dela começou a tocar. Ela conferiu o número. Will sentiu o carro desacelerar. Amanda parou no acostamento. Ela atendeu, escutou, e então apertou o botão de destrancar a porta. — Um pouco de privacidade, por favor?

Will saiu da SUV. O clima estava maravilhoso no dia anterior, mas naquele momento estava nublado e quente. Ele caminhou na direção da esquina do centro comercial. Havia um restaurante rústico perto da entrada da rua. Ele chutou, pela cadeira de balanço pintada na placa, que fosse algum estabelecimento de cozinha do interior. Estranhamente, pensar em comida não fez o estômago de Will roncar. A última coisa que ele havia comido era uma tigela de mingau instantâneo que ele se forçou a engolir de manhã. Estava sem apetite, coisa que só tinha experimentado uma vez antes na vida — da última vez que passara um tempo com Sara Linton.

Will se sentou no meio-fio. Carros passavam rápido atrás. Ouvia fragmentos de músicas que vinham dos rádios deles. Um olhar para Amanda lhe disse que ela ia demorar um tempo. Estava gesticulando com as mãos, o que nunca era bom sinal.

Ele pegou o celular e passou pelos números. Ele devia ligar para Faith, mas não tinha nada para relatar e a conversa da noite anterior não tinha acabado bem. O que quer que tivesse acontecido com Evelyn não ia melhorar as coisas. Não importava qual fosse a manobra verbal ardilosa de Amanda, ainda existiam alguns fatos que ela não podia contornar só usando lábia. Se os asiáticos realmente estavam tentando tomar o mercado de drogas dos Texicanos, então Evelyn Mitchell devia estar no centro do negócio. Hector podia se chamar de vendedor de carros, mas ainda tinha a tatuagem que o ligava à facção. Ainda tinha um primo na prisão liderando aquela mesma organização. Seu sobrinho tinha levado um tiro e morrido na casa de Evelyn, e o próprio Hector estava morto no porta-malas dela. Não tinha motivo para uma policial, especialmente aposentada, estar metida com esse tipo de criminoso, a não ser que estivesse rolando alguma sujeira.

Will baixou os olhos para o celular. Treze horas. Ele devia ir até o menu de configurações e tentar descobrir como voltar ao mostrador normal, mas não tinha paciência naquele momento. Em vez disso, rolou os contatos até o número de Sara, que tinha três oitos. Ele tinha ficado olhando fixamente para os números tantas vezes nos últimos meses que estava surpreso de eles não estarem gravados a fogo em suas retinas.

A não ser que se contasse o mal-entendido infeliz com a lésbica que morava em frente à casa dele, Will nunca tivera um encontro de verdade. Ele estava com Angie desde os oito anos de idade. Em algum momento, houve paixão e, por um tempo curto, algo que parecia próximo a amor, mas ele não conseguia se lembrar de um período na vida em que tivesse se sentido feliz de estar com ela. Ele vivia com medo de ela aparecer na porta. Sentia um alívio enorme quando ela ia embora. Onde ela o conquistava era o meio do caminho, aqueles raros momentos de paz em que ele tinha um vislumbre de como uma vida tranquila poderia ser. Eles comiam juntos, iam ao mercado e cuidavam do jardim — ou Will cuidava e Angie ficava olhando —, e então, à noite, iam se deitar e ele se via na cama com um sorriso, porque a vida era assim para o resto do mundo.

E então, quando ele acordava de manhã, ela tinha ido embora.

Eles eram próximos demais. Esse era o problema. Tinham passado por coisas de mais, visto horrores de mais, compartilhado medo, ódio e pena de mais para se verem como algo mais do que vítimas. O corpo de Will era como um monumento a essa infelicidade: as marcas de queimadura, as cicatrizes, os vários golpes que ele sofrera. Por anos, ele quisera mais de Angie, mas, recentemente, Will tinha chegado à dura conclusão de que não tinha nada mais que ela pudesse dar.

Ela não ia mudar. Ele sabia dessa verdade mesmo quando finalmente se casaram, o que acontecera não depois de um planejamento cuidadoso, mas porque Will havia apostado com Angie que ela não iria até o fim com aquilo. Mesmo sem a aposta, ela nunca veria estar com Will como outra coisa senão um porto seguro, na melhor das hipóteses, e um sacrifício, na pior. Tinha um motivo para ela nunca tocar nele a não ser que quisesse algo. Tinha um motivo para ele não tentar ligar quando ela desaparecia.

Ele deslizou o polegar para dentro da manga e sentiu o início da longa cicatriz que subia por seu braço. Era mais grossa do que ele lembrava. A pele ainda era sensível ao toque.

Will tirou a mão. Angie tinha se encolhido da última vez que seus dedos acidentalmente tocaram o braço exposto dele. As reações dela a ele sempre eram intensas, nunca medianas. Gostava de testar o limite dele. Era seu esporte favorito: quão ruim ela precisava ser até Will se encher e a abandonar igual a todas as outras pessoas da vida dela?

Eles tinham muitas vezes andado nessa corda bamba, mas, por algum motivo, ela sempre conseguia puxá-lo de volta no último segundo. Mesmo naquele momento, Will sentia o puxão. Ele não via Angie desde a morte da mãe dela. Deidre Polaski era viciada e prostituta e tinha tomado uma overdose que a deixara num coma vegetativo quando Angie tinha onze anos. O corpo dela havia durado vinte e sete anos antes de finalmente entregar os pontos. Quatro meses tinham se passado desde o velório. Não era muito, considerando o restante — Angie já desaparecera por um ano inteiro uma vez —, mas Will sentia um arrepio na espinha que lhe dizia que havia algo errado. Ela estava com problemas, ou machucada, ou chateada. O corpo dele sabia, assim como sabia que precisava respirar.

Eles sempre estiveram conectados desse jeito, mesmo quando eram crianças. Especialmente quando eram crianças. E, se tinha uma coisa que Will sabia sobre a esposa, era que ela sempre o procurava quando as coisas iam mal. Ele não sabia quando ela apareceria, se seria um dia depois ou na semana seguinte, mas sabia que em algum momento, no futuro próximo, ia voltar do trabalho e encontrar Angie sentada em seu sofá, comendo seus potinhos de flan e fazendo comentários depreciativos sobre a cachorrinha dele.

Era por isso que Will tinha ido à casa de Sara na noite anterior. Estava se escondendo de Angie. Estava lutando contra o inevitável. E, para ser sincero, estava louco para rever Sara. O fato de ela ter comprado a desculpa dele sobre a casa estar de cabeça para baixo o fazia pensar que talvez também o quisesse lá. Quando criança, Will havia treinado a si mesmo para não desejar o que não podia ter — os brinquedos mais novos, sapatos que realmente servissem, refeições caseiras que não saíssem de uma lata. Seu poder de negar coisas a si mesmo desaparecia no que dizia respeito a Sara. Ele não conseguia parar de pensar na sensação da mão dela em seu ombro quando estavam na rua, no dia anterior. O polegar dela havia acariciado a lateral do seu pescoço. Ela tinha levantado os calcanhares para ficarem da mesma altura e, só por um segundo, ele achara que ela o beijaria.

— Ah, não — gemeu Will.

Ele visualizou a carnificina na casa de Evelyn Mitchell, o sangue e a massa encefálica espirrados na cozinha e na área de serviço. E então tentou esvaziar a mente, porque tinha quase certeza de que serial killers começavam justamente com essa história de pensar em sexo e depois imaginar cenas de violência.

A SUV deu ré num solavanco. Amanda abriu a janela. Will se levantou.

Ela disse:

— Era uma fonte na polícia de Atlanta. Parece que nosso tipo B negativo apareceu na caçamba de lixo do Grady. Inconsciente, quase sem respirar. Acharam a carteira dele em um dos sacos de lixo. Marcellus Benedict Estevez. Desempregado. Mora com a avó.

Will se perguntou por que Sara não tinha ligado para ele para contar aquilo. Talvez já tivesse saído do trabalho. Ou talvez não fosse obrigação dela mantê-lo informado.

— Estevez falou alguma coisa?

— Ele morreu faz meia hora. Vamos passar no hospital depois disso aqui.

Will achou que era uma viagem inútil, considerando que o cara estava morto.

— Tinha alguma coisa com ele?

— Não. Entre.

— Por que a gente vai...

— Não tenho o dia todo, Will. Limpe a terra da sua vagina e vamos logo.

Will entrou na SUV.

— Eles confirmaram que o tipo sanguíneo de Estevez é B negativo?

Ela pisou no acelerador.

— Sim. E as digitais dele foram identificadas como sendo um dos oito conjuntos encontrados na casa de Evelyn.

De novo, havia alguma coisa que ele não estava sabendo.

— Foi uma conversa longa para só essa mínima informação.

Pelo menos desta vez ela foi direta:

— Recebemos uma ligação sobre Chuck Finn. Por que você não me disse que falou com o oficial de condicional dele ontem à noite?

— Acho que eu estava ressentido.

— Bom, você certamente me deu o troco, hein. O oficial de condicional foi fazer uma fiscalização surpresa hoje de manhã. Chuck sumiu há dois dias.

— Espere aí. — Will se virou para ela. — O oficial de Chuck me disse ontem à noite que sabia onde ele estava. Disse que Chuck nunca deixava de se apresentar.

— Com certeza o escritório de condicional do Tennessee está tão sobrecarregado e sem pessoal quanto o nosso. Pelo menos, ele teve coragem de falar a verdade hoje de manhã. — Ela lançou um olhar sério para ele. — Chuck Finn assinou a própria saída do centro de tratamento há dois dias.

— Centro de tratamento?

— Ele estava na Healing Winds. Está sóbrio há três meses.

Will se sentiu levemente vingado.

— Também foi na Healing Winds que Hironobu Kwon se tratou. Estiveram lá ao mesmo tempo.

Will precisou ficar em silêncio por um momento.

— Quando você descobriu tudo isso?

— Agorinha, Will. Não faça bico. Tenho uma velha amiga que trabalha com registros lá no tribunal de dependentes químicos. — Aparentemente, Amanda tinha uma velha amiga em todo canto. — Kwon foi enviado a Hope Hall quando era réu primário. — Esse era o centro de tratamento hospitalar do tribunal de dependentes químicos. — O juiz não estava muito propenso a lhe dar uma segunda chance às custas do Estado, então a mãe interveio e disse que tinha conseguido uma vaga na Healing Winds.

— Onde ele conheceu Chuck Finn.

— É uma clínica grande, mas tem razão. Seria forçar a barra dizer que esses dois homens em particular estavam lá ao mesmo tempo por acaso.

Will ficou chocado de ouvi-la concordar, mas seguiu em frente:

— Se Chuck falou para Hironobu Kwon que Evelyn tinha dinheiro guardado... — Ele sorriu. Finalmente, algo fazia sentido. — E o outro cara? O B negativo que apareceu no Grady. Tem alguma ligação com Chuck ou Hironobu?

— Marcellus Estevez nunca foi preso. Nascido e criado em Miami, Flórida. Há dois anos, se mudou para Carrollton para estudar na West

Georgia College. Largou no trimestre passado. Não teve contato com a família desde então.

Outro jovem de vinte e poucos anos que tinha se metido com gente muito ruim.

— Você pelo jeito sabe muito sobre Estevez.

— A polícia de Atlanta já falou com os pais dele. Registraram um boletim de ocorrência de pessoa desaparecida assim que a universidade informou que o filho deles não estava indo às aulas.

— Desde quando Atlanta está compartilhando informação com a gente?

— Vamos dizer que eu falei com algumas amigas.

Will estava começando a formar uma imagem de uma rede de velhinhas duronas e frias que ou deviam um favor a Amanda, ou tinham em algum momento da longa carreira trabalhado com Evelyn.

Ela disse:

— A questão é que não sabemos como o tipo B, Marcellus Estevez, se encaixa nisso. Exceto por Hironobu Kwon e Chuck Finn, não tem nem sombra de ligação entre mais ninguém na casa. Todos fizeram ensino médio em lugares diferentes. Nem todos fizeram faculdade, mas os que fizeram não estudaram juntos. Não se conheceram na prisão. Nenhum deles fazia parte da mesma facção ou do mesmo grupo social. Todos têm históricos diferentes, origens em povos diferentes.

Will sentiu que, pelo menos nisso, ela estava sendo sincera. Em qualquer investigação envolvendo múltiplos criminosos, a chave era sempre descobrir como eles haviam se conhecido. Os seres humanos tinham hábitos muito previsíveis. Descobrindo onde se conheceram e como, ou o que os unira, em geral dava para achar alguém de fora do grupo, mas relativamente próximo, que quisesse falar.

Will disse a ela o que estava pensando desde que vira a casa revirada de Evelyn:

— Parece uma vingança pessoal.

— A maioria das vinganças é mesmo.

— Não, estou falando que parece ter a ver com algo mais do que só dinheiro.

— Vai ser uma das muitas perguntas que vamos fazer a esses babacas quando metermos as algemas neles. — Amanda girou o volante, fazendo uma curva repentina que jogou Will para o lado. — Desculpe.

Ele não conseguia se lembrar de alguma vez que Amanda tivesse se desculpado por qualquer coisa. Ficou olhando para ela, que estava de perfil. O maxilar estava mais proeminente que o normal. A pele estava pálida. Ela parecia realmente acabada. E tinha dado a ele mais informação nos últimos dez minutos do que nas vinte e quatro horas anteriores.

— Tem mais alguma coisa rolando?

— Não.

Ela parou na frente de um grande armazém comercial com seis docas de carregamento. Não havia caminhões de carga, mas vários veículos estavam parados na frente dos portões. Qualquer um dos veículos teria custado mais que o salário anual de Will — BMWs, Mercedes, até um Bentley.

Amanda deu uma volta no estacionamento, garantindo que não houvesse surpresas. O espaço era grande o suficiente para um veículo semipesado manobrar e descer para as docas, facilitando a carga e a descarga. Ela fez um retorno preguiçoso, voltando pelo mesmo caminho. O carro cantou pneu quando ela virou o volante com tudo, entrando na vaga disponível mais distante do prédio, fora da grama. Amanda desligou o motor. A SUV estava diretamente em frente ao que parecia a recepção. Cerca de cinquenta metros de espaço aberto os separavam do prédio. Um lance de degraus de concreto caindo aos pedaços levava a uma porta de vidro. O corrimão estava tão enferrujado que havia tombado para o lado. A placa na entrada tinha um conjunto de armários de cozinha pregado na frente. Uma bandeira dos confederados balançava com a brisa. Will leu a primeira palavra da placa, depois chutou o resto:

— Southern Cabinets, os Armários do Sul? Que fachada de drogas diferente.

Amanda estreitou os olhos para ele.

— Ver você é que nem assistir a um cachorro andando com as patas traseiras.

Will saiu do carro. Encontrou Amanda atrás da SUV. Ela usou o controle para abrir o porta-malas. Em Valdosta, de manhã, eles tinham trancado as armas antes de entrar na cadeia. A SUV preta seguia os regulamentos da GBI, o que significava que toda a parte de trás era tomada por um grande armário de aço com seis gavetas. Amanda digitou a senha na fechadura digital e abriu a gaveta do meio. A Glock dela estava guardada num saquinho de veludo roxo bem escuro com o logo da Crown Royal bordado na bainha. Ela o jogou na bolsa enquanto Will prendia o coldre no cinto.

— Espere um pouco.

Amanda pôs a mão no fundo da gaveta e puxou um revólver de cinco tiros. Esse tipo particular de Smith and Wesson era chamado de "das antigas", porque a maioria das pessoas das antigas usava. A arma era leve, com um cão interno que a tornava fácil de esconder. Apesar do logo "Lady Smith" gravado logo acima do gatilho, o coice podia deixar um hematoma feio na mão inteira. A Smith and Wesson de Evelyn Mitchell era de um modelo similar, com cabo de cerejeira, em vez do cabo customizado de nogueira de Amanda. Will ficou se perguntando se as duas teriam adquirido aquele modelo de arma ao sair juntas para fazer umas comprinhas.

Amanda instruiu:

— Fique reto. Tente não reagir. Estamos bem à vista da câmera.

Will tentou seguir essas ordens enquanto Amanda colocava a mão por baixo da jaqueta dele, nas costas, e enfiava o revólver dentro da calça. Ele ficou olhando para o armazém à frente. Era de metal, mais largo do que fundo, e tinha mais ou menos a metade do tamanho de um campo de futebol americano. O prédio todo ficava numa fundação de concreto que levantava a altura do térreo em pelo menos um metro e duzentos, a altura padrão de uma doca de cargas. Fora os degraus íngremes de concreto que levavam à porta da frente, não tinha outro jeito de entrar e sair. A não ser que você estivesse disposto a se içar até a doca de cargas e abrir no muque os portões de metal.

Ele perguntou:

— Cadê os caras que você botou para ficarem de olho aqui?

— Doraville precisou de ajuda. Estamos sozinhos.

Ele viu a câmera acima do portão ir para a frente e para trás.

— Ah, parece uma ótima ideia o que estamos fazendo.

— Fique reto. — Ela deu um tapa nas costas dele, para garantir que a arma estivesse bem apertada no corpo. — E, pelo amor de Deus, não murche a barriga, senão ela vai cair direto no chão. — Ela precisou ficar na ponta dos pés para fechar o porta-malas. — Não sei por que você usa o cinto tão solto. Ele é inútil se você não usar direito.

Will caminhou atrás dela em direção à entrada. A caminhada foi rápida, cinquenta metros de exposição. A câmera tinha parado sua varredura para acompanhar o avanço deles. Era como se tivessem alvos no peito. Ele se concentrou no topo da cabeça de Amanda, na forma como o cabelo dela formava um redemoinho na coroa, parecendo um presunto redondo assado.

A porta de vidro se abriu quando eles chegaram aos degraus de concreto da entrada. Amanda protegeu os olhos do sol, olhando para um homem asiático mal-encarado. Ele era enorme, o corpo composto aparentemente por partes iguais de gordura e músculo. O cara ficou parado sem falar nada, segurando a porta aberta enquanto os via subir os degraus. Will entrou depois de Amanda. Seus olhos levaram algum tempo para se ajustar ao ambiente da recepção minúscula e abafada. O carpete era marrom de um jeito que causaria repulsa num homem mais meticuloso. O lugar todo cheirava a serragem e gasolina. Will ouvia máquinas ligadas no armazém: pinadores pneumáticos, compressores, tornos mecânicos. O rádio tocava Guns N' Roses.

Amanda disse ao homem:

— A Sra. Ling deve estar me esperando.

Ela sorriu para a câmera montada acima da porta.

O homem não se mexeu. Amanda enfiou a mão na bolsa como se procurasse um batom. Will não sabia se ela estava pegando a arma ou se só precisava mesmo de batom. Sua resposta veio quando a porta foi aberta por uma mulher alta e esguia com um sorriso no rosto.

— Mandy Wagner, há quanto tempo.

A mulher parecia quase contente. Era asiática, mais ou menos da idade de Amanda, com o cabelo cheio de fios grisalhos. Era magra como uma adolescente. Sua regata mostrava braços torneados. Ela falava com um sotaque distinto e arrastado do Sul. Havia algo felino na forma como se movia, ou talvez isso tivesse a ver com o cheiro de maconha grudado no corpo dela. A mulher usava mocassins com miçangas em cima, o tipo de souvenir que se encontraria numa loja para ludibriar turistas em frente a uma reserva indígena.

— Julia. — Amanda deu um sorriso convincente. — Que bom ver você.

Elas se abraçaram e Will viu a mão da mulher se demorar na cintura de Amanda.

— Este é Will Trent, meu colega. — Ela colocou a mão por cima da de Julia enquanto se virava para Will. — Espero que não se importe de ele vir junto. Está em treinamento.

— Que sorte poder aprender com a melhor — elogiou Julia. — Fale para ele deixar a arma no balcão. Você também, Mandy. Continua usando aquele saco velho da Crown Royal?

— Ele evita que os fiapos entrem no percussor.

A arma fez um baque quando ela jogou a bolsa no balcão. O homem sisudo conferiu o conteúdo, depois fez um aceno de cabeça para a chefe. Will não obedeceu tão rápido. Não se sentia confortável em abrir mão de sua arma.

— Will — disse Amanda. — Não me envergonhe na frente dos meus amigos.

Ele soltou o coldre do cinto e colocou sua Glock no balcão.

Julia Ling riu e fez sinal para passarem pela porta. O armazém era ainda maior do que parecia por fora, mas a operação era pequena, o tipo de coisa que caberia numa garagem de dois carros. Tinha pelo menos uma dúzia de homens montando armários. Will não conseguia saber se eram orientais, hispânicos ou alguma outra coisa, porque estavam com o boné puxado bem para baixo e o rosto virado. Quem quer que fossem, obviamente estavam trabalhando. O cheiro de cola era pungente. Havia serragem por todo o chão. Uma bandeira gigantesca dos confederados servia como divisória entre a área de trabalho e os fundos do prédio, que pareciam vazios. As estrelas eram amarelas, em vez de brancas.

Julia os levou por outra porta e eles chegaram num escritório de fundos pequeno, mas bem mobiliado. O tapete era fofo. Havia dois sofás com almofadas bem preenchidas. Um chihuahua gordo se sentava numa poltrona reclinável perto da janela, de olhos fechados para o pouco sol que entrava pelo vidro. Barras pesadas de metal emolduravam a vista do beco de serviços atrás do prédio.

— Will tem uma chihuahua — comentou Amanda, porque Will não tinha sido emasculado o suficiente por um dia. — Como ela se chama mesmo?

Will sentia um arame farpado preso na garganta.

— Betty.

— É mesmo? — Julia pegou o cachorro e se sentou com ele no sofá. Deu um tapinha no assento ao seu lado, e Amanda se sentou. — Este é Arnoldo. É uma coisinha gorducha. A sua é de pelo longo ou curto?

Will não sabia o que mais fazer. Ele estendeu a mão para trás para puxar a carteira, lembrando-se tarde demais do revólver de Amanda. A arma se mexeu perigosamente e Will se sentou no sofá em frente às mulheres, abrindo a carteira para mostrar a foto de Betty.

Julia Ling fez um som de *tsc* com a língua.

— Que coisinha adorável.

— Obrigado. — Will pegou a foto de volta e guardou a carteira no bolso do casaco. — O seu também é.

Julia já tinha dessintonizado Will. Ela passou a mão pela perna de Amanda.

— O que traz você aqui, docinho?

Amanda também fez um bom trabalho excluindo Will.

— Imagino que tenha ficado sabendo sobre Evelyn.

— Sim — disse Julia, estendendo a palavra. — Pobre Almeja. Espero que sejam delicados com ela.

Will se segurou para não deixar o queixo cair. Evelyn Mitchell era Almeja.

Amanda colocou a mão por cima da de Julia. Em vez de tirá-la de seu joelho, ela a manteve ali.

— Será que você não ouviu nada sobre onde ela pode estar?

— Nem um pio, mas você sabe que, se eu tivesse ficado sabendo, procuraria você na hora.

— Obviamente, estamos fazendo tudo para garantir que ela volte em segurança para casa. Eu mexeria uns pauzinhos consideráveis para fazer isso.

— Sim — repetiu Julia. — Ela é avó agora, né? De novo, quero dizer. Que família fértil. — Ela riu como se fosse uma piada interna. — Como está aquela menina querida e doce?

— É um momento difícil para todos da família.

— Sim.

Pelo jeito, "sim" era a palavra favorita dela.

— Você deve ter ficado sabendo de Hector.

— Coitadinho. Eu estava pensando em pegar um Cadillac, mais simples que o meu carro.

— Achei que os negócios estavam indo bem, não?

— É que não é hora de ficar dirigindo algo tão chamativo. — Ela abaixou a voz: — Sequestros-relâmpago.

— Terrível — disse Amanda, balançando a cabeça.

— Esses jovenzinhos são um problema sério. — Ela fez *tsc* com a língua. Will acreditava ter entendido pelo menos parte da conversa. Julia Ling estava se referindo aos jovens que tinham invadido a casa de Evelyn. — Eles veem todos os gângsteres na TV e acham que é muito fácil. Scarface. O poderoso chefão. Tony Soprano. Dá para ver a cabecinha deles girando. Logo ficam com umas ideias e saem atirando sem pensar nas consequências. — De novo, ela estalou a língua. — Acabei de perder um dos meus funcionários por causa desse tipo de ação descuidada.

Ela estava falando de Benny Choo, o homem de camisa havaiana. Will tinha razão. Julia Ling havia mandado o capanga dela para limpar a bagunça feita por Ricardo e seus amigos. E, aí, Faith o matara.

Amanda devia saber disso também, mas foi com cuidado:

— Esse ramo de negócios tem riscos. O Sr. Choo entendia isso tanto quanto qualquer um.

Julia Ling hesitou o suficiente para fazer Will se preocupar com Faith, mas então soltou lentamente:

— Sim. O preço dos negócios. Acho que vamos deixar Benny descansar em paz.

Amanda pareceu tão aliviada quanto Will.

— Ouvi dizer que seu irmão está aprendendo a lidar com o novo ambiente.

— Sim — falou ela. — "Lidar" é uma boa palavra. Roger nunca gostou do calor. Savannah é praticamente *tropical*.

— Sabe, tem uma vaga na D&C. Quer que eu veja se eles aceitam Roger? Talvez seja bom ter uma mudança de ambiente.

Ela fingiu considerar a oferta.

— Ainda um pouco quente demais. — Ela sorriu. — Que tal a Phillips?

— Bom, *é* um lugar bem bacana. — Também era onde Ignatio Ortiz estava cumprindo sua pena por homicídio. Amanda balançou a cabeça como se sentisse muitíssimo em dizer que aquele destino específico de férias já havia sido reservado por outra família. — Não parece a melhor opção.

— Baldwin é mais perto para eu ir de carro.

— Baldwin não combina muito com o temperamento de Roger. — Provavelmente porque a prisão só aceitava detentos de segurança mínima e média. — Augusta? Fica perto, mas não demais.

Ela franziu o nariz.

— Com o site que divulga criminosos sexuais?

— Bem pensado. — Amanda pareceu refletir, embora provavelmente já tivesse feito o acordo com a promotoria. — Sabe, Arrendale começou a aceitar alguns presidiários de segurança máxima. Só com bom comportamento, lógico, mas com certeza Roger consegue isso.

Ela deu uma risadinha.

— Ah, Mandy. Você conhece Roger. Ele vive se metendo em encrenca.

A oferta de Amanda foi firme.

— Mesmo assim, eu consideraria Arrendale. Com certeza podemos fazer com que a transição seja agradável. Evelyn tem vários amigos que só querem que ela volte em segurança para casa. Roger pode muito bem conseguir algo no processo.

Julia fez carinho no cachorro.

— Vou ver o que ele diz da próxima vez que eu for visitá-lo.

— Uma ligação talvez seja melhor. — Amanda acrescentou: — Com certeza ele vai querer saber de Benny por você, não por um estranho.

— Que Deus o tenha. — Ela apertou a perna de Amanda. — É horrível perder pessoas de quem a gente gosta.

— É, sim.

— Eu sei que você e Evelyn eram próximas.

— Ainda somos.

— Por que você não se livra do Tonto aí para podermos nos consolar?

A risada de Amanda soou genuinamente alegre. Ela deu uns tapinhas no joelho de Julia, e então se levantou do sofá.

— Ah, Jules. Que bom ver você de novo. Queria que a gente pudesse se ver mais.

Will começou a se levantar, mas aí se lembrou do revólver. Ele colocou as mãos nos bolsos para manter a calça justa o bastante para segurá-lo no lugar. Era só o que faltava, ele quebrar esse joguinho de Amanda derrubando uma arma pela perna da calça.

Amanda diz:

— Me dê um retorno sobre Arrendale. É realmente um lugar muito bacana. As janelas têm dez centímetros a mais na área de segurança máxima. Muito sol e ar fresco. Acho que Roger vai amar.

— Avisarei a decisão dele. Acho que podemos concordar que incerteza é ruim para os negócios.

— Diga a Roger que estou à disposição.

Will abriu a porta para Amanda. Eles atravessaram juntos a oficina. A equipe claramente tinha feito uma pausa. As máquinas estavam desligadas e as estações, vazias. O volume do rádio tinha sido abaixado e só emitia um zumbido. Ele murmurou para Amanda:

— Foi bem interessante.

— Vamos ver se ela faz a parte dela. — Ele via que ela estava esperançosa. Tinha voltado a caminhar com um gingado. — Apostaria minha perna esquerda que Roger sabe exatamente o que aconteceu ontem na casa de Eve. Provavelmente foi a própria Julia quem contou.

Ela nunca teria deixado a gente pisar aqui dentro se não estivesse disposta a negociar. Vamos saber de alguma coisa em uma hora. Escute o que eu digo.

— A Sra. Ling parece querer muito agradar você.

Ela parou e o olhou.

— Você acha mesmo? Nunca sei se ela está só sendo carinhosa ou...

Em vez de terminar a frase, Amanda deu de ombros.

Ele achou que ela estava brincando, depois percebeu que não.

— Acho. Quer dizer... — Ele sentiu que estava começando a suar. — Você nunca...

— Vê se cresce, Will. Eu *fiz* faculdade.

Ele ainda conseguia ouvi-la dando uma risadinha enquanto caminhavam para a porta da frente. Will imaginou que passaria a vida inteira amaldiçoado com essa mulher o manipulando como um fantoche. Ele estava estendendo a mão para a porta quando ouviu o primeiro estouro, quase como uma garrafa de champanhe sendo aberta. Então, sentiu a orelha arder, viu a porta lascar à sua frente e soube que era uma bala. E mais uma. E mais uma.

Amanda foi mais rápida que Will. Tinha puxado a arma da parte de trás da calça dele, girado e disparado dois tiros antes de ele se jogar no chão.

O som de uma metralhadora rasgou o ar. Balas passaram a centímetros da cabeça dele. Não dava para saber de onde estava vindo o ataque. O fundo do armazém estava escuro. Podia ser de Ling-Ling, dos homens que estavam trabalhando nos armários ou de ambos.

— Vai! — gritou Amanda.

Will abriu a porta da recepção com o ombro. Claro que as armas tinham sumido do balcão. O homem asiático carrancudo que os deixara entrar estava morto no chão. Will sentiu algo duro bater na nuca. Ficou atordoado por uns segundos antes de perceber que Amanda tinha jogado a bolsa nele.

Will a enfiou debaixo do braço e bateu a porta da frente. O sol repentino e forte o cegou tanto que ele tropeçou descendo os degraus de concreto. O corrimão velho envergou sob o peso dele, suavizando o que podia ter sido uma queda catastrófica. Rapidamente, ele se endireitou e atravessou direto o estacionamento em direção à SUV estacionada. O conteúdo da bolsa de Amanda foi caindo enquanto ele procurava a chave. Ele apertou o botão e, quando chegou à traseira do veículo, o porta-malas já estava aberto. Will digitou a senha da fechadura. A gaveta se abriu deslizando.

Na experiência de Will, tinha quem preferisse escopeta e quem preferisse rifle. Faith preferia a escopeta, o que era contraintuitivo considerando a estatura diminuta dela e o fato de que o coice de uma escopeta podia rasgar seu manguito rotador. Will gostava do rifle. Era direto, firme e extremamente preciso, mesmo a quase cinquenta metros — o que era bom, já que era a distância aproximada entre a SUV e a entrada do prédio. A GBI dava aos agentes o Colt AR-15A2, que Will apoiou no ombro na hora que a porta abriu num estouro.

Ele colocou o olho na mira. Amanda lidou com o sol melhor do que ele. Sem perder o ritmo, ela voou pela escada de concreto, atirando para trás, mas as balas não atingiram o homem atarracado que a perseguia. Ele estava de óculos escuros, com uma metralhadora na mão. Em vez de dar um tiro nas costas enquanto ela corria, ele levantou a arma para o ar enquanto pulava os degraus. Era coisa de caubói, o que deu a Will a oportunidade de também fazer algo do tipo. Ele puxou o gatilho. O homem deu um solavanco para trás e caiu no chão.

Will abaixou o rifle. Procurou Amanda. Ela estava voltando na direção do homem no chão. Ela estava segurando a própria arma ao lado do corpo. Devia estar sem munição. Will pressionou de novo o olho na mira para dar cobertura a ela, caso mais alguém saísse do prédio. Ela chutou a metralhadora para longe. Ele via sua boca se mexendo.

Sem aviso, Amanda mergulhou atrás dos degraus de concreto. Will tirou o olho da mira para poder localizar a nova ameaça. Era o homem no chão. Inacreditavelmente, ele continuava vivo. Estava com a Glock de Will apontada para a SUV. Disparou três vezes seguidas, muito rápido. Will sabia que o armário de metal espesso o protegeria, mas, mesmo assim, se abaixou enquanto um metal atingia o outro.

O tiroteio parou. O coração de Will estava batendo tão forte que ele sentia a pulsação no estômago. Arriscou um olhar para o prédio. O atirador devia estar escondido atrás da Mercedes, provavelmente do lado oposto ao tanque de gasolina. Will alinhou o rifle, torcendo para o cara fazer alguma coisa idiota, como mostrar a cara. Em vez disso, apareceu a Glock. Will atirou, e a arma rapidamente recuou.

— Polícia! — gritou Will, porque precisava dizer isso. — Mãos ao alto!

O cara atirou cegamente na direção da SUV, errando por vários metros. Will murmurou algumas palavras feias. Olhou para Amanda como que perguntando qual era o plano. Ela balançou a cabeça, não para negar nada a ele, mas exasperada. Se Will tivesse acertado o primeiro tiro, não estariam tendo aquela conversa.

Ele não conseguia pensar num jeito de gesticular para ela que ele tinha, sim, acertado o tiro — não sem ser demitido —, então apontou para o pente saindo de seu rifle como forma de questionar. Ela estava sem balas? O revólver dela tinha cinco cartuchos. A não ser que ela tivesse pegado o carregador rápido da bolsa, não podia fazer muita coisa.

Mesmo à distância, ele viu a cara de irritação dela. Claro que ela tinha pegado o carregador da bolsa. Provavelmente também tinha parado para passar um batom e dar uns telefonemas. Ele conferiu de novo a Mercedes, escaneando os pontos pelo contorno do sedã grande. Quando olhou de novo para Amanda, ela já havia aberto a Smith and Wesson, jogado os projéteis no chão e recarregado. Ela acenou com a mão para ele andar logo.

— Senhor! — gritou Will. — Estou dando mais um aviso para se entregar.

— Vai se foder!

O homem atirou de novo na direção de Will, acertando o painel da porta do SUV.

Amanda foi andando agachada até a beirada dos degraus de concreto, então abaixou a cabeça perto do chão, tentando ver onde o homem estava escondido. Voltou a se sentar. Não olhou para Will. Não parou para alinhar a mira. Simplesmente apoiou a mão no terceiro degrau e apertou o gatilho.

A televisão tinha feito um grande desserviço aos bandidos. Não mostrava que balas podiam atravessar paredes de reboco e portas de metal dos carros. Também não explicava que um ricocheteio não era nada parecido com uma bola de borracha. Balas saíam em altíssima velocidade e queriam seguir em frente. Atirar para o chão não fazia com que a bala pulasse de volta no ar. Atirar no chão embaixo de um carro faria a bala ricochetear baixo no pavimento, furar o pneu e, se você estivesse sentado do jeito certo, se alojar na sua virilha.

Que foi exatamente o que aconteceu.

— Puta que pariu! — gritou o homem.

Will ordenou:

— Mãos ao alto!

Duas mãos se levantaram.

— Eu me rendo! Eu me rendo!

Desta vez, Amanda estava com a arma bem apontada para o homem ao caminhar até o carro. Chutou a Glock para longe, depois enfiou o joelho nas costas dele, o tempo todo de olho na porta da recepção.

Ela estava observando a porta errada. Uma das portas de carga se abriu com tudo. Uma van preta saiu tão acelerada que parecia estar voando. Saíram faíscas quando ela deslizou no asfalto. A borracha queimou. As rodas derraparam antes de ganhar tração. Will viu dois jovens na cabine. Estavam os dois de jaqueta esportiva preta e boné preto. A van momentaneamente bloqueou sua visão de Amanda. Will levantou o rifle, mas não podia atirar — não sem arriscar que a bala atravessasse a van e atingisse Amanda. Soaram mais dois estouros rápido. Tiros. A van foi embora cantando pneu.

Will correu para o estacionamento para alinhar a mira. Ele parou. Amanda estava no chão.

— Amanda? — Ele sentiu o peito apertar. Sua voz não queria sair. — Amanda? Você está...

— Puta merda! — gritou ela, rolando para poder se sentar. Seu rosto e peito estavam cobertos de sangue. — Puta *merda*.

Will pôs um joelho no chão e a mão no ombro dela.

— Você foi atingida?

— Estou bem, seu idiota. — Ela deu um tapa para tirar a mão dele. — Este aqui está morto. Atiraram na cabeça dele duas vezes enquanto fugiam.

240

Will conseguia ver. O rosto do homem estava acabado.

— É um puta disparo certeiro saindo de um carro em movimento. — Ela o olhou com raiva enquanto ele a ajudava a se levantar. — Bem melhor que o seu. Quando foi sua última vez no estande? Isso é inaceitável. Absolutamente inaceitável.

Will sabia que era melhor não discutir com ela, mas, se ele fosse de discutir, talvez tivesse mencionado o quanto tinha sido má ideia deixar as armas no balcão ou o quanto era imbecil, para começo de conversa, entrar naquele lugar sem reforços.

— Juro por Deus, Will, quando isso aqui acabar... — Ela não terminou a frase. Saiu andando a passos largos, pisando no estojo de pó compacto de plástico que tinha caído da bolsa. — Puta merda!

Will se ajoelhou na frente do morto. Por hábito, checou a pulsação. Havia um buraco na jaqueta esportiva preta dele, a cerca de cinco centímetros do coração. Era grande o bastante para Will enfiar o dedo. Ele puxou o zíper e revelou a parte de cima de um colete à prova de balas de nível militar. O projétil encamisado tinha se expandido com o impacto, batendo na placa balística e se achatando como um cachorro tentando rastejar para baixo de um sofá.

Na mosca, bem no meio do peito.

Amanda estava de volta. Olhou para o morto sem falar uma palavra. Devia estar contra o vento quando ele foi atingido. Havia pedaços de massa cinzenta grudados na cara dela. Um pedaço de osso estava preso no colarinho de sua blusa.

Will se levantou. Só conseguiu pensar em oferecer seu lenço.

— Obrigada. — Ela limpou o rosto com a mão firme. O sangue se espalhou como maquiagem de palhaço. — Graças a Deus que tenho uma muda de roupas no carro. — Ela levantou os olhos para ele. — Seu paletó está rasgado.

Ele olhou a manga. Havia um pequeno rasgo onde o ombro tinha batido no asfalto.

— Você sempre tem que ter uma muda de roupas no carro. Nunca se sabe o que vai acontecer.

— Sim, senhora.

Will descansou a mão na coronha do rifle.

241

— Ling-Ling se mandou. — Amanda secou a testa. — Ela saiu com aquele cachorro idiota debaixo do braço. Com as armas disparando. Não tenho nenhuma impressão de que estivesse tentando me salvar, mas pareceu bem óbvio que também estavam tentando matá-la.

Will tentou processar essa nova informação.

— Eu supus que os atiradores estivessem trabalhando para Ling--Ling.

— Se Julia quisesse nos matar, teria atirado em nós dois na sala dela. Você não viu a espingarda de cano curto embaixo da almofada do sofá?

Will fez que sim, embora não tivesse visto a arma, e pensar nela naquele momento o fez suar frio.

— Os atiradores trabalhavam na oficina dela. Eu os reconheci de quando entramos. Estavam montando armários. Por que tentaram matar Julia? Ou a gente, aliás?

— Não é óbvio? — Finalmente, Amanda percebeu que não era. — Eles não queriam que ela falasse comigo. Com certeza não querem que ela fale com Roger. Ela deve saber de alguma coisa.

Will tentou encaixar as peças.

— Julia falou que os jovens estavam se precipitando. Tentando ser gângsteres. Não imagino que um bando de caras de vinte e poucos anos, cheios de testosterona, queiram receber ordens de uma mulher de meia-idade.

— E eu achando que os homens amavam isso. — Amanda olhou para o morto. — Ele está suando que nem um porco. Com certeza estava usando alguma coisa.

Alguma coisa que o fazia ser capaz de suportar o impacto de uma bala encamisada de calibre .223 de 55 gramas no peito e pular segundos depois como pão na torradeira.

Amanda cutucou o homem com a ponta do sapato, empurrando-o para poder pegar a carteira dele.

— Esses jovenzinhos pelo jeito não gostam de deixar testemunhas. — Ela pegou a carteira de motorista do homem. — Juan Armand Castillo. Vinte e quatro anos. Mora na Leather Stocking Lane, em Stone Mountain.

Ela mostrou o documento a Will. Castillo parecia professor de escola, não o tipo de cara que perseguiria agentes da GBI num estacionamento com uma metralhadora.

Amanda abriu o resto da jaqueta de Castillo. A Glock dela estava enfiada na calça dele. Ela a pegou, dizendo:

— Bem, pelo menos ele não atirou em mim com a minha própria arma.

Will a ajudou a soltar as fivelas laterais do colete Kevlar.

— E ele está fedendo também. — Amanda levantou a camiseta, para ver o peito dele. — Sem tatuagem. — Olhou os braços. — Nada.

— Olhe as mãos.

Castillo estava com os punhos fechados. Ela abriu os dedos dele com a própria mão, o que tecnicamente era contra todos os procedimentos oficiais, mas Will já era cúmplice, então não tinha muita importância. Ela disse:

— Nada.

Will olhou o estacionamento. Só havia dois carros naquele momento, o Bentley e a Mercedes.

— Você acha que tem mais alguém lá dentro?

— O Bentley é de Ling-Ling. Imagino que ela mantenha outro carro por perto e o esteja usando agora para se esconder o máximo possível. A Mercedes é de Perry. — Ela explicou: — O homem morto na recepção.

— Você parece mesmo conhecer muito essa gente. Mandy.

— Não estou a fim disso agora, Will.

— Julia ocupa uma posição alta no bando. Está praticamente no topo.

— Tem algum motivo para você estar falando que nem o Frangolino?

— Estou só dizendo que precisa ter muita coragem ou uma estupidez tremenda para tentar matar alguém influente como Julia Ling. O irmão dela não vai deixar por isso mesmo. Você mesma me disse que ele é praticamente louco. Atirar na irmã dele é uma declaração de guerra.

— Finalmente, um argumento relevante. — Ela devolveu o lenço dele. — Você conseguiu ver bem os homens da van?

Ele fez que não.

— Jovens, acho. Óculos. Boné. Jaqueta. Mais nada que eu possa jurar que vi.

— Não estou pedindo para você jurar. Estou pedindo para... — O ar foi invadido pelo som de sirenes. — Até que enfim.

Will chutava que fazia menos de cinco minutos que o primeiro tiro havia sido disparado. Pelos seus cálculos, era um tempo de reação bastante bom.

Ele perguntou:

— *Você* conseguiu ver os caras?

Ela fez que não.

— Pelo jeito, estamos procurando alguém com experiência em atirar de um carro em movimento.

Ela tinha razão sobre os tiros. Acertar alguém na cabeça, duas vezes, de um veículo em movimento, mesmo a uma distância curta, não era sorte. Exigia prática, e obviamente o assassino de Castillo não estava preocupado com a possibilidade de errar.

Will perguntou:

— Por que eles não atiraram em você?

— Você está reclamando ou fazendo uma pergunta? — Amanda espanou algo do braço. Baixou os olhos para Castillo. — Acho que, agora, só faltam dois. Pelo menos nossas chances estão melhorando.

Ela estava falando das digitais encontradas na casa de Evelyn.

— São três.

Ela fez que não, ainda olhando o cadáver.

Ele contou nos dedos.

— Evelyn matou Hironobu Kwon. Faith se encarregou de dar um fim em Ricardo Ortiz e Benny Choo. Marcellus Estevez morreu no Grady, e Juan Castillo aqui completa cinco. — Ela não falou nada. Ele ficou preocupado de ter feito a conta errado. — Oito conjuntos de digitais na casa da Evelyn, menos cinco homens mortos, dá três.

Ela observou as viaturas vindo em velocidade pela estrada.

— Dois — disse a ele. — Um tentou matar Sara Linton há uma hora

11

Dale Dugan entrou correndo na sala de descanso médico.

— Eu vim assim que me permitiram.

Sara fechou os olhos enquanto trancava seu armário. Tinha passado quase duas horas repassando seu depoimento para a polícia de Atlanta. Em seguida, os diretores do hospital a cercaram por mais uma hora, supostamente para ajudar, mas Sara logo percebeu que estavam mais preocupados com a possibilidade de serem processados. Assim que ela assinou um papel os absolvendo de qualquer responsabilidade, foram embora tão rápido quanto haviam chegado.

Dale perguntou:

— Quer que eu pegue alguma coisa para você?

— Obrigada, mas estou bem.

— Quer que eu leve você para casa?

— Dale, eu...

A porta se abriu com um baque. Will estava lá com uma cara de pânico.

Por alguns segundos, nada mais importava. Sara ficou cega a todo o resto na sala. Sua visão periférica desapareceu. Tudo se afunilou para Will. Ela não viu Dale indo embora. Não ouviu a confusão constante de sirenes de ambulância e telefones tocando e pacientes gritando.

Ela só viu Will.

Ele deixou a porta se fechar, mas não foi na direção dela. Sua testa estava suando. A respiração dele estava ofegante. Ela não sabia o que dizer a ele, o que fazer. Só ficou ali parada, olhando para ele como se fosse mais um dia normal.

Ele perguntou:

— É uma roupa nova?

Ela riu, e o som ficou preso na garganta. Ela tinha colocado o uniforme hospitalar. Suas roupas eram evidências para a polícia.

O canto da boca dele se levantou num sorriso forçado.

— Destaca o verde dos seus olhos.

Sara mordeu os lábios para impedir as lágrimas de caírem. Tinha desejado ligar para ele na hora em que tudo aconteceu. O celular estava na mão dela, o número dele na tela, mas ela guardou o aparelho na bolsa porque sabia que, se visse Will antes de estar pronta, ela se estilhaçaria que nem uma peça delicada de porcelana.

Amanda Wagner bateu na porta ao entrar na sala.

— Odeio interromper, Dra. Linton, mas podemos dar uma palavrinha?

O rosto de Will mostrou raiva.

— Ela não...

— Está tudo bem — interrompeu Sara. — Não tenho muito a dizer.

Amanda sorriu como se fosse uma reuniãozinha social.

— Qualquer coisa vai ser bem-vinda.

Sara tinha falado tanto do assunto nas últimas horas que recitou os acontecimentos de forma mecânica. Deu a eles a versão abreviada de seu depoimento, sem entrar numa descrição detalhada da viciada que aparentemente era como qualquer outra que Sara já tivesse visto. Também não descreveu o lixo ao redor da caçamba, nem os paramédicos, nem a lista de procedimentos que seguiu. Foi direto ao ponto: o jovem que a olhou de trás da cortina. Ele tinha dado um soco no peito dela. Tinha atirado duas vezes na cabeça do paciente. Era magro, caucasiano, de vinte e cinco a trinta anos, usava uma jaqueta esportiva preta e boné de time de beisebol. No curto tempo transcorrido desde que ela o vira pela primeira vez até a morte dele, o homem não dissera uma só palavra. O único som que ela havia escutado fora um gemido, seguido pelo ar saindo com um assovio do pescoço dele enquanto sua respiração escapava.

Ela terminou:

— Ele estava com a mão em torno da minha. Não consegui impedir. Ele está morto. Os dois estão mortos.

Will pareceu ter dificuldade de falar.

— Ele machucou você.

Sara só conseguia assentir com a cabeça, mas sua mente conjurou a imagem que ela vira no espelho do banheiro: um hematoma feio alongado acima do seio direito, onde ela tinha levado o soco.

Will pigarreou.

— Tudo bem. Obrigado pela sua cooperação, Dra. Linton. Eu sei que você deve querer ir para casa.

Ele se virou para sair, mas Amanda não fez menção de se mexer.

— Dra. Linton, notei uma máquina de refrigerante na sala de espera. Quer tomar alguma coisa?

Sara foi pega de surpresa.

— Eu...

— Will, pode pegar uma Sprite Diet para mim e... Desculpe, Dra. Linton. O que deseja?

O maxilar de Will se apertou como uma roda dentada. Ele não era idiota. Sabia que Amanda estava tentando ficar sozinha com Sara, assim como Sara sabia que Amanda não ia desistir até conseguir o que queria. Ela tentou facilitar para Will, dizendo:

— Uma Coca seria bom.

Ele não cedeu tão fácil.

— Certeza?

— Sim. Certeza.

Ele não estava feliz, mas saiu da sala.

Amanda conferiu o corredor, para garantir que Will tinha ido. Virou-se para Sara.

— Estou torcendo por você, sabe.

Sara não fazia ideia do que ela estava falando.

— Will — explicou. — Tem filhas da puta de mais na vida dele, e eu não vou a lugar nenhum.

Sara não estava a fim de piada.

— O que você quer, Amanda?

Ela foi direta:

— Os corpos continuam lá embaixo no necrotério. Preciso que você os examine e me dê sua opinião profissional. — Ela completou: — Uma opinião de legista.

Sara sentiu um frio na espinha só de pensar em rever o homem. Toda vez que piscava, conseguia ver o rosto sem expressão dele pairando acima dela. Não conseguia segurar a própria mão sem sentir os dedos dele ao redor dos dela.

— Não posso abrir os corpos.

— Não, mas pode me responder algumas perguntas.

— Tipo?

— Uso de drogas, afiliações a facções e se um deles está ou não com a barriga cheia de heroína.

— Que nem Ricardo.

— É, que nem Ricardo.

Sara não se permitiu tempo para pensar no pedido.

— Tudo bem. Eu faço.

— Faz o quê?

Will tinha voltado. Devia ter ido e voltado correndo. Estava ofegante de novo, segurando dois refrigerantes com uma mão só.

— Ah, olhe você aí — disse Amanda, como se estivesse surpresa em vê-lo. — Estávamos descendo ao necrotério.

Will olhou para Sara.

— Não.

— Eu quero fazer isso — insistiu Sara, embora sem saber o porquê.

Nas últimas três horas, ela só conseguia pensar em ir para casa. Mas com Will ali, naquele momento, pensar em voltar a seu apartamento vazio era inimaginável.

— Não precisamos disso. — Amanda pegou as latas de refrigerante e jogou no lixo. — Dra. Linton?

Sara os levou pelo corredor em direção aos elevadores, sentindo como se uma vida inteira tivesse se passado desde que fizera aquele mesmo trajeto de manhã. Uma maca ocupada passou, com paramédicos gritando números e médicos dando ordens. Sara estendeu o braço, guiando Will para se encostar na parede de modo que o paciente pudesse passar. Sua mão pairou bem na frente da gravata dele. Ela sentiu o tecido sedoso roçando na ponta dos dedos. Ele estava usando terno, seu uniforme normal de trabalho, mas sem o colete de sempre. O paletó era azul-escuro, a camisa, um tom mais claro da mesma cor.

O policial. Sara tinha esquecido o policial.

— Eu não...

— Espere um pouco — disse Amanda, como se estivesse com medo das paredes terem ouvidos.

Enquanto esperavam o elevador, Sara estava puta consigo mesma. Como tinha esquecido o policial? Qual era o problema dela?

As portas se abriram. O elevador estava lotado. Levou um tempo interminável para as polias e roldanas velhas começarem a funcionar com um rangido. Eles desceram um andar e a maioria das pessoas saiu. Dois auxiliares de enfermagem jovens foram com eles até o subsolo. Eles desceram e se dirigiram à escada, provavelmente para um encontro amoroso ilícito.

Amanda esperou até estarem bem longe e não poderem ouvir.

— O que foi?

— Tinha um homem aqui no hospital quando entramos, vindo da caçamba. Eu quase o atropelei. Mandei sair do caminho e ele mostrou um distintivo. Parecia um distintivo. Não sei dizer com certeza. Ele estava agindo como policial.

— Em que sentido?

— Agia como se tivesse todo o direito de me interrogar e ficou irritado quando não respondi imediatamente.

Sara lhe deu um olhar de quem sabia do que estava falando.

— Parece um policial mesmo — admitiu Amanda, irônica. — O que ele queria?

— Saber se o paciente ia ou não sobreviver. Falei que talvez, apesar de ser óbvio que... — Sara deixou a voz sumir, tentando ao máximo lembrar. — Ele estava de terno cinza-escuro. Camisa branca. Era muito magro, quase emaciado. Fedia a fumaça de cigarro. Continuei sentindo o cheiro mesmo depois de ele ir embora.

— Você viu para onde ele foi?

Ela fez que não.

— Branco? Negro?

— Branco. Cabelo grisalho. Era mais velho. Parecia mais velho. — Ela pôs a mão no rosto. — As bochechas eram encovadas. E os olhos tinham as pálpebras bem caídas. — Ela se lembrou de mais uma coisa. — Ele estava usando um boné. Um boné de time de beisebol.

— Preto? — quis saber Will.

— Azul — respondeu ela. — Do Atlanta Braves.

— Provavelmente vamos conseguir boas imagens do topo do boné nas câmeras de segurança — comentou Amanda. — Vamos ter que compartilhar essa informação com a polícia de Atlanta. Eles talvez queiram que você fale com um artista de retrato falado.

Sara faria o que fosse preciso.

— Desculpe não ter lembrado antes. Eu não sei o que...

— Você estava em choque. — Will parecia pronto para dizer mais. Olhou de soslaio para Amanda, depois indicou as portas duplas na outra ponta do corredor. Ele disse: — Acho que é por aqui.

No necrotério, Júnior e Larry não estavam em canto algum. No entanto, havia duas macas, cada uma com um corpo, cada uma com um lençol branco cobrindo um cadáver. Sara supôs que um fosse o homem que ela encontrara na frente da caçamba de lixo e o outro, o homem que tinha atirado primeiro e tentado matá-la depois.

Havia uma mulher mais velha apoiada na porta da câmara frigorífica. Quando eles entraram, ela levantou os olhos do BlackBerry. O crachá do hospital estava guardado no bolso da calça. Sem jaleco, só um tailleur preto bem cortado. Ela claramente trabalhava na administração do hospital. Era mais velha, tinha mais cabelos brancos do que pretos. Afastou-se da câmara e foi até eles. Sua postura era reta como uma vara e o peito grande se estufava à frente como a proa de um navio.

Ela não parou para apresentações. Puxou um caderninho espiral do bolso do paletó e começou a ler:

— O nome do atirador é Franklin Warren Heeney. A polícia de Atlanta encontrou a carteira com ele. Um garoto da região, mora em Tucker com os pais. Largou a Perimeter College no segundo ano. Sem registro de empregos. Sem histórico de prisão como adulto, mas, aos treze anos, passou seis meses no reformatório por quebrar janelas. Tem uma filha de seis anos que mora com uma tia lá em Snellville. A mãe da criança está na cadeia do condado por roubar uma loja e ter um saquinho de metanfetamina dentro da bolsa. Foi só o que consegui descobrir dele. — Ela indicou o outro corpo. — Marcellus

Benedict Estevez. Como falei ao telefone, a carteira dele foi achada na caçamba de lixo. Imagino que vocês já o tenham investigado, não é? — Amanda fez que sim, e a mulher fechou o caderno. — Só tenho isso por enquanto. Não chegou mais nada pela escuta.

Amanda assentiu de novo.

— Obrigada.

— Ganhei uma hora para vocês antes de os meninos dos cadáveres chegarem. Dra. Linton, as imagens que você pediu de Estevez estão no malote. Já reuni algumas ferramentas que podem ser úteis. Lamento não poder fazer mais.

Ela tinha feito bastante. Sara olhou as quatro mesas de Mayo dispostas ao lado dos corpos. Quem quer que fosse a mulher, tinha algum conhecimento médico e um cargo alto o bastante na hierarquia do Grady para atacar o armário de depósito sem disparar alarmes.

— Obrigada.

A mulher acenou em despedida e saiu da sala.

Quando Will fez uma pergunta a Amanda, foi num tom sarcástico:

— Me deixe adivinhar, uma das suas velhas amigas?

Amanda o ignorou.

— Dra. Linton, podemos começar?

Sara precisou se forçar a se mexer, ou teria só ficado lá presa ao chão até o prédio ruir ao seu redor. Havia um pacote de luvas estéreis pendurado num gancho na parede. Ela pegou um par e as forçou a entrar nas mãos suadas. O pó se amontoou em bolinhas que se grudaram como massa na mão dela.

Sem preâmbulo, ela puxou o lençol que cobria o primeiro corpo, revelando Marcellus Estevez, o homem que ela achara ao lado da caçamba de lixo. Ele tinha dois buracos de bala na testa, um perto do outro. Queimaduras de pólvora tatuavam a pele. Ela sentiu cheiro de cordite, o que era impossível, porque o homem tinha sido alvejado horas antes.

Amanda falou:

— Duas balas no meio da testa, que nem nosso carro do armazém.

Will falou baixo:

— Você não precisa fazer isso.

— Estou bem. — Sara se forçou a andar logo com aquilo, começando pela parte fácil, murmurando: — Ele tem aproximadamente vinte e cinco anos. Entre um e setenta e três a um e setenta e cinco. Uns oitenta quilos. — Ela pressionou os olhos para abri-los, sentindo que estava entrando na rotina do exame. — Marrom. Ictérico. A ferida estava séptica. A necrópsia provavelmente vai mostrar infiltração nos órgãos maiores. Estava em choque sistêmico quando o encontramos.

Ela abaixou mais o lençol para poder olhar de novo a barriga, desta vez procurando uma avaliação forense em vez de um tratamento.

O homem estava nu, suas roupas tinham sido cortadas quando ele fora trazido ao pronto-socorro. Sara via claramente a ferida penetrante da facada no quadrante inferior do abdome. Ela pressionou os dois lados do corte para ver se conseguia discernir o caminho da lâmina.

— O intestino delgado foi perfurado. Parece que a faca entrou num ângulo ascendente. Golpe com a mão direita em posição supinada.

Amanda perguntou:

— Ele estava em cima dela?

— É que eu suponho. Estamos falando de Evelyn, certo? — Will continuava estoico, mas Amanda confirmou com a cabeça. — A lâmina entrou num ângulo oblíquo às linhas de Langer do abdome, ou a direção natural da pele. Se eu reorientar as bordas assim — ela torceu a pele na posição que estava quando o homem foi esfaqueado —, dá para ver que o ponto de penetração sugere que Evelyn estava deitada de barriga para cima, provavelmente no chão, com o agressor em cima dela. Ele estava levemente dobrado na altura da cintura. A faca entrou assim. — Sara estendeu a mão para um bisturi na bandeja, mas mudou de ideia e, em vez disso, pegou uma tesoura. Ela ilustrou a ação, segurando a mão ao lado do quadril, com a tesoura virada para cima. — Foi mais defensivo do que deliberado. Talvez tenham lutado e caído ao mesmo tempo. A faca entrou. O homem rolou para o lado enquanto a lâmina continuava alojada. Dá para ver como a ferida tem uma incisão significativamente maior na borda lateral, indicando movimento.

— Faca de cozinha? — perguntou Amanda.

— Estatisticamente, é a arma mais provável, e a briga aconteceu na cozinha, então, faz sentido. Vão precisar fazer uma comparação no IML para ter certeza. Eles acharam a arma na cena do crime?

— Acharam — respondeu ela. — Tem certeza disso? Ela estava deitada de barriga para cima?

Sara viu que Amanda não estava contente com a avaliação. Queria que a amiga fosse uma lutadora, não alguém que só deu sorte.

— A maioria das facadas fatais acontecem na região esquerda do tronco. Se você quer matar alguém, tem que mirar no coração, de cima para baixo, direto no peito. Isto foi defensivo. — Ela indicou a palma da mão do homem, cortada. — Mas Evelyn não se entregou fácil. Em algum momento, deve ter atacado diretamente, porque ele agarrou a lâmina da faca.

Amanda só pareceu levemente apaziguada por essa informação.

— Tem alguma coisa na barriga dele?

Sara estendeu a mão para baixo da maca e puxou o malote destinado ao legista de Fulton County. Krakauer tinha preenchido a maioria das informações enquanto Sara estava sendo interrogada pela polícia. O formulário era padrão. O legista que fizesse a autópsia precisava saber das drogas usadas, procedimentos feitos, quais marcas vinham do hospital e quais tinham origens mais nefastas. Sara achou uma reprodução de imagem térmica das radiografias na última página. Ela disse:

— A barriga parece não ter corpos estranhos. Vão ter certeza quando abrirem, mas estou supondo que a quantidade de heroína de que estamos falando, pela qual valeria a pena morrer, seria fácil de ver.

Will pigarreou. Parecia relutante ao perguntar:

— Teria muito sangue em Evelyn depois de esfaquear esse cara?

— Pouco provável. A maior parte do sangramento aconteceu dentro da barriga, mesmo depois de a faca ter sido puxada. Tem o ferimento defensivo na mão dele, mas as artérias ulnar e radial estão intactas e nenhuma artéria digital foi comprometida. Se o corte na mão dele fosse mais fundo ou se um dos dedos tivesse sido aberto ou arrancado, seria de se esperar uma perda de sangue importante. Mas não é o caso de

Estevez, então estou supondo que Evelyn teria uma quantidade mínima de sangue nas roupas.

Will continuou:

— Tinha muito sangue no chão. Dava para ver pegadas indo e voltando nos azulejos.

— Qual era o tamanho do espaço?

— Do tamanho de uma cozinha — disse ele. — Maior que a sua, mas não muito, e fechada. A casa é mais antiga, estilo rancho.

Sara pensou.

— Eu teria que ver as fotos da cena do crime, mas tenho quase certeza de que, se tinha sangue suficiente no chão para sugerir uma luta, esse sangue não veio da mão ou da barriga de Estevez. Pelo menos não todo ele.

— Estevez conseguiria simplesmente se levantar sozinho e sair andando depois desses ferimentos?

— Não sem ajuda. Qualquer tipo de dano à parede abdominal dificulta a respiração, quanto mais o movimento. — Sara pôs a mão na barriga. — Pense em quantos músculos têm que ser ativados só para se sentar.

Amanda perguntou a Will:

— O que você está querendo saber?

— Estou só me perguntando quem lutou com Evelyn se este cara não conseguia se levantar depois de levar uma facada e se não havia muito sangue do ferimento dele.

Sara seguiu o raciocínio.

— Você acha que Evelyn estava ferida.

— Pode ser. Eles fizeram tipagem sanguínea na cena, mas não analisaram tudo, e o resultado do DNA só vai chegar daqui a alguns dias. — Ele deu de ombros. — Se Evelyn estava ferida, e Estevez não sangrou muito, isso pode explicar o sangue a mais.

— Com certeza, se ela está ferida, não é nada sério — disse Amanda, afastando a teoria de Will como se espantasse uma mosca.

Qualquer pessoa racional já teria aceitado a possibilidade mais que real de que as chances de sobrevivência de Evelyn Mitchell eram bem pequenas, considerando o tempo que havia passado. Amanda parecia estar se apegando à teoria oposta.

Sara é que não ia contrariar.

Havia uma lupa grande em uma das bandejas. Sara puxou a lâmpada do teto e voltou ao exame, analisando o cadáver dos pés à cabeça em busca de vestígios, marcas de agulha, qualquer coisa incomum que pudesse levar a uma pista. Quando foi hora de virar o corpo, Will pôs um par de luvas cirúrgicas e ajudou.

— Olha, que interessante — comentou Amanda, com sua tendência de sempre ao eufemismo.

Estevez tinha uma tatuagem grande de anjo nas costas. A imagem cobria os ombros e se estendia até o final do sacro, tão intrincada que parecia mais um entalhe.

— Gabriel — disse Sara. — O arcanjo.

Will perguntou:

— Como você sabe?

Ela apontou para a trombeta na boca do anjo.

— Não tem fundamento bíblico, mas algumas religiões acreditam que o Dia do Juízo Final virá quando Gabriel tocar a trombeta. — Sara sabia que Will nunca tinha frequentado a igreja. — É o tipo de coisa que ensinam às crianças na escola dominical. E combina com o nome dele, Marcellus Benedict, acredito que sejam os nomes de dois papas diferentes.

Amanda quis saber:

— Você diria que a tatuagem foi feita recentemente?

A pele na lombar ainda estava irritada da agulha.

— Uma semana, talvez cinco dias? — Ela se aproximou para olhar os arabescos mais de perto. — Ela foi feita em etapas. Quem fez deve ter levado muito tempo. Provavelmente meses. Não é algo que se esquece fácil, e imagino que tenha sido bem cara.

Will segurou a mão do morto.

— Você viu isto embaixo das unhas dele?

— Eu vi que estão sujas — admitiu ela. — É bem comum para um homem dessa idade. Não posso tirar amostra. O IML iria surtar e qualquer coisa que eu achasse seria descartada porque não estabelecemos a cadeia de provas.

Will aproximou o nariz dos dedos do homem.

— Para mim, tem cheiro de gasolina.

Sara também cheirou.

— Não consigo dizer. A polícia me falou que conferiu as câmeras de segurança externas. Não são estáticas. Elas varrem todo o estacionamento, o que os criminosos obviamente sabiam, porque conseguiram não ser pegos largando o corpo. O horário diz que Estevez estava na caçamba havia pelo menos doze horas. O cheiro pode ser de qualquer coisa. — Ela virou a mão para mostrar a Will. — Isto é mais interessante. Estevez obviamente fazia trabalhos manuais. Tem um endurecimento da pele na eminência tenar e na lateral do indicador. Ele segurava algum tipo de ferramenta por períodos longos de tempo. A ferramenta devia ter um peso razoável e ele devia fazer bastante movimento com ela.

Ele perguntou a Amanda:

— Você disse que ele estava desempregado?

— O registro do Estado mostra que ele está recebendo seguro-desemprego há quase um ano.

Sara pensou em outra coisa.

— Pode me passar isso? — Ela apontou para a lupa. Will a pegou e esperou enquanto Sara abria a boca de Estevez à força. O maxilar estava duro. O tendão estourou quando ela abriu os lábios. — Segure aqui — pediu a Will, indicando que ele devia focar nos dentes de cima. — Está vendo essas endentações minúsculas nas bordas inferiores dos dentes superiores frontais? — Will chegou mais perto, depois deixou Amanda olhar. — São impressões repetitivas. Elas acontecem quando se segura algo constantemente entre os dentes. A gente vê esse tipo de coisa em costureiras que mordem as linhas ou marceneiros que põem os pregos na boca.

— E que fazem armários? — perguntou Will.

— É possível. — Sara olhou de novo a mão de Estevez. — Esses calos podem vir de segurar uma pistola de pregos. Eu teria que ver a ferramenta para comparar, mas, se você me dissesse que ele é marceneiro, eu concordaria que as mãos mostram sinais de trabalho nesse ramo. — Ela pegou a mão esquerda do homem. — Está vendo essas cicatrizes no indicador? Elas combinam com ferimentos comuns em marceneiros. Um martelo que escorrega. Um prego que fura a pele. Uma rosca que arranca a camada superior da derme. Está vendo essa cicatriz descendo pela linha central da unha? — Will fez que sim. — Ela corta a cutícula também. Marceneiros usam facas utilitárias para cortar bordas ou marcar a madeira. Às vezes, a lâmina escorrega pela unha ou arranca a pele da lateral do dedo. Muitas vezes eles usam a mão não dominante para alisar massa de vidraceiro ou calafetar, o que causa um desgaste nas pontas dos dedos. As digitais dele mudariam de uma semana para a outra, às vezes de um dia para o outro.

Amanda perguntou:

— Então, ele está fazendo esse trabalho há um tempo?

— Eu diria que, seja qual for o trabalho que tenha causado essas marcas, vem sendo feito há uns dois ou três anos.

— E Heeney, o atirador?

Sara estendeu a mão por baixo do lençol para ver as mãos do outro homem. Não queria olhar de novo o rosto dele.

— Ele era canhoto, mas chutaria que trabalhava no mesmo ramo de Estevez.

Will falou:

— Existe uma ligação, pelo menos. Os dois trabalhavam para Ling-Ling.

Sara perguntou:

— Quem é Ling-Ling?

— Uma suspeita desaparecida. — Amanda olhou o relógio. — Preciso correr com isso. Dra. Linton, pode examinar nosso outro amigo aqui?

Sara não se permitiu tempo para pensar. Puxou o lençol com um movimento rápido. Era a primeira vez que olhava a cara de Franklin Warren Heeney desde que ele havia tentado matá-la. Seus olhos estavam abertos. Os lábios estavam fechados em torno do tubo que tinha sido inserido na garganta para ajudá-lo a respirar. Uma crosta de sangue circulava o pescoço dele, no ponto em que a carne se abrira. Ele ainda estava vestido da cintura para baixo, mas a jaqueta e camiseta tinham sido cortadas para que a equipe do pronto-socorro pudesse tentar salvar a vida dele. Era só uma formalidade, o homem tinha

257

cortado a própria jugular. Tinha perdido quase metade do volume de sangue do corpo antes mesmo de conseguirem pegá-lo do chão e colocá-lo na maca. Sara sabia, porque ela tinha sido a médica dele.

Ela levantou os olhos. Tanto Amanda quanto Will olhavam para ela.

— Me desculpem. — Ela precisou pigarrear antes de falar de novo. — Ele tem mais ou menos a mesma idade de Estevez. De vinte e cinco a trinta anos. Magro demais para sua constituição. — Ela apontou para as marcas de agulha no braço. O acesso que ela inseriu ainda estava grudado na pele. — Usuário recente, pelo menos de forma intravenosa. — Ela achou um otoscópio e verificou o interior do nariz do homem. — Tem cicatrizes importantes nas passagens nasais, provavelmente de cheirar pó. — Ela enfiou o instrumento mais fundo. — Ele fez cirurgia para reparar o septo, então, estamos falando de cocaína ou metanfetamina, talvez oxicodona. Todos são extremamente corrosivos à cartilagem.

Will perguntou:

— E heroína?

— Ah, heroína, lógico. — Sara pediu desculpa de novo: — Me desculpem, a maioria dos usuários de heroína que eu vejo fumam ou injetam. Os que cheiram em geral vão direto para o necrotério.

Amanda cruzou os braços.

— E o estômago dele?

Sara não precisou olhar a pasta. Não tinham feito radiografias. O homem havia expirado antes de poderem pedir qualquer exame. Em vez de continuar a avaliação, Sara se viu olhando de novo para o rosto dele. Franklin Heeney não tinha exatamente cara de coroinha, mas aquela pele marcada de acne e aquelas bochechas encovadas eram reconhecíveis para alguém no mundo. Ele tinha mãe. Tinha pai, uma filha, talvez irmã ou irmão, pessoas que, naquele momento, provavelmente estavam recebendo a notícia de que seu ente querido estava morto.

O ente querido que tinha matado um homem a sangue-frio e socado Sara com tanta violência que ela não conseguira respirar. Ela sentiu o hematoma no peito começando a latejar com aquela lembrança. Ela também tinha mãe — uma irmã, um pai —, e toda a sua família ficaria horrorizada de saber o que havia acontecido com Sara naquele dia.

Amanda perguntou:

— Dra. Linton?

— Perdão. — No tempo que levou para caminhar até a caixa de luvas e colocar um novo par, ela conseguiu se recompor. Ignorou a cara de preocupação de Will e pressionou os dedos na barriga do cadáver. — Não sinto nada de incomum. Os órgãos estão na posição certa e são do tamanho normal. Sem inchaço ou compactação do intestino ou do estômago. — Ela tirou as luvas e as jogou no lixo. A água da pia estava gelada, mas Sara lavou as mãos mesmo assim. — Não posso mandar para bater a radiografia porque vão precisar da identidade do paciente e, sinceramente, não vou fazer uma pessoa viva esperar para satisfazer uma curiosidade. O IML vai dar uma resposta definitiva. — Ela jogou álcool gel na palma, lutando para manter a voz estável. — Então é isso?

— Sim — respondeu Amanda. — Obrigada, Dra. Linton.

Sara não se importou com a resposta dela. Ignorou Will. Ignorou os dois corpos. Manteve os olhos na porta até atravessá-la. No corredor, concentrou-se no elevador, no botão que apertaria, nos números que se acenderiam acima da porta. Ela só queria pensar nos próximos passos, não nos passos que ficavam para trás. Precisava sair daquele lugar, ir para casa, se embrulhar num cobertor no sofá, colocar os cachorros no colo e esquecer aquele dia infeliz.

Houve passos atrás dela. Will estava correndo de novo. Ele a alcançou rápido. Ela se virou. Ele parou a alguns metros.

— Amanda está mandando um alerta geral sobre a tatuagem.

Por que ele estava ali parado? Por que ele ficava correndo até ela sem fazer absolutamente nada?

Ele continuou:

— Talvez a gente encontre...

— Eu realmente não estou nem aí.

Ele ficou olhando, com as mãos no bolso. A manga do paletó estava apertada no braço. Havia um pequeno rasgo no tecido.

Sara apoiou o ombro na parede. Não tinha notado antes, mas havia um corte recente no lóbulo da orelha dele. Ela queria perguntar sobre aquilo, mas ele provavelmente diria que se cortou fazendo a barba.

Talvez ela não quisesse saber o que tinha acontecido. A Polaroid da boca machucada dele ainda estava gravada a fogo em sua memória O que mais tinham feito com ele? O que mais ele tinha feito consigo mesmo?

Will falou:

— Por que nenhuma das mulheres na minha vida me liga quando precisa da minha ajuda?

— Angie não liga para você?

Ele baixou os olhos para o chão entre eles.

Ela disse:

— Desculpe. Não foi justo. Foi um dia muito cansativo.

Will não levantou os olhos. Em vez disso, segurou a mão dela. Seus dedos se entrelaçaram aos dela. A pele de Will estava morna, quase quente. Ele passou o polegar pelo interior da palma dela, pela cartilagem entre seus dedos. Sara fechou os olhos enquanto ele explorava lentamente cada centímetro de sua mão, acariciando as linhas e reentrâncias, pressionando o polegar delicadamente contra a pulsação no punho dela. Seu toque era paliativo. Ela sentiu o corpo começando a relaxar. Sua respiração ganhou a mesma cadência que a dele.

As portas do necrotério se abriram. Sara arrancou a mão ao mesmo tempo que Will. Nenhum dos dois se olhou. Eram dois adolescentes pegos no banco de trás de um carro estacionado.

Amanda levantou o celular no ar, triunfante.

— Roger Ling quer conversar.

12

Faith estava o mais perto que já estivera na vida de um colapso nervoso. Seus dentes não paravam de bater, apesar de o suor pingar pelo corpo. Ela tinha vomitado o café da manhã e precisava se forçar a almoçar. Sua cabeça doía tanto que era sofrido até fechar os olhos. Sua glicemia estava igualmente frágil. Precisara ligar para o consultório da médica para saber o que fazer. Eles haviam ameaçado colocá-la no hospital se não conseguisse controlar os níveis de glicose. Faith tinha prometido voltar a dar notícias, depois tinha ido ao banheiro, ligado o chuveiro na temperatura mais quente que conseguia suportar e chorado de soluçar por meia hora.

A mesma série de pensamentos ficava passando por sua cabeça como pneus abrindo um sulco numa estrada de cascalho. Eles tinham entrado na casa dela. Tinham mexido nas coisas dela. Nas coisas de Jeremy. Sabiam quando ele tinha nascido. Sabiam em quais escolas ele havia estudado. Sabiam do que ele gostava e não gostava. Tinham planejado aquilo — tudo aquilo, até o último detalhe.

A ameaça parecia uma sentença de morte. Boca fechada. Olhos abertos. Faith não se achava capaz de abrir mais os olhos nem fechar mais a boca. Tinha revistado a casa duas vezes. Não parava de olhar o celular, o e-mail, o Facebook de Jeremy. Eram três da tarde. Ela estava presa em casa que nem um animal enjaulado havia quase dez horas.

E ainda nada.

— Ei, mãe?

Jeremy entrou na cozinha. Faith estava sentada à mesa, olhando o quintal, onde os investigadores Taylor e Ruivo estavam conversando seriamente com o chão. Ela via pela atitude entediada dos dois que estavam só esperando notícias do chefe para poder voltar ao trabalho normal. Até onde sabiam, o caso tinha sofrido uma parada brusca. Horas de mais haviam se passado. Ninguém entrara em contato. Ela lia a verdade nos olhos deles. Eles acreditavam sinceramente que Evelyn Mitchell estava morta.

— Mãe?

Faith esfregou o braço de Jeremy.

— O que foi? Emma acordou?

A bebê tinha dormido demais na noite anterior. Estava manhosa e irritada, e havia gritado quase uma hora antes de finalmente se entregar à soneca da tarde.

— Ela está bem — respondeu Jeremy. — Eu ia dar uma volta. Sair de casa por um minuto. Respirar um ar fresco.

— Não. Não quero que você saia de casa.

A expressão dele mostrou a Faith o quanto sua voz estava rígida. Ela apertou o braço dele.

— Quero que você fique aqui, tudo bem?

— Estou cansado de ficar preso.

— Eu também, mas quero que você me prometa que não vai sair de casa. — Ela manipulou as emoções dele. — Já tenho que me preocupar com a sua avó. Não me obrigue a colocar você na minha lista.

A relutância dele era óbvia, mas ele disse:

— Tudo bem.

— Faça alguma coisa com seu tio Zeke. Vão jogar baralho ou algo do tipo.

— Ele fica emburrado quando perde.

— Você também.

Faith o mandou embora da cozinha. Acompanhou o trajeto dele pela casa até o quarto no andar de cima pelos rangidos familiares das tábuas e das escadas. Ela devia botar Zeke para fazer os vários pequenos consertos de que ela precisava. Claro que isso envolveria falar de fato com ele e Faith estava dando tudo de si para evitar o irmão. Milagrosamente, ele parecia estar fazendo o mesmo. Fazia três horas que ele estava na garagem, trabalhando no laptop.

Faith se levantou da mesa e começou a andar de lá para cá na esperança de gastar um pouco da energia ansiosa. Não durou muito. Ela se debruçou na mesa e mexeu no teclado do próprio laptop para acender a tela. Usou o mouse para atualizar o Facebook de Jeremy. A roda colorida começou a girar. Jeremy devia estar jogando alguma coisa lá em cima e deixando a rede lenta.

O telefone tocou. Faith deu um pulo. Ficava sobressaltada com qualquer barulho inesperado. Estava nervosa como um gato. A porta dos fundos se abriu. O Ruivo esperou enquanto ela tirava o telefone do gancho. Ela via pela cara cansada do homem que ele achava que aquilo era não só uma mera formalidade, mas um serviço abaixo de seus talentos.

Ela levou o telefone ao ouvido.

— Alô?

— Faith.

Era Victor Martinez. Ela dispensou o Ruivo com um aceno.

— Oi.

— Oi.

Depois que a parte fácil tinha acabado, nenhum dos dois parecia capaz de falar. Ela não conversava com Victor havia treze meses, desde que lhe enviara uma mensagem dizendo que ele precisava tirar as coisas da casa dela, senão ia largar tudo na rua.

Victor quebrou o silêncio.

— Alguma notícia da sua mãe?

— Não. Nada.

— Faz mais de vinte e quatro horas, né?

Ela não confiava que conseguiria falar. Victor tinha o hábito de apontar o óbvio e seu amor por séries criminais significava que ele sabia tanto quanto Faith que o tempo estava contra eles.

— Jeremy está bem?

— Está. Obrigada por trazê-lo para casa ontem. E por ficar com ele. — Ela teve a ideia de perguntar: — Você não viu nada de incomum enquanto estava aqui, né? Ninguém rondando a casa?

— Claro que não. Eu teria falado para a polícia.

— Quanto tempo você ficou aqui antes de eles chegarem?

— Não muito. Seu irmão veio mais ou menos uma hora depois e eu fui embora.

O cérebro exausto de Faith teve dificuldade de fazer a conta. Os sequestradores de Evelyn não hesitaram. Haviam vindo direto da casa dela para cá. Estavam familiarizados o bastante com o espaço para subir direto para o quarto de Faith e plantar o dedo embaixo do travesseiro dela. Talvez estivessem vigiando a casa mesmo antes disso. Talvez tivessem escutado suas ligações ou conferido seu calendário do laptop e soubessem que ela não estaria em casa. Nada ali era protegido por senha, porque ela sempre partira do pressuposto de que era um lugar seguro.

Faith não ouviu algo que Victor falou.

— É o quê?

— Falei que seu irmão é meio babaca.

Faith se irritou:

— Não é exatamente um momento fácil para ele, Victor. Nossa mãe está desaparecida. Só Deus sabe se está viva ou morta. Zeke largou tudo para ficar com Jeremy. Lamento se você achou que ele foi grosso. Está meio difícil ser simpático agora.

— Segure a onda, tá? Me desculpe. Eu não devia ter dito isso.

A respiração dela estava acelerada outra vez. Faith tentou recuperar o controle. Queria gritar com alguém. Essa pessoa provavelmente não precisava ser Victor.

— Está aí? — perguntou ele.

Faith não podia mais arrastar aquilo.

— Eu sei que Jeremy mostrou uma foto de Emma para você.

Ele pigarreou.

— O que você está pensando sobre ela... — Faith pressionou as pálpebras fechadas com as pontas dos dedos. — Você tem razão.

Ele ficou em silêncio pelo que pareceu uma eternidade. Finalmente, falou:

— Ela é linda.

Faith abaixou a mão. Olhou para o teto. Seus hormônios estavam tão doidos que mesmo a coisa mais idiota do mundo seria capaz de fazê-la explodir. Ela segurou o telefone com o ombro e tentou atualizar o Facebook de Jeremy de novo.

— Quando tudo isso acabar, eu gostaria de conhecê-la.

Faith viu a roda girar na tela do computador enquanto o processador trabalhava. Ela não conseguia pensar em ver Victor com Emma.

Pegando a bebê no colo. Fazendo carinho no cabelo dela. Comentando que olhar para aqueles olhos castanho-claros era como se ver no espelho. Faith só podia pensar no agora e em como cada segundo que passava tornava menos provável que Evelyn Mitchell fosse ver o aniversário de um ano da neta.

— Sua mãe é uma guerreira — disse Victor. E continuou, quase melancólico: — Que nem você.

A página finalmente carregou. GoodKnight92 tinha postado um comentário oito minutos atrás.

— Tenho que ir.

Faith desligou o telefone. Sua mão pairou acima do laptop. Ela ficou olhando as palavras na tela. Tinham algo de familiar.

Você deve estar se sentindo preso. Por que não sai de casa e respira um ar fresco?

Eles tinham entrado de novo em contato com Jeremy, e o filho, o menininho dela, tinha estado a ponto de sair pela porta e colocar a vida em risco para recuperar a avó.

Ela levantou a voz, chamando:

— Jeremy?

Faith esperou. Não ouviu passos lá em cima, nenhum rangido na escada ou nas tábuas.

— Jeremy? — ela chamou de novo, entrando na sala. Uma eternidade se passou. Faith agarrou as costas do sofá para não cair. Sua voz vibrou de pânico. — Jeremy!

O coração dela deu um pulo com o som surdo vindo lá de cima, passos pesados pelo chão. Mas foi Zeke quem chamou de cima do patamar.

— Meu Deus, Faith, o que foi?

Faith mal conseguia falar.

— Onde Jeremy está?

— Eu disse que ele podia dar uma volta.

O Ruivo veio da cozinha com uma cara confusa. Antes que ele conseguisse falar alguma coisa, Faith agarrou a arma do ombro dele e saiu voando. Não registrou nada na mente enquanto abria a porta da frente e corria para fora da casa. Só parou quando estava no meio da rua. Ela viu um vulto lá na frente. Ele estava prestes a dobrar a esquina da próxima rua. Alto, magrelo, calça jeans larga e um moletom amarelo da Georgia Tech.

— Jeremy! — ela gritou. Um carro parou no cruzamento, a alguns metros do filho dela. — Jeremy!

Ele não a escutou. Andou na direção do carro.

Faith correu, balançando os braços, batendo no asfalto com os pés descalços. Agarrou a arma com tanta força que parecia fazer parte de sua pele.

— Jeremy! — ela berrou. Ele se virou. O carro estava na frente dele. Cinza-escuro. Quatro portas. Ford Focus modelo novo com detalhes em cromo. A janela se abriu. Jeremy se virou de volta para o carro e se debruçou para olhar lá dentro. — Pare! — Faith berrou, sentindo um aperto na garganta. — Saia de perto do carro! Saia de perto do carro!

A motorista estava inclinada para Jeremy. Faith viu uma adolescente boquiaberta atrás do volante, obviamente aterrorizada com uma louca armada correndo pela rua. O carro saiu cantando pneu assim que Faith alcançou o filho. Ela deu um encontrão nele, quase o derrubando no chão.

— Por quê? — perguntou ela, agarrando o braço dele com tanta força que seus dedos doeram.

Ele se afastou, esfregando o braço.

— Caramba, mãe, qual é seu problema? Ela estava perdida. Pediu informação.

Faith estava zonza de medo e adrenalina. Ela se curvou e pôs a mão no joelho. Estava com a arma ao lado. O Ruivo também estava ali. Ele tomou a arma de volta.

— Agente Mitchell, isso não foi bacana.

As palavras dele a encheram de raiva.

— Não foi bacana? — Ela bateu no peito dele com a palma da mão aberta. — Não foi bacana?

— Agente.

O tom de voz dele deixava implícito que ela estava histérica, o que só serviu para amplificar sua fúria mais um pouco.

— E deixar meu filho sair pela porta quando você foi designado para cuidar dele? Também não foi bacana? — Ela o empurrou de novo. — E você e seu parceiro parados coçando o saco enquanto meu menino some? — Outro empurrão. — Isso é bacana?

O Ruivo levantou as mãos, rendendo-se.

— Faith — disse Zeke. Ela não tinha notado o irmão ali parado, talvez porque, para variar, ele não estivesse piorando tudo. — Vamos só voltar para casa.

Ela estendeu a mão para Jeremy, com a palma para cima.

— Me dê o iPhone.

Ele pareceu chocado.

— Quê?

— Agora — ordenou ela.

— Todos os meus jogos estão nele.

— Não estou nem aí.

— O que eu vou ficar fazendo?

— Leia um livro! — ela berrou, com a voz aguda. — Só fique offline. Escutou? Sem internet!

— Meu Deus.

Ele olhou ao redor procurando apoio, mas Faith não queria saber nem se o próprio Deus descesse e pedisse para ela pegar leve com o garoto.

Ela disse:

— Se precisar, eu amarro você com uma corda na minha cintura.

Ele sabia que não era brincadeira, ela já tinha feito aquilo antes.

— Não é justo.

Ele bateu o telefone na mão dela. Faith o teria jogado no chão e pisoteado se aquela porcaria não tivesse sido tão cara.

— Sem internet — repetiu Faith. — Sem ligações. Nenhum tipo de comunicação, e fique dentro da porra da casa. Escutou?

Ele andou em direção à casa, dando as costas para ela. Faith não ia liberá-lo tão fácil.

— Escutou?

— Escutei! — gritou ele. — Caramba!

O Ruivo enfiou a arma de volta no coldre, ajustando as alças como uma animadora de torcida arrogante. Seguiu Jeremy rua afora. Faith foi mancando atrás dele. Seus pés estavam machucados do asfalto pedregoso. Zeke caminhou ao lado dela. Seu ombro roçou no da irmã. Faith se preparou para algum tipo de sermão, mas ele ficou compassivamente em silêncio enquanto subiam a entrada de carros e entravam na casa.

Faith jogou o iPhone de Jeremy na mesa da cozinha. Lógico que ele queria sair. O lugar estava começando a parecer uma prisão. Ela apoiou o peso do corpo na cadeira. O que ela estava pensando? Como algum deles podia ficar seguro ali? Os sequestradores de Evelyn conheciam a planta da casa. Obviamente tinham escolhido Jeremy como alvo. Qualquer um podia estar naquele carro. Podiam ter aberto a janela, apontado uma arma para a cabeça dele e puxado o gatilho. Ele podia ter sangrado até morrer no meio da rua e Faith só saberia que tinha alguma coisa errada quando a porcaria do Facebook dele carregasse.

— Faith? — Zeke estava parado no meio da cozinha. O tom indicava que não era a primeira vez que ele a chamava. — O que está acontecendo com você?

Faith cruzou os braços.

— Onde você anda se hospedando? Você não estava dormindo na casa da mamãe. Eu teria visto suas coisas.

— Na Dobbins.

Ela devia ter imaginado. Zeke sempre amou o anonimato sem personalidade do alojamento na base, mesmo que a Reserva de Dobbins ficasse a uma hora de carro do hospital de veteranos em que ele estava trabalhando.

— Preciso que você me faça um favor.

Ele ficou cético na mesma hora.

— O quê?

— Quero que você leve Jeremy e Emma para a base com você. Hoje. Agora. — A polícia de Atlanta não era capaz de proteger a família dela, mas a Força Aérea dos Estados Unidos era. — Não sei por quanto tempo. Só preciso que você fique com eles na base. Não deixe nenhum dos dois sair até eu liberar.

— Por quê?

— Porque preciso ter certeza de que eles estão seguros.

— Seguros do quê? O que você está planejando?

Faith olhou para o quintal para conferir se os investigadores não estavam ouvindo. O Ruivo a olhou com o maxilar tenso. Ela se virou de volta para o irmão.

— Preciso que você confie em mim.

Zeke soltou uma risada de desdém.

— Por que eu começaria a fazer isso agora?

— Porque eu sei o que estou fazendo, Zeke. Eu sou policial. Fui treinada para esse tipo de coisa.

— Que tipo de coisa? Correr na rua descalça como se estivesse fugindo do hospício?

— Eu vou trazer a nossa mãe de volta, Zeke. Nem que eu morra. Vou trazê-la de volta.

— Você e mais qual exército? — zombou ele. — Vai chamar a tia Mandy e sujar a cara de todos eles de batom?

Ela deu um soco na cara dele. Ele pareceu mais chocado do que ferido. Pelo que ela estava sentindo, os nós dos dedos dela talvez tivessem quebrado. Apesar disso, ela teve alguma satisfação ao ver uma linha fina de sangue pingar no lábio superior dele.

— Meu Deus — murmurou ele. — Para que isso?

— Você vai precisar pegar meu carro. Não dá para colocar a cadeirinha no Corvette. Posso dar algum dinheiro para gasolina e compras de mercado e eu...

— Espere aí.

A voz dele foi abafada pela mão enquanto ele tateava o nariz, avaliando os danos. Ele a olhou — olhou de verdade — pela primeira vez desde que ela havia entrado pela porta da própria casa. Faith já tinha batido antes no irmão. Já o tinha queimado com um fósforo. Já tinha dado uma surra nele com um cabide. Até onde se lembrava, era a primeira vez que qualquer violência entre os dois parecia funcionar de fato.

— Tudo bem. — Ele usou a torradeira para ver seu reflexo. O nariz não estava quebrado, mas um hematoma roxo forte estava começando a se formar embaixo do olho. — Mas não vou pegar seu Mini. Já vou parecer bem retardado do jeito que estou.

13

Will demorava a sentir raiva, mas, quando sentia, segurava esse sentimento como um sovina com um pote de ouro. Não jogava coisas nem usava os punhos. Não se enfurecia nem levantava a voz. Na verdade, acontecia o contrário. Ele ficava quieto — completamente em silêncio. Era como se suas cordas vocais ficassem paralisadas. Ele guardava tudo porque, por sua vasta experiência com pessoas raivosas, Will sabia que botar para fora significava que alguém podia acabar muito machucado.

Não que essa expressão de raiva em especial não tivesse suas desvantagens. Seu silêncio teimoso o fizera ser suspenso da escola mais de uma vez. Anos antes, Amanda o transferira para as partes baixas das montanhas do norte da Geórgia por sua recusa em responder às perguntas dela. Uma vez, ele parou de falar com Angie por três dias inteiros, por medo de dizer algo que não conseguiria retirar. Eles moravam juntos, dormiam juntos, jantavam juntos, faziam tudo juntos, e ele não dirigiu uma palavra a ela por setenta e duas horas completas. Se tivesse uma categoria nas Paraolimpíadas para analfabetos funcionais mudos, Will não teria dificuldade de ganhar o ouro.

Tudo isso para dizer que não falar com Amanda durante o trajeto de cinco horas até a Prisão Estadual Coastal não era nada. O preocupante era que a intensidade da raiva de Will não diminuía. Ele nunca odiara outro ser humano mais do que quando Amanda lhe dissera que, aliás, Sara quase tinha sido assassinada. E esse ódio não ia embora. Ele ficava esperando sentir aquele alívio, a panela indo de fogo alto a baixo, mas não vinha. Mesmo naquele momento, enquanto Amanda andava de lá para cá na frente dele, indo de uma ponta a outra da sala de espera de visitantes vazia, como um pato no tiro ao alvo, ele sentia a fúria queimando por dentro.

A pior parte era que ele queria falar. Ansiava por falar. Queria explicar tim-tim por tim-tim e ver o rosto dela desabar ao perceber que Will a desprezava verdadeira e irrevogavelmente pelo que ela lhe tinha feito. Ele nunca havia sido um homem vingativo, mas queria muito, muito feri-la.

Amanda parou de andar. Colocou as mãos na cintura.

— Não sei o que andaram falando para você, mas ficar emburrado não é atraente num homem.

Will olhou para o chão. Havia marcas no linóleo das mulheres e crianças que tinham passado seus fins de semana ali esperando para visitar os homens dentro das celas.

Ela continuou:

— Como regra, só deixo alguém me chamar daquele nome uma vez. Acho que você escolheu um momento adequado.

Então, ele não tinha ficado completamente mudo. Quando Amanda lhe contara sobre Sara, ele a tinha chamado pela palavra que parecia com o nome dela. Mas não em espanhol.

— O que você quer, Will, um pedido de desculpas? — Ela soltou uma risada. — Tudo bem, peço desculpas. Me desculpe por não deixar você ficar distraído do seu trabalho. Me desculpe por evitar que sua cabeça entrasse em parafuso. Me desculpe...

A boca dele se mexeu por vontade própria.

— Dá para você só calar a boca?

— Como é que é?

Ele não se repetiu. Não estava nem aí se ela havia escutado, ou se seu emprego corria algum risco, ou se ela ia acabar com a raça dele por confrontá-la. Will não conseguia se lembrar da última vez que havia experimentado uma agonia como a daquela tarde. Eles tinham ficado sentados naquela merda de armazém por uma hora inteira até a polícia de Doraville os liberar. Will entendia, racionalmente, por que os investigadores queriam falar com eles. Havia dois corpos e buracos de bala por todo lado. Havia uma pilha de metralhadoras ilegais numa prateleira nos fundos. Havia um cofre enorme na sala de Julia Ling, com a porta aberta e notas de cem dólares espalhadas pelo chão. Não dava para só chegar nessa cena do crime e liberar as duas testemunhas. Havia formulários a preencher, perguntas a responder. Will tivera que prestar depoimento. Tivera que esperar enquanto Amanda prestava o dela. E, pelo jeito, ela levou todo o tempo do mundo. Ele ficou sentado no carro, vendo-a falar com os investigadores, sentindo um terremoto no peito.

Ele pegava e soltava o celular mil vezes. Devia ligar para Sara? Devia deixá-la em paz? Ela precisava dele? Mas será que não ligaria se precisasse? Ele tinha que vê-la. Se a visse, saberia como reagir, saberia do que ela precisava e como ajudá-la. Ele a abraçaria. Beijaria a bochecha dela, o pescoço, a boca. Ele faria tudo ficar bem.

Ou só ficaria lá parado no corredor que nem um trouxa, molestando a mão dela.

Amanda estalou os dedos, chamando a atenção dele. Will não levantou a cabeça, mas ela falou do mesmo jeito.

— Seu contato de emergência é Angela Polaski. Ou, melhor dizendo, Angie Trent, suponho, já que ela é sua esposa. — Ela fez uma pausa para criar um efeito. — Ela ainda *é* sua esposa?

Ele fez que não. Nunca tinha tido tanta vontade na vida de socar uma mulher.

— O que você queria que eu fizesse, Will?

Ele continuou balançando a cabeça.

— Então, eu falo que a sua... sei lá, o que a Dra. Linton é para você atualmente? Amante? Namorada? *Amiguinha?* Eu falo para você que ela está com um problema, e aí? A gente larga tudo para você poder ficar olhando apaixonado para ela?

Will se levantou. Ele não ia mais ficar ali. Pediria carona na estrada para voltar para Atlanta se fosse necessário.

Ela suspirou como se o mundo estivesse contra ela.

— O diretor vai chegar a qualquer minuto. Preciso que você cresça para eu poder preparar você para sua conversa com Roger Ling.

Will a olhou pela primeira vez desde que tinham saído do hospital.

— Eu?

272

— Ele pediu especificamente por você.

Era algum tipo de truque, mas ele não conseguia entender aonde aquilo ia dar.

— Como é que ele sabe meu nome?

— Imagino que a irmã tenha contado.

Até onde Will sabia, Julia Ling continuava foragida.

— Ela ligou para ele na prisão?

Ela cruzou os braços.

— Roger Ling está na solitária por ter escondido uma lâmina no reto. Ele não recebe ligações. Não recebe visitas.

O isolamento nunca impediu o sistema de mensagens da prisão. Havia tantos celulares ilegais dentro das paredes que no ano anterior, durante uma greve de presidiários no estado inteiro, o *New York Times* tinha sido inundado de ligações de detentos fazendo suas exigências.

Mesmo assim, Will falou:

— Roger Ling pediu para falar comigo especificamente?

— Sim, Will. O pedido veio pelo advogado dele. Ele pediu para falar com você especificamente. — Ela admitiu: — Mas, claro, ligaram para mim primeiro. Ninguém sabe quem raios você é. Só Roger, pelo jeito.

Will se recostou na cadeira. Sentiu que apertava o maxilar com força. O silêncio queria voltar. Sentia-o como uma sombra pairando sobre ele.

Ela perguntou:

— Quem você acha que é o policial que confrontou a Dra. Linton no hospital?

Ele balançou a cabeça. Não queria mais pensar em Sara. Ficava enjoado toda vez que pensava no que ela tinha passado naquele dia. Sozinha.

Amanda se repetiu:

— Quem você acha que é o policial?

De novo, ela estalou os dedos para chamar a atenção dele.

Ele levantou a cabeça. Queria quebrar a mão dela.

— Isso não tem a ver comigo. É pela Faith, para trazer de volta a mãe dela. Agora, quem você acha que é o policial?

Ele pigarreou para tirar a sensação de vidro da garganta.

— Como você conhece toda essa gente?

— Que gente?

— Hector Ortiz. Roger Ling. Julia Ling. Perry, o guarda-costas que dirige uma Mercedes. Por que você trata toda essa gente pelo nome?

Ela ficou em silêncio, obviamente ponderando se deveria responder. Enfim, cedeu.

— Você sabe que eu cresci nesse trabalho junto com Evelyn. Fomos cadetes juntas. Fomos parceiras antes de cansarem de ver a gente resolvendo todos os casos deles. — A lembrança a fez balançar a cabeça. — Esses são os bandidos que estavam do outro lado. Drogas. Estupro. Homicídio. Agressão. Negociação de reféns. Crime organizado e corrupção. Lavagem de dinheiro. Eles estão aí há tanto tempo quanto nós. — Ela completou, pesarosa: — Ou seja, muito, muito tempo.

— Você trabalhou em casos contra eles?

Havia cinquenta cadeiras na sala, mas ela se sentou bem ao lado dele.

— Ignatio Ortiz e Roger Ling não chegaram fácil ao topo. Eles subiram passando por cima de cadáveres. Muitos e muitos cadáveres. E a parte triste é que, em algum momento, foram seres humanos. Eram pessoas normais e bacanas que iam à igreja todo domingo e batiam cartão no emprego durante a semana.

Amanda balançou de novo a cabeça, e Will via que suas palavras evocavam memórias que ela preferia esquecer. Mesmo assim, ela disse:

— Sabe, a palavra *marginalidade* se refere à parte da sociedade que nunca é vista, mas também quer dizer a parte vulnerável. A parte fraca. É disso que monstros como Roger Ling e Ignatio Ortiz se aproveitam. Vício. Ganância. Pobreza. Desespero. Quando esses caras descobriram como explorar essas pessoas, nunca mais olharam para trás. Começaram arrombando carros para traficantes aos doze anos. Mataram antes de terem idade para comprar bebida num bar legalmente. Cortaram gargantas e espancaram velhinhas até a morte e fizeram tudo o que era necessário para chegar ao topo e manter esse poder. Então, quando você me pergunta por que eu chamo todos pelo nome, é porque eu *conheço* essa gente. Eu sei quem são. Vi a escuridão da alma deles. Mas garanto a você que não é uma via de mão dupla.

274

Eles não fazem a mais puta ideia de quem eu sou, e passei minha carreira mantendo as coisas assim.

Will estava cansado de ser cauteloso.

— Eles conhecem Evelyn.

— Sim — admitiu Amanda. — Acredito que conheçam.

Ele se recostou na cadeira. Era uma confissão chocante. Ele não sabia como reagir. Infelizmente — ou talvez felizmente —, ela não deu a ele essa oportunidade.

Amanda juntou as mãos. A hora do desabafo tinha acabado.

— Vamos falar desse policial que confrontou Sara no hospital.

Will ainda estava tentando entender o que tinha acabado de acontecer. Por um breve momento, havia se esquecido completamente de Sara.

— Chuck Finn — anunciou ela.

Will apoiou a cabeça na parede. Sentiu bloco de concreto gelado contra o couro cabeludo dele.

— Ele era policial. Algumas coisas não se perdem, independentemente da quantidade de heroína injetada. Ele é alto. Provavelmente perdeu muito peso por causa do vício. Sara não o teria reconhecido pela foto de identificação criminal. Suponho que ele seja fumante. A maioria dos viciados é.

— Então, no hospital: você acha que Chuck Finn entendeu, pelo que Sara falou, que Marcellus Estevez talvez sobrevivesse, e por isso mandou Franklin Heeney lá para matar o cara.

— Você não acha?

Amanda não respondeu rápido. Ele percebeu que o que ela havia dito sobre Evelyn Mitchell estava pesando em sua consciência.

— Não sei mais o que eu acho, Will. E juro por Deus que é verdade.

Ela parecia cansada. Seus ombros estavam curvados. Havia uma espécie de distanciamento nela. Ele repassou conversa dos dois e se perguntou o que finalmente a tinha feito admitir que Evelyn Mitchell não era exatamente limpa. Nunca na vida tinha visto Amanda desistir de nada. Parte dele tinha pena e outra parte percebeu que ele talvez nunca mais tivesse aquela oportunidade.

Ele atacou enquanto ela estava de guarda baixa.

— Por que eles não atiraram em você na frente do armazém?

— Eu sou vice-diretora da GBI. É um cargo muito importante.

— Eles já sequestraram uma policial condecorada. Tentaram atirar em você no armazém. Eles mataram Castillo. Por que não mataram você?

— Eu sei lá, Will. — Ela esfregou os olhos. — Acho que a gente deve ter ficado no meio de alguma guerra.

Will olhou o pôster da Campanha contra a Metanfetamina na parede. Uma mulher sem dentes com pele cheia de escaras o olhava de volta. Ele ficou pensando se aquela seria a aparência da viciada que tinha avisado Sara sobre o homem largado ao lado da caçamba de lixo. Quanto tempo havia levado até Marcellus Estevez estar morto e Franklin Henney estar lutando com Sara no chão, ameaçando rasgar a cara dela com um bisturi?

Minutos. Talvez dez, no máximo.

Will não conseguia evitar. Ele colocou os cotovelos nos joelhos e apoiou a cabeça nas mãos.

— Você devia ter me contado. — Ele ouviu uma voz distante na cabeça gritando para ele calar a boca. Mas não conseguia. — Você não tinha direito de esconder isso de mim.

Amanda deu um suspiro pesado.

— Talvez eu devesse ter contado a você, sim. Ou talvez tivesse razão de esconder. Se for a primeira opção, me desculpe. Se for a segunda, pode ficar bravo comigo depois. Preciso que você repasse a situação comigo. Preciso descobrir o que está acontecendo. Se não por mim, pela Faith.

A voz dela tinha o mesmo desespero que ele sentia. O dia a tinha derrotado por completo. Will não conseguia evitar. Por mais que a odiasse naquele momento, não podia ser cruel.

E, em algum ponto em meio a tudo aquilo, o alívio veio. Ele não tinha notado, mas, em algum momento dos últimos dez minutos, a raiva dele tinha começado a diminuir aos poucos, então, naquele instante, quando pensava no assunto, quando considerava o que Amanda tinha feito em relação a Sara, Will sentia uma raiva purulenta em vez de um ódio ardente.

Ele respirou fundo e, devagar, soltou o ar enquanto voltava a se sentar.

— Tudo bem. Temos que supor que todos os homens mortos trabalhavam na oficina de Julia. Alguns oficialmente, outros não, todos atuando nas duas frentes do negócio dela.

— Você acha que Ling-Ling mandou Ricardo Ortiz à Suécia para comprar heroína?

— Não, acho que Ricardo se precipitou. Acho que animou os jovenzinhos, achando que podiam tomar o negócio de Ling-Ling. Decidiu por conta própria ir para a Suécia. — Will olhou o relógio. Eram quase sete. — Ele foi torturado, provavelmente por Benny Choo.

— Então, por que não só o cortaram para tirar as drogas de dentro dele e acabaram logo com o assunto?

— Porque ele falou que sabia onde poderiam conseguir mais dinheiro.

— Com Evelyn.

— Foi o que eu disse antes. — Ele se voltou para ela. — Chuck Finn mencionou em uma das sessões de grupo com Hironobu Kwon na Healing Winds que a antiga chefe dele estava sentada numa montanha de dinheiro. Corta para ontem de manhã. Ricardo com a barriga cheia de heroína e Benny Choo acabando com ele. O amigo Hironobu Kwon fala que sabe onde podem arrumar dinheiro para sair daquela situação. — Will deu de ombros. — Eles vão para a casa de Evelyn. Benny Choo vai junto para não deixar os dois darem no pé. Só que não conseguem encontrar o dinheiro, e Evelyn se recusa a entregar.

— Talvez não estivessem esperando encontrar Hector Ortiz lá. Ricardo reconheceria o primo do pai.

Will queria perguntar o que Hector Ortiz estava fazendo na casa de Evelyn para começo de conversa, mas não queria fazer Amanda mentir para ele naquele momento.

— Ricardo Ortiz sabia que matar Hector causaria algum problema. Ele já estava dando as costas ao próprio pai contrabandeando heroína. Ling-Ling está atrás da cabeça dele, porque descobriu que Ricardo também a traiu. O grupo dele não consegue encontrar o dinheiro na casa de Evelyn. Ela se recusa a falar. Ricardo neste ponto deve perceber que sua vida não vale muita coisa. Ele está entupido de balõezinhos de heroína e não consegue evacuar. Foi espancado até quase a morte. Benny Choo está apontando uma arma para a cabeça dele. — Will repassou o depoimento de Faith sobre o confronto dela com Choo e Ortiz. — A última palavra de Ricardo foi "Almeja". Foi assim que Julia Ling chamou Evelyn, certo? Como Ricardo saberia disso?

— Imagino que, se sua teoria se provar correta, de que tudo isso veio de Chuck Finn, então foi daí.

— Por que o nome de Evelyn seria a última palavra na boca de Ricardo?

— É o nome de guerra dela. Eu ficaria surpresa se Ricardo soubesse o nome real. — Ela explicou: — Não são só os bandidos que se dão apelidos. Se você trabalhar um tempo com tráfico de drogas, eles inventam uma gíria para falar de você. Às vezes, isso vaza para o esquadrão. "Hump" e "Hop" obviamente eram abreviações dos sobrenomes. Boyd Spivey era Marreta. Chuck Finn era chamado de Peixe, provavelmente porque não conseguiam lembrar o nome de um lemingue. — Ela sorriu, mais uma piada interna. — Roger Ling ficou com o crédito por inventar "Almeja", o que pareceu curioso na época até percebermos que ele não falava nadinha do idioma dos pais. Mandarim, caso você queira saber.

— E você?

— Eu não trabalho com tráfico de drogas.

— Mas eles conhecem você.

— Wag — ela disse. — Abreviação de Wagner.

Will não acreditou nela.

— Por que Roger Ling pediu para falar comigo?

Ela deu uma risada, surpresa.

— Você não pode achar mesmo que é o único homem nesta prisão que me despreza neste momento.

Houve um zunido alto e um estrondo de portões se abrindo e fechando. Dois guardas entraram na sala de espera, seguidos por um homem mais novo com óculos de Harry Potter e um corte de cabelo desleixado para combinar. Definitivamente não era uma das velhas amigas de Amanda. Havia remendos de veludo nos cotovelos da jaqueta de cotelê dele. A gravata era de malha de algodão. A camisa tinha uma mancha no bolso. Ele cheirava a panqueca.

— Jimmy Kagan — apresentou-se, apertando a mão de cada um.

— Não sei que pauzinhos você mexeu, vice-diretora, mas é a primeira vez nos meus seis anos como diretor aqui que sou chamado para voltar ao trabalho tão tarde da noite.

Amanda tinha voltado facilmente à sua antiga personalidade. Era como ver uma atriz entrando na personagem.

— Agradeço por sua cooperação, diretor Kagan. Todos temos que fazer nossa parte.

— Eu não tive muita escolha — admitiu Kagan, indicando que os guardas deviam abrir a porta principal da prisão. Ele os levou por um longo corredor a passos rápidos. — Eu não vou atrapalhar todo o meu sistema, não importa que contatos você tenha. Agente Trent, você vai ter que entrar na área das celas. Ling está na solitária há uma semana. Pode falar com ele pela abertura da porta. Você deve saber com que tipo de pessoa está lidando, mas digo desde já que eu não entraria numa sala com Roger Ling nem que apontassem uma arma para a minha cabeça. Na verdade, tenho pavor de que um dia aconteça justamente isso comigo.

Amanda levantou uma sobrancelha para Will.

— Pelo jeito que você fala, parece que os primatas estão cuidando do zoológico.

Kagan olhou para ela como se achasse que ela estava delirando ou era maluca. Ele disse a Will:

— Em todos os períodos da existência do sistema prisional dos Estados Unidos, pelo menos metade da população de detentos foi diagnosticada com algum tipo de doença mental.

Will assentiu com a cabeça. Já tinha ouvido essa estatística. Todas as prisões do país juntas compravam mais Prozac do que qualquer outra instituição.

Kagan continuou:

— Alguns são piores do que outros. Ling é o pior dos piores. Devia estar numa ala psiquiátrica. Trancado. Com a chave jogada fora.

Outro portão se abriu e fechou.

Kagan listou as regras.

— Não chegue perto da porta. Não ache que está seguro só porque está a um braço de distância. Esse homem é cheio de recursos e tem muito tempo livre. A lâmina que achamos enfiada na bunda dele estava num embrulho feito à mão com fios puxados dos lençóis da cama. Ele levou dois meses para fazer. E trançou uma estrela da Yellow Rebel, como forma de zombaria. Deve ter tingido com urina.

Kagan parou em mais uma porta e esperou que ela se abrisse.

— Não tenho ideia de como ele conseguiu a lâmina. Ele fica na cela vinte e três horas por dia. O tempo dele no pátio é separado; ele fica sozinho. Não tem visitas com contato e os guardas todos morrem de medo dele. — A porta se abriu e ele continuou andando. — Se dependesse de mim, ia deixar o cara apodrecendo naquele buraco. Mas não decido isso. Ele vai ficar confinado por mais uma semana, a não ser que faça alguma coisa horrível. E, pode acreditar, ele é capaz de coisas horríveis.

O diretor parou num conjunto de portas de metal. A primeira fez um som metálico ao se abrir, e eles entraram.

— Da última vez que o trancamos no buraco, o guarda que o mandou para lá foi atacado no dia seguinte. Nunca achamos o responsável, mas o homem perdeu um olho. Foi arrancado com a mão.

A porta atrás deles se fechou e a da frente se abriu com um baque. Kagan falou:

— Vamos ter câmeras observando vocês, Sr. Trent, mas devo alertá-lo que nosso tempo de reação é de sessenta e um segundos, pouco mais de um minuto. Não conseguimos acelerar mais do que isso. Estou com uma equipe de ação completa, equipada e de prontidão, caso aconteça alguma coisa. — Ele deu um tapinha nas costas de Will. — Boa sorte.

Tinha um guarda esperando para levar Will. O homem parecia cheio do terror que se via no rosto de um detento no corredor da morte. Era como olhar um espelho.

Will se virou para Amanda. Tinha quebrado seu silêncio na sala de espera para que ela explicasse o que ele devia dizer a Roger Ling, mas só naquele momento ele percebia que ela não dera conselho nenhum.

— Quer me ajudar aqui?

Ela disse:

— *Quid pro quo*, Agente Starling. Não volte sem alguma informação útil.

Will lembrou de novo que a odiava.

O guarda fez sinal para ele atravessar a porta, que se fechou atrás deles.

O homem disse:

— Fique perto das paredes. Caso veja algo vindo na sua direção, cubra os olhos e feche a boca. Provavelmente é merda.

Will tentou andar como se seus testículos não tivessem se encolhido para dentro do corpo. As luzes das celas estavam apagadas, mas o corredor estava bem iluminado. O guarda ficou perto da parede, longe dos presidiários do outro lado. Will fez o mesmo. Sentia um novo par de olhos o acompanhando a cada vez que passava em frente de uma cela. Havia um som de algo se arrastando atrás dele: pedacinhos de papel amarrados em linhas, bilhetes contrabandeados deslizando pelo chão de concreto. Mentalmente, Will listou todos os possíveis contrabandos nas celas. Navalhas feitas de escovas de dente e pentes. Lâminas moldadas a partir de pedaços de metal roubados da cozinha. Fezes e urina misturadas numa caneca para criar bombas de gás. Fios de um lençol trançados para formar um chicote, com lâminas amarradas nas pontas.

Mais um conjunto de portas duplas. As primeiras se abriram. Eles atravessaram e elas se fecharam. Alguns segundos se passaram. As portas duplas seguintes se abriram rangendo.

Chegaram a uma porta sólida com um pedaço de vidro no nível dos olhos. O guarda pegou um molho pesado de chaves e achou a certa. Enfiou-a numa fechadura na parede. Houve um *tá-tum* de um ferrolho que se abriu. Ele se virou e olhou para a câmera acima. Os dois esperaram até haver um clique de resposta do guarda que os observava de uma sala de exibição remota. A porta se abriu deslizando.

Confinamento. A solitária. O buraco.

O corredor tinha cerca de nove metros de comprimento e três de largura. De um lado, oito portas de metal. Do outro, uma parede de concreto. Não havia janelas. Sem ar fresco. Sem luz do sol. Sem esperança.

Como Kagan explicou, esses homens tinham todo o tempo lıvre do mundo.

Ao contrário do resto da prisão, todas as luzes do teto estavam acesas na solitária. O brilho das lâmpadas fluorescentes causou em Will uma dor de cabeça instantânea. O corredor estava quente e úmido. Havia uma espécie de pressão no ar, uma sensação pesada. Ele sentia que estava no meio de um campo esperando um tornado chegar.

— Ele está na última — disse o guarda, de novo se mantendo perto da parede, com o ombro roçando o concreto.

Will via que a tinta estava gasta de os guardas deslizarem o ombro por alı durante anos. As portas em frente estavam bem trancadas. Cada uma tinha uma janelinha estreita, no nível dos olhos, como num bar secreto. Havia uma fenda embaixo para passar refeições e colocar algemas. Todas as portas e todos os painéis estavam fechados com ferrolhos e rebites pesados.

O guarda parou na última porta. Pôs a mão no peito de Will e garantiu que as costas dele estivessem bem encostadas na parede.

— Não preciso mandar você ficar aqui, né, grandão?

Will fez que não.

O homem pareceu reunir coragem antes de ir até a porta da cela. Fechou as mãos no ferrolho que cobria o painel de visualização.

— Sr. Ling, se eu puxar esta chapa, você vai me causar algum problema?

Houve um som abafado de rısada atrás da porta. Roger Ling tinha o mesmo sotaque pesado do sul que a irmã.

— Acho que por enquanto você está seguro, Enrique.

O guarda estava suando. Agarrou o ferrolho e o puxou, saindo do caminho tão rápido que seus sapatos rangeram no chão.

Will sentiu uma gota de suor rolando pelo pescoço. Roger Lıng estava visivelmente em pé com as costas encostadas na porta. Will vıa a lateral do pescoço dele, a parte de baixo da orelha e uma ponta do uniforme laranja da prisão que cobria o pescoço. As luzes lá dentro estavam acesas, mais fortes do que no corredor. Will via os fundos da cela, a beirada de um colchão no chão. O espaço era menor que o de uma cela normal, menos de dois metros e meio de profundidade, provavelmente um e vinte de largura. Devia ter uma privada, mas nada mais. Sem cadeira. Sem mesa. Sem nada que o fizesse se sentir um ser humano. Os cheiros normais de uma prisão — suor, urina, fezes — aqui eram mais pungentes. Will percebeu que não havia gritos. Em geral, uma cadeia era barulhenta como uma escola de ensino fundamental, especialmente à noite. Os bilhetinhos tinham feito seu trabalho. O lugar todo havia parado porque Roger Ling tinha um visitante.

Will esperou. Conseguia ouvir o coração batendo, o som da respiração entrando e saindo dos pulmões.

Ling perguntou:

— Como vai Arnoldo?

O chihuahua de Julia Ling. Will pigarreou.

— Vai bem.

— Ela está deixando ele engordar? Eu disse para ela não deixar.

— Ele parece... — Will se esforçou para achar uma resposta. — Ela não o está deixando passar fome.

— Naldo é um carinha muito legal — disse Ling. — Eu sempre digo que um chihuahua sempre vai ser tão nervoso quanto o dono. Você concorda?

Will nunca tinha pensado muito nisso, mas falou:

— Acho que faz sentido. A minha é bem tranquila.

— Como ela se chama mesmo?

Tudo aquilo tinha um motivo, na verdade. Ling queria confirmar se estava falando com o cara certo.

— Betty.

Ele tinha passado no teste.

— Prazer em conhecê-lo pessoalmente, Sr. Trent.

Ling mudou de posição e Will viu boa parte da nuca dele. Uma tatuagem de dragão subia pelas vértebras. As asas se estendiam pela cabeça raspada. Os olhos eram de um amarelo vivo.

Ling disse:

— Minha irmã está bem surtada.

— Imagino.

— Aqueles merdinhas tentaram matar ela. — A voz dele estava dura, exatamente o tipo de tom que se esperaria de um homem que havia mutilado e matado duas mulheres. — Eles não estariam bancando os durões se eu não estivesse aqui trancado. Eu ia acabar com a raça deles. Sacou?

Will olhou para o guarda. O cara estava tenso como um bulldog pronto para lutar. Ou fugir, que parecia a opção mais inteligente. Will pensou na equipe de ação esperando e se perguntou o que Roger Ling conseguiria fazer em sessenta e um segundos. Muita coisa, provavelmente.

Ling continuou:

— Você sabe por que eu pedi para falar com você?

Will foi sincero.

— Não faço ideia.

— Porque eu não confio em nada que aquela filha da puta fala.

Obviamente, ele estava falando de Amanda.

— Provavelmente faz bem.

Ele riu. Will escutou o som ecoando na cela. Não tinha alegria no ruído. Era gélido, quase maníaco. Will se perguntou se as vítimas de Ling tinham ouvido aquela risada enquanto estavam sendo estranguladas até a morte com a coleira de Arnoldo.

Ling continuou:

— Precisamos acabar com isso. Sangue demais nas ruas é ruim para os negócios.

— Me diga como posso fazer isso acontecer.

— Tive notícia de Ignatio. Ele entende que a Yellow não está por trás disso. Ele quer paz.

Will não era exatamente especialista em facções, mas duvidava que o líder dos Texicanos daria a outra face depois de o filho ser espancado e morto. Ele disse a Ling:

— Eu pensei que o Sr. Ortiz fosse querer vingança.

— Nada, cara. Sem vingança. Ricardo cavou a própria cova. Ignatio sabe disso. Diga isso para Faith também. Ela fez o que tinha que fazer. Família é família, né?

Will não gostava do fato de aquele homem saber o nome de Faith e certamente não confiava nas palavras dele. Ainda assim, falou:

— Digo, sim.

Ling ecoou as palavras da irmã.

— Esses jovens são doidos, cara. Não têm noção do valor da vida. Você se mata para dar uma vida boa para eles. Dá carro novo, manda para escola particular e, no minuto que eles estão sozinhos, *pá*, se viram e arrebentam você.

Will achou "*pá*" um baita eufemismo, mas guardou isso para si.

— Ricardo estudou na Westminster — disse Ling. — Sabia?

Will estava familiarizado com a escola particular, que custava mais de vinte e cinco mil dólares por ano. Também sabia, pelos registros, que Hironobu Kwon tinha estudado na Westminster com uma bolsa de matemática. Então, havia mais um ponto de conexão ali.

Ling disse:

— Ignatio achou que podia comprar uma vida diferente para o filho, mas aqueles riquinhos mimados fizeram o menino ficar viciado em óxi.

— Ricardo foi para a clínica de reabilitação?

— Caralho, o carinha *morava* na clínica. — Ele se mexeu de novo. Will ouviu o tecido duro da camisa laranja roçar na porta de metal.

— Você tem filho?

— Não.

— Não que você saiba, né? — Ele riu como se fosse engraçado. — Eu tenho três. Duas ex-mulheres que vivem me enchendo para conseguir dinheiro. Mas eu dou. Elas colocam meus meninos na linha, não deixam minha filha se vestir que nem puta. Ficam fora de confusão. — Ele levantou um dos ombros. — Mas vai fazer o quê, né? Às vezes, está no sangue. Não importa quantas vezes você mostre o caminho certo, eles chegam numa certa idade e botam ideia na cabeça. Acham que de repente não precisam trabalhar até chegar no topo. Veem o que os outros têm e acham que podem só ir lá e pegar.

Ling parecia saber muito sobre os problemas de Ignatio Ortiz como pai. Estranho, especialmente considerando que os dois estavam trancados em prisões diferentes que ficavam a quase um estado inteiro de distância. Boyd Spivey estava errado. Os amarelos não estavam fazendo uma jogada para roubar os hispânicos. Os amarelos estavam trabalhando para eles.

Will falou:

— Você tem uma relação comercial com o Sr. Ortiz.

— É uma afirmação justa.

— Ignatio pediu para Julia dar ao filho um emprego no lado legítimo do negócio.

— É bom um jovem ter profissão. E Ricardo gostou. Ele tinha talento para o trabalho. A maioria deles fica só montando caixas, prendendo portas. Ricky era diferente. Era esperto. Sabia botar as pessoas certas no trabalho. Poderia ter a própria oficina um dia.

Will começou a entender.

— Ricardo montou uma equipe: Hironobu Kwon e os outros trabalhavam na oficina da sua irmã. Talvez tenham visto o dinheiro entrando pelo lado menos legítimo do negócio e achado que mereciam uma parcela maior. Ortiz nunca aprovaria uma facção novata tomando parte do que era dos Texicanos, mesmo que fosse do próprio filho.

— Começar um negócio é mais difícil do que parece, especialmente uma franquia. Tem que pagar as taxas.

— Você ficou sabendo da viagem de Ricardo para a Suécia.

— Caceta, todo mundo soube. — Ele riu como se aquilo fosse engraçado. — O problema de ter essa idade é que você não sabe quando ficar de boca calada. Jovem, burro e pensa com a cabeça de baixo.

— Seu pessoal falou com Ricardo sobre a viagem dele. — Will não disse que provavelmente estavam torturando o jovem durante a conversa. — Ricardo mencionou que talvez tivesse um jeito de resolver o problema, pagando bem. — Will imaginou que Ricardo estaria disposto a dar a própria mãe em troca quando terminaram de torturá-lo.

— Ele disse a vocês que podia conseguir uma grana. Muita grana. Quase um milhão de dólares. Em dinheiro vivo.

— Parece um acordo que nenhum empresário recusaria.

Tudo estava se encaixando. Ricardo tinha levado seus caras à casa de Evelyn, onde encontraram bem mais resistência do que esperavam.

Eles mataram Hector. Mesmo que Amanda estivesse certa e Hector Ortiz fosse só vendedor de carros, não havia como contornar o fato de que ele era primo de Ignatio Ortiz.

— Ricardo levou os homens para a casa de Evelyn para pegar o dinheiro. Só que não contavam que ela fosse resistir. Fizeram vítimas demais. Precisavam se reagrupar. E aí chegou Faith.

Ling perguntou:

— Você já ouviu essa história?

Will continuou falando.

— Eles levaram Evelyn a algum lugar para interrogá-la.

— Parece um bom plano, cara.

— Só que ela não entregou o dinheiro. Se tivesse entregado, nós não estaríamos aqui.

Ele riu.

— Não sei, não, cara. Você parece ter perdido alguma coisa nessa história.

— Como assim?

— Pensa bem.

Will ainda estava perdido.

— O único jeito de matar uma cobra é cortar a cabeça.

— Tá.

Ele continuava sem entender.

— Até onde eu sei, a velha cobra continua por aí se contorcendo.

— Você está falando de Evelyn?

— Caralho, você acha que aquela vaca velha ia conseguir fazer um bando de crianças seguir ela? A puta não conseguiu manter ordem nem na casa *dela*. — Ele estalou a língua num *tsc* do mesmo jeito que a irmã fazia. — Nada, cara, isso é trabalho de homem. Como você acha que eles superaram minha irmã? As minas não têm culhão para esse tipo de coisa.

Will não ia discutir com isso. Facções criminosas eram o maior clube do bolinha do mundo — mais patriarcais que a Igreja Católica. Julia Ling só estava na liderança para satisfazer às vontades do irmão. Generais não iam para a batalha. Mandavam peões para a linha de frente. Hironobu Kwon levou um tiro minutos depois de invadir a casa.

Ricardo Ortiz fora deixado para trás. Benny Choo apontou uma arma para a cabeça dele. O homem tinha sido derrotado. Abandonado. Era dispensável.

Outra pessoa tinha dado a dica sobre Evelyn. Outra pessoa estava liderando a facção.

Will disse:

— Chuck Finn.

Ling riu como se o nome o surpreendesse.

— Chuckleberry Finn. Achei que esse mano já estava morto. Peixe dormindo com os peixes.

— Ele está por trás disso?

Roger não respondeu à pergunta.

— E o velho Marreta também foi derrubado. Pelo que escutei, fizeram um favor para o cara. Saiu que nem homem em vez de esperar ser abatido que nem um cachorro. Não dá para dizer que não saiu nada de bom disso.

— Quem está por trás...

— Ó, acabou aqui. — Roger Ling bateu na porta da cela. — Enrique, fecha aí.

O guarda começou a deslizar de volta o painel. Will estendeu a mão para impedi-lo. Como uma cobra dando o bote, Ling botou a mão para fora da fenda e agarrou o pulso de Will. Ele puxou com tanta força que o ombro de Will bateu na porta. A lateral do rosto dele ficou pressionada contra a superfície fria de metal. Ele sentiu um hálito quente na orelha.

— Sabe por que você está aqui, mano?

Will puxou o corpo para trás com toda a força que tinha. Empurrou com a perna, tentou apoiar o pé na parte de baixo da porta.

Ling estava segurando com muita força, mas sua voz não demonstrava esforço.

— Diga para Mandy que Evelyn já era. — A voz dele ficou mais baixa. — Pá, pá. Dois na cabeça. Ding-dong, Almeja morreu.

Ling o soltou. Will caiu para trás, batendo com os ombros na parede de concreto. O coração dele estava batendo como um metrônomo. Ele olhou de novo para a porta da cela. Houve um barulho de metal deslizando em metal. O painel de visualização se fechou, mas não antes de Will ver os olhos de Roger Ling. Eram totalmente pretos, sem alma. Mas tinha mais uma coisa ali. Um flash de triunfo mesclado com sede de sangue.

— Quando? — berrou Will. — Quando foi isso?

A voz de Ling estava abafada atrás da porta.

— Fala para Mandy usar alguma coisa bonita no velório. Eu sempre gostei dela de preto.

Will espanou o corpo para tirar a sujeira. Caminhando pelo corredor, perguntou-se o que era pior: sentir o hálito quente de Roger Ling no pescoço ou ter que falar para Amanda e Faith que Evelyn Mitchell estava morta.

14

Faith pegou um dos carrinhos que ficavam enfileirados do lado de fora do supermercado. Achou uma lista antiga na bolsa e a segurou com força enquanto entrava no lugar, fingindo que era só mais um dia de compras. A polícia de Atlanta tinha levado a Glock dela para fazer análise balística, mas eles não sabiam da Walther P99 que Zeke mantinha carregada no porta-luvas. Sentiu o peso dela na bolsa enquanto levantava a alça do ombro, para tirá-la. A arma de fabricação alemã era adequada para o irmão, que nunca tinha entrado em combate. Era volumosa e cara, o tipo de coisa que a pessoa carregava para se exibir. Mas também era capaz de derrubar um homem a quase cem metros e, no fim das contas, era só disso que Faith precisava.

Ela começou pela seção de frutas e verduras, levando mais tempo do que o normal para avaliar o frescor das laranjas empilhadas no expositor. Botou algumas num saco plástico, depois foi para o setor de padaria.

Devia ter saído de casa horas antes, mas queria esperar a ligação de Zeke dizendo que Jeremy e Emma estavam abrigados em segurança nos aposentos para oficiais em visita na Base Aérea da Reserva de Dobbins. Só para colocar todos no Impala de Jeremy tinha levado um século. Zeke havia gritado com a cadeirinha de bebê. Jeremy continuava de bico por causa do iPhone confiscado. Emma não tinha chorado, porque o irmão mais velho estava lá para acalmá-la, mas Faith soluçara igual a um bebê no minuto em que o carro desaparecera no fim da rua.

Faith supunha que os homens que levaram a mãe dela fossem tão habilidosos quanto eram atrevidos. Taticamente, sempre estiveram em vantagem, fosse para levar Evelyn ou invadir a casa de Faith. Mas, com dois policiais na cozinha dela e o irmão de um metro e oitenta e dois andando por lá como um valentão atrás de briga, não tinha como eles tentarem entrar de novo.

Eles tinham ido atrás de Jeremy, que, exceto por Emma, era o elo mais fraco. Faith sentiu a respiração falhar ao pensar nos filhos. Tinha estado tão preocupada com a mãe que deixou o resto da família exposta. Isso não iria mais acontecer. Ela manteria todo mundo seguro ou morreria tentando.

Faith sentiu uma presença olhando por cima de seu ombro. Alguém a estava observando. Sentia que estavam de olho nela desde o momento em que saíra de casa. Casualmente, Faith se virou. Viu um menino com uniforme da Elma Chips empilhando sacos de biscoito na prateleira. Ele sorriu para ela. Faith sorriu de volta e empurrou o carrinho pelo corredor.

Quando Faith era pequena, o homem da marca Charles Chips vinha toda segunda encher as latas de metal marrom com batatinhas. Às terças e quintas, o caminhão da Mathis Dairy parava em frente à sua casa enquanto Petro, o motorista, colocava leite fresco na prateleira de metal ao lado da porta da garagem. Dois litros custavam noventa e dois centavos. Suco de laranja era cinquenta e dois centavos. Leitelho, o favorito do pai dela, quarenta e sete centavos. Se Faith fosse boazinha, a mãe a deixava contar o trocado para pagar Petro. Às vezes, Evelyn comprava achocolatado, por cinquenta e seis centavos, para ocasiões especiais. Aniversários. Notas boas no boletim. Vitória em jogos. Apresentações de dança.

Cosméticos. Vitaminas. Xampu. Cartões comemorativos. Livros. Sabonete. Faith não parava de empilhar coisas no carrinho, convidando quem quer que estivesse ali a fazer contato. Ela diminuiu o passo. O carrinho estava quase cheio. Ela conferiu o iPhone de Jeremy. Não havia novas mensagens no Facebook dele, nem e-mails de GoodKnight92. Faith fez o caminho de volta pela loja, devolvendo o xampu e as vitaminas, olhando as revistas mais uma vez. Olhou o relógio. Tinha passado quase uma hora ali sem ninguém a abordar. O Ruivo provavelmente estava começando a se perguntar por que ela estava demorando tanto. O jovem investigador não pareceu se incomodar quando ela disse que ia ao mercado sozinha. Ainda estava lambendo as feridas por Faith ter pegado a arma dele. Ela não sabia bem se ainda havia espaço para forçar a barra com ele sem gerar uma reação em resposta.

Ela contornou com o carrinho um idoso que tinha parado no meio do corredor de cereais. Faith sabia que eles a queriam no estacionamento. Queriam que estivesse sozinha. Era melhor ceder logo e acabar com aquilo. Ela colocou a mão na bolsa, pronta para tirá-la do carrinho. A razão interveio. Eles não podiam sequestrá-la no meio do supermercado. Podiam tentar, mas Faith não iria a lugar nenhum. Teriam que negociar com ela ou atirar. Ela não ia sair daquele mercado sem um acordo para trazer a mãe de volta.

Faith parou na frente do banheiro e deixou o carrinho ao lado da porta. Era a terceira vez que ia, desde que chegara ao mercado. Não era só para tentar atraí-los. Um dos vários benefícios da diabetes atacada era que a bexiga parecia cheia o tempo todo. Ela abriu a porta do banheiro feminino e segurou a respiração por causa do cheiro. As paredes de aço inoxidável e o piso de azulejo tinham uma camada de sujeira. O ar parecia gorduroso. Se tivesse escolha, Faith teria esperado até chegar em casa, mas não tinha esse luxo.

Ela conferiu as quatro cabines, e entrou na destinada a pessoas com deficiência, que ainda era a menos nojenta. As coxas doíam enquanto ela ficava suspensa acima da privada. Aquilo exigia equilíbrio. Ela precisava segurar a bolsa próxima da barriga, porque não tinha onde pendurar e ela receava que o couro falso ficasse grudado no chão.

A porta do banheiro se abriu. Faith olhou por baixo da cabine. Viu um par de sapatos femininos. Saltos baixos. Tornozelos gordos enfiados em meias marrons de compressão. A torneira foi ligada. O suporte de toalhas de papel rangeu. A torneira foi desligada. A porta voltou a se abrir, depois se fechou lentamente.

Faith fechou os olhos e murmurou uma oração de alívio. Terminou de fazer xixi, deu a descarga e pendurou de novo a bolsa no ombro. A porta da cabine não fechava direito. Estava sem a peça de girar o trinco. Ela precisou enfiar o dedo mindinho na abertura quadrada e girar o eixo de metal para abrir a porta.

— *Hola.*

Na mesma hora, Faith catalogou tudo o que podia sobre o homem à sua frente. Porte mediano, alguns centímetros mais alto que Faith, em torno de oitenta quilos. Pele marrom. Cabelo escuro. Olhos azuis. Band-Aid no indicador esquerdo. Tatuagem de cobra do lado direito do pescoço. Calça jeans de um azul desbotado com buracos nos joelhos. Jaqueta esportiva preta com uma saliência na frente que só podia ser de uma arma. A aba do boné preto estava puxada bem para baixo. Mesmo assim, ela conseguia ver o rosto dele. Os pelos faciais esparsos. A pinta na bochecha. Ele tinha mais ou menos a idade de Jeremy, mas não era em nada parecido com o filho dócil e amoroso dela. Parecia irradiar ódio. Faith conhecia esse tipo, com o qual já havia lidado muitas vezes. Pavio curto e dedo rápido no gatilho. Cheio de maldade. Jovem demais para ser esperto, idiota demais para envelhecer.

Faith colocou a mão na bolsa.

Ele pressionou a saliência sob a blusa.

— Se eu fosse você, não faria isso.

Faith sentiu o aço frio da Walther. O cano estava apontado na direção do homem. O dedo dela, perto do gatilho. Ela podia atirar de dentro da bolsa antes mesmo de ele pensar em levantar a jaqueta.

— Onde está minha mãe?

— "*Minha* mãe" — repetiu ele. — Cê fala como se fosse só sua.

— Deixe minha família fora disso.

— Cê não manda nada aqui.

— Preciso saber se ela está viva.

Ele levantou o queixo e estalou a língua uma vez na parte de trás dos dentes. O gesto era familiar, a mesma reação que Faith arrancara de absolutamente todo bandido que já havia prendido.

— Tá segura.

— Como eu vou saber disso?

Ele riu.

— Não vai, vaca. Cê não vai saber nada.

— O que você quer?

Ele esfregou o polegar nos outros dedos.

— Grana.

Faith não sabia se era capaz de segurar o blefe de novo.

— Só me diga onde ela está e a gente acaba com isso. Ninguém precisa se machucar.

Ele riu de novo.

— Pô, cê acha que eu sou idiota?

— Quanto você quer?

— Tudo.

Uma onda de xingamentos lhe veio à mente.

— Ela nunca pegou dinheiro nenhum.

— Essa historinha que ela me contou já era, piranha. Já deu. Me dá a porra da grana e eu te entrego o que sobrou dela.

— Ela está viva?

— Por pouco tempo, se você não fizer o que eu mandar.

Faith sentiu uma gota de suor escorrendo pelas costas.

— Consigo arrumar o dinheiro amanhã. Meio-dia.

— Qual é, tá esperando o banco abrir?

— É um cofre de segurança bancário. — Ela estava inventando tudo na hora. — Cofres. São três. Pela cidade toda. Preciso de tempo.

Ele sorriu. Um dos dentes estava coberto de um metal prateado. Platina, provavelmente valia mais do que aquilo que Faith tinha na conta corrente.

— Sabia que você ia negociar. Falei para a mamãe que a bebezinha não ia largar ela.

— Preciso saber se ela está viva. Nada disso vai acontecer até eu ter certeza de que ela está bem.

— Eu não diria que bem, mas, da última vez que vi, a filha da puta ainda estava respirando.

Ele tirou um iPhone do bolso, um modelo mais novo do que o que ela tinha conseguido comprar para Jeremy. O homem pôs a língua entre os dentes e mexeu na tela com os polegares. Achou o que estava procurando e mostrou o celular a Faith. A tela mostrava a imagem da mãe dela segurando um jornal.

Faith ficou olhando a foto. O rosto da mãe estava inchado, quase irreconhecível. A mão dela estava amarrada com um trapo ensanguentado. Faith apertou os lábios. A bile que subiu fez sua garganta queimar. Ela lutou contra as lágrimas que ardiam nos olhos.

— Não consigo saber o que ela está segurando.

Ele usou os dedos para aumentar a imagem.

— É um jornal.

— Eu sei que é um *USA Today* — irritou-se ela. — Isso não prova que ela está viva agora. Só prova que, em algum momento depois de os jornais serem entregues hoje de manhã, você a obrigou a segurar isso.

Ele olhou para a tela. Ela percebeu que ele estava preocupado. Ele mordeu o lábio inferior como Jeremy fazia sempre que ela o pegava fazendo algo de errado.

O homem falou:

— Isso é prova de vida. Você precisa negociar comigo se quiser manter as coisas assim.

Faith notou que a gramática dele tinha melhorado. A voz também havia subido uma oitava. Tinha algo familiar no tom, mas ela não conseguia identificar. Só precisava que ele continuasse falando.

— Você acha que eu sou idiota? — questionou ela. — Isso não prova nada. Minha mãe já pode estar morta. Não vou entregar a você uma pilha de dinheiro só por causa de uma porcaria de uma foto. Você pode ter feito no Photoshop. Não sei nem se é ela mesmo.

Ele chegou mais perto, estufando o peito. Seus olhos eram amendoados, azul-escuros com pontos verdes. De novo, ela teve a sensação de conhecê-lo.

— Eu já prendi você uma vez.

— Caralho. — Ele bufou. — Você não sabe porra nenhuma de mim.

— Preciso de uma prova de que minha mãe está viva.

— Se você continuar com essa palhaçada, ela não vai continuar viva por muito tempo.

Faith teve aquela sensação familiar da gota d'água fazendo tudo transbordar dentro dela. Toda a raiva e a frustração dos últimos dias saíram com tudo.

— Você já fez isso antes, por acaso? É um amador? Não dá para aparecer assim sem prova real. Caralho, eu sou policial há dezesseis anos. Você acha que eu vou cair nesse truque barato? — Ela o empurrou para trás com força suficiente para mostrar que estava falando sério. — Eu vou embora.

Ele bateu a cara dela na porta. O golpe deixou Faith atordoada. Ele se virou num movimento brusco e pressionou o pescoço dela com o braço esquerdo. A mão direita dele agarrou o rosto de Faith, com os dedos apertando o crânio dela. Ele falou cuspindo:

— Você quer que eu deixe mais um presente embaixo do seu travesseiro? Quem sabe os olhos dela? — Ele pressionou o polegar com mais força no globo ocular de Faith. — Os peitos, de repente?

A porta pressionou as costas de Faith. Alguém estava tentando entrar no banheiro.

— Oi? — disse uma mulher. — Licença, está aberto?

O homem ficou olhando Faith como uma hiena estudando a presa. A mão dele tremia pela força com que segurava o rosto dela. Os dentes de Faith estavam cortando o interior da bochecha. Seu nariz começou a sangrar. O homem podia quebrar o crânio dela se quisesse.

— Amanhã de manhã — disse ele. — Eu mando instruções. — Ele chegou tão perto que os traços deles ficaram borrados aos olhos de Faith. — Não é para contar isso para ninguém. Não é para contar para sua chefe. Nem para aquele maluco que trabalha com você. Nem para o seu irmão, nem mais ninguém da sua adorada *família*. Ninguém. Escutou?

— Sim — sussurrou ela. — Sim.

Parecia impossível, mas ele apertou mais forte.

— Eu não vou te matar de primeira — alertou ele. — Vou cortar suas pálpebras. Tá me escutando? — Faith fez que sim. — Vou te obrigar a olhar enquanto arranco a pele do seu filho. Pedaço por pedaço, vou cortar a carne dele até você só conseguir ver os músculos e ossos e só conseguir ouvir aquele bebezinho chorando que nem o veadinho mimado que ele é. E aí vou para a sua filha. A pele dela vai ser mais fácil, que nem desgrudar um papel. Você me entendeu? Sacou o que eu estou falando? — Ela fez que sim de novo. — Não me irrita, piranha. Você não tem ideia de como eu tenho pouco a perder.

Ele a soltou tão rápido quanto a havia agarrado. Faith caiu no chão. Ela tossiu e sentiu gosto de sangue na garganta. Ele a chutou para fora do caminho para poder abrir a porta. Ela pôs a mão na bolsa. Seus dedos sentiram o contorno da arma. Ela devia se levantar. Precisava se levantar.

— Senhora? — chamou uma mulher. Ela espiou pela porta e olhou para baixo, vendo Faith. — Quer que eu chame um médico?

— Não — sussurrou Faith.

Ela engoliu o sangue da boca. O interior da mandíbula estava rasgado. Mais sangue escorreu do nariz.

— Tem certeza? Eu posso ligar...

— Não — repetiu Faith.

Não havia para quem ligar.

15

Will parou na entrada de carros e esperou a porta da garagem se abrir. Todas as luzes da casa estavam apagadas. Betty provavelmente estava flutuando que nem um balão da Macy's no desfile de Ação de Graças, de tanto que devia estar com a bexiga cheia. Pelo menos ele esperava que sim. Will não estava nada a fim de limpar sujeira do chão.

Ele sentia que tinha matado Amanda. Não literalmente, não com as próprias mãos, como ele havia sonhado em fazer pela maior parte do dia. Contar a ela o que Roger Ling havia dito, que Evelyn Mitchell estava morta, era quase como dar um tiro no peito dela. Ela tinha desinflado na frente dele. Toda a sua bravata sumira. Toda a arrogância e crueldade e mesquinharia saíram voando dela, e a mulher à frente dele era só uma casca.

Will tivera o bom senso de esperar até saírem da prisão para transmitir a notícia. Ela não tinha chorado. Em vez disso, para seu horror, os joelhos dela haviam cedido. Foi aí que ele a abraçou. Ela era surpreendentemente ossuda. O quadril era pontiagudo sob a mão dele. Os ombros eram frágeis. Ela parecia dez, vinte anos mais velha quando ele pôs o cinto de segurança nela e fechou a porta do carro.

O trajeto de volta tinha sido sofrido. O silêncio de Will no caminho até lá não era nada em comparação àquilo. Ele tinha se oferecido para parar no acostamento, mas ela mandou não fazer isso. Bem perto de Atlanta, ele viu a mão dela segurar a porta. Will nunca tinha ido à casa de Amanda antes. Ela morava num condomínio fechado no meio de Buckhead. Todas as casas tinham aparência majestosa, com cantos decorados de tijolos e janelas de borda pesada. Ela o direcionara para uma unidade nos fundos.

Will tinha colocado o carro em ponto morto, mas ela não saíra. Ele estava pensando se devia ou não ajudá-la de novo quando ela dissera:

— Não conte para Faith.

Ele tinha ficado olhando a porta da frente. Havia uma bandeira hasteada num mastro na entrada. Flores primaveris. Uma decoração sazonal. Amanda nunca lhe parecera uma pessoa que curtisse bandeiras. Ele não a imaginava parada na varanda de salto e terninho, na ponta dos pés para prender a bandeira apropriada no mastro.

— Precisamos verificar isso — dissera ela, apesar de a fala de Roger Ling ter sido a mera confirmação de uma verdade que Will vinha intuindo quase o dia todo.

Amanda também devia saber. Era a única explicação para a confissão que havia feito mais cedo na sala de espera da prisão. Ela tinha admitido que Evelyn era corrupta porque sabia que não tinha mais motivo para proteger a amiga. A marca de vinte e quatro horas já havia passado. Não houvera contato dos sequestradores. Tinha sangue por todo o chão da cozinha de Evelyn, e boa parte dele — talvez a maior parte — era da própria Evelyn. Os jovens com quem estavam lidando tinham mostrado ser assassinos sem remorso, nada mais que matadores, mesmo quando se tratava de membros da própria equipe.

As chances de Evelyn Mitchell ter sobrevivido àquela noite eram próximas de zero.

Will dissera a ela:

— Faith precisa saber.

— Eu conto quando tiver certeza. — A voz dela parecia insípida, sem vida. — A gente se encontra amanhã, às sete. A equipe toda. Se chegar um minuto atrasado, melhor nem ir.

— Vou estar lá.

— Vamos encontrá-la. Preciso ver com meus próprios olhos.

— Tudo bem.

— E, se o que o Roger falou for verdade, vamos achar os caras que fizeram isso e acabar com a raça deles. De cada um. Vamos mandar todos para o inferno.

— Sim, senhora.

A voz dela estava tão baixa e cansada que ele mal a escutava.

— Não vou descansar até cada um deles estar morto. Quero ver enfiarem a agulha nesses homens e assistir até os pés deles terem espasmo, os olhos revirarem e o peito deles congelar. E, se o Estado se recusar a matá-los, eu mesma mato.

Amanda tinha aberto então a porta e saído do carro. Will vira o esforço que ela tinha feito para manter as costas eretas e subir as escadas. Se dependesse de Amanda, se houvesse uma forma da amiga estar viva só com a força da vontade dela, não haveria dúvidas da sobrevivência de Evelyn.

Mas simplesmente não era o caso.

O portão da garagem terminou de se abrir. Will entrou e apertou o botão para fechá-lo. A garagem não era parte da casa originalmente. Will tinha adicionado aquela estrutura na época em que o bairro estava em transição, quando viciados batiam na porta dele querendo saber se ali ainda era uma boca de fumo de crack. A entrada da garagem era estranha e dava no primeiro quarto. Betty levantou a cabeça da almofada ao ver Will. Havia no canto uma poça sobre a qual nenhum dos dois estava pronto para conversar.

Will acendeu as luzes enquanto andava pela casa. O ar estava gelado. Ele abriu a porta da cozinha para Betty poder sair. Ela hesitou.

— Está tudo bem — disse ele, usando o tom mais reconfortante que conseguiu.

As feridas dela estavam cicatrizando, mas a cachorrinha ainda se lembrava da semana anterior, quando um gavião tinha descido voando no jardim e tentado pegá-la. E Will ainda se lembrava da risada incontrolável do tosador quando ele contou que um gavião tinha confundido a cachorra dele com um rato.

Betty enfim saiu, mas não sem um olhar desconfiado por cima do ombro. Will pôs a chave do carro no gancho e a carteira e a arma na mesa da cozinha. A pizza do dia anterior continuava na geladeira. Will pegou a caixa, mas só conseguiu ficar olhando os pedaços gelatinosos.

Ele queria ligar para Sara, mas, desta vez, suas motivações eram puramente egoístas. Queria contar a ela o que tinha acontecido naquele dia.

Queria perguntar se era certo esperar para contar a Faith que a mãe estava morta. Queria descrever para ela a sensação de ver Amanda tão para baixo. Falar que tinha ficado assustado de vê-la cair tão longe de seu pedestal.

Em vez disso, ele guardou a caixa de pizza de volta na geladeira, conferiu se a porta continuava entreaberta e foi tomar banho. Era quase meia-noite. Ele estava de pé desde as cinco da manhã, tendo dormido apenas algumas horas na noite anterior. Will parou embaixo do fluxo de água quente, tentando lavar tudo daquele dia. A sujeira da Prisão Estadual de Valdosta. O armazém onde haviam tentado atirar nele. O Grady, onde ele ficara zonzo de medo. A Coastal, onde ele havia suado tanto que ainda tinha manchas redondas de suor nas axilas da camisa.

Will pensou em Betty enquanto secava o cabelo. Ela ficara presa em casa o dia todo. A poça era uma responsabilidade dos dois. Por mais tarde que fosse, ele não conseguia pensar em dormir. Devia levá-la para passear. Esticar as pernas ia ser bom para os dois. Ele pôs uma calça jeans e uma camisa social gasta demais para continuar usando no trabalho. O colarinho estava puído. Um dos botões estava quebrado, pendurado por um fio.

Ele entrou na cozinha para pegar a coleira de Betty.

Angie estava sentada à mesa.

— Bem-vindo de volta, amor. Como foi seu dia?

Will preferia dirigir de novo até a Coastal e enfrentar Roger Ling mais uma vez do que falar com a esposa naquele momento.

Ela se levantou e pôs os braços em torno dos ombros de Will. Levou a boca para perto da dele.

— Você não vai me dar oi?

As mãos dela acariciando seu pescoço não se pareciam em nada com as de Sara.

— Pare.

Ela se afastou e fingiu fazer biquinho.

— Isso é jeito de cumprimentar sua esposa?

— Por onde você andou?

— Desde quando você liga para isso?

301

Ele pensou bem. Ela tinha feito uma pergunta legítima.

— Não ligo, na verdade. Eu só... — As palavras saíram com mais facilidade do que ele imaginava. — Não quero você aqui.

— Humm. — Ela abaixou o queixo e cruzou os braços. — Bem, acho que isso era inevitável. Pelo jeito, não posso deixar você sozinho.

Ela havia fechado a porta dos fundos. Ele a abriu. Betty entrou correndo. Ela viu Angie e rosnou.

Angie falou:

— Pelo jeito, nenhuma das mulheres da sua vida fica feliz em me ver.

Ele sentiu os pelos da nuca se arrepiarem.

— Do que você está falando?

— Sara não contou para você? — Angie fez uma pausa, mas ele não conseguia respondê-la. — É Sara, né? É esse o nome dela? — Ela deu uma risada ofegante. — Preciso dizer, Will, ela é um pouquinho simplória para você. Quer dizer, aqui em cima ela é aceitável, mas não tem bunda nenhuma e é quase mais alta do que você. Achei que você gostasse de mulheres mais femininas.

Will ainda não conseguia falar. Seu sangue tinha congelado nas veias.

— Ela estava aqui quando cheguei em casa ontem, fazendo qualquer coisa no quarto. Ela não contou para você?

Sara não tinha contado. Por que não tinha contado?

— Ela tinge o cabelo. Você sabe, né? Aqueles reflexos não são naturais.

— O que você...?

— Estou só avisando que ela não é o anjinho perfeito que você imagina.

Will forçou as palavras a saírem.

— O que você falou para ela?

— Perguntei por que ela estava trepando com o meu marido.

O coração dele parou. Era por isso que Sara tinha chorado na tarde do dia anterior. Explicava sua frieza inicial quando ele aparecera à noite na casa dela. O coração de Will se apertou como se estivesse em um torno.

— Você não tem permissão para falar com ela nunca mais.

— Você está tentando protegê-la? — Angie riu. — Nossa, Will. É hilário, considerando que eu estou tentando proteger você.

— Você não...

— Ela tem uma tara por policiais. Você sabe, né? — Ela balançou a cabeça em reação à estupidez dele. — Eu pesquisei quem era o marido dela. Era um partidão. Trepava com tudo que respirava.

— Que nem você.

— Ah, vá. Se esforce mais do que isso, amor.

— Eu não quero me esforçar. — Ele finalmente disse as palavras nas quais vinha pensando no último ano. — Só quero que isso acabe. Quero que você saia da minha vida.

Ela riu na cara dele.

— Eu *sou* a sua vida.

Will ficou olhando para ela. Angie estava sorrindo. Seus olhos praticamente reluziam. Por que ela só parecia feliz quando estava tentando magoá-lo?

— Não consigo mais continuar.

— O nome dele era Jeffrey. Sabia? — Will não respondeu. Claro que ele sabia o nome do marido de Sara. — Ele era inteligente. Fez faculdade... uma de verdade, não uma qualquer por correspondência que cobra a mais para mandar seu diploma. Liderava um departamento inteiro da polícia. Eles eram apaixonados pra caralho, ela ficava até vesga nas fotos. — Angie pegou a bolsa da cadeira. — Quer ver? Eles saíam no jornal daquele fim de mundo semana sim, semana não. Quando ele morreu, fizeram a porra de uma colagem na primeira página.

— Por favor, só vá embora.

Angie soltou a bolsa.

— Ela sabe que você é burro?

Ele pôs a língua entre os dentes da frente.

— Ah, lógico que sabe. — Ela quase parecia aliviada. — Isso explica tudo. Ela tem pena de você. O coitadinho do Willy não sabe ler.

Ele balançou a cabeça.

— Vou falar uma coisa para você, Wilbur. Você não é um ótimo partido, não. Não é bonito. Não é inteligente. Não está nem na média. E não chega nem perto de ser bom de cama.

Ela já tinha falado aquilo tantas vezes que as palavras não tinham mais sentido.

— Você vai chegar a algum lugar com isso?

— Estou tentando impedir que você se machuque. É aí que eu vou chegar.

Ele baixou os olhos para o chão.

— Não faça isso, Angie. Só desta vez... não faça.

— Não fazer o quê? Falar a verdade? Porque você obviamente está com a cabeça tão enfiada no cu que não consegue enxergar o que está rolando. — Ela aproximou o rosto a centímetros do dele. — Você não sabe que toda vez que ela beija você, toda vez que ela toca, fode ou abraça você, ela está pensando nele? — Ela pausou como se esperasse uma resposta. — Você é só um substituto, Will. Você só está alı até chegar alguém melhor. Outro médico. Um advogado. Alguém que consiga ler um jornal sem ficar com a boca cansada.

Will sentiu a garganta apertando.

— Você não entende nada.

— Eu entendo as pessoas. Entendo as mulheres. Bem melhor do que você.

— Entende, sim, tá bom.

— Entendo mesmo. E entendo você, acima de tudo. — Ela parou para analisar o dano. Obviamente, não era o suficiente. — Você está esquecendo que eu estava lá, amor. Todo dia de visita, todo evento de adoção, você ficava lá parado na frente daquele espelho penteando o cabelo, conferindo suas roupas, se arrumando todo para, quem sabe, uma mamãe e um papai vissem você e o levassem para casa com eles. — Ela começou a balançar a cabeça. — Mas nunca levaram, né? Ninguém nunca o levou para casa. Ninguém nunca quis você. E sabe por quê?

Ele não conseguia respirar. Seus pulmões começaram a doer.

— Porque tem alguma coisa em você, Will. Alguma coisa errada. Alguma coisa estranha. Deixa as pessoas nervosas. Faz com que queiram se afastar de você o máximo possível.

— Só pare. Tá? Pare.

— Parar o quê? De apontar o óbvio? O que você acha que vai acontecer com ela? Vocês vão se casar e ter bebês e viver uma vida normal? — Ela riu como se fosse a coisa mais ridícula que tinha escutado. — Você já pensou que talvez goste do que a gente tem?

Ele sentiu gosto de sangue na ponta da língua. Imaginou uma parede entre eles. Uma parede grossa de concreto.

— Existe um motivo para você me esperar. Existe um motivo para você não sair com ninguém, nem ir a bares, nem pagar por uma boceta que nem todos os outros homens da face da Terra.

A parede ficou mais alta, mais firme.

— Você gosta do que a gente tem. Você sabe que não pode ficar com mais ninguém. Não de verdade. Você não pode ir até a beira desse precipício. Não pode se abrir desse jeito com alguém, porque sabe que, no fim das contas, as pessoas *sempre* abandonam você. E é isso que sua preciosa Sara vai fazer, amor. Ela é adulta. Já foi casada antes. Teve uma vida real com outra pessoa. Alguém que era digno de ser amado e que sabia amá-la de volta. E ela vai ver bem rápido que você não é capaz disso. E aí vai chutar sua bunda e se mandar.

O gosto de sangue na boca dele ficou mais forte.

— Você é um desesperado do caralho por atenção. Sempre foi assim. Grudento. Patético. Carente.

Ele não suportava mais Angie tão perto. Foi até a pia e encheu um copo de água.

— Você não sabe nada de mim.

— Você contou para ela o que aconteceu com você? Ela é médica. Ela sabe como é uma queimadura de cigarro. Sabe o que acontece quando alguém segura dois fios desencapados na sua pele. — Will tomou a água de um gole só. — Olhe para mim. — Ele não levantou os olhos, mas ela continuou falando mesmo assim. — Você é um projeto para ela. Ela tem pena de você. Coitadinho do Will, órfão. Você é a Helen Keller e ela é aquela vaca que não sei quem é, que a ensinou a ler. — Ela agarrou o queixo dele e o obrigou a virar para ela. Mesmo assim, Will desviou o olhar. — Ela só quer curar você. E, quando se cansar de tentar consertá-lo, quando ela perceber que não tem pílula mágica que vai acabar com a sua burrice, vai jogar você de volta no lixo onde ela o achou.

Algo dentro dele ruiu. Sua determinação. Sua força. Suas paredes frágeis.

— E depois? — gritou ele. — Eu vou voltar rastejando para você?

— Como sempre.

— Prefiro ficar sozinho. Prefiro apodrecer sozinho num buraco do que ficar preso a você.

Ela deu as costas para ele. Will pôs o copo na pia e usou o dorso da mão para secar a boca. Angie não chorava muito, pelo menos não de verdade. Cada criança com que Will fora criado tinha uma tática de sobrevivência diferente. Meninos usavam os punhos. Meninas viravam bulímicas. Algumas, como Angie, usavam o sexo e, quando o sexo não funcionava, usavam as lágrimas e depois, quando as lágrimas não funcionavam, achavam outra coisa para atingir seu coração.

Quando Angie se virou, estava com a arma de Will na boca.

— Não...

Ela puxou o gatilho. Ele fechou os olhos, levantou as mãos para proteger o rosto dos pedaços de cérebro e crânio.

Mas nada aconteceu.

Devagar, Will baixou os braços e abriu os olhos.

A arma continuava na boca de Angie. Disparo seco. O eco do cão clicando era como uma agulha perfurando o tímpano dele. Ele viu o pente na mesa. A bala que ele mantinha na câmara estava ao lado.

A voz de Will tremeu:

— Nunca mais você...

— Ela sabe do seu pai, Will? Você contou para ela o que aconteceu?

O corpo todo dele tremia.

— Nunca mais faça isso de novo.

Ela colocou a arma de volta na mesa e pôs as mãos no rosto dele.

— Você me ama, Will. Você sabe que me ama. Você sentiu quando eu puxei o gatilho. Sabe que não pode viver sem mim.

Os olhos dele se encheram de lágrimas.

— Nós não somos pessoas completas se não estivermos juntos. — Ela acariciou a bochecha e a sobrancelha dele. — Você não sabe disso? Não lembra o que fez por mim, amor? Você estava disposto a abrir mão da sua vida por mim. Você nunca faria isso por ela. Nunca se cortaria por ninguém, só por mim.

Ele se afastou dela. A arma continuava na mesa. Sentiu o pente gelado em sua mão. Ele o encaixou no lugar. Puxou o ferrolho para carregar uma bala no tambor. Ele estendeu a arma para ela, com o cano apontado para o próprio peito.

— Vamos, atire em mim. — Ela não se mexeu. Ele tentou pegar a mão dela. — Atire em mim.

— Pare. — Ela levantou as mãos. — Pare com isso.

— Atire em mim — repetiu ele. — Ou você atira em mim, ou me deixa ir embora.

Ela pegou a arma e a desmontou, jogando as partes na bancada. Quando suas mãos ficaram livres, deu um tapa na cara dele. Depois mais um. E então seus punhos começaram a voar. Will agarrou os braços dela. Angie se contorceu, virando-se de novo para ele. Ela odiava que a segurassem. Ele pressionou o corpo contra o dela, forçando-a a encostar na pia. Ela lutou furiosamente, gritando e o arranhando.

— Me solte! — De costas, ela o chutou, enfiando o calcanhar no pé dele. — Pare com isso!

Will apertou mais forte. Ela se encostou nele. Toda a raiva e frustração dos últimos dois dias se acumularam num lugar. Ele sentiu o corpo respondendo a ela, ansiando pelo alívio. Ela conseguiu se virar de novo. Levou a mão atrás do pescoço dele, puxando-o para mais perto. Colocou os lábios nos dele. Abriu a boca.

Will se afastou. Ela avançou para abraçá-lo de novo, mas ele deu mais um passo para trás. Sua respiração estava pesada demais para falar. Essa era a dança deles. Raiva. Medo. Violência. Nunca compaixão. Nunca carinho.

Ele pegou a coleira de Betty no gancho. Aos pés dele, a cachorrinha saltitou. As mãos de Will tremiam tanto que ele quase não conseguiu encaixar a guia na coleira. Tirou as chaves do gancho e guardou a carteira no bolso de trás.

— Não quero você aqui quando eu voltar.

— Você não pode me deixar.

Ele montou de novo a arma e prendeu o coldre na calça jeans.

— Eu preciso de você.

Ele se virou para olhar Angie. O cabelo dela estava desgrenhado. Ela parecia desesperada, disposta a qualquer coisa. Ele estava exausto daquilo. Completamente exausto.

— Você não entende? Eu não quero que alguém precise de mim. Quero ser desejado.

Ela não tinha uma boa resposta para isso, então escolheu uma ameaça.

— Juro que vou me matar se você sair por aquela porta.

Will saiu da cozinha.

Ela foi atrás dele pelo corredor.

— Eu vou tomar comprimidos. Vou cortar os pulsos. É um dos seus métodos favoritos, né? Vou cortar os pulsos e você vai chegar em casa e me achar. E aí, como vai ser, Wilbur? Como você vai se sentir se voltar para casa depois de foder a sua médica adorada e eu estiver morta no banheiro?

Ele pegou Betty no colo.

— Annie Sullivan.

— Quê?

— Foi a mulher que ensinou Helen Keller.

Will entrou na garagem e fechou a porta atrás de si. A última coisa que viu foi Angie parada no corredor, com os punhos fechados à frente. Ele entrou no carro. Esperou o portão da garagem abrir. Saiu de ré e esperou o portão fechar.

Betty se acomodou no banco ao lado dele enquanto ele dirigia. Ele abriu a janela para ela poder curtir o ar da noite. Will só percebeu para onde estava indo quando chegou na frente do prédio de Sara. Ele pegou a cachorra e a levou à porta da frente. Sara morava no último andar. Ele tocou o interfone. Não precisou falar nada. Houve um zumbido de resposta e a fechadura se abriu com um clique.

Betty se contorceu quando entraram no elevador. Ele a colocou no chão. Quando chegaram ao último andar, ela saiu correndo para o corredor. A porta de Sara estava aberta. Ela estava parada no meio da sala. Seu cabelo estava solto, caindo pelos ombros. Estava usando calça jeans e uma camiseta branca fina que não escondia muito bem o que havia por baixo.

Will fechou a porta. Queria dizer tantas coisas a ela, mas, quando finalmente conseguiu falar, não saiu nada.

— Por que você não me disse que encontrou Angie?

Ela não respondeu. Só ficou lá olhando para ele. Will não conseguiu parar de olhar de volta. A camiseta era justa. Ele via o volume dos seios dela, os mamilos pressionando o tecido fino.

Ele disse:

— Me desculpe. — A voz dele falhou. Ele nunca ia se perdoar por levar Angie para a vida de Sara. Era a coisa mais horrível que ele já havia feito com alguém. — Pelo que ela falou para você. Eu não queria...

Sara foi até ele.

— Me desculpe, de verdade.

Ela pegou a mão dele e virou a palma para cima. Os dedos de Sara se moveram ágeis nos botões do punho da camisa dele.

Will queria puxar o braço. Precisava fazer aquilo. Mas não conseguia se mexer. Não conseguia fazer os músculos funcionarem. Não conseguia impedir as mãos dela, nem os dedos, nem a boca.

Ela pressionou os lábios no pulso exposto dele. Era o beijo mais delicado que ele já experimentara. A língua dela percorreu levemente a pele, traçando a cicatriz dele braço acima. Will sentiu uma corrente passando pelo corpo de um jeito que, quando ela beijou sua boca, ele já estava pegando fogo. O corpo dela se encaixou no dele com uma curva. O beijo se aprofundou. Ela fechou a mão na nuca dele, raspando as unhas pelo cabelo. Will estava zonzo. Estava em queda livre. Não conseguia parar de tocá-la — os quadris estreitos, a curva da lombar, os seios perfeitos.

Ele prendeu a respiração quando Sara deslizou a mão para dentro da camisa dele. Os dedos dela roçaram o peito e a barriga dele. Ela não se esquivou. Não vacilou. Em vez disso, grudou a testa na dele, olhou-o nos olhos e disse:

— Respire.

Will soltou a respiração que sentia estar segurando a vida inteira.

SEGUNDA-FEIRA

16

Sara acordou com o som do chuveiro ligado. Ela se virou na cama. Sua mão percorreu a reentrância que tinha ficado no travesseiro. Os lençóis estavam retorcidos em seu corpo. Seu cabelo estava uma zona. Ela ainda sentia o cheiro de Will no quarto, o gosto dele em sua boca, lembrava a sensação dos braços dele em volta dela.

Não conseguia se lembrar da última vez que não quisera sair da cama por um bom motivo. Obviamente, acontecia quando Jeffrey era vivo, mas, pela primeira vez em quatro anos e meio, Jeffrey era a última coisa em que ela estava pensando. Seu pior medo sempre fora que o fantasma do marido fosse segui-la no quarto. Mas isso não tinha acontecido. Só havia Will e a alegria absoluta que ela sentia por estar com ele.

Sara tinha uma vaga lembrança de que suas roupas estavam em algum lugar entre a cozinha e a sala de jantar. Ela puxou um robe de seda preto do armário e saiu pelo corredor. Os cachorros deram um olhar preguiçoso do sofá quando ela entrou na sala. Betty estava dormindo numa almofada. Billy e Bob estavam amontoados num formato de lua crescente em torno da cachorrinha. Will precisava estar no trabalho dali a uma hora, senão Sara teria ido tomar banho com ele. No dia anterior, ela tinha dito à equipe do hospital que não precisava de um tempo de folga depois do tormento pelo qual passara, mas, naquela manhã, ficou feliz por terem insistido. Ela precisava processar o que tinha acontecido. E queria estar em casa quando Will voltasse do trabalho.

As roupas dela estavam bem dobradinhas na bancada. Sara sorriu, pensando que enfim tinha achado um bom uso para a mesa de jantar. Ligou a cafeteira. Havia um Post-it amarelo na parede em cima das tigelas dos cachorros. Will tinha desenhado uma carinha sorrindo no meio. Ela viu outro bilhete com o mesmo símbolo acima das coleiras. Que coisa maravilhosa um homem que alimentava os cachorrinhos e os levava para passear enquanto Sara estava dormindo. Ela ficou olhando a tinta azul, o arco de um sorriso e os dois pontos como olhos.

Sara nunca tinha ido atrás de um homem antes. Sempre estivera na posição de ser conquistada. Mas, na noite anterior, tinha percebido que nunca ia acontecer nada se ela não tomasse a iniciativa. E ela queria que acontecesse alguma coisa. Queria Will como havia muito tempo não queria nada.

No início, ele tinha ficado um pouco tímido. Obviamente tinha vergonha do corpo, o que era risível, considerando o quanto era lindo. As pernas dele eram fortes e definidas. Seus ombros eram musculosos. O abdome poderia estar facilmente num anúncio de cuecas no meio da Times Square. Mas não era só isso. As mãos dele sabiam exatamente onde tocá-la. A boca dele era uma delícia. A língua era uma delícia. Tudo nele era uma delícia. Estar com ele era como uma chave se encaixando na fechadura. Sara nunca sonhara que algum dia se abriria tanto a outro homem.

Se tinha alguma comparação a fazer, era entre Sara e sua personalidade de antigamente. Algo tinha se alterado dentro dela e não era só a bússola moral. Ela se sentia diferente com Will. Não precisava saber imediatamente tudo sobre esse homem com quem dividira sua cama. Ela não sentia necessidade de exigir respostas sobre os óbvios maus-tratos que ele tinha sofrido. Pela primeira vez na vida, Sara se sentia paciente. A garota que tinha sido expulsa da escola dominical por discutir com a professora e enlouquecera os pais, a irmã e, por fim, o marido com o desejo incansável de entender cada detalhezinho de tudo no mundo finalmente estava aprendendo a relaxar.

Talvez ter visto a Polaroid da boca suturada de Will a tivesse ensinado a não bisbilhotar. Ou talvez só fizesse parte da natureza da vida aprender com erros do passado. Por ora, Sara estava contente por simplesmente estar com Will. O resto viria com o tempo. Ou não. De todo modo, ela se sentia extremamente satisfeita.

Houve uma batida insistente na porta, provavelmente de Abel Conford, que morava no apartamento da frente. Ele era advogado e tinha nomeado a si mesmo como czar do estacionamento. Toda reunião de condomínio a que Sara já tinha ido começava com Abel reclamando de visitantes parando nas vagas erradas.

Sara apertou o robe enquanto abria a porta. Em vez do vizinho, encontrou Faith Mitchell.

— Desculpe incomodá-la.

Faith já foi entrando no apartamento. Estava com um casaco azul-marinho volumoso, e a cabeça coberta pelo capuz. Óculos de sol obscureciam metade do rosto dela. Calça jeans e All-Star de cano alto completavam o look. Ela parecia exatamente o que uma mãe da Associação de Pais e Mestres imaginaria como sendo um gatuno.

Sara só conseguiu perguntar:

— Como você entrou?

— Falei para o seu vizinho que eu era policial e ele me liberou.

— Que ótimo — murmurou Sara, se perguntando quanto tempo levaria para todo mundo no prédio achar que ela estava sendo presa. — O que houve?

Faith tirou os óculos. Havia cinco minúsculos hematomas em torno do rosto dela.

— Preciso que você ligue para Will por mim. — Ela foi até a janela e olhou o estacionamento lá embaixo. — Pensei nisso a noite toda. Não consigo fazer isso sozinha. Acho que não sou capaz. — Ela protegeu os olhos com a mão, apesar de o sol ainda não ter nascido. — Eles não sabem que eu estou aqui. O Ruivo dormiu. Taylor foi embora ontem à noite. Eu saí de fininho. Pelo quintal dos fundos. Peguei o carro de Roz Levy. Eu sei que eles grampearam meus telefones. Estão me observando. Não podem saber que estou fazendo isso. Não podem saber que falei com alguém.

Ela era uma garota-propaganda de hipoglicemia. Sara sugeriu:

— Não quer se sentar?

Faith continuou empoleirada olhando o estacionamento.

315

— Mandei meus filhos embora. Eles estão com meu irmão. Ele nunca nem trocou uma fralda. É responsabilidade demais para Jeremy.

— Tá. Vamos conversar. Venha aqui e se sente comigo.

— Preciso trazê-la de volta, Sara. Não quero nem saber o que vai me custar. O que vou ter que fazer.

A mãe dela. Will tinha contado a Sara sobre a viagem à Prisão Estadual de Coastal e a conversa com Roger Ling.

— Faith, sente-se.

— Não posso me sentar, senão nunca mais vou levantar. Preciso do Will. Pode por favor ligar logo para ele?

— Eu vou chamá-lo para você. Prometo, mas você precisa se sentar. — Sara a guiou para a banqueta na bancada da cozinha. — Você tomou café da manhã?

Ela fez que não.

— Meu estômago está revirado demais.

— Como está sua glicemia?

Ela parou de balançar a cabeça. A cara de culpa era resposta suficiente.

Sara deixou a voz firme.

— Faith, não vou fazer nada até controlarmos sua taxa de glicose. Entendeu?

Faith não discutiu, talvez porque parte dela soubesse que precisava de ajuda. Ela tateou os bolsos da jaqueta e puxou um punhado de balas duras que jogou no balcão. Em seguida, colocou uma arma grande, depois a carteira, um molho de chaves em um chaveiro com L dourado em letra cursiva e, finalmente, o kit para teste de glicemia.

Sara conferiu as estatísticas no histórico do medidor. Faith obviamente tinha passado os últimos dois dias brincando de roleta russa do doce. Usar doces para sair dos pontos baixos e suportar os altos era um truque comum entre diabéticos. Era um bom jeito de superar um momento difícil, mas um jeito ainda melhor de acabar em coma.

— Eu devia levar você para o hospital agora. — Sara agarrou o monitor. — Sua insulina está aí?

Faith procurou de novo nos bolsos e colocou quatro canetas de insulina descartáveis na bancada. Começou a tagarelar:

—Eu comprei na farmácia hoje de manhã. Não sabia quanto tomar. Eles me mostraram, mas eu nunca usei antes e são tão caras que eu não queria errar. Minhas cetonas estão ok. Eu usei uma fita ontem à noite e hoje de manhã. Acho que eu devia colocar uma bomba.

—Uma bomba de insulina não seria má ideia. —Sara deslizou uma fita de teste para dentro do monitor. —Você jantou ontem à noite?

—Mais ou menos.

—Vou entender como um não — murmurou Sara. —E lanches? Alguma coisa?

Faith apoiou a cabeça na mão.

—Não consigo pensar direito sem Jeremy e Emma. Zeke ligou hoje de manhã. Disse que estão acomodados, mas eu percebi que ele está irritado. Ele nunca foi bom com crianças.

Sara pegou o dedo de Faith e alinhou a lanceta.

—Quando isso acabar, vamos ter uma longa conversa sobre sua falta de disciplina. Eu sei que dizer que este momento é estressante para você é um belo eufemismo, mas sua diabetes não é uma coisa que dá para magicamente interromper e deixar de lado. Sua visão, sua circulação, suas habilidades motoras... — Sara não terminou a frase. Tinha dado sermão em tantos diabéticos sobre esse mesmo problema que se sentia lendo um roteiro. —Você tem que se cuidar para não acabar cega, numa cadeira de rodas ou coisa pior.

Faith disse:

—Você está diferente.

Sara ajeitou o cabelo, que estava para cima na parte de trás.

—Está praticamente reluzindo. Você está grávida?

Sara riu, surpresa com a pergunta. Uma gravidez ectópica aos vinte e poucos anos a tinha levado a uma histerectomia parcial. Will não era tão milagreiro assim.

—Você usa cento e trinta?

—Cento e trinta e cinco.

Sara girou a dosagem correta na caneta.

—Você vai injetar isso, depois eu vou fazer café da manhã e você não vai fazer mais nada até ter comido tudo.

— Esse fogão custa mais do que a minha casa. — Faith se debruçou na bancada para ver melhor. Sara a empurrou de volta. — Quanto você ganha?

Ela pegou a mão de Faith e colocou os dedos dela em volta da caneta de insulina.

— Você faz isso e eu vou buscar Will.

— Você pode ligar para ele daqui. Eu sei o que você vai dizer.

Sara não parou para se explicar, em especial porque Faith obviamente estava tendo dificuldade de processar informações. Ela pegou as próprias roupas da bancada e entrou no quarto. Will estava parado na frente da cômoda, vestindo a camisa. Ela viu o peito largo dele refletido no espelho, a mancha escura de queimaduras elétricas descendo pela barriga e desaparecendo dentro da calça jeans. Sara tinha colocado a boca em cada centímetro daquele corpo no dia anterior, mas ali parada, à luz do dia, sentiu-se desconfortável com ele.

Ele a olhou pelo espelho. Sara apertou mais o robe na cintura. Ele tinha feito a cama. Os travesseiros estavam empilhados organizadamente contra a cabeceira. Não era assim que ela tinha imaginado aquela manhã.

Ele perguntou:

— O que houve?

Ela colocou as próprias roupas dobradas na cama.

— Faith está aqui.

— Aqui? — Ele se virou. Parecia quase em pânico. — Por quê? Como ela soube?

— Ela não sabe. Me pediu para ligar para você. Ela está apavorada porque o telefone dela está grampeado.

— Ela ficou sabendo da mãe?

— Acho que não. — Sara colocou a mão no peito, acinturando de novo o robe, sentindo cada pedacinho de sua nudez embaixo. — Ela disse que tem gente observando. Está paranoica. A glicemia dela está altíssima. Está tomando insulina agora. Depois que ela comer alguma coisa, deve se acalmar.

— Eu preciso ir comprar café da manhã?

— Posso fazer alguma coisa.

— Eu posso... — Ele parou, parecendo extremamente desconfortável. — Talvez eu devesse fazer isso. Para Faith, quero dizer. Depois, você pode cozinhar alguma coisa para mim.

Então, a lua de mel tinha acabado. Pelo menos, ela agora sabia por que Bob estava com cheiro de ovos mexidos naquela noite.

— Eu fico aqui para vocês terem um pouco de privacidade.

— Você pode... — Ele hesitou. — Pode ser melhor se você estiver junto. Vou precisar dar a notícia sobre a mãe dela.

— Achei que Amanda tinha dito para esperar.

— Amanda diz muita coisa com que eu não concordo.

Ele indicou que ela devia sair do quarto antes dele. Sara caminhou pelo corredor, sentindo Will bem perto. Apesar do que tinha acontecido naquela noite — algumas partes bem ali, no corredor —, ele parecia um estranho para ela. Sara apertou mais o robe, desejando ter parado para colocar uma roupa de verdade.

Faith continuava sentada na bancada da cozinha. Um pouco da energia ansiosa tinha se dissipado. Ela viu Will e disse:

— Ah.

Ele pareceu envergonhado. Sara também se sentia assim. Talvez isso explicasse o humor distante dele. Parecia errado estarem juntos considerando o que tinha acontecido com Evelyn Mitchell.

Apesar disso, Faith falou:

— Está tudo bem. Estou feliz por vocês.

Will ignorou o comentário.

— A Dra. Linton disse que você precisa comer.

— Preciso falar com você primeiro.

Will olhou para Sara. Ela fez que não.

— Você precisa tomar café da manhã primeiro.

Will abriu a lava-louças e pegou a frigideira. Achou os ovos e o pão no lugar certo. Faith o observou fazendo café. Não falou nada. Sara não sabia se era por ela estar tendo uma queda de glicemia ou se não sabia o que dizer. Provavelmente um pouco dos dois. De sua parte, Sara nunca se sentira tão desconfortável na própria casa. Ficou assistindo a Will quebrar os ovos e passar manteiga nas torradas. O maxilar dele estava rígido. Ele não a olhou. Ela podia muito bem ter ficado no quarto.

Will pegou três pratos do armário e os encheu de comida. Sara e Faith se sentaram no bar. Embora houvesse uma terceira cadeira, Will ficou de pé, apoiado na bancada. Sara ficou remexendo a comida. Faith comeu metade dos ovos e um pedaço de torrada. Will limpou o prato, depois terminou a torrada de Faith e a de Sara antes de raspar o resto para o lixo e empilhar os pratos na pia. Ele enxaguou a tigela em que tinham estado os ovos, passou uma água na frigideira e lavou as mãos.

Finalmente, ele disse:

— Faith, preciso contar uma coisa.

Ela balançou a cabeça. Devia saber o que estava por vir. Ele estava de pé, de costas para a bancada. Não se inclinou nem pegou as mãos dela. Não se aproximou nem se sentou ao seu lado. Só deu a notícia direto.

— Ontem à noite, eu estava na Prisão Estadual de Coastal. Conversei com um homem que tem um cargo bem alto no tráfico. Roger Ling. — Ele manteve os olhos focados nos dela. — Não tem outra forma de dizer isto. Ele me falou que sua mãe foi morta. Com dois tiros na cabeça.

De início, ela não reagiu. Ficou ali sentada com os cotovelos na bancada, mãos penduradas para baixo, boca aberta. No fim, falou:

— Ela não está morta, não.

— Faith...

— Vocês acharam o corpo?

— Não, mas...

— Quando foi isso? Quando ele falou com você?

— Tarde, lá pelas nove da noite.

— Não é verdade.

— Faith, é verdade. Esse cara sabe do que está falando. Amanda disse...

— Não quero nem saber o que Amanda disse. — Ela procurou algo nos bolsos de novo. — Mandy não sabe do que está falando. Não sei quem é esse cara que falou com você, mas estava mentindo.

Will olhou Sara de canto de olho.

— Dê uma olhada — disse Faith. Estava segurando um iPhone. — Está vendo isso? É o Facebook de Jeremy. Eles estão mandando mensagens.

Will se afastou da bancada.

— Quê?

— Encontrei um deles ontem à noite. No supermercado. Ele fez isso. — Ela indicou os hematomas no rosto. — Eu falei para ele que precisava de uma prova de vida. Hoje de manhã, ele me mandou um e-mail pela conta do Facebook de Jeremy.

— Quê? — repetiu Will. Ele estava sem cor no rosto. — Você se encontrou com ele sozinha? Por que você não me ligou? Ele podia...

— Veja isso aqui.

Ela mostrou o telefone. Sara não conseguia ver a imagem, mas ouviu o som.

— É segunda de manhã. Cinco e trinta e oito. — Evelyn fez uma pausa. Havia um barulho de fundo. — Faith, me escute. Não faça nada que eles mandarem. Não confie neles. Só fique longe. Você, seu irmão e as crianças são minha família. Minha única família... — De repente, a voz ficou mais forte. — Faith, é importante. Preciso que você se lembre do nosso tempo juntas antes de Jeremy...

Faith disse:

— Pare bem aí.

Will perguntou:

— Do que ela está falando? Do tempo antes de Jeremy?

— De quando eu estava grávida. — Ela ficou corada, embora tivessem se passado quase vinte anos. — Minha mãe ficou comigo. Ela foi... — Faith balançou a cabeça. — Eu não teria conseguido sem ela. Ela só ficava me falando para ser forte, que um dia aquilo ia passar e que ia ficar tudo bem.

Sara pôs a mão no ombro de Faith. Ela não podia imaginar a dor que a outra estava sentindo.

Will olhou o iPhone.

— O que está passando na televisão atrás dela?

— *Good Day Atlanta*. Eu confirmei com a emissora. É o quadro do clima que eles transmitiram faz meia hora. Dá para ver o horário em cima do logo da emissora. Recebi o arquivo dois minutos depois.

Ele entregou o celular a Sara, mas ainda não a olhava nos olhos.

Curiosidade sempre fora a fraqueza dela. Os óculos de leitura de Sara estavam na bancada. Ela os colocou para poder ver os pequenos detalhes. A tela mostrava Evelyn Mitchell sentada ao lado de uma televisão de plasma grande. Estava sem som, mas Sara viu a moça do tempo apontando para a previsão de cinco dias. Evelyn olhava para fora da câmera, provavelmente para o homem que a filmava. O rosto dela era um caos ensanguentado. Ela começou, enrolando as palavras:

— Hoje é segunda de manhã.

Sara deixou o vídeo seguir, depois soltou o telefone.

Faith a observava atentamente.

— Como ela parece estar?

Sara tirou os óculos. Não conseguia exatamente dar uma opinião médica com base num vídeo granulado, mas era óbvio para qualquer um que Evelyn tinha tomado uma surra feia. Apesar disso, ela falou:

— Parece estar aguentando firme.

— Foi o que eu achei. — Faith se virou para Will. — Eu disse que me encontraria com eles ao meio-dia, mas o e-mail diz meio-dia e meia. Na casa da minha mãe.

— Na casa da sua mãe? — repetiu ele. — Ainda é uma cena do crime ativa.

— Talvez tenha sido liberada. A polícia de Atlanta se recusa a me dizer qualquer coisa. Me deixe encontrar o e-mail. — Faith moveu os polegares pela tela de novo e entregou o celular a Will. — Ah — disse ela, estendendo a mão para o aparelho. — Esqueci...

— Pode deixar. — Will pegou os óculos de Sara da bancada e os colocou. Ficou olhando o telefone por alguns segundos. Sara não conseguia saber se ele tinha lido o e-mail ou só chutando ao dizer: — Eles querem dinheiro.

Faith tirou o celular dele.

— Não tem dinheiro.

Will só ficou olhando para ela.

— Não é verdade — falou Faith. — Nunca foi verdade. Você não conseguiu provar nada. Ela não era corrupta. Boyd e o resto estavam no esquema, mas minha mãe nunca aceitou nada.

— Faith — disse Will. — Sua mãe tinha uma conta bancária.

— E daí? Todo mundo tem conta bancária.

— Uma conta bancária em outro estado. Está no nome do seu pai. Ela ainda tem. Até onde eu sei, entraram e saíram uns sessenta mil. Pode ter outras contas em outros estados, com outros nomes. Vai saber.

Faith balançou a cabeça.

— Não. Você está mentindo.

— Por que eu mentiria sobre isso?

— Porque não consegue admitir que estava errado em relação a ela. Ela não era corrupta. — Os olhos dela se encheram de lágrimas. Ela tinha a expressão de quem sabia a verdade, mas não conseguia aceitar. — Não era.

Houve outra batida na porta. Sara supunha que Abel Conford finalmente tinha notado os carros a mais no estacionamento. Errada de novo.

— Bom dia, Dra. Linton.

Amanda Wagner não parecia feliz de estar parada no corredor. Seus olhos estavam vermelhos. A maquiagem parecia ter sido esfregada e tirada do nariz. A pele estava mais escura nos pontos da bochecha cobertos por base e blush.

Sara abriu mais a porta. Apertou de novo o roupão, perguntando-se de onde tinha vindo aquele tique nervoso. Talvez fosse porque ela estava completamente nua por baixo e a seda preta fosse fina como papel crepom. Ela não tinha planejado ser anfitriã de uma festa naquela manhã.

Faith pareceu irritada ao ver Amanda.

— O que você está fazendo aqui?

— Roz Levy telefonou. Disse que você roubou o carro dela.

— Eu deixei um bilhete.

— Que ela estranhamente não interpretou como a forma correta de se pedir permissão. Felizmente, consegui convencer a mulher a não chamar a polícia. — Ela sorriu para Will. — Bom dia, Dr. Trent.

Will fingiu ter uma fascinação repentina pelos azulejos do piso da cozinha.

— Espere aí — disse Faith. — Como você sabia onde eu estava?

— Roz tem um rastreador no carro. Cobrei uns favores na central.

— Rastreador? É um Corvair de novecentos anos. Vale cinco dólares.

Amanda tirou o casaco e o entregou a Sara.

— Desculpe por atrapalhar sua manhã, Dra. Linton. Adorei o que você fez no seu cabelo.

Sara forçou um sorriso enquanto pendurava o casaco no armário.

— Quer um café?

— Aceito, obrigada. — Ela se virou para Will e Faith. — Eu devia ficar magoada por não ter sido convidada para esta festa?

Ninguém parecia querer responder. Sara pegou três canecas do armário e colocou café em cada uma. Escutou a voz de Evelyn Mitchell no iPhone enquanto Faith mostrava o vídeo para a nova convidada.

Amanda pediu que ela desse play de novo, depois uma terceira vez, e então perguntou:

— Quando chegou isso?

— Há pouco mais de meia hora.

— Leia para mim a mensagem que veio junto.

Faith leu:

— "Meio-dia e meia na rua João Pequeno, 339. Leve o dinheiro numa mala de lona preta. Não avise a ninguém. Estamos observando você. Se não seguir essas instruções, ela vai morrer, e você e sua família também. Lembre o que eu disse."

— Roger Ling. — A voz de Amanda tinha uma fúria contida. — Eu sabia que aquele filho da puta estava mentindo. Não dá para confiar numa puta palavra que nenhum deles diz. — Ela pareceu perceber o significado mais amplo de suas palavras. Sua boca se abriu em surpresa. — Ela está *viva*. — Ela riu. — Ah, meu Deus, eu sabia que a velhota não ia se entregar sem lutar. — Ela levou a mão ao peito. — Como eu pensei por um minuto que...

Amanda balançou a cabeça. Seu sorriso estava tão largo que ela acabou cobrindo a boca com a mão.

Will fez a pergunta mais importante:

— Por que eles iam querer encontrar você na casa da sua mãe? Não é segura. Eles não vão ter vantagem. Não faz sentido.

Faith respondeu:

— É um local conhecido. É fácil de vigiar.

Will disse:

— Mas não tem como a cena de crime ter sido liberada. Vai levar dias para analisar tudo.

Amanda opinou:

— Os sequestradores devem saber de alguma coisa que nós não sabemos.

— Pode ser um teste — contrapôs Will. — Se tirarmos a equipe forense, vai ficar óbvio que Faith falou com a polícia. Ou com a gente. — Ele disse a Faith: — Chegando na casa, você vai estar exposta. Se entrar, vai estar indo direto para as mãos deles. O que os impede de atirarem em você e pegarem o dinheiro? Principalmente se não conseguirmos colocar uma equipe tática para isolar a área.

— Podemos dar um jeito — insistiu Amanda. — Só tem três rotas de entrada e saída do bairro. Eles virão de alguma das direções e vamos estar com armas em punho.

Will ignorou a bravata. Abriu a gaveta ao lado da geladeira e pegou uma caneta e um bloco de papel. Segurou a caneta de um jeito desajeitado com a mão esquerda, prendendo-a entre os dedos do meio e anelar. Sara o observou cobrir a página com um T grande, depois desenhar dois quadrados de forma irregular — um no braço do T, outro na base. Sua noção espacial era melhor do que Sara poderia imaginar, mas, também, ele provavelmente já tinha ido várias vezes à casa de Faith.

Ele explicou:

— A casa de Faith fica nesta esquina. A de Evelyn é aqui na João Pequeno. — Ele traçou uma linha em formato de L entre as duas casas. — Temos todo esse espaço aberto. Eles podem bloquear o cruzamento aqui e levá-la. Podem estacionar uma van no mesmo ponto e atirar à distância. Ela pode parar na entrada de carros aqui e vir a van preta. Dois na cabeça, como Castillo no armazém, ou podem pegá-la e chegar na interestadual ou na Peachtree Road em cinco minutos. Ou eles podem facilitar e montar tudo aqui... — Ele desenhou um retângulo ao lado da casa de Evelyn. — A garagem de Roz Levy. Ali tem uma mureta onde eles podem apoiar um rifle. A janela do banheiro da casa de Evelyn dá para a da Sra. Levy. Fica num declive. Da casa dela, dá para ver até depois da porta da cozinha da casa de Evelyn, sem ninguém saber. Faith entra pela porta e é derrubada.

325

Amanda pegou a caneta e transformou a base do T num círculo.

— A João Pequeno é uma rua que dá uma volta completa. O bairro todo se dobra em si mesmo. — Ela desenhou mais arcos. — Aqui é a Nottingham. Frei Tuck. Robin Hood. Beverly. Lionel. — Ela desenhou grandes Xs nos pontos finais. — A Beverly aqui dá na Peachtree, onde todo carro do mundo acaba passando. A outra ponta joga você de volta no loop infinito de Ansley Park. A Lionel faz a mesma coisa. São gargalos. A maioria das casas nessas rotas têm vagas de estacionamento na rua. Podemos colocar dez carros em cada ponto e ninguém notaria.

Will disse:

— Não estou preocupado com as rotas de saída deles. Estou preocupado com Faith entrando sozinha naquela casa. Se eles estiverem mesmo observando o lugar, no minuto em que aparecer alguém que não devia estar lá, eles vão saber. Tiveram quase três dias inteiros para mapear o bairro, talvez mais. Mesmo se os caras da unidade de perícia criminal saírem, vão estar contando o número que sai e o número que entra.

Amanda virou o papel. Desenhou uma planta grosseira de uma casa, indicando os cômodos.

— Faith entra pela cozinha. O hall de entrada fica aqui, dando para a sala de estar. Aqui fica a estante de livros à esquerda; minha esquerda. Ocupa a parede toda. O sofá fica encostado aqui. A poltrona *bergère* está aqui à direita. Tem algumas outras cadeiras aqui e aqui. O móvel do toca-discos aqui. Portas de vidro de correr na frente do hall de entrada. — Ela bateu a caneta no que devia ser o quarto principal. — Eles vão segurar Eve aqui até Faith chegar com o dinheiro, depois vão trazê-la para a sala. É o lugar óbvio para a troca.

— Não tem nada óbvio aqui. — Ele tomou a caneta. — Não podemos cobrir as janelas da frente, porque não sabemos quem está observando a casa. Não podemos cobrir os fundos porque o quintal é aberto para o dos vizinhos e eles vão ver movimento em qualquer janela. Ainda não sabemos quantos caras sobraram na equipe. Pode ser um, podem ser cem. — Ele jogou a caneta. Seu tom era firme: — Não gosto dessa ideia, Faith. Você não pode ir lá. Não nos termos deles.

Vamos achar outro jeito de fazer isso. Vamos sugerir um local que possamos isolar com antecedência para garantir que você vai estar segura.

O tom de Amanda deixou sua irritação evidente:

— Deixe de ser tão fatalista, Will. A gente tem seis horas. Todos nós conhecemos a planta da casa, então temos tanta vantagem quanto eles. Eu conheço todas as velhas daquele bairro. É uma rua residencial. Tem gente praticando corrida, entregadores, caminhões de TV a cabo, leitores de parquímetro, carteiros e passantes vespertinos que podemos usar. Posso enfiar quatro equipes nas próximas horas e ninguém vai nem notar. Não somos um bando de Guardas Keystone. Damos conta disso.

— Eu vou — ofereceu-se Will, e Sara sentiu o coração pular na garganta.

— Você não vai conseguir se passar por Faith.

— A gente manda um e-mail para avisar que eu vou fazer a troca. Roger Ling sabe como eu sou. Mesmo que ele não esteja envolvido nisso, obviamente está curtindo o show. Ele sabe quem são esses caras. Pode falar para confiarem em mim.

Sara sentiu uma onda de alívio ao ver Amanda começar a fazer que não com a cabeça antes mesmo de ele terminar de falar.

Ele insistiu:

— É mais seguro assim. Mais seguro para Faith.

Como sempre, Amanda não aliviou:

— É uma das coisas mais idiotas que já ouvi saindo da sua boca. Pense no que a gente viu nos últimos dias. É um monte de amador. Julia Ling praticamente desenhou isso para nós. Estamos lidando com um bando de meninos jovens e burros que acham que sabem brincar de polícia e ladrão. Vamos pôr todos de quatro ou na cova antes mesmo de se darem conta do que está acontecendo.

Will não estava convencido.

— Eles podem ser jovens, mas são destemidos. Mataram muita gente. Correram muitos riscos idiotas.

— Nenhum mais idiota do que mandar você em vez de Faith. É *assim* que as pessoas são mortas. — Amanda decidiu: — Vamos fazer do meu jeito. Vamos descobrir como colocar nossa gente de forma estratégica. Vamos manter os olhos em Faith o tempo todo. Vamos esperar até os sequestradores aparecerem com Evelyn. Faith vai fazer a troca, e aí vamos pegá-los quando tentarem fugir.

Will não cedia. Estava irredutível.

— Ela não pode fazer isso. Não pode entrar lá sozinha. Ou você me deixa ir, ou vamos achar outro jeito.

Faith falou:

— Se eu não estiver sozinha, minha mãe vai morrer.

Will olhou para o chão. Obviamente achava que ainda havia uma possibilidade real de Evelyn Mitchell estar morta. Sara se viu concordando silenciosamente com ele. Aquilo não parecia um plano para trazer Evelyn de volta. Parecia um plano para matar Faith. Amanda estava tão obcecada em salvar a amiga que não conseguia ver o dano colateral.

Sara tinha se esquecido do café. Ficou com um para si, depois passou as outras canecas para Amanda e então para Will.

— Obrigado — disse Will, sem graça, e aceitou a sua. Era como se ele estivesse tentando garantir que suas mãos não se tocassem.

Faith falou:

— Ele não toma café. Pode ficar para mim.

Sara sentiu as bochechas começando a queimar.

— Você provavelmente não deveria ingerir cafeína agora.

Will pigarreou.

— Não tem problema. Eu gosto, às vezes.

Ele deu um gole da caneca e praticamente fez uma careta ao engolir. Sara não ia conseguir aguentar aquilo muito mais tempo. A única forma de ficar mais deslocada seria puxando um acordeão e começando a cantar polca.

— Melhor eu dar um pouco de privacidade a vocês.

Amanda a impediu.

— Se não se importa, Dra. Linton, eu gostaria da opinião de alguém de fora.

Estavam todos olhando para ela. Parecia impossível, mas Sara se sentiu ainda mais nua do que antes. Ela olhou para Will em busca de ajuda, mas a expressão neutra dele devia ser a mesma que ele dava à mulher do banco ou ao cara que levava o lixo reciclável.

Não tinha o que fazer. Ela se sentou ao lado de Faith. Amanda ocupou o outro assento.

— Tudo bem, vamos repassar o que já sabemos para estarmos todos atualizados. Will, faça um resumo para nós.

Ele apoiou a caneca de café na bancada e começou a falar. Contou a Faith tudo o que acontecera desde que Evelyn tinha sido levada, detalhando a cena do crime, a visita a Boyd Spivey na D&C e os ex-colegas dele calados na Prisão Estadual de Valdosta. Os lábios de Faith se abriram em surpresa quando ele contou a ela sobre as fotografias tiradas por Roz Levy do namoradinho de Evelyn. Apesar disso, continuou em silêncio enquanto ele detalhava o tormento de Sara no hospital e o tiroteio no armazém de Julia Ling. Sara sentiu o aperto familiar no peito quando ele chegou à última parte. O corte na orelha dele. Uma bala tinha passado raspando a menos de três centímetros de seu crânio.

Will falou:

— Ricardo Ortiz e Hironobu Kown se conheciam da escola. Os dois estudaram na Westminster. Muito provavelmente estavam trabalhando juntos na oficina de armários de Ling-Ling. Botaram na cabeça que queriam abrir o próprio negócio. Obviamente formaram uma equipe com os outros caras da oficina. Ricardo foi à Suécia e comprou heroína para venderem. Segundo Roger Ling, todos os meninos estavam se gabando disso. Benny Choo, capanga dos Yellow Rebels, pegou Ricardo e espancou o cara. Estava prestes a acabar com aquilo, mas Ricardo, ou talvez Hironobu, disse a ele onde podiam conseguir um dinheiro.

Faith estava absorvendo tudo em silêncio, mas, naquele momento, murmurou:

— Minha mãe.

— Isso — confirmou Will. — Chuck Finn e Hironobu Kwon ficaram na mesma clínica de reabilitação por pelo menos um mês. Chuck deve ter contado para Hironobu sobre o dinheiro. Ricardo estava prestes a morrer, então, Hironobu diz: "Eu sei onde conseguir quase um milhão em dinheiro." Benny Choo aceita a oferta.

Amanda continuou a história:

— Era isso que estavam procurando na casa de Evelyn. Acharam que tinha dinheiro lá. Quando ela não entregou, foi levada.

Sara achou conveniente Amanda ter pulado o fato de que Hector Ortiz, primo de um dos mais poderosos chefões do tráfico em Atlanta, estava morto no porta-malas de Evelyn. Devia ter ficado calada, mas estavam na casa dela, que tinham invadido sem aviso prévio, e Sara estava cansada de ser educada.

— Isso não explica por que Hector Ortiz estava lá.

Amanda levantou uma sobrancelha.

— Não, não explica, não é mesmo?

Sara não trabalhava para aquela mulher. Não ia ficar pisando em ovos.

— Você não vai responder à pergunta?

Havia um sorriso falso nos lábios de Amanda.

— A questão mais importante aqui é que eles fizeram tudo isso porque querem dinheiro. Com gente que quer dinheiro, dá para negociar.

Will contrariou:

— Isso não tem a ver com dinheiro.

— Não temos tempo para a intuição da sua mulher — irritou-se Amanda.

A voz dele parecia cansada, mas ele não cedeu:

— Estão tentando prender Faith naquela casa por um motivo. Se entrarmos lá sem saber esse motivo, não vai acabar bem. Para nenhum de nós. — O que ele disse parecia perfeitamente racional, mas Sara via que Amanda não estava convencida. Mesmo assim, ele seguiu tentando. — Olha, se fosse só por dinheiro, eles teriam pedido resgate no primeiro dia. Não estariam com esse vaivém pelo Facebook. Não iam arriscar encontrar Faith pessoalmente no supermercado. Seria uma transação simples. Fazer a ligação. Pegar o dinheiro. Largar a refém em algum lugar e se mandar.

De novo, uma suposição racional. De novo, Amanda o ignorou e disse:

— Não tem um objetivo secreto aqui. Eles querem dinheiro. Vamos dar dinheiro a eles. Vamos enfiar tão no fundo da garganta deles que vão cagar as notas no caminho inteiro até a prisão.

— Ele tem razão. — Durante a maior parte do diálogo, Faith tinha ficado olhando para o nada, mas, com a hipoglicemia finalmente controlada, ela tinha voltado a pensar como investigadora. — E a conta bancária?

Amanda se levantou para pegar mais café.

— A conta não importa.

Will parecia pronto para discordar, mas, por razões próprias, ficou quieto.

Amanda disse a Faith:

— Seu pai apostava.

Faith fez que não com a cabeça.

— Não é verdade.

— Ele jogava pôquer todo fim de semana.

— Apostando moedinhas. — Ela continuou balançando a cabeça. — Meu pai era corretor de seguros. Ele odiava riscos.

— Ele não estava arriscando nada. Tomava muito cuidado. — Amanda contornou a ilha da cozinha e se sentou ao lado de Faith. — Quantas vezes ele e Kenny foram a Las Vegas quando você era pequena?

Faith ainda não estava convencida.

— Era para congressos de trabalho.

— Bill era metódico. Ele era metódico com tudo. Você sabe disso. Ele sabia blefar e sabia quando parar. Kenny não era tão esperto, mas essa é uma história para outra hora. — Ela encarou Will. — Bill não pagava impostos sobre o dinheiro. É por isso que a conta era um segredo.

Sara via sua própria confusão refletida no rosto de Will. A partir de certa quantia, não dava para só sair andando de um cassino de Las Vegas, de qualquer cassino legal nos Estados Unidos, sem pagar impostos.

Faith não percebeu isso.

— Não imagino meu pai correndo esse tipo de risco. Ele odiava apostas. Vivia pegando no pé de Kenny por causa disso.

— Porque Kenny era um idiota com dinheiro — contrapôs Amanda. A pontada amarga na voz dela fez Sara lembrar que os dois tinham namorado por muitos anos. — Para Bill, era só diversão, um jeito de relaxar, e às vezes ele ganhava muito dinheiro, e às vezes perdia um pouco, mas sempre sabia quando parar. Não era um vício para ele. Era um esporte.

Will finalmente falou.

— Por que Evelyn não me disse isso quando estava sendo investigada?

Amanda sorriu.

— Ela não contou um monte de coisa para você, sobre vários assuntos, quando estava sendo investigada.

— Não — concordou ele. — Mas ela podia facilmente ter se livrado da suspeita se...

— Não tinha suspeita — interrompeu Amanda. Ela direcionou as palavras a Faith: — Foi sua mãe que denunciou a equipe. É por isso que a chamavam de Almeja. Ela era uma delatora.

— Quê? — A confusão de Faith era quase palpável. Ela olhou para Will como se ele tivesse as respostas. — Por que ela não me contou?

Amanda disse:

— Porque ela queria proteger você. Quanto menos você soubesse, mais segura estaria.

Will questionou:

— Então por que está contando isso para ela agora?

Amanda obviamente estava irritada.

— Porque você não larga o osso daquela porcaria de conta, apesar de eu ter dito mil vezes para você que ela não tem importância.

Will tinha colocado a caneca de café na bancada. Devagar, girou a alça para ficar paralela à parede atrás da pia.

Faith fez a pergunta que Sara estava pensando:

— Como ela descobriu que estavam desviando dinheiro?

Amanda deu de ombros.

— E isso importa?

— Importa — respondeu Will, que obviamente queria ouvir a história para poder encontrar os buracos.

Amanda respirou fundo antes de começar:

— Teve uma apreensão no sul, num dos conjuntos habitacionais de East Point. Evelyn liderou a equipe de operações que entrou no apartamento. De manhã cedinho. Os bandidos ainda estavam dormindo, de ressaca da noite anterior, com uma pilha de dinheiro largada na mesa de centro e cocaína suficiente para derrubar um elefante. — Amanda começou a sorrir, claramente curtindo a história. — Eles reuniram todos e os fizeram desfilar na rua. Estavam com as mãos atrás das costas, de joelhos, olhando para as portas das viaturas, para que lembrassem quem é que mandava. Aí veio a mídia, e Boyd nunca conseguia resistir. Ele alinhou a equipe para fotos, com os bandidos atrás. Coisa de *As panteras*. Sua mãe sempre odiou essa parte. Em geral, ela saía, voltava ao escritório para cuidar da papelada quando a imprensa chegava. Dessa vez, a rua estava bloqueada, então ela voltou ao apartamento e olhou tudo. — Amanda apertou os lábios. — A primeira coisa que ela notou foi que a pilha de dinheiro não estava igual a antes. Ela disse que, quando derrubaram a porta, estava em formato de pirâmide. Você sabe que sua mãe sempre era a primeira a entrar. — Faith fez que sim. — Ela disse que notou a pirâmide de cara, porque Zeke sempre...

— Colocava tudo em forma de pirâmide — completou Faith. — Quando ele tinha dez ou onze anos, começou a empilhar coisas, livros, Legos, carrinhos Matchbox, em pirâmide.

— Sua mãe achou que ele fosse autista. Talvez tivesse razão. — Amanda continuou: — Enfim, ela notou a pilha, é isso que importa. Quando ela voltou ao apartamento, a pirâmide era um quadrado. Depois disso, ela começou a observar a equipe mais de perto, ficando de orelha em pé, rastreando quais casos davam certo e quais se desfaziam porque provas eram perdidas ou as testemunhas sumiam. Foi só quando ela teve certeza que ela me procurou.

Will falou:

— Você me disse que a denúncia era anônima.

— Evelyn precisava ser investigada como todos os outros. Não estávamos lidando com coroinhas de igreja. Boyd e a equipe estavam acumulando toneladas de dinheiro. Também estavam sendo pagos para fazer vista grossa. Não dá para interferir nesse tipo de coisa sem arriscar a vida. Eve tinha que ser protegida. Então, decidimos que íamos chamar de denúncia anônima e colocá-la à prova igual a todo mundo.

Faith falou:

— Mas eles devem ter suspeitado que a denúncia veio da minha mãe. Ela era a única que não estava envolvida.

— Tem um abismo entre suspeitar e saber. — A voz dela demonstrou exaustão. — E Boyd Spivey a protegeu. Deixou claro que ela estava fora de alcance. Ele sempre a defendeu. Acho que foi por isso que mataram o cara. Eles podiam aguentar a GBI e a polícia de Atlanta no pé deles, mas alguém com a influência de Boyd Spivey poderia atingi-los de um jeito que nós não conseguimos.

Faith estava quieta, provavelmente pensando no homem morto que tinha protegido sua mãe. De sua parte, Sara estava pensando no tempo e no dinheiro investidos mandando matar um homem que estava no corredor da morte. Aquilo tudo tinha sido cuidadosamente planejado e executado por gente que conhecia os pontos fracos de Evelyn Mitchell: Boyd Spivey, o capanga dela; Faith, a filha; Amanda, a melhor amiga. Estava parecendo cada vez mais um ataque por vingança e menos uma busca por dinheiro. Sara notou que Will tinha feito as mesmas conexões. Mas, como sempre, quando ele finalmente falou, não mencionou o óbvio. Em vez disso, perguntou a Amanda:

— Você censurou a conta bancária no meu relatório?

— Nós não somos a Receita Federal. — Ela deu de ombros. — Não tem por que punir alguém que fez a coisa certa.

Sara via que Will estava bravo, mas mesmo assim ele não falou nada. Nem ficou enfurecido. Só enfiou as mãos nos bolsos e se recostou na bancada. Ela nunca tinha discutido com ele. Àquela altura, não tinha certeza de que um dia isso fosse acontecer, mas Sara imaginava que seria um grande exercício em vão.

Por sua vez, Faith parecia alheia aos buracos na história de Amanda. Considerando que sua glicemia andava disparando e despencando que nem uma bola de pingue-pongue nos últimos dias, era surpreendente até ela conseguir ficar sentada direito. Foi por isso que Sara teve certeza de ter ouvido errado quando Faith enfim falou:

— Eles deixaram o dedo dela embaixo do meu travesseiro.

Amanda nem piscou.

— Cadê o dedo?

— No meu armário de remédios. — Faith levou a mão à boca. Pareceu que ia vomitar. Sara ficou de pé num pulo e pegou a lata de lixo, mas Faith fez sinal de que não precisava. — Estou bem.

Ela respirou fundo algumas vezes. Sara pegou um copo do armário e o encheu de água.

Faith bebeu avidamente, a garganta fazendo barulho ao engolir.

Sara encheu o copo novamente e o colocou na frente dela. Depois se recostou na bancada e ficou de olho em Faith. Will estava a alguns metros de distância, ainda com as mãos nos bolsos. Sara sentia a distância entre eles como uma onda de ar frio.

Faith tomou um gole de água antes de contar:

— Eles tentaram pegar Jeremy. Eu o mandei embora com meu irmão. Emma também. Depois, fui ao supermercado e o cara me encurralou no banheiro.

Amanda perguntou:

— Como ele era?

Faith deu uma descrição muito detalhada da altura, do peso, da roupa e da gramática.

— Acho que era hispânico. Tinha olhos azuis. — Ela olhou para Sara. — É normal?

— Não é comum, mas também não é raro. — Sara explicou: — O México foi colonizado por espanhóis. Alguns se casaram com indígenas. Nem todos os mexicanos têm pele marrom e cabelo escuro. Alguns têm cabelo loiro e pele mais clara. Alguns têm olhos azuis ou verdes. É um gene recessivo, mas aparece.

Amanda perguntou:

— Mas esse cara tinha olhos azuis?

Faith fez que sim.

— Sem tatuagem?

— Uma cobra no pescoço.

Foi a vez de Amanda assentir com a cabeça.

— Podemos colocar um alerta. No mínimo, vamos conseguir uma lista de homens hispânicos entre dezoito e vinte anos que têm olhos azuis. — Ela pareceu se lembrar de uma coisa. — Não tivemos sorte na busca por estúdios de tatuagem. A pessoa que fez a tatuagem do arcanjo Gabriel em Marcellus Estevez ou está fora do estado, sem registro, ou não quer falar.

— Tinha algo de familiar nele — disse Faith. — Achei que talvez já tivesse prendido o cara, mas ele me disse que não.

— Com certeza estava falando a verdade. — Amanda pegou o BlackBerry e começou a digitar enquanto falava. — Vou pedir para o departamento de registros olhar seus relatórios. Conheço uma pessoa na polícia de Atlanta que pode entrar discretamente nos seus casos antigos, de antes de começar a trabalhar com a gente.

— Duvido que achem alguma coisa. — Faith esfregou a têmpora. — Ele tem a idade de Jeremy. Talvez conheça meu filho. Talvez tenham estudado juntos. Sei lá.

Amanda terminou o e-mail.

— Você perguntou para Jeremy?

Faith fez que sim.

— Dei uma descrição aproximada ontem à noite. Ele não conhece ninguém que se encaixe no perfil. Pelo menos ninguém de quem consiga se lembrar.

Will perguntou:

— Tem mais alguma coisa que você lembre?

Obviamente, havia algo. Faith parecia reticente.

— É uma coisa bem boba. Talvez... — Ela olhou para Sara. — Minha glicemia anda louca. Está me fazendo alucinar.

Sara questionou:

— Em que sentido?

— Eu só... — Ela balançou a cabeça. — É bobeira. Tinha alguma coisa errada com a gaveta de talheres. — Ela riu de si mesma. — É muito bobo. Deixem para lá.

— Continue — pediu Sara. — O que tinha de errado?

— Os garfos estavam virados para o lado errado. E as colheres. E minhas canetas estavam na gaveta errada. Eu sempre as coloco no mesmo lugar, e... Depois eu entrei na sala e os globos de neve estavam todos virados para a parede. Em geral ficam virados para a frente. Eu tomo muito cuidado com eles. Eram do meu pai. Jeremy não pode nem encostar. Zeke não chegaria perto. É que... — Ela balançou a cabeça. — Sei lá. Pode ser que eu tenha feito isso ontem à noite e não me lembre. De repente só achei que estavam virados para o lado errado. Mas eu me lembro de virá-los de volta, então... — Ela apoiou a cabeça nas mãos. — Minha mente anda uma bagunça desde que tudo isso aconteceu. Não tenho certeza do que é real e do que não é. Talvez eu só esteja enlouquecendo. Eu posso estar alucinando?

Sara disse a ela:

— Seus níveis de glicemia estão erráticos, mas não apontam para uma descompensação metabólica. Você não está tão desidratada, mas com certeza está muito estressada. Está se sentindo gripada ou com uma infecção?

Faith fez que não.

— Eu esperaria confusão, que você demonstrou, e paranoia, que é compreensível, mas não alucinações de fato. — Ela sentiu a necessidade de acrescentar: — Virar os globos de neve parece mais uma coisa que uma criança faria para chamar atenção. Tem certeza de que não foi seu filho?

— Eu não perguntei. Tenho vergonha até de falar nisso. Com certeza não é nada.

Amanda estava balançando a cabeça.

— Jeremy não faria uma coisa dessas, especialmente com o que está acontecendo. Ele não iria querer causar ainda mais estresse em você. E ele tem quase vinte anos. É maduro demais para esse tipo de coisa.

— Pode ser que eu só tenha imaginado — disse Faith. — Por que esses caras virariam todos os globos de neve? — Ela pareceu se lembrar de outra coisa. — E desrosqueariam as lâmpadas?

Amanda suspirou.

— Não tem importância, Faith. O que importa é que precisamos chegar juntos a um plano. — Ela olhou o relógio. — São quase sete horas. Precisamos botar a cabeça para pensar.

Faith comentou:

— Will tem razão. Estão observando a casa da minha mãe. Eu sei que estão observando a minha. Se levarmos a polícia...

— Não tenho nenhuma intenção de fazer uma idiotice dessas — interrompeu Amanda. — Ainda não sabemos se Chuck Finn está envolvido ou não. — Faith abriu a boca para protestar, mas Amanda levantou a mão para impedi-la. — Eu sei que você acha que Chuck foi levado a uma vida de crime enquanto os outros mergulharam nela voluntariamente, mas para a lei é bem preto no branco. Ele ficou com o dinheiro. Ele gastou. Confessou os crimes e está solto em algum lugar com um vício bem sério que custa um dinheirão. Você também precisa lembrar que Chuck ainda tem amigos na polícia de Atlanta e, onde não tem amigos, talvez tenha dinheiro para comprar alguns. Eu sei que você não quer ouvir isso, mas não tem como contornar o fato de que ou ele deu a dica para Hironobu Kwon, ou está mexendo os pauzinhos nesse novo grupo de jovens.

Faith contestou:

— Não parece algo que Chuck faria.

— Tirar dinheiro de apreensões também não parece algo que Chuck faria, mas foi o que aconteceu. — Ela disse a Will: — Você mencionou o ponto de observação da casa de Roz Levy. Não tem como eles montarem nada ali. Ela atiraria neles no segundo em que pusessem o pé na entrada.

— É verdade — concordou Faith. — A Sra. Levy observa a rua que nem um gavião.

Will opinou:

— Exceto quando alguém está levando um tiro ou sendo sequestrado na casa ao lado.

Amanda ignorou o comentário.

— A questão, Will, é que podemos explorar a posição tão facilmente quanto os sequestradores. A menos que mandemos você dentro da maior caixa do mundo, precisamos descobrir como colocar você e seu rifle dentro da garagem de Roz Levy sem ser visto. — Ela olhou para Faith. — Tem certeza que não seguiram você até aqui?

Faith fez que não com a cabeça.

— Eu tomei cuidado. Não fui seguida.

— Boa garota — disse Amanda. Estava de volta em seu habitat natural, quase alegre com a tarefa em mãos. — Preciso dar uns telefonemas para descobrir o que está acontecendo na casa de Evelyn. Nossos bandidos não teriam sugerido um encontro lá se achassem que a Unidade de Perícia Criminal de Atlanta estaria trabalhando no local. Vamos ver se Charlie consegue fazer umas perguntas também. Fora isso, acho que tenho mais uns favores no bolso com umas velhas amigas da Zona Seis que adorariam mostrar para os novinhos como é que se faz. Dra. Linton?

Sara ficou surpresa de ouvir seu nome.

— Sim?

— Obrigada pelo seu tempo. Posso confiar que vai guardar segredo sobre esta festinha, certo?

— Lógico.

Faith se levantou atrás de Amanda.

— Obrigada — disse ela. — De novo.

Sara a abraçou.

— Tome cuidado.

Depois foi a vez de Will. Ele estendeu a mão.

— Dra. Linton.

Sara abaixou os olhos, perguntando a si mesma se estava tendo uma das alucinações de Faith. Ele estava realmente se despedindo dela com um aperto de mão.

Ele falou:

— Obrigado pela ajuda. Desculpe pelo incômodo desta manhã.

Faith murmurou algo que Sara não conseguiu ouvir.

Amanda abriu o armário. Sara supôs que o sorriso na cara dela não fosse por estar feliz de ver seu casaco.

— Eu conheço vários vizinhos de Evelyn. A maioria é aposentada e acho que, com exceção da velha megera da casa da frente, ninguém vai se importar em emprestar a casa. Vou precisar arranjar algum dinheiro. Acho que consigo, mas vai ser em cima da hora. — Ela colocou o casaco. — Faith, você precisa ir para casa e esperar notícias nossas. Imagino que, em algum momento, vamos precisar que você vá a um ou dois bancos. Will, volte para casa e troque essa camisa. O colarinho está puído e um botão caiu. Aproveite para começar a construir um cavalo de Troia ou inventar um plano para seduzir Roz Levy. Ela estava prestes a mandar prender Faith uma hora atrás. Só Deus sabe que bicho mordeu aquela bunda enrugada hoje de manhã.

— Sim, senhora.

Sara abriu a porta para eles. Amanda começou a ir na direção do elevador. Will, sempre cavalheiro, deu um passo para o lado para Faith sair primeiro.

Sara fechou a porta atrás de Faith.

— O que... — começou Will, mas ela pôs um dedo nos lábios dele.

— Meu bem, eu sei que você tem que trabalhar e sei que vai ser perigoso, mas, nada do que você fizer hoje vai ser de perto tão arriscado quanto fazer tudo aquilo ontem à noite comigo e depois achar que pode se safar com um aperto de mão na manhã seguinte. Tá bom?

Ele engoliu em seco.

— Me ligue mais tarde.

Ela deu um beijo de despedida nele e abriu a porta para ele ir embora.

17

Will assinava muitas revistas de carros. Comprava principalmente pelas fotos, mas, às vezes, sentia-se compelido a ler as
reportagens. Era por isso que sabia que o sedã Chevrolet Corvair 700
verde-abacate de 1960 de Roz Levy valia bem mais do que a avaliação
de cinco dólares de Faith.

O carro era uma beleza, o tipo de clássico pelo qual as montadoras
americanas eram conhecidas antigamente. O motor traseiro boxer de
seis cilindros de alumínio, com refrigeração a ar, tinha sido desenhado
para concorrer diretamente com os modelos europeus compactos mais
populares que estavam chegando ao mercado. O design era reconhecido por sua inovadora suspensão traseira por eixo de torção, que
ganhou seu próprio capítulo no livro *Unsafe at Any Speed*, de Ralph
Nader. O pneu reserva ficava no porta-malas dianteiro, onde em geral
era o motor dos outros carros, bem do lado de um aquecedor a gasolina para a cabine de passageiros. Embora o inverno tivesse terminado,
o tanque continuava cheio, e Will sabia disso porque estava com o
rosto apertado contra o cilindro de metal enquanto Faith o levava até
a casa da Sra. Levy. O som da gasolina se agitando era como ondas
quebrando na praia. Ou como um combustível altamente volátil sendo
revirado a menos de um milímetro de ferrugem da cara dele.

O carro tinha sido construído bem antes de a Administração de
Segurança no Trânsito das Rodovias Nacionais exigir que todos os
fabricantes instalassem uma alça de liberação de emergência que
brilhava no escuro caso alguém ficasse preso no porta-malas. Will
não tinha certeza se conseguiria alcançar uma alça, mesmo que ela

existisse. O compartimento era fundo, mas não largo, parecia uma boca de pelicano. Ele estava dobrado num espaço onde devia caber um pneu reserva e talvez umas poucas malas — malas de 1960, não as modernas de rodinha que as pessoas ultimamente usavam para levar a casa toda numa viagem de fim de semana para a montanha.

Em resumo, tinha uma possibilidade bem real de ele morrer ali antes de Roz Levy lembrar que devia abrir a porta da mala para ele.

Um feixe fino de luz entrava pela vedação de borracha rachada em torno da dobradiça. Will levantou o celular para ver a hora. Ele estava no porta-malas havia quase duas horas e ainda faltava pelo menos mais meia hora. O rifle estava enfiado no meio de suas pernas de um jeito que já não era mais agradável. Seu coldre estava virado de forma que a Glock cutucava a lateral do corpo dele como um dedo insistente. Fazia um bom tempo que a garrafa de água que Faith lhe dera já tinha virado só uma garrafa de plástico reciclado. Estava fazendo aproximadamente seis mil graus dentro daquela tumba de metal. Suas mãos e seus pés estavam dormentes. Will estava começando a achar que aquilo era uma péssima ideia.

Ele tinha se inspirado nas palavras "cavalo de Troia". Uma ligação para Roz Levy fora suficiente para perceber que ela não ia facilitar para eles. Ainda estava puta por Faith ter pegado o carro dela. Tinha se recusado a deixar qualquer um entrar em sua casa. Fora Will quem sugerira então aquela idiotice para ele mesmo fazer, o que não era comum. Faith devolveria o Corvair à garagem. Ele se esconderia no porta-malas até alguns minutos antes do horário combinado. A Sra. Levy levaria o lixo para fora e destrancaria o porta-malas no caminho. Em seguida, Will sairia rastejando para dar cobertura a Faith.

O fato de Roz Levy ter concordado com esse plano alternativo tão facilmente o fez suspeitar que ela talvez não cooperasse, mas aí mais uma hora se passou e eles não tinham mais muita escolha.

Havia também outros cavalos de Troia — a maioria mais inteligente que o de Will. O bom das velhas amigas de Amanda era que eram mulheres idosas, o que, nessa situação em particular, ia contra os estereótipos. Quem quer que estivesse observando o bairro estaria esperando jovens com armas e cheios de testosterona, com o dedinho ansioso no gatilho e cabelo curto. Amanda tinha mandado seis amigas a várias casas do quarteirão. Elas estavam segurando assadeiras e boleiras, com a bolsa pendurada no braço. Algumas carregavam a Bíblia. Para qualquer um que estivesse olhando, pareceriam visitantes.

O perímetro externo estava coberto por um caminhão de TV a cabo, uma van de pet shop móvel e um Prius amarelo-vivo que nenhum policial de respeito jamais dirigiria. Com os três veículos, dava para monitorar todo o tráfego que entrava e saía das duas vias que davam acesso à parte do bairro onde a família Mitchell morava.

Mesmo com tudo aquilo, Will ainda não estava feliz com o plano. Era dos males o menor, sendo que o mal maior era não ter presença policial nenhuma. Ele não gostava da ideia de Faith tão vulnerável, embora ela estivesse armada e tivesse provado para qualquer pessoa que quisesse ver que não hesitaria em atirar em alguém. Ele sentia no âmago que Amanda estava errada. Aquilo não tinha a ver com dinheiro. Talvez no nível mais superficial. Pode ser que até os próprios sequestradores achassem que era tudo por dinheiro, pura e friamente. Mas, no fim das contas, o comportamento deles deixava a motivação aparente. Era pessoal. Tinha alguém agindo por rancor. Chuck Finn parecia o suspeito mais provável. Seus subalternos queriam o dinheiro. Chuck queria vingança. Era uma situação em que todo mundo saía ganhando, menos Faith.

E o idiota preso num Corvair 1960.

Will fez uma careta ao tentar mudar de posição. Suas costas doíam. Seu nariz coçava. A sensação na bunda era como se ele tivesse pressionado o peso todo do corpo contra um pedaço duro de metal por duas horas. Em retrospecto, enfiar Will num porta-malas parecia mais o tipo de ideia que Amanda teria. Dolorosa. Humilhante. Com altas chances de acabar mal para ele. Will devia ter algum tipo de desejo de morte. Ou talvez só quisesse passar mais umas horas cozinhando no calor porque era o único jeito de ter tempo para pensar no que tinha se metido.

E não estava falando do carro.

Will nunca tinha fumado um cigarro. Nunca tinha usado nenhum tipo de droga ilegal. Odiava o gosto das bebidas alcoólicas. Quando criança, tinha visto como o vício podia arruinar vidas e, como policial, via como podia acabar com elas. Ele nunca tinha sentido tentação de se embriagar. Nunca entendeu como as pessoas podiam ficar tão desesperadas pelo próximo barato que estavam dispostas a trocar a vida e tudo que importava por mais uma onda. Elas roubavam. Entravam na prostituição. Abandonavam ou vendiam os filhos. Assassinavam pessoas. Faziam qualquer coisa para evitar a abstinência, aquele ponto em que o corpo desejava tanto a droga que se virava contra si mesmo. Cãibras musculares. Pontadas na barriga. Dores de cabeça ofuscantes. Boca seca. Palpitações cardíacas. Mãos suadas.

O desconforto físico de Will não era causado apenas pelo espaço apertado do Corvair da Sra. Levy.

Ele estava em abstinência de Sara.

Em seu favor, ele percebia que sua reação a ela era completamente desproporcional ao que um ser humano normal devia estar sentindo naquele momento. Ele ia fazer papel de trouxa. Mais do que já tinha feito. Ele não sabia se comportar perto dela. Pelo menos não quando não estavam transando. E tinham transado muito, então Sara havia levado um tempo até presenciar em primeira mão a burrice espetacular de Will. E que show ele tinha dado. Apertando a mão dela como se fosse um corretor mostrando uma casa. Estava surpreso por ela não ter dado um tapa nele. Até Amanda e Faith ficaram sem saber o que dizer enquanto esperavam o elevador. A idiotice dele tinha chegado a deixar as duas sem palavras.

Will começava a se perguntar se havia algo fisicamente errado com ele. Talvez ele fosse diabético que nem Faith. Ela vivia gritando com ele por causa do pãozinho doce da tarde, do segundo café da manhã, do amor pelos *nachos* cheios de queijo da máquina de comida. Ele repassou os sintomas. Estava suando muito. Seus pensamentos estavam acelerados. Estava confuso. Estava com sede e precisava muito, muito urinar.

Sara não parecia brava com ele ao se despedir. Ela o chamara de meu bem, um apelido que só tinham usado com ele uma vez, e também tinha sido ela. Ela o havia beijado. Não era um beijo apaixonado — era mais um selinho. O tipo de coisa que se via em séries de 1950 logo antes de o marido pôr o chapéu e sair para trabalhar. Ela tinha pedido para ele ligar mais tarde. Será que queria mesmo que ele ligasse ou só estava querendo provar alguma coisa? Will estava acostumado às mulheres de sua vida querendo provar algo às suas custas. Mas o que definia "mais tarde"? Era mais tarde naquele dia ou mais tarde no dia seguinte? Ou mais para o fim da semana?

Will soltou um gemido. Era um homem de trinta e quatro anos com um emprego e uma cachorrinha para cuidar. Precisava se controlar. Não ia ligar para Sara de jeito nenhum. Nem mais tarde naquele dia, nem mesmo na próxima semana. Ele era simplório demais para ela. Não tinha traquejo social. Estava desesperado demais para ficar com ela. Will tinha aprendido do jeito mais difícil que o melhor a se fazer quando se queria realmente alguma coisa era parar de pensar naquilo, porque nunca ia conseguir. Ele precisava fazer isso com Sara naquele momento. Precisava fazer isso antes de tomar um tiro ou acabar levando Faith à morte por agir que nem uma menina apaixonada.

A pior parte era que Angie tinha razão em tudo.

Bom, talvez nem tudo.

Sara não tingia o cabelo.

O telefone dele vibrou. Will tentou não se castrar com o próprio rifle enquanto enfiava o fone Bluetooth na orelha. O porta-malas era bem isolado, mas mesmo assim ele manteve a voz num sussurro.

— Alô?

— Will? — Era disso que ele precisava: a voz da Amanda no seu ouvido. — O que você está fazendo?

— Suando — cochichou ele de volta, perguntando-se se ela poderia ter feito uma pergunta mais inútil.

Ele tivera a ideia de sair pulando do porta-malas que nem um super-herói. Depois de tanto tempo, percebia que provavelmente já ia ser vantagem não sair rolando no chão que nem um pedaço de língua.

— Já montamos tudo na casa de Ida Johnson. — A vizinha de quintal de Evelyn. Will não tinha certeza de como Amanda havia levado a mulher na lábia e a convencido a deixar um bando de policiais ficar na casa dela. Talvez tivesse prometido que Faith não atiraria em mais nenhum traficante no quintal dela. — Acabei de ouvir no rádio que teve um tiroteio de veículo em movimento no leste de Atlanta. Dois mortos. Ahbidi Mittal e a equipe dele acabaram de sair da casa de Evelyn para fazer a perícia no carro. Vai ter visibilidade. Uma mulher com a filha. Branca, loira, classe média, bonita.

Então, agora eles sabiam como os sequestradores planejavam liberar a casa de Evelyn. Amanda tinha dado alguns telefonemas discretos mais cedo e descoberto que a equipe da Unidade de Perícia Criminal tinha pelo menos mais três dias na casa. Sabiam que os sequestradores de Evelyn tinham experiência em atirar de um carro em movimento. Obviamente, esses bandidos em especial não tinham medo de matar transeuntes inocentes e sabiam exatamente qual o perfil certo de vítima para garantir que todas as emissoras de Atlanta parassem a programação para cobrir os acontecimentos ao vivo na cena do crime.

Para Will, a parte mais perturbadora era que isso provava que eles não tinham problema em assassinar uma mãe e sua filha.

Amanda continuou:

— O quintal de Evelyn está todo escavado.

Talvez fosse o calor, mas Will imaginou um cachorro procurando um osso.

— Ela deve ter dito que o dinheiro estava no quintal. Tem buraco por todo lado.

Tinha sido um dos primeiros chutes de Will. Ele agora via como era uma bobagem. As pessoas não escondiam mais dinheiro assim. Até Evelyn tinha uma conta bancária. Ultimamente tudo ficava num arquivo digital.

Ele manteve a voz baixa.

— A Sra. Levy viu quando estavam cavando?

Amanda ficou em silêncio, o que não era comum.

— Amanda?

— Ela não está atendendo o telefone no momento, mas deve estar só tirando uma soneca.

Ele não conseguia engolir. Agora que talvez aquilo realmente acontecesse, não tinha mais graça.

— Ela deve ter colocado o alarme para despertar.

Will se perguntou como a velha ia ouvir o alarme se não conseguia ouvir o telefone. Então parou de se preocupar, porque ia desmaiar de insolação bem antes de aquilo acontecer.

Amanda falou:

— Tenho duas amigas comigo e mais uma das antigas na rua. Ela vai ficar de olho em Faith enquanto estiver indo para a casa. Bev está com o Serviço Secreto. Ela confiscou um caminhão do correio.

Will queria ter ficado mais surpreso com essa informação. Se Amanda tivesse dito que havia ligado para uma velha amiga na Casa Branca e pedido emprestado os códigos nucleares, ele ia só assentir com a cabeça.

— Está tudo se alinhando. — Amanda sempre ficava tagarela logo antes de resolver um caso, e agora não era exceção. — Faith está esperando em casa. Foi em três bancos diferentes hoje de manhã para dar credibilidade à história dos cofres. Pedimos para um dos gerentes entregar o dinheiro para ela no último. Todas as notas estão registradas. No forro da mala de lona tem um rastreador. — Ela ficou um momento em silêncio. — Acho que ela vai ficar bem. Por enquanto, Sara estabilizou a taxa dela de glicose. Estou preocupada por ela não estar se cuidando.

Will também estava preocupado com isso. Sempre pensou que Faith fosse indestrutível. Ela parecia capaz de lidar com qualquer crise. Talvez por ter sido jogada na maternidade antes de estar pronta. As palavras da Sra. Levy sobre o escândalo da gravidez abalando o bairro não paravam de voltar à cabeça dele. Faith obviamente ainda tinha alguma vergonha. Tinha ficado corada ao explicar as palavras da mãe a Sara, embora fosse claro que Evelyn estava só usando o que possivelmente eram suas últimas palavras à filha para tirar um pouco dessa culpa. A vida toda de Faith tinha sido arruinada pela gravidez. Mas, de algum jeito, ela conseguira se reerguer. Evelyn estivera junto para oferecer apoio, mas o trabalho pesado fora todo de Faith. Concluir o supletivo. Entrar para a Academia. Voltar à faculdade. Criar o filho. Ela era uma das mulheres mais fortes que Will já conhecera. Em alguns sentidos, era mais forte até do que Amanda.

E merecia a verdade.

Will sussurrou:

— Por que você mentiu para Faith dizendo que o pai dela apostava?

Amanda não respondeu.

Ele começou a pergunta de novo:

— Por que você...

— Porque ele apostava mesmo — disse Amanda. — Eu imaginava que, depois da manhã de hoje, você seria capaz de reconhecer que um homem pode apostar outras coisas que não dinheiro.

Will engoliu o restinho de saliva na boca. Não estava a fim das charadas de Amanda no momento.

— Evelyn fazia parte do esquema.

— Ela cometeu um grande erro há muito tempo e está pagando desde então.

Ele teve dificuldade de manter a voz baixa.

— Ela aceitou dinheiro...

— Vou prometer uma coisa para você, Will. Se tirarmos Evelyn dessa, ela vai contar a você a verdade completa sobre tudo. Você pode ficar com ela uma hora inteira. Ela vai responder a todas as suas perguntas.

Ele olhou o porta-malas, o feixe de luz entrando pela vedação de borracha rachada.

— E se não a tirarmos dessa?

— Aí, não vai mais importar, né? — Ele escutou uma conversa no fundo. — Preciso ir. Ligo de novo para você quando tiver notícias.

Will mudou o rifle de posição de novo para poder desligar. Fechou os olhos e tentou clarear a mente. Uma gota de suor escorreu por suas costas. Ele sentiu um ardor perto da base da coluna, onde tinha sido arranhado por Sara.

Will chacoalhou a cabeça, tentando fazer a imagem sumir antes que o rifle fizesse uma denúncia de abuso sexual. Pensou em como seria o rifle no banco de testemunhas, usando o gatilho para secar uma lágrima que caía da mira.

Ele balançou a cabeça outra vez. O calor o estava afetando mesmo. Para focar a mente, começou a repassar o caso. Amanda sempre queria que ele narrasse tudo desde o começo. Era o melhor jeito de ver o que tinham deixado passar. No calor do momento, era difícil encaixar as peças. Naquele momento, Will relembrou os últimos dias, passo a passo, examinando todos os ângulos, revisando todas as mentiras e meias verdades que os bandidos haviam contado a eles, além das mentiras e meias-verdades inventadas por Amanda.

Como antes, a mente de Will sempre voltava a Chuck Finn. Era um processo de eliminação. Chuck era o único homem da antiga equipe de Evelyn que eles não sabiam onde estava. Ele tinha se tratado na Healing Winds com Hironobu Kwon. Obviamente conhecia Roger Ling, que o chamara de Chuckleberry Finn.

Roger também tinha falado em cortar a cabeça da cobra. Tinha de haver um líder. Chuck podia muito bem ser essa pessoa. Ele cumpria muitos requisitos: tinha uma vingança pessoal contra Evelyn Mitchell por denunciá-lo. Sua vida na prisão não tinha sido moleza. Ele tinha passado de policial respeitado a alguém que precisava tomar cuidado na hora de tomar banho.

O homem provavelmente havia adquirido o vício dentro da cadeia, e no minuto em que recebera liberdade condicional, tinha feito a festa. Heroína e crack eram um hábito caro. Mesmo que Chuck estivesse limpo nos últimos tempos, já não teria mais nenhum dinheiro. De todos os policiais que Will investigou, Chuck era o que menos tinha bens depois dos crimes. Ele havia torrado tudo em viagens de luxo, vendo cada canto do mundo no estilo dos multimilionários. Só a viagem à África havia custado uns cem mil dólares. A única pessoa que Will entrevistara que realmente parecia chateada com as acusações contra Chuck Finn era o agente de viagens dele.

Will imaginou que logo descobriria se Chuck estava ou não por trás de tudo aquilo. Ele escutou a garagem se abrindo e pantufas se arrastando pelo concreto. O porta-malas se abriu e a luz do sol se derramou sobre ele como água. Ele viu a Sra. Levy passar a passos leves com um saco de lixo branco na mão. Ouviu o som plástico de uma lixeira de rua quando ela jogou o lixo fora.

Will agarrou o rifle com uma das mãos e segurou a tampa do porta--malas com a outra. Seu movimento foi como tinha previsto — parecia mais uma língua preguiçosa caindo no concreto do que o Super-Homem entrando em ação. Roz Levy passou bem ao lado dele. Olhava para a frente, muito tranquila. Estendeu a mão, e sem esforço fez o movimento curto de fechar o porta-malas. Ela voltou para dentro de casa e fechou a porta sem sequer olhar para Will, que ficou ali largado, pensando que era perfeitamente possível que aquela velha tivesse a calma necessária não só para matar o marido, mas para mentir sobre isso na cara de Amanda durante a última década.

Will se deitou por uns segundos no concreto, curtindo a sensação gelada na pele, engolindo o ar fresco e limpo com notas do cheiro do óleo vazando da traseira do Corvair. Apoiou-se nos cotovelos. Sua memória da garagem, embora precisa, era praticamente inútil. Era um espaço totalmente aberto na frente e atrás, como um viaduto, só que mais perigoso. A casa de Roz Levy ficava de um dos lados da estrutura. Do outro, havia uma mureta de tijolos, de mais ou menos um metro e vinte de altura, com uma coluna ornamentada de metal de cada lado para sustentar o teto. Por debaixo do carro, Will conseguia ver a rua, mas não tinha uma posição estratégica para saber se estava ou não sendo vigiado.

Ele olhou para o lado. A lixeira ficava equidistante entre a mureta e o carro. Will imaginou que o borrão de movimento seria óbvio a qualquer um que observasse, mas não tinha muita escolha. Ele se agachou bem baixo. Prendeu a respiração, pensando que não havia tempo a perder, e voou para trás da lixeira grande.

Sem balas. Sem gritos. Nada além de seu coração batendo no peito.

Ainda havia pouco menos de um metro para ele percorrer até a mureta. Will se preparou para sair, mas aí parou, porque provavelmente tinha um jeito melhor de fazer aquilo do que ficar sentado apoiado na parede, com uma placa de néon apontando para sua cabeça. Devagar, ele empurrou a lixeira, andando agachado e reduzindo a distância entre o carro e a mureta. Pelo menos ele tinha alguma cobertura visual, embora não proteção, de qualquer um na rua. Do outro lado do quintal, a história era outra. A mureta podia protegê-lo de tiros vindos da casa de Evelyn, mas ele era basicamente um alvo fácil para qualquer um que se aproximasse dele vindo do quintal.

Will não podia continuar agachado daquele jeito para sempre. Ele dobrou um joelho e arriscou olhar por cima da mureta. O espaço estava livre. A casa de Evelyn ficava numa elevação mais baixa. Mesmo se tivesse planejado, ele não conseguiria ter alinhado melhor a janela do banheiro. Ficava bem alta na parede, provavelmente dentro do box do chuveiro. A abertura era estreita o bastante para passar uma criança, mas, infelizmente, não um homem adulto. Sobretudo um homem gigante. A persiana estava aberta. Will tinha uma boa visão do corredor. Com a mira do rifle no olho, ele conseguia enxergar as fibras da madeira da porta que levava à garagem de Evelyn. Estava fechada. Pó preto cobria o ambiente branco nos locais onde os técnicos da unidade de perícia criminal tinham coletado digitais.

Eles já tinham resolvido. Quando Faith entrasse na casa, era para entrar por aquela porta.

O telefone de Will vibrou. Ele apertou o fone Bluetooth.

— Estou em posição.

— A van preta acabou de ser vista na Beverly. Eles vieram do lado da Peachtree.

Will segurou mais forte a empunhadura.

— Onde está Faith?

— Acabou de sair de casa. Está a pé.

Ele não precisou falar nada. Os dois sabiam que aquilo não fazia parte do plano. Era para Faith ir de carro, não dar um passeio a pé.

Ele ouviu um barulho de motor na rua. A van preta parou perto do meio-fio. Não estavam exatamente disfarçados. Os painéis laterais estavam lotados de buracos de bala. Will deslizou a alavanca na lateral do rifle para a posição de atirar. Mirou no meio da van enquanto a porta lateral se abria. Ele olhou o interior, surpreso pelo que encontrou.

Will sussurrou para Amanda.

— Só tem dois deles. Estão com Evelyn.

— Você está autorizado a atirar.

Ele não via como fazer aquilo. Os dois jovens de cada lado de Evelyn Mitchell estavam com as armas apontadas para a cabeça dela. Era impressionante, mas, se um deles puxasse o gatilho, não ia matar só

Evelyn — a bala atravessaria direto o crânio dela e entraria na cabeça do amiguinho. Amanda teria chamado aquilo de provisão divina se a melhor amiga dela no mundo não estivesse no meio dos dois Einsteins.

Eles puxaram Evelyn da van, garantindo que o corpo dela desse cobertura para eles. Ela gritou de dor, o som atravessando a tarde tranquila. Não estava amarrada, mas Evelyn Mitchell não podia exatamente correr para buscar segurança. Uma de suas pernas estava com uma tala grosseira feita com dois cabos de vassoura quebrados. Fita adesiva os mantinha no lugar. Era óbvio que ela estava gravemente ferida. Era óbvio que seus sequestradores não estavam nem aí.

Os dois garotos estavam usando jaqueta e boné preto. Caminhavam em fila única, com Evelyn espremida no meio. O de trás mantinha uma Glock pressionada nas costelas dela, estimulando-a a seguir como se fosse um cavalo. Ela claramente não conseguia caminhar sozinha. O braço do cara da Glock estava em torno da cintura dela. Ela se recostava nele a cada passo e seu rosto era uma máscara de dor. O da frente mantinha os joelhos dobrados ao caminhar. A mão de Evelyn estava cravada no ombro dele, tentando se equilibrar. O homem não vacilou. Ficava varrendo a frente da casa com uma Tec-9. O dedo estava no gatilho, que era terrivelmente sensível. Will não via uma Tec-9 desde que a proibição federal de semiautomáticas — não mais em voga nos dias atuais — tinha falido o fabricante. A arma tinha sido usada durante o massacre de Columbine. O fato de ser semiautomática praticamente não tinha importância quando se tinha cinquenta balas no pente.

Por um segundo, Will tirou o olho da mira e observou a rua. Estava vazia. Nada de Chuck Finn. Nada de jovens com jaquetas esportivas e bonés pretos. Ele olhou de novo pela mira. Sentiu o estômago se revirar. Não podia ter só dois deles.

A voz de Amanda estava tensa.

— Você consegue fazer o disparo?

A visão de Will estava alinhada com o peito do cara da Tec-9. Talvez os dois garotos não fossem completos amadores, afinal. O da Tec-9 estava diretamente na frente da Evelyn, garantindo que qualquer bala que o atravessasse também a atingisse. O mesmo valia para o da Glock, grudado atrás dela. Um tiro na cabeça estava fora de cogitação. Mesmo que houvesse um jeito de derrubar o da Tec-9, o da Glock botaria uma bala em Evelyn antes de Will conseguir realinhar a mira. Ele podia muito bem acabar matando a prisioneira junto, ao atirar em um de seus captores.

— Sem disparo — sussurrou para Amanda. — É arriscado demais.

Ela não contra-argumentou.

— Mantenha a linha de mira livre. Eu aviso quando Faith chegar na casa.

Will rastreou as três figuras até desaparecerem dentro da garagem. Ele girou, direcionando o rifle para a porta da cozinha, prendendo a respiração enquanto esperava. A porta foi aberta com um chute. Will manteve o dedo no gatilho enquanto Evelyn Mitchell entrava tropeçando na cozinha. O da Glock continuava atrás dela. Ele a levantou e a carregou, com um esforço visível no rosto. O da Tec-9 continuava à frente, ainda caminhando abaixado. O topo do boné aparecia no nível do peito de Evelyn. Will analisou o rosto dela. Um dos olhos estava fechado de tão inchado. A pele da bochecha estava com um ferimento aberto.

Eles estavam no hall de entrada. Evelyn fez uma careta de dor quando o da Glock soltou a cintura dela para colocá-la no chão. Era uma mulher magra, mas praticamente um peso morto. O garoto atrás dela estava ofegante. Ele pressionou a cabeça nas costas dela. Assim como o da Tec-9, ele ainda era mais um adolescente que um homem.

A luz no hall de entrada tinha mudado. O lugar estava mais escuro. Eles certamente tinham fechado as cortinas que cobriam as janelas da frente. Eram de vinil, feitas para filtrar a luz, não para bloqueá-la por completo. Will ainda conseguia ver claramente todos os três. Evelyn foi meio carregada, meio empurrada, desta vez para a sala. Ele viu o boné preto, com a Tec-9 balançando no ar. Depois, sumiram. A linha de mira dele estava livre até a cozinha.

— Eles estão na sala — disse ele a Amanda. — Todos eles.

Ele não ressaltou que o plano óbvio dela já estava descarrilando. Evelyn não tinha sido levada para o quarto dos fundos. Eles queriam que ela estivesse bem na frente e no meio do lugar quando Faith entrasse na casa.

353

Amanda falou:

— Estão usando Eve como escudo enquanto fecham as cortinas dos fundos. Não consigo ter mira. — Ela murmurou um xingamento. — Não consigo ver nada.

— Onde está Faith?

— Deve chegar logo.

Will tentou relaxar o corpo para os ombros não doerem. Nada de Chuck Finn. Nada de esconderem Evelyn. Os dois garotos não tinham vistoriado a casa para ver se havia policiais escondidos. Não tinham protegido o local. Não tinham barricado a porta da frente nem tomado qualquer precaução para garantir que sua fuga fosse tão fácil quanto a entrada.

Cada item que não ticavam da lista era uma forca se apertando no pescoço de Faith.

E só o que Will podia fazer naquele momento era esperar.

18

Antes de sair de casa, Faith usou o iPhone de Jeremy para fazer um vídeo para os filhos. Disse a eles que os amava, que eram tudo para ela e que, independentemente do que acontecesse naquele dia, deviam sempre saber que ela adorava cada fio de cabelo na cabeça preciosa deles. Ela disse a Jeremy que ficar com ele fora a melhor decisão que tinha tomado na vida. Que ele *era* a vida dela. Disse a Emma a mesma coisa e acrescentou que Victor Martinez era um bom homem e que ela estava feliz que a filha ia conhecer o pai.

Dramática, Zeke teria dito. Ela fez um vídeo para ele também. Suas palavras ao irmão a surpreenderam, principalmente porque a expressão "seu babaca" não havia surgido nenhuma vez. Ela disse a ele que o amava. Disse que sentia muito pelo que o fizera passar.

Depois disso, tentou deixar um vídeo para a mãe. Faith tinha parado e recomeçado a gravação pelo menos umas doze vezes. Havia tanto a dizer. Que ela sentia muito. Que torcia para Evelyn não estar decepcionada com as escolhas que Faith fizera. Que cada pedacinho de coisa boa dentro de Faith tinha vindo dos pais. Que seu único objetivo na vida fora ser uma policial tão boa, uma mãe tão boa, uma mulher tão boa quanto a própria mãe.

No fim, desistiu, porque a probabilidade de Evelyn Mitchell ver a gravação um dia era mínima.

Faith não era completamente iludida. Sabia que estava entrando numa armadilha. Mais cedo, na cozinha de Sara, Amanda não estava escutando Will, mas Faith estava. Ela entendia a lógica do que ele estava dizendo, de aquilo ser mais do que uma busca por dinheiro.

Amanda estava contaminada pela emoção da caçada, a oportunidade de dizer para aqueles novatos filhos da puta que tinham tido a cara de pau de levar a melhor amiga dela que não iam se safar dessa. Will, como sempre, via a situação mais claramente. Sabia fazer as perguntas certas, mas também sabia como ouvir as respostas, o que era igualmente importante.

Ele era um homem racional, não se deixava levar pela emoção — pelo menos Faith achava que não. Não dava para saber o que se passava naquela cabeça dele. Que Deus ajudasse Sara Linton na tarefa hercúlea que teria pela frente. O aperto de mão daquela manhã não seria a pior parte. Mesmo que Sara conseguisse tirar Angie Trent do jogo, o que Faith duvidava ser possível, ainda tinha a teimosia imutável de Will. A última vez que Faith tinha visto um homem se fechar tão rápido foi quando contou ao pai de Jeremy que estava grávida.

Ou talvez Faith estivesse errada em relação a Will. Ela lia tão bem o parceiro quanto ele lia um livro. A única coisa que Faith podia garantir era a habilidade sinistra que Will tinha de entender o comportamento emocional alheio. Faith supunha que isso vinha de ser criado num lar de acolhimento, tendo que discernir rapidamente se a pessoa à sua frente era amiga ou inimiga. Ele era um mestre em arrancar fatos de pistas sutis que as pessoas normais tendiam a ignorar. Ela sabia que era só questão de tempo até Will descobrir o que acontecera com Evelyn tantos anos antes. A própria Faith só tinha descoberto naquele dia de manhã, quando, talvez pela última vez, revirara as coisas de Jeremy.

Claro, ela não podia depender completamente da telepatia investigativa de Will. Faith, sempre maníaca por controle, tinha escrito uma carta delineando tudo o que havia acontecido e por quê. No último banco em que esteve, ela enviara a carta por correio para a casa de Will. A polícia de Atlanta veria os vídeos no iPhone de Jeremy, mas Will nunca contaria o que Faith tinha escrito na carta.

Nisto ela confiava com todo o seu ser: Will Trent sabia guardar um segredo.

Faith bloqueou os pensamentos sobre a carta enquanto saía pela porta de casa. Parou de pensar na mãe, em Jeremy, Emma, Zeke — qualquer um que pudesse entorpecer sua mente. Ela estava armada até os dentes. Tinha uma faca de cozinha dentro da mala de lona, escondida debaixo do dinheiro. A Walther de Zeke estava enfiada na frente da calça. Ela estava usando um coldre de tornozelo com uma das Smith and Wesson reservas de Amanda pressionada firmemente contra a pele. O metal estava irritando a região. Tinha a sensação de algo evidente e volumoso ali, de forma que ela precisava se concentrar para não mancar.

Faith passou pelo Mini. Recusava-se a ir com seu carro para a casa da mãe. Era parecido demais com qualquer outro dia normal em que ela carregava Emma e suas coisas e dirigia um quarteirão e meio até a casa da mãe. Faith tinha sido teimosa a vida toda e não ia mudar isso naquele momento. Ela queria fazer pelo menos uma coisa do seu jeito naquele dia.

Ela virou à esquerda no fim da entrada de sua casa, depois pegou a direita para a casa da mãe. Observou o longo trecho da rua. Havia carros parados em garagens abertas e fechadas. Ninguém estava na varanda da frente, embora isso não fosse lá incomum. Era um bairro com varandas nos fundos. Na maior parte do tempo, cada um cuidava da própria vida.

Pelo menos até aquele momento.

Havia um caminhão de entregas estacionado à sua direita. A entregadora saiu quando Faith passou. Faith não reconheceu a mulher — uma hippie mais velha com um rabo de cavalo grisalho caindo pelas costas tipo Crystal Gayle. O cabelo foi balançando enquanto ela caminhava até a caixa de correio do Sr. Cable, onde enfiou um bando de catálogos de lingerie.

Faith mudou a mala de lona de mão enquanto virava à esquerda na rua da mãe. A mala com o dinheiro dentro era muito pesada, quase sete quilos no total. O dinheiro estava em seis blocos, cada um com cerca de dez centímetros de altura. Eles tinham combinado 580 mil dólares, tudo em notas de cem, principalmente porque era a quantia de dinheiro que Amanda podia tirar do arquivo de provas. Parecia uma quantia crível se Evelyn estivesse envolvida na corrupção que derrubou seu esquadrão.

Mas ela não estava envolvida na corrupção. Faith nunca tinha duvidado da inocência da mãe, então a confirmação de Amanda não trouxera muita paz. Parte de Faith devia ter intuído que havia mais coisa na história. Havia outras coisas em que a mãe estava metida e que eram igualmente condenáveis, mas Faith, sempre a filha mimada, tinha fechado bem os olhos por tanto tempo que parte dela não conseguia mais acreditar na verdade.

Evelyn chamava esse tipo de negação de "cegueira voluntária". Normalmente, estava descrevendo um tipo específico de pessoa idiota — uma mãe que insistia que o filho merecia mais uma chance, apesar de ele ter sido condenado duas vezes por estupro. Um homem que não parava de insistir que a prostituição era um crime sem vítimas. Policiais que achavam que tinham o direito de aceitar dinheiro sujo. Filhas que estavam tão envolvidas nos próprios problemas que não se davam o trabalho de olhar ao redor e ver que os outros também estavam sofrendo.

Faith sentiu uma brisa no cabelo ao chegar na entrada da casa da mãe. Tinha uma van preta na rua, exatamente na frente da caixa de correio. O interior estava vazio, pelo menos até onde ela conseguia ver. Não havia janelas atrás. Havia buracos de bala no metal, em um dos lados. O identificador era discreto. Havia um adesivo desbotado da campanha Obama/Biden no para-choque de cromo.

Ela levantou a fita amarela de cena do crime que estava bloqueando a entrada de carros. O Impala de Evelyn continuava estacionado na garagem aberta. Faith havia brincado de amarelinha na frente daquela casa. Tinha ensinado Jeremy a jogar uma bola de basquete na cesta velha e enferrujada que Bill Mitchell pregara no beiral. Havia deixado Emma ali quase todos os dias nos últimos meses, dando um beijo na bochecha de sua mãe e de sua filha antes de ir para o trabalho.

Faith apertou mais forte a mala ao entrar na garagem. Estava suando e a brisa fria da área coberta lhe deu um arrepio. Ela olhou ao redor. A porta do quarto de ferramentas continuava aberta. Era difícil acreditar que só dois dias tinham se passado desde que Faith tinha visto Emma na pequena construção pela primeira vez.

Ela se virou para a casa. A porta da cozinha tinha sido aberta com um chute. Estava torta, soltando nas dobradiças. Ela viu a marca de sangue da mão da mãe, o espaço vazio onde o dedo anelar dela devia ter pressionado a madeira. Faith segurou a respiração enquanto empurrava a porta, esperando levar um tiro na cara. Chegou a fechar os olhos. Não veio nada. Só o espaço vazio da cozinha e sangue por todo lado.

Ao entrar na casa dois dias antes, Faith estava tão focada em achar a mãe que não tinha processado de verdade o que estava vendo. Agora, entendia a batalha violenta que havia acontecido. Ela já tinha visto cenas de crime suficientes para entender. Sabia como era uma briga. Mesmo já tendo muito tempo que o corpo havia sido removido da área de serviço, Faith ainda conseguia se lembrar da posição dele, do que ele estava vestindo, da forma como sua mão estava aberta no chão.

Will lhe tinha contado o nome do garoto, mas ela não conseguia se lembrar. Não conseguia se lembrar de nenhum deles — nem do homem em quem ela havia atirado no quarto, nem do homem que ela tinha matado no quintal da Sra. Johnson. Depois do que fizeram, eles não mereciam que ela soubesse o nome deles.

Faith voltou a atenção à cozinha. A passagem estava vazia. Ela via até o corredor. Era meio da tarde, mas a casa parecia estar na penumbra. As portas do quarto estavam fechadas. As cortinas que cobriam as grandes janelas de cada lado da porta da frente também. A única luz que entrava livremente vinha da janela do banheiro. A persiana estava levantada. Faith passou pela sala de jantar e foi para o hall de entrada. Ficou parada com o corredor à direita e a cozinha à esquerda. A sala de estar estava à sua frente. Ela devia pegar a arma, mas não achava que fossem atirar nela. Ainda não.

O cômodo estava na penumbra. As cortinas tinham sido fechadas, mas eram mais transparentes do que opacas. Uma brisa suave balançava o tecido onde a porta de vidro tinha sido quebrada. O cômodo ainda estava de cabeça para baixo. Faith não conseguia lembrar como era antes, apesar de ter morado dezoito anos de sua vida ali. As estantes de livros lotadas cobriam a parede esquerda. As fotos de família emolduradas. O móvel com o toca-discos e seus alto-falantes de som chiado. O sofá excessivamente estofado. A poltrona *bergère* em que o pai dela se sentava para ler. Naquele momento, era Evelyn quem estava sentada ali, com a mão esquerda embrulhada numa toalha ensopada de sangue. A direita estava tão inchada que podia pertencer a um manequim. Havia dois cabos de vassoura presos com fita adesiva na perna dela, mantendo-a esticada à frente. A blusa branca estava manchada de sangue. O cabelo estava grudado na lateral da cabeça. Um pedaço de fita adesiva cobria sua boca. Seus olhos se arregalaram ao ver Faith.

— Mãe — sussurrou Faith.

A palavra ecoou em seu cérebro, conjurando todas as memórias de Faith dos últimos trinta e quatro anos. Ela tinha amado a mãe. Tinha brigado com ela. Gritado com ela. Mentido para ela. Chorado no colo dela. Fugido dela. Voltado para ela. E, então, aquilo.

O jovem do supermercado estava na outra ponta da sala, apoiado na estante. Sua posição era estratégica, o topo de um triângulo. Evelyn estava abaixo e à esquerda dele. Faith estava a quatro metros e meio da mãe, formando o segundo ângulo da base. Ele estava na sombra, mas a arma em sua mão era fácil de ver. O cano de uma Tec-9 estava apontado para Evelyn. O pente com cinquenta balas se projetava em pelo menos trinta centímetros para baixo da base da arma. Outros carregadores estavam visíveis no bolso da jaqueta dele.

Faith soltou a mala de lona no chão. Sua mão queria alcançar a Walther. Ela queria descarregar o pente todo no peito dele. Não ia mirar na cabeça. Queria ver seus olhos, ouvir seus gritos, enquanto as balas o despedaçavam.

— Eu sei o que você está pensando. — Ele sorriu, o dente de platina reluzindo na pouca luz que havia na sala. — "Consigo puxar minha arma antes dele apertar o gatilho?"

— Não.

Faith era rápida no gatilho, mas a Tec-9 já estava apontada para a cabeça da mãe. A matemática estava contra ela.

— Pegue a arma dela.

Ela sentiu o metal frio de um cano pressionando sua cabeça. Alguém estava atrás dela. Outro homem. Ele arrancou a Walther da cintura de sua calça jeans, depois pegou a mala de lona. Então, abriu o zíper. A risada dele era como a de uma criança na manhã de Natal.

— Caralho, cara, olha quantas verdinhas! — Ele saltitou na ponta dos pés enquanto caminhava até o amigo. — Puta que pariu, mano!

Estamos ricos! — Ele jogou a Walther na mala. Estava com a Glock enfiada na parte de trás da calça. — Puta que pariu! — repetiu, mostrando a mala para Evelyn. — Tá vendo isso, vadia? Curtiu? A gente conseguiu de qualquer jeito.

Faith manteve os olhos no garoto do supermercado. Ele não estava feliz como o parceiro, mas era de se esperar. Nunca tinha sido por dinheiro. Will havia acertado horas antes.

O homem perguntou a Faith:

— Quanto tem aí?

Ela respondeu:

— Pouco mais de meio milhão.

Ele deu um assovio baixo.

— Ouviu isso, Eve? Você roubou muito dinheiro.

— Pois é. — O parceiro abriu uma pilha de notas em leque. — Dava para ter acabado com isso tudo dois dias atrás, vaca. Acho que chamam você de Almeja com razão.

Faith não conseguia olhar a mãe.

— Pegue — disse ela ao homem. — Foi o acordo. Pegue o dinheiro e vá embora.

O amigo estava pronto para fazer exatamente isso. Soltou a mala ao lado da poltrona de Evelyn e pegou um rolo de fita adesiva do chão.

— Pô, cara, vamos direto para Buckhead. Vou comprar um Jaguar e...

Dois tiros seguidos soaram. A fita adesiva caiu no chão. Rolou para de baixo da poltrona onde Evelyn estava, depois o corpo do garoto caiu estatelado ao lado dela. Parecia que alguém tinha batido na parte de trás da cabeça dele com um martelo. O sangue jorrava no chão, formando uma poça em torno dos pés da poltrona e da mãe dela.

O jovem disse:

— Ele falava demais. Não acha?

O coração de Faith batia tão alto que ela mal conseguia ouvir a própria voz. O revólver escondido no coldre de tornozelo parecia quente, como se queimasse a pele dela.

— Você acha mesmo que vai sair vivo daqui?

Ele continuou apontando a Tec-9 para a cabeça da mãe dela.

— O que faz você pensar que eu quero sair daqui?

Faith se permitiu olhar a mãe. Pingava suor do rosto de Evelyn. A borda da fita adesiva estava desgrudando da bochecha dela. Não a tinham amarrado. A perna quebrada garantia que ela não fosse a lugar nenhum. Mesmo assim, estava ereta na poltrona. Ombros para trás. Mãos unidas no colo. A mãe dela nunca se encurvava. Nunca deixava transparecer nada — exceto naquele momento. Havia medo em seus olhos. Não medo do homem com a arma, mas medo do que seria contado para sua filha.

— Eu sei — disse Faith à mãe. — Está tudo bem. Eu já sei.

O homem virou a arma para o lado, apertando os olhos enquanto abaixava a mira na mãe dela.

— Sabe o quê, vadia?

— De você — falou Faith para ele. — Eu sei quem você é.

19

Will estava com o olho pressionado na mira do rifle quando a Tec-9 disparou. Ele viu primeiro os flashes, dois estrobos claros. Um milissegundo depois, registrou o som. Ele se encolheu, não conseguiu evitar. Quando voltou a olhar pela mira, viu Faith. Ela continuava parada no hall de entrada, de frente para a sala de estar. O corpo dela vacilou. Ele esperou, contando os segundos, para garantir que ela não ia cair.

Ela não caiu.

— Que porra aconteceu?

Roz Levy estava do outro lado do Corvair. Ele olhou por baixo do carro e descobriu que admirava a ponta do cano de um Colt Python com acabamento brilhante de níquel. Will não sabia como ela tinha conseguido manter aquele negócio estável. O cano da arma tinha pelo menos quinze centímetros. A munição Magnum .357 podia produzir choque hidrostático, o que significava que o impacto de um ferimento no peito era grande o bastante para causar hemorragia cerebral.

Ele tentou manter a voz calma.

— Dá para, por favor, apontar esse negócio para outro lado?

Ela recolheu a arma e desengatilhou o cão.

— Puta que pariu — murmurou, apoiando as mãos para se levantar. — Lá vem Mandy.

Will viu Amanda correndo pelo quintal. Ela estava descalça, com o walkie-talkie numa das mãos e a Glock na outra.

— Faith está bem — informou ele. — Ainda está na casa. Não sei quem...

— Venha — ordenou Amanda, passando pelo Corvair e entrando na casa de Roz Levy.

Will não obedeceu. Em vez disso, usou a mira para conferir de novo o corredor de Evelyn. Faith continuava lá parada. Estava com as mãos estendidas à frente, palmas para baixo, como se tentasse argumentar com alguém. Será que os flashes tinham sido tiros de alerta ou tiros fatais? O atirador do veículo em movimento gostava de dois tiros, um logo após o outro. Se tivessem matado Evelyn, Faith não estaria ali parada com as mãos estendidas. Will sabia no seu âmago que, se algo acontecesse com a mãe, ela estaria ou no chão, ou em cima dos assassinos.

— Will! — rosnou Amanda.

Ele manteve o rifle perto do corpo enquanto passava correndo pelo carro e entrava na casa. As duas mulheres estavam paradas no que, em algum momento, devia ter sido uma varanda fechada, mas que tinha virado uma área de serviço. Antes que ele pudesse fechar a porta, Roz Levy começou a berrar com Amanda.

— Me devolva isso! — exigiu a velha.

Amanda estava com o Python.

— Você podia ter matado todo mundo. — Ela abriu a câmara e ejetou a munição de .38 Specials em cima da secadora. — Eu devia prender você agora.

— Adoraria ver você tentando.

Não era só Roz Levy que estava puta. Will sentiu um aperto na garganta pelo esforço que fazia para não gritar.

— Você disse que seria uma troca simples. Você disse que eles iam pegar o dinheiro e entregar Evelyn.

— Cale a boca, Will.

Amanda girou o cilindro vazio de volta no revólver e o jogou em cima da lavadora.

Ela devia ter entendido o silêncio de Will como obediência às ordens, mas a verdade era que ele estava tão furioso que não confiava em si mesmo para falar. Discutir não ia mudar o fato de que Faith estava presa naquela casa sem um plano claro de saída. Não podiam fazer nada naquele momento exceto esperar a SWAT aparecer e fingir que era uma negociação de refém, não uma missão suicida.

A não ser que o próprio Will entrasse. Ele agarrou o rifle. Devia entrar lá. Devia fazer exatamente o que Faith tinha feito dois dias antes, arrombar a porta e começar a atirar.

A mão de Amanda se fechou no pulso dele.

— Nem ouse sair deste cômodo — alertou ela. — Eu mesma atiro em você se precisar.

Os dentes de Will começaram a doer de tanto que os estava apertando. Ele se afastou dela e bateu numa cadeira de jardim de metal no meio do cômodo. Não pôde deixar de observar o entorno. Havia uma câmera de alta velocidade montada num tripé, virada para o vidro da porta. Roz Levy tinha coberto aquele vidro com cartolina preta, deixando um furinho para a lente se encaixar. Uma espingarda ficava ao lado. Não era de surpreender ela não ter deixado Will entrar na casa. Não queria que ele obstruísse a visão dela.

Will olhou pelo visor da câmera. A lente era mais nítida que a mira dele. Ele via o suor escorrendo pela lateral do rosto de Faith. Ela ainda estava falando. Estava tentando argumentar com o atirador.

Um atirador. Só restava um homem.

Dois bandidos entraram naquela casa. Os dois estavam com jaqueta e boné pretos. Um tinha sido morto a tiros. Disso, pelo menos, Will tinha certeza. Ele tinha visto os dois garotos forçando Evelyn a atravessar o gramado e entrar na casa. O de trás fazia todo o esforço sozinho. Era descartável, como Ricardo, como Hironobu Kwon, como todos os outros homens que tinham tentado botar as mãos no dinheiro de Evelyn Mitchell.

Mas nunca tinha sido por dinheiro. Chuck Finn não estava mexendo os pauzinhos. Não tinha mago por trás da cortina. Ali estava a cabeça da cobra de Roger Ling: um garoto irado de olhos azuis, com uma Tec-9 e algum rancor que estava decidido a guardar.

Will falou entre dentes:

— Agora é só ele. É o que ele queria o tempo todo.

— Ele nunca vai conseguir gastar um centavo daquele dinheiro.

Ele teve dificuldade de manter a voz baixa:

— Ele não liga para o dinheiro.

— Então, ele liga para quê? — Ela agarrou o ombro dele e o puxou para longe da câmera. — Vamos, gênio. Me diga o que ele quer.

A Sra. Levy murmurou:

— Você sabe o que ele quer.

Ela estava carregando os cartuchos de volta no revólver.

— Silêncio, Roz. Já cansei de você por hoje. — Amanda olhou Will com raiva. — Por favor, me ilumine, Dr. Trent. Sou toda ouvidos.

— Ele quer matá-la. Quer matar as duas. — Will finalmente soltou o maior "eu avisei" da vida dele. — E, se você tivesse se dignado a me ouvir uma vez na vida, nada disso estaria acontecendo.

A fúria iluminou os olhos de Amanda, mas ela disse:

— Continue. Pode desabafar.

No fim, a gota d'água para ele foi a anuência dela.

— Eu avisei que era melhor ir devagar. Eu avisei que a gente precisava descobrir o que eles realmente queriam antes de mandarmos Faith com um alvo nas costas. — Ele reduziu o espaço entre os dois, deixando-a acuada contra a máquina de lavar. — Você estava tão obcecada por provar que tem o pau maior que o meu que nem parou para pensar que eu podia ter razão em alguma coisa. — Will se aproximou o suficiente para sentir a respiração dela no rosto. — Todo sangue derramado está nas suas mãos, Amanda. *Você* fez isso com Faith. Você fez isso com todos nós.

Amanda virou a cabeça para o outro lado. Não respondeu Will, mas ele viu a verdade nos olhos dela. Ela sabia que ele tinha razão. Sua aceitação silenciosa não era consolo, mas mesmo assim Will recuou. Ele estava em cima dela como um valentão, agarrando o rifle com tanta força que as mãos tremiam. A vergonha afastou a raiva. Ele afrouxou um pouco as mãos e relaxou o maxilar.

— Rá. — A Sra. Levy riu. — Você vai deixar o rapaz falar assim, Wag? — Ela tinha recarregado o Python. Encaixou o cilindro, dizendo a Will: — Era assim que a gente a chamava: Wag, porque ela calava a boca e abanava o rabo que nem uma *vagabunda* toda vez que tinha um homem perto.

Will ficou chocado com as palavras da mulher, principalmente porque não conseguia imaginar nada mais distante da verdade.

A Sra. Levy levantou o Python com as duas mãos. Disse a Amanda:

— E falando em botar o pau na mesa, você poderia ter acabado com isso há vinte anos se tivesse colhão de forçar a Eve a...

366

Amanda chiou:

— Me poupe das suas liçõezinhas de merda, Roz. Se não fosse por mim entre você e sua receita de biscoito, você estaria agora no corredor da morte.

— Eu avisei quando aquilo aconteceu. Não dá para misturar pombo com azulão.

— Você não sabe que porra está falando. Nunca soube. — Amanda latiu mais ordens no walkie-talkie. Sua voz tremeu, o que preocupou Will tanto quanto tudo o que havia acontecido nos últimos dez minutos. — Derrubem aquela van preta. Quero os quatro pneus vazios. Liberem o quarteirão o mais rápido possível. Chamem a polícia de Atlanta para entrar discretamente e me deem uma previsão da SWAT nos próximos cinco minutos ou é melhor nem aparecerem amanhã para trabalhar.

Will posicionou o olho de volta na câmera. Faith continuava falando. Pelo menos, sua boca estava se mexendo. Ela estava de braços cruzados. Will se pegou pensando na escolha de palavras levemente racista de Roz Levy: pombos e azulões. A Sra. Levy era cheia de ditados, como o que dissera a ele dois dias antes: uma mulher corre mais rápido com a saia levantada do que um homem com a calça arriada. Era uma coisa estranha a se dizer sobre uma garota grávida de catorze anos que tinha tido um bebê aos quinze.

Will perguntou à velha:

— Por que você não levou esse Python para a casa de Evelyn quando ouviu tiros no outro dia?

Ela baixou os olhos para a arma. Tinha um pouco de petulância em seu tom.

— Eve me mandou não ir lá, não importava o que acontecesse.

Will não achava que ela fosse do tipo de seguir ordens, mas talvez fosse do tipo que ladra e não morde. Envenenamento era uma escolha covarde, assassinato a sangue-frio sem o inconveniente de sujar as mãos. Ele tentou pressioná-la até chegar na verdade.

— Mas você ouviu tiros.

— Supus que Evelyn estivesse resolvendo algum problema antigo. — Ela apontou para Amanda com o polegar. — Pode notar que ela não ligou para *essa aqui* pedindo ajuda.

Amanda descansou o queixo no walkie-talkie. Estava observando Will como se esperasse uma panela ferver. Estava sempre dez passos à frente dele. Sabia onde o cérebro dele ia antes dele mesmo.

Ela disse à Sra. Levy:

— Eu sabia que Evelyn estava saindo de novo com Hector. Ela me contou faz meses.

— Contou o cacete. Você ficou tão chocada de ver aquela foto quanto eu quando tirei.

— E tem importância, Roz? Depois de tanto tempo, tem alguma importância?

A velha parecia achar que sim.

— Não é culpa minha ela estar disposta a jogar a vida fora por dez segundos de prazer.

Amanda riu, incrédula.

— Dez segundos? Não é à toa que você matou seu marido. Era so isso que aquele velho babaca conseguia dar a você, dez segundos?

O tom dela era mordaz, pesaroso, o mesmo que ela tinha usado ao telefone meia hora antes.

Um homem pode apostar outras coisas que não dinheiro.

Ela estava falando de Will e Sara. Estava falando dos riscos inerentes ao amor.

Will se virou de novo para a câmera. Faith continuava falando. Será que Roz tinha montado a câmera naquele mesmo dia ou ela ficava ali o tempo todo? A visão da casa era clara. O que ela teria visto dois dias atrás? Evelyn fazendo sanduíche. Hector Ortiz trazendo compras do mercado. Eles estavam confortáveis um com o outro. Tinham uma história. Uma história que Evelyn estava tentando esconder da família.

Pombos e azulões.

Will tirou os olhos da câmera.

— Ele é filho de Evelyn.

As duas pararam de falar.

Will continuou:

— Hector é o pai, certo? Foi esse o erro que Evelyn cometeu há vinte anos. Ela teve um filho de Hector Ortiz. A conta bancária era usada para ajudar a sustentar o garoto?

Amanda suspirou.

— Eu já disse que a conta não tem importância.

Roz fez um som de desgosto.

— Bem, eu não vou mais guardar segredo. — Alegremente, ela contou a Will: — Não dava para ela criar um bebê de pele escura, né? Eu sempre disse para ela trocar com o de Faith. Aquela menina era doida. Ninguém teria ficado surpreso de ela estar metida com um chicano. — Ela gargalhou com a expressão chocada de Will. — E, vinte anos depois, ela fez isso de qualquer forma.

— Dezenove anos — corrigiu Amanda. — Jeremy tem dezenove. — Ela olhou o cômodo, finalmente percebendo o que Roz Levy andava fazendo. — Cacete — murmurou. — Devíamos ter cobrado a você o assento na primeira fila.

Will perguntou:

— O que aconteceu?

Amanda olhou pelo visor da câmera.

— Evelyn deu o bebê para uma garota que trabalhava com a gente. Sandra Espisito. Ela era casada com outro policial. Eles não conseguiam ter filhos.

— Podemos trazê-los aqui? Talvez consigam conversar com ele.

Ela fez que não com a cabeça.

— Paul foi morto em serviço faz dez anos. Sandra morreu ano passado. Precisava de um transplante de medula. Teve que explicar para o filho por que ele não podia ser doador. — Ela se voltou para Will. — Ele pesquisou primeiro o lado da família paterna. Sandra deve ter achado que seria mais fácil. Hector convidou o menino para uma reuniãozinha. Foi assim que ele conheceu Ricardo. Foi assim que se envolveu com os Texicanos. Ele começou a usar drogas. Primeiro maconha, depois heroína, e aí não tinha como voltar atrás. Evelyn e Hector viviam colocando e tirando o garoto da clínica.

Will sentiu uma ardência no estômago.

— A Healing Winds?

Ela fez que sim.

— Da última vez, pelo menos.

— Ele conheceu Chuck Finn lá.

— Não sei os detalhes, mas imagino que sim.

Se Will soubesse disso antes, não teria deixado de jeito nenhum Faith entrar sozinha naquela casa. Ele a teria amarrado. Teria enfiado Amanda no porta-malas da Sra. Levy. Teria chamado a SWAT de todas as forças policiais do país.

Amanda disse:

— Vamos, pode falar. Eu mereço.

Will já tinha gastado tempo suficiente gritando com ela.

— Como são os fundos da casa?

Ela não conseguiu processar a pergunta.

— O quê?

— Os fundos da casa. Faith está parada no hall de entrada. Está olhando para a sala de estar. Toda a parede dos fundos é de janelas e uma porta de correr de vidro. Você disse que as cortinas estavam fechadas. São de algodão fino. Dá para ver alguma coisa, tipo uma sombra ou movimento?

— Não. Está claro demais do lado de fora e, lá dentro, a luz está apagada.

— Quando a SWAT vai chegar?

— O que você está pensando?

— Precisamos do helicóptero.

Dessa vez, ela não questionou. Ligou o walkie-talkie e contactou diretamente o comandante da SWAT.

Will olhou pela câmera enquanto Amanda negociava o pedido. Faith continuava parada no hall. Não estava mais falando.

— Tem algum motivo para você não ter me contado que Evelyn tinha um filho ilegítimo com Hector Ortiz?

— Porque isso mataria Faith — Amanda respondeu, aparentemente sem perceber a ironia. Suas palavras seguintes foram mais direcionadas a Roz: — E Evelyn não queria que ninguém soubesse, porque não é da porcaria da conta de ninguém.

Will pegou o celular.

— O que você está fazendo?

— Ligando para Faith.

20

O celular de Faith vibrou no bolso. Ela não se mexeu. Só ficou olhando para mãe. Tinha lágrimas escorrendo pelo rosto de Evelyn.

— Está tudo bem — disse Faith a ela. — Não tem importância.

— Não tem importância? — ecoou o homem. — Valeu, maninha.

Aquela palavra fez Faith se encolher, desconfortável. Como ela tinha sido cega. E egoísta. Fazia tanto sentido agora. A licença extensa que a mãe havia tirado do trabalho. As viagens profissionais repentinas e os silêncios irritados do pai dela. A cintura de Evelyn sempre aumentando, sendo que ela nunca tinha estado acima do peso, nem antes, nem depois. As férias que ela havia tirado com Amanda um mês antes do nascimento de Jeremy. Faith tinha ficado furiosa quando, depois de quase oito meses de prisão compartilhada, Evelyn anunciara que ia de carro para a praia para se divertir com a tia Mandy. Faith se sentira traída. Abandonada. E, agora, se sentia muito idiota.

Preciso que você se lembre do nosso tempo juntas antes de Jeremy...

Era o que Evelyn tinha dito no vídeo. Ela estava dando uma pista a Faith, não relembrando uma época. *Lembre-se daquela época. Tente se lembrar do que estava acontecendo de verdade — não só com você, mas comigo.*

Na época, Faith estava tão envolvida consigo mesma que só ligava para sua própria infelicidade, sua própria vida arruinada, suas próprias oportunidades perdidas. Olhando então em retrospecto, ela via os sinais óbvios. Evelyn se recusava a sair durante o dia. Não atendia a porta. Acordava de madrugada para fazer compras num mercado do outro lado da cidade. O telefone tocava muito, mas Evelyn se recusava a atender. Ela tinha se fechado. Tinha se isolado do mundo. Dormia no sofá e não na cama com o marido. Exceto por Amanda, não conversava com ninguém, não via ninguém, não procurava ninguém. E, o tempo todo, tinha dado a Faith a única coisa que todo filho secretamente deseja: cada segundo de sua atenção.

E aí tudo mudou quando Evelyn voltou das férias com Amanda. Ela tinha chamado aquilo de "meu tempo longe", como se tivesse ido às fontes termais se curar. Estava diferente, mais feliz, como se um peso tivesse sido tirado de seus ombros. Faith tinha espumado de inveja de ver a mãe tão diferente, tão aparentemente despreocupada. Antes da viagem, elas se refestelavam numa infelicidade compartilhada e Faith não conseguia entender como a mãe conseguira superar aquilo tão facilmente.

Faltavam semanas para Faith dar Jeremy à luz, mas a vida de Evelyn havia voltado ao normal — ou o mais normal que se podia esperar com uma adolescente mal-humorada, mimada e gravidíssima em casa. Ela voltara a fazer compras no mercado de sempre. Tinha perdido uns quilos durante o tempo longe e começara a perder o restante com uma dieta restrita e exercícios. Forçava Faith a fazer longas caminhadas depois do almoço e em algum momento começou a ligar para velhos amigos, o tom de voz indicando que tinha sobrevivido ao pior e, agora que chegava ao fim, estava pronta para voltar à luta. Seu travesseiro já não ficava no sofá, mas na cama que ela dividia com o marido. Ela avisou à prefeitura que iria voltar depois do nascimento de Jeremy. Fez um corte de cabelo novo, curtinho. Em geral, começou a agir como ela mesma de novo. Ou pelo menos uma nova versão dela mesma.

Havia rachaduras na fachada feliz, algo que Faith só percebia naquele momento.

Nas primeiras semanas da vida de Jeremy, Evelyn chorava toda vez que o pegava no colo. Faith se lembrava de encontrar a mãe soluçando na cadeira de balanço, segurando Jeremy tão forte que ela tinha medo de o bebê não conseguir respirar. Como em todo o resto, Faith tinha ciúme do laço entre eles. Buscou formas de punir a mãe, afastando Jeremy dela. Ficava na rua com ele até tarde. Levava-o ao shopping, ao cinema, ou a um sem-número de lugares que não eram para bebê — só para se vingar. Só para ser cruel.

E, todo aquele tempo, Evelyn estava sofrendo e desejando não só um bebê, mas o bebê *dela*. Esse jovem raivoso e sem alma que naquele momento apontava uma arma para sua cabeça.

Faith sentiu o telefone parar de tocar. E, logo depois, recomeçou. Ela disse à mãe:

— Desculpe por não ter apoiado você.

Evelyn balançou a cabeça. Não tinha importância. Mas tinha, sim.

— Me perdoe, mamãe.

Evelyn olhou para baixo, depois de novo para Faith. Ela estava sentada na beirada da cadeira, com a perna machucada estendida à frente. O homem morto estava deitado no chão a menos de sessenta centímetros dela. A Glock continuava presa na parte de trás da calça dele. Podia muito bem estar a quilômetros de distância. Evelyn não podia exatamente pular e agarrar a arma. Mesmo assim, dava para ela ter levantado a mão e tirado a fita que cobria a boca. O adesivo já estava desgrudando. Os cantos da fita adesiva prateada estavam dobrando para trás. Por que ela estava fingindo estar silenciada? Por que estava sendo tão passiva?

Faith ficou olhando para a mãe. O que ela queria que a filha fizesse? O que ela *podia* fazer?

Um *tum* pesado chamou a atenção delas. As duas olharam para o homem. Um a um, ele jogou no chão os livros que sobravam nas prateleiras.

— Como foi crescer aqui?

Faith continuou quieta. Ela se recusava a ter aquela conversa.

— Mamãe e papai em volta da lareira. — Ele chutou a Bíblia no chão. As páginas se esvoaçaram enquanto ela voava pela sala. — Devia ser bem da hora chegar em casa todo dia para tomar leite com biscoito. — Ele manteve a arma ao lado do corpo enquanto ia na direção de Evelyn. Na metade do caminho, virou-se para trás, andando em linha reta. De novo, esqueceu as gírias de rua. — Sandra tinha que trabalhar todo dia. Não tinha tempo de ir para casa ver se eu tinha feito a lição.

Nem Evelyn. Bill trabalhava de casa. Era o pai que garantia que eles tivessem lanche e fizessem as resenhas sobre os livros.

— Você guardava um monte de merda dele no seu armário. Fazia essa parada para quê?

Ele estava falando de Jeremy. Faith continuou sem responder. Evelyn a obrigara a guardar tudo porque sabia que, um dia, Faith ia adorar aquilo mais que tudo, e o mesmo valia para as coisas de Emma.

Ela olhou para a mãe.

— Me desculpe.

Evelyn olhou de novo o homem morto, a Glock. Faith não sabia o que a mãe queria que ela fizesse. Ele estava a mais de quatro metros de distância.

— Eu fiz uma pergunta. — Ele tinha parado de andar para lá e para cá. Parou no meio do corredor, bem na frente de Faith. A Tec-9 estava apontada bem para a cabeça de Evelyn. — Responda.

Ela não ia falar a verdade, então, entregou a última pista que tinha feito tudo se encaixar.

— Você trocou a mecha de cabelo.

O sorriso dele gelou o sangue de Faith. Ela tinha percebido naquele dia de manhã que a mecha de cabelo de Jeremy não havia escurecido com o tempo. O laço azul de bebê que segurava os fios era diferente do outro. As bordas estavam retas, não puídas no local onde Faith os esfregara como um talismã nos últimos meses de sua gravidez de Emma.

Os talheres. As canetas. Os globos de neve. Sara tinha razão. Era algo que uma criança faria para chamar atenção. Quando Faith conheceu pela primeira vez o homem, no banheiro, estava tão preocupada em lembrar a descrição dele que não processou o que estava vendo. Ele tinha a idade de Jeremy. Mais ou menos a altura de Faith. Tinha mordido o lábio igual a Jeremy. Tinha a arrogância de valentão de Zeke. E os olhos azuis de Evelyn.

O mesmo formato amendoado. O mesmo azul-escuro com pontos verdes.

Faith disse:

— Sua mãe obviamente amava você. Ela guardou uma mecha do seu cabelo.

— Qual mãe? — perguntou ele, e Faith ficou sobressaltada com a pergunta.

Será que Evelyn tinha guardado uma mecha do cabelo dele por tantos anos? Faith imaginou a mãe no hospital, segurando o bebê sabendo que seria pela última vez. Fora Amanda quem havia pensado em arrumar uma tesoura? Será que ela tinha ajudado Evelyn a cortar um pedaço do cabelo e amarrar num laço azul? Será que Evelyn tinha guardado a mecha consigo nos últimos vinte anos, pegando-a de vez em quando para sentir os fios macios e fininhos de bebê entre os dedos?

Claro que sim.

Não tinha como entregar um filho e não pensar nele todo dia, a todo momento, pelo resto da vida. Não era possível.

Ele perguntou:

— Você não quer nem saber meu nome?

Os joelhos de Faith estavam tremendo. Ela queria se sentar, mas sabia que não conseguiria se mover. Estava parada no hall de entrada. A porta da cozinha ficava à esquerda. A porta principal da casa, atrás dela. O corredor, à direita. No fim do corredor, ficava o banheiro. Depois do banheiro, estavam Will, seu Colt AR-15A2 e sua mira excelente, se ela conseguisse fazer aquele bastardo vir na direção dela.

Ele virou a arma de lado, no estilo de gângster, enquanto alinhava a mira.

— Pergunte meu nome.

— Qual é seu nome?

— Qual é seu nome, *irmãozinho*?

Ela sentiu gosto de bile na boca.

— Qual é seu nome, irmãozinho?

— Caleb — respondeu ele. — Caleb. Ezekiel. Faith. Acho que a mamãe gosta de nomes inspirados na Bíblia.

Gostava mesmo, por isso o segundo nome de Jeremy era Abraham e o primeiro nome de Faith era Hannah. Por que Faith tinha escolhido o nome de Emma baseada na beleza, em vez de honrar a tradição da mãe? Evelyn tinha sugerido Elizabeth, Esther ou Abigail, e Faith fora teimosa só porque não sabia como agir de outro jeito.

— Foi aqui que ele cresceu também, né? — Caleb balançou a arma, indicando a casa. — Seu precioso Jeremy?

Faith odiava o nome do filho na boca dele. Queria dar um soco no homem para enfiar o nome do filho de volta garganta abaixo.

— Assistiu à TV. Leu uns livros. Jogou uns jogos. — O armário debaixo da estante de livros estava aberto. Ele manteve um olho em Faith enquanto puxava os jogos de tabuleiro e os atirava no chão. — Banco Imobiliário. Detetive. Jogo da Vida. — Ele riu. — Foi mal!

— O que você quer da gente?

— Caceta, você fala igualzinho a ela. — Ele se virou de volta para Evelyn. — Não foi isso que cê me disse, mamãe? "O que você quer de mim, Caleb?" Como se pudesse me pagar para sumir. — Ele olhou de novo para Faith. — Ela me ofereceu dinheiro. Que tal? Dez mil dólares para me mandar.

Faith não acreditava nele.

— Ela só queria saber de proteger você e seu filhinho mimado de merda. — O dente de platina brilhou na luz fraca. — Você agora tem dois filhos, né? A mamãe não pode ficar com o bebezinho escuro dela, mas você não tem problema nenhum de ficar com a sua.

— É diferente hoje em dia — respondeu ela. A condição de Evelyn podia ter sido segredo, mas Faith havia envergonhado a família o suficiente por uma vida toda. O pai tinha perdido clientes de longa data. O irmão fora forçado a se exilar. O que teriam achado de Evelyn Mitchell criando um filho que obviamente não era do marido? Não existia opção boa. Faith não conseguia nem imaginar como a mãe tinha sofrido. — Você não faz ideia de como era na época.

— Dois pontos para vocês. A mamãe disse a mesma coisa. — Ele apontou para o bolso dela. — Não vai atender?

O telefone dela tinha voltado a vibrar.

— Você quer que eu atenda?

— POP — disse ele. Procedimento Operacional Padrão. — Eles querem saber minhas exigências.

— Quais são suas exigências?

— Atenda o telefone e a gente descobre.

Ela esfregou a mão na perna para secar o suor, depois puxou o celular.

— Alô?

Will disse:

— Faith, esse cara é...

— Eu sei quem ele é. — Ela olhou para Caleb, torcendo para ele enxergar cada grama de ódio que ela sentia por ele. — Ele tem exigências.

Ela estendeu o telefone para Caleb, rezando para ele se aproximar para pegar.

Ele continuou fincado no mesmo lugar.

— Eu quero leite com biscoito. — Ele parou, como se estivesse pensando um pouco mais. — Quero minha mãe em casa todo dia quando eu voltar da escola. Quero um dia sem ser arrastado para a missa de manhã cedo e sem meus joelhos ficarem doloridos de ter que rezar toda noite. — A mão dele fez um arco na direção da estante. — Quero que minha mãe leia livros sobre cabrinhas felizes e luas. Você fez isso com Jaybird, né?

Faith mal conseguia falar.

— Não fale o nome dele.

— Você levou Jayzinho para o parque, para o Six Flags, para a Disney e para a praia.

Ele devia ter memorizado cada foto na caixa de lembranças de Jeremy. Quanto tempo ele tinha passado na casa dela? Quantas horas tinha passado colocando as patas nas coisas de Jeremy?

— Pare de falar o nome do meu filho.

— Senão o quê? — Ele riu. — Diga para eles que é isso que eu quero. Quero que vocês todos me levem para a Disney.

O braço de Faith tremia de segurar o telefone.

— O que você quer que eu fale para ele?

Ele bufou, com desdém.

— Caramba, não preciso de nada agora. Tenho minha família comigo. Minha mãe e minha irmã mais velha. Vou precisar de mais o quê? — Ele voltou para perto da estante e se apoiou nas prateleiras. — A vida é boa.

Faith pigarreou. Colocou o telefone de volta no ouvido.

— Ele não tem exigências.

Will perguntou:

— Você está bem?

377

— Eu...

— Viva-voz — falou Caleb.

Faith baixou os olhos para o celular para poder encontrar o botão certo. Ela disse a Will:

— Ele está ouvindo você.

Will hesitou.

— Sua mãe está confortável? Ela consegue se sentar?

Ele estava pedindo pistas.

— Ela está na poltrona do meu pai, mas estou preocupada com ela. — Faith respirou fundo. Continuou olhando nos olhos da mãe. — Se isso se arrastar, talvez eu precise de insulina. — Caleb tinha visto a geladeira de Faith. Ele certamente sabia que ela era diabética. — Minha glicemia estava em mil e oitocentos hoje de manhã. Minha mãe só tem o suficiente para mil e quinhentos. Eu tomei minha última dose ao meio-dia. Vou precisar da próxima às dez no máximo, senão minha glicemia vai começar a oscilar pra lá e pra cá.

— Tudo bem — concordou ele, e ela rezou para ele ter entendido a mensagem e não ter dado só uma resposta rápida.

Ela disse:

— Seu telefone... — A mente dela não estava rápida o bastante. — A gente liga para ele se precisar de alguma coisa? Para o seu celular?

— Sim — pausou ele. — Conseguimos mandar sua insulina em cinco minutos. Só nos avise. Me avise.

Caleb apertou os olhos. Ela estava falando demais, e nem Faith, nem Will eram bons naquilo.

— Tome cuidado. — Faith não precisou fingir que estava assustada. A voz tremeu sem nenhum esforço. — Ele já matou o parceiro dele. Ele tem uma...

— Desligue — mandou Caleb

Faith tentou achar o botão.

— Desligue! — gritou ele.

O celular escorregou da mão dela. Faith se apressou para pegá-lo no chão. Ela se lembrou do revólver no tornozelo. A Smith and Wesson estava gelada sob seus dedos.

— Não! — gritou a mãe dela.

Sua boca tinha se aberto tanto que uma parte da fita adesiva finalmente se soltou. Caleb estava com a arma enfiada nas costelas dela. Com a mão livre, ele pressionava a perna quebrada.

— Não! — guinchou Evelyn.

Faith jamais ouvira outro ser humano fazer um som daquele tipo. O fato de estar vindo da mãe dela era como se a mão de alguém estivesse sendo enfiada dentro de seu peito e arrancando seu coração.

— Pare! — Faith implorou, ficando de pé e mostrando as mãos. — Por favor, pare! Por favor, só... por favor!

Caleb aliviou a pressão, mas manteve a mão acima da perna quebrada.

— Chute essa arma pra cá. Devagar, senão eu mato essa vadia de qualquer jeito.

— Está tudo bem. — Ela se ajoelhou. Um tremor passou por todo o seu corpo como uma convulsão. — Estou fazendo o que você mandou. Estou fazendo exatamente o que você mandou. — Ela levantou a calça da perna e pegou a arma entre o polegar e o indicador. — Não a machuque mais. Olhe só.

— Devagar — alertou ele.

Ela deslizou a arma pelo chão na diagonal, rezando para Caleb voltar para onde estava antes. Ele deixou a arma passar, e continuou ao lado de Evelyn.

Ele falou:

— Tente de novo uma coisa dessas, vadia.

— Não vou tentar — respondeu Faith. — Eu juro.

Ele apoiou a Tec-9 nas costas da cadeira, inclinando o cano para baixo, na direção da cabeça de Evelyn, que estava com a fita adesiva pendurada na boca. Ele a arrancou.

Ela puxou o ar com força. A respiração entrava e saía do nariz quebrado fazendo chiado.

Ele avisou:

— Não fique muito acostumada com o ar fresco.

— Deixe-a ir embora. — A voz de Evelyn estava rouca. — Não é ela quem você quer. Ela não fazia ideia. Era criança.

— Eu também era criança.

Evelyn tossiu, cuspindo sangue.

— Só a deixe ir, Caleb. Sou eu quem você quer punir.

— Você alguma vez pensou em mim? — Ele manteve a arma na cabeça dela enquanto se ajoelhava ao seu lado. — Todas as vezes que pegou aquele bebezinho bastardo dela, você por acaso pensou em mim?

— Eu nunca parei de pensar em você. Não passou um dia sem...

— Porra nenhuma.

Ele se levantou de novo.

— Sandra e Paul amavam você como a um filho de sangue. Eles adoravam você.

Ele desviou o olhar dela.

— Eles mentiram para mim.

— Eles só queriam que você fosse feliz.

— Eu pareço feliz agora? — Ele indicou o homem morto no chão. — Todos os meus amigos estão mortos. Ricky, Hiro, Dave. Todos eles. Eu sou o último que sobrou. — Ele parecia estar esquecendo seu próprio papel na carnificina. — Meu pai falso está morto. Minha mãe falsa está morta.

Evelyn disse:

— Eu sei que você chorou no velório dela. Eu sei que você amava Paul e...

Ele deu um tapa de mão aberta atrás da cabeça dela. Faith se moveu sem pensar. Ele balançou a arma na direção dela e ela parou.

Faith olhou a mãe. A cabeça de Evelyn estava caída para a frente. Pingava sangue de sua boca.

— Eu nunca esqueci você, Caleb. No fundo do seu coração, você sabe disso.

Desta vez, ele bateu mais forte nela.

— Pare — implorou Faith. Não sabia se estava falando com a mãe ou com Caleb. — Por favor, só pare.

Evelyn sussurrou:

— Eu sempre amei você, Caleb.

Ele levantou o rifle e deu uma coronhada na lateral da cabeça dela. O impacto fez a cadeira vırar. Evelyn caiu com força no chão. Ela gritou de dor quando a perna se retorceu. A tala de cabo de vassoura se quebrou ao meio. O osso da coxa dela ficou exposto.

— Mãe!

Faith começou a ir na direção dela.

Houve um som de silvo. Madeira voou do chão. Faith congelou. Não conseguia saber se tinha sido atingida. Só conseguia ver a mãe no chão e Caleb parado em cima dela com o punho fechado. Ele chutou Evelyn. Com força.

— Por favor, pare — suplicou Faith. — Eu juro...

— Cala a boca.

Ele olhou o teto. De início. Faith não reconheceu o som. Era um helicóptero. As hélices cortavam o ar, estremecendo os tímpanos dela.

Caleb estava então apontando a Tec-9 para Faith. Ele precisou falar alto para ser ouvido.

— Foi um tiro de alerta — disse a ela. — O próximo vai ser no meio da sua testa.

Ela baixou a cabeça para o chão. Tinha um buraco na madeira. Ela deu um passo atrás, engoliu o grito que queria sair da garganta. O som das hélices diminuiu quando o helicóptero parou.

Faith mal conseguia falar.

— Por favor, não a machuque. Pode fazer qualquer coisa comigo, mas, por favor...

— Ah, eu vou machucar você já, já, irmãzinha. Vou machucar pra valer. — Ele levantou os braços como se estivesse num palco. — Essa que é a parada toda, pô. Vou mostrar pro seu bebezinho precioso como é crescer sem a mamãe. — Ele manteve a arma em Faith. — Você fez bem de sair correndo atrás dele na rua ontem. Se estivesse um pouquinho mais perto, eu ia matar o moleque bem ali.

O vômito subiu na boca de Faith.

Ele empurrou Evelyn com o tênis.

— Pergunta por que ela não ficou comigo.

Faith não confiava que conseguisse abrir a boca.

— Pergunta por que ela não ficou comigo — repetiu Caleb, e levantou o pé, pronto para chutar a perna quebrada da mãe.

— Tá bom! — berrou Faith. — Por que você não ficou com ele?

Caleb falou:

— Por que você não ficou com ele, *mãe*?

— Por que você não ficou com ele, mãe?

Evelyn não se mexeu. Estava de olhos fechados. Assim que o pânico começou a crescer em Faith, a boca da mãe se abriu.

— Eu não tive escolha.

— Pô, cê não passou o último ano me falando isso, mãe? Que todo mundo tem escolha?

— Era uma outra época. — O olho bom dela se abriu. Os cílios estavam grudados. Ela olhou para Faith. — Desculpe, meu amor.

Faith balançou a cabeça.

— Você não precisa se desculpar por nada.

— Ah, que beleza. Um encontrinho de mãe e filha aqui. — Ele empurrou a cadeira com tanta força na parede que a perna traseira quebrou. — Ela tinha vergonha de mim, foi por isso. — Ele foi até a estante e voltou. — Não podia explicar como um bebezinho de pele escura tinha saído de dentro dela. Diferente de você, né? Outra época. — Ele voltou a andar. — E você acha que seu papai era tão bonzinho quando você era criança. Conta o que ele disse para você, mãe. Conta o que ele obrigou você a fazer.

Evelyn estava deitada de lado, de olhos fechados e braços estendidos à frente. O movimento superficial do peito dela era a única coisa que indicava que ainda estava viva.

— Seu paizinho disse para ela que era ele ou eu. Que tal? O Sr. Corretor do Ano dos Seguros Galveston por seis anos seguidos disse para sua mamãe que ela não podia ficar com o bebê dela, porque, se ficasse, nunca mais veria os outros filhos.

Faith teve dificuldade em não demonstrar que ele finalmente tinha conseguido atingir o ponto certo. Ela adorava o pai, idolatrava-o como qualquer filhinha do papai mimada, mas, adulta, conseguia facilmente imaginar Bill Mitchell dando esse ultimato a Evelyn.

Caleb tinha voltado à sua posição original perto da estante. A arma estava abaixada ao lado do corpo, mas ela sabia que, a qualquer momento, ele podia levantá-la. Ele estava de costas para a porta de correr de vidro. Evelyn estava à esquerda dele. Faith estava na diagonal, a cerca de três metros e meio e esperando o alvoroço começar.

Ela rezava para Will ter entendido a mensagem. A sala era um relógio. Faith estava em mil e oitocentos, ou seis horas. Evelyn estava em mil e quinhentos, três horas. Caleb estava indo e vindo entre dez e doze.

Faith tinha se oferecido pelo menos vinte vezes no último mês para tirar o celular de Will do horário militar. Ele sempre recusava porque era teimoso e sentia uma mistura estranha de vergonha e orgulho no que dizia respeito ao seu distúrbio. Will estava, naquele momento, observando-a pela janela do banheiro. Ele tinha dito para ela dar um sinal. Ela passou os dedos pelo cabelo, colocando o polegar e o indicador num sinal de okay.

Faith olhou a mãe jogada no chão. Evelyn a observava com o olho bom. Será que tinha visto Faith dar o sinal a Will? Era capaz de entender o que estava para acontecer? Ela estava respirando com dificuldade. Seus lábios estavam cheios de bolhas. Ela obviamente tinha sido estrangulada. Havia hematomas escuros no pescoço. Tinha um corte na lateral da cabeça. Saía sangue de uma abertura feia na bochecha. Faith sentiu uma onda de amor dominá-la, transbordando em direção à mãe. Era como uma luz saindo de seu corpo. Quantas vezes Faith tinha procurado aquela mulher pedindo ajuda? Quantas vezes tinha chorado no ombro dela?

Tantas vezes que Faith perdera a conta.

Evelyn levantou a mão. Seus dedos tremeram. Ela cobriu o rosto. Faith se virou. Uma luz clara ofuscante entrou pelas janelas da frente. Atravessou as cortinas finas, jogando um holofote dentro da casa.

Faith se abaixou. Talvez a memória muscular se lembrasse de algum exercício de treinamento de anos antes. Talvez fosse instinto humano se encolher o máximo possível quando sentia que estava para acontecer algo de ruim.

Nada aconteceu de imediato. Segundos se passaram. Faith se pegou contando:

— Dois... três... quatro...

Ela levantou a cabeça para olhar Caleb.

O vidro se estilhaçou. Ele deu um solavanco como se tivesse levado um soco no ombro. Sua expressão era uma mescla de dor e choque.

Faith se esforçou para se levantar do chão. Voou na direção de Caleb. Ele apontou a arma para a cara dela. Ela olhou bem dentro do cano curto raiado, e o buraco escuro da ponta da arma a encarou de volta. A raiva a dominou, queimando suas entranhas, impelindo-a à frente. Ela queria matar aquele homem. Queria rasgar a garganta dele com os próprios dentes. Queria arrancar o coração do peito dele. Queria ver a dor em seus olhos enquanto ela fazia com ele tudo o que ele tinha feito com sua mãe, sua família, com a vida de todos eles.

Mas ela nunca teria oportunidade de fazer isso.

A lateral da cabeça de Caleb explodiu. Seus braços se levantaram num solavanco. Balas disparadas da Tec-9 fizeram chover gesso branco do teto. Memória muscular. Dois tiros, bem rápido, um depois do outro.

Devagar, ele caiu no chão. A única coisa que Faith conseguia ouvir era o som do corpo dele batendo no piso. Primeiro o quadril, depois o ombro, depois a cabeça estourando contra a madeira maciça. Os olhos dele continuaram abertos. Azul-escuros. Tão familiares. Tão sem vida.

Até nunca mais.

Faith olhou para a mãe. Evelyn tinha conseguido se sentar apoiada na parede. Ainda estava com a Glock na mão direita. O cano da arma começou a abaixar. O peso era demais. Ela soltou o braço. A arma caiu com um estrépito no chão.

— Mãe...

Faith mal conseguia ficar de pé. Ela meio andou, meio rastejou até a mãe. Não sabia onde tocá-la, qual parte do corpo dela não estava machucada ou quebrada.

— Venha aqui — sussurrou Evelyn. Ela puxou Faith para o colo. Acariciou as costas dela. Faith não conseguiu evitar. Começou a soluçar que nem criança. — Está tudo bem, meu amor. — Evelyn pressionou os lábios no topo da cabeça de Faith. — Vai ficar tudo bem.

QUINTA-FEIRA

21

Will pôs as mãos nos bolsos enquanto descia pelo corredor até o quarto de Evelyn Mitchell no hospital. Estava quase inebriado de exaustão. Sua visão estava tão aguçada que o mundo era seu Blu-ray. Havia um zumbido agudo em seus ouvidos. Ele sentia cada um dos poros de sua pele. Era por isso que ele nunca tomava café. Will estava ligado o suficiente para dar energia a uma cidade pequena. Tinha passado as últimas três noites com Sara. Seus pés mal tocaram o chão.

Ele parou na frente do quarto de Evelyn, perguntando-se se devia ter trazido flores. Will tinha dinheiro na carteira. Deu meia-volta, retornando para os elevadores. Podia pelo menos comprar um balão da loja de presentes. Todo mundo gostava de balões.

— Ei. — Faith abriu a porta da mãe. — Aonde você vai?

— Sua mãe gosta de balões?

— Devia gostar quando tinha sete anos.

Will sorriu. Da última vez que vira Faith, ela estava chorando no colo da mãe. Parecia um pouco melhor agora, mas não muito.

— Como ela está?

— Bem. Essa noite foi um pouco melhor que a anterior, mas a dor ainda está forte.

Will só podia imaginar.

Evelyn tinha sido levada às pressas para o Grady com uma escolta policial completa. Ficou em cirurgia por mais de dezesseis horas. Tinham colocado metal suficiente na perna dela para encher uma maleta enorme de ferramentas.

Ele perguntou:

— E você?

— É muita coisa para absorver. — Faith balançou a cabeça, como se ainda não conseguisse entender. — Eu sempre quis outro irmão, mas era porque eu achava que ele poderia dar um pau no Zeke.

— Parece que você sabe se cuidar.

— Dá bem mais trabalho do que você pensa. — Ela apoiou o ombro contra a parede. — Deve ter sido tão difícil para ela. O que ela passou. Nem imagino abrir mão de um dos meus filhos. Preferia arrancar meu coração.

Will desviou o olhar, encarando o nada atrás dela.

— Desculpe. Eu não estava pensando em...

— Não tem problema — disse ele. — Sabe, um número surpreendente de órfãos acaba no sistema penitenciário. — Ele deu alguns dos melhores exemplos: — Albert DeSalvo. Ted Bundy. Joel Rifkin. Filho de Sam.

— Acho que Aileen Wuornos também foi abandonada pelos pais.

— Vou avisar os outros. É bom ter uma mulher na lista.

Ela riu, mas obviamente sem muita vontade. Will olhou de novo por cima do ombro dela. Havia uma enfermeira grande com um buquê de flores vindo pelo corredor.

Faith falou:

— Eu tinha certeza de que não íamos sair vivas daquela casa.

Alguma coisa na voz dela indicava que o que acontecera com a família ainda não tinha sido superado. Talvez nunca fosse. Algumas coisas nunca nos deixavam, não importava o quanto tentássemos.

Will disse:

— Precisamos realmente combinar um código melhor, caso algo assim aconteça de novo.

— Eu estava apavorada de você não entender. Graças a Deus que tivemos todas aquelas discussões sobre tirar seu telefone do horário militar.

— Na verdade, eu não entendi.

Ele sorriu com a expressão de choque dela. Will tinha deixado o celular no viva-voz enquanto conversava com Faith. Assim que a ligação acabou, Roz Levy tinha dado sua opinião, explicando a eles que a sala era um relógio e que ela ficaria mais do que contente de correr até lá com seu Python e acabar com o delinquente na posição de meio-dia.

Will disse a Faith:

— Eu gosto de pensar que, em algum momento, teria entendido.

— Você sabe que uma glicemia de mil e oitocentos provavelmente significaria que eu estava ou morta, ou num coma irreversível, né?

— Lógico que eu sabia disso.

— Meu Deus do céu — sussurrou ela. — Parece que não somos uma máquina tão bem-ajustada.

Ele sentiu a necessidade de contar a ela.

— O helicóptero fui eu. A câmera infravermelha mostrou para a gente onde vocês estavam, confirmou que o parceiro dele estava morto. — Ela não pareceu impressionada, então Will completou: — E as luzes foram ideia minha.

Eles tinham alinhado duas viaturas e ligado o farol de xênon forte na direção das janelas da frente. A sombra de Caleb contra as cortinas tinha dado algo em que mirar.

— Bem, obrigada de todo jeito por atirar nele. — Ela obviamente conseguiu ler a expressão dele. — Ah, Will, não foi você?

Ele soltou uma expiração longa.

— Amanda me jurou que ia devolver um dos meus testículos se eu a deixasse atirar.

— Espero que você a tenha feito colocar isso por escrito. Porque ela também não acertou em cheio.

— Ela culpou meu rifle. Algo a ver com o fato de eu ser canhoto.

A empunhadura era universal, mas Faith não discutiu.

— Bem, que bom você estava lá. Eu me senti mais segura.

Ele sorriu, embora tivesse quase certeza de que tudo aquilo podia ter acontecido sem a presença dele. Amanda era engenhosa e, basicamente, Will tinha ficado escondido atrás de um muro enquanto Faith arriscava a própria vida.

Ela disse:

— Estou feliz por você estar com Sara.

Ele tentou suprimir o sorriso bobo que queria abrir.

— Só estou por perto até ela perceber que consegue alguma coisa melhor.

— Queria acreditar que você está brincando.

Will também. Ele não entendia Sara. Não sabia o que a motivava nem por que ela estava com ele. Mas ela estava. E não só isso — parecia feliz. Sara estava sorrindo tanto de manhã que quase não conseguira fazer biquinho para dar um beijo de despedida nele. Will tinha achado que talvez tivesse papel higiênico grudado na cara, no local em que se cortara fazendo a barba, mas ela havia dito que estava sorrindo porque ele a fazia feliz.

Ele não sabia o que fazer com aquilo. Não fazia sentido.

Mas Faith sabia como acabar com o sorriso dele.

— E Angie?

Ele deu de ombros, como se Angie não tivesse deixado tantas mensagens no telefone fixo e no celular até as duas caixas postais ficarem lotadas. Cada mensagem era mais desagradável que a outra. Cada ameaça era mais grave. Will tinha escutado todas. Não conseguia evitar. Ainda via Angie com a arma na boca. Ainda sentia seu coração acelerar com a ideia de abrir a porta do banheiro um dia e achá-la sangrando até a morte na banheira.

Felizmente, Faith não focou muito tempo no negativo.

— Você contou para Sara que morre de medo de chimpanzés?

— O assunto não surgiu.

— Mas vai surgir. É o que acontece em relacionamentos. Todo assunto surge, você gostando ou não.

Will assentiu rápido com a cabeça, esperando que isso a calasse. Não teve tanta sorte.

— Olhe só. — Ela usou a voz de mãe, que empregava quando ele não andava com as costas retas ou usava a gravata errada. — O único jeito de você estragar tudo é se continuar se preocupando em estragar tudo.

Will preferia estar preso de novo no porta-malas da Sra. Levy do que ter aquela conversa.

— Estou preocupado com Betty.

— Aham.

— Ela está muito apegada.

Isso era verdade. A cachorrinha tinha se recusado a deixar o apartamento de Sara naquela manhã.

— Só prometa que vai esperar pelo menos um mês antes de falar que está apaixonado por ela.

Ele soltou uma respiração longa, com saudade do isolamento dentro do Corvair.

— Você sabia que a Bayer tinha a marca registrada da heroína?

O subterfúgio a fez balançar a cabeça.

— A empresa que faz aspirina?

— Eles perderam o registro da marca depois da Primeira Guerra Mundial. Está no Tratado de Versalhes.

— A gente aprende uma coisa nova todo dia.

— A Sears vendia seringas carregadas de heroína no catálogo. Duas por um e cinquenta.

Ela colocou a mão no braço dele.

— Obrigada, Will.

Ele deu um tapinha na mão dela, depois outro, porque um só provavelmente não era suficiente.

— Você devia agradecer a Roz Levy. Foi ela quem descobriu tudo.

— Ela não é exatamente uma velhinha fofa, né?

Era um eufemismo. A velhota tinha assistido ao pior pesadelo de Evelyn se desenrolar como se fosse um esporte.

— Ela é meio diabólica.

— Ela deu a você o sermão sobre pombos e azulões?

Faith se virou quando ouviu mais vozes. A porta do quarto de Evelyn se abriu. Jeremy saiu, seguido por um homem alto com corte de cabelo militar e uma mandíbula quadrada que imediatamente trazia à mente a palavra *milico*. Estava com Emma no colo, apoiada em um dos ombros largos. A bebê parecia um saco de ervilha congelada pendurado de um arranha-céu. O corpo dela deu um pequeno solavanco ao soluçar.

— Isso vai ser divertido. — Faith se afastou da parede com um gemido. — Will, este é meu irmão Zeke. Zeke, este é...

— Eu sei quem é esse babaca.

Will estendeu a mão.

— Ouvi falar muito de você.

Emma soluçou. Zeke olhou com raiva. Não apertou a mão de Will. Will tentou uma conversa leve.

— Que bom que sua mãe está melhor.

Ele continuou olhando com raiva. Emma soluçou outra vez. Will sentiu pena do homem. Como dono de uma chihuahua, ele sabia como era difícil parecer durão segurando uma coisa incrivelmente minúscula.

Jeremy os salvou do concurso de quem encarava mais tempo.

— Oi, Will. Obrigado por vir.

Will apertou a mão dele. Era um menino magrelo, mas tinha um cumprimento forte.

— Fiquei sabendo que sua avó está melhor.

— Ela é durona. — Ele passou o braço pelos ombros de Faith. — Igual a minha mãe.

Emma soluçou de novo.

— Vamos, tio Zeke. — Jeremy o pegou pelo cotovelo. — Falei para a vovó que íamos colocar minha cama no andar de baixo para minha mãe poder cuidar dela quando ela sair do hospital.

Zeke demorou para quebrar o contato visual. Os soluços contínuos de Emma deviam ter influenciado sua decisão de seguir o sobrinho pelo corredor.

— Desculpe — Faith falou. — Ele é meio escroto, às vezes. Não sei como, mas Emma o adora.

Devia ser porque não conseguia entender uma palavra do que ele dizia.

Faith perguntou:

— Quer falar com a minha mãe?

— Eu só vim ver como você estava.

— Ela já perguntou por você algumas vezes. Acho que ela quer conversar.

— E não pode conversar com você?

— Eu já entendi o básico. Não tem por que eu saber os detalhes sórdidos. — Ela forçou um sorriso. — Amanda disse para ela que prometeu a você uma hora de conversa.

— Não achei que isso fosse acontecer de verdade.

— Elas são melhores amigas há quarenta anos. Cumprem as promessas uma da outra. — Ela deu um tapinha no braço dele de novo e começou a ir embora. — Obrigada por vir.

— Espere. — Will colocou a mão no bolso do casaco e puxou o envelope que tinha chegado pelo correio naquela manhã. — Nunca recebi uma carta antes. Quer dizer, além dos boletos.

Ela analisou o envelope fechado.

— Você não abriu.

Will não precisava. Faith nunca saberia o quanto era importante para ele o fato de ela acreditar que ele seria capaz de ler a carta.

— Você quer que eu abra?

— Claro que não. — Ela arrancou o objeto da mão dele. — Já é bem ruim Zeke e Jeremy terem visto aqueles vídeos que eu fiz. Eu não tinha ideia de que ficava tão feia chorando.

Will não podia discordar.

— Enfim. — Ela olhou o relógio. — Preciso tomar minha insulina e comer alguma coisa. Vou estar na lanchonete se precisar de mim.

Will ficou olhando Faith seguir pelo corredor. Ela parou na frente do elevador e se virou para olhá-lo. Enquanto ele observava, ela rasgou a carta ao meio, depois rasgou de novo. Will bateu uma continência para ela, depois empurrou a porta do quarto de Evelyn e entrou. Quase todas as superfícies estavam cobertas de flores variadas. Will sentiu o nariz começando a coçar com o perfume forte.

Evelyn Mitchell virou a cabeça para ele. Estava deitada na cama. A perna quebrada estava elevada, com parafusos no estilo Frankenstein saindo do gesso. A mão estava apoiada num apoio de espuma. Havia gaze no espaço onde devia estar o dedo anelar. Tubos entravam e saíam de seu corpo. O corte na bochecha estava fechado com curativo de ponto falso. Ela parecia menor do que ele se lembrava, mas, também, tudo pelo que ela tinha passado era capaz de reduzir o tamanho de uma pessoa.

— Agente Trent.

— Capitã Mitchell.

Ela mostrou a ele o gatilho da bomba de morfina.

— Estava adiando tomar isso porque queria conversar com você.

— Não precisa. Não quero lhe causar mais dor.

— Então, sente-se, por favor. Meu pescoço dói de ficar olhando para você aí em cima.

Já havia uma cadeira ao lado da cama dela. Will se sentou.

— Que bom que você está bem.

Os lábios dela mal se mexiam.

— Ainda falta um pouco para eu chegar a ficar bem. Vamos só dizer que estou aguentando firme.

— Melhor que o contrário.

Ela disse:

— Mandy me contou sobre seu papel em tudo isso. — Will imaginava que tinha sido uma conversa bem curta. — Obrigada por cuidar da minha filha.

— Acho que você tem mais crédito por isso do que eu.

Os olhos dela se encheram de lágrimas. Ele não tinha certeza se era de dor ou de pensar em perder Faith.

Só então lembrou que ela também tinha perdido outro filho.

— Meus sentimentos.

Ela engoliu com evidente dificuldade. A pele de seu pescoço estava quase preta de hematomas. Evelyn Mitchell, por duas vezes, tinha sido forçada a escolher entre a família com Bill Mitchell e o filho que tivera com Hector Ortiz. Em ambas, tomou a mesma decisão. Apesar de Caleb ter facilitado bastante para ela dessa última vez.

Ela disse:

— Ele era um jovem muito perturbado. Eu não sabia como ajudar. Ele tinha tanta raiva.

— Não precisa falar disso.

Ela soltou uma risada rouca do fundo da garganta.

— Ninguém quer que eu fale dele. Acho que prefeririam que ele só desaparecesse. — Ela indicou o copo d'água na mesa. — Você pode...

Will pegou o copo e inclinou o canudo para que ela pudesse beber. Ela não conseguia levantar a cabeça. Delicadamente, Will estendeu o braço e a apoiou.

Ela bebeu por quase um minuto inteiro antes de soltar o canudo.

— Obrigada.

Will se sentou de novo. Ficou olhando o buquê de flores na mesa à sua frente. Havia um cartão de visita preso no laço branco. Ele reconheceu o logo da polícia de Atlanta.

Evelyn contou:

— Hector era IC. — Informante confidencial. — Entregou o primo. Eles eram de uma facção, começou como uma coisa pequena, um motivo para invadir carros e roubar bolsas para poderem jogar videogames, mas depois ficou cruel bem rápido.

— Los Texicanos.

Ela fez que sim.

— Hector queria sair. Ele continuou falando e eu continuei ouvindo, porque era bom para a minha carreira. — Ela acenou com a mão boa. — E, aí, uma coisa levou à outra. — Seus olhos se fecharam. — Eu era casada com um corretor de seguros. Era um homem muito gentil e um ótimo pai, mas... — Quando ela suspirou, a respiração saiu aos poucos dos lábios. — Sabe como é quando você está lá na rua perseguindo bandidos e seu coração está batendo forte e você sente que o mundo todo está aos seus pés, e quando chega em casa... faz o quê? O jantar? Passa camisas e dá um banho nas crianças?

— Você estava apaixonada pelo Victor?

— Não. — Ela foi firme na resposta. — Nunca. E o mais estranho é que só percebi o quanto era apaixonada pelo Bill quando o magoei tanto que achei que fosse perder meu marido.

— Mas ele ficou com você.

— Ditando as regras — disse ela. — Na época, eu fui cortada das negociações. Ele se encontrou com Hector. Eles chegaram a um acordo de cavalheiros.

— A conta bancária.

Ela voltou os olhos para o teto. Devagar, fechou-os. Ele achou que Evelyn tivesse dormido, até ela voltar a falar.

— Sandra e Paul tinham muitas dívidas por ajudarem a família dela. Não tinham dinheiro para filhos, mesmo que conseguissem engravidar. Parte do dinheiro na conta era de Hector. Parte era meu. Dez por cento de cada salário meu ia para Caleb. Era como o dízimo, só que não para a igreja... apesar de ainda ser uma penitência. — O canto de sua boca se levantou de leve em algo parecido com um sorriso. — Se bem que acho que Sandra dava boa parte desse dinheiro para a igreja toda semana. Eles eram muito religiosos. Católicos, mas isso não me incomodava tanto quanto incomodava Bill. Achei que fossem dar ao menino uma base moral forte. — Ela deu uma risada. — Parece que não.

— Caleb descobriu sobre você quando Sandra ficou doente?

Ela olhou para Will.

— Recebi uma ligação dela. Parecia que estava me alertando, o que, na época, não fazia sentido, então, ignorei. A primeira vez que o vi já adulto foi no velório dela. — A memória a fez balançar a cabeça. — Meu Deus, ele era igualzinho a Zeke naquela idade. Mais bonito, se quiser saber a verdade. Mais raivoso, o que foi o problema. — A cabeça dela continuava se movendo de um lado para o outro. — Eu só vi o quanto ele era raivoso quando já era tarde demais. Não fazia ideia.

— No velório, você conversou com Caleb?

— Tentei começar uma conversa, mas ele saiu andando. Umas semanas depois, eu estava faxinando a casa e notei umas coisas fora do lugar. Meu escritório tinha sido revistado. Ele fez um ótimo trabalho. Eu não teria notado se não estivesse procurando uma coisa específica. — Ela explicou: — Eu tinha uma mecha do cabelo de bebê dele escondida num lugar que meus filhos não conheciam. Fui procurar e não estava lá. Ali eu já devia ter percebido. Devia ter notado como ele estava obcecado por mim. Como me odiava.

Evelyn parou para recuperar o fôlego. Will via que ela estava cansada. Apesar disso, ela continuou:

— Eu liguei para Hector e pedi para ele me encontrar. A gente estava em contato desde a doença de Sandra. Não tínhamos muito tempo para colocar as coisas em dia. Íamos num Starbucks perto do aeroporto para ninguém nos ver. Era como antigamente, tudo às escondidas. Mentindo para minha família não descobrir. — Ela fechou os olhos de novo. — Caleb vivia metido em problemas. Tentei de tudo com ele, até ofereci dinheiro para ele poder fazer faculdade. Faith está tendo a maior dificuldade para ajudar Jeremy com as mensalidades, e eu estava lá oferecendo uma bolsa integral para o garoto. Ele só riu na minha cara. — O tom dela ficou ácido, irritado. — No dia seguinte, recebi uma ligação de um velho amigo do esquadrão de narcóticos. Eles tinham pegado Caleb com uma quantidade séria. Precisei pedir para Mandy mexer uns pauzinhos. Ela não queria. Disse que eu já tinha dado chances demais para ele. Mas eu implorei.

— Heroína?

— Cocaína — corrigiu ela. — Heroína estaria além do meu alcance, mas cocaína dava para resolver. Eles derrubaram o caso porque concordamos em mandá-lo para a clínica.

— Vocês o mandaram para a Healing Winds.

— Hector mora a poucos quilômetros de lá. O filho do primo dele, Ricardo, tinha ficado internado na mesma instituição. E Chuck estava lá. Coitado do Chuck. — Ela parou e engoliu para limpar a garganta. — Ele me ligou no começo deste ano para fazer as pazes. Já está sóbrio há oito meses. Eu sabia que ele estava fazendo terapia na Healing Winds e achei que Caleb ficaria seguro lá.

— Chuck contou a história dele para os garotos.

— Aparentemente, isso é um dos passos da reabilitação. Ele contou para eles do dinheiro. E, lógico, apesar de Chuck ter garantido que eu não tinha nada a ver com aquilo, eles não acreditaram.

— Era Chuck aquele dia no hospital. Era ele o policial que havia perguntado a Sara se o menino ia sobreviver.

Ela fez que sim.

— Ele viu o que tinha acontecido comigo no noticiário e veio ver se podia ajudar. Não parou para pensar que, com a ficha dele, ninguém ia querer ajuda. Pedi para Mandy tentar resolver as coisas com o oficial de condicional dele. Fui eu que meti o cara em problema. Meus homens sempre me defenderam, mesmo quando não era bom para eles.

— Na sua opinião, Caleb achava que você tinha desviado dinheiro igual aos outros?

Ela obviamente ficou surpresa com a pergunta.

— Não, agente Trent. Não acredito que ele achasse isso, não. Ele tinha uma noção preconcebida de que eu era fria e insensível, a mãe que nunca o tinha amado. Disse que a única coisa que herdou de mim foi meu coração obscuro.

Will se lembrou da música que estava tocando quando Faith chegou na casa da mãe.

— "Back in Black."

— Era a música dele. Ele ficava insistindo para eu prestar atenção na letra, mas quem é que vai saber o que são todos aqueles berros?

— Fala sobre se vingar das pessoas que desistiram de você.

— Ah. — Ela pareceu aliviada de enfim entender. — Ele tocou aquilo sem parar no rádio da cozinha. E aí Faith chegou e a música parou. Fiquei apavorada. Acho que nunca prendi a respiração por tanto tempo. Mas eles não queriam Faith. Não a turma de Caleb, pelo menos. Benny Choo falou que ia cuidar de tudo. Ficou para trás com Ricardo. A heroína dentro dele era valiosa demais, mas ele mandou os outros caras me pegarem e irem embora, então, eles obedeceram.

Will queria ter certeza da ordem dos acontecimentos.

— Caleb estava lá ao mesmo tempo que Faith?

— Ele olhou para ela pela janela. — A voz de Evelyn estremeceu. — Nunca fiquei com tanto medo na vida. Pelo menos não antes disso.

Will estava mais do que familiarizado com esse tipo de medo.

— O que aconteceu antes de Faith chegar? Você estava fazendo sanduíche, certo?

— Eu sabia que Faith ia se atrasar. Essas sessões de treinamento em geral demoram. Tem sempre um babaca na primeira fila que quer aparecer. — Ela ficou um momento em silêncio, reunindo os pensamentos. — Hector foi me pegar no mercado. Ele conhecia minha rotina. Era esse tipo de homem. Quando eu falava alguma coisa, ele prestava atenção. — Ela ficou um momento em silêncio, talvez em homenagem ao ex-amante. — Ele tinha ido visitar Caleb na clínica e foi avisado de que ele tinha saído por conta própria. Eles não trancam ninguém. Caleb simplesmente saiu. A gente não devia ter se surpreendido. Eu já tinha dado uns telefonemas e descoberto que Ricardo estava se metendo com umas coisas que não iam ser boas para nenhum deles.

— Heroína.

Ela soltou uma expiração lenta.

— Hector e eu montamos o quebra-cabeça enquanto eu dirigia com ele de volta para casa. Sabíamos que Ricardo estava trabalhando na oficina de Julia, e também sabíamos que não sairia nada de bom desses meninos se unindo. *Folie à plusieurs.*

Will já tinha ouvido a expressão. Referia-se a uma síndrome em que um grupo de pessoas aparentemente normais desenvolvia uma psicose compartilhada quando estavam juntas. A Família Manson. O Ramo Davidiano. Sempre tinha um líder instável no meio da doença. Roger Ling o havia chamado de cabeça da cobra. E um homem como Roger Ling devia saber.

Evelyn disse:

— Parte de mim queria que Faith voltasse para casa mais cedo. Eu queria que ela encontrasse Hector, para eu ser obrigada a explicar tudo.

— Caleb matou Hector?

— Acho que só pode ter sido ele. Foi sorrateiro e covarde. Eu ouvi a arma, porque depois de ouvir o som de um silenciador a gente não esquece, e olhei na garagem. O porta-malas estava fechado e não tinha ninguém lá. Não pensei duas vezes. Talvez eu já soubesse que aquilo fosse acontecer. Peguei Emma e a levei para o quarto de ferramentas. Voltei com minha arma e tinha um homem na área de serviço. Atirei antes de ele conseguir abrir a boca. Quando eu me virei, Caleb estava lá.

— Você lutou com ele?

— Eu não podia atirar nele. Ele não estava armado. Era meu filho. Mas eu levei a melhor. — Ela olhou a mão machucada. — Acho que ele não esperava que eu fosse reagir de um jeito tão agressivo à tentativa de cortar meu dedo.

— Ele cortou lá mesmo?

Will tinha imaginado que aquilo fosse parte de alguma negociação posterior.

— Um dos outros garotos ficou sentado nas minhas costas enquanto Caleb cortava. Ele usou a faca de pão. Serrou para frente e para trás que nem um tronco de árvore. Acho que ele gostou de me ouvir gritar.

— Como você arrancou a faca dele?

— Nem sei. É uma dessas coisas que acontecem sem você pensar. Na verdade, não me lembro da maior parte das coisas que aconteceram depois, mas me lembro do outro garoto caindo em cima de mim e da sensação daquela faca entrando na barriga dele. — Ela exalou forte. — Eu corri para a garagem para pegar Emma e me mandar de lá. Foi quando escutei Caleb gritando. — "Mamãe, mamãe." — Ela pausou por mais um momento. — Ele parecia machucado. Não sei o que me fez voltar lá dentro. Foi instinto, que nem com a faca, mas antes tinha sido por autopreservação, e aquilo seria autodestruição. — A memória obviamente era dolorosa. — Eu sabia o quanto era errado. Lembro de pensar muito claramente, quando passei correndo pelo meu carro e entrei de volta na casa, que era uma das coisas mais idiotas que eu faria na vida. E eu tinha razão. Mas não consegui parar. Eu o escutei me chamando e só entrei correndo.

Ela parou de novo para respirar. Will viu que a posição do sol tinha mudado e estava nos olhos dela. Ele se levantou e virou a persiana para baixo.

Exausta, ela soltou um "Obrigada".

— Quer descansar?

— Quero terminar isso e depois não quero falar sobre esse assunto nunca mais.

Parecia exatamente o tipo de coisa que Faith diria. Will sabia que era melhor não discutir. Ele se sentou na cadeira, esperando que ela continuasse.

Evelyn não recomeçou imediatamente. Por um minuto, só ficou ali deitada, o peito subindo e descendo com a respiração.

Finalmente, ela falou:

— Por uns três anos, depois que ele nasceu, mais ou menos uma vez por mês, eu dizia para Bill e as crianças que precisava cuidar de alguma burocracia no escritório. Em geral, aos domingos, quando eles estavam na igreja, por ser mais fácil. — Ela tossiu. Sua voz estava ficando mais rouca. — Mas na verdade eu ia até o parque no fim da rua e ficava sentada sozinha no banco ou, se estivesse chovendo, eu ficava no carro e só chorava sem parar. Nem Mandy sabia disso. Eu dividi tudo da minha vida com ela, mas isso, não. — Ela deu um olhar sério para Will. — Você não sabe como foi difícil para ela com Kenny. Ela não conseguia dar filhos a ele e ele queria uma família. Do próprio sangue. Ele insistia muito nisso. Contar para ela o quanto eu sentia saudade de Caleb seria cruel.

Will se sentia meio desconfortável de ouvir algo tão pessoal sobre a chefe. Tentou fazer Evelyn voltar ao dia do sequestro.

— Caleb enganou você para que voltasse para a casa. Foi por isso que você não pegou Emma e fugiu?

Ela ficou em silêncio por tempo suficiente para mostrar a ele que tinha percebido que ele estava mudando de assunto.

— Não dá para enganar quem não quer ser enganado.

Will não concordava muito, mas, mesmo assim, assentiu com a cabeça.

— Eu entrei correndo na cozinha. Benny Choo estava lá. Claro que era Benny Choo. Carnificina por todo lado. Ele estava em seu habitat natural. A gente lutou um pouco, ele venceu, principalmente porque teve ajuda. Ele queria o dinheiro. Todo mundo queria o dinheiro. O lugar estava lotado de homens raivosos exigindo dinheiro.

— Menos Caleb — chutou Will.

— Menos Caleb — confirmou ela. — Ele só ficou sentado no sofá comendo frios direto do saco, vendo os outros correndo e revirando minha casa de cabeça para baixo. Acho que ele adorou. Acho que foi a maior diversão da vida dele ficar me vendo lá sentada, morta de medo, enquanto os amigos dele corriam que nem galinha sem cabeça procurando uma coisa que ele sabia que não existia.

— E o A embaixo da cadeira?

Ela deu uma risada instável.

— Era uma flecha. Imaginei que os peritos fossem achar. Eu queria que eles soubessem que o principal culpado estava sentado no sofá. Caleb deve ter deixado cabelo, fibras, digitais.

Will ficou pensando se a equipe de Ahbidi Mittal teria entendido a mensagem. Will com certeza tinha feito tudo errado.

Ela perguntou:

— Me diga uma coisa, eles realmente escavaram meu quintal?

Will percebeu que ela estava falando dos homens de Caleb, não dos de Ahbidi Mittal.

— Você disse que o dinheiro estava lá?

Ela riu, provavelmente pensando nos garotos correndo para lá e para cá no escuro com pás.

— Achei que parecia plausível, de tanto que acontece nos filmes.

Will não confessou que ele próprio tinha visto muitos filmes daquele tipo.

Abruptamente, o comportamento de Evelyn mudou. Ela olhou o teto outra vez. Os azulejos estavam manchados de marrom. Não era uma vista muito bonita. Will reconhecia a técnica de evitação quando via uma.

Ela sussurrou:

— Eu não paro de pensar que matei meu filho.

— Ele ia matar você. E Faith. Ele matou muito mais gente.

Ela continuou olhando os azulejos do teto.

— Mandy me disse para não falar com você sobre isso.

Will sabia que a morte de Caleb Espisito estava sendo revisada pela polícia, mas supunha que, em poucos dias, Evelyn seria liberada, como Faith tinha sido.

— Foi legítima defesa.

Ela soltou uma expiração lenta.

— Acho que ele queria que eu escolhesse entre os dois. Entre ele e Faith.

Will não confirmou que tinha a mesma opinião.

— Ele podia perdoar o pai. Hector tinha uma vida boa, mas nunca se casou, nem teve outro filho. Mas, quando Caleb viu o que eu tinha... o que eu tinha lutado para reconstruir com Bill e as crianças... ele se ressentiu demais. Ele me odiou tanto. — Os olhos dela brilhavam com lágrimas. — Lembro que uma das coisas que eu disse para ele antes de tudo isso acontecer foi que guardar um rancor assim era como beber veneno e esperar que a outra pessoa morresse.

Will imaginou que fosse o tipo de conselho que as mães davam aos filhos. Infelizmente, ele teve que aprender essa lição do jeito mais difícil.

— Você se lembra de alguma coisa do lugar onde ficou presa?

— Era um armazém. Abandonado, com certeza. Eu gritei o suficiente para acordar os mortos.

— Quantos homens estavam lá?

— Na casa? Acho que oito. Ficaram apenas três no armazém, contando Caleb. Eles se chamavam Juan e David. Tentaram não usar os nomes verdadeiros, mas não eram muito sofisticados, se é que você me entende.

Juan Castillo tinha tomado um tiro na frente do armazém de Julia Ling. David Herrera tinha sido morto a sangue-frio na frente de Evelyn e Faith. Benny Choo, Hironobu Kwon, Hector Ortiz, Ricardo Ortiz. No total, oito pessoas foram mortas por causa do rancor que um homem havia guardado por vinte anos.

Evelyn devia estar pensando a mesma coisa. Sua voz assumiu um tom de desespero.

— Você acha que eu podia tê-lo impedido?

A não ser que ela matasse Caleb antes de tudo aquilo acontecer, Will não via como.

— Um ódio desses não passa.

Ela não parecia reconfortada.

— Bill achava que o que tinha acontecido com Faith era culpa minha. Disse que, por eu estar com Hector, parei de olhar as crianças. Pode ser que ele tivesse razão.

— Faith é bem decidida a fazer o que ela quer.

— Você acha que ela puxou a mim. — Ela fez um aceno com a mão, para Will nem protestar. — Não, ela é *exatamente* como eu. Que Deus a ajude.

— Existem coisas piores.

— Hum.

Evelyn fechou os olhos de novo. Will ficou olhando para o rosto dela. Suas feições estavam quase obscurecidas pelo inchaço. Ela tinha mais ou menos a idade de Amanda, era o mesmo tipo de policial, mas não o mesmo tipo de mulher. Will passou boa parte da vida tendo inveja dos pais de outras pessoas. Era um desperdício de tempo pensar no que poderia ter sido. Mas, conversando com Evelyn Mitchell e sabendo os sacrifícios que ela tinha feito pelos filhos, Will não conseguia deixar de sentir um pouco de inveja.

Ele se levantou, pensando em deixá-la dormir, mas Evelyn abriu os olhos. Ela apontou para o jarro com água. Will a ajudou a beber com o canudo. Desta vez, ela não estava com tanta sede, mas Will viu a mão dela se fechar em torno do gatilho da morfina.

— Obrigada.

Ela pôs a cabeça de volta no travesseiro e apertou mais uma vez o gatilho.

Will não se sentou.

— Quer que eu traga mais alguma coisa para você antes de ir embora?

Ou ela não ouviu a pergunta, ou escolheu ignorar.

— Eu sei que Mandy é dura com você, mas é porque ela te ama.

Will sentiu suas sobrancelhas se levantando. A morfina tinha começado a fazer efeito rápido.

— Ela tem muito orgulho de você, Will. Fica se gabando de você o tempo todo. Como você é inteligente. Forte. Você é como um filho para ela. Mais do que imagina.

Ele sentiu a necessidade de olhar para trás, caso Amanda estivesse rindo lá da porta.

Evelyn continuou:

— E ela *tem mesmo* que se orgulhar. Você é um bom homem. Eu não ia querer minha filha sendo parceira de mais ninguém. Fiquei tão feliz quando vocês se juntaram. Só queria que tivesse virado algo mais.

Ele conferiu a porta novamente. Nada de Amanda. Quando voltou a se virar, Evelyn estava olhando direto para ele.

Ela perguntou:

— Posso ser sincera com você?

Ele fez que sim, embora se perguntasse se até aquele momento, então, ela não tinha sido.

— Eu sei que você teve uma vida difícil. Sei o quanto você se esforçou para virar uma pessoa boa. E sei que você merece ser feliz. E não vai ser com a sua esposa.

Como sempre, o primeiro impulso de Will foi defender Angie.

— Ela sofreu muito.

— Você merece algo muito melhor.

Ele sentiu a necessidade de dizer a ela:

— Eu também tenho os meus demônios.

— Mas os seus são bons, do tipo que deixa você mais forte. — Ela tentou sorrir. — "Se eu me livrasse dos meus demônios, perderia os meus anjos."

Ele chutou longe:

— Hemingway?

— Tennessee Williams.

A porta se abriu. Amanda deu uma batidinha no relógio.

— Tempo encerrado.

Ela acenou para que ele saísse.

Will olhou o relógio do celular. Ela tinha dado a ele exatamente uma hora.

— Como é que você sabia que eu estava aqui?

— Fale enquanto anda. — Ela juntou as mãos. — Nossa garota precisa descansar

Will tocou o cotovelo de Evelyn, porque era o único lugar que não estava com curativos ou preso em alguma coisa.

— Obrigado, capitã Mitchell.

— Se cuide, agente Trent.

Amanda empurrou Will enquanto ele saía do quarto. No corredor, ele quase derrubou uma enfermeira.

Amanda disse:

— Você a deixou cansada.

— Ela queria falar.

— Ela passou por muita coisa.

— Vai dar algum problema ela ter atirado em Caleb Espisito?

Amanda fez que não.

— A única pessoa que devia estar preocupada é Roz Levy. Se fosse por mim, ela seria presa por obstrução de justiça.

Will não discordava, mas a Sra. Levy tinha aperfeiçoado o papel que fazia de velhinha. Nenhum júri no mundo a condenaria.

— Um dia eu pego aquela velhaca — prometeu Amanda. — Ela parece um liquidificador. Está sempre agitando as coisas.

— Certo. — Will tentou acabar com aquilo. Sara tinha saído do trabalho cinco minutos atrás. Naquela mesma manhã, ele havia sugerido que eles almoçassem juntos, mas não tinha certeza de que ela fosse lembrar. — Vejo você amanhã.

Ele caminhou em direção ao elevador. Para seu desânimo, Amanda o seguiu.

Ela perguntou:

— O que Evelyn contou para você?

Ele alongou os passos, tentando despistá-la ou, pelo menos, obrigá-la a se esforçar.

— A verdade, espero.

— Certamente havia alguma bem no fundo, sim.

Will odiava a facilidade que ela tinha de colocar dúvidas na cabeça dele. Evelyn Mitchell era a melhor amiga de Amanda, mas as duas não se pareciam em nada. Evelyn não fazia joguinhos. Não tinha prazer em humilhar os outros.

— Acho que ela me contou o que eu precisava saber. — Ele apertou com força o botão de descer. Não conseguiu resistir: — Disse que você tem orgulho de mim.

Amanda riu.

— Bem, isso não é nem um pouco a minha cara.

— Não.

Um pensamento ocorreu a Will. Talvez Evelyn estivesse, afinal, contornando a verdade. Será que ela tinha secretamente dado uma pista a ele? Will sentiu uma onda de náusea o dominando.

Você é como um filho para ela. Mais do que imagina.

Ele se virou para Amanda, preparando-se para o pior dia da sua vida.

— Você vai me contar que na verdade é minha mãe?

A risada dela ecoou pelo corredor. Ela se apoiou na parede para não cair.

— Tá bom. — Ele apertou de novo o botão do elevador. E de novo. E aí pela terceira vez. — Já entendi. Muito engraçado.

Ela secou lágrimas dos olhos.

— Ah, Will, você acha mesmo que um filho meu ia virar um homem igual a você?

— Quer saber? — Ele se curvou para poder olhá-la nos olhos. — Vou entender isso como um elogio, e você não pode me impedir.

— Deixe de ser ridículo.

Ele se encaminhou para a escada de emergência.

— Obrigado, Amanda, por me dizer uma coisa tão legal.

— Volte aqui.

Ele empurrou a porta.

— Vou guardar para sempre no coração.

— Não ouse sair andando.

Will fez exatamente isso, descendo dois degraus de cada vez, tranquilo por saber que os pezinhos dela não conseguiriam alcançá-lo.

22

Sara tirou os óculos de leitura e esfregou os olhos. Fazia pelo menos duas horas que ela estava sentada à mesa da sala de descanso médico. O prontuário do paciente no tablet à sua frente estava começando a virar um borrão. Ela tinha dormido um total de seis horas nos últimos quatro dias. Seu nível de exaustão lembrava a residência, quando ela dormia numa cama dobrável de hospital no quartinho de material de limpeza que ficava atrás do posto de enfermagem. A cama ainda estava lá. O Grady tinha passado por uma reforma de um bilhão de dólares desde a última vez que Sara trabalhara no pronto-socorro, mas nenhum hospital gastava dinheiro para facilitar a vida dos residentes.

Nan, a estagiária de enfermagem, estava no sofá de novo. Tinha uma caixa de biscoitos pela metade de um lado e um saco de batatinhas do outro. Mal dava para ver seus polegares digitando furiosamente no iPhone. De poucos em poucos minutos, provavelmente quando chegava um e-mail novo, ela dava uma risadinha. Sara considerou se era possível a menina estar ficando mais jovem diante de seus olhos. Seu único consolo era que, em alguns anos, as porcarias que Nan amava tanto comer iam começar a fazer diferença.

— O que foi? — perguntou Nan, largando o celular. — Tudo tranquilo?

— Tranquilo

Sara estava estranhamente aliviada de a menina ter voltado a falar com ela. Nan andava emburrada desde que percebera que Sara não ia contar os detalhes suculentos de sua participação no episódio do tiroteio do hospital.

A jovem ficou de pé, tirando as migalhas do uniforme.

— Quer almoçar? Acho que Krakauer ia fazer um pedido na Hut.

— Obrigada pelo convite, mas tenho planos.

Sara olhou o relógio. Era para Will levá-la para almoçar. Aquele seria o primeiro encontro deles, o que dizia bastante sobre como andava a vida de Sara ultimamente, considerando que ele era o motivo de ela não estar dormindo.

— A gente se vê.

Em vez de empurrar a porta, Nan a abriu jogando o corpo contra ela.

Sara tirou um momento para curtir a paz e o silêncio da sala de descanso. Pôs a mão no bolso e puxou um pedaço de papel dobrado. Tinha esquecido os óculos no carro de manhã e precisara subir de novo as escadas até o estacionamento para pegá-los. Foi quando achou o bilhete preso no para-brisa. Estranhamente, não era a primeira vez que alguém deixava a palavra *vaca* no carro de Sara. Ela imaginou que devia agradecer por, desta vez, não terem riscado na lataria.

Sara não precisava consultar um especialista em caligrafia para saber que a mensagem era de Angie Trent. Outro bilhete tinha sido deixado no carro de Sara na manhã anterior, embora daquela vez a saudação a esperasse logo na saída do apartamento. Angie estava melhorando. Esse segundo bilhete era mais criativo do que o "puta" do dia anterior.

Sara fez uma bolinha com o papel e a jogou na lata de lixo. Claro que errou a mira. Levantou-se para pegar. Em vez de jogar no lixo, onde era seu lugar, ela voltou a desdobrar o papel e ficou olhando a palavra. Com certeza era desagradável, mas Sara não conseguia deixar de achar que merecia. No calor do momento, ela nunca se permitira pensar na aliança no dedo de Will. À luz fria do dia, porém, era outra coisa. Ele era um homem casado. Mesmo sem a designação legal, ainda havia um laço entre ele e Angie. Os dois estavam conectados de uma forma que Sara jamais entenderia.

E estava bem claro que Angie não ia se retirar graciosamente. A única questão era quanto tempo levaria para essa mulher conseguir arrastar Sara para a sarjeta junto com ela.

Houve uma batida na porta.

Sara se certificou de que o bilhete estava no lixo antes de abrir. Will estava ali, com as mãos nos bolsos. Apesar de terem estado juntos de todas as maneiras possíveis, os primeiros dez minutos entre eles sempre eram estranhos. Era como se ele estivesse eternamente esperando Sara tomar a iniciativa, dar algum sinal de que ainda não tinha se cansado dele.

Ele perguntou:

— Você está ocupada?

Ela abriu completamente a porta.

— Não estou, não.

Ele olhou o espaço.

— Eu tenho permissão de entrar aqui?

— Acho que podemos abrir uma exceção.

Ele parou no meio da sala, mantendo as mãos nos bolsos.

Sara perguntou:

— Como está Evelyn?

— Está bem. Pelo menos, eu acho. — Ele tirou as mãos dos bolsos, mas só para começar a girar a aliança no dedo. — Faith vai tirar um tempo de folga do trabalho para cuidar dela. Acho que vai ser bom para as duas terem um tempo juntas. Ou muito ruim. Vai saber.

Sara não conseguiu evitar. Olhou em direção ao bilhete amassado na lixeira. Por que ele continuava usando a aliança? Provavelmente pelo mesmo motivo de Angie continuar deixando bilhetes no carro de Sara.

Will perguntou:

— O que foi?

Ela indicou a mesa.

— Podemos sentar?

Ele esperou que ela se sentasse primeiro, depois ocupou a cadeira em frente a ela e falou:

— Não parece coisa boa.

— Não — concordou ela.

Ele batucou na mesa.

— Acho que eu sei o que você vai falar.

Ela falou mesmo assim:

410

— Eu gosto de você, Will. Eu gosto muito, muito de você.

— Mas?

Ela tocou a mão dele, pousando o dedo na aliança de casamento.

— É — disse ele.

Sem explicação. Sem desculpa. Sem oferta de tirar a aliança e jogar pela janela. Ou, no mínimo, enfiar dentro da porcaria do bolso.

Sara se forçou a continuar:

— Eu sei que Angie é uma parte importante da sua vida. Eu respeito isso. Respeito o que ela significa para você.

Ela esperou uma resposta, mas não parecia que viria. Em vez disso, Will pegou a mão dela. Passou o polegar pelas linhas de sua palma. Sara não conseguiu impedir a reação de seu corpo ao toque dele. Baixou os olhos para as mãos dos dois. Deixou o dedo deslizar para dentro do punho da camisa dele. A beira da cicatriz estava áspera contra sua pele. Ela pensou em tudo o que não sabia sobre ele — a tortura que ele havia suportado. A dor que havia causado a si mesmo. E tudo tinha acontecido com Angie ao lado dele.

— Não consigo competir com ela — admitiu Sara. — E não consigo ficar com você estando preocupada de você querer ficar com ela.

Ele pigarreou.

— Eu não quero ficar com Angie.

Ela esperou que Will dissesse que queria, na verdade, ficar com ela, Sara. Mas ele não fez isso.

Sara tentou outra vez.

— Não posso ficar em segundo lugar. Não posso achar que, não importa o quanto eu precise de você, você sempre vai correr primeiro para Angie.

De novo, ela esperou que ele falasse alguma coisa — qualquer coisa — que a convencesse de que ela estava errada. Os segundos se passaram. Pareceu uma eternidade.

Quando ele enfim falou, sua voz estava tão baixa que ela mal escutou.

— Ela dava muito alarme falso. — Ele umedeceu os lábios. — Quando a gente era pequeno, estou falando. — Ele levantou os olhos para ver se Sara estava ouvindo, depois voltou a olhar as mãos dos dois. — Uma vez nos colocaram juntos. Era um lar de acolhimento.

411

Parecia mais uma fazenda de confinamento. Estavam fazendo aquilo pelo dinheiro. Pelo menos a esposa. O marido estava fazendo pelas meninas adolescentes.

Sara sentiu um aperto na garganta. Lutou contra o impulso de se compadecer por Angie.

— Então, como eu falei, Angie dava muitos alarmes falsos. Quando ela acusou o cara de molestá-la, a assistente social não acreditou. Nem registrou ocorrência. Não me ouviu quando falei que, daquela vez, ela não estava mentindo. — Ele deu de ombros. — Eu a escutava durante a noite às vezes. Gritando quando ele a machucava. Ele a machucava muito. Nenhuma das outras crianças ligava. Acho que ficavam felizes de não estar acontecendo com elas. Mas para mim... — Ele não completou a frase. Viu seu polegar se mover pela parte de trás dos dedos dela. — Eu sabia que, se um de nós fosse ferido, eles teriam que abrir uma investigação. Ou se a gente se ferisse de propósito. — Ele apertou a mão dela com mais força. — Então, falei para Angie: vou fazer isso. E eu fiz. Peguei uma lâmina do armário de remédios e me cortei. Eu sabia que não dava para ser pela metade. Você viu. — Ele deu uma risada pesarosa. — Não foi pela metade.

— Não — concordou ela.

Era difícil entender como ele tinha conseguido não desmaiar com a dor.

— Então — continuou Will —, isso tirou a gente daquela casa, e eles a fecharam, e as pessoas que a administravam não puderam mais receber crianças. — Ele levantou os olhos e piscou alguma vezes para afastar as lágrimas. — Sabe, uma das coisas que Angie me disse outra noite foi que eu nunca faria isso por você... que eu nunca me cortaria desse jeito. E acho que ela tinha razão. — Havia uma tristeza no sorriso dele. — Não porque eu não gosto de você, mas porque você nunca me colocaria nessa situação. Você nunca me pediria para fazer essa escolha.

Sara olhou nos olhos dele. O sol que entrava pelas janelas deixava os cílios de Will brancos. Ela não conseguia imaginar pelo que ele tinha passado, o nível de desespero que o levara a pegar aquela lâmina.

— Melhor eu deixar você seguir seu dia. — Ele se debruçou e beijou a mão dela, deixando o lábio ficar ali por uns segundos. Quando se endireitou, algo nele tinha mudado. Ele estava mais firme, mais determinado. — Você precisa saber que, se precisar de mim, vou estar aqui. Não importa o que aconteça. Eu vou estar aqui.

Tinha um tom decisivo no que ele disse, como se tudo estivesse resolvido. Ele parecia quase aliviado.

— Will...

— Está tudo bem. — Ele deu uma de suas risadas desconfortáveis. — Acho que você é imune ao meu charme espantoso.

Sara sentiu um nó na garganta. Não conseguia acreditar que ele estava se entregando tão fácil. Queria que ele lutasse por eles. Queria que ele batesse o punho na mesa e dissesse para ela que aquilo não era o fim, de jeito nenhum, que ele não ia abrir mão dela assim sem mais nem menos.

Mas ele não fez isso. Só tirou a mão dele da dela e se levantou.

— Obrigado. Eu sei que parece bobo. — Ele a olhou de relance, depois olhou a porta. — Só... obrigado.

Ela ouviu os passos dele cruzando o piso, depois o barulho vindo do corredor quando a porta se abriu. Sara apertou os olhos com os dedos, tentando conter as lágrimas. Não conseguia superar o tom de resignação dele, sua aceitação fácil ao que ele claramente considerava inevitável. Ela não fazia ideia de qual era o objetivo daquela história sobre Angie. Será que Sara devia ter pena da mulher? Devia achar romântico Will estar disposto a se matar para salvá-la?

Ela percebia então que Will era mais parecido com Jeffrey do que ela queria admitir. Talvez Sara tivesse uma tara por bombeiros, não policiais. Os dois tinham mostrado uma alta propensão a entrar correndo em prédios pegando fogo. Só na última semana, Will tinha sido alvejado por gângsteres, ameaçado por um psicopata, intimidado por três mulheres pelo menos, emasculado na frente de estranhos, se enfiado no porta-malas de um carro por horas a fio e se voluntariado para entrar numa situação em que sabia que tinha alta probabilidade de ser morto. Ele estava tão decidido a resgatar todo mundo da face da

Terra que Will não percebia que precisava ser resgatado dele mesmo. Todo mundo tirava vantagem dele. Todo mundo explorava sua boa vontade, sua decência, sua gentileza. Ninguém pensava em perguntar a Will do que ele precisava.

Tinha passado sua vida inteira nas sombras, o menino estoico sentado no fundo da sala, com medo de abrir a boca e ser descoberto. Angie o mantinha no escuro para servir a suas necessidades egoístas. Sara rapidamente percebeu, em sua primeira vez com Will, que ele nunca tinha estado com uma mulher que soubesse amá-lo. Não era de surpreender que ele tivesse desistido tão fácil quando ela falou que era o fim. Will tinha certeza de que nada de bom em sua vida ia durar. Era por isso que ele parecia tão aliviado. Estava com os dedos na beira do precipício. Tinha medo demais de saltar porque nunca tinha caído de fato.

Sara sentiu a boca se abrir, surpresa. Ela era tão culpada quanto o restante das pessoas. Estava tão desesperada para Will lutar por ela que nunca lhe ocorrera que Will esperava que Sara lutasse por ele.

Antes que sua razão pudesse intervir, ela já tinha atravessado a porta e estava correndo pelo corredor. Como sempre, o pronto-socorro estava lotado. Enfermeiras corriam com bolsas de soro. Macas passavam voando. Sara deu um pinote até o elevador. Apertou o botão uma dezena de vezes, implorando em silêncio para as portas se abrirem. As escadas davam nos fundos do hospital. O estacionamento ficava na frente. Quando ela conseguisse contornar o prédio, Will já estaria em casa. Sara olhou o relógio, pensando em quanto tempo tinha desperdiçado tendo pena de si mesma. Will provavelmente já estava do outro lado da plataforma. Três estruturas. Seis andares de carros. Mais, se ele tivesse usado uma das plataformas da universidade. Ela devia esperar na rua. Sara tentou mapear mentalmente as ruas. Bell. Armstrong. Talvez ele tivesse estacionado no Centro de Detenção Grady.

As portas finalmente se abriram. George, o segurança, estava lá parado, apoiando uma das mãos na arma. Will estava ao seu lado.

George perguntou:

— Tudo bem, doutora?

Sara só conseguiu assentir.

Will saiu do elevador, com uma cara meio acanhada.

— Esqueci que Betty está na sua casa. — Ele deu aquele sorriso familiar e desconfortável. — Correndo o risco de parecer um cantor de música country, eu diria que você pode levar meu coração, mas não pode levar minha cachorrinha.

Sara levou um encontrão de um paramédico que passava atrás dela. Apoiou as palmas das mãos no peito de Will para não cair. Ele só ficou ali parado com as mãos nos bolsos, sorrindo para ela com uma cara curiosa. Quem já tinha ficado ao lado desse homem? Não sua família, que o abandonara aos cuidados do Estado. Não os pais dos lares de acolhimento, que achavam que ele era descartável. Não os médicos que tinham feito experimentos com o lábio estourado dele. Não os professores e assistentes sociais que entenderam sua dislexia como burrice. E especialmente não Angie, que tinha apostado a vida dele com tanta facilidade. Aquela vida preciosa.

— Sara? — Will parecia preocupado. — Você está bem?

Sara subiu as mãos até os ombros dele. Sentiu o músculo duro familiar por baixo da camisa, o calor de sua pele. Ela tinha beijado as pálpebras dele de manhã. Ele tinha cílios delicados, loiros e macios. Ela o havia provocado, beijando suas sobrancelhas, seu nariz, seu queixo, deixando o cabelo cair no rosto e no peito dele. Quantas horas Sara tinha passado no último ano se perguntando como seria a sensação da cicatriz da boca dele em seus próprios lábios? Quantas noites ela havia sonhado em acordar em seus braços?

Tantas horas. Tantas noites.

Sara ficou na ponta dos pés para olhar nos olhos dele.

— Você quer ficar comigo?

— Sim.

Ela se deleitou com a certeza dele.

— Eu também quero ficar com você.

Will balançou a cabeça. Parecia estar esperando o fim de uma piada muito ruim.

— Não entendi.

— Deu certo.

— O que deu certo?

— Seu charme espantoso.

Ele estreitou os olhos.

— Que charme?

— Eu mudei de ideia.

Ele ainda não parecia acreditar nela.

— Me dê um beijo — disse ela a Will. — Eu mudei de ideia.

Agradecimentos

Como sempre, agradeço imensamente a Victoria Sanders, minha agente, e às minhas editoras Kate Miciak e Kate Elton. Angela Cheng Caplan também deveria estar aqui presente. Gostaria ainda de agradecer a todos em minhas editoras pelo apoio contínuo. Gina Centrello e Libby McGuire, foi um prazer conhecê-las. Adam Humphrey, agradeço por ter me deixado matá-lo. E bater em você. E humilhá-lo. E todas as outras coisas às quais Claire não dá valor.

Obrigada ao incomparável Vernon Jordan por me presentear com histórias da Atlanta dos anos 1970. O senhor é uma lenda. David Harper, este é pelo menos o seu décimo ano me ajudando a fazer com que Sara pareça médica. Como sempre, sou imensamente grata por sua ajuda e peço desculpas por quaisquer erros que tenham sido cometidos a serviço da história. Agente especial John Heinen, o mesmo se aplica a você. Quaisquer erros com armas são de minha responsabilidade. Tenho que agradecer a muitas pessoas da Georgia Bureau of Investigation, incluindo Pete Stuart, Wayne Smith, John Bankhead e ao diretor Vernon Keenan. Vocês são tão generosos cedendo seu tempo e tão apaixonados pelo que fazem que é um prazer estar na companhia de vocês. Presidente David Ralston, agradeço por seu apoio contínuo.

Os papais não recebem muita atenção neste livro, mas gostaria de agradecer ao meu por ser um pai tão maravilhoso. Eu escreveria uma história sobre você, mas ninguém acreditaria no quanto você é bom. E por falar em bondade, DA — como sempre, você é meu coração.

Aos meus leitores, observem que esta e uma obra de ficção. Embora eu seja moradora de Atlanta por mais da metade da minha vida, também sou escritora e mudei ruas, projetos de prédios e bairros para atender às minhas necessidades perversas. (Ah, vá, Sherwood Forest, você sabe que merece!)

Este livro foi composto na tipografia Sabon LT Std,
em corpo 11/15, e impresso em
papel off-white no Sistema Cameron da
Divisão Gráfica da Distribuidora Record.